THE WAR YEARS

A Chronicle of Washington State in World War II

By James R. Warren

THE WAR YEARS

A Chronicle of Washington State in World War II

By James R. Warren

Published by History Ink

in association with

**University of Washington Press
Seattle & London**

ISBN 0-295-98076-1

Published by History Ink, Seattle, in association with University of Washington Press,
Seattle and London.

Distributed by the University of Washington Press, P.O. Box 50096, Seattle, WA 98145-5096.

Designed by Marie McCaffrey, Crowley Associates, Inc. Edited by Priscilla Long and Walt Crowley,
History Ink. Indexed by Gwen Warren, Proofread by Gail Warren and D. Darlene Secord.

First printing November 11, 2000

Library of Congress Catalogue No. 00-108416

A HistoryLink Book

To learn more about local history, visit www.historylink.org

TABLE OF CONTENTS

FOREWORD

From today's perspective World War II seems to be ancient history. Present generations understandably have difficulty sensing the emotions, the effort, the glory, and the sorrow of those four years when American youth fought and died on battlefields around the world.

During these war years Americans had no trouble identifying the enemy. Dictator Hitler and his well-armed Nazi troopers invaded neighboring countries, killing and pillaging in what they called their "blitzkrieg" or lightning war. Mussolini of Italy took Ethiopia by force and threatened other countries, though not with the success of Hitler. The Italian dictator was often parodied as a *poseur* with his chin stuck out and his chest heavy with medals. Across the Pacific Ocean the Japanese Prime Minister, General Hideki Tojo, initiated attacks on China, Southeast Asia and many Pacific islands. In October 1941 he played a leading role in negotiating the Tripartite Pact with Italy and Germany that formed what became known as the Axis. Tojo assumed three roles — Prime Minister, War Minister and Chief of Army Staff—and therefore he was largely responsible for Japanese activity during the war, including the attack on Pearl Harbor.

Aging World War II veterans frequently speak before school assemblies and various organizations on Veterans' Day, Independence Day and other patriotic holidays. These audiences seem most interested in stories of battlefield experiences and of life on the home front. They usually are surprised at the question: "Did you know that during World War II, the State of Washington reportedly produced more war materiel per capita than any other state?" The 1940 census counted 1,736,191 Washington residents, whereas today's population is more than five million. That comparatively small population of the early 1940s produced thousands of warships, bombers, tanks and transport vehicles. Plutonium for the atom bomb was purified at Hanford; tons of aluminum were produced at newly built mills in Spokane, Vancouver and Tacoma; and huge quantities of vital foodstuffs, wood products and minerals resulted from Washington State's war effort. Tens of thousands of service personnel from all branches of the armed forces were trained at scores of army and navy installations located in the state, some of them among the largest in the country. Many times during the war years government and military representatives acknowledged the tremendous effort of Washington's residents and businesses.

Perhaps the most telling wartime statistic is the number of youthful citizens who gave their lives in the fight to preserve our freedoms. The names of more than 6,000 Washington war dead are listed in the back of this book. Washington State citizens in uniform were awarded thousands of medals for bravery in battle. Twenty-five of them were presented the nation's highest award for valor, the Medal of Honor. Many of the medals were awarded posthumously.

This book was first suggested in 1995 at a meeting of the "Victory '95 Committee" that planned the celebration of the 50th anniversary of the end of World War II. We thank the Boeing Company and Patsy Bullitt Collins for their donations toward the cost of publishing the book.

We who lived in Washington State in the early 1940s retain vivid memories of the war years; one objective of this book is to help the reader sense some of the emotions we felt during the war. It also describes some of the efforts of Washington State residents, businesses and organizations to help the Allied nations achieve victory over the Axis

INTRODUCTION

Washington State Prepares for War

The nation's first peacetime draft took effect on October 16, 1940. During that one day more than 16 million American males aged 21 to 35 registered. In the photo, eight University of Washington students stride toward their registration location. Seattle Post-Intelligencer Collection, 28732, MOHAI.

The Great Depression decade that preceded World War II was hellish for most families in ways vastly different from the war years. After the 1929 stock market crash, panic swept west across the country. Agricultural prices dropped, lumber sales nearly zeroed out, family incomes dropped precipitously, banks and other businesses began to fail. In Washington State an estimated one-quarter of the employed lost their jobs. With hundreds of hungry families, Seattle mayor Robert Harlin formed a "Commission on Improved Employment" and a million-dollar bond issue was voted to finance the effort, but that funding soon was depleted. Other state leaders struggled to find ways to counter the depression.

In 1932 Democrats swept into power across the country and in Washington State captured all congressional seats. With Franklin D. Roosevelt in the White House many federal programs were funded to provide jobs for the unemployed wage earners.

The Depression continued until the last two years of the decade when the country began to reconsider its isolationist urges to stay out of Europe's wars. When the media began reporting on Hitler's *blitzkrieg* attacks on France and other European countries and on Japan's army advances in China and Southeast Asia, Americans gradually changed their minds and began aiding England and France. The U.S. began seriously to develop defensive protections. Within a few months, thousands of jobs became available in defense industries. Rural residents began migrating to cities where defense industries were located. Urgent contracts for armaments, military equipment and supplies were signed by Washington State industries. The Japanese attack on Pearl Harbor hardened the resolve of Washington State residents to adopt a total commitment to the war effort.

Those of us who reside in the northwest corner of the 48 contiguous states tend to consider the Pacific Ocean as our front porch. We were stunned and outraged when, on a quiet Sunday, December 7, 1941, the Japanese navy, without warning, sent bombers, fighter planes and midget submarines to attack Pearl Harbor, Hawaii. That enemy assault made us realize that our home state was vulnerable to similar attacks. We also realized that our country had only recently begun to build defenses against such dangers. Our resentment grew as the damage to Pearl Harbor was revealed. The two-hour attack by 360 enemy warplanes sank or damaged eight battleships and 14 smaller warships, obliterated about 200 aircraft on the ground, killed 2,400 Americans and wounded 1,300.

After the attack, the public demand for war information resulted in sold-out newsstands, a shortage of newsmagazines and huge audiences for radio newscasts and movie theater newsreels depicting scenes of battle. The daily war news provided subject matter for daylong discussions. Defeat of the Axis powers—dictator-led Germany, Japan and Italy—became the all-consuming objective of Americans everywhere. Furthermore, the war began to etch vivid pictures on the memory pages of Washington State residents, many of them proud memories, some of them painful and all in full color.

The U.S. was officially at war from December 8, 1941 to September 2, 1945, nearly four years. At first the allies were forced to retreat on most fronts. But America's armed forces and civilian workers, along with the country's developing industrial might, helped the Allied nations gradually turn the tide of battle.

America Mobilizes

The first peacetime program of compulsory military service in U.S. history was enacted in September 1940. It called for all males aged 18 to 64 to register under the Selective Service Act, but only those 38 and younger were actually drafted.

The day after the December 7 attack on Pearl Harbor, the U.S. declared war on the Axis and draft boards were ordered to defer only irreplaceable employees in vital war industries

During the Great Depression, many "soup kitchens" fed unemployed men who had migrated to the cities seeking the few available jobs. By 1939, defense work in cities like Seattle was making such relief a thing of the past. MOHAI Collection, 17794.

and agriculture. A few professionals such as clergy and doctors whose services were required on the home front also could defer joining the armed forces, as could men with proven family hardship cases, and those physically or mentally unable to serve. Many men eligible for deferment volunteered to join the armed services anyway.

The country moved quickly to full mobilization for the war effort. The War Manpower Commission, established in April 1942, moved to effectively utilize the nation's labor resources. Thousands migrated from rural areas to the cities where entire families became involved in the production of ships, planes,

tanks and other war equipment and materiel. Manpower shortages soon became apparent.

The U.S. War Manpower Commission, established to organize labor resources, soon realized women might be the solution to the growing labor shortages. Before the war, only a small percentage of women worked outside the home, but as war efforts increased thousands of women became involved in production of ships, airplanes, tanks and other combat equipment. They also filled most positions in offices and retail outlets.

And thousands of American women served in the Armed Forces. Beginning on May 15, 1942, women could enlist for non-combat duties in the Women's Auxiliary Army Corps (WAAC), later more simply called Women's Army Corps, or WAC, and Women in the Air Force (WAF). The other services followed suit: the Navy with the Women Appointed for Voluntary Emergency Service (WAVES), the Coast Guard with Semper Paratus Always Ready Service (SPARS) and the Marine Corps Women's Reserve. Members of the Women's Air Force Service Pilots (WASPs) flew all types of aircraft from factories to designated service destinations. In addition, thousands of women served as nurses, Red Cross aides, USO hostesses, volunteers in rationing efforts and war bond desks and in dozens of other ways that helped gain the eventual victory.

President Roosevelt on February 9, 1943 established a minimum work-week of 48 hours with overtime pay for hours over 40. To prevent employers from raiding the workforces of other companies, seven million war workers were frozen in their jobs.

In June 1942, the War Production Board instituted a system of priorities for strategic materials. The listing and decisions were classified so as not to provide information to the enemy. Three months later, a $4 billion program was funded

The Depression garbage dumps south of downtown Seattle attracted hungry vagrants in town seeking employment. Every load of garbage was searched for returnable bottles, edible foods, usable clothing, anything that might be of value. Seattle P-I Collection, 86.5, MOHAI.

to increase the production of synthetic rubber to compensate for the natural rubber supply being choked off by Japanese advances in the South Pacific. Beginning in December 1941, auto tires were rationed.

Production of fuel, especially petroleum and coal, was placed under government control. A Small War Plants Corporation was established in June 1942 to help finance war efforts of smaller companies. Early in 1942, price controls were ordered on commodities and on rents in defense-crowded cities to prevent consumer gouging, and sugar, coffee, and gasoline were added to the rationed list. Meats, fats and oils, butter and cheese, processed foods and shoes required ration stamps beginning in 1943. These efforts to control prices and to maintain a supply of required commodities were successful. During the World War II years prices rose 31 percent, compared to 62 percent during World War I.

Most labor problems were mediated by the National War Labor Board and settlement was usually reached without work stoppages. The national government organized dozens of other war agencies, among them the Office of Civilian Defense, the Office of War Information, the Office of Scientific Research and Development, the Office of Lend-Lease Administration, the War Shipping Board and the National Housing Agency.

In August 1942, planning for development of the atomic bomb commenced with establishment of three centers of activity: a Uranium 235 separation plant at Oak Ridge, Tennessee; a bomb development laboratory at Los Alamos, New Mexico; and a plutonium production works at Hanford, Washington. All were operated in such extreme secrecy that even those who helped develop the weapon did not know what the end product of their labors would be. The first atomic bomb was successfully tested July on 16, 1945, at Alamogordo, New Mexico and on August 6 and 9 the first two atom bombs dropped on Japan decimated two cities. The powerful new weapon soon forced Japan to surrender unconditionally, bringing the war to a conclusion. Only then was it revealed that the secret weapon was an atom bomb.

Washington State's Important Role in World War II

Washington, a comparatively small and undeveloped state, played an increasingly important role in efforts to improve U.S. defense capabilities. Census takers in 1940 counted 1,736,191 Washington residents. The war effort quickly attracted a quarter million more.

Congress authorized enlistment of women into the armed services in the spring of 1942. Within a year 100,000 women were in uniform. These members of the Women's Army Corps are shown marching in 1944 at Seattle's Fort Lawton. MOHAI Collection, 876.

The Washington Secretary of State, Belle Reeves, in January 1943 issued a report titled "War Production in Washington" that opened with these words:

> No State has been more profoundly affected economically by the expansion of war industries than has Washington. By the middle of 1941, migration of war workers was already at full tide and the relation of prime military contracts in the Puget Sound Area to the value of manufacturing products in 1939 was relatively five times greater than for the country as a whole. This relationship of war work to normal activity has been about twice as great as for Los Angeles and four times greater than for San Francisco.

Her lengthy report cannot be included here in entirety but several parts of it are quoted below to indicate how the war brought rapid changes to Washington State.

Secretary Reeves noted that the Seattle-Tacoma-Bremerton area received a tremendous impact from war contracts and quickly became one of the major war production centers of the nation. The War Production Board in August 1942 revealed that by July 1, 1942, more than $1 billion in contracts had been awarded Seattle's aircraft industry and $709 million had been awarded to Seattle shipyards. The city ranked as one of the first three in the country in war contracts per capita, and the state was one of the first two in the nation for war contracts per capita.

Secretary of State Reeves pointed to the fact that in 1939 the value of the state's manufactured goods, including lumber products, totaled only $637 million, an amount smaller than the value of contracts awarded to just the State's shipbuilding through the middle of 1942. The value of airplane and ship contracts in 1943-44 equaled the total of all manufacturing in the state in 1939. She added:

> The immensity of the shift to war industry is further emphasized by comparison with pre-war shipbuilding. In 1939 this particular industry had shrunk from its World War I expansion to a value of less than $6,500,000. The present value of contracts for approximately 200 vessels of all kinds in the 16 private and one government plant in the Puget Sound Area is over $700,000,000 and represents an increase of more than 100 times the figure for shipbuilding [in 1939].

> Since contracts for military planes now exceed one billion dollars, these orders, placed in the past three years, are nearly double in value the total of all Washington's manufactured products in 1939. Floor space of Seattle airplane plants had been increased from 800,000 square feet to 2,400,000 by the first of 1942 and has since been increased another 1,700,000 square feet. Boeing Aircraft company employment jumped from about 7,500 persons in 1940 to more than 22,000 two years later.

She reported on population growths, mentioning that King County's 1940 population of 504,980 had increased by an estimated 100,000 in 1941-42. She expected the 1940 Seattle-Tacoma-Bremerton population of about 750,000 to increase to one million persons by the end of 1943. Between 1940 and mid-1942, Kitsap County's population increased 90 percent, King County's 20 percent, Mason County's 28 percent, and Pierce County's 10 percent. In Clark County, the population jumped more than 40 percent between 1940 and 1943, due in large part to shipbuilding and

In 1941, battles spread around the world. The U.S., though still officially neutral, was sensing danger. Virginia Mason Hospital in Seattle graduated this class of nurses on March 12, 1941. Seattle P-I Collection, 23614, MOHAI.

aluminum production. The state population was expected to increase from 1,736,191 in 1940 to more than 2,000,000 by 1944.

No aluminum had been produced in Washington State before 1940. Two years later, with power from the new Bonneville and Grand Coulee Dams, the state was producing one-third of all the aluminum refined in the country. This production was centered in the Longview, Vancouver, Spokane and Tacoma areas. Because of unprecedented demands for all metals, the state increased production of such strategic minerals as lead, zinc, copper and tungsten.

The importance of Grand Coulee Dam during the war effort cannot be overemphasized. With electricity generated by this dam, then the largest in the world, the metals for the B-17s and B-29s were created, the plutonium at Hanford was purified, the shipyard welding machines were powered, and the homes of thousands of new residents were electrified. President Harry Truman remarked that without Grand Coulee Dam "it would have been almost impossible to win this war."

Lumber, one of the state's most important products, also was in great demand. Many billions of board feet were utilized in construction projects varying from barracks to minesweepers. Specialized lumber products were developed to substitute for critically scarce metals. For example, water-resistant plywood was produced for construction of many different war needs including training planes and barges. New products were developed including cork made from fir bark, tannic acid extracted from hemlock bark and a fireproof wood to meet special construction needs.

Throughout the war years, Washington continued as a leading agricultural state. In 1941 state farm production increased in value to approximately $250,000,000 and in 1942 agricultural production reached an all-time high. In addition, victory gardens grown by individual families helped provide food for the growing wartime population. Fortunately, advancements in food preservation, such as dehydration of fruits, vegetables, milk and eggs, allowed foods to be transported to distant war fronts. In 1943 the burgeoning numbers of men and women in the armed services increased the need for powdered eggs to 400,000,000 pounds, whereas the year before only 250,000,000 pounds had been produced.

During the war years, Washington's fishing industry was one of the most productive in the country. Salmon, halibut and a variety of other products of the sea were harvested. Virtually all of the canned salmon produced in Washington and Alaska was purchased by the Army and Navy.

In 1941 nearly $100 million was spent on construction in the Pacific Northwest, much of it used to build factories and mills that would produce aircraft, ships and aluminum. Also, huge contracts were let for construction of facilities to house the armed services and the workers at defense industries. Vancouver's McLoughlin Heights project in 1942 provided homes for more than 12,000 persons. In two years the population of Bremerton doubled from 15,000 to 30,000. Renton, with a population of 5,000 before the war, more than tripled that number in four years. Major construction projects changed the demographics of Spokane, Pasco, Yakima, Walla Walla, Ephrata and several other cities.

With wartime housing in short supply, families moving to the state to work in war industries often lived in temporary quarters such as this trailer park in Bremerton. Kitsap Regional Library, 2710.

The population in most Eastern Washington counties remained comparatively stable during the years of war. However, major problems developed when better paying war industry jobs caused a severe shortage of workers to harvest fruit and field crops. Local people in those areas labored heroically to save the produce, often aided by high school students released from their classrooms.

A shortage of telephone services developed as the number of newcomers escalated and the demands of the armed services increased. During 1941, Pacific Telephone and Telegraph Company reported an 11 percent increase in the number of telephones in service and a delay of several months was common for new installations. In those days before natural gas had been piped into the area, electric companies met most of the increased demand for power. Coal production was augmented in order to overcome fuel shortages, especially in Seattle and Tacoma, and wood stoves remained the source of heat in many homes.

Secretary of State Reeves' January 1943 report was prepared when the U.S. had been at war for 14 months. The conflict would last another 38 months before victory was achieved. She concluded her report with a prediction that proved to be fairly accurate.

> The year 1943 will be another period of tremendous productivity in the successful prosecution of the war. Many serious problems in industry and agriculture will be encountered and solved, and the people of this state will meet the challenge with the same resourcefulness that they have shown in the past.

The Report on the Schools

The biennial report of Pearl Wanamaker, State Superintendent of Public Instruction, issued on June 30, 1942, mentioned problems educators faced early in the war. A sudden influx of pupils into areas where war industries were situated created an acute shortage of educational facilities. Funding was provided in 1941 for construction of several new schools, but a shortage of critical building materials slowed these efforts. As a result more and more students were crowded into each classroom and some schools taught two shifts a day. Schools that normally required ten teachers, Mrs. Wanamaker reported, now required twenty. The State Department of Public Instruction, she explained, "was able to inaugurate a combined state and federal plan of emergency aid to the districts where the crowding was most severe."

A second major education problem soon became apparent. The drafting of male teachers and the appeal of better-paying industry jobs resulted in a severe shortage of teachers just as enrollments were ballooning. As a result, War

Emergency Certificates were issued in the districts where regularly certified teachers were not available.

Many older teenagers left school to work in war industries. After their 18th birthday males could be drafted or could enlist in the armed services. Educators and parents feared these young people would find their loss of education especially difficult when they returned to civilian life after the war. Industries were urged to arrange four-hour shifts to allow youth to work part-time and still attend classes. In farm communities where student help was needed during harvest season, schools adjusted their schedules to meet local conditions. During summer months the U.S. Employment Service registered city youth for farm work, forest fire prevention and other employment.

Because new school busses were not available during the war, districts were forced to utilize and maintain older equipment. Some students walked two miles to the nearest school bus stop. Many schools staggered opening and closing times to allow each bus to serve twice as many students. With more women employed in war industries, the need for nursery schools and childcare centers became critical. The federal government helped fund nursery schools operated by school districts near factories vital to the war effort.

Rationing of scarce necessities called for every family to acquire ration books. Teacher and parent volunteers manned tables at public schools in every community to distribute ration cards and stamps. In addition, during the 18 months following Pearl Harbor, intensified vocational programs provided by public schools trained 110,000 Washington State men and women for work in aircraft construction, shipbuilding and in dozens of semi-technical positions.

The U.S. Treasury Department, in cooperation with the schools, inaugurated a stamp and bond savings program to help fund the war effort. Students at many schools hoped to fund a jeep or small plane with their purchases of savings stamps. Every pupil had

a booklet with pages printed for war stamps of various denominations. Once filled, the book could be turned in for a war savings bond that earned interest until cashed.

State Colleges and Universities

The University of Washington became involved in the war effort. Hundreds of service personnel were trained on campus. The Navy established a V-12 unit there, housing the men in residence halls and feeding them in the former student commons in the Home Economics building. Army R.O.T.C., Quartermaster and Air Force pre-meteorology classes were scheduled. Members of the home economics staff trained students to prepare foods in quantity for in-plant and armed services dining facilities.

The University's chemistry department found ways to utilize waste from pulp mills, worked on developing new explosives, and established a laboratory for chemical warfare. The Oceanography Department undertook classified investigations for the U. S. Weather Bureau, the Navy, and the Coast and Geodetic Survey. The Department of Mines' laboratory assisted with intensive research for minerals and experimented with processes of extraction and refinement of aluminum from Northwest clays. Engineers perfected welding magnets to

With war rationing in effect, applicants for ration books crowded into schools across the state on May 12, 1942. This scene at Oak Lake School in Seattle shows schoolteachers and volunteers helped with the paper work. Seattle P-I Collection, 23059, MOHAI.

be used in newly developed methods of shipbuilding, and built wind tunnel testing tools used in the design of B-29 bombers. In the summer of 1943, the University created an Applied Physics Laboratory that helped the Navy develop better proximity fuses to use against submarines.

In many ways it was a different Husky campus during the war. Civilian enrollment dropped by more than 3,500 as students and more than 100 faculty took leave to enter the armed services or some special branch of government. Newly established adult education courses were offered on and off campus. The Far Eastern Department developed intensive language-area study programs to familiarize students with the cultures and languages of China, Japan, Russia and Korea. Refresher courses in nursing and first aid and special instruction in a number of academic subjects benefited many employees of war industries. In May 1944, the Washington State Medical Association, aware of the need for more doctors and dentists, discussed with its members and with University regents the possibility of establishing a Medical School on the campus. The 1945 legislature followed through and appropriated nearly $4 million for the first building. The School of Health Sciences became the first major addition after the war.

Wartime restrictions did curtail University summer school programs. Several physical education classes were dropped, as were numerous vocational tours. Restrictions on gas and tires caused cancellation of auto tours to Seattle's Skagit power plant and other such sites.

A typical wartime program scheduled on campus was the Associated Women Student's United Nations Heroes Assembly at which war heroes from various allied countries spoke. A Soviet Girl in uniform who was credited with killing 309 Nazis appeared, as did women from the Dutch Navy and the British Royal Navy and Air Force. Mrs. Franklin D. Roosevelt introduced the speakers.

At Washington State College in Pullman, the war's impact was obvious beginning in 1942. At men's dormitories and fraternities, stripped beds and suitcases piled at the door were common sights. Instead of football rallies, students gathered at the Pullman train depot to say good-bye to friends. Many male students did not study hard because they doubted they would be on campus long enough to earn a degree. Others applied themselves with vigor in hopes of qualifying for officers' candidate school or pilot training or other personal objectives. Before the 1942 fall semester ended, the men's dorms and fraternities were almost vacant.

They weren't empty long, for military personnel soon began appearing on campus for special training. The college contracted with the War Department to conduct Army Signal Corps instruction, Army veterinary education, Japanese language training, and preflight schooling for bomber crews. At one point, more than 1,900 military trainees trod the campus. Men in uniform filled Ferry, Stimson, and McCroskey Halls and several fraternity houses. They brought a new pace of living to the campus. Future bomber crews formed intramural teams to compete in campus sports, learned to operate radios and other technical equipment, and to fly small aircraft. They met coeds, threw farewell dances and were gone within four months. Within days they were replaced by a new batch of servicemen.

By the fall of 1944, the campus newspaper noted that nearly all college-age males on campus marched in step to meals and classes. And sometimes, when they passed an attractive woman, the officer in charge would order: "Eyes right!"

Central Washington State College in Ellensburg quickly developed plans for campus defense and evacuation of living quarters in case of attack. CWSC also became involved in solving the labor shortage when students voted in 1942 to close the school for three days to help harvest the Eastern Washington apple crop. Of 540 students and faculty, 375 volunteered for this "battle of the orchards."

The college attempted to maintain the usual social program on campus but soon discovered there were too few male partners for the usual Wednesday night dances. Occasionally men were imported from the nearby Air Base for special functions and the coeds often attended dances at the USO. This situation changed after a Civilian Pilot Training unit was stationed on the campus. During the 21-month session, 263 men were trained and most served in the Armed Forces during the war. Then, during 1943, Central Washington became a training school for units of the Air Force. The first problem was to find housing for 400 cadets. Kamola Hall was the right size, but was occupied by women students. To solve the housing problem, a three-way switch was arranged. The 55 men students in Munson Hall were moved to the downtown Antlers and Webster Hotels. The women students moved to Munson Hall, leaving Kamola Hall for Air Force cadets. The five-month Air Corps program included mathematics, physics, history, English, physical education, medical aid and civil air regulations. The objective was to "diminish education differences for subsequent Air Force training." Twenty-four instructors were assigned to teach these fledgling airmen.

As was the case in all colleges, during the war years, fewer regular students enrolled at Central. The nadir in 1944 found only 248 civilian students on campus, and only eight of them were men. Enrollment, however, picked up rapidly after the war ended. The first veterans, 13 of them, enrolled under the G. I. Bill in the autumn of 1945. This number jumped to 119 for winter quarter. Of these 24 were married and 10 had children. By the beginning of the 1946-47 school year, housing for veterans with families was a real problem. The college acquired pre-fabricated army surplus apartments, a complex soon known as "Vetville." To house single veteran students, three temporary dormitories were acquired from the Ellensburg Army Airport when it was declared surplus. Three of these dormitories were named for former student leaders who had been killed in combat—Courtland Carmody, Douglas A. Munro, and Hamilton J.

Montgomery. Another was named for a faculty member, Clifton Alford, who was killed in the war.

The experience at Central and at other colleges and universities in the state proved that an educational institution designed for civilian students could adjust quickly to meet the needs of the country in time of war.

During the war colleges often found it difficult to secure construction materials. A wartime story describes how a determined Dr. Frank F. Warren, President of Whitworth College in Spokane, overcame one of his wartime frustrations. It seems the President, for several years, had wanted to replace the "temporary" gymnasium on the campus. He launched a funding campaign in January 1941. By October, the Board of Trustees agreed that construction could commence, and excavation started on December 1. A week later Pearl Harbor was attacked and the country was at war. Government priorities for building materials immediately were reserved for the armed forces and the Whitworth gymnasium project was delayed. But Dr. Warren was not to be denied. When construction faltered for lack of nails, the good doctor, while on promotion trips to small towns throughout the state, would stop by local hardware and building supply stores and purchase a few pounds of nails from each. He also managed to scrounge up a needed carload of cement just hours before the government issued a "freeze" order on all such building materials. Enough of the gymnasium was completed to allow its use, though it was not formally finished until after the war.

Cities and Towns

Every city, every county, every region in the state was involved in the war effort. Every individual, every company, every public service agency felt the effects of the war in dozens of ways. The war was constantly on every mind and each day the war news motivated citizens to work long and often unusual hours. Many companies scheduled three eight-hour shifts each day. Most families had members serving in the armed services and the thought that victory would bring them back motivated the home front.

Urban areas experienced great population growth during the early war years, and the population numbers in some small rural towns also increased markedly, especially if war industries or military bases had been established nearby. Villages near cities were transformed into major suburbs almost overnight. Several of these suburbs did not incorporate until after the war, but soon were numbered among the larger cities in the state. After victory had been achieved, many of the migrant war-workers and service personnel who had sampled life in Washington State decided to make their homes here.

The Spokane Area

As with other cities and towns, Spokane faced rapid change after the U.S. entered the war. Blackouts were ordered so that enemy planes could not identify large cities. *The Spokesman Review* hung heavy blinds in its windows since many of its employees worked at night. The Davenport Hotel covered its skylight with black tar. Merchants blanked out their lights in various ways. Young men anxious to enlist in the Army, Navy and Marine Corps thronged

recruiting stations. War bonds sold so rapidly that supplies at some banks were depleted.

Within a few months of the outbreak of war, Spokane's streets began to fill with uniformed personnel. Fort Wright and Felts Field had been established before the war, and within months of Pearl Harbor other bases were added. Almost overnight Geiger Field and Galena (later Fairchild Air Force Base) were built; Baxter Hospital was caring for 1,500 war-wounded; and Velox Naval Supply Depot was being guarded 24 hours a day by more than a hundred Marines and Navy men.

The largest number of service personnel in the Spokane region were stationed at Farragut Naval Station, located across the Idaho border on Lake Pend Oreille. It became the second largest naval training center in the U.S. with facilities for more than 45,000.

In the beginning few recreational facilities were available for service personnel near Spokane, but the city soon remedied that situation. By 1943 several centers welcomed servicemen and women, including the USO Lutheran Service Center, a second USO Club located in a building that had served as headquarters for the Depression WPA, and the George Washington Carver Club for black servicemen. The Victory Shop, with aid of the Community Chest, the Council of Church Women, and several downtown businessmen's clubs sponsored a Soldier Service Center. At this center, service personnel could find information about Spokane homes that welcomed servicemen for dinner. Several church groups in the Spokane area sponsored frequent dances and dinners.

As in other cities, many of Spokane's downtown buildings were leased for the war effort. Spokane Army Air Depot's administrative headquarters at first were located in the Hutton Building, but it soon proved to be too small and the headquarters moved to 1011 West First. After a time, these offices also proved to be insufficient and the headquarters personnel occupied a recently closed department store building.

The Navy Velox Supply Depot east of Spokane opened on January 1, 1943. More than 2,700 were employed in its 32 warehouses that enclosed 86 acres. Spokane's Industrial Park now occupies the site of the former Navy Depot. Cheney Cowles Museum, Spokane, L93-18.78.

Spokane residents quickly shifted into war work. Large construction crews were recruited to build military facilities. Thirty thousand Spokane residents helped construct the huge Farragut Naval Base in 1942. More than a hundred buildings were erected at Geiger Field in just 29 days. In one year at Galena, 262 buildings were completed. Crews working seven days a week, 24 hours a day erected the aluminum plant at Trentwood in one year. The result was one of the largest buildings under one roof in the country at that time. A second new plant, this one at Mead, also began producing aluminum for warplanes and Quonset huts.

As the shortage of workers increased, the number of women employees surged. They drove city buses and moved into manufacturing and office jobs that previously had not been open to them. Before the war only unmarried women were hired as teachers, but as the war progressed, married women were more than welcome in the classrooms. Teenagers also were issued special work permits. With all members of the family working, stores changed their hours to accommodate them. For example, on Mondays they served customers from noon to 9 p.m.

All this activity resulted in unprecedented population growth. The 1940 census counted 122,001 Spokane residents; the 1950 census counted 161,721.

On September 2, 1945, the day World War II officially ended, Spokane's downtown streets were thronged with people. Automobiles sounded their horns, fire sirens shrieked, and crowds went wild with emotion, some people crying, others cheering, and others solemn with thoughts of a loved one whose name was on the long list of casualties.

Tacoma

"During the war, everything Tacoma produced was in demand, especially soldiers." Northwest historian Murray Morgan penned those words for his book *Puget's Sound*. He added: "Fort Lewis, Madigan Army Hospital and McChord

Air Field, which had been acquired by the War Department in 1938, expanded hugely, while the tideflats sprouted shipyards."

World War II affected the Tacoma area much as had World War I, but on a larger scale. McChord Air Field construction was begun in 1938 by WPA Depression workers who cleared and graded a landing strip. Soon B-17s and B-24s of the 17th Bombardment Group were using the facility. Then B-25s became the predominant planes at McChord. Some of the airmen involved in the Doolittle 1942 raid on Tokyo were trained there. By 1943, McChord was the largest bomber-training base in the country.

Fort Lewis had been largely ignored by the Army during the 1920s and 1930s, causing Tacoma and Pierce County officials to remind the military that the property was given to the government during World War I with the understanding it would be developed as a major base. When this did not occur, the county and city began insisting that the Army either utilize the property or return it to local control. Conscious of the value of Camp Lewis, as it was then called, the Army elevated it to the level of a Fort and adopted a 10 year development plan. In 1937, Fort Lewis was the site of the largest military exercise in the U.S. More than 7,500 Third Division soldiers were trained there under several officers who became famous in World War II among them, General George C. Marshall, Major Mark Clark and Major Dwight D. Eisenhower.

By 1941, all across America, defense facilities were under construction. That year these barracks were erected at West Geiger Field in Spokane. Cheney Cowles Museum photo L87-1.20192-41.

Tacoma Shipyard in Tacoma was busy during the war, as this May 1945 photograph indicates. Washington State Historical Society, Tacoma.

As war spread throughout Europe, the numbers of Army men at Fort Lewis and McChord Field increased from 7,000 to 26,000. When the military draft act became law in September 1941, $14 million was allotted to construction at North Fort Lewis. After Pearl Harbor, more than 50,000 soldiers at a time were trained at the Fort.

The war also increased the need for hospital space and the Fort Lewis Hospital was transformed into Madigan Medical Center. Hundreds of the most gravely wounded and mentally war-damaged servicemen were treated there. By war's end, the population of army personnel in Pierce County equaled half the population of Tacoma.

During depression days the Tacoma waterfront was aided by a state law empowering public port districts to develop new industrial areas. An area south of Eleventh Street was deeded to the Port by the city and in 1940 a bureau was formed to recruit tenants. The U.S. became involved in the war shortly after the streets, utilities, and rail connections were completed in the port area.

Tenants began clamoring for additional space as thousands of troops from Fort Lewis were being shipped to Pacific war fronts through the Port of Tacoma. The demand for space was so heavy that the port took over adjacent private docks. All sorts of materials flowed over the Tacoma piers, including flour for Army kitchens, wool blankets bound for the Aleutian Islands and ammunition for various Pacific island battlefields.

To load the heavier materials, the Port needed new equipment. The government paid for this expensive machinery to speed the loading of cargo. Forklifts toted pallets of war supplies from warehouse to dock where cranes swung heavy slings into the holds. The new Victory ships, built with a single massive hold, allowed cargo, even bundles of logs, to be quickly loaded. This modern equipment helped Puget Sound ports to thrive during the years following World War II.

Most Tacoma businesses were involved in the war effort. A few examples:

- Three shifts of employees at National Blower and Sheet Metal Company worked round the clock producing metal building materials for military base construction.

- The Fick Foundry Company produced iron casting and for a time turned out hand grenades urgently needed by the armed services.

- The wartime demand for gloves caused the North Star Glove Company to drastically increase production and to open a branch in Orting.

- Selden Furniture and Carpet could not replace their stock because materials were required for the war effort. However, the fear of air raids created a demand for blackout blinds. At one point early in 1942,

The pristine Lake Washington Floating Bridge has opened a few weeks before this 1940 photograph was taken. The bridge proved vital during the war years by drastically reducing the mileage between the suburban areas and farms east of the lake and the the factories and shipyards in Seattle. PEMCO, Webster-Stevens Collection, MOHAI.

the company had a backlog of orders for 30,000 window shades for wartime housing. The firm increased production to a shade every 45 seconds, 16 hours a day, six days a week. The company secured government contracts allowing them access to materials to produce furniture and linoleum. One contract called for them to lay 96 rail cars full of asphalt tiles in government buildings.

- Banks in Tacoma helped finance shipyards and other war industries, while meeting the banking needs of growing numbers of customers.

The Bellevue-Kirkland-Redmond Area

Bellevue serves as a prime example of the wartime effect on the suburbs. The estimated population of unincorporated Bellevue in 1930 was 3,000, with most people living on farm and orchard properties or in summer homes on the Lake Washington shore. In the 1930s and 1940s, a few Japanese families moved in as tenant farmers and tilled large fields of produce, especially berries. As a result, Bellevue's major celebration each year was the Strawberry Festival. During 1942, the 55 Japanese-American farmers and their families living in the Bellevue-Midlakes area, about 300 families in all, were trucked to Kirkland where they were loaded onto railroad cars bound for relocation camp at Tule Lake, California, just south of Klamath Falls, Oregon. Some of these people

had lived on the East Side for more than 40 years and had worked at developing berry and vegetable fields covering more than 470 acres. They had formed their own Christian Church, basketball team, and produce warehouses that shipped vegetables to Eastern markets. While a few of their Bellevue neighbors took advantage of these families when they were forced to leave on short notice, others were supportive and helpful. After the war, fewer than half the Japanese-American families returned, and some who did felt unwelcome.

During the early war years volunteers staffed an aircraft observation tower atop the hill in today's Vuecrest neighborhood. Twenty-four hours a day, these volunteers watched for enemy aircraft. In case of an air raid, church and school bells were to be rung, sirens were to sound, and automobile horns were to blow three short and one long beep. In case incendiary bombs were dropped, all homes were instructed to have on hand a bucket of dry sand, long-handled shovels and rakes, heavy gloves, goggles, and blankets to be dipped in water to throw on flames. Nursing courses were scheduled and 4 bed emergency first aid clinics were established at several locations. A drive to raise funds for the Red Cross was soon in progress.

The Bellevue American newspaper promoted scrap drives. Rags, rubber goods and old tires, paper, rope and all types of metal were collected to help overcome basic shortages.

Piles of scrap metal were gathered at Bellevue schools for Army trucks to carry to local smelters

The American Pacific Whaling Company fleet, moored in Meydenbauer Bay just south of Bellevue's Main Street, was taken over by the Coast Guard. The whaling vessels were overhauled, painted and armed for shore patrol. The docking facility was converted to a repair base for Coast Guard vessels.

With Seattle housing in short supply, many defense worker families found shelter in East Side buildings, some inhabiting former summer cabins or converted farm structures. As these new families crowded onto what had been farm and orchard properties, problems became apparent. There was little recreation available and families missed the amenities of city life. As a result many moved to Seattle as soon as they found shelter there. During the early war years, Kemper Freeman, Sr., and his father Miller, aware of the population growth and the need for more retail outlets and services, began buying property north of Main Street. They purchased 10 acres from James Ditty and a number of acres from the Burrows family whose farm was located on the site of the present Bellevue Shopping Square. The Freemans found they faced a dilemma: All building materials were reserved for the war effort except in cases of emergency. Eventually the government, understanding the need for East Side recreation facilities, permitted construction of the Bell-Vue Theater, the first structure to be completed in Bellevue Square.

At Kirkland and Houghton (then separate towns), growth had been fairly continuous since the turn of the century. The shipyard at Houghton, founded in 1901, had been purchased by John Anderson in 1906 and renamed Lake Washington Shipyard. During the war years, many ferries and merchant and Navy vessels were built and repaired there by more than 6,000 employees. That is one reason Kirkland's 1940 population of 2,084 more than doubled in the decade. Another reason for the population surge: Thousands of young men discharged from the services in 1945 and 1946 were soon purchasing family homes in the suburbs.

In Redmond, as was the case in other cities, citizens united in the war effort. Employees willingly worked overtime. Children collected scrap, old newspapers and metal for recycling. The first Redmond aircraft lookout was situated near Avondale Road and Redmond Way in an unused storage building that happened to have a telephone, a scarce convenience during the war years. In 1942 a 20-foot-high structure was built, forcing volunteers to climb a steep stairway to a lookout platform with a railing but no roof. Later the tower was enclosed and a stove installed. Women volunteered for the daylight hours, often bringing their babies or knitting. Men kept watch at night.

Olympia

Civilian pilot training commenced at Olympia airport as early as 1939. After Pearl Harbor, the Olympia airport became an adjunct of McChord Air Force Base and housed P-38 fighter planes. A ground school at St. Martin's College trained more than a thousand pilots, radio operators and mechanics as part of a national program. The Port of Olympia in the late 1930s became a lend-lease shipping facility and by 1942 large quantities of war cargo flowed through Olympia bound for Russia. Early in the war Puget Sound Shipbuilding and Olympia Shipbuilding relocated on port property.

Following the Pearl Harbor attack, a roof

Before the war William Schupp's American Pacific Whaling fleet, moored on Meydenbauer Bay, was said to be the largest business in small, unincorporated Bellevue. During the war, the Army requisitioned one whaler and the Coast Guard leased the others as patrol boats and used the Bellevue wharves and buildings as a repair station. The Bellevue Yacht Club and Yacht Basin now occupy part of the former whaling station property. MOHAI Collection, 83.10.3976.

siren on the building housing radio station KGY was to sound in case of air attack. A group of women volunteered to serve as plane spotters and as a Red Cross motor corps. A club was organized in the old capitol building for soldiers from nearby Fort Lewis. During the war, an USO club was built on East Fourth Street. Scrap metal and grease drives were organized.

Walla Walla

Residents of Walla Walla realized war was threatening when two local National Guard units were mobilized in September 1940 and sent to Fort Lewis for training. Many government projects were also obvious in the area.

On December 27, 1941, three weeks after the attack on Pearl Harbor, the Army announced Walla Walla was to be the site of the Army's Northern Defense headquarters, but a year later it was moved to Seattle. In January 1942, final approval was given for construction of Walla Walla Air Base. The Second and Fourth Air Forces trained a total of 8,000 officers and men at that base. In 1947 it was declared surplus and became the municipal airport.

Also in 1942, Walla Walla was selected as site of a 1,000-bed Army hospital that soon was expanded to 1,850 beds. Named in honor of Walter D. McCaw, a World War I general, the faculty served some 16,000 patients during the war.

German prisoners of war, under guard, worked in canneries late in the war, helping

harvest and can the famed Walla Walla green peas. Patriotic activities were staged at the city's Victory Center and movie stars and other celebrities sold war bonds there. In those days when the services were segregated, two USOs were developed in the city, one for white service personnel and one for black.

One of the city's most famous guests arrived a month after the war ended. Jonathan M. Wainwright, the General captured by the Japanese on Corregidor in 1942, was born in Walla Walla in 1883. His Army officer father was stationed there during the Nez Perce War. Jonathan Wainwright had moved away while still a youth and had not been back until his visit in November 1945.

Vancouver, Washington

Vancouver provides another illustration of wartime urban growth. During the 1940s this port city across the Columbia River from Portland, Oregon, became the site of major wartime industries including a large Kaiser shipyard. In 1940 Vancouver was home to 18,788; census takers in 1950 counted 41,664 residents. This growth that started during the war continued and by the mid-1990s, incorporation of outlying areas had increased the population to nearly 150,000, a figure surpassing Bellevue as the fourth largest city in the state.

Tri-Cities Area

World War II activities caused the Tri-Cities area to flourish. Richland, Pasco and Kennewick became almost instant cities after January 1943, the date U.S. Army engineers took control of 560 square miles on the banks of the Columbia River in Central Washington. Much of this property was sand dunes and sagebrush but hundreds of acres had been converted to

Walla Walla-born General Jonathan "Skinny" Wainwright was captured by the Japanese early in the war. Freed at war's end, he recuperated briefly in Hawaii and in November 1945 visited the city of his birth. Photo from Whitman College Library.

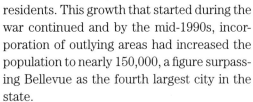

Employee housing was scarce in Hanford, where plutonium was purified for the first atomic bombs. More than 4,000 trailers were moved there to shelter 12,000 new residents, and some families made their own artistic improvements. Washington State Historical Society, Tacoma, Album 51.

Women quickly learned to construct sheet metal ductwork that was commonly used on ships of all types. This photo was taken at the Puget Sound Naval Shipyard in Bremerton. Kitsap Regional Library Image 613.

valuable irrigated orchards and farmlands. Construction crews soon arrived and began building a huge secret installation. Employees were selected carefully and had no idea what the fruits of their labor would be . They were forbidden to talk about their work, and military intelligence personnel monitored phone calls and censored mail.

Security was so effective that although the first atom bomb was successfully tested in New Mexico in July 1945, Hanford employees like the rest of the world, did not learn of the test until after the atom bomb had been dropped on Hiroshima, Japan, three weeks later. Only then did they realize that the plutonium purified at Hanford was an important ingredient in that bomb.

For a time the Tri-Cities region was listed as one of the fastest growing areas in the United States. Much of the growth occurred during the war years and immediately after, a time when activities at the Hanford Atomic Works were intense. Just how rapidly the three small towns added residents is indicated in the population figures below.

	1920	1940	1950	1960	1997
Richland	279	247	22,000	23,548	36,550
Kennewick	1,684	1,918	10,106	14,244	49,090
Pasco	3,362	3,913	10,228	14,522	25,300

Kitsap County

During the war, activity increased dramatically at the Puget Sound Navy Shipyard in Bremerton. The streamlined ferry *Kalakala*

made several trips a day transporting Seattle residents to and from the shipyard at Bremerton. By 1943, the Bremerton Navy yard and 16 private yards around Puget Sound held $700 million in contracts to build 200 ships and were recruiting workers from all over the country. The Keyport Torpedo Station and Bangor Naval Ammunition Depot also added employees. As a result, rural Kitsap County's population increased about 90 percent between 1940 and 1942.

Port Angeles and the Strait of Juan de Fuca

At the outset of the war, the U.S. feared a Japanese invasion and hastily fortified Puget Sound. The Army purchased Port Crescent west of Port Angeles, demolished the few buildings there and replaced them with Camp Hayden. Barracks were built and a powerful searchlight was placed on a peak east of Crescent Bay, allowing personnel stationed there to log the names of passing ships day and night. Concrete bunkers protected the Camp's two 45-foot rifled cannons, the largest ever produced in the United States. These guns were fired just once in practice, then were scrapped after the war.

Port Angeles also was the site of the U.S. Coast Guard Air Station on Ediz Hook. Originally the station was built in 1934 to counter smuggling operations and to provide protection of life and property at sea. The oldest Coast Guard Station on the Pacific Coast, it played a strategic wartime role in the coastal defense plan. The added responsibilities resulted in several temporary buildings at the base. A gunnery school was established to train aerial gunners and local defense forces. During 1942, most of the Coast Guard planes were busy investigating reports of enemy submarines in the Strait of Juan de Fuca and offshore waters. Other planes were used to convoy ships along the coast and to tow targets for the gunnery school. The Air Station was responsible for Coast Guard anti-submarine and rescue activities down to the California border and had aircraft and boats stationed at Neah Bay, Quillayute, Astoria and South Bend.

Everett

Snohomish County during the war attracted many Midwest families, about half of them for work in defense industries. Robert Humphrey, in his book *Everett and Snohomish County*, wrote:

> This was a time of great social change. The new freedom of having a job that paid well was especially appreciated by women. Women readily handled jobs once regarded as being the province of men. I remember the shock of seeing a small five-foot-tall woman driving a huge bus, whipping in and out of traffic, opening and closing doors, making change, asking you to 'Please stand back in the bus,' — and doing it very well. The term 'Rosie the Riveter' was born. It was to let the world know that women had come to join the work force. Never again were they to be ignored.

McNeil Island

McNeil Island Federal Penitentiary was an unusual community to be involved in the war effort, but the inmates there performed important work. They manufactured open-mesh rope cargo nets for the Navy, producing as many as 65 of these 14-foot square nets each day. Prison workers salvaged 85 tons of scrap cable each month from ships damaged at Pearl Harbor. They stripped off the insulation and returned the cable to the navy in reusable condition.

The staff and inmates had skills learned in the prison's long-time boat building and repair program and built three tugboats for the army in Alaska. They also produced foodstuffs in huge quantities. The prison farm grew tons of potatoes and, as a wartime measure, developed a plant that produced up to 6,000 pounds per day of dehydrated potatoes for the army. The large prison cannery turned out immense quantities of fruits and vegetables. The acreage the government acquired for the Hanford Atomic Research Reservation included several orchards. To keep the fruit from being wasted,

a branch prison camp was established at Benton City where, at times of peak harvesting activity, two hundred or more inmates were housed in Quonset huts near the orchards.

The War is Remembered in Small Towns, Too

At Chewelah, south of Colville, slag heaps and rusting buildings mark the remains of a huge vital magnetite plant during the war. Magnetite was needed to produce high-grade steel. Here more than 800 workers refined the ore carried from the mine by aerial tram.

The village of Warden, south of Moses Lake, was proud of its rural electrification until, during the War, airforce aviators mistook the town's bright lights for their practice target on a nearby bombing range and dropped sand-filled bombs. A citizen, realizing what was happening, raced to the powerhouse to turn off the streetlights, while the mayor worriedly called the sheriff. The sheriff, meantime, rang up the commander of the Ephrata Air Base, and offered to surrender the town of Warden.

South of Okanogan is the little town of Malott. During World War II, captured German soldiers were kept in a nearby camp, where under guard they worked in the orchards, filling a need for more manpower. Apparently their P.W. experiences weren't all that bad for, after the war, a few returned to settle there.

In 1940 Oak Harbor on Whidbey Island was a sleepy village of 376. In 1942 the nearby Naval Air Station was dedicated as a rearming facility for patrol planes operating in defense of Puget Sound. Within a few years the population of Oak Harbor had grown to nearly 1,200. After the Naval Station was enlarged in postwar years, the population increased to more than 12,000.

Had the event not been kept secret, a 1945 occurrence near Chimacum, south of Port Townsend, would have made headlines. A 35-

As the war was winding down, armed guards escorted German prisoners of war to the Wenatchee area to help with the apple harvest. "PW" was printed on the prisoners' jackets in large letters, and they were not supposed to communicate with civilians. Seattle P-I Collection, 28266, MOHAI.

foot, bomb-laden balloon, one of more than 9,000 released from Japan, landed harmlessly in the vicinity. The enemy was hoping these air-borne armaments would set American forests ablaze and negatively affect morale. The U.S. strictly censored any information about these balloons lest the Japanese know they were reaching America and release more of them. An estimated 25 of these balloons did travel on prevailing winds across the Pacific Ocean to Washington State, but caused no damage. In Oregon, however, on May 5, 1945, one of these balloons caused casualties. Five young people and the wife of a pastor on a church picnic were killed when they touched a bomb balloon stuck on the lower limb of a tree.

Every city, town and hamlet that existed in Washington State during the war has its memories of local wartime events and activities, especially those near military installations. *The World Almanac and Book of Facts* for 1944 listed the following military posts in Washington. A disclaimer at the outset reads: "The following list does not include all military installations as there are certain installations which are not released for publication." Each installation name is followed by the nearest post office (in parenthesis).

- ARMY BASES: Camp Angeles (Port Townsend); Barnes General Hospital (Vancouver); Fort Casey (Whidbey Island); Fort Ebey (Whidbey Island); Fort Flagler (Marrowstone Island); Fort Hayden (Neah Bay); Fort Lewis (had its own post office); McCaw General Hospital (Walla Walla); Pasco Engineer Depot (Pasco); Seattle Port of Embarkation (Seattle); Seattle Army Service Forces Depot (Seattle); Striped Peaks Military Reservation (Joyce in Clallam County); Fort Townsend (Port Townsend); Vancouver Barracks (Vancouver); Fort Worden (Port Townsend).

- ARMY AIR FORCE STATIONS: Arlington Navy Airport (Arlington); Boeing Field (Seattle); Ellensburg Army Air Field (Ellensburg); Felts Field (Spokane); Geiger Field (Spokane); Gray Field (Fort Lewis); Kitsap County Airport, (Bremerton); McChord Field (had its own post office); Moses Lake Army Air Field (Moses Lake); Mount Vernon Navy Airport (Mt. Vernon); Okanogan Flight Strip (Okanogan); Olympia Army Air Field (Olympia); Paine Field (had its own post office); Port Angeles Army Air Field (Port Angeles); Quillayute Navy Airport (Quillayute,Clallam County); Seven Mile Bombing and Gunnery Range (Spokane); Shelton Navy Airport (Shelton); Spokane Army Air Field (Spokane): Walla Walla Army Air Field (Walla Walla); Fort George Wright (Spokane); Yakima Army Air Base (Yakima).

- NAVY SHORE ESTABLISHMENTS: Puget Sound Navy Yard (Bremerton); Navy Station (Manchester, Kitsap County); Sand Point Naval Air Station (Seattle, with auxiliary fields in Shelton, Mount Vernon, Arlington and Quillayute).

Not included in the list were several newer facilities such as the Whidbey Island Naval Air Station and the Hanford Atomic Works in Central Washington.

The War Effort Touched Every Business

The war effort touched every business in Washington State. This fact is demonstrated in the following few examples selected from company histories. The Boeing Airplane Company, Pacific Car and Foundry, the shipyards, and other major producers of war materials are mentioned often in the monthly reports of wartime events that make up the next chapters. The excerpts that follow were selected to indicate how the war affected diverse businesses, including small ones, during those years.

Longview Fibre Company

This pulp and paper mill produced many products for the war effort. Perhaps their best known container was what they called "Victory

Boxes." Composed of 5-ply solid-fiber paperboard that was asphalt laminated to resist water and other rigors of war use, Victory Boxes delighted the soldiers in the South Pacific who could hardly believe how hardy they were. During assaults on South Pacific islands, these supply boxes were often tossed into the surf from landing craft so they could float ashore on the tide. After this saltwater dunking, the boxes then smoldered in the hot sun until the beach was secured and forces moved inland. Through all this mistreatment—soaking in salt water, dry heat, stacking, and rough handling, the Longfibre containers stayed intact, protecting vital foods and other items needed by the troops.

Longview Fibre also developed other shipping containers such as waxed lettuce-crate liners, waxed butter-cube bags and various fiber wrappings. Their containers were used for "passing the ammunition" to front line gunners, and armed forces sleeping bags were packaged in their corrugated boxes. The boxes met unprecedented government specifications that required bursting strength of 750 pounds per square inch when dry and 500 pounds after being immersed in water for 24 hours. The company produced thousands of cases of paper towels for the Army and Navy, aircraft plants, shipyards and medical supply depots. Scores of different types of bags were utilized during the war for widely diversified uses including the protection of powder for munitions and, packing dry ice.

Various other wartime efforts were initiated at Longview including emphasis on salvaging critical materials such as bronze, brass, steel and felt from the scrap yard.

Recycling Became a Big Business

During the war years scarcities were a fact of life, in part because the German submarine attacks on Atlantic convoys interrupted the supply of raw materials such as tin and aluminum, and Japanese advancements cut off supplies of rubber and other raw materials from the South Pacific. Copper was in such short supply that the government began issuing zinc pennies, reserving copper for shell casings and wiring. Toothpaste and shaving cream tubes in those days included tin or lead in their manufacture and, for a time, an empty tube had to be exchanged when a full one was purchased. Children peeled the tinfoil from cigarette packages and gum wrappers and molded it into rolls to be deposited in school collection barrels.

An average of nearly 30 million tons of scrap metal was consumed each year at steel foundries. Tin was so important to the war effort that the War Production Board urged all Americans to rinse out used cans, flatten them, and turn them in for recycling.

The War Production Board salvage chief complimented Washington State in June 1943 for its outstanding salvage campaign. During a meeting with the Seattle recycle committee headed by Leo Weisfield, he said that Washington led the nation in the total amount as well as per capita in the collecting of nylon and silk for the war effort and also in the amount of scrap metal recycled.

The late Josie Razore in 1992 reminisced about the recycling business. His first garbage contract was in Bellingham in 1928 and he received the garbage collection contract in Seattle in 1938, and later expanded to the suburbs. During the war his company, Rabanco, was involved with the recycling of usable

Early in the war, aluminum was in short supply and scrap metal was collected. Here on Seattle's University Street in front of the Olympic Hotel a sign over the repository reads: "Over the Top! Aluminum round-up exceeds quota! 35,000 pounds in this corral alone. Enough to build 5 fighter planes!" Seattle P-I Collection, 28148, MOHAI.

discards and developed into one of the largest privately held disposal companies in the U.S. Today, metals, glass and other reusable materials are collected much as they were during the war.

Nordstrom Shoe Company

After war was declared, prices were frozen and business assumed a new complexion. For example, Elmer Nordstrom wrote in his book, *The Winning Team*:

> The Nordstrom Company, then exclusively in the shoe business, could sell as many shoes as were obtainable. The problem was their scarcity and the fact they were rationed. Customers paid ration stamps along with cash for shoes. The stamps were deposited in the bank until more shoes were ordered. Leather was scarce because of military needs, forcing manufacturers to use rubber soles on all civilian shoes. Wingtips, which required extra leather, were not made during the war. The trick was to travel the country, usually by train to find shoes for Nordstrom to sell.

The Coolidge Propeller Company

During the early years of the war, Coolidge Propeller was supplying 14 shipyards with urgent production schedules. Its 1937 work force of seven had increased to 60 by 1941. Fred Dobbs, aware of the painstaking process of preparing molds, decided to find an easier, faster way. He developed the hinged foundry flask which could cast 15 to 20 propellers from a single mold. During the war years he invented a hydraulic pitching and adjusting machine with which to alter pitch and repair blades. He patented a hydraulic positioning and balancing machine which eliminated the inefficient method of laboriously balancing heavy propellers. All of these innovations sped the process of launching the many ships being built in local yards.

People's National Bank

In 1937 People's Bank and Trust Company became known as People's National Bank of Washington, and two years later had nine outlets. During the war, more than 70 of the bank's 300 employees served in the armed forces. Mostly women were hired to replace them. Joshua Green, the long-time president, noted that they "not only proved to be efficient and faithful workers, they added beauty and attractiveness." When the war ended, returning veterans were reinstated in positions for which they were best qualified, with salary increases equal to those they would have received had their employment at the bank not been interrupted.

Fisher Flouring Mill Company and KOMO Radio

In 1942, Kenneth Fisher, then in charge of grocery product sales, came across a flaked cereal in the mill laboratory that he liked. He gave the product a market test and found that customers also liked it. In 1943, the new hot cereal hit the market with a free colored war map of the Far East given as a premium. It so happened that on launch day, General MacArthur landed in Lingayen Gulf. Both the map and Zoom cereal were immediately successful.

The Fisher's radio station KOMO had been on the air since 1926. In 1933, they leased KJR from the National Broadcasting Company and purchased it in 1941. Thus, the Fisher companies operated two of Seattle's major radio stations to which thousands tuned each day for war news.

Continental, Inc.

This company began as a mortgage and loan operation in the 1920s and had grown to where, during World War II, it played a major role in providing funding for housing in the war-crowded Puget Sound area.

By the time the U.S. entered World War II, the depression was fast sinking beneath a flood of defense orders and war workers were streaming into the area to fill jobs at the shipyards, Boeing, the Port of Seattle, and elsewhere. Of the 48 states, Washington experienced the second greatest percentage population gain during the war years.

After war was declared, the government placed restrictions on construction. Certain materials were designated "essential" to the war effort, and this stopped most civilian building activity except in those areas designated as war production centers. Seattle, home to several major defense contractors, was allowed considerable wartime housing construction. Continental worked with four contractors to build 50 family residences on Columbia Ridge atop Beacon Hill. By 1944, Continental ranked as third largest among King County mortgage institutions and that year placed more than $5 million in mortgages.

W. Walter Williams, President of Continental, during the war years, served as Chairman of the Washington State Defense Counsel and was honored as Seattle's First Citizen in 1945.

General Construction

The General Construction Company had been busy during the Depression years constructing dams and bridges, many of them in the Northwest. During the war years, General Construction became involved in building ships in the Northwest and in Texas with such partners as the South Portland Shipbuilding Corporation, Houston Shipbuilding Corporation and the Oregon Shipbuilding Corporation, where J .A. McEachern was president and Edgar Kaiser, Executive Vice President. Henry J. Kaiser wrote the following statement:

> We and the McEacherns were in competing camps for several years. Then, during the building of Bonneville Dam, our respective groups bid for and each got parts of the same job. This threw us together. We worked side by side, learning about e ach other, and it resulted in respect and friendship. Later the McEacherns also joined us as one of the founding stockholders of Kaiser Aluminum.

In December 1941, General Construction started building Pier B in Seattle for the U.S. Army and in February 1942 signed a contract to build a large dry dock at the Bremerton Navy Yard. The next year the Navy had them construct a huge floating wooden dry dock, the largest ever built. In 1944, General Construction was engaged to build a rail line between Bremerton and Shelton.

Lumber Businesses

James Stevens in his book *Green Power* wrote:

> World War II, with its enormous demands for cantonments, shipyards and other military construction, made business for even the most 'haywire' sawmill. Overcutting on private timberland was a patriotic duty. Hundreds of thousands of acres of accessible young forest growth were sacrificed to war needs for lumber in the years 1940-45.

The history of Pope and Talbot during the war in many ways sums up the situation with all mill companies. Edwin Coman and Helen Gibbs, authors of *Time, Tide and Timber*, the story of that company, wrote:

> If the shipping arm of Pope & Talbot was taxed to the limit by the war effort, lumber was nevertheless a vital commodity in the forties and the company's mills therefore ran at peak capacity for the duration. The company's lumber appeared all over the South Pacific... Over 60 percent of the Port Gamble production from 1940 to 1945 — 150 million feet — went into the construction of three naval housing projects at Bremerton, Washington. At the same time, the St. Helens mill in Oregon shipped 30 million feet of lumber to what were to be the atomic bomb plants in Richland and Hanford, Washington.

Pacific Car and Foundry

PACCAR received defense contracts beginning in 1940. The first was a joint venture with Lake Washington Shipyards to build flotation devices for use with anti-submarine nets spread across Puget Sound and to produce six small seaplane tenders. A few weeks later, the Navy ordered 15 steel barges. Then Pacific

During the war, Pacific Car and Foundry manufactured Sherman tanks at its Renton plant and developed a vehicle to recover damaged tanks from battlefields. They also produced tractors, cranes, trucks and logging equipment, all vital to the war effort. This August 1943 photo did not appear in the newspaper, perhaps for security reasons. Seattle P-I Collection, 86.5.6759.4, MOHAI.

Car's neighbor, the Boeing Airplane Company, hired it as a sub-contractor to fabricate aluminum wing spars for B-17s.

Next came an order for General Sherman M4-A1 tanks. It took some doing to begin production of these large tanks in the small foundry. However, the men on the production line were able to switch from the manufacture of heavy railway cars to tanks without too much difficulty. The first Sherman tank was delivered to Army Ordnance in May 1942. The letter of acceptance called it "the very best that had been at the Proving Center." The initial success resulted in the government building a modern foundry that allowed Pacific Car to cast heavy tank hulls and turrets. When finished in 1943 this was the largest electric steel furnace foundry in the U.S. In all, Pacific Car produced 926 Sherman tanks.

In 1943 the company was awarded a contract to produce a tank recovery vehicle, the M-26 truck tractor, for the Army. Until this vehicle was produced, there was no adequate way to recover tanks that were disabled on the battlefield. However, the government had classified Seattle as a critical labor area and demanded the company move to a new site to manufacture the M-26. PACCAR found a location on the fairgrounds at Billings, Montana, and established an assembly line there. They turned out a total of 1,372 of these tank recovery vehicles at Billings, and also used the site to rehabilitate hundreds of trucks needed in the war effort.

Paul and William Pigott, Jr. also entered the shipyard business. In 1942 they capitalized the Everett Pacific Company and transformed a stretch of tidal wasteland into a major shipbuilding facility. First they built an 18,000-ton floating dry dock and then began filling a contract for 10 net layers. The Bureau of Ships ordered 51 auxiliary vessels including barrack ships, cargo barges and steel harbor tugs, and by the beginning of 1944, the Everett yard had completed nearly $50 million in U.S. Navy contracts and employed 5,500, about one-fourth of them women. Pacific Car and Foundry purchased all of the Everett Pacific stock in 1944.

Near the end of 1944, Pacific Car bought controlling stock in Kenworth Motor Truck Corporation. Kenworth was turning out trucks and wreckers when the War Department declared Seattle a critical labor area and asked Kenworth to move to some site where employees would be readily available. They quickly moved part of the production to Yakima. During 1944 Kenworth employed 800 workers, including 507 in Seattle, 415 of them women. Kenworth employees turned out 3,000 assemblies and subassemblies for B-17 and B-29 bombers during the war and in 1944 Kenworth manufactured 716 vehicles for the military and 217 for commercial use. In March 1945, with the conflict in Europe nearing its climax, the government began canceling contracts, and PACCAR started planning for peacetime production.

Puget Power

For Puget Power the outset of World War II brought a truce in the war with consumer-owned utilities such as Seattle City Light. Puget Power, like other companies, struggled to maintain its work force. Of the 577 Puget Power employees called into military service, more than 50 were wounded and 13 killed. As the war progressed, more women were hired and performed well in positions previously held only by men.

American Telephone and Telegraph Co.

Long distance telephone calling first became common during World War II. With millions of men and women in the armed services, telephoning was a way to keep in touch with loved ones during those turbulent years. Government needs for long-distance phone circuits also escalated. As a result, the armed services and government were given priority over civilian businesses and residential callers.

Between 1939 and 1945 the number of interstate long-distance calls tripled. In 1943 the volume was 50 million calls higher than anticipated. Phone subscribers were asked to limit all calls to a five-minute maximum and to keep long-distance lines clear from 7 a.m. to 10 p.m. The telephone network was straining to meet the demand, despite the fact that during the war years only about half of the homes had telephones. In those days before direct dialing, long distance calls required speaking with an operator who then contacted another distant operator to complete the call. In 1945, the Bell System employed 171,439 operators who, on average, completed about 600,000 long-distance calls each day.

By V-J Day, the telephone company had a backlog of more than two million applications for telephone service. The production facilities of Western Electric switched from producing wartime gear such as radar systems, anti-aircraft gun electronic aimers and a variety of special telephone systems for battlefield equipment, and began producing telephones, transmission equipment and switches to provide the service the public demanded.

Legal Firms

Lawers also were involved in the war effort. The firm known presently as Gordon, Thomas, Honeywell, Malanca, Peterson and Daheim existed as four independent small Tacoma law offices during the war years. While the men

involved were too old for service in the active forces, they were actively engaged in the war effort. Some served on Selective Service Boards, others represented draftees appearing before those boards, and one worked as personnel director at Todd Pacific Shipyards where more than 28,000 employees turned out more than 50 aircraft carriers during the war. Other lawyers headed up local war bond drives and were active in supervising the entertainment facilities for thousands of service personnel stationed at McChord Air Field and Fort Lewis, and several volunteered to assist Army personnel at both bases with their legal problems.

The Perkins Coie Law Partnership during the war years was known as Todd, Holman, Sprague & Allen. Members of the firm were involved in the war effort in many ways. For example, William M. (Bill) Allen served as general counsel for The Boeing Company. As a result the law firm was involved in all aspects of Boeing's wartime roles. The lawyers prepared and negotiated contracts to acquire land for plant expansion, and arranged bank loans to acquire new machinery and equipment needed to produce aircraft for the U.S. and its allies. License agreements were negotiated with other aircraft manufacturers for second source

After serving overseas, service men and women arriving in the U.S. flocked to available telephones to call home. These booths on a New York City pier were typical of those reserved for members of the armed forces. AT&T Archives.

production of B-17 Flying Fortresses and B-29 Superfortresses. Three days after the war with Japan terminated, William M. Allen was elected president of the Boeing Company and directed the redeployment of company assets and personnel, thereby laying the foundation for The Boeing Company we know today.

Frank Holman served as chairman of the Alien Enemy Hearing Board for the Western District of Washington. Elmer Todd withdrew from the firm in 1942 to become publisher of *The Seattle Times*. Several members of the firm accepted commissions in the military. Lowell Mickelwait joined the Army Air Corps, DeForest Perkins and Calhoun Shorts the Navy, Francis Holman, Thomas Todd and John Blair, the Army.

Farm Organizations

The Yakima Fruit Growers Association published the *Big Y Bulletin* during the war and in it described some of the wartime activities in the valley. Here are a few quotes from the February-March 1942 edition.

> Without a doubt, the Yakima Valley is one of the greatest fruit producing areas in the world. And production from Yakima farms — of commodities other than fruits — are also of vital importance to the state and nation . . .The new 1942 goals call for the greatest production in the history of American agriculture, and for putting every acre of land, every hour of labor, and every bit of farm machinery, fertilizer, and other supplies to use which will best serve the nation's needs. The coming production season is the most crucial in the history of American agriculture.

> What is Yakima Valley's place in this all-out program to win the war? What part will it play? Did you know that the army, navy and marine corps have already been utilizing thousands of tons of Yakima canned and dried fruits, and the lend-lease program has bought heavily of the 1940 and 1941 production for shipment to Britain? . . . The processed fruit crops of Yakima County, as well as the berry pack from Western Washington counties constitutes an item in

feeding our military forces that cannot be underestimated. Troops can do very well for awhile on "goldfish and hardtack," or on a better diet of meats, starches, and some vegetables. But most dietitians will agree that to put the real fighting edge on our troops in the field or in camp, the addition of fruit to the daily ration is highly important. The war emergency places Yakima horticulture in position to do a definite service for the nation.

Examples of the war's effect on businesses could continue for pages. Every business, no matter how small, was involved in the effort to win the victory.

This introductory chapter concludes with a quote from a 1942 *National Geographic Magazine* article titled "Wartime in the Pacific Northwest." The author, Frederick Simpich, Sr., explains in an introductory sentence that the article had been censored and included no details that might be helpful to the enemy.

> This Pacific Northwest, by the Great Circle route through the Aleutians, is only about 4,700 miles from Tokyo. . . . Portland, Seattle, Tacoma, Vancouver are all exposed to the risk of air raids. But now their all-out defense works, and grim evidence of aggressive warfare meets you at every turn . . . New bombers, pursuit planes, merchant ships, long barges for landing invasion troops, mine sweepers and mine layers; destroyers, seaplane tenders, crash boats, carriers and transports made by converting freighters; uniforms, sleeping bags by the thousands, knockdown houses for use in Alaska; skis, dog sleds and dog harness; gas mask fillers, incendiary bomb casings; cartridge clips, preserved foods, propellers, marine steering engines by hundreds — these are but a few of the things now made here....

> Today this fairly new country that used to thrive on fish, fruit and fresh-cut lumber sees its former ways of life utterly upset. By tens of thousands men have quit what they were doing yesterday and now hold jobs in the new mushroom wartime shops. . . . For Seattle, the Klondike gold rush itself was a quiet, sleepy event compared with today's unparalleled excitement.

THE WAR YEARS

A Chronicle of Washington State in World War II

By James R. Warren

CHAPTER ONE

Washington Goes to War

December 7, 1941–December 31, 1942

On July 9, 1942, these Washington State men were photographed as they voiced the Navy oath at Seattle's newly built Victory Square. Service personnel, World War I veterans, and several hundred family members and friends attended the event. Seattle P-I Collection, 28251, MOHAI.

We who experienced those war years may now be considered "old folks," but our recollections of those memorable days are still with us, many of them painful, many of them proud, and all in full color. Those were emotional years for all Americans.

We hope the information that follows will elicit a small measure of those same emotions in the reader, for to truly understand the war, one must sense the sentiments of the time.

Organizing Civil Defenses in Washington State

After Pearl Harbor, the development of a defense against possible air attack received highest priority. Lookout stations situated all along the coast were manned 24 hours a day by volunteer spotters scanning the skies for enemy aircraft. Coast Guard and Navy ships and planes, members of the State National Guard, and citizens donating private pleasure craft patrolled the Washington coast. The Defense Command indicated that Puget Sound and the Grays Harbor areas were the most likely sites for an enemy attack.

The day after Pearl Harbor, coastal cities were ordered blacked out and radio stations were silenced during certain hours to prevent enemy planes and ships from following the lights and radio signals to locate populated areas. A couple of days later, the 2nd Interceptor Command shifted the start of the blackout time back from midnight to 1:30 a.m. and motorists were delighted to hear they would be permitted to use normal headlights after 5 a.m. The two days of driving to work in near total darkness had resulted in several accidents. On December 12 the military eased the situation even more by announcing that blackouts and radio silences would be necessary only in cases of emergency. Information of any possible attack would be aired on all radio stations broadcasting at the time.

Several months earlier, Seattle had ordered air raid sirens in sufficient quantity to install one in each neighborhood, but none arrived until weeks after the country was at war. Meantime, police and fire sirens were to be used as the air raid warning system.

Several false alarms scared residents in those early days of the war. Five days after Pearl Harbor, the Navy reported it had followed up on rumors of arrows of fire in burning fields that pointed to Seattle but no such flames were located. They also checked reports of Japanese warships in the Strait of Juan de Fuca but sighted only Canadian and U.S. vessels in those waters.

Industry Moves to Full War Schedules

As New Year's Day, 1942, approached, most of the state's war industries announced that their employees had agreed to work a full schedule on the holiday.

During the war years, government censorship prevented publication of industry production statistics. In December, however, with the war only a few weeks old, newspapers frequently mentioned increases in the state's manufacturing output. Puget Sound shipyards, they noted with some pride, had 161 vessels under construction. The contracts were reported to be worth $400 million, not counting the additional millions used to enlarge several of the shipyards.

- The Puget Sound Navy Yard in Bremerton held contracts worth $75 million for eight destroyers, four seaplane derricks, one submarine tender, four seaplane tenders, and six escort vessels.

- Seattle-Tacoma Shipbuilding Corporation was building 25 Navy destroyers worth $172 million. Associated Shipbuilders of Seattle was producing four Navy seaplane tenders worth $18 million, six Navy wooden minesweepers worth $1,980,000, and a Navy self-propelled lighter worth $350,000.

- Tacoma Boatbuilding Corporation, J. M. Martinac Shipbuilding of Tacoma, Ballard Marine Railway, and Bellingham Marine Railway and Boatbuilding each held $1,350,000 contracts to construct four 135-foot minesweepers.

- Birchfield Boiler Company of Tacoma was building a 65-foot Coast Guard tender and

Headlines:
December 1941

December 7:
JAPAN ATTACKS PEARL HARBOR, HAWAII

December 8:
JAPAN INVADES PHILIPPINE ISLANDS

December 10:
JAPAN CAPTURES ISLAND OF GUAM

December 23:
AMERICANS ON WAKE ISLAND SURRENDER TO JAPANESE

December 25:
BRITISH SURRENDER HONGKONG TO JAPANESE

*Headlines:
January 1942*

January 11:
JAPANESE INVADE DUTCH
EAST INDIES

January 20:
HITLER APPROVES "FINAL
SOLUTION" TO EXTERMINATE
THE JEWS

six 100-foot tugs for the Marine Corps at a cost of $1,800,000.

- Seattle Shipbuilding and Dry Dock Company had four 135-foot Navy minesweepers under construction at a cost of $1,328,000. They also were building a $60,000 dredge for the Army Engineers.

- Lake Washington Shipyard in Houghton had agreed to produce four Navy submarine net tenders for $1,916,000, a Coast and Geodetic Survey ship for $1,279,000, and six Navy seaplane tenders for $2,700,000.

- Lake Union Dry Dock and Machine Works had signed contracts to build six 135-foot Navy minesweepers for $1,992,000.

- Winslow Marine Railway and Shipbuilding had agreements to build four steel navy minesweepers for $7,600,000.

- Western Boat Building of Tacoma had accepted a $670,000 contract to produce two 135-foot mine sweepers.

- Several smaller Seattle yards including Sagstad Shipyards, N. J. Blanchard Boat Company, and Shain Manufacturing Company, had signed smaller contracts.

According to the maritime publication, *The Log,* by December 1, 1941, sixteen Puget Sound plants had signed contracts to build 138 vessels at a cost of $366,716,000. These and other state shipyards would sign additional contracts as the war effort proceeded.

January 1942

Strengthening Civil Defense

Major Willard A. Johnston, speaking to air-raid wardens, policemen, firemen and other key persons in civil defense, on January 2 explained that the anti-aircraft guns being installed in the Puget Sound region did not indicate the area was safe from enemy bombers. He added, "If we have air raids now, they will be token raids carried out at long distance just because the Japanese want to show us they can do it. But if the outer defenses — the Philippines, Hawaii and Alaska fall, then the war might well come closer to this coast." He also mentioned that the anti-aircraft guns were being located to protect specific industrial plants.

State Civilian Defense Chief W. Walter Williams, President of Seattle's Continental, Inc., was a busy man. *The Seattle Times* reported him to be on the way to the nation's capital, his fourth trip east in the seven months since his appointment. On this trip he was scheduled to meet with Mrs. Eleanor Roosevelt, the assistant director of civilian defense efforts; Charles F. Palmer, a defense housing coordinator; and with Fred Catlett, a former Seattle businessman who worked with the

Early in the war as enemy invasions and bombing raids were believed possible, eight Civil Defense Rescue Service vehicles were acquired by Seattle. In this 1942 photo, they are lined up in front of the County-City Building. MOHAI, 7298.

Barrage balloons and smoke screens were not unusual sights on Puget Sound during the war. This photo was taken near Bremerton. Kitsap Regional Library, 1946.

Federal Home Loan Bank. He would also inquire as to what action had been taken on the House bill to appropriate $100 million for purchase of fire-fighting equipment, gas masks and helmets for use in defense areas.

While he was away, some Seattle north-end residents received a scare. Before families in the Crown Hill and Blue Ridge neighborhoods were alerted that an air raid siren was being installed, it was tested. The unfamiliar loud moan frightened nearby families, sent children crying to their mothers, and caused dogs to howl. Within a week, 17 sirens were in working order in Seattle and five more were soon activated. All during the war years, they were tested each day exactly at noon, and residents soon were setting their clocks by these sirens.

Barrage Balloons

Barrage balloons were a wartime addition to the Puget Sound skyline. Shortly after Pearl Harbor, Army engineers began asking certain householders living on hills near major war equipment factories if they would lease ground to the army "for the duration." Once approval was received, graders leveled sites for the equipment that would control the balloons. Army trucks rumbled through the streets carrying troops and equipment and soon the

huge rubber whales rose silently into the sky firmly tethered to earth by thin steel cables intended to slice the wings off any low flying attacking enemy planes. The troops operating the gas-filled behemoths lived in tents beneath the balloons. Most of these men happened to be from Brooklyn and appreciated the friendliness of the Northwest families in whose yards they lived. The families frequently provided cookies and coffee for the soldiers, and perhaps more importantly, bathing facilities.

A June 1942 windstorm ripped several of the huge balloons from their moorings and their metal cables were dragged across several power lines, disrupting electric service in King and Kitsap counties.

Transportation

Transportation facilities, so vital in time of war, received immediate attention after the U.S. became involved in the conflict. One of the first objectives in Washington State was to complete the Stevens Pass Highway east from Gold Bar to the summit and west to Everett and Bothell. This major artery had remained unfinished during the Depression years, but now it became a necessity in case enemy attacks forced families living in the coastal areas to quickly evacuate inland. It was also needed as a military route to potential battle zones and as a way to transport Eastern Washington produce to port cities for shipment.

Air travel, used by few Americans previous to this time, increased rapidly during the early months of the war. On January 9, 1942, the government temporarily reserved Boeing Field for Army use, forcing all commercial flights to use the Air Force's new Paine Field near Everett. Twenty days later, the federal government sent word it might increase its $1 million allotment for an air terminal in the Seattle metropolitan area. Two sites were under consideration, one between Lake Sammamish and Lake Washington and the other near Bow Lake on the hill south of Seattle. Tacoma and Seattle appeared to be near an agreement to jointly operate the air terminal. Though the airport, now called Sea-Tac, was not completed until 1949, some runways were in use earlier.

The Army Transport Service in Seattle expanded rapidly early in the war. In January 1941, the total staff consisted of two Army officers and eight civilians. A year later the shore staff consisted of 24 commissioned officers and 330 civilian personnel. In addition, Army transports and chartered ships based in Seattle employed 583 crewmen, and local stevedores busily loaded vessels 24-hours a day.

The Office of Production Management (OPM) made several difficult decisions in January 1942. They prohibited the sale of new automobiles and trucks to civilians. OPM explained that "the job now is to put the country's Army on wheels and to give them guns, planes, and tanks to fight with." Furthermore the government reserved for the war effort the 450,000 passenger cars in dealers' inventories. Local auto dealers predicted this drastic curtailment of their businesses would force staff reductions.

Funding the War

President Roosevelt received enthusiastic support from Congress when he presented a program calling for half the national income to be dedicated to the war effort. Democrats and Republicans alike agreed Congress would honor every qualified request for funds to strengthen the nation's fighting power. They also agreed that higher taxes were necessary and that heavy borrowing against the nation's credit would continue.

The Boeing Airplane Company

The Boeing Company received national attention early in 1942 after announcing its production of B-17 bombers had increased by 70 percent. The bombers already were recognized as "the deadliest offensive aerial weapon in America's arsenal." President Philip G. Johnson explained that the company was producing at top speed, 24 hours a day, seven days a week, including every holiday. Chief of the Air Corps, General George C. Kenney, sent him a telegram that read: "The Boeing Company has responded to the emergency in an unparalleled manner and each and every man in the organization is to be congratulated on his part in increasing the plant's output." A month later, the General probably would have said "every man and woman" deserves to be congratulated, for by then, many women had been hired.

Early in the war the Seattle area was fearful of enemy air attacks. What appears from the air to be a residential neighborhood was actually camouflage over the Boeing's Seattle B-17 bomber factory. Boeing Management Co.

Few Draft Exemptions Allowed

On January 8 the office of the Undersecretary of War told draft and occupational board advisers that the day was past when employers could compete with the Army for physically fit men. He told them it was their responsibility, aided by government training programs, to help fill industry positions with those not eligible for the draft. "Eventually the only labor supply will be women," he concluded. Two weeks later the Army began seeking 12,000 women to work as telephone operators, clerks, machine operators, welfare workers, cooks, laundresses and air-raid wardens. An Army spokesman noted that some women might be sent to American defense outposts overseas, but that subject was still under discussion.

Late in January, nearly two months after Pearl Harbor, statistics indicated that Seattle and Tacoma business income had increased by more than 50 percent during 1941, a larger increase than in most other U.S. cities. Projections for 1942 showed that even greater increases could be expected.

Wartime Shortages

The war effort immediately began causing shortages and serious consideration of rationing. In late January the Retail Grocers' Association reported that stores were limiting purchases of sugar to five and ten pound sacks and some stores had sold all they had in stock. The Office of Price Administration warned that continued heavy runs on sugar supplies would compel the government to begin rationing within a month. Washington State's production of sugar beets helped counter the shortage by increasing the harvest in 1942. The U and I Sugar Company plant in Toppenish, one of the largest in the west, processed 225,000 tons of beets into 660,000 hundred-pound sacks of sugar and was signing up additional beet farm acreage for 1943.

Auto tires were in limited supply after Japanese advances in the South Pacific cut the raw rubber supply routes. Highest priority for tires went to the armed services, forcing tire

rationing to begin early in January. Governor Arthur B. Langlie appointed members to serve on 111 state boards that decided which citizens had priority in purchasing the 4,919 new tires allotted to the state for the month of January. Later, the government also rationed re-treads. Tires became so valuable that citizens were advised to keep them in safe storage. Even so, many were stolen, including 12 tires taken by thieves from a service station on Broadway in Seattle.

The shortage of rubber threatened to limit production of girdles and corsets, but on January 25 the War Production Board relented and released limited amounts of Lastex for production of foundation garments.

Nearly every town and city on Puget Sound with a pier became involved in wartime shipping. This 1942 photo shows the Mukilteo munitions pier lined with explosives. MOHAI, 830.

Early in the war, after the enemy blocked raw rubber supplies from the South Pacific, women's foundation garments were in short supply. After methods of producing synthetic rubber were discovered, a Frederick and Nelson show widow proudly displayed new products, an indication the shortage was ending. Pemco, Webster-Stevens Collection, MOHAI.

*Headlines:
February 1942*

February 9:
TO BOOST WAR PRODUCTION,
U.S. ADOPTS DAYLIGHT
SAVING TIME

February 13:
GERMANS DECIDE AGAINST
TRYING TO INVADE ENGLAND

February 15:
THE JAPANESE CAPTURE
SINGAPORE

Housing

During January additional government housing became available. More than 1,500 low-income families moved into Seattle's Yesler Terrace and 150 families of Naval enlisted men occupied Navy housing near Sand Point Air Station. Facilities to house 3,618 additional Seattle families were under construction. To the south in Vancouver, Washington, the government was building 6,000 homes for shipyard workers and in Tacoma $22 million was provided to fund 1,020 new housing units for war workers. At Ephrata, 100 family units, 30 apartments for couples, and 375 dormitory rooms were under construction.

The War Production Board halted all private construction jobs costing more than $500, except for remodeling of family homes to provide housing for war workers. Across the state thousands of basements, attics and garages were converted and rented to newcomers employed in war industries.

Sometimes the war caused residents to lose their homes. Early in 1942, more than 100 residents living in the Smith Cove area were evicted from houses built on property owned by the Northern Pacific Railroad. The Navy needed the space for enlarging Piers 90 and 91.

Even businesses were sometimes forced to move. The Seattle Stock Exchange, Grain Exchange and Merchants' Exchange were forced out of the Exchange Building when the 13th Naval District took it over to house their headquarters.

With housing increasingly scarce, National Price Administrator Leon Henderson took action to curb inflationary rentals in boomtowns. Communities across the country were placed on 60-day notice to reduce all rents to government recommended levels.

February 1942

Effects of the Wartime Draft

The draft rapidly removed young men from the hometown scene. By 1942, so many had been inducted that training camps were full. Later draftees were told that a short wait was necessary before they could be called to active service.

Most young Washington State men were anxious to serve their country. Those physically and mentally qualified, when called to active duty, were given 10 days to close their private affairs. On the appointed day, in groups of 100 or so, they gathered at designated places, each with a small suitcase of personal belongings and usually with family members or friends along to say goodbye. They boarded trains or buses bound for a nearby facility where they were sworn into the service. Many in Washington State were inducted into the Army at Fort Lewis, where they learned to make a cot, to salute properly, and were provided their first uniforms. Within a few days they were on their way to a training facility, usually in some distant state. For many of these young men, having been raised during the Depression, this was their first journey to a distant place.

At training camps, the recruits quickly lost their civilian identities. They memorized their personal serial numbers, learned to march at a cadence of 128 steps per minute, practiced the manual of arms with real rifles, and discovered that kitchen police (KP) was a common experience for privates. Major emphasis was on bodybuilding and on developing mental strengths needed in combat. After a month or two of exhaustive basic training, most inductees began hoping the war would end quickly so they could return home and continue with their lives. Many of the men called to active duty early in the war, if they survived combat, would spend four years in the service.

Fearing the country's food supplies would suffer if farm youth were conscripted, Senators from the mid-west promoted deferments for essential farm laborers. At the same time General Hershey, the officer in charge of the draft, was criticized by many for exempting motion picture actors, directors, and others in that industry. He argued that movies were an essential morale building activity. Nonetheless, several top male stars, including James Stewart, volunteered to serve in the armed services.

Victory Gardens helped combat wartime food shortages. Ballard High School students and faculty tilled this large Seattle garden tract in 1940. Seattle P-I Collection, 28244, MOHAI.

Volunteers

Civilian volunteers played an increasingly important role in wartime Washington State. Hundreds of women graduated from the six-week training program to become Red Cross Volunteer Nurses' Aides. They served without pay, supplementing the work of professional nurses who were being shifted to Army and Navy hospitals. The Seattle-King County Red Cross also involved hundreds of volunteer donors to provide blood plasma for emergency use in case of local disaster.

Volunteers continued to occupy aircraft observation posts scattered across the state. The Army, after declaring this a vital activity, assumed control of the effort. During the daytime, when most men were working, women filled in as observers. In many cases, observation posts were located in homes, stores, or business buildings. Some were comfortable, including one in a penthouse, but most were primitive. The Army made certain that all were heated since the volunteers represented all age groups from high school students to senior citizens.

Other volunteers helped with selective service registration. In February the draft age, originally 21 to 35, was widened to include men from 20 to 44 years of age. Many Japanese Americans, both native-born and foreign-born, anxious to show their patriotism by fighting for the United States, were among the first registrants.

Victory Gardens

All over the state, citizens began planting victory gardens. Seattle Mayor Earl Millikin appointed Ernest W. Campbell, assistant school superintendent, as Chairman of a committee to develop gardening activities. Homegrown foodstuffs became an important part of the wartime food supply.

Business News

Most businesses quickly became involved in the war effort. Leo Weisfield explained how American jewelers produced jewels tiny enough to be used in watches and other instruments vital to war industries. Previously such jewels were produced exclusively in Switzerland.

Headlines: March 1942

March 1:
ALLIED NAVAL SQUADRON NEARLY WIPED OUT IN EFFORTS TO INTERCEPT JAPANESE INVASION FORCE BOUND FOR JAVA

March 7:
JAPANESE CAPTURE RANGOON, BURMA

March 9:
JAPANESE TAKE JAVA AND CAPTURE 100,000 ALLIED TROOPS

March 11:
GENERAL MACARTHUR ESCAPES FROM PHILIPPINES AS JAPANESE CLOSE IN

March 13:
GERMANS CANCEL PLANS TO INVADE ENGLAND BECAUSE OF A LACK OF NAVAL POWER

March 15:
BRITISH SURRENDER SINGAPORE TO THE JAPANESE

March 19:
JAPANESE PLANES ATTACK DARWIN, AUSTRALIA

With wartime production requiring employees to work seven days a week and on holidays, little time remained for recreation. However, all-work-and-no-play schedules caused worker fatigue. To help remedy this, the Chicago-Milwaukee Railroad scheduled a 6 p.m. Wednesday train to transport skiers to Snoqualmie Summit Ski Bowl. This allowed three hours of skiing and a 1 a.m. arrival back in Seattle. Some 200 Boeing employees were among the first to take advantage of this opportunity. Roller skating rinks and movie theaters began staying open from 1 to 5 a.m. to serve those working 4 p.m. to midnight swing shifts.

A Few of the Many Heroes of February

Two Washington State men who joined the Flying Tiger Squadron before Pearl Harbor were among the first American war heroes mentioned by the media, but they were difficult to identify. News dispatches from Burma early in February told of two pilots named Bob who had distinguished themselves in action over Rangoon when their squadron of pursuit planes guarding the Burma Road shot down 11 of 22 Japanese attack planes. No last names were given in the dispatch, but the young wife of one of the "Bobs" lived in Seattle and she recognized her husband, 27-year-old Robert Neale as one of them. She explained that the two Bobs met while students at Washington State College in 1938. The other man, she said, was her husband's best pal, Robert Little of Spokane. Bob Neale soon advanced to squadron leader and raised his number of downed enemy planes to 20.

Later in the month, listings of casualties at Pearl Harbor and of early battles of the war were released by the military. On February 10, the name of James B. Payne was one of the local men mentioned. He was missing in action in an undisclosed combat area. This 38-year-old Warrant Officer had been in the Navy for more than 20 years. He, his wife and daughter were living at Pearl Harbor at the time of the Japanese attack. His family was evacuated home to Seattle while Payne continued on duty. Warrant Officer Payne later was declared dead.

Listed as dead by the Navy Department were: Marines Eugene W. Wade of Seattle, Harold F. Drain of Sedro Woolley, Otto N. Lund of Benge, Richard B. White of Anacortes and Richard P. Jobb of Moclips. The location and cause of death were often not included in early casualty lists for fear such information would aid the enemy in assessing effects of battle. Notice the hometowns listed above; even small communities were feeling the effects of war.

Lieutenant Jack N. Finley, son of a prominent Seattle dentist, was killed when his Army fighter plane collided with another in mid-air in the vicinity of McKenna, southeast of Olympia. The planes were on a routine training flight from McChord Field.

March 1942

Relocating Japanese-American Families

The major local news story of the month concerned the moving of Washington residents of Japanese heritage to inland relocation centers. Since the Pearl Harbor attack, local Japanese, including those born in the U.S., were considered suspect by many of their neighbors. Demands surfaced insisting they be removed from defense areas to sites east of the Rocky Mountains. The Japanese-Americans responded that they did not want to become wards of the government and hoped their racial group could help lead the offensive against the Empire of Japan. But still many white citizens distrusted them.

On Vashon Island, FBI agents and deputy sheriffs searched Japanese homes for short wave radios, firearms and other contraband, but most families had turned in all such items earlier. Only a few white citizens made known their disapproval of government actions that ignored the fact that many of these people were American citizens. Even the comic strips entered the argument when Joe Palooka, who had joined the Army, was shown saluting a young Japanese American soldier. The

On March 30, 1942, an Army truck backed up to a farmhouse on Bainbridge Island to load a Japanese American family and what belongings they could carry with them to relocation camps. Seattle P-I Collection, 28044, MOHAI.

Reverend Thomas Gill, a Catholic priest, declared any evacuation of Japanese Americans should be for military necessity only. Floyd Schmoe of the American Friends Service committee argued that evacuation should be to a nearby site where these people could continue with their occupations.

Among those calling for the evacuation of both alien and native-born Japanese was publisher Miller Freeman and State Attorney General Smith Troy. When queried about immigrants from other Axis countries, Troy replied that Germans and Italians should also be evacuated from defense areas.

On March 12, 1942, news headlines proclaimed that all Japanese would be relocated away from coastal regions. Later in March, the Army ordered a curfew requiring German and Italian aliens and all person of Japanese ancestry, aliens and citizens alike, to remain in their homes between 8 p.m. and 6 a.m. The Japanese living on Bainbridge Island were the first in the state to be registered for evacuation. And once registered they were not allowed

visitors of Japanese extraction unless they were residents of the island.

On March 30, Army trucks moved the first 237 Bainbridge residents off the island. Another 287 had moved of their own volition to eastern sites. As they climbed into Army trucks, the Japanese Americans pointed proudly to their tilled land. Each strawberry field was in order and pea fields were sprouting neat green rows. F.O. Nagatani explained that these families had worked hard to prepare the land for production. "We won't be here to harvest the crops but they will be as good or better than any previous crops. We hope this will aid the war effort."

More than 5,000 of these Japanese Americans were moved to flimsy temporary quarters on the Puyallup Fair Ground's parking lots. They were housed there until more permanent camps were constructed further inland.

Most Japanese Americans complied with the orders without complaint but it was a wrenching experience. Tearful teenagers said goodbye to high school friends. Where one spouse was not of Japanese extraction,

Many of the families left in tears. Here a solemn mother carries her sleeping child toward the ferry that will take them to Seattle, the first step of a long journey. Seattle P-I Collection, 28050, MOHAI.

On March 31, 1942, Soldiers escorted Japanese American families down the Eagledale Dock on Bainbridge Island to the ferry. Note how soldiers helped tote the heavy luggage. Seattle P-I Collection, 28055, MOHAI.

married couples were separated by the relocation. Most families lost the bulk of their belongings since they were restricted to taking only a few suitcases. They were given only a couple of weeks to sell or dispose of possessions they could not carry. Many Nisei businessmen lost their investments. Not one Japanese-American was found guilty of spying or in any way supporting the enemy. Indeed, many of the young males joined the Army 442nd all Japanese American Regiment that became one of the most decorated units of the war. Many men of the 442nd died fighting the Germans in Europe. Other Japanese Americans were lauded for their service as Army and Navy interpreters on the Pacific war front.

After the Japanese were removed from the area, the Civil Control Administration and local Chambers of Commerce scrambled to find manpower to operate their former farms. Even before the last Japanese American farmers were relocated, dozens of stalls were empty in the Pike Place Market because all Japanese Americans were forbidden to enter the central business zone of Seattle. When the last families had departed, a total of 10,600 acres of farmland in Pierce and King Counties were without care until replacements were found. To attract new operators, half a million dollars became available as loans to those assuming the responsibility for the crops. That year the usual early strawberries from California did not arrive because the Japanese Americans there also had

These Nisei families occupied temporary quarters at the Puyallup Fairgrounds for five months during 1942, while internment facilities were built inland. Seattle P-I Collection, 29078, MOHAI.

The all-Japanese American 442nd Battalion earned more awards than any other U.S. unit of the same size, including Medals of Honor, 44 Silver Stars, and 1,000 Purple Hearts. The unit sustained more than 9,000 casualties. Here veterans escort the body of a buddy from Seattle's Buddhist Church after funeral services. Seattle P-I Collection, 28194, MOHAI

As the war continued to draft males, women were hired to fill major positions such as Bremerton crane operator. Kitsap Regional Library, 608.

This photo shows mechanics assembling propeller engines for Boeing Bombers in the Seattle factory early in the war. Seattle P-I Collection, 23926, MOHAI.

been evacuated. Instead berries were imported from Missouri, but customers complained of the price, a then astronomical $7 per 24 one-quart cups. In Bellevue, where the annual Strawberry Festival was a major event, some vegetable and fruit crops were wasted because the Japanese Americans were gone. The call went out for help during both early harvesting and late planting of Bellevue acreage.

Business News of the Month

On March 15, 1942, members of the Seattle machinist Local 79 agreed to work seven days a week at Washington Iron Works, Pacific Car and Foundry, Western Gear and other companies. The agreement provided a 12 percent cost-of-living increase and the same salary shift differentials as in the shipyards — 10 percent extra for the 4 to midnight shift and 15 percent extra for the midnight to 8 a.m. shift.

The Puget Sound Navy Yard sent out a call for 1,000 women to be employed as mechanical learners. They were needed to speed up production and relieve men to serve in the armed forces. The Navy Yard offered the women ratings and classifications for which they had not been eligible in the past. The starting wage was $4 a day and the Navy estimated that eventually this could rise to $10 a day, an appealing income to families that had recently survived the 1930s Depression.

Price controls were in effect and Seattle landlords were warned to reduce their rents to levels of April 1941 or the federal government supervisor from the Office of Price Administration would enforce the law. Landlords violating the act, which Congress had recently passed, could receive a maximum sentence of a year in jail and a fine of $5,000.

Atop Beacon Hill in Seattle, Columbia Ridge, a privately financed upscale housing development was nearing completion. The 207 homes, ranging in price from $4,200 to $4,800, were located south of Jefferson Golf Course on curving streets and irregular-shaped lots. The location, near the Boeing plants, attracted hundreds of potential purchasers to a March 9 open house.

In Seattle's South End, a huge former industrial plant was taken over by the Army Quartermaster Corps. There hundreds of carloads of food, clothing, medical supplies and barracks equipment were warehoused for immediate fulfillment of orders received from military bases. The 1,148 feet long structure covered seven acres. Behind closely guarded gates 1,000 Army and civilian employees kept this Seattle General Army Depot operating day and night.

Smaller Seattle businesses that singly had experienced trouble acquiring war contracts decided to combine their bids. One example: Seattle furniture and textile manufacturers submitted applications to the War Production

Board and began successfully bidding as a pool. The Chamber of Commerce and officers of Seattle's General Depot encouraged such action.

The Boeing Airplane Company in March announced that after years of net losses while the B-17 bomber was being developed, company profits for 1941 were more than $6 million, due in large part to production of those bombers. President P. G. Johnson explained that the company's agreement with the federal government provided for a review of costs after delivery of a certain number of units. In line with this understanding, Boeing advised the government that a substantial downward revision in price could be expected.

While the home folks were prospering, the boys in uniform were missing the gravy train. Army and Navy inductees were paid $21 a month minus $2.85 for laundry and about $3 for dry cleaning. The government's induction gift of a razor, five blades, a toothbrush and toothpaste was one-time only. After that, inductees paid for their own toilet articles. Also, a quarter dollar a month was deducted for up-keep of Old Soldiers' Homes. The few dollars remaining paid for admission to view a few movies in the base theater, bought a few snacks and tobacco at the PX and paid bus fare for a visit to the nearest town. Congress began discussions about perhaps doubling the private's pay to $42 and raising officers' stipends also. Republican Senator Gurney of North Dakota was against such a salary increase, arguing that once the nation's fighting forces reached the goal of 6 million, such a boost would increase war costs $750 million a year. He agreed that some pay increase might be proper, but concluded: "If you look at the taxpayers' pocketbook, the suggested military pay increase is not justified

Medical Advances

A professor of clinical surgery at the University of Oregon Medical School, Dr. Louis P. Gambee, spoke to the Surgical Society at Harborview County Hospital in Seattle on March 13, 1942. He informed them that improved surgical

techniques on the battlefield were saving wounded men, but that even more were being saved by the new sulfa drugs that reduced bacteria and infections. The wounded were also being helped by improved methods of treating shock, the administration of plasma, and better anesthesia. Specialists such as Dr. Gambee often traveled to Seattle to lecture since there was no medical school in the state.

A Few of the Many Heroes of March

A graduate of the University of Washington, Lieutenant James W. Boundy of Seattle risked his life to save others. He leaped into a raging sea amid gale winds and freezing temperatures in an effort to carry a line ashore from the Navy stores ship *Pollux* after it ran aground off the rocky coast of Newfoundland. Boundy lived but 92 officers and men died in the disaster.

Two Navy men from Seattle, Ensign Robert W. Granston and Lieutenant Trose E. Donaldson were awarded the Navy Cross for heroism during the first Japanese aerial bombardment of the Cavite Naval Base in the Philippines. Trose Donaldson was killed later in the war.

April 1942

Wartime Effects On Local Education

Colleges and universities across the land were busy training service personnel and undertaking war research. The University of Washington campus was closed to the public at night because of secret research projects; some of them so closely guarded that professors involved were forbidden to tell even their department heads about their laboratory activities.

Five months after Pearl Harbor, the University of Washington enrolled 1,000 persons in evening engineering, economics and business courses. The College of Forestry was involved in extensive research to find ways to use waste materials from logging and sawmill operations. One effort by Professor Frederick Wangaard resulted in a method of using parts

Headlines: April 1942

April 9:
JAPANESE NAVY SINKS 120,000 TONS OF BRITISH MERCHANT SHIPPING

April 9:
ALLIED FORCES ON LUZON SURRENDER

April 18:
GENERAL JAMES DOOLITTLE LEADS AIR RAID ON JAPAN

April 29:
JAPANESE TAKE CONTROL OF THE BURMA ROAD, THE ONLY ROUTE TO CHINA

of Douglas Fir bark to manufacture a cork substitute that helped overcome the war-caused shortage of cork from the Mediterranean area.

Meantime, the availability of high-paying jobs and the urgency of the draft resulted in dropping enrollments at state universities and colleges. At the University of Washington, 4,950 students registered for spring quarter, 2,000 fewer than a year earlier.

Business News Stories of the Month

War Production Board efforts to keep the state's smaller manufacturers busy met with considerable success in 1942. While lists of these contracts were not released because of censorship, it was noted that local sheet-metal fabrication, machine assembly and valve assembly companies had recently signed war contracts.

The results of the first year of the nation's production of Liberty ships were published in April. During the previous 12 months, contracts to build 1,488 of these cargo carriers had been signed by 17 shipyards. Pacific Coast shipyards were building 673 of them and the Maritime Commission expected to order 56 additional tankers plus 60 Liberty ships. Thirty of these Liberty ships would be built at the Kaiser shipyards in Vancouver, Washington.

Later in April, the government took control of all American merchant marine vessels still in private hands. The requisitioned vessels, including 48 in Seattle, continued to be operated by the original owners acting as agents for the War Shipping Administration.

Polls of The American Institute of Public Opinion found that the American public wanted a tough and drastic wartime program to control prices and wages, something legislators had hesitated to tackle. The people wanted the government to control both labor unions and business profits.

The war years were profitable for motion picture studios. War films and comedies attracted the biggest crowds. In April, at Seattle's Orpheum Theater, James Cagney starred in an aviation drama, *Captains of the Clouds*. At the Music Hall, the musical comedy *The Fleet's In* starred Dorothy Lamour and William Holden. At the 5th Avenue, full houses were enjoying *To the Shores of Tripoli*, an action comedy with John Payne and Maureen O'Hara. The Paramount advertised a double feature: *Song of the Islands*, a musical comedy starring Betty Grable and Victor Mature, plus *Secret Agent of Japan*, a spy thriller with Preston Foster. Many theaters included newsreels from the war fronts depicting actual battle scenes. Theaters scheduled features for swing shift workers, too, and some stayed open all night.

Radio stations attracted listeners with several newscasts a day. National networks fed local stations the news of the world and in the evening broadcasts of live music of big bands such as Glen Miller, Tommy Dorsey, Guy Lombardo, Duke Ellington and Louis Armstrong. On Saturday night during the war years, most radios were turned to "Your Hit Parade" that featured the week's most popular songs. Often a sentimental war ballad was the Number One Hit.

Women War Workers

Many newspapers carried the series of articles from WorldWide Press that heralded women as the solution to the manpower shortage. The War

"Rosie the Riveter," real name unknown, is shown working on a Boeing Flying Fortress on September 2, 1943. Hundreds of Washington State women helped build thousands of these giant bombers that played a major role in winning the war. Seattle P-I Collection, 23930, MOHAI.

16

Production Board estimated that, of the expected two million new workers needed in 1942, most would be women. One housewife was quoted as saying, "I don't want to roll bandages or learn to spot airplanes. I want a war job. I want to feel I am making something real, a piece of an airplane or a tank, or a gun or a shell that the boys on the front line will use against the enemy." At the time women held only one of every 10 war jobs. That statistic was about to change. Experts estimated that a third of all jobs in aircraft assembly plants could be performed satisfactorily by women, including much of the riveting, drilling, countersinking, dimpling and bucking. All they needed was training. Americans soon recognized "Rosie the Riveter" as a wartime heroine.

Veterans of World War I joined those registering now that draft age was extended to include men 45 to 65. These older men were to be called to duty only if needed. Among those registering was 58-year-old Edgar Akers, an employee at the Seattle Port of Embarkation. As a young Lieutenant in 1918, shrapnel and machine-gun bullets had crippled Akers right arm. Now, 25 years later, he still could not shake hands without pain, but he favored the registration of older men. So did William J. (Wee) Coyle, another World War I veteran who signed up that day. Coyle was a famed Husky football player before he fought in the First World War and afterwards he was a well-known car dealer.

A Few of the Many Heroes of April

Two privates preparing to serve breakfast at the large Army Air Corps mess hall at Paine Field were killed when a pursuit plane stationed at the field crashed on take-off and plowed through the building. If the accident had occurred a few minutes later, several hundred men would have been eating breakfast in the building. The pilot of the plane was seriously injured.

Two days later an Army pursuit plane exploded over Possession Point, killing the pilot. On that same day, in a residential area near Olympia, a plane from McChord Field crashed into the Arthur Thompson home, killing the pilot and slightly injuring Mrs. Thompson. Such accidents occurred frequently in the state during the war.

Mrs. Ralph Rings of Seattle faced a double tragedy on April 4. That day the Navy informed her and her husband that their 26-year-old son, Lieutenant (j.g.) Glen R. Rings, was missing. Ralph Rings was in the transfer business and had a meeting in Walla Walla. He decided to drive over and that evening suffered a fatal heart attack at age 49. Their son, who had graduated from Queen Anne High School and the University of Washington, was later listed as killed in action.

May 1942

Victory Square is Dedicated

One of the more memorable and colorful sites in Seattle during the war years was Victory Square on University Street between Fourth and Fifth Avenues in front of the Olympic Hotel and Metropolitan Theater. Several well-known businessmen were involved with activities there. Russell W. Young, a newspaper executive, chaired the operations committee; George Weber, of the Seattle Advertising Club, coordinated activities for the King County War Savings Committee; Stanly W. Donogh headed the King County Minute Man sale of war bonds at Victory Square; Dietrich Schmitz chaired the county war-savings bond committee; and the theater and musician unions supported the effort.

A replica of Jefferson's home, Monticello, served as the speakers' stand at the west end of Victory Square. At the east end of the block stood a 75-foot-high replica of The Washington Monument on which were inscribed a growing list of King County war dead.

A huge crowd jammed the area for the dedication ceremonies on May 2. An army band on a truck rode through the city center playing patriotic music to remind citizens of the event. Trucks filled with sailors waving

Headlines: May 1942

May 7:
CORREGIDOR SURRENDERS TO THE JAPANESE; GENERAL WAINWRIGHT AND 15,000 ALLIED TROOPS ARE TAKEN PRISONER

May 31:
JAPANESE MIDGET SUBS TORPEDO NAVAL SHIP IN SYDNEY, AUSTRALIA, HARBOR, KILLING 19 SEAMEN.

During the war years, many large businesses recognized hardworking employees. Edward Bufmyer was selected mechanic of the month at Isaacson Iron Works, and was presented the award on July 27, 1942, at Victory Square by local newsman Dick Keplinger and movie actress Ginger Rogers. MOHAI, 16980.

On a damp October 3, 1942, Bob Hope entertained a crowd and sold war bonds at Seattle's Victory Square on University Street between 4th and 5th Avenues. The Metropolitan Theater on the right was later demolished to make room for the drive-in entrance of the Four Seasons Olympic Hotel. Seattle P-I Collection, 28264, MOHAI.

their caps followed the band. Noted operatic tenor John Charles Thomas, in town for a concert, sang the national anthem. The audience was reminded several times that a major war bond sale was starting. While the entertainment was underway, Corporal Phillip Horan, a member of the local Transport Guard approached the bond booth and declared, "I want some bonds." When asked how many, he laid down $100 in currency and asked, "As much as that will buy." He was told it would purchase bonds worth $125 at maturity. "Fine," he responded. When a nearby reporter asked where he had earned the money, Horan explained that it represented some savings from the year he had been stationed in Seattle plus "a bit of luck."

During the war, many famous movie stars and musicians appeared at Victory Square during bond rallies. Bob Hope was there several times, as was Bing Crosby. Among the dozens who appeared were Betty Grable and Lana Turner. Famous bandleaders and their musicians entertained the crowds. Local celebrities also attracted audiences that purchased millions of dollars worth of war bonds each year at Victory Square.

The Navy Secretary Visits Puget Sound

Navy Secretary Frank Knox visited Seattle on May 7. A large crowd at Victory Square heard him praise Seattle's war effort. He exclaimed, "No city has a greater role to play in the war than Seattle." Later he reviewed hundreds of bluejackets on parade at Sand Point Naval Air Station and visited the Bremerton Navy Yard.

The Costs of War

Fiscal officials in the nation's capitol disclosed that in less than a year the United States had paid out as much for World War II as was spent during the entire First World War. From July 1, 1940, to May 1, 1942, war costs approached 26 billion U.S. dollars.

The Need to Shelter Visitors

Hundreds of service personnel arrived in Seattle each weekend on furlough, visiting relatives and friends, or sightseeing. To house and feed them became an obvious challenge. In May, 53 soldiers and youth began construction of an Army recreation center at 15th Avenue South and Dakota Street near Jefferson Park. The plans called for housing 1,000 in 55 cottages, 73 winterized tents, a large concessions building, a recreation hall, a women's reception room, officers quarters and a large bathhouse. Delays developed however, and over the July 4th holidays, 855 soldiers had to sleep in old barns and tool houses, and some even slept under the stars. The Major in charge of construction called for city assistance in order to complete the Jefferson Park camp.

Meantime in the Field Artillery Armory, 500 cots equipped with bedding went unused because no sponsor had been found. The Service Men's Club said it could not assume financial responsibility for Armory operations because all its funds were allotted. Eventually an agreement was reached and they began to provide the Armory beds for visiting service personnel.

Late in May the City Council provided $10,000 to equip a "Negro" Y. M. C. A. building at 23rd Avenue and East Olive Street. In those days the armed services were segregated and black soldiers visiting the area were quartered at Collins Fieldhouse. They soon requested these quarters be moved closer to where their people lived.

Homes for families were rapidly being erected throughout the region. At Renton Highlands, one of the largest Federal Public Housing Authority projects in the area, 500 houses had been completed and 1,500 more were under construction. In Seattle, the federal government supplied $19 million for five housing projects with 3,768 family units at Sand Point, Yesler Terrace, High Point, Holly Park and Rainier Vista.

A Few of the Many Heroes of May

Charles Fagan of Seattle and Robert Nelson of Aberdeen were bound for Europe to serve as ambulance drivers with the American Field Service. Their ship was hardly at sea when a German torpedo smashed into the hull and it began to sink. One man was flung into the ocean by the explosion but was pulled into a lifeboat crowded with 20 survivors. A Norwegian schooner that stopped to take the men aboard was bound for a distant destination, so those in the lifeboat decided they preferred returning to the U.S. They asked that their gasoline tank be filled and headed west toward home. Just before their boat nosed into the sands at Cape Cod, the motor sputtered through the last drops of fuel, forcing all aboard to wade ashore. When Fagan called his mother in Seattle to describe his experience, he expressed his satisfaction at the fact that not one person was lost in the sinking.

During the month the Navy reported 88 men from the state of Washington were missing in action. The list covered the period from Pearl Harbor Day to April 25, 1942. A majority of the men later were reported as killed in action, dead of wounds, or prisoners of war. About a quarter of those listed as missing survived to return home.

The story of Clarence M. Formoe of Seattle became known during the month. He was at Pearl Harbor when the Japanese raided. Under a rain of bullets from enemy planes, he managed to set up his machine gun and fire back. He lost his life in the effort and was decorated posthumously for extraordinary heroism. Formoe was a graduate of Queen Anne High School and had attended the University of Washington. His widow was employed at the Boeing Aircraft Company. The Navy later named a ship in his honor.

Headlines:
June 1942

June 6:
JAPANESE TROOPS INVADE
ALASKA'S ALEUTIAN
ISLANDS

June 7:
U.S. WINS FIRST MAJOR
NAVAL BATTLE NEAR
MIDWAY

June 20:
GERMAN FORCES TAKE
TOBRUK IN NORTH AFRICA

June 28:
GERMANS BEGIN SUMMER
OFFENSIVE IN RUSSIA

On June 22, 1942, an army officer at what appears to be the Seattle Armory instructed a group of businessmen on the proper use of gas masks. Seattle P-I Collection, 27963, MOHAI.

June 1942

The Japanese Attack on Dutch Harbor, Alaska

Early on the morning of June 3, four Japanese bombers and 15 fighters attacked Dutch Harbor on Unalaska Island in the Aleutian chain where air and submarine bases were under construction. Unalaska is separated from the mainland by Unimak Pass, the route to Nome, Bristol Bay and other Bering Sea and Arctic points. The Great Circle ship route across the Pacific from Puget Sound to the Orient used this waterway. During this Dutch Harbor attack, the first enemy aerial bombs in history fell on North America.

About 1,700 civilian personnel were working at Dutch Harbor, a large percentage of them from the state of Washington, so a lot of worrying followed news of the attack. Fearing further enemy incursions, a radio silence of several hours was imposed along the entire West Coast to prevent enemy airmen from

homing in on radio signals to American targets. Air raid wardens and other defense personnel were ordered to stand by, and scores of Coast Guard Auxiliary civilian volunteers headed their craft into Puget Sound for an all-night vigil.

On July 17, the casualty statistics resulting from the Alaska attack were published. The bombing and strafing of Dutch Harbor, nearby Fort Mears and the Army post at Fort Glenn some 70 miles west of Dutch Harbor killed 44 American Army and Navy men and wounded 49. On July 25 a bullet-scarred Army transport, a survivor of the attack, arrived in Seattle with the wounded and women and children from the Dutch Harbor vicinity.

We now know that the Japanese raid on Dutch Harbor and the occupation of two Aleutian Islands were diversionary tactics, an attempt to draw the U.S. Navy to Alaska while the Japanese fleet attacked Midway. But on May 14, American code breakers had intercepted enemy messages and the U.S. Navy was on alert at Midway. The June 5-7 naval battle near Midway Island resulted in a decisive defeat of the enemy. News headlines on June 11 announced "Flying Fortresses Struck First Blow at Two Jap Fleets." The B-17s and other U. S. forces scattered two large Japanese fleets, sank many of their largest warships, beat off an attack by 180 enemy planes and may have prevented an invasion of the Hawaiian Islands.

General Hap Arnold, Commander of American Air Forces, sent a telegram to the Boeing Company praising the B-17s for their long-range scouting missions in the Aleutians and for keeping contact with the enemy under adverse weather conditions. He added that Flying Fortresses flying at 20,000 feet had scored hits on Japanese aircraft carriers during the Battle of Midway.

While the Midway battle was under way, Japanese troops occupied the Aleutian Islands of Kiska and Attu. In return, the U.S. Navy bombarded Kiska and Attu every month or two. On May 11, 1943, the U.S. 7th Division landed on Attu and, in several vicious battles, slowly advanced across the island until on May 30 they gained complete control. In the bloody fighting, 2,350 Japanese died (including suicides) and 28 were wounded. American losses were 600 killed and 1,200 wounded. The Japanese, still occupying Kiska, were bombarded on July 6 and 22 and they quietly evacuated the island. The Americans shelled the island a couple of times to soften it up for the August 15th landing of 34,000 soldiers. To their surprise, they found the enemy had vacated Kiska.

Exchange of Civilians

June brought an exchange of Japanese and American nationals. More than a thousand citizens of Japan and Thailand were traded for 629 American citizens held by the Japanese. Included in the exchange were several missionaries and businessmen from Washington State, including Irving N. Linnell of Medina, an American consul general stationed in the Far East. That same month the Swedish liner *Gripsholm* docked at New York with twelve persons from Washington State who had escaped from Axis-dominated European countries.

Large Navy Building Projects Near Completion

In Pasco, amidst sand and sagebrush, a thousand men sweating on machines leveled and surfaced the largest Naval Reserve Air Training Station in the Pacific Northwest. Here, far from the sea, the Navy would train thousands of men to take off and land on carriers and to pilot torpedo planes and long-range patrol bombers. Scattered around the large T-shaped main field were 16 practice fields where scores of pilots could practice landings simultaneously.

At the south end of Seattle's Lake Union, a large, gray structure, the Naval Armory, was

In June 1942 the Bon Marche proudly noted that 1156 of its 1200 employees were buying a war bond a week. An army band and a black jazz group provided music for the Victory Square award ceremony. Seattle P-I Collection, 28252, MOHAI.

By mid-1942, war shipping on Seattle's waterfront required additional wharf space. Three short years earlier, the area where this large pier is being constructed was the location of a Depression era shack town housing hundreds of destitute unemployed. PEMCO, Webster-Stevens Collection, MOHAI.

dedicated in June. During the war it housed a training school and after the war became headquarters for the Naval Reserve.

Share the Ride

After citizens were urged to share their cars to save rubber and gas, four well-known residents of the Highlands decided to ride together to downtown Seattle. Almost every morning for the duration, they gathered at the home of the designated driver of the day. The four were George H. Greenwood, President of Pacific National Bank; Mrs. A. Scott Bullitt, President of Stimson Realty; Hamilton Rolfe, manager of the Hoge Building; and Lewis L. Stedman, Seattle attorney.

A Few of the Many Heroes of June

Thirty-five miles off Neah Bay in early June a Japanese submarine torpedoed a cargo ship that immediately began to sink. The 56 American seamen climbed aboard a lifeboat and two rubber rafts, fully expecting the sub to

surface and machine-gun them. If it did they hoped to give the enemy a surprise. Young First Officer E. W. Nystrom, as he abandoned the sinking freighter, paused long enough to detach a 30-caliber machine gun from the bridge rail and grab nine drums of ammunition. He said he hoped to kill two of the Japanese enemy for his father's sake. His father, Fred Nystrom, had commanded the steamship *H. F. Alexander* before being captured by the Japanese and imprisoned in Hong Kong.

However, the Japanese sub did not surface and, as the wind rose, weather became the enemy. The struggling men could see the peaks of the Olympic Mountains on the horizon. After 26 hours of rowing and bailing, a fishing schooner sighted the lifeboat and carried the exhausted and freezing men to Neah Bay. There, as they warmed up, they helped the Coast Guard plot the probable location of the two life rafts. Both were located and all aboard were saved except for the 56-year-old cook, who perished of exposure.

July 1942

Events of July 4th

All across the state, thousands turned out for the parades and patriotic events to celebrate the first Independence Day since the U.S. declared war on the Axis. Sidewalks were jammed along parade routes and citizens tossed confetti from crowded windows. Military bands led marching service personnel, a sight that elicited applause and cheers as they marched in perfect step behind the flag bearers. Civilian groups, too, were part of the parade, including air-raid wardens in white helmets and gas masks. In Seattle the crowd was surprised at the unscheduled appearance of eight new P-38 fighter planes that zoomed low over the rooftops. The reviewing stand in front of the Seattle Public Library was surrounded by a milling mass of humanity saluting the military units passing in review.

Holiday entertainment was planned for the hundreds of service personnel in town. The Poggie Club arranged for service men to try their hand at Puget Sound fishing. Hundreds of young ladies from the surrounding area were bused to Fort Lewis to celebrate with soldiers who were not given leave over Independence Day. To their surprise they found the young men to be very shy. A young Seattle woman, Virginia Bruce, realized something needed to be done to warm up the party. She found a microphone and said, "What is this? We've traveled 50 miles to show you boys a good time. And what happens? Nothing! Come on, boys, let's get acquainted." The master of ceremonies took his cue and challenged the soldiers, "What would sailors do at a time like this?" Soon a baseball game and swimming races were under way, a huge picnic supper was being served, and the dance floor was full of jitterbugging couples.

Testing the Sea Ranger

The Navy announced on July 9 that the Boeing Airplane Company was testing a huge new seaplane bomber, the XPBB1 "Sea Ranger." The plane, the largest twin-engine flying boat ever built in the U.S., tested well during initial flights. However, production of the initial order of 57 Sea Rangers was canceled after it became apparent that existing land-based planes could do the job as well. And the one prototype was dubbed the "Lone Ranger." The large plant in Renton built by the Navy for Boeing to produce the Sea Ranger was transferred to the Army for production of the huge new Boeing B-29 bombers.

Increase of Business

At a July 25 meeting, Seattle civic leaders labeled the growth of Seattle and environs since Pearl Harbor as nothing less than phenomenal. D.K. MacDonald, Chamber of Commerce president, estimated some 65,000 persons had settled in Seattle during the year. Employment numbers were way up. Women actively at work in war production plants numbered about 20,000 and another 60,000 women volunteers and paid workers were engaged in all phases of war activities. More than 75 percent of city businesses capable of conversion to war work had received contracts and the remainder were converting rapidly. With much greater amounts of money in circulation, department stores reported a 36 percent increase in sales during the first five months of 1942 compared to a year earlier.

MacDonald offered some predictions for the future. He suggested that giant cargo planes pulling trains of gliders across the Pacific were not a fantasy. They would be built by Boeing, he thought, and would take up any slack from the loss of Flying Fortress construction at war's end. He said Boeing would also be building what he called "flivver" planes. He thought the U.S. would become the world's policeman after the war and therefore the shipyards would switch from warships to cargo ships. He believed that most of the trade with China and other parts of the world would be in dehydrated foods, a rapidly developing product of the Evergreen State.

Names in the News

Seattle Mayor William F. Devin appointed Kenneth B. Colman to administer the

July 4:

GERMANS CAPTURE SEVASTOPOL AND 90,000 RUSSIAN PRISONERS

July 15:

FIRST FLIGHTS "OVER THE HUMP" CARRY SUPPLIES TO CHINESE ALLIES

July 19:

IMPROVED ATLANTIC CONVOY SYSTEM SAVES SHIPS AND LIVES

July 29:

JAPANESE TAKE KOKUDA AIRFIELD IN NEW GUINEA

maintenance of vital war transportation. His major duties included finding ways to conserve automotive equipment, rubber and gasoline through elimination of needless transportation and by careful operation of equipment.

Washington Senator Mon C. Wallgren accompanied by Senators Carl A. Hatch of New Mexico and Harold H. Burton of Ohio, three members of the Truman Committee, investigated how expeditiously war expenditures were being handled. They visited Boeing Airplane plants, McChord Field and Bremerton, and earlier had spent time at Grand Coulee Dam and in Spokane. Senator Burton said the legislators were pleased with the progress made in the aluminum rolling mill at Spokane and predicted that a magnesium plant would soon be operating there. He was struck by the foresight that had resulted in the construction of Grand Coulee and Bonneville dams. "It seems like the beneficent intervention of Providence that those two projects were ready and waiting just when they were needed most," he said.

Concerns About the Draft

In mid-July, Secretary of War Stimson warned the country that in his opinion young married men and youths aged 18 and 19 would be drafted into the armed services before the Axis was vanquished. Also, he was concerned about the many medical practitioners leaving private practice to enter the service, and mentioned that the 50th General Hospital, a Seattle unit including 48 prominent physicians and surgeons, seven dentists, nine administrative officers and 120 nurses, had been placed on alert for overseas duty.

More Women Become Involved

The Navy late in July called for 1,000 single women to volunteer as officer candidates. If accepted, they had to agree not to marry in the course of their training. These women served in the newly created organization called Women Appointed for Volunteer Emergency Service (WAVES).

Isabel Kane was the first Tacoma woman to enlist in the Women's Auxiliary Army Corps (WAAC) and was assigned to Fort Des Moines, Iowa, for training. Miss Kane, a University of Washington graduate, also held a master's degree from the University of California and had been a faculty member at Central Washington College of Education.

Several Bellevue women pitched in to make the annual Bellevue Strawberry Festival successful, then planted acres of tomatoes, peas, beans and helped harvest orchard fruits. Heavy rains helped produce bumper crops just as Japanese-American farmers were sent to relocation centers. Without the help of the women, much of the crop would have been lost.

The Seattle Times published an article titled "Hail, Women of Seattle!" It described the variety of jobs the women were filling and added: "Women, making home a safe and sane place for their families, carry on while sons and husbands, fathers and sweethearts do their jobs 'somewhere over there' or on the home front." The article stated that more than 60,000 local women were working in war activities, about 10 thousand of them in defense plants ringing Puget Sound.

A Few of the Many Heroes of July

Captain Francis E. (Bud) Nestor, 23, pilot of an American Army bomber in the African war theater, was reported missing in action. He had played football at Seattle Preparatory School, St. Martin's College in Olympia, and the University of Washington. He later was declared killed in action.

Dr. Clyde L. Welsh, a prominent Seattle physician and Navy lieutenant commander was listed as missing in action in the Philippines. He had been on duty at Canacao Hospital near Cavite Naval Base when the Japanese struck. Though the enemy was closing in, many doctors stayed in Manila to care for the wounded. After the war, it was found that Dr. Welsh had died as a prisoner of war.

Ensign Albert E. (Bud) Mitchell was 27 when killed in aerial combat with the enemy.

JOHN THOMAS LANCASTER RONALD LAWRENCE ARLET
MELVIN GRANT JOHNSON HOMER BILYEU
VICTOR MARVIN GADDOW ALBERT EDWARD MITCHELL
CLARENCE MELVIN FOEMOE ROBERT L. HOLSBO
MARSHAL GEORGE DUNFEE ROBERT CHARLES ELY
WILLIAM JOHN DAY ARTHUR LIONEL TAYLOR
ERNEST EUGENE CONEY GLEN ALLEN SUMMERS
JAMES WARREN CASEY HARDY WILBUR PETERSON
ROBERT N. BROOKS GEORGE LAWRENCE PARIOIS
KENNETH DAY BRARKE HUGH KENNETH NAFF
WILLIAM EUGENE BLANCHARD JAMES CERNIE MYERS
ALTON WALTER WHITSON HENRI CLAY MAXON
CLARENCE MERTON CASKEY JOHN DOUDIE LEGGET
GEORGE LELAND HUTCHINSON

WE HERE HIGHLY RESOLVE
THAT THESE DEAD SHALL
NOT HAVE DIED IN VAIN
Lincoln

His mother and wife received word of his death on June 11 and concluded that he died during the Japanese attack on Dutch Harbor, Alaska. Mitchell was a graduate of Seattle's Broadway High School, and had attended the University of Washington. Another local man believed killed in the Alaska battles was 19-year-old Seaman Frank Edward Birks, a Ballard High graduate, who for a time was a member of the Coast Patrol Squadron at Sand Point Naval Air Station.

Brigadier General William F. Marquat, who had worked at *The Seattle Times* before the war, was awarded the Distinguished Service Cross for extraordinary heroism while serving with General MacArthur in the Philippines. When the General was ordered to Australia as the Japanese were about to take Corregidor, he took General Marquat with him. Word was received in July that General Marquat had volunteered as observer on a hazardous four-

plane aerial combat mission over Port Moresby in New Guinea. Eight Japanese planes attacked the American aircraft, damaging all four and killing one man, but all planes managed to limp back to their base. For displaying marked coolness during the air battle, the General was awarded the Silver Star medal.

On Friday, July 16, King County solemnly honored its heroic war dead as the first 40 names were inscribed on the front panel of the replica of Washington's monument at Victory Square. Special invitations to attend were mailed to relatives of those to be listed. Throughout the war, as casualties were reported, the names of the dead were added. By the time victory was won four years later, several thousand names were inscribed on the monument.

The final heroic story for the month of July has a happy ending. Lieutenant Leo Hawel, a young pilot from Seattle who had rowed with

"Hero's Day" at Victory Square on July 21, 1942, honored the first King County war dead, several of whom were killed at Pearl Harbor. Their names had recently been inscribed on the Washington Monument replica. Before the war ended the monument was covered by names of those who gave their lives in World War II. Seattle P-I Collection, 28257, MOHAI.

Headlines:
August 1942

August 7:
U.S. TROOPS LAND ON GUADALCANAL; VICTORY IS ACHIEVED IN SIX MONTHS OF BATTLES THAT KILL 16,000 JAPANESE AND 1,600 AMERICANS.

August 11-13:
A SUPPLY CONVOY HEADED TO MALTA LOSES MANY SHIPS IN A GERMAN AIR AND SEA ATTACK

August 17:
FIRST ALL-U.S. BOMBING RAID ON EUROPE HITS ROUEN, FRANCE.

August 31:
GERMAN TROOPS MOVE TO WITHIN 16 MILES OF STALINGRAD

During World War II Lana Turner, a favorite movie star and pinup girl, traveled around the country selling war bonds. In 1942 she appeared in Seattle and other Puget Sound cities. While being welcomed at the Puget Sound Navy Yard in Bremerton, she was presented a bouquet of roses. Kitsap Regional Library, 1948.

Husky crews at the University of Washington, was nervous and tense as he piloted a Boston bomber on one of the first American air raids on German-occupied territory. As he skimmed along at rooftop level over The Hague in Nazi-occupied Holland, he glanced out a side window and caught a glimpse of two young women seated at their breakfast table staring back at him with startled looks on their faces. The experience made him chuckle and released some of the tension, he told his father in a V-mail letter.

August 1942

Business and Industry

On August 3 the Boeing Airplane Company's huge war factory was quiet for half an hour as employees and executives gathered on the apron in front of Plant 2 to receive an award for outstanding production, the Army and Navy "E" pennant. Boeing was the first aircraft manufacturer to be so honored. At the ceremony, broadcast coast to coast on radio, President Philip G. Johnson told the audience that Boeing could increase production 40 percent if they had more materials.

The state's lumber business was thriving. At an August 8 auction of Olympic Peninsula spruce, the State Land Board opened bids for 4,700,000 board feet of timber for war uses. Three blocks of state timber in the Hoh River area produced bids ranging from $7.31 to $13.29

per thousand feet, considerably higher than anticipated. The war effort's increasing demands for wood products caused sawmills and logging camps to operate night and day. The shortage of labor caused lists of unfilled orders to lengthen. One logging operation that employed 975 men in January could find only 420 to hire in July. Among orders marked high priority were lumber for Navy sub-chasers, gliders and training planes; wood parts for combat aircraft; timbers for battleship planking and decking; construction supplies for military bases; and scores of wood items for secret and experimental military work. Only two mills on the West Coast, one in Lewis County, the other in Oregon, could produce the 126-foot knotless, clear-lumber keel timbers needed for sub-chasers. Both mills were operating at capacity while the Navy anxiously waited for the last half of the keels it had ordered. In addition, Army and Navy bases from Arctic wastelands to tropical swamps were calling for Douglas fir lumber from Western Washington.

Washington had not previously been a major producer of metal ores, but war demands were causing the mining industry to develop. The state, it was found, had deposits of virtually every metal in demand, including gold, silver, copper, lead and zinc, all of which were being produced, plus small amounts of tungsten, antimony, mercury and manganese. Chromium, important for military uses and in making special varieties of steel, had been located in several sections of the state. Iron ore finds were reported in 13 counties. As part of the war effort, the state government promoted exploration and development of mineral resources.

Major war bond sales were constantly promoted throughout the state. In October, Bing Crosby, one of the country's favorite crooners and movie actors, visited Tacoma, his hometown during the first 12 years of his life. He drew a huge crowd to a bond rally there, where he crooned the popular ballad, "Any Bonds Today?" After entertaining the Tacoma crowd, he, bandleader Phil Harris and others in the

Headlines:
September 1942

September 10-14:
NAZI U-BOATS HIT ALLIED ATLANTIC CONVOY, SINK 12 FREIGHTERS AND A DESTROYER, LOSE ONLY ONE SUB.

September 17:
GEN. LESLIE GROVES NAMED TO HEAD ALL U.S. ATOMIC RESEARCH

September 25:
U.S SHIPYARDS BUILD 488 CARGO SHIPS IN ONE YEAR

company traveled to Fort Lewis to perform several shows for soldiers. Two days later he attracted 15,000 , the largest crowd to that date, at Seattle's Victory Square, where $177,000 worth of war bonds were sold in two hours.

Wartime Art Exhibit

The Seattle Art Museum's major August exhibit was titled, "The Fire Blitz of London, 1940." English artists produced the paintings while serving as volunteer firemen during the devastating aerial raids. Three of the artists were honored in person at a reception as the exhibit was opened.

New Navy Hospital Dedicated

On August 22 an 800-bed Navy hospital opened at 15th Avenue Northeast and East 50th Street, north of Seattle. Following the dedication ceremony, Captain F. F. Murdoch, commander of the hospital, inspected the 44-building establishment, then attended a buffet luncheon in the Enlisted Men's Recreation Center. (After the war, this property housed Firlands Tuberculosis Sanatorium and Fircrest School for the Retarded. Later Shorecrest High School was constructed on a portion of the property.)

A Few of the Many Heroes of August

Major Alexander S. Caplan, 33, a former Seattle lawer and the youngest man ever elected to a Washington Superior Court judgeship, on January 22 died of wounds received in the Philippine Islands. He left a wife; a four-year-old son, Allan; and a year-old daughter, Carla Marie, whom he had never seen.

Lieutenant Frank Guberlet was home visiting his young wife during August. He had met her when both played violas in the University of Washington symphony. The Lieutenant was in charge of an aircraft carrier repair crew during the Coral Sea and Midway battles and the Gilbert and Marshall Island raids. He explained that most of his experiences were below deck where he could hear the battles but not see them.

September 1942

Women in the Service

Edna L. Cox of Seattle, the first officer assigned in the new Women's Auxiliary Army Corps, was sent to cooking school at Fort Riley, Kansas. She formerly was assistant dietitian at Harborview County Hospital. Other WAACs from the state were assigned to Fort Des Moines, Kansas, and to Washington, D.C. Miss Jane Bogue, Seattle's first WAVE and one of the first women to earn the Navy rank of Lieutenant (j.g.), was assigned to the Naval Procurement Office to recruit applicants for the WAVES.

After the Pearl Harbor attack, air raid wardens appointed in Western Washington neighborhoods learned how to react to incendiary bombs and gas attacks. On August 2, 1942, Seattle's Madrona neighborhood wardens drilled in their gas masks. Seattle P-I Collection, 27965, MOHAI.

Education

The Seattle Public Schools in conjunction with the United States Civil Service Commission offered several new training courses beginning in September. High school youth, after passing aptitude tests, were admitted to classes on aircraft-engine repair, parachute packing, aircraft-instrument repair or machine shop skills. These "mechanic learners" were paid $50 per month. Most classes lasted six months, and after graduation from high school, the trainees were assigned to Army air depots at a beginning salary of $100 per month.

Many students in the Army Enlisted Reserve were drafted before they could graduate. The Secretary of War on September 10 explained that increasing war demands made it necessary to call them to active service at age of 20, the lowest draft age.

The Story of "The Swoose"

Lieutenant General George H. Brett, chief of Army Air Forces in the Southwest Pacific, traveled on his favorite Flying Fortress named *Swoose* (half swan, half goose). The Boeing bomber, veteran of battles in the Philippines, Java and Australia, had more flying time to its

credit than any other plane in the Army. On September 1, it arrived at the airport of its birth, Boeing Field. The General asked that the plane be ready to depart at 9 the next morning. At the appointed time, mechanics wound up the starter and the pilot flipped the ignition switch, but the *Swoose* told them it didn't want to leave home again. It backfired — shooting flaming gasoline onto the concrete and leaving fire in the engine cowling which was doused with carbon dioxide from a fire extinguisher.

The *Swoose* had been involved in several record-breaking flights and more than once was used as a hospital ship. It wore bandages on tail, wings and fuselage to cover wounds inflicted by enemy bullets. C. L. Egtvedt, chairman of the board of the Boeing Company, offered to trade a new B-17 for the *Swoose* but the General refused. He suggested the new plane be given to someone who really needed it. The *Swoose* was good enough for him. Hearing that fond acclamation, the beloved old B-17 took off without a hitch, carrying the General and his party to the East Coast.

Business News Stories

Wartime shortages resulted in several new businesses being started. One challenge was to find a substitute for steel that was in short supply. The Army needed housing that could be quickly constructed in distant places. Giant half-cylinder Quonset Huts, manufactured in Quonset, Rhode Island, filled the bill, but they were made of steel. Several local men formed a new company called Pacific Huts to produce shelters made of wood. The wall sections had strong ribs of laminated spruce with inner and outer skin coverings of a pressed wood product. Flooring was plywood. Manufacturing 1,000 huts of this type saved 15,000 tons of steel. And they could be assembled with half the labor. Soon after perfecting the hut, the company received a $1 million contract from the Army.

When Japanese advances in the South Pacific interrupted the supply of raw rubber, the U.S. was forced to begin recycling rubber products. These Seattle residents on November 10, 1942, brought in used tires for the rubber drive. Seattle Post Intelligencer Collection, 28171, MOHAI.

Labor Day 1942 found labor and management working together across the state. Management-labor committees conferred frequently and settled most disputes before they reached the stop-work stage. And nearly every company, small or large, received war contracts. Webster-Brinkley produced steering engines for the huge freighters sliding down the ways in shipyards across the country. Western Gear Works manufactured reduction gears, aircraft and boat cranes and other machinery for all types of vessels. Isaacson Iron Works produced propeller shafting and other equipment for the Navy and Maritime Commission. Boat yards were busy, too. Washington Boat Works was building 12 small Navy craft. Barbee Marine Yards in Ballard was working on 10 small vessels. Ballinger Boat Works in Kirkland had contracts to build 68 picket boats for the Coast Guard. Small boat works in Bremerton, Everett and Renton also held defense contracts.

No matter how small the business, it faced government regulations. Gene Nelson, owner of Loyal Fuel Company, sold cordwood in the Seattle area. He requested permission to raise his retail price by 50 cents to $5.75 a cord. The OPA officer hesitated, then, after Nelson explained that without this wood, residents of South Park would be mighty chilly during the winter, he gave permission for the increase in cost.

The Seattle Fleet Post Office

Mail was vitally important to the morale of servicemen, most of whom were stationed a distance from their families. The large fleet post office in Seattle handled 3,500 sacks of mail each week, each filled with letters and packages bearing addresses of ships and stations of the U.S. Navy beyond the continental limits. Lieutenant Neil Williams and his crew of 11 enlisted men, many with post office experience, sorted and dispatched the mail as it arrived from all 48 states. Twice a day, trucks arrived with loads of gray canvas mailbags. The men, who were rated specialists, sorted tens of thousands of items each day to

be delivered to the many stations and vessels of the 13th Naval District.

September Draft News

In mid-September information was released to all eligible single men in Washington State who had registered in the first three draft calls to report to their draft boards by October 1. Childless married men up to age 45, except those in essential occupations, were warned to expect a call to active duty, and all married men were told reclassification was underway and they could expect a 1-A rating.

People in the News

Dr. Richard E. Fuller, Director of the Seattle Art Museum, philanthropist and geologist, on September 9 was commissioned as a major in the Army Specialist Corps. He served as senior procurement officer of the Pacific Northwest personnel division. Major Fuller had served overseas in World War I as an ambulance driver for the French army and later, after the U.S. entered the war, served as a second lieutenant in the 42nd Division Heavy Field Artillery.

Norman A. (Jim) Archibald was an air force hero of World War I. He had crash landed behind the enemy lines, spent 81 miserable days as a German prisoner, and wrote a book about these

As the U.S. moved to full war production, critical shortages of paper developed. Improved chemical processes allowed newspaper to be recycled. All during the war the State's Cub Scouts salvaged truckloads of paper and cardboard. Seattle P-I Collection, 28175, MOHAI.

Headlines: October 1942

October 3:
FDR FREEZES WAGES, RENTS AND FARM PRICES

October 16:
JAPANESE LAND IN FORCE ON GUADALCANAL

October 31:
50 NAZI BOMBERS HIT CANTERBURY, DESTROY FAMED CATHEDRAL

experiences titled *Heaven High-Hell Deep*. It became a best seller in 1935. Wanting to help with World War II, Archibald, who had been working at the Boeing Airplane Company, was commissioned a captain in the U.S. Air Force and sent to Miami for technical training. Though nearly half a century old, Archibald declared himself "excited, thrilled and delighted" to be serving his country a second time.

October 1942

Should 18-Year-Olds be Drafted?

All through October Congress debated whether men as young as 18 should be drafted. As the bill was being written, amendments would have barred 18 – and – 19 year-old youth from being assigned to foreign battlefields before being trained for a year on American soil. General George C. Marshall, Army Chief of Staff, opposed any such training requirements. Several days of heated debate followed. Senator Johnson of California told his colleagues that he opposed "the calling of children to fight our battles," and that he would not stand idly by while that generation was decimated. The Senate passed the bill to draft youth aged 18 and 19 but agreed that the teenagers should experience a year of training in this country before being sent overseas. They also agreed to exempt farm youth from the draft until proper replacements had been located.

General Hershey, when asked how many 18 and 19 year olds would be drafted,

This 1942 Frederick and Nelson show window, titled "Get in the Scrap," urged the salvaging of used tires, waste paper, rags, and scrap metal. Pemco Webster & Stevens collection, MOHAI.

responded that approximately 2,400,000 had registered the previous June 30 and another 1,800,000 had reached age 18 since that date and would be eligible for the draft. How many would pass physicals and how many had already enlisted was unknown. He concluded that more than two million of that number would probably be classified 1-A.

Labor Shortages Continue

Washington's orchardists wore furrowed brows in early October because of a shortage of pickers. On October 3, President Roosevelt allocated $1 million to pay for transporting 8,000 Midwestern farm workers to Eastern Washington to help harvest the multi-million dollar apple crop. On October 5, a train arrived in Wenatchee with 193 men, women, boys and girls from Chicago. On October 18, Seattle high school juniors and seniors were given a three day weekend to help pick and pack apples.

The Victory Tax Raises Hardly a Whimper

On October 27 citizens across the country learned that beginning January 1, 1943, in addition to the regular income tax, a victory tax of 5 percent would be assessed on incomes over $12 per week or $624 a year. This victory tax was withheld from paychecks of those on wages or salary. Businessmen, self-employed, domestic and farm laborers and public officials remitted this Victory Tax with their other taxes on March 15.

Scrap Metal Pickup

On October 7, a two-week scrap metal drive in Seattle's business district resulted in equipment of many sorts being piled on the sidewalk in front of hotels, office buildings, theaters and retail outlets. Army trucks manned by stalwart soldiers transported the often-heavy items to a steel mill repository to be melted down for the war effort. One newspaper article advised: "Don't hesitate to pile it on the sidewalk. A few pedestrians may bark their shins, but that pile of metal of yours may keep some American boy from dying."

The University on a War Footing

The University of Washington's wartime activity policy called for curtailment of nonessential functions. The Student Council on October 1 voted to cancel the varsity ball and junior prom, the University's biggest social events of the year. Kirby Torrance, presiding over the session, proposed establishing a student war council to coordinate campus war activities.

Recognizing that the armed services required physically fit youth, the University in 1942 developed a physical-education program for male students. Six quarters of physical training were required and all upper-division students had to pass a stiff physical fitness test before they were excused from any of these training periods.

A Few of the Many Heroes of October

Lieutenant (j.g.) Lawrence H. Young was reported missing in the performance of duties in the submarine service. He was a graduate of Roosevelt High School in Seattle and of the University of Washington where he was senior manager of the tennis and swimming teams. His father was a leading architect and engineer and his mother was educational director of the Seattle Art Museum. He later was listed as killed in action.

Robert C. Bower of Seattle, attached to the Civilian Technical Corps and posted to the Royal Navy, was involved in the Dieppe raid on the French coast on August 19. The raid, involving about 6,000 men, was designed to provide battle experience and to gain information about German defenses, but it ended in disaster. Losses totaled 3,600 men and 106 aircraft, a destroyer and 33 landing craft. Robert Bower, after returning to the U.S., was furloughed to his mother's home to recover from injuries suffered at Dieppe.

The mother of Marine Pfc. John Robert Himelrick, who was captured at Wake Island on December 23, received a letter telling her that he was being held in a prisoner of war camp near Shanghai. He reported: "I am in good

This 1942 photo of the black 32nd Aviation Squadron at Spokane's Geiger Field illustrates how completely the armed services were segregated during World War II. Cheney Cowles Museum, Spokane, L96-1.10.

Headlines:
November 1942

November 11:
ALLIED FORCES LAND IN NORTH AFRICA

November 15:
JAPANESE LOSE 28 WARSHIPS AT GUADALCANAL

November 21:
THE 1,500-MILE ALCAN HIGHWAY OPENS

November 25:
RUSSIANS ENCIRCLE GERMANS AT STALINGRAD

health and getting along all right. We have started a garden. Tell my friends hello. I think of you often and hope you don't worry about me." Private Himelrick later died in prison camp.

Four young Navy officers, one a former University of Washington student, were cited at Sand Point Naval Air Station for "heroic and distinguished service during an attack by dozens of frantic enemy planes." While piloting dive-bombers attacking a crippled and burning Japanese aircraft carrier, the sky filled with enemy fighters from the carrier. Despite this, the Navy flyers managed to send the carrier to the bottom. The Washington man involved was Lieutenant Robert P. Williams, 24, a resident of Snoqualmie.

On October 2, 15 men from the state were involved in a successful Flying Fortress raid on an aircraft factory and airfield in Northern France. Crewmen included Lieutenant Hardin W. Cheney and Sergeants Walter T. Ross and Lee A. Varner from Seattle. The flotilla of bombers was led by Colonel Ronald Walker of Spokane. Others from Spokane on the long flight were Lieutenants Chris Tolenaars and John N. McGee, and Sergeants Kempster M. Hashells and John A. Bianca. Lieutenant Walter M. Riess of Klickitat; Lieutenant Jared G. Crimp of Ellensburg; Sergeants Eutene B. Fleming, Port Angeles; Francis D. Crossman, Bellingham; Herman E. Zimmerman, Longview; Jim D. Reed, Kennewick; and Lusius Birbeck, Vancouver, were also on the raid. Not a B-17 was lost in this 13th raid to be made by the Boeing bombers. The flyers reported that their bombs burst on target and that they destroyed five Nazi fighter planes.

Mrs. Margaret Hetzler was a lonesome mother. Both her sons had been captured by the Japanese. The younger boy, 23-year-old Melvin, was captured when the Japanese took Guam on December 10. He wrote his mother in June and the letter arrived in October, telling her he was interned in a prison camp in Japan. Luckily, the complete medical staff from the naval station on Guam was in the same camp

and the Americans were in good health at the time. Melvin apparently survived. Her older son, Marvin, on Corregidor when it fell, was listed as missing. His name did not appear on any Japanese list of American dead, but it was known they often refused to release names of prisoners. Marvin Hetzler later was reported to have died in prison camp. Both the Hetzler boys were popular graduates of Sumner High School.

Navy Lieutenant Henry M. McDowell, 27, was awarded the Distinguished Flying Cross before 22,000 spectators on Navy Day at the Miami Orange Bowl for contributing to the destruction of Japanese ships attempting to flee from the Battle of Midway. He piloted a scout bomber into heavy anti-aircraft fire and bombed and strafed the ships. Lieutenant McDowell attended school in Aberdeen and was a student at Washington State College before entering the service in 1939.

November 1942

Two November Holidays

The Victory Square Veterans' Day rally, the largest to date at that patriotic shrine, featured representatives from all veterans' organizations. Service personnel gathered at Third and Madison with banners and flags flying and marched to Victory Square where patriotic band music filled the air. After a brief ceremony ended with the sounding of Taps, more names of servicemen who died in the war's early battles were inscribed on the replica of the Washington Monument.

On Thanksgiving Day many Washington residents were too busy with the war effort to take the day off, but all over the state, families gave thanks for the plenty that existed despite rationing. And they prayed for the safety of loved ones engaged in the war and for an early victory and a lasting peace. Across the state, hundreds of servicemen were invited to private homes for holiday dinners. In Seattle, many Laurelhurst homes were opened to soldiers and sailors who, after the holiday feast, were invited to a dance in the fieldhouse.

Japanese Submarines in the Northwest

During the fall months of 1942 the Japanese sent several of their long-range submarines across the ocean to feed on Pacific Coast shipping. They knocked out such well-known freighters as the Coastwise Line's *Coast Trader* near Cape Flattery and the tanker *Camden* off Willapa Bay. There were other ships torpedoed but the enemy activity subsided after 1942 as the enemy concentrated its fleets in the South Pacific and near the Aleutian Islands.

More Housing

An $8 million federal allotment for construction of 2,500 temporary homes for war workers in the Seattle area was received in early November. The homes were built on city and county-owned property within walking distance of war plants. Strictly temporary, all were planned for easy removal after the war.

The Armed Services Take Over Resort Areas

During November, 500 Coast Guard recruits were being physically conditioned in the foothills of the Cascades. The regimen in muscle building was tough, but the housing was comfortable. The Coast Guard leased the favorite vacation spot of tourists, hunters and fishermen called the Big Four Inn. The 45 sleeping rooms in the main building and 30 cottages accommodated a couple of hundred trainees. The dining hall seated 145, and chief commissary steward, Sam Rubin, from the Portland Club, served memorable meals to four shifts of Coast Guardsmen.

Another resort, the Pacific Beach Hotel near Moclips, became a training center occupied by blue-jacketed men of the Navy. The rambling white building, with its broad verandah facing the Pacific Ocean, was transformed into a Navy barracks housing 350 men. The Navy, after taking over the building in August, added a two-story north wing. Officers lived in six cottages on the grounds.

Business News of the Month

William F. Boni, Associated Press Military

Editor, on November 10 described the Boeing Flying Fortress as a fine airplane. "It combines utility with pleasing design. It flies like a dream and hits like a nightmare. It has the grace of a palomino and the durability of a Percheron. It is in the words of Lieutenant General Henry H. (Hap) Arnold, chief of the Army Air Forces, 'the guts and backbone of our world-wide aerial offensive.'" Boni added that Boeing's latest model "has a top speed of over 300 miles an hour, has a ceiling of 35,000 feet or better, can fly anywhere up to 4,000 miles, though not with peak load, and its armament of 10 or more machine guns make it a wicked foe for Japanese Zero or Nazi Focke-Wulfe."

On November 18, 1942, *The Seattle Times* carried a profile of "towering, gray-eyed" H.W. McCurdy, President of Associated Shipbuilders, a company that combined Puget Sound Bridge and Dredging Company with Lake Union Drydock and Machine Works. Behind McCurdy's office on Harbor Island an inferno of activity was apparent as workers came and went in their colored and numbered hard hats. McCurdy explained that Puget Sound Bridge and Dredge years before had actually built Harbor Island by filling in the tideflats there. His company built other things, too, such as

With most men in the family in the armed services or working long hours in war industries, many women felt it necessary to learn how to perform some of the former male duties. This 1942 Red Cross demonstration taught women how to change and rotate auto tires. Seattle P-I Collection 23620, MOHAI.

Headlines:
December 1942

December 2:
FIRST SUCCESSFUL SELF-
SUSTAINING ATOMIC CHAIN
REACTION OCCURS AT THE
UNIVERSITY OF CHICAGO

December 21:
SEVERE WINTER WEATHER
AND RUSSIAN TROOPS FORCE
NAZI ARMIES INTO RETREAT

December 31:
GERMANS FAIL TO STOP
ALLIED ARCTIC CONVOY
TAKING SUPPLIES TO RUSSIA

December 31:
ALLIES FORCE GERMANS TO
RETREAT IN LIBYA

the Dexter Horton Building and University Stadium. McCurdy introduced his general manager, George H. Stebbins, by describing him as baptized in whale oil back in New England where he was raised. Stebbins, all business at the moment, said: "We've got to have a thousand more men right away. Three thousand pretty soon. Look at these charts. We're desperately shorthanded." Stebbins and McCurdy returned to the office to lay out a "men wanted" advertising campaign to publish in the Spokane papers.

Volunteers

When Seattle voters went to the polls to vote on November 3, they were asked to bring books to donate to service men in Alaska and the Pacific Northwest, where many men were stationed in dreary outposts without adequate reading material. More than 45,000 books were collected at voting places, many of them bestsellers of the past three years. These books were taken to a School District warehouse to be picked up by Army trucks for distribution.

During the month, coeds at the University of Washington presented a series of dances for men in uniform. At the November Halloween dance, called the "Ghost Guard Glide," 200 Coast Guardsmen were entertained at the women's gymnasium on the campus. There was a grand march, identification favors, apple bobbing and a waltz contest with music provided by a nine-piece Coast Artillery dance band. Punch and wafers were served at intermission. Because of the 10:30 p.m. campus curfew, the dance began early.

A Few of the Many Heroes of November

Chief Machinist's Mate Cornelius Cremer, a career Navy man with 15 years of service, was listed as dead and the Navy asked his widow not to reveal details of his death until the ship on which he served had arrived in a safe port. Cremer's wife and 6-year-old daughter had recently moved to Seattle from Anacortes.

Machinist George B. Gooding, while attached to a minesweeper at Cavite Naval Base in the Philippines, had injured his arm. Gangrene infection set in, and doctors sent him to a Manila hospital the day before the Japanese conquered the city. Nothing more was heard from Gooding, though the Navy later reported he had died as a prisoner of the Japanese.

When Navy ship *Jarvis* was lost without a trace, two Seattleites went down with it. Warren J. Newgard had graduated from Ballard High School two years earlier. The other Seattle man who died on the *Jarvis* was Chief Machinist's Mate Erwin A. Kerndl. His wife, Helen Mae, worked at the Naval Supply Depot at Mare Island, California, and their 6-and 11-year-old daughters were in Seattle visiting Kerndl's mother when news of his death arrived.

Major Jack R. Cram, born in Raymond, Washington, was a Husky track star during the late 1920s. After graduation he trained as a Marine pilot at Sand Point, and was called to active duty in 1941. On October 15, a critical day in the defense of Guadalcanal, he and his crew were flying a Catalina Flying Boat on patrol when they spotted a Japanese transport sailing toward the Solomon Islands. Major Cram had never been in combat before and his crew had never fired a shot at the enemy. Nevertheless, he maneuvered the lumbering aircraft into a dive and, though enemy Zeros were firing at them, the crew released two torpedoes. One sank the enemy transport. Marine Corps and Navy fighter pilots who observed the sinking verified the feat. The flying boat returned with both fuel tanks and an oil tank riddled with bullet holes, one tire flat and the tail sieved with holes.

Three Seattle servicemen were home in late November. Lieutenant James F. Standard, a Seattle physician serving with the Navy, and Sergeant Dick Chayka and Pfc. Leonard Deuel Jr., both of the Marine Corps, were enjoying furloughs. All three had survived battles on Guadalcanal. Private Deuel described a Trappist monk who was in his outfit. "Amid all the battle, with us hiding behind a rock the size of a cabbage, this Trappist monk would stand up serene amid the confusion. He had absolute faith in God, and just his standing there gave courage to us all."

By November 1942, Robert E. Galer was one of the most decorated marines of World War II and had made headlines across the country. Residents of Washington State had long been familiar with his name. Born in Seattle in 1913, he graduated from Queen Anne High School where he was a noted athlete. After breaking several basketball scoring records at the University of Washington, he was named to the Pacific Coast all-star basketball team. In October 1942 he downed 11 Japanese planes and would add two more before the war ended. He was shot down four times himself. He was awarded many medals including the most coveted, the Medal of Honor. For a more detailed biography see the appendix where all Washingtonians who were awarded the Medal of Honor during World War II are listed.

December 1942

Business Stories of the Month

The local Kirsten Pipe Company, producers of the internationally popular patented smoking pipe with a metal stem and briar bowl, in December shifted its entire work force to the production of 300 different light metal parts needed in the manufacture of major war equipment.

Leon Morel said that he asked no questions when his Morel Foundry received unusual orders for ship parts from the Navy. His employees were busy turning out valves and castings for ships of all allied nations.

The Doran Company of Seattle produced the largest ship propellers made on the Pacific Coast. These huge 23-ton solid bronze propellers were trucked to shipyards that were building or repairing cargo vessels. Doran also turned out smaller propellers of various sizes.

During the month the state ordered manufacturers of ice cream to reduce their output by 20 percent because butterfat was needed for butter, which was increasingly in short supply.

Names in the News

WAAC Third Officer Hazel Milbourn of Seattle was assigned to head the new administrative office for the eight Western states of the Ninth Service Command. Lieutenant Milbourn had been with the first group of Seattle WAAC officer candidates to leave the area for training.

Seattle's only professional anatomical artist, Miss Jessie Phillips, transferred her skill to Navy hospitals after joining the WAVES on December 1. She continued utilizing her abilities as a Navy anatomical illustrator.

In December, Miss Karen Falkenburg became the first "lady lead man" to work at Associated Shipbuilders. A graduate of the University of Washington, she was hired at the shipyard in September and moved up rapidly. Before the war she had been a millinery designer.

Education

As 1942 ended, 200 naval aviation cadets arrived at the University of Washington to enroll in pre-flight training classes. They were housed in a women's dormitory on campus after the coeds they displaced were moved into sororities.

At West 933 Third Avenue in Spokane, a USO facility served servicemen and women with reading material, places to write letters home, and young ladies to chat with in a homey atmosphere. The photo is dated December 1942. Cheney Cowles Museum, Spokane, L87-1.26355-42.

Young hostesses and servicemen danced to the big band sound at a Seattle USO dance on New Years Eve, 1942. After the dance was over, dating was not allowed and the young women were chaperoned home. Seattle P-I Collection, 28212, MOHAI.

Christmas 1942

The holiday season brought sustained efforts to provide Christmas cheer for service personnel stationed far from home. On December 20, the Junior Chamber of Commerce launched a Seattle-wide campaign urging citizens to help make servicemen in the area feel welcome. Ralph Benaroya, Activities Chairman of the Junior Chamber, urged citizens to invite servicemen to their homes for Christmas dinner or host groups of them to the theater or other entertainment. Collection bins to hold gifts for service personnel were placed in leading stores throughout the area. Cookies, cakes, candies and other delicacies were delivered to service men's clubs where daily open houses were planned from December 24 to January 1.

The Red Cross collected gifts for men confined to Army and Navy hospitals in the state. Gray Lady Units wrapped the presents in bright paper and attached the names of the men to whom the gifts were given. Christmas trees were decorated in each ward and Daughters of the Pioneers made dozens of holly wreaths and other

Christmas decorations for assembly rooms. Ambulatory wounded took a keen delight in assisting with the holiday preparations. One exclaimed: "Gee, next to being home, this is working up to be the best Christmas." The Washington State Defense Council on Christmas Day assured citizens, "There is no doubt that every service man spending Christmas in Washington has been remembered with a Christmas gift. A generous and friendly spirit of cooperation prevailed in all parts of the state and the last minute swamping of Victory Canteens with gifts assured success in the effort to take the holidays to all the men and women stationed here."

A Few of the Many Heroes of December

Naval Reserve Lieutenant Commander Albert L. Lloyd was a well-known insurance company executive in Washington State before being called to active duty. On November 13 he was listed as missing in action. His wife Ruth and son Wayne were residing in Bremerton when the Navy informed them that the Commander had lost his life at sea.

Tacoma's Richard F. Breckenridge, a husky submarine sailor, received the Navy Cross on December 30 for battling a torrent of water while attempting to close the conning tower hatch as his submarine dived hurriedly to escape destruction in enemy waters. When the commanding officer ordered the conning tower abandoned, all hands but Breckenridge immediately dropped down into the control room. The conning tower hatch jammed as Breckenridge struggled to close it and the lower hatch slammed shut below, trapping him. He succeeded in freeing the hand wheel that allowed him to manually wind the top hatch closed just before water had completely filled the conning tower. Had he not succeeded he would have drowned between the two hatches. His heroism saved valuable instruments and allowed the submarine to sail on.

A black Navy hero worked in the naval barracks at Seattle-Tacoma Shipbuilding for three weeks before a local reporter heard of his exploits and sought him out. Not even his commanding officer realized that Charles Jackson French had saved the lives of seven shipwrecked and wounded comrades.

The destroyer *Gregory*, on which French served as mess attendant, was sunk in a battle near the Solomon Islands. When ordered to abandon ship, French carried a wounded comrade to a lifeboat and safety, but the boat was packed so full there was no room for French. He dropped into the water and began to swim. Just then a raft floated into sight, spinning in circles as the men aboard tried to paddle against a strong tide. French, afraid to climb aboard for fear his weight would sink the raft, swam to one side and began to push and tow. He kept swimming until daybreak six hours later. That was when a search plane spotted the raft and radioed for help. Ensign Robert Adrian, wounded and on the raft, gave French credit for saving his life and the lives of the others. After the story made the papers, French was feted in the Armistice Day parade in Omaha, Nebraska, and was invited to speak before a crowd at City Hall Square. His next stop was in Hollywood, where he met several movie stars including Charles Laughton and Rochester (Eddie Anderson) the black comedian. And most satisfying of all, he was given time to visit his family in Arkansas, after which he returned to the Navy to help win the war.

CHAPTER TWO

War Production Surges

January 1, 1943 ~ December 31, 1943

*The Puget Sound Navy Yard in Bremerton sponsored this 1943 bond rally. A sign above
the stage pictured the three Axis dictators beneath a slogan that reads "Help Bat their
Heads Together! Buy Bonds!"* Kitsap Regional Library, 642y.

Personal bankruptcies increased for a time in 1943 because during the Depression years lenders learned it was worthless to sue persons with little or no income. After the debtors found employment, their wages sometimes were impounded or garnisheed. As a result, some could not meet their daily obligations and were forced into bankruptcy. After a few months, especially in families where wives also found employment, debts were soon paid. With wartime rationing and a dearth of civilian goods on the market, there was little to buy and savings began to accumulate, much of which was invested in war bonds.

As the war progressed, alcoholic beverages became scarce in Washington State liquor stores. When it was announced on January 2 that the government would prohibit the manufacture of liquor, thousands rushed to stock up, quickly depleting the supply of popular brands. Because Washington State stores had received only $2 million worth of a $14 million liquor order, their supplies were short to begin with. The government soon announced there was no need to hoard liquor because a five-year supply existed in distillers' warehouses. When customers still bought heavily, the State Liquor Board instituted a weekly quota system that brought many customers to the stores each week. Later the rule was changed to allow purchase of two-week allotments per visit.

Seattle's historic Frye Hotel became part of the war effort when the Army leased it in 1943 to house the 4th Fighter Command. The 326 rooms were furnished with Army cots and footlockers and enlisted men were billeted on the first 10 floors, officers on the top three floors. The hotel dining room and coffee shop served three meals a day and the men billeted there reported they had never been so well fed.

The Army and the Navy on January 17 honored the Webster-Brinkley Company for out-standing war production. The Army-Navy "E" pennant was presented to George Gunn, Jr., company president, by Captain Spencer S. Lewis, assistant commandant of the 13th Naval District. Employee representatives Jay Longmire, a machinist, and Marian Lewis Lambert, a shop employee, accepted the award for all company employees

On January 20, snowflakes began drifting down and soon eight inches covered the Puget Sound region. Airplane factories and shipyards were forced to suspend operations, paralyzing vital war manufacturing. When more snow was forecast, frustrated employees voiced criticism of the transit system and of the people responsible for plowing the streets. Even leading city politicians were unable to reach their offices because of the snow. Two days later the temperature moderated and rain fell, allowing citizens to return to working the usual long hours demanded by the war effort.

Drafting Husbands

Members of the Selective Service Board warned that the state's manpower quota for February was the highest since the draft began and would total more than four times the quota for January. They anticipated this would remove many younger workers from jobs in war industries. They also predicted that all married men without children would be in the service by summer, and that married men with children would be drafted later.

Wartime Activities

Lieutenant E. T. Litchfield made it clear in an article he wrote for the *Spokesman Review* that the State Guard was the first line of defense behind the regular army and came into being only when the national guard had been called to war duty. State guard members received no pay, but every Tuesday night at 8 o'clock after roll call at the armory, they perfected drills, were involved in hand grenade practices, performed guard duty, and learned to fire machine guns and other weapons. State guard regulations did not allow use of these troops outside the state, but in the event of riots, sabotage, enemy action or disaster, they were to be called into action.

January 1:
ALLIED AIR OFFENSIVE CONCENTRATES ON GERMAN U-BOAT BASES

January 3:
SOVIET ARMIES GAIN GROUND IN CAUCASUS

January 14-24:
ROOSEVELT AND CHURCHILL AGREE ON PRIORITIES AT CASABLANCA

January 22:
GERMANS FORCED OUT OF TRIPOLI, LIBYA

January 30:
U.S. FORCES ADVANCE ON GUADALCANAL

The First battalion, Fifth Washington Infantry, the state guard unit of Spokane and the Inland Empire, taught hundreds of men what the army was all about. Their commander was Colonel Lester M. Kauffman, operator of one of the largest automobile firms in the Spokane area. Besides the three state guard companies in Spokane, he commanded companies in Walla Walla, Wenatchee, Yakima, Pullman and Mason City.

In January, the new $12 million Spokane Naval Supply Depot was dedicated. More than 2,500 attended the impressive ceremony undertaken by officer personnel, the marine guard detail, and the Pasco Negro Navy Band. The supply depot was busy during the war years supplying the Farragut Naval Station, the Navy airfields at Pasco, and other Navy activities east of the Cascades.

Also in January 1943, Army engineers completed a $4 million medical center on outskirts of Spokane. This 1500-bed cantonment-type hospital operated by the Army Medical Corps was named Baxter General Hospital.

Names in the News

Movie Actor Clark Gable, after receiving the silver wings of an aerial gunner, was assigned to the Second Air Force at Fort George Wright, Spokane. He was not expected to stay there long, but his future assignments were not divulged.

Early in 1943, Congressman Warren Magnuson lost his secretary to the Coast Guard. When Miss Mary Turnbull, who had worked in the Congressman's office for five years, joined the SPARS, the Congressman, a Navy Reserve officer, was philosophical about the matter. With a grin on his face he quipped, "I regret I have but one secretary to give to my country."

Avis Lyche Leslie's job meant more to her than her monthly paycheck. She was secretary at the King County War Savings Bond Office and, with pride, told a reporter about her six Lyche brothers, four of them in the Navy, one in the Air Force, and the sixth about to be inducted.

Two had been wounded. Her oldest brother, though he had a wife and child, had recently been reclassified 1-A. Her husband, Burt Leslie, worked for the Army Engineers and his two brothers were in the armed services. These, she said, were some of the motivations behind her avid interest in selling war bonds.

On January 9, President Roosevelt left the White House on a secret mission. At Miami two Boeing Pan American Clippers, huge seaplanes under charter to the Navy, were waiting. He was hoisted aboard the Dixie Clipper and he and his party flew to Casablanca to meet Winston Churchill. There they and their advisers established priorities for continuing the war and agreed to demand unconditional surrender from Germany, Italy and Japan. Three weeks later the President returned aboard the Boeing Clipper.

Miscellaneous News of the Month

The Seattle Symphony and the Russian Ballet, for the first time in entertainment history, joined to provide a performance for swing-shift workers and their families. The mid-day program included two popular ballets, *Bluebeard* by Offenbach and *Princess Aurora* by Tchaikowsky. Symphony president Henry Judson, said, "We believe war workers, and particularly those on the swing shifts, deserve the highest type of entertainment, and we are planning to help them get it."

On January 10, 29 men from various countries stood before U.S. District Judge Lloyd L. Black and were sworn in as U. S. citizens. These emigrants from Poland, Britain, the Philippines, Italy, Germany, Czechoslovakia, Nigeria and Mexico had all joined the U.S. Army and took the oath of allegiance standing proudly in their olive drab uniforms.

The President told Congress on January 13 that $109 billion would be needed to pay for fighting the war in 1943. That brought the total cost of World War II from Pearl Harbor through June 30, 1944 to $196 billion, an amount that surpassed the costs of all other wars combined from the Revolutionary War through World War I.

American film critics selected *Mrs. Miniver*, a drama of wartime English family life, as the best picture of 1942. It starred Greer Garson, Walter Pidgeon and Teresa Wright, and for several weeks drew crowds to the Fifth Avenue Theater in Seattle.

A Few of the Many Heroes of January

With increasing numbers of U.S. Service personnel on the World War fronts, casualty lists were growing longer and increasing numbers of Washington's service personnel were being recognized for heroic actions. Here are a few of the many heroes of January 1943.

Fighter pilots Stanley G. Huey of Seattle and Othen Nelson Carlos of Auburn were awarded Air Medals for accompanying bombers on a hazardous 500 mile over-water flight to the Aleutian island of Kiska to hit the Japanese invaders. The mission of the fighter pilots was to keep enemy planes at a distance and to divert anti-aircraft fire. After the bombing run was completed, Huey and Carlos continued to strafe Japanese installations with remarkable success, the Alaska Defense Command reported. All planes returned safely.

In January 487 Navy men and Marines, wounded while fighting in the steaming swamps of Guadalcanal and on ships of war in the South Pacific, arrived in Seattle. Their train pulled into Smith Cove at 2:45 a.m., January 9, and the men were carried on stretchers to buses and ambulances to be transported to the new naval hospital north of Seattle.

The Navy and Marine Corps medal was awarded Arthur W. Glauer, a chief gunner's mate from Seattle, for heroic and courageous conduct during salvage efforts on a U.S. merchant ship. The citation stated simply that he was the diver who was instrumental in restoring the 10,000-ton ship to service.

Lieutenant (j.g.) Marvin Hart, a 23-year-old member of the Navy's Patrol Wing 4, received the Distinguished Flying Cross for his actions while defending the Aleutians after the Japanese attack of June 1942. Pilot of a Catalina Patrol boat, he volunteered for several dangerous missions to demolish enemy supplies and war craft while facing "an almost incredible succession of obstacles." His wife and baby daughter lived on Bothell Way.

On January 15, the Army Air Corps announced that five Washington State men had been awarded the Air Medal for outstanding service in the Middle East. Three were from Seattle: Captain B. Carl Del Missier, Staff Sergeant Lyle C. Winchell and Sergeant Keith P. McJunkins. Others were Technical Sergeant Robert Starsevich of Bremerton, Staff Sergeant Alvin Hall of Yakima, Major Max R. Fennel of Stanwood and Captain John N. Laven of Spokane. McJunkins, 24, was radio operator on a heavy bomber that struck enemy targets all the way from Bizerte on the Mediterranean to Bangkok in Thailand. Earlier Captain Del Missier had received the Silver Star for a bombing raid against Japanese warships in the Indian Ocean, and a few days later was awarded the Distinguished Service Cross for aerial operations in the Middle East.

A B-17 crew made news at a bomber station in England. The plane, called *Dry Martini*, took part in a raid on a steel factory in Lille, France. The Americans had just dropped their bombs when German fighters attacked. A shell crashed through the *Dry Martini* cockpit killing the pilot and wounding the co-pilot. The officer leading the flight of B-17s watched the *Dry Martini* dive 2,500 feet and considered it lost. The wounded co-pilot, however, managed to regain control and join a later formation of American planes headed for England. German fighters attacked this group of planes, firing cannon shots through the fuselage and nose of "Dry Martini." One shell knocked the oxygen mask off the navigator, 2nd Lieutenant Robert H. Nye of Bellevue. He grabbed a spare mask and continued with his duties. The co-pilot maneuvered the wounded bird safely to an English airfield, then was rushed to a hospital, where he recovered from his wounds.

On January 2, 1943, several Washington men participated in the second biggest bombing raid of the North African battle area to that date. Flying Fortresses and P-38 fighters pounded docks and other objectives at both Tunis and Bizerte. They managed to destroy at least 10 German aircraft with the loss of no American planes. Named in the dispatch were Sergeants Alex Pauline and John R. Blanca of Spokane and John D. Reed of Kennewick. Each of the three was credited with downing an enemy plane. Others participating were Everett M. Woolum and Kempster M. Lashells of Spokane, John W. Leluning of Zillah and Richard H. Granstrang of Ellensburg.

Seattle Lieutenant Norman Kossis, Broadway High School cheerleader and University of Washington graduate, enlisted in the Army Air Corps and was assigned as a bombardier on a Flying Fortress based in England. In December he mailed a letter home describing how on a raid over the Continent the nose of his plan was shot off and he almost froze to death before reaching the home

On February 18, 1943, one of the four engines on a prototype B-29 bomber caught fire as the plane rose from Boeing Field on a test flight. Pilot Edmond Allen could not gain altitude and narrowly missed the Exchange Building in downtown Seattle as he wrestled the plane out over Elliott Bay and nosed it toward the runway. The huge bomber slammed into the Frye Packing plant at 2203 Airport Way, just short of the field, killing all 11 crewmembers and 20 packing plant employees. Seattle P-I Collection 20230, MOHAI.

airfield. On January 3, while his plane was one of seven heavy bombers attacking the St. Nazaire submarine base in France, the Lieutenant's luck did not hold. His family later learned that he did not survive the St. Nazaire raid.

Lieutenant Theodore R. Hokenstad, coxswain on the University of Washington's 1937 championship freshman crew, was involved in one of the first American B-17 raids on Nazi-occupied France in late 1942. Later, the 26-year-old navigator was listed as missing during action in North Africa. In January his father, a Lutheran minister in Bremerton, was informed that his son was dead.

Several Washington State men served with the Royal Air Force in the months before the U.S. became involved in the fighting, and several of them died while flying. One of them, Lieutenant Lawrence H. Kiskaddon, 27, died January 27 when his bomber crashed in South Carolina. He had joined the RAF in 1941 and later transferred to the U.S. Air Force. Raised in Seattle, he had graduated from the University of Washington, and was a nephew of W. Walter Williams, Chairman of the Washington State Defense Council.

Emerson H. Kieswetter, a Lincoln High School graduate, also served with the Royal Air Force. The 24-year-old Sergeant was killed when his plane was destroyed on a raid over Northwestern Germany.

Ballard High School graduate Murray Duda joined the Royal Canadian Air Force shortly before the attack on Pearl Harbor. He was ordered to England in the fall of 1942 where he learned to fly a Spitfire. He was killed on January 16, 1943, during a raid on Berlin.

February 2:
LAST GERMAN TROOPS IN
STALINGRAD SURRENDER

February 17:
GERMANS DESTROY TWO-
THIRDS OF U.S. FIRST
ARMORED DIVISION IN
TUNISIA

February 28:
NORWEGIAN PARATROOPERS
FROM BRITAIN DAMAGE
NORSK POWER STATION
WHERE GERMANS PRODUCE
HEAVY WATER FOR ATOMIC
RESEARCH

February 28:
DURING FEBRUARY GERMAN
U-BOATS OVERWHELMED THE
ALLIED ATLANTIC OCEAN
CONVOY SYSTEM; SINK 120
MERCHANT SHIPS

Lieutenant Donald D. Manchester of Spokane, was bombardier on the lead plane of a January raid on Wake Island. A radio newsman in the Pacific Theater interviewed him after the raid and a Spokane station broadcast his statements. His wife and her parents heard him admit that he had been nervous and a little scared. When the announcer asked him why, he explained that it was his first time in combat and that the other fellows felt the same way. He praised his crew, saying that the reason he had been able to unload all his bombs on the objective was because the pilot, Colonel Matheny, flew perfectly and the navigator located the completely blacked-out island. It was a moonlit night, he said, and they left a blaze visible for 75 miles.

February 1943

Boeing Bomber Crashes Into Meat Packing Plant

On February 28, 1943, a prototype Boeing plane was being tested. Five minutes after lifting off from Boeing Field, fire flared in number one engine. Eddie Allen, Boeing's best-known test pilot, feathered the propeller of the engine and the crew activated the carbon dioxide extinguisher. Allen radioed the control tower that he was returning to the field. As he turned over Lake Washington, the wing of the aircraft began to burn. Allen fought to keep the craft in the air over downtown Seattle. At about 1,000 feet, two crewmen bailed out but their parachutes did not have time to open. Shortly after they jumped, the huge plane crashed into

An aerial view of the February 1943 B-29 crash scene at the Frye Packing Company plant in Seattle. The Army quickly recovered the remnants of the secretly developed test model of the giant bomber, and news reports of the tragedy were censored.
Boeing Management Co.

the three-story Frye Packing Company plant and fire exploded through the building.

Eddie Allen and the ten crewmembers, all highly skilled engineers and technicians, were instantly killed. Fortunately it was lunchtime for packing plant employees and comparatively few were on the top floor where the plane hit. Still — 30 workers died as a result of the crash and fire.

Soldiers passing in an Army truck witnessed the accident and rushed to the flaming building to help survivors. News reports prominently mentioned one of the soldiers, Private Sam Morris, a black 26-year-old heavyweight boxer from Florida, who saved four Frye employees. As the workers scrambled out of the building, Morris and other Army men rushed inside and up the stairs. Morris, on hands and knees in dense smoke, located two men, one on the floor unconscious, the other staggering in circles. He wrapped his overcoat over their heads and carried both out. He then yelled at an employee hanging from a window of the burning third story to jump and he'd catch him. This he did. He later broke the fall of

During the war hundreds of wounded Navy men and Marines arrived on a rail siding at Lake Forest Park, where they were transferred to ambulances and transported to the U.S. Naval Hospital (later Firlands Tuberculosis Hospital) north of Seattle. Seattle P-I Collection, 28178, MOHAI.

another man who jumped. He then grabbed a fire hose and helped douse the fire.

On April 3, the nation's First Lady, Eleanor Roosevelt, awarded the Soldier's Medal to the five enlisted men involved in saving at least 10 persons trapped in the blazing Frye Company plant. As they stood at attention in the County-City Building Square in Seattle, the medals were presented to each of the men for outstanding heroism performed outside actual battle. The men, four of whom were black members of a local anti-aircraft crew, were considered true heroes after their stories appeared in the local press.

Because of wartime secrecy, news reports did not mention the type of plane involved. As a result, some time passed before the public was told that the plane that crashed was an experimental model of a huge new Boeing bomber called the B-29.

The Coast Guard and the Navy Keep Busy

The local Coast Guard Auxiliary showed its worth during the war years. Members who owned pleasure craft were involved in saving lives and property during big storms, such as the high wind of mid-January. The gale pried open log booms and swept heavy timbers into moorage areas, isolating families on Hood Canal. Auxiliary members carried food and emergency supplies to homes isolated by the storm. One cold February night when waves were 12 to 15 feet high and decks and windows were coated with frost, auxiliary members patrolled Puget Sound in what they called "The Refrigerator Express." In the cold, they managed to retrieve several washed-out docks and boats that were adrift.

When the Seattle Fire Department was faced with the prospect of retiring the 323-ton

fireboat *Duwamish* for lack of a crew, the U.S. Coast Guard agreed to man the vessel. The city paid their regular Coast Guard salaries and maintained the fireboat and the government supplied the fuel. In addition to keeping the fireboat in service, the plan reduced city expenses by $1,500 per month.

At the new Naval Hospital in North Seattle, construction of a 500-bed addition was started in February. When completed, the number of beds located in the hospital's several one-story frame structures totaled 1,500. The additional beds were needed because other Naval Hospitals in Seattle and Bremerton were filled to capacity.

With so many wounded Navy and Marine Corps men recuperating in the area, providing recreation for them became a challenge. The Interchange Business Club and the University of Washington drama department scheduled performances of the play *The Farmer's Wife* for Navy hospital patients. One hundred of them arrived by bus at the University's Showboat Theater on the Ship Canal at the edge of the campus where they enjoyed the sprightly English comedy. Glenn Hughes of the University Drama Department said the student cast gladly volunteered for these special performances.

Business Items

The State Office of Price Administration disclosed on February 3 that an investigation discovered that all but 27 of the 459 retail meat markets had over-charged customers or otherwise violated regulations. The Seattle Meat Dealers' Association responded that their markets could not operate under present government ceilings and, if retail prices were not adjusted upward, many would be forced to close their doors.

February found Seattle's 21 textile plants without sufficient raw materials to meet civilian needs. Many owners feared they would be forced out of business after the regional War Manpower Commission in San Francisco refused to issue new contracts in the Puget

Sound area because of the critical labor shortage. After local Chambers of Commerce took steps to inform the War Manpower Commission about the true situation in Western Washington, new contracts were forthcoming.

On February 21, the Puget Sound Navy Yard announced that 10,000 more men were needed in Bremerton and at the Keyport Torpedo Station to replace the 40 percent of personnel taken by the draft. Two weeks earlier Selective Service had partially lifted the ban on drafting fathers and abolished deferments for men engaged in 29 formerly exempt occupations. Paul V. McNutt, War Manpower Commissioner, told the House Military Affairs Committee that he expected 10 of every 14 able-bodied men between 18 and 38 would be wearing an Army or Navy uniform by the end of the year.

Not all business stories of the month were serious. One reporter found that tattoo artists were busy in Seattle now that many servicemen were visiting the city. However, the style of artwork was changing. Patriotic designs were most popular, in part because the Navy had banned unclad figures. One tattoo artist noted that much of his recent business was drawing clothes on former nudes.

Seattle's Pike Place Meat Market was busy on February 20, 1943. Most meats were rationed and, as the signs indicate, the government had established ceiling prices. Seattle P-I Collection, 28110, MOHAI.

Headlines:
March 1943

March 5:
443 ALLIED AIRCRAFT ATTACK ESSEN IN THE FIRST OF 43 RAIDS ON RUHR VALLEY FACTORIES THAT WILL COST 1,000 ALLIED BOMBERS

March 11:
U.S. LEND-LEASE TO THE ALLIES IS EXTENDED; THE TOTAL NOW EXCEEDS $9.6 BILLION

March 18:
GERMANS PUSH DEEPER INTO RUSSIA BUT LOSE A MILLION SOLDIERS IN WINTER BATTLES

March 29:
ALLIED ARMIES ADVANCE IN NORTH AFRICA, AND ON NEW GUINEA

Auto dealers also were facing lean times. Pontiac dealers met in the Olympic Hotel with Verne Murray, national general sales manager for the company. He found that local dealers understood the need to maintain essential transportation in their communities. He added, "When it is remembered that 79 percent of all war workers get to their jobs by automobile, the enormous responsibility involved in keeping those cars in running condition is apparent."

On February 22, regulations were published describing how local rationing boards were to distribute 340,000 new passenger automobiles. Only persons listed in 14 high priority groups, including physicians, nurses, veterinarians, clergymen, firemen and policemen, were eligible for consideration.

Higher Education in Wartime

A majority of students on the University of Washington campus were serving in the enlisted reserve programs of the Army and Navy. Rigid physical conditioning courses were compulsory for both men and women students and numerous technical courses were inaugurated to train students for work on the war effort. Following University President L. P. Sieg's call for students to take part-time jobs to alleviate the increasing labor shortage, a campus manpower commission was formed to advise students of employment opportunities.

A Few of the Many Heroes of Febuary

Radioman Frank E. English, after a year's experience aboard a U.S. submarine in the South Pacific, arrived on furlough at his parent's home in rural King county. The 25-year-old former University of Washington student proudly told a reporter that the submarine on which he served had sunk 11 Japanese ships.

In February, four Washington State Navy men were awarded the Air Medal for heroism in the North Pacific. Their names: Lieutenant (j.g.) Dewey A. Ostrom of Seattle; Lieutenant (j.g.) George T. King of Woodway Park; Ensign Leonard A. Dobler of Rockford in Spokane County; Lieutenant (j.g.) Louis W. Fisher of Seattle; and Lieutenant (j.g.) Edward Arnold of Bremerton. All were in their twenties and three had recently married.

The Air Medal awarded to Colonel Ted S. Faulkner was the third decoration he had earned in less than a year. He previously received a Purple Heart and the Distinguished Flying Cross. He served with the 19th Bombardment Group in the Southwest Pacific, one of the most noted Air Force units. The group was on duty in the Philippines at the outbreak of war and experienced a year of active service without a leave. The Colonel's proud mother lived in Kirkland.

The King County Humane Society inducted a different type of hero on February 16. Eleven of the "boys" were classified 1-A and outfitted with G. I. traveling compartments and 50 pounds of food, then taken aboard a train bound for basic training camp. This was the first group of "Dogs for Defense" to be recruited locally. The largest hounds were trained in Helena, Montana, as sled dogs, and 25 others were sent to Fort Robinson, Nebraska, to learn how to assist soldiers in combat.

March 1943

Boeing Workers Seek Raises

Late in February, the workers at the Boeing Airplane factory walked out because of their low pay at a time when, despite government controls, living costs were increasing. At the time, beginners at Boeing earned 63 cents per hour, a wage raised to 70 cents after three months and to 78 cents after six months. The union was requesting a 95-cent starting wage. Employees rated as mechanics earned from 88 cents to $1.17 per hour. Two days after the walkout, the War Labor Board agreed to consider their wage demands and all workers returned immediately to their jobs.

To give some perspective to those salaries, Safeway, in March advertised bread at 9 cents a loaf, oranges at 7 cents a pound, sugar at 5 pounds for 34 cents, flour at 25 pounds for 96 cents, and potatoes at 3 cents per pound. Beer sold for 10 cents per 11-ounce bottle. Fine men's suits at Frederick and Nelson cost $45 and a suit-dress for women was priced at $7.95.

A Changed Rationing System

The new system of rationing food that became effective on March 1 was more complicated than earlier systems and caused considerable delay at the grocery stores. Called the "point system," it allowed 48 points per person during March. The number of points allotted to a can of food depended in part on its weight. Smallest cans ranged from 1 to 4 points. One pound cans were worth 6 to 13 points. Foods in short supply were worth more points than that readily available. As one newspaper reported: "Grocers' foreboding of being inundated by floods of confused questions and probably hard to take feeble jokes on point rationing were well founded."

Shortly after the point system was inaugurated, M. L. Bean, Tradewell Stores' general manager, announced a "Victory Food Sale." At the 35 Tradewell outlets, displays emphasized non-rationed foods and free recipes were available explaining how to use these foods in balanced diets. Also offered was a class to teach housewives five steps that helped keep track of ration points.

The Armed Services Purchase Property in Washington State

Between July 1, 1940, and January 15, 1943, the U.S. Navy paid $7.5 million for 80,000 acres of land in the Pacific Northwest. Among the 38 pieces of property were a radio station and 160 acres of land on Bainbridge Island; 996 acres in Clallam, Snohomish and Skagit Counties; an ammunition storage facility on Indian Island; a 390-acre Marine Corps training area in Kitsap County; a 200-acre auxiliary airfield for the Seattle Naval Air Station; a 76-acre storage facility in Seattle; 4,324 acres for a Whidbey Island Naval Air Station; and a rifle range, turret shop, and shipfitters' shop at Bremerton Navy Yard. Other properties were purchased for Everett shipbuilding facilities; a Pacific Beach

Anti-Aircraft Training Station; the Pasco Naval Reserve Air Base; the Harbor Island Receiving Station; the Seattle Naval Reserve Armory; and the Spokane Naval Supply Depot.

The Army on March 1 leased St. Mark's Cathedral in Seattle to house a training school. The building had stood vacant since the Depression years when the congregation could not pay off the $266,000 mortgage held by a trust company. The lenders had foreclosed and the congregation had shifted services to St. Barnabus' Chapel. The wartime economy soon made it possible for the Episcopalians to repay the loan and repossess the cathedral.

Over in Eastern Washington, residents in and near the tiny settlement of Richland were amazed at what was happening nearby. The federal district court had condemned 193,833 acres, an act that interfered with ranching and farming activities that had been producing $500,000 worth of agricultural products each year. The residents sent a 12-man delegation to Olympia to discuss the situation with Governor Langlie. At the State capital they were advised to "sit tight" and to disregard rumors about why the property had been condemned for defense purposes. Not until after World War II did it become known that the Hanford Reservation was the site of plutonium production for the atom bomb.

Business News

Northwest Airlines developed an advertising slogan that read "Every Minute Counts," and proudly reported that their planes could fly a Seattle traveler to Chicago in just 13 hours and 10 minutes and to Washington D.C. in just 17 hours and 35 minutes.

Congressman Warren G. Magnuson and other members of the Washington State delegation began an effort in March to establish autonomy for the Pacific Northwest and to develop direct communication with the War Production Board. At the time, all communication had to be routed through the San Francisco office and local politicians sensed that California companies were receiving favored treatment.

The Puget Sound area constantly had been described as having a critical labor shortage and, as a result, new contracts were being withheld. In August Senator Mon C. Wallgren confirmed that the Seattle office of the War Production Board would become an independent headquarters representing Washington, Oregon, Alaska and part of Idaho.

The Frederick and Nelson Department Store displayed a Treasury Department "Victory Flag" in its tearoom on March 7. This emblem indicated that 90 percent of the store's 2,000 employees had invested at least 10 percent of their salaries in war bonds. In the store's auditorium, a traveling exhibit displayed 80 photographs of 49 different Royal Air Force and American aircraft involved in the United Nations' round-the-clock bombing raids on Nazi-held territory.

The Rotogravure section of *The Seattle Times* featured photos and an article that compared the present Bremerton and its shipyard with what it was like 24 years earlier during World War I. After studying the photographs, the author concluded that "the old Bremerton — city and yard alike — appear primitive when compared to the modern scene."

A reporter visiting Simpson Logging Company's Camp 5 in northern Grays Harbor County found it heavily involved in the war effort. "Tin-pants" loggers were bouncing logs down the hillsides to where trucks could load and carry them to mills. The lumber was critical in the building of ships and army camps. This literally was a "guns, not butter" operation, the reporter wrote. Because of rationing, no butter was available in the mess hall, but as one logger said, "It's swell to have butter on hotcakes but if we ain't got it, we ain't got it." Other favorite foods were missing, too, but the loggers didn't grumble as they consumed plenty of whatever foods were available.

On March 30 the Army released about 12 million cases of canned fruits, juices and vegetables to the Food Distribution Administration to ease civilian shortages. The FDA also agreed that the Agriculture Department should release an additional two million cases of canned fruits and vegetables to augment the food supplies in the nation's retail outlets.

Local People in the News

Miss Joanna Eckstein was elected president of the Seattle Visiting Nurse Service at their March meeting. Mrs. Dietrich Schmitz, the retiring president, said, "Furthering the services of the visiting nurses in this defense city is a most essential war work." These nurses cared for widows, wives and families of service men and newcomers who moved to the Northwest in search of work, and provided needed health guidance. The Visiting Nurse Service was successful because it provided care where needed and it was needed more than ever in time of war. In 1942 they made more than 13,000 home visits to the ill, a figure that took on added importance during the wartime shortage of health professionals.

Attractive red-haired Mrs. Gwendolyn Orchard was one of the first women to learn how to drive a Seattle transit bus through the downtown business district. When Mrs. Orchard swung the big vehicle into the loading zone, let off the passengers, then calmly moved back into the traffic stream, a seasoned male driver sitting nearby commented that she was better at it than many men folks and mentioned that 11 women were being taught to drive the regular service routes.

Notes from the Education Scene

In March the Seattle Public Schools opened two additional nursery schools, both in Methodist churches. The need for such services increased as more mothers found wartime jobs.

The parents of Roosevelt High School students complained to the Seattle School Board about the intense recruiting of 17- and 18-year-old youths by the Naval Air Service. It was one thing to test the students for possible participation in the Navy's specialized training program, the parents believed, but they did not like the emotional appeals made to "immature

17-year olds" that frequently tempted them to enlist in the service before completing their high-school studies.

The University of Washington's emergency war training program was extended through the 1943 spring quarter. During the previous two quarters more than 5,000 persons enrolled in classes teaching naval architecture and ship drafting, mechanical drawing, blueprint reading, fundamentals of aerodynamics, and design and operation of radio equipment. Several of these classes had been formulated especially for women.

Men students at Seattle Pacific College who were active in the Army Enlisted Reserve Corps were ordered to active duty during March. Dr. C. Hoyt Watson, armed-services representative at the college, said they would report for active duty at Fort Lewis on April 10. A larger group of University of Washington reservists had been called to active duty the week before.

The Washington State College Victory Bell on College Hill in Pullman was rung each evening during the semester, not to boast of athletic triumphs but to honor students leaving to join the armed services. Crowds of townspeople, students, and the college military band gathered at the railway station to wish each student a safe and speedy return.

On the evening of March 3, a spacious recreation building was dedicated at Fort Lawton. The Federal Government paid construction costs and the Joint Council of Teamsters furnished the interior. In an impressive ceremony, Teamsters president Dave Beck tendered the gift to General Eloy Denson, commanding general of the Seattle Port of Embarkation, who in turn presented it to Colonel H. L. Branson, Fort Lawton commander. Some 1,500 servicemen watched the ceremony and afterward took advantage of the new facility that included a library of 5,000 volumes, a large dance floor, a cafeteria with a soda fountain just like the one in the drugstore at home. Jerry Morris, local radio personality whose real name was Morrie Alhadeff, was in charge of the dedication. After the program,

the cafeteria hostess served pie and coffee for 15 cents. Full meals were available the next day. Officers and men mingled freely at the dedication, but from then on the club served only enlisted men.

A Few of the Many Heroes of March

Major Robert E. Galer, a former University of Washington basketball star, received the Medal of Honor from President Roosevelt on March 24. Galer was presented this highest of awards for heroic conduct during battles over the Solomon Islands. (See appendix for details about Medal of Honor winners.)

Early in the 1930s, Hans L. Pollitz and his mother escaped the Nazis in Germany and immigrated to the United States. In 1937, they moved to Seattle where they enjoyed the freedom and the Northwest scenery. Pollitz volunteered to serve in the Army shortly after the U.S. declared war, and in March 1943 he died in action on a New Guinea battlefield.

The local press published daily casualty lists as increasing numbers of Americans were shipped to battle areas. Early in March four Washington Navy men, Roscoe S. Roundy of Seattle, Harland V. Swanson of Bothell, Everett A. Green of Bremerton, and Edward Martin of Everett were reported missing and all later were declared dead.

April 1943

The Business Picture

Washington State's post-war business prospects were a major subject for discussion during the month. Seattle Chamber of Commerce President D. K. MacDonald predicted the city population would rise to one million. He did not mention the suburbs but his figure must have included them. He saw tremendous growth in trade with Russia, China and the Territory of Alaska. He felt the Seattle-Tacoma Airport, when completed, would open trade doors to the Orient. Home construction and renovation would boom as the region attempted to catch up after 10 years of

Headlines: April 1943

April 1-30:
ALLIED BOMBERS DROP 10,000 TONS OF BOMBS DURING 10 MAJOR ATTACKS ON GERMANY

April 7:
180 JAPANESE PLANES ATTACK U.S. FORCES ON GUADALCANAL, SINKING THREE ALLIED SHIPS INCLUDING A DESTROYER

April 17:
OF 115 B-17S SENT TO ATTACK BREMEN AIRCRAFT FACTORIES, 16 ARE LOST TO ENEMY FIRE

April 18:
AFTER THE U.S. LEARNS TO DECIPHER ENCODED ENEMY MESSAGES, ADMIRAL YAMAMOTO, COMMANDER OF THE JAPANESE FLEET, IS LOCATED AND DIES WHEN HIS PLANE IS SHOT DOWN

April 24:
SS TROOPERS SLAUGHTER MANY JEWISH FAMILIES IN THE WARSAW GHETTO; SEND THE REST TO EXERMINATION CAMPS

April 26-May 6:
AN ATLANTIC CONVOY UNDER CONSTANT ATTACK BY 51 U-BOATS LOSES 13 OF 42 VESSELS WHILE DESTROYING 7-U-BOATS AND DAMAGING 17

During the war, with gasoline and tires rationed and new automobiles not available, bus services were vital. The Boeing Airplane Company employees came from all parts of the county. Buses such as those in the photograph carried hundreds to work each morning and home each evening. Boeing Management Co. P3221

depression and years of war. The State's vast power resources would attract new industries. He believed magnesium and aluminum plants would continue production and reclamation projects in Central Washington would add 1,700,000 acres of rich farmlands.

Boeing President Philip Johnson predicted his company's top engineers would develop new products in many fields. He even suggested that the helicopter and automobile might be combined to produce an entirely new type of vehicle. Spokesmen for mining industries predicted the light metals industry would prove the biggest boon in post-war development. Lumbermen foresaw prosperity ahead because of the huge housing shortage.

On April 11, Boeing again was advertising for more workers to manufacture Flying Fortresses. Perhaps, with production of the still-secret B-29 under way, they realized their labor shortage would grow more acute. They sought 3,000 more employees immediately. In answer to a reporter's query, the company representative responded that the total number of planes needed to meet military requirements was a military secret.

Gross sales at Boeing for the previous year topped $390 million, more than four times the 1941 sales of $97 million. However, profits dropped from $6 million to $5 million because of increased taxes and lowered prices for the planes.

An Edmonds lumberyard had successfully transformed itself into a shipyard in two years. The plant, owned by Pointer-Willamette Company, was founded only a few months before it began assembling steel barges for the Army. The final barge, built in only six and one half days, was launched ahead of schedule.

Though the government attempted to control them, real estate prices were increasing. A five-room bungalow with full basement, hot air heating and two-car garage on a large lot in north Seattle was advertised for $5,500. A South End home with six rooms and double plumbing was available for $3,000. One of the more expensive homes advertised at $14,000 was seven years old and located in the "finest restricted district." It was situated on a large well-landscaped lot with a Sound view. Four years earlier these homes would have cost about one-third less.

Education

During the war years, the Alaska Communications System trained hundreds of operators in their second floor classrooms in a downtown Seattle office building. A series of classes for 300 students were in session three shifts a day teaching fundamentals of radio theory, how to send and receive Morse code messages, how to read coded tape, and how to operate teletypes. After graduation, the students were assigned to duty in Alaska, Canada, or in the War Department's Seattle message center.

Early in the war, all Washington State colleges lost instructors to the armed services. Four professors from the University of Washington School of Journalism serve as examples. Lieutenant Vernon McKenzie and Lieutenant Byron H. Christian, when they finished basic training with the Army Air Forces in Florida, were assigned to West Coast bases. Lieutenant Merrit Benson left the campus to teach at a naval base and Lieutenant Robert Mansfield was stationed at Miami Beach.

The Broadway High School Technical Shop was a whirring, humming classroom where students learned by actually repairing equipment under the tutelage of George Muench and other instructors. Typical challenges: how to repair an automobile generator, a washing machine, a vacuum cleaner, a mangle, a waffle iron or a toaster. Because most electrical appliances were unavailable during the war, learning to repair them was a worthwhile venture. In the process, the students learned math, how to use tools, and how common appliances such as radios and electric stoves worked. Many of the students at the Broadway High School Technical Shop later entered the armed services with specialist ratings.

Local Residents in the News

In April seven young women who had been deaf since birth were hired as junior inspectors in the electrical wiring department at Boeing. Mildred and Helen Catron, Elma Tuggle, Mrs. Edith Cook, Mrs. Frances Frederickson, Elsie Spencer and Betty Voelker were directed by considerate instructors who helped them interpret printed instructions that detailed how to inspect wires, terminals and other electrical connections. Their digital talents proved to be highly valuable in examining the intricate parts of giant four-motored bombers. Because of their deafness, factory noises did not distract them. Officials noted that a growing number of physically handicapped persons were employed at Boeing.

The first 25 WACS to be stationed in the Northwest were warmly welcomed at Fort Lawton during April. Lieutenants Ida Stoller and Dorine Goldberg, commanders of the group, explained that additional Army women would soon arrive. The officers said they were a self-sufficient group in many ways. The "handywoman" of the group, according to the Lieutenants, was Auxiliary Specialist Alma Denham, 22, of Chickasha, Oklahoma. Among her several talents was serving as hairdresser for the group. "She's good at it, too. We're supposed to keep our hair up off our collars." Auxiliary Denham interposed: "I'm not a trained hairdresser. I'm ranked as a cook's helper in the

Army, but in civilian life, I was a truck driver. Drove anything they'd give me up to a ten-ton job. I thought the Army would be able to use that experience, so I joined the Army, and what did they do? Instead of assigning me a truck to drive, they assign me as a cook's helper. This is the Army, Mrs. Jones."

Increasing numbers of Coast Guard women also arrived in the State during April to take over "shore-side" duties that would free men for battle stations. These SPARS operated typewriters and switchboards and performed duties requiring mechanical skills and precision. Young, eager and enthusiastic, they were anxious to complete training so they could begin contributing to the war effort by flashing messages to planes, performing microscopic measurements on plane parts, working at airport control towers, rigging parachute harnesses and operating radio sets.

Jack Chan, for 20 years a Chinese-American interpreter at the Seattle Immigration and Naturalization Office, proudly spoke of having four sons, two daughters and seven nephews serving in the armed services. "All are third-generation Chans in America," he said. "I was born in this country — never been out of it except on a trip to Canada — and all my children were born here. My parents were born in California. My grandfather came to this country. This is our land."

Mrs. John Loor Locke, chairman of the King

Many women members of the U.S. Marine Corps attended ordnance school at the Marine Corps Air Station in Quantico, Virginia. These two are learning to attach a depth bomb to an airplane's bomb rack. National Archives 86-WWT-59-3

County Women's War Savings Division, announced that movie star Barbara Stanwyck would sell bonds and sign autographs on April 28 at Victory Square. After that appearance Miss Stanwyck was scheduled to attend a war-bond rally at Seattle-Tacoma Shipbuilding. Her husband, handsome movie star Robert Taylor, at the time a lieutenant (j.g.) in the Navy, did not accompany her.

Following a brief mid-April furlough at home, Captain John Evans, former University of Washington crew manager and holder of the Distinguished Service Cross and Air Medal, was assigned to the First Troop Command in Indianapolis. Before returning to duty, he retired his best friend, Corporal Blackout, from the service. Corporal Blackout had 500 hours of flight time to his credit and seven months experience with the transport command. He was aboard the plane one dawn when Captain Evans flew a load of needed supplies to much-bombed Malta. He also accompanied the Captain on the non-stop 1,500-mile trip that carried the first paratroopers to Oran. "He's been through a lot, "Captain Evans said, as he gave the Corporal a fond farewell cuff on the ear. "He's retiring from active service, now. He was the runt of seven puppies belonging to a WAAF stationed in Scotland. I took a shine to him and she let me have him. He's been a great companion and a good soldier. Now he can stay home and enjoy his dog food."

Miscellaneous April Items

Barnes General Hospital, biggest Army installation of its kind in the Northwest, consisted of 80 buildings on 50 acres at Fort Vancouver on the Columbia River. At Barnes, almost 1,000 civilians, Army personnel, nurses and administrative workers cared for soldiers wounded on the battlefield. The patients stayed only a short time at Barnes, a reception and evacuation hospital for men destined for other health care facilities nearer their homes.

A reed-filled acreage bordering Seattle's Union Bay was transformed into family garden plots for the war effort. Dubbed "Lagoon Farm Unincorporated," it was one of several community ventures in cooperative gardening. It was located on a strip of land at Surber Drive and East 41st Street that originally was intended to become additional greens for the University of Washington golf course. During the spring planting season, university professors were seen spading earth side-by-side with Boeing workers while a postman tilled asparagus near a high school senior planting corn. It truly was a neighborhood effort.

The Seabees, newest branch of the Navy family, began recruiting 2,400 officers in April. The men selected were given ranks ranging from warrant officer to lieutenant commander. The duty of the Seabees was to closely follow fighting marines during invasions and build advance bases, barracks, hospitals, airfields, gun emplacements, fuel oil stations and tank farms. Men with a background of field construction experience were urged to apply.

A Few of the Many Heroes of April

Lieutenant (j.g.) Vernon F. Sorenson, 23, holder of the Navy Medal for gallantry in action, was listed as missing in action in April. Lieutenant Sorenson was a graduate of the University of Washington and Broadway High School. At age 21, before entering the Navy, he had worked as the youngest Seattle skipper of a halibut schooner. His wife and daughter were living in Seattle when the telegram was delivered. Lieutenant Sorenson was later listed as dead.

The casualty lists grew longer each week. On April 15, Harry W. Ryan of Seattle was reported dead. An aviation machinist's mate, he was aboard a big patrol bomber on a tactical mission out of California when it disappeared over the Pacific. Ryan, 22, was a Queen Anne High School graduate.

Walter Raleigh Veth, whose wife lived in Seattle, also was listed as missing by the Navy, as were Philmer Gustav Zier of Davenport in Lincoln County and Albert G. Kapel of Veradale, Spokane County. All later were declared deceased.

Lieutenant (j.g.) Carl R. Heussy, 37, a

Seattle attorney and son of a Seattle physician, died on April 6 at a Port Angeles hospital of injuries received in the crash of a Coast Guard patrol plane on the Olympic Peninsula. A second Washington man, T. E. Kesner, aviation radioman from Port Angeles, also was killed in the accident.

Coastguardsmen rescued 53 Russian men and women after their freighter ran aground on the rocky North Pacific coast. The ship lay on her side at the base of a cliff with monstrous waves hammering at the hull. The coastguardsmen, two of whom spoke some Russian, made a line from bootlaces supplemented with strips of cloth found on the beach. When it was long enough they tossed one end to the Russians to be tied to a heavier line that was then pulled from the ship back to the cliff. The survivors, eight of them women, were then hauled one by one up the precipitous cliff to the top, then lowered down the other side to safety. The Coast Guard praised an Army medical unit that provided valuable assistance during the rescue.

Harry Anderson, a West Seattle High School graduate, was resting at home in April after surviving his second merchant ship sinking. Enemy bombers sank the first ship off Port Darwin, Australia, forcing him to swim a mile to safety. The second freighter, the *Lahaina,* was sunk December 11 by a submarine some distance off the Hawaiian Islands. The 37 survivors piled into a lifeboat hoping to reach safety. Besides Anderson, only two others — Kenneth Madison from Renton and Roderick Cameron of Tacoma — lived through the ordeal. When Anderson arrived at a hospital on one of the Hawaiian Islands, the Navy sent his mother a terse message saying he was safe. With her son now sitting near her, Mrs. Anna Anderson told a reporter, with a happy laugh, "The last I'd heard of him, he was in Houston, Texas, working as a shipping clerk. It is good to have him home."

Colonel William W. Momyer of Seattle led a group of P-40 pilots in an air battle against Nazi planes over Tunisia in April. In one day the Colonel knocked down four Stukas and his group raised their victory numbers to 34 German planes.

Not all war deaths occurred overseas. Two Seattle flyers, both sons of prominent Seattle businessmen, were killed April 21 in a Navy training plane accident over desolate desert country near the Tri-Cities. One of the dead was Aviation Machinist's Mate John G. Dupar, 22, son of Mr. and Mrs. Frank A. Dupar. His father was president of Palmer Supply Company and secretary of Western Hotels. Young Dupar's widow, five brothers and two sisters survived him. The other Seattle man who lost his life was Lieutenant William C. Haas, 26, a University of Washington graduate who learned to fly at the Sand Point Naval Air Station. He had been an instructor at the Pasco Navy Airfield for nine months.

May 1943

Business News

The Tri-Cities were booming. In the crowded town of Pasco near the Hanford Engineering Project, newly hired DuPont Company employees, including engineers, construction foremen and specialists, frantically searched for living quarters. With the new Navy airfield nearby, officers and enlisted men crowded into town. In nearby Kennewick, lodgings also were virtually unobtainable. Tiny Richland almost overnight became the largest of the three towns. The 1940 population of the Tri-cities was about 6,000. A few years later the population exceeded 40,000.

During May, the Office of Price Administration was busy investigating prices from one end of the country to the other in an effort to prevent inflation and price gouging. In Seattle the OPA cracked down on restaurant prices. Henry B. Owen, the district OPA head, remarked, "the nickel cup of coffee seems to be a thing of the past and the ten-cent sandwich is extinct." The investigators even searched for hidden price increases such as reducing the size of portions. Owens added that the objective was

Headlines:
May 1943

May 1-31:
DURING MAY, ALLIES LOSE 58 SHIPS ON THE ATLANTIC BUT SINK 41 ENEMY U-BOATS

May 12-25:
ROOSEVELT AND CHURCHILL MEETING IN WASHINGTON, DC—COMMIT TO A CROSS-CHANNEL INVASION OF EUROPE IN MID-1944

May 13:
GERMANS SURRENDER IN TUNISIA; 250,000 TAKEN PRISONER

May 17:
GERMANS BEGIN 5TH OFFENSIVE AGAINST TITO'S YUGOSLAV PARTISANS

to protect war workers, clerks and white-collar workers, many of whom were forced to live in hotels or single rooms and had to eat all their meals out.

Good news arrived in early May with the announcement that the first 9,000-foot concrete runway at Seattle-Tacoma Airport would be completed by mid-summer, relieving the pressure on Boeing Field. Plans called for an administration building and perhaps as many as 10 hangers to be built later on the site.

Rhodes Department Store in Seattle inaugurated a five-day Tuesday through Saturday workweek beginning May 17. This released 8,000 man-hours per week for employees to become involved in essential war work. Store employees readily agreed to the plan.

Everett Pacific Shipbuilding Company was authorized to enlarge its plant in order to accommodate repair work on ships up to 10,500 tons and was awarded $3.5 million by the government to build an 18,000-ton dry-dock.

During the month, a new shipyard took shape at Kennydale on the eastern shore of Lake Washington. It was touted as the largest shipbuilding plant on the Pacific Coast dedicated to construction of wooden vessels. Besides new buildings constructed on the site, Barbee Plant No. 2 was floated in on scows. The Seattle-Renton Mill building, purchased by the Barbee Company, also was moved across to Kennydale.

Thousands of American citizens of Japanese descent were hired in essential jobs during May. More than 8,000 of these people labored on farms in the three West Coast states and 4,000 others served as unpaid volunteer farm workers. In addition, about 1,000 Japanese-Americans were involved in various professions, more than 7,000 were managing farms, and 10,000 were employed in clerical, sales and similar positions or were employed as craftsmen. The Office of War Information now described the inland camps where 110,000 Japanese-Americans were relocated as "temporary way stations." More than two-thirds of the people held there were American citizens by birth. Japanese-American adults who met behavior and attitudinal requirements, the report stated, were now eligible to leave the centers.

In May, Merchant Mariners were provided a Seattle recreation center in the Vitucci building located a half block north of Pine Street on Fourth Avenue. The United Seamen's Service leased the entire second floor and appointed Roland H. Vivian manager. Crew members of merchant ships returning to Seattle after sailing in war zones found entertainment, social and recreational relaxation, and advice and counsel there.

The Coast Guard leased two floors of the Assembly Hotel at Eighth and Madison for the exclusive use of SPARS. The young women lived under military discipline, and had their own kitchen, dining room and recreation area.

Former residents of the New Richmond Hotel, some of whom had lived there for 20 years or more, were re-settled in private homes, in rooming-houses, in other hotels or with relatives when the 300-room hotel, located on Fourth Avenue South between Jackson and Washington Streets, was taken over by the Army Medical Corps. Those who were forced out reported they truly missed the friendly atmosphere of their former home.

Hundreds of Washington State mothers on Mothers' Day, May 9, received flowers from sons stationed all over the world. This was made possible through the Army Exchange Service in cooperation with the Florists' Telegraph Delivery Association. Men overseas referred to a list available at every Post-Exchange, selected the type of bouquet to be sent and paid a reduced price. These orders were sent to an office in Detroit, sorted by city, and then were telegraphed to florists throughout the country.

On the night of May 30, a $350,000 fire destroyed three large buildings at the Nettleton-Baldwin Construction Company in Seattle. A man working at Pacific Huts factory adjoining the construction company called in the alarm. A 69-year-old night watchman, Fred W. Morton, was badly burned when he tried to extinguish the flames with a hose that uncoupled from the water pipe.

Education

Seattle School Superintendent Worth McClure traveled East on business and returned home with a full realization of the moral hazards that confronted youth left long hours to their own devices while both parents worked. He heard about communities where juvenile delinquency had become a huge problem and urged local parents to make full use of the school system's program for out-of-school care. Funding was available for such care under provisions of the Federal Lanham Act.

He also reported enrollment at Van Asselt School had increased from 160 students to 560 because of the influx of families of war workers. An estimated 700 students were expected to register there by the opening of school in the fall. Six new double portables were already in use at Van Asselt and three additional portables were on order.

At the University of Washington 32 young men, all 17-years-old, were sworn into the Navy in May as cadets in the V-12 program. They had passed intelligence tests with high scores and were enrolled in accelerated courses at approved colleges and universities. The plan was to train needed naval doctors, dentists, engineers, chaplains and general deck officers. The V-12 cadets were expected to maintain above-average grades and those who did not were transferred to active duty as apprentice seamen. The Army Specialized Training Programs (ASTP) was activated about the same time with similar objectives.

Draft Deferments are Suspended

Colonel Walter J. DeLong, State Director of Selective Service, announced on May 21 that married men with children were not likely to be called before 1944. However, the State was expected to provide 24,000 men needed by the Army and Navy during the next six months. Only 96,000 men in Washington, including married men with children, were available for the draft. To meet the State's quota, about 3,000 men a month would be inducted. The Colonel indicated that 90 percent of the men on the deferred list would be called to serve within a year. Even the 35 percent of men found to be physically unqualified for the armed forces were likely to be called to limited service.

Army Recreational Center Addition

The Seattle Jefferson Park Army Recreational Center opened a new 43-room guesthouse on May 8. The structure provided free housing for women in uniform and low-cost housing for wives of servicemen. Major Ralph Sitts, the commanding officer at the Center, expressed appreciation for the whole-hearted cooperation of the Seattle Rotary Club in providing the building materials. Army personnel did the construction work. Seattle, Ballard, Renton, and Salmon Bay Aeries of the Fraternal Order of Eagles supplied furnishings. The 43 rooms included single quarters for visiting service women, rooms for husbands and wives, and shower, laundry, ironing, and trunk storage facilities, plus a large lounge.

Parts of Seattle Declared Off-Limits

A rising problem with venereal disease caused military authorities at McChord Field to declare 74-square blocks south of Yesler Way in Seattle to be off limits to their men. Earlier Paine Field officers had barred their men from this area. The Navy joined the cry by demanding a "clean-up of vice conditions in Seattle." Dr. Ragnar Westman, city health commissioner, charged that 50 establishments were operating intermittently as houses of prostitution. The Seattle Police Chief was criticized by the local press and responded that his men were fighting the problem. Conditions later were reported to be improving.

Civilian Prisoners of Japanese

On May 24, the names of 34 Washington State civilians captured by the Japanese in the Philippines were published in local newspapers.

A group of young women called "Minute Maids" (a name suggested by the famed Minute Men of the Revolutionary War) were introduced at Victory Square on May 23, 1943, and assigned to sell war bonds and stamps at downtown locations. Seattle P-I Collection, 28265, MOHAI.

Of these 15 were from Seattle and 19 from elsewhere in the state. Several couples with children were listed. In some cases only a wife was named, the status of the husband not being known at the time. A few examples: Mrs. Blanche Yankey, Jr. of Seattle was listed but the names of her husband and two sons were not included, a situation that caused considerable concern among relatives. Her husband, J. F. Yankey, Jr., had managed a construction and engineering business in the Philippines since 1929. Donald E. McCann, a 25-year-old University of Washington engineering graduate, had worked in Manila for a commercial airline for five months before war broke out. Maxine Miller was serving as a U.S Navy secretary in Manila. Mrs. Edward Stewart, born in Seattle as Dorothy Belyon, a niece of Otto and Victor

E. Rabel, had gone to Manila to marry an Englishman. Seven Tacomans, including three married couples, were on the lists as were a man and wife from Kelso, another pair from Sedro Woolley and single persons from Auburn, Everett, Renton, Seaview, Washougal, Bremerton and Cheney. Most were repatriated during the war.

Japanese-American Privates Visit Seattle

Six U.S. Army privates of Japanese ancestry, four of them former Seattle residents, visited their old hometown on furlough on May 20. Despite warnings that such visits might result in racial violence, the soldiers, wearing their U.S. Army uniforms, dined in Seattle restaurants and no unusual incidents occurred. The young men, unnamed in the brief news item, were described as circumspect in their actions.

War Bonds Sales Continue

During special noonday ceremonies, with a Hitler dummy hanging in effigy above workers building ships, the Seattle-Tacoma Shipbuilding Corporation received the Treasury Department's "T" award for war bond purchases. During the Second War Loan campaign, 2,400 of the newer shipyard employees had joined the payroll-deduction plan with a combined subscription of $17,000 per week. The "T" award was presented to firms where at least 90 percent of the employees dedicated more than 10 percent of their pay to purchasing bonds.

A Few of the Many Heroes of May

All through the month, casualty lists contained names of American servicemen previously listed as missing in action, but reclassified as prisoners of the Japanese in the Philippines. Many of these men died in prison camps. Master Sergeant Harold A. Fuller of Seattle, a UW graduate, had served in the Army as a secretary on the staff of General MacArthur. Fuller was captured on Corregidor and later died as a prisoner of war. In the same list were three other Washington State men who did not survive Japanese captivity: First Lieutenant Chester O. Bennett of Opportunity, Spokane County; 2nd Lieutenant Harold Johnson of Tacoma; and 2nd Lieutenant Donald D. Robins of Woodland.

Two days later, the press noted that Lieutenant Commander Clyde L. Welsh, who earlier was reported missing, had officially been declared a prisoner of the Japanese. He had served as an eye-nose-and-ear specialist in Seattle for eight years before being called to active duty at Canacao Hospital near Cavite in April 1941. The doctor did not survive his prisoner-of-war experiences.

On May 14, papers carried a list of 44 Washington State men captured by the Japanese, nine of whom died in prison camp. Among the deceased were: Lieutenant (j.g.)

William R. Kaye, 26, a University of Washington and West Seattle High School graduate; and Lieutenant (j.g.) Charles J. Lightfoot, 26, the grandson of a former governor of Hawaii. Also dead were: Lieutenant (j.g.) Charles M. Wilkins, graduate of Queen Anne High School and the University of Washington, who had been in charge of supplies at Cavite; Machinist's Mate Douglas Allen of Clarkston; Lieutenant Vance C. Prewitt of Walla Walla; Machinist's Mate David W. Crawford of Husum, Klickitat County; Lieutenant (j.g.) Charles F. Letson of Southworth, Kitsap County; Electrician's Mate Thomas L. Morrissey, of Bellingham; and Seaman Robert E. Trowbridge, of Everett. Later Private Jay Ripley, 23, of Seattle, a tank-battalion mechanic on Bataan was reported to have succumbed in prison camp.

Navy Signalman James M. Myler was awarded two presidential citations for bravery at Cavite, both delivered to his parents, Mr. and Mrs. Clyde Myler of Lake Forest Park, on Christmas Eve 1942. The former Broadway High School student was 34 years old when he died in Japanese captivity. He had served with the Navy since 1926. His brother, David T. Myler, a Navy storekeeper listed as missing after the November 1942 sinking of the *U.S. S. Juneau* also later was declared dead. The two sailors were the only sons in the family.

Many of the first American casualties of the war in the Pacific were reported in May and with them arrived lists of Americans killed in North African battles. On May 27, it was announced that Staff Sergeant Clarence P. Somers was missing in North Africa. He later was listed as killed in action. Sergeant Somers, 25, had graduated from Duvall High School.

Often the families of men reported missing in action waited anxious months before further information was received. Those were agonizing times not knowing whether the loved one was dead or a prisoner. Lieutenant Joe Klaas serves as an example. The 23-year-old Klaas joined the American Eagle Squadron of the Royal Air Force before the U.S. was officially at war. After Pearl Harbor, he transferred to the Army Air

*Farm Day, June 28,
1943, at Victory
Square recognized
the vital agricultural
contributions of the
State. Youth involved with
agricultural pursuits in
or near Bothell, Auburn,
Kent and Bellevue helped
celebrate the event.*
Seattle P-I Collection,
28266, MOHAI.

Force and flew in North Africa until reported missing on April 6. On May 10, his mother, who lived at the Windsor Apartment Hotel at Sixth and Union in Seattle, received a telegram from the War Department stating that her son was a prisoner of war in Italy. For the first time she knew he was still alive and her mind was eased because the Italians were believed to treat their prisoners better than the Nazis. But on May 27, a corrective telegram arrived stating that her son was a prisoner of war in Germany and had been wounded when captured. Mrs. Klaas received about 25 letters from persons east of the Rocky Mountains who had heard her son's name listed as a prisoner on short wave radio from Europe. Joe Klaas lived to come home and write about his experiences.

Many familiar names are found among lists of war dead from Washington State. Major Cheney Cowles, who had been managing editor of *The Spokane Chronicle* and earlier had served as executive editor of *The Spokesman Review,* was killed when a bomber crashed in Alabama. Major Cowles was serving as an

intelligence officer at Shreveport, Louisiana. The medium bomber reportedly broke up in the air, killing the four men aboard. The major's widow and two-year-old daughter survived him.

Lieutenant Leland J. Flower of Seattle was listed as missing in action after a bombing raid over the Continent. His parents later were informed that he had died of his wounds. Flower was a Roosevelt High School and University of Washington graduate who was called into the service in 1941 and served in North Africa before being transferred to England. He was navigator on a plane shot down during a raid on St. Nazaire, France.

Forrest D. Hedington, a member of a medical detachment in an armored infantry regiment, had been in the Army less than a year when his parents in Seattle received word that he had been missing since November 8, 1942. Technician Hedington's mother told a reporter that she and her husband had thought of all sorts of things that might have happened to him. But she felt "he must be all right — he just must." She had asked the Red Cross to help find out what had happened to her son. Young Hedington was later declared dead.

The number of American war casualties was escalating. More than 80,000 battle casualties had occurred during the first 17 months of war. The Navy, Marine and Coast Guard casualty numbers totaled 24,000, Army casualties totaled 56,942, and Merchant Marine casualties from September 1941 to May 7 totaled 4,455.

Captain Thomas Reese, 23, one of the lucky ones, wrote home from Guadalcanal that he and a crew of two had just taken off when they hit foul weather. Their plane's engine conked out at 2:30 a.m. on a dark and stormy night, the plane lost altitude quickly, hit the water, and sank in about 20 seconds. Two of the three men aboard managed to escape before the plane submerged. They grabbed an uninflated rubber lifeboat, pulled it from its storage bag and inflated it, but it was upside down. After swallowing mouthfuls of sea water, they managed to right it, climbed aboard and found both water and emergency rations had been dumped into the sea. At dawn they sighted a couple of distant islands. Reese had kept his parachute and the two men rigged it into a haphazard sail. They reached the first island 17 hours later but found it barren with no coconuts or water, so they sailed on toward the next island where they found a few green coconuts with milk to quench their thirst. They described their stay there as long enough to be able to count their ribs before a search plane from their squadron spotted the rubber raft and sent a torpedo boat to rescue them.

June 1943

Business News of the Month

During the month the Boeing Company began importing women workers from all over the country. To provide them living quarters while they were in training, the Federal Housing Administration built temporary barracks in the Denny Regrade area.

Meat packers in Seattle worked through the month to overcome the acute shortage of meat. For a time, half of Seattle's 450 markets had closed their doors for lack of beef and pork. Part of the problem resulted from confusion over government price rollbacks and subsidy payments. As a result, three packing firms established closer ties with retail outlets in hopes of preventing future shortages.

A state law guaranteeing women equal pay status with men became effective on June 7. After that, any employer who discriminated in any way between the sexes or who paid any female lower wages in time, piecework, or salary than was being paid similarly employed men could be charged with a misdemeanor.

The new wartime $5 auto-use tax stamps went on sale June 7 at post offices and Internal Revenue offices. By law every car was to display one on the windshield after June 30.

Sixty farm families were confused and bewildered when the military forced them from some of the finest soil in the White River Valley. Most of the evacuees became more understanding when told the 500 acres taken by the military would become the site of an $11 million lend-lease storage depot. After June 30 when the owners were remunerated for their property, several depot structures began rising just south of Auburn.

On June 13, Washington Boat Works on Lake Union launched its 59th vessel, a 45-foot Navy picket boat. Since establishing the plant in 1939, the company had signed contracts with the government totaling more than $1 million and had finished 14 patrol boats for the Coast Guard, 10 aircraft-rescue boats for the Navy and 34 training craft for the Maritime Commission.

With tires rationed during the war, Spokane's Goodrich Tire Store served as an official inspection station to verify tire wear and the need for new tires. Cheney Cowles Museum, Spokane, L96-1.22.

Headlines: June 1943

June 1-30:
ALLIES ARE WINNING BATTLE OF THE ATLANTIC, SINK 17 ENEMY SUBS, LOSE ONLY 20 MERCHANT SHIPS

June 1:
"GONE WITH THE WIND" BRITISH MOVIE STAR LESLIE HOWARD, DIES IN PLANE SHOT DOWN BY THE GERMANS

June 8:
PRESIDENT ROOSEVELT THREATENS DESTRUCTIVE BOMBING RAIDS IF GERMANS USE POISON GAS

June 10:
ALLIES PLAN YEARLONG BOMBER OFFENSIVE IN EUROPE THAT WILL LAST THROUGH D-DAY

June 12:
JAPANESE FORCES LOSE MAJOR AIR BATTLE NEAR GUADALCANAL

June 14:
ALLIES SEIZE THREE SICILIAN ISLANDS IN THE MEDITERRANEAN

June 30:
AMERICAN FORCES SUCCESSFULLY INVADE ISLANDS OF NEW GUINEA

In 1943 Native Americans were transported to Vashon Island farms to harvest the berry crop. All Japanese Americans previously involved in the harvest had been relocated inland a year earlier. Seattle P-I Collection, 23857, MOHAI.

The first synthetic rubber tires arrived in Seattle on June 23. A product of American ingenuity, the tires were the first indication of the success of the vital program that began when the Japanese cut off the supply of natural rubber from the South Pacific. The state's initial allotment consisted of 50 tires. Most consumers found it difficult to distinguish the synthetic from the virgin rubber tires unless they noted a small red rubber inset in the synthetic sidewall bearing the symbol S-3.

The farm labor supervisor at Washington State College reported that 125 Japanese from the Hart Mountain, Wyoming, relocation center had been moved to the town of Dayton in Columbia County to work for Blue Mountain Canning Company. This was the first group of Japanese-Americans employed in Washington State under the new farm-labor program authorized by Congress. The Japanese harvested the pea fields and were housed in the company's farm labor camp. Earlier the War Relocation Authority had expressed faith in the loyalty of 12,000 Japanese-Americans released from custody and said any accusations that spies and saboteurs had been freed were "irresponsible and ignorant." Not one instance of disloyal activity had been reported from the 12,000 given leave from relocation centers, they said.

With the population of the Seattle area rising rapidly, the post office announced the city was among the larger communities in the United States where zone delivery numbers would be required. For example, the address might read "Seattle 99, Wash."

The fishing reports for June indicated one of the best catches of salmon and halibut in years. This was a surprise considering the fact that Japanese hostile action in the Bristol Bay area of Alaska had prevented fishing there.

Edgar F. Kaiser testified in a shipyard labor hearing in Portland in early June that his father, Henry J. Kaiser, before building three shipyards in the Portland-Vancouver area, spent a lot of time at Seattle-Tacoma Shipbuilding Corporation learning the fundamentals of ship construction. At first he had projected 6,000 to 8,000 workers would be needed in their

Columbia River shipyards. This turned out to be a major underestimate. By June 1943 the three yards employed nearly 85,000 workers.

Motion picture theaters were a major source of entertainment during the war years. In June, movies advertised in local newspapers included Clark Gable in *Wings Up*, John Garfield in *Air Force*, James Cagney and Joan Leslie in *Yankee Doodle Dandy*, and George Murphy and Pat O'Brien in *Navy Comes Through*. One of the most popular features at the Paramount, Music Box and Blue Mouse Theaters was a newsreel depicting the U.S. efforts to retake Attu Island in Alaska from the Japanese invaders.

As a result of the manpower shortage, the governors and parole boards of every state were asked to release more prisoners to help in the war effort. Many first offenders with good records were inducted into the Army.

News Concerning Service Personnel

Across the state the number of marriage licenses broke all records as young couples wed before one or both went off to the armed services. On June 1 in King County, 96 applied for marriage licenses, a one-day record. Another statistic was likewise rising: the number of divorces. Many of the "quicky" marriages did not last and war-related separations often aggravated the situation.

The Coast Guard warned Puget Sound mariners that during the first week of June, coastal defense practice would result in shells being fired up to 5,000 yards northwest of Point Wilson, up to 20,000 yards northwest of Angeles Point, 5,000 yards northwest of Admiralty Head, and 5,000 yards northeast of Morrowstone Point. Ships and pleasure craft were advised to stay clear of those areas. The Coast Guard also reported that Canadian authorities had issued a warning about an unexploded depth charge found in the Strait of Juan de Fuca and provided its approximate location.

The United Seamen Service Center at 1616 Fourth Avenue in Seattle opened in June. Both licensed and unlicensed men of the American Merchant Marine were welcome to use the center for rest and recreation. A lounge, game room, library and snack bar were available. The Center was busy from the day it opened.

In late June, the 300 WAVES in the Seattle area celebrated the first anniversary of the founding of their organization. They invited Navy enlisted men and officers and representatives of several Navy organizations to a celebration at the Masonic Temple at Harvard and Pine. A huge birthday cake was served after the premiere showing of the motion picture titled *Women in Blue*. The film highlighted WAVES working at jobs they had taken over to relieve men needed on the war fronts.

The government announced on June 22 that the families of servicemen would receive increased government financial support. The $62 a month allowance was raised to $78, a figure that included $22 deducted from the husband's military pay

A Few of the Many Heroes of June

Major Everett Holstrom of Tacoma was with the famed Colonel Jimmy Doolittle raiding party that took off from the Aircraft Carrier Hornet on April 18, 1942, to bomb Tokyo. All planes but one had been lost when they ran out of fuel, but the crews bailed out. Some were captured

Navy WAVES learn to repair airplane engines in a July 1943 class at Naval Training School in Norman, Oklahoma. U.S. Naval Historical Center.

Headlines:
July 1943

July 1-18:
THE BATTLE OF KURSK,
INVOLVING 6,000 TANKS,
RESULTS IN RUSSIAN ARMIES
GAINING THE INITIATIVE
OVER THE GERMANS

July 10:
ALLIES LAND ON SICILY AND
THE ISLAND FALLS TO THE
ALLIES ON AUGUST 17

July 17:
ON NEW GUINEA THE 41ST
DIVISION, THE WASHINGTON
STATE NATIONAL GUARD
UNIT, ADVANCES AGAINST
THE JAPANESE

July 19:
700 AIRCRAFT BOMB ROME
AND DROP THOUSANDS OF
LEAFLETS URGING ITALIANS
TO SURRENDER

and executed by the Japanese. Now, 13 months after that experience, Major Holstrom and his wife were enjoying his two-week furlough at their home in Tacoma. He told a reporter, "We were lucky when our crew bailed out. It was raining and we landed on top of a mountain in China. Two days later guerrillas found us and during the next six days managed to guide us to a railroad. Soon after that we were in India where we gorged ourselves with ice cream." The Major concluded with a prediction that "The next bombing of Tokyo probably won't be just a single raid but a sustained bombing."

Joseph Merlino, Seattle macaroni manufacturer, experienced a strange coincidence. His son, Ernest Merlino, was being trained at Officers' Candidate School at Camp Wolters, Texas. Then on June 23, a letter came from his nephew, also named Ernest Merlino, saying he was in Texas. This nephew, whom Joseph had last seen on a visit to Italy in 1933, had been drafted into the Italian army, was taken prisoner in Tunisia, and had posted the letter to his uncle from a prisoner of war stockade at Camp Harford, Texas. The Italian Ernest wrote that he was delighted to be in America. His brief censored letter did not contain any political sentiments but his uncle said that his nephew obviously wanted to remain in the U.S. when the war was over.

Private James Jensen was born in Onalaska, Lewis County. He enlisted in the Army in March 1941 and was sent to the Philippines. His mother, Mrs. Henry Geier of Centralia, received word that her 25-year-old son, James, was missing after Bataan fell to the Japanese. A year went by before she learned that the Japanese had captured him. Then three months later she was notified of his death in prison camp.

July 1943

Business News of the Month

On July 1 the Navy announced it would award contracts for a $1,129,900 expansion of the Seattle Naval Station at Piers 90 and 91 at Smith Cove. The project included building barracks for 700 men, quarters for 80 bachelor officers, a training school and other buildings. All of the structures were erected on the reclaimed area north of the Garfield Street Bridge. In addition, quarters for 224 enlisted WAVES and 58 of their women officers were constructed on Magnolia Bluff on a point of land south of the bridge originally designated as a city park.

Thirty coeds and a college man became participants in the "Students-in-Industry" project in Seattle. All of those involved were from small towns and were students at colleges in Montana, Idaho, Oregon and Washington. The aim of the project was to allow students to relieve manpower shortages while earning tuition money and sociology credits. This program was activated in a dozen large American cities. Twelve of the girls in the Seattle program were working as rivet buckers and mechanics at Boeing. They were amazed at the lack of housing, the crowded buses and the casual air about possible air raids. The lone male was from Gooding, Idaho, and was placed at City Light. He remarked that the most valuable lesson he had learned in the program was "how to get along with 30 women."

Seattle officials and War Manpower Commission representatives met on July 30 to consider allowing city jail prisoners to be employed in war jobs. Some incarcerated males received suspended sentences if they agreed to work in war plants. Chronic drunks were ordered to rehabilitation in a municipal work camp in hopes that they, too, could later join the war effort.

Kenworth Motor Truck Corporation of Seattle developed two new vehicle assembly programs for the War Production Board. On July 7, the company delivered the first of 100 heavy-duty trucks ordered. The firm also was one of 14 in the nation contracted to produce 75,000 highway trucks, and one of five to participate in the construction of 241 off-highway vehicles that would be too heavy or too wide to be driven on standard highways.

The 10,000 members of Washington's 4-H Clubs did their part in the war effort. In every nook and corner of every county, the youth clubs were active in efforts to overcome food shortages. The groups salvaged tin cans, collected games to send to soldiers, and gathered "junk jewelry for service men to trade to South Seas natives." All sorts of 4-H gardens were cultivated and backyard poultry and rabbit projects were common. The youngsters also raised cows, ducks and goats. In Cowlitz County a group contracted with a cannery to produce two acres of beans and the eleven 4-H clubs on Bainbridge Island helped harvest the strawberry crop.

Seattle added another regional war-agency office when the Pacific Northwest headquarters of the Small War Plants Corporation opened on July 23. General Robert W. Johnson, chairman of the S.W.P.C., came to town to set up the office that assumed some of the duties formerly performed in San Francisco. The Seattle office was responsible for Washington, Oregon and most of Idaho. Rear Admiral E. H. Campbell (retired) of Medina was named regional director. The objectives of the Small War Plants Corporation included the spreading of contracts across the region and helping small plants to succeed.

With the increasing population on Lake Washington's East Side, the 1942 toll revenues from the Mercer Island Floating Bridge increased by more than $74,000 over receipts of the previous year, more than enough to fund retirement of the $320,000 in bonds payable in 1943.

The War Labor Board in July denied a pay boost to more than one million U.S. shipyard workers but did recommend that a study be made of the wage rates and classifications in

the industry. The previous May, shipyard workers on the Pacific Coast had been allowed a wage increase of 8 cents an hour.

July Stories about Northwest People

Mrs. Mary Larson, 66, worked full-time at Lake Washington Shipyards in Houghton during 1943. Her 11 children all were members of the armed services or engaged in occupations supportive of the war effort. After the last of her flock left home, she sought employment at the shipyard and was hired as a scaler. She remarked, "My contribution may not be important but I make an even dozen Larsons working to win the war. And we are all putting 10 percent of our pay into war bonds." Mrs. Larson was described as prim and sedate but said she disliked being called 'a little old lady.'"

On July 20, First Lady Eleanor Roosevelt visited the Seattle Naval Hospital, accompanied by her daughter Mrs. Anna Roosevelt Boettiger, a Mercer Island resident. Mrs. Roosevelt talked with a 19-year-old man recuperating from war

During the war years, the Naval Supply Depot and 13th Naval District headquarters were located at Seattle's Smith Cove. Four large piers were numbered 88 through 91 and north of the Magnolia Bridge large barracks buildings, office structures and storage facilities were constructed. MOHAI collection, 2025.

The Lake Washington Floating Bridge shortened the former commute from East Side towns to Seattle by about 20 miles, helping conserve rationed gasoline and making it easier for suburbanites to work in war industries. This 1942 photo shows the bridge's Mercer Island tollbooths. MOHAI Collection.

wounds received in the battle for the Aleutians. She explained, "I am very interested in wartime's curious coincidences. My son, Elliott, wrote me recently of two such coincidences. Only 15 minutes after he landed in England the tail dropped off his plane. And on the return trip to Africa, the wind blew his plane into a transport ship, completely demolishing the plane, but my son was not injured. More than ever, I say, 'It's all luck.'" Commander M. H. Tibbetts, the hospital orthopedic surgeon introduced Mrs. Roosevelt to the veterans. She stood by their beds as the men told her how they were wounded. She wished each of them a speedy recovery.

Clay Blackstock, after two years as a business administration student at the University of Washington, decided to volunteer for the U.S. Corps of Engineers. His own father, Nehemiah Blackstock, chairman of Seattle Draft Board No. 1, affixed his signature to papers certifying that his son was volunteering before being drafted. Young Blackstock served as a forest products' talleyman, a position he qualified for because of his experience working with his father at the Blackstock Lumber Company.

In July the first German, Italian and Japanese prisoners of war arrived at Spanaway

to be housed briefly in a former Civilian Conservation Corps barracks adjacent to Fort Lewis. The 12-acre tract in a pine grove on the Fort Lewis prairie was made secure before the enemy soldiers were incarcerated there. The prisoners were photographed, identified, entered in official lists, medically examined and properly outfitted. Because the camp was located in a critical war area, the prisoners were only processed there before being assigned to inland camps for the duration.

Press and Navy officers waited patiently in Room 1023 of the Olympic Hotel to interview a subject who arrived 25 minutes late. When she walked in, red-haired, freckled, dressed in an olive green print dress, clanking a large bracelet on her wrist, they forgave her for keeping them waiting. Movie star Ginger Rogers had no trouble facing the cameras. In the background, looking shyly at the floor, was Private Jack Briggs of the Marine Corps, outranked by several uniformed officers in the room. The Navy public relations officer announced that Private Briggs would not be included in any of the pictures even though he was the husband of the actress. The tall and red-haired husband had played small parts in "Life With Father" and other movies. He said he liked being a Marine, then stepped farther back into the shadows to allow attention to focus on Miss Rogers, who was in Seattle to help the WAVES celebrate their first anniversary.

A Few of the Many Heroes of July

A list of 20 Washington State men reported to be prisoners of the Japanese was published in local newspapers on July 1. Of the 20, six were later reported to have died in prison camp. Among them was Seattle Marine Sergeant Richard A. Yarrow, a Queen Anne High School graduate, who had enlisted in 1935 and fought in early battles in the Philippines. He was awarded the Distinguished Service Cross for bravery on Bataan where he was wounded in January 1942. Other prisoners who died in captivity were Lieutenant Kenneth I. Bunn of Wenatchee, Lieutenant Colonel Harland R.

Burgess of Vancouver, Lieutenant Colonel W. T. Holloway Cook of Steilacoom, Major Allen L. Peck of Spokane, and Technical Sergeant Einar Wilson of Tacoma.

On July 30 Staff Sergeant Budd R. Schmidt, 24, of Brewster, Okanogan County, tail gunner on a Flying Fortress, downed a JU-88 during a raid over Oschersleben, Germany. On an earlier raid he shot down two enemy fighter planes. In a letter to a friend he described the experience:

We were over France on a regular bombing mission when a motor conked out about 15 minutes from the target. The pilot turned around to head for home flying about 20 feet above the ground. Over the English Channel about 25 Focke-Wulfs attacked us and during the resulting scramble, we downed nine of them. The only thing that saved us was the low altitude, because Jerry couldn't hit us from below and he had to be careful when diving at us to keep from crashing in the water. We landed with about 500 bullet holes in our B-17. I got two Jerries for my share and incidentally I was scared as hell.

August 1943

Local News of the Armed Services

On August 8 in a ceremony on the lawn of the County-City Building in Seattle, General Edward Morris, commander of the Fourth Fighter Command, officiated at the ceremony where former WAACs became WACs as the word "Auxiliary" was dropped and its members were resworn into the Women's Army Corps. When the half-hour ceremony ended, the "new" WACs hurried back to their jobs.

A new warplane was introduced early in August — the P-51B Mustang. A high altitude fighter, it was said to be the fastest aircraft ever flown. Details of the plane were restricted information but in fly-overs reporters witnessed it streak out of sight in seconds.

With the Allies winning battles, fear of Japanese attacks on the West Coast began to dissipate. The Coast Guard relieved its volunteers of many duties, returning many of

the privately owned pleasure craft to their owners to use in more pleasurable cruising. The Coast Guard's several new harbor craft assumed all such duties.

August 4, 1943, marked the 153rd birthday of the U.S. Coast Guard, which was founded in 1790 as the Revenue Cutter Service. During World War II, coastguardsmen joined other fighting forces in the South Pacific, Greenland, North Africa and Australia. They manned rapid-fire guns aboard troop transports and cargo ships, drove invasion barges onto hostile shores under enemy fire, guarded convoys carrying war materials to the fighting Allies, and protected U.S. coasts against landings of enemy troops and saboteurs.

U.S. civilians appreciated what American service personnel were accomplishing and tried to provide them recreational activities. The Women's University Club in Seattle, for example, sold cookbooks and gave teas to provide funds to outfit a clubmobile for troops in Alaska. At a fundraising tea at the Broadmoor home of Mr. and Mrs. Cassius Gates, the empty clubmobile was parked in the driveway. The women present agreed to furnish it with a movie projector, a radio and record player, a doughnut-making machine and other luxuries needed to make this "home on wheels" for the men up north. It was the first of its kind to be sent to Alaska.

During the previous 18 months, Washingtonians donated more than 538,000 pounds of magazines and 100,000 books to Army troops through the Liberty Committee of the Civilian War Commission.

An item on the front page of many papers urged that airmail packages containing Christmas gifts and food for prisoners of war or interned civilians in the Far East be sent no later than August 24 to assure delivery by the holidays.

August Business News Items

The $7.5 million destroyer *Pritchett* was sent down the ways at the Seattle-Tacoma Shipbuilding Corporation on August 1. This

On September 21, 1943, workmen at Seattle's Boeing Airplane Company plant were completing the interior shell of a Flying Fortress. Seattle P-I Collection, 23931, MOHAI.

ship, the 18th World War II destroyer built by the Corporation, was christened by Mrs. Dorothy Prichett Tucker of Seattle, a distant cousin of Commander James M. Prichett of the U.S. Navy who had commanded the gunboat *Tyler* during the Civil War. A second cousin of Commander Prichett, J.B. Prichett, 94, one of the few surviving Confederate veterans, was a guest of honor. The old gentleman explained: "While Commander Pritchett won distinction with the Union forces, I served with the Confederacy in a Georgia regiment toward the close of the Civil War."

Throughout August, much effort was given to locating 9,000 additional employees for the Boeing Company. The entire state now was aware that the government was withholding war contracts because of reputed regional manpower shortages. The Seattle Chamber of Commerce took up the cudgels and President D. K. MacDonald wired the Secretary of War stating that a community effort to find the needed workers was underway. He received a response from Undersecretary of War Robert

Patterson stating that only the normal number of cancellations would be forthcoming as long as the drive to recruit 9,000 new Boeing workers was progressing.

The Boeing Airplane Company kept trying to improve employee services at its plants. They rebuilt employee cafeterias to provide hot meals for 1,600 people at a time. Restrooms were enlarged and brief entertainment was provided during noon lunch periods. The company continued efforts to convince the government to increase the regulated pay scales. Beginners at Boeing were paid 67 cents per hour while the shipyard scale started at 95 cents an hour.

Boeing purchased full-page advertisements in several newspapers to explain how the company was working to overcome the manpower shortage. One ad was headlined "Here's What Boeing is Doing About the Manpower Situation:"

> Over 40 percent of the Fortress job was bid out to subcontractors; 20 percent more was transferred to branch plants. Since before Pearl

Harbor Boeing has subcontracted many major parts of the Fortress. For even then it was anticipated that future demands for Flying Fortresses would require production schedules which would exceed the manpower potential in Seattle.

Now, with a critical shortage of manpower in this area, Boeing is completely revising its production operation to transfer all possible assemblies to branch plants in out-of-town locations. In addition, Boeing is placing further sub-contracts in the Seattle area, with those plants having facilities and personnel suitable to this type of work.

Likewise, the Branch Plant program is being expanded far beyond original plans. Plans are now being set up in Aberdeen, Everett, Tacoma, Bellingham and Chehalis, and planned for Shelton and possible other locations where manpower is available.

Today 157 major subcontractors are building parts for the Flying Fortress. They are located in 20 different states. Their plants vary in size — employ from less than 10 people to thousands. They supply 10,473 separate parts for the Fortress, each one of which Boeing would otherwise have to make itself. In addition, 1,500 direct suppliers and vendors contribute thousands of other parts . . .

But even with the comprehensive subcontracting and branch plants program, the Boeing company still needs several thousand additional employees for its Seattle plant to meet the constantly increasing schedules which the government has assigned Boeing for the production of the Flying Fortress — the weapon which is spearheading the allied attack on the Axis.

One of the causes of the sudden need for more manpower, the start of B-29 production, was top secret and could not be mentioned in any of the news releases.

The Navy Torpedo Station at Keyport in Kitsap County was seeking 500 more employees. Keyport was established in 1914 to overhaul and modernize torpedoes. During World War II the activities at the station were expanded and it became one of the Navy's prime torpedo assembly plants.

During August, a "Share the Home" project was inaugurated in the State's metropolitan areas in an effort to find living space for additional employees hired by war industries. In peacetime, a family moving to a new community could build or buy a home, but during the war, with labor and construction materials not available for building private homes, newcomers were forced to find quarters in existing structures. The war-housing office in the Douglas Building helped new workers find shelter with Washington families who had basements or upstairs rooms to rent. Sometimes the homeowner provided both room and board.

Washington tavern owners, facing a shortage of beer during the summer months, met to discuss their difficulties. The suggestion of one tavern owner that they restrict patrons to one glass of beer an evening was met with hollow silence. Then the publicans agreed to close their establishments only after the last drops of beer had run from their taps. The attorney for the Washington Brewers Institute explained that the shortage was the result of the military taking 15 percent of the output of all breweries, a shortage of metal for caps and glass for bottles and the war preventing the importation of brews. At the meeting, the tavern keepers learned that future wine supplies also were not assured because winemaking was not considered a vital war industry.

The price for haircuts increased from 75 cents to $1 on August 13. The cause, according to the Barbers' Union, was the rising cost of living and because customers tended to wait longer between trims, which resulted in each haircut taking longer.

People in the News

Former Democratic national chairman James A. Farley arrived in Seattle on August 3 on a business trip and to speak to the Seattle Rotary Club. He told a reporter that "The German people will not be able to withstand the pounding of the Allies. During the First World War, the

German homeland was not damaged but already in the present war, many German cities have been reduced to rubble." He hoped the war would end before the next election because, fighting the Axis enemy resulted in the American people having little time for politics.

Colonel W. R. Lovelace managed to break an altitude record when he bailed out of a Flying Fortress at 40,200 feet over Eastern Washington. This was the first public indication that the B-17 could operate effectively above 35,000 feet.

The traditional Ladies Day at the Seattle Yacht Club occurred on August 8. It usually was preceded by two days of men's races, but in 1943 most of the men were in the service or too busy at war work to go sailing. A sufficient number of younger women appeared to allow star boats, sloops and flatties to race. A number of the older women continued with their Red Cross sewing projects as they watched from the Yacht Club's sunny verandah overlooking Lake Union.

On August 14, Staff Sergeant Edward B. Loughran married Dorothy Michlitch in a ceremony at the Mayflower Hotel. The couple had been engaged for some time, but wedding plans were delayed until the Sergeant received an unexpected furlough. Social consultants traditionally spent a week arranging for a society wedding, but during the war years ceremonies were often planned in a day or two. In record time, Mrs. D.E. McEacheran arranged for this wedding and a nuptial breakfast for 60 people at the Mayflower Hotel. Seattle's wartime housing shortage created a problem for such events. Banquet halls were often converted at night into sleeping rooms for service men, who otherwise would have no place to stay. Mrs. McEacheran said, "Sometimes we have to waken people early so we can move the beds out and the banquet tables in. But these days, nobody minds that."

Cebert Ballargeon, Seattle banker, chaired the King County Third War Loan drive during August. His duty was to sell a sufficient number of bonds to meet King County's share of the $15 billion national quota. Eighteen civic leaders agreed to help him. "We can count on them," Ballargeon said, "as we do on our men in the South Pacific and in Europe, to succeed gloriously."

A Few of the Many Heroes of August

A battalion of Seabees from Alaska arrived in Seattle on August 19. With rifles slung over their shoulders, the 1,300 men of the Navy's 13th Construction Battalion filed ashore from a large transport. During their year at Dutch Harbor these men had salvaged several ships, and constructed warehouses, storage quarters, water works and roads. Also aboard the transport were varied Army personnel, including Air Force detachments, returning to the lower 48 states for new assignments.

Flight Officer Barlow D. Brown of Seattle, co-pilot of the Flying Fortress named *Impatient Virgin II*, participated in the American air attack on Bonn in the Ruhr Valley on August 12. He said they ran into plenty of anti-aircraft shells but saw few fighters. Earlier, in a raid over Hanover, his B-17 was badly shot up but managed to limp back to its field. Another Fortress co-pilot on the Bonn raid, Captain Boardman C. Reed of Tacoma, described the affair as a "milk run." His formation encountered only six German fighters, he said, and they made one pass and then vanished.

William C. Brown returned home on furlough after 15 months of service with the British Army and three months as an American Field Service volunteer ambulance driver in Tunisa. While visiting with his mother in Medina, his eyes lit up when he saw the dinner she had prepared. "Someone has been exaggerating the conditions at home," he said. "Rumors on the front lines suggested a U. S. food shortage. I haven't tasted food like this since I left the States, and after what I'd heard, it's beyond my wildest dreams." Asked about the kind of duties he had performed, he responded: "When the Eighth Army was attacking the Jerries, the British lost a lot of stretcher-bearers through enemy action and called on our lads to help. Every one of them volunteered for the dangerous duty, and though several were killed and a few wounded, they did a swell job."

Mercer Island Deer Season

To close the news of the month of August, here is a story that illustrates how life in the Northwest has changed since the war years. Early in August 1943, Prosecutor Lloyd Shorett warned the King County Commissioners they were sitting on a powder keg. It seems the State Game Commission had decreed an open deer-hunting season during September on Mercer Island and on the eastern shore of Lake Washington. Shorett reported that Bainbridge Island families earlier had protested against such an open season there. But the farmers on Mercer Island were complaining that deer were damaging victory gardens and crops. The Game Commission plan allowed hunting only through the sparsely populated center of Mercer Island, not on the busier shorelines. Even so, Shorett felt it was a potentially dangerous situation and asked that the plan be reconsidered.

September 1943

Labor Day, September 6

Labor Day was nationally recognized but President Roosevelt called on Americans to observe it not as a holiday but as a day to increase the output of war materials. Across the state workers heeded his plea.

Congressman Warren G. Magnuson conversed with War Department personnel about plans to overcome the manpower shortage in the Puget Sound area. He argued against transferring part of the Boeing Airplane Company operations to other locations to increase B-17 production; he believed a wiser plan would be to dislocate other smaller local industries. Tom Smith, Chairman of the King County Democrats, sent a telegram to Paul V.

McNutt, Director of the War Manpower Commission, explaining that cancellation of other war contracts in the state in order to provide manpower for Boeing would instead result in an exodus of skilled workers to other parts of the country. Smith suggested that Boeing could be fully manned "if the great wage differential existing between it and other war industries in the area were reduced, and if working conditions on the job were substantially improved."

An area production emergency committee was formed to find solutions for the manpower shortage. They described Seattle's efforts as being of the utmost importance to the war effort because of the role local industries played in meeting requirements of both the Army and the Navy. Local shipyards released a few employees in an effort to help Boeing. Boeing gained 772 employees after the War Labor Board adjusted wage schedules, raising the minimum wage to 82 + cents an hour and the top wage to $1.60 an hour. The airplane company also continued to open branch plants in other Washington towns including Chehalis, where 400 persons were soon assembling Flying Fortress parts. Previously Boeing had organized subassembly plants in Aberdeen, Everett, Bellingham and Tacoma.

The state's shipyards were more productive than ever during the month. On September 4, Ballard Marine Railway Company sent two ships down the ways in a double ceremony. One, a sturdy wooden minesweeper, the 12th ship of the type to be launched from the yard, completed a $4 million government contract. The second was a trim little wooden sub-chaser, the first of two ordered by the Navy.

On September 11 the Ames Shipbuilding and Dry-dock Company in Seattle launched a huge steel caisson into the West Waterway. The all-welded caisson was built to use as a floodgate on a Navy dry dock.

The shortage of workers again made for a difficult harvest in the fruit orchards of Central Washington. A September call went out for 25,000 persons to pick and pack the more than three billion apples ripening on the trees. Chambers of Commerce across the state were asked to help recruit workers.

The families streaming into Seattle found few, if any, empty living quarters. Hotels and rooming houses were more than full. To ease the situation, early in September the former Immigration and Naturalization Service Building at 84 Union Street was transformed. Where once aliens were detained and where, during the Depression, indigent families were provided free shelter, the Seattle Housing Authority opened a reception center for recently arrived war workers; men who could find no other lodging were provided a comfortable bed in a dormitory. Also available were a safe in which they could secure their valuables, lockers for luggage and clothes, laundry facilities, and a recreation room with pool and ping-pong tables. The charge was 75 cents a night. These were temporary arrangements while the men were helped to find permanent rooms or apartments.

Milk consumption in the cities increased rapidly during the fall of 1943. Again, population increase was the major cause. Because fluid milk sales were more profitable, butter and cheese shortages developed. The government warned that milk sales might be limited in urban areas if consumption continued to increase.

The Seattle Times Sunday magazine section on September 5 carried a lengthy article describing the contributions of Northwest Indians to the war effort. In defense plants, Indian youth were learning the trades of welding and riveting. They were found working in the holds of partially constructed ships, in construction crews at the airport, and on the assembly lines at Boeing. Many Native American young men had entered the services; more than 60 members of the small Lummi Reservation near Bellingham had enlisted. The tribes in Washington State were united with one objective; to see the war quickly won. Like all

Americans, they dreamt of a future that would allow them to return to peacetime pursuits.

A Shortage of Health Professionals

Hospital administrators and directors of nursing schools in the state joined the U.S. Public Health Service campaign to recruit 65,000 cadet nurses to replace nurses serving in the armed forces. The local shortage of nurses was acute and the Army and Navy were asking for 2,500 additional nurses each month. To attract cadet nurses, the government offered tuition, uniforms, fees and a monthly stipend to young women who would join the cadet nurse corps to be trained at established institutions across the country.

Commander M. E. Lapham, executive officer of the procurement and assignment service of the War Manpower Commission visited Seattle on September 3. The Commission was considering ways to assure an equitable distribution of doctors and dentists. The Commander told reporters that Washington State had contributed all the doctors and dentists it could spare to the country's armed forces. "Washington is a critical area of war work with an expanding population," he said. "The state, district, and county committees have done commendable work. It is now apparent that full consideration should be given to the welfare of the civilian population."

Miscellaneous Items from September

During September, physical training at the University of Washington was developing strong bodies for future officers of the Navy and Marine Corps who were completing the V-12 program. The men also learned commando tactics such as wrestling, judo and boxing to prepare them for potential hand-to-hand encounters with the enemy.

On September 14, the 10 p.m. curfew for youth 16 and younger was expanded to cover 17-year-olds as well. The law made it a misdemeanor, punishable by fine or jail sentence, for youngsters under 18 to be away from their homes after curfew unless they carried a written excuse stating it was a necessity. Parents could be fined or jailed for allowing their offspring to break the law. Youth were not allowed in public places, including theaters, after ten p.m. unless with a parent.

A Few of the Many Heroes of September

Chief Gunner's Mate James C. Ogden, whose wife and daughter lived in Centralia, was awarded two medals in a ceremony at the Pearl Harbor submarine base. Admiral Chester W. Nimitz, commander of the Pacific Fleet, presented him with the Silver Star and the Navy and Marine Corps medal for silencing several enemy guns while on submarine patrol duty.

The parents of 19-year-old Leland Camp were notified that their son was killed in action in Italy. Young Camp had entered the Army seven months earlier, had been sent to North Africa and then to the front in Italy. He had been an outstanding athlete at Lacross High School. His grandfather was serving as mayor of Lacross when the telegram arrived telling of Leland Camp's death.

A September 20 news release from U.S. Headquarters in the South Pacific called attention to a new Marine Corps flying ace, Major Gregory Boyington. During raids on Japanese bases in the Solomons, Boyington set a record by shooting down five Zeros in a single engagement. The 30-year-old Major called Okanogan and Seattle home. He was a University of Washington graduate and while on campus excelled in swimming and wrestling. Boyington later was awarded the Congressional Medal of Honor and emerged as one of the most colorful and famous soldiers of the war. (For details see the Medal of Honor winners in appendix.)

Lieutenant Robert H. Adams of Pomeroy, a former student at Washington State College, was awarded an Oak Leaf cluster for his Air Medal for outstanding work while on an escort mission to Wau, New Guinea. He was ordered to intercept a superior number of enemy planes and managed to shoot one down in flames. The

news of the award was delayed and did not reach his parents until September 22. Eleven days later his parents received another telegram notifying them their 23-year-old son was missing. He later was listed as killed in action.

Lieutenant Hoge Sullivan was home on furlough during September after more than 200 hours of strafing, dive-bombing, high and low escort missions and sea sweeps. In addition he had instructed other P-38 pilots in the combat tactics he had learned by experience over North Africa, Sicily and Italy. His decorations included the Air Medal with 11 Oak-Leaf Clusters, the Silver Star and the Distinguished Flying Cross. Hoge Sullivan's grandfather, James D. Hoge, was the Seattle banker for whom the Hoge Building was named.

Head wounds received in the Battle of Attu incapacitated Sergeant Bernard Cook. With his medical discharge in his pocket, Cook returned to his home in Tennessee, anxious to find a job that paid enough to allow him to marry his fiancée. Together they visited a Boeing employment representative in Nashville who quickly hired them and arranged their transportation to Seattle. They were married in mid-September at the bride's home in Kentucky and left the following day for the Pacific Northwest. A few hours after arriving they reported at the Boeing plant. "We can't get to work building Flying Fortresses soon enough to suit us," Cook said.

October 1943

A Few Business Items of the Month

Interior Secretary Harold Ickes announced that sufficient steel had been allocated to build 26 refineries to produce high-octane aviation gasoline. This would double the nation's output of the much-needed fuel.

Paul Hoffman, Chairman of the National Committee for Economic Development and President of the Studebaker Corporation, visited the Northwest in late October. He said, "Of all the 48 states, Washington faced the third most

Headlines: October 1943

October 1:
HITLER ORDERS HIS ARMY TO HOLD THE LINE SOUTH OF ROME

October 12:
THE FIFTH AIRFORCE DROPS 350 TONS OF BOMBS ON RABAUL, NEW BRITIAN

October 13:
ITALY DELCARES WAR ON ITS FORMER ALLY GERMANY

October 14:
SCHWEINFURT BALL BEARING FACTORY IS HEAVILY DAMAGED BY 291 B-17 BOMBERS; GERMANS DOWN 60 OF THE PLANES AND DAMAGE 140

October 31:
SOVIET ADVANCES CUT ALL GERMAN RAIL LINES LEADING TO THE CRIMEA

serious postwar problem. Michigan had a 59 percent increase in its working population due to war activities. Connecticut had a 48 percent increase and Washington had an increase of 45 percent." He suggested that plans be formulated for postwar employment and for out-migration of workers that might occur at war's end.

During the month, State Liquor Control Board enforcement officers cracked down on taxicab drivers who sold liquor to departing soldiers at railroad stations for as much as $18 a fifth. Those caught in the act were charged with illegal sale of liquor by the bottle. Officers said six drivers were arrested in two days.

It was noted in a national news dispatch that women were delighted by the War Production Board's decision to double the production of hairpins. One young lady noted that "It was time somebody recognized the fact that there is no substitute for a bobby pin." Beauty shop operators reportedly breathed a great sigh of relief. One reported that she watched all her customers after one woman tried to walk out of her shop with her hair jammed full of the scarce bobby pins.

On October 15, news releases from the nation's capital informed the world that a new super bomber, one larger than Liberators and Flying Fortresses, was on the way to war fronts. To quote the release: "The mystery plane is known as the Boeing B-29, with a greater bomb-carrying capacity, range and fighting power than any existing bomber."

Another government release mentioned that a modification of the previously secret Norden bombsight permitted precision bombing from a much higher altitude. About 300 bombsights a month were being manufactured at a cost of $11,000 each. Many were installed in Boeing B-17 and B-29 bombers.

Beginning in late October lend-lease supplies and war materials destined for shipment to allies by way of the Pacific Northwest ports were stored in 12 huge warehouses surrounded by 41 miles of railroad siding in Auburn. The depot was one of the largest of the nine re-consignment operations in the country. The depot relieved congestion at Seattle, Tacoma and Portland piers. Located in a huge field half a mile wide by two and a half miles long, the depot provided 2 million square feet of closed storage plus railroad track space for 1,400 freight cars.

The new Marine Hospital overlooking Seattle from the north end of Beacon Hill was described as one of the most modern in the nation. The large structure had capacity to care for 5,800 Coast Guard, Merchant Marine and Army transport patients.

Wartime Life in Washington State

On October 9, military developments permitted West Coast dim-out restrictions to be relaxed. Normal night driving lights were permitted, as were field lighting for nighttime sports, normal lighting in store windows, and a more "carefree" lighting of homes. Streetlights, however, continued to be shielded. The Western Defense command warned that if Japanese submarines should attack coastal shipping, the dim-out would be reinstated immediately.

What was described as the "biggest crowd ever to assemble in Seattle" appeared at the University of Washington Stadium on October 3 to view spectacular demonstrations of military might. An hour before the program began, the stadium was filled to capacity and tens of thousands were turned away. The major objective of the display was to aid the drive to recruit 9,000 Boeing workers. General Hap Arnold, Chief of the Army Air Forces, was in the reviewing stand. A mock invasion was staged by Army troops wading ashore from landing craft that beached at the open end of the stadium. Bob Hope and his company of entertainers put on a show similar to those they presented for service personnel. The thousands turned away were invited to attend a repeat performance hurriedly arranged for the next evening with all performers present except for the Bob Hope ensemble, which had other engagements.

Across the state, colleges and school districts provided all sorts of night vocational classes to train people to work in war industries. Several thousand Seattle adults attended classes at Broadway-Edison Public Evening School, including a large number of service personnel stationed locally who were allowed to enroll without paying the usual fees.

WACS stationed in the Seattle area hundreds of miles from their homes complained to a reporter that they were lonesome and received few invitations to visit Northwest families. They described the cold atmosphere of their barracks as monotonous. They liked their work and felt they were aiding the war effort but hoped to become acquainted with local families. After the article appeared, invitations flooded in. "When I went to dinner," Sergeant Ellen McQuaid of Michigan said, "the people treated me as if I was their own daughter. They want me to come back again, and I am certainly going to do so at the first opportunity." Many other young women told similar stories. It seems that none as yet had accepted male "dates," but a few were thinking of responding positively to recent invitations.

Many wives of military men gave birth during the war while their husbands were fighting on some distant war front. These fathers often did not see their children until months, sometimes years later. And hundreds of these fathers did not survive the war and never saw these new sons and daughters. For the lucky ones, newspaper photos with articles about their new babies were clipped and mailed to the fathers on the warfronts. Army Lieutenant Gerald Lehan was in England when he received a clipping with a photo of his wife and 14-month-old son Robert. Captain G. C. Johnson, whose daughter was five days old in the photo he received, was with a Merchant Marine ship in Australia. Aviation Machinist's Mate James Revier had been three months overseas when he received a photo of his wife and 12-day-old son James. These men were from Seattle and none of their names appear on casualty lists, so they apparently returned to become acquainted in person with their children.

Several wives whose Army officer husbands were interned in Asian prison camps formed an informal luncheon club to boost one another's spirits and exchange any meager bits of information. They met monthly at Hotel Edmund Meany. The group also chose projects that would help with the war effort. One wife lost her husband, Colonel Jasper Brady, when he died in prison camp.

People in the News

On October 14, several Washington State families received the good news that the Japanese were repatriating several Washington civilians by way of Portuguese India. Listed from Seattle were: Paul Lutey, who had worked for American President Lines; George Otto Rockholtz, former oil company employee in Hong Kong; Bergman B. Lee and his wife Clara, missionaries in the Orient; and Winifred Englund, the 11-year-old daughter of the Reverend and Mrs. William Englund, who were presumed to be still in Japanese hands. Also listed as being repatriated were Seattleites Margaret Mary Eason, Joseph Martin, Laurist Valdmere, Walter Irving, D. W. Bruins, Sadie M and Paula Wilholt and Robert Prescott Leonard.

Tacomans being freed were George J. McCarthy, former traffic manager of American President Lines; and William Misner Portrude and Martha Ann Wilson. Also listed were Herbert C. Balleti from Tenino, Frederick G. Harris from Kelso, Wallace M. Larson of Dayton, Gaelen D. Litchfield from Vancouver, Ada A Matthias from Olympia, Mary Naomi Peyton of Garfield, Martha Henrietta Phillips of Mount Vernon, and Hazel Marie Rothrock of Tonasket. Six names of Wenatchee residents were on the list: Edith C. Coffin; Winnie S. and Myra E. Brown; and Francis M., Beatrice C., and Theodore H. Smith. Bellingham residents listed were Nathan E., Lois A, Barbara A, Nathan T. and Lois V Walton; and Elden C, Marian C, Lorna L, Dwight W, and Elden C. Whipple, Jr. This was the second group of Washingtonians to be traded for Japanese nationals held in the U.S.

Headlines: November 1943

November 1:
U.S. TROOPS LAND ON BOUGAINVILLE IN THE SOLOMON ISLANDS

November 6:
SOVIET ARMIES RETAKE THE MAJOR CITY KIEV FROM THE GERMANS

November 18:
RAF BEGINS "BATTLE OF BERLIN" THAT EVENTUALLY WILL INCLUDE 16 MAJOR AIR ATTACKS ON THE GERMAN CAPITOL

November 20-23:
U.S. TROOPS WIN TARAWA BATTLE AT A COST OF 1,000 AMERICANS KILLED AND 2,000 WOUNDED

November 25:
GLIDER BOMB SINKS A BRITISH TROOPSHIP IN THE MEDITERRANEAN; 1000 MEN ARE LOST

November 28:
CHURCHILL, ROOSEVELT, AND STALIN MEET AT TEHERAN TO PLAN THE INVASION OF SOUTHERN FRANCE

On October 1, Seattle shipyard employees selected Mrs. Frances Nevitt, a tiny blond beauty, to be Queen of the shipyards. She was introduced at three bond-selling movie premieres at the Orpheum Theater. When she shyly explained that she worked as a pipefitter's helper, the audience just laughed and refused to believe it. Queen Frances laughed in return, a habit of hers that first convinced fellow swing-shift workers to nominate her. When they asked her to enter the contest, she refused, but her friends donated money and purchased a formal gown for her. After that she could find no way to refuse them a second time. Mrs. Nevitt, 21, had joined the shipyard crew just three weeks earlier after her husband of one month, Lieutenant Robert Nevitt, left for overseas. Although Frances was born in Seattle, her parents, Mr. and Mrs. J. J. Schrag, lived on a ranch near Monroe. She said, "Boy, will they be shocked when they hear about this." When asked if she would use the honor of being selected Queen as a first step to greater laurels, she responded "No. I'm just waiting for Bob to come home. And I'll work my shift tonight."

The 25 families brought from eastern Oklahoma to the White River Valley in April 1943 by the Farm Security Administration to keep farmland there productive had quickly settled in. They found other farm folk of the valley to be friendly and the soil rich and productive. Some, however, did not enjoy living in the thin-walled two-room cabins, the only shelters available. Others did not like the dampness of the Puget Sound fall season, but many of the families already were planning to become permanent residents.

A Few of the Many Heroes of October

Marine Captain Robert Vaupell on October 8 was awarded the Air Medal for heroism over the Solomons. He previously had received two citations and the Navy Cross for his part in the battle of Midway. The citation for his Air Medal credited him with downing an enemy plane although wounded in the arm. He then survived Zero fighter attacks during the 90-mile flight down the coast of Santa Isabel Island and, despite his injury and considerable damage to his plane, sent contact reports until his radio was disabled. He finally brought his fighter to a safe landing on his home field. He was sent home to his wife, Ellen, in Seattle to recover from his wounds.

In Spokane Seaman Robert Lawrence Louks' mother received his posthumously awarded Purple Heart in mid-October. He had joined the Navy the day after Pearl Harbor when only 17 years old. He was killed in the Japanese raid on Dutch Harbor, Alaska, in June 1942. Mrs. Loucks had received little information about how her son lost his life until the medal arrived. With it was a letter describing how Robert Loucks had manned a gun with a crew that succeeded in keeping the enemy from reaching the objective. Just as the action appeared to be over, eight enemy bombers flew over to drop bombs. One exploded in front of the gun, killing the entire crew.

Lieutenant Robert T. Roberts, a marine fighter pilot with the Hell Hawk Squadron in the South Pacific was reported missing in action in October. A graduate of Spokane's West Valley High School, he attended Washington State College for two years before enlisting. His parents later were informed he had been killed in action.

Yank, the Army weekly, in October dedicated its first five pages to the battle on New Georgia Island that involved several Washington State heroes. These men fought for 12 days from Munda airfield to the sea, during which one company, with a single rifleman in a favorable firing position, passed loaded weapons to him until he forced the enemy to stop attacking. The company commander was Captain Don Downen of Pullman, a 1936 W.S.C. graduate.

The article also mentioned a hill named "O'Brien" for Lieutenant Robert M. O'Brien of Everett, who died in the New Georgia fighting. Another hill was named for Lieutenant Louis K. Christian of Pullman who died early in the battle. Others mentioned in the article were

Sergeant Orville Cummins and Captain Ralph Phelps of Spokane, Lieutenant Bob Brown of Bellingham, Sergeant Elmer McGlynn and Private Charles Boughner of Seattle, and Sergeant Bob Isaman of Chewelah.

Captain Everett E. Blakeley of Seattle and the crew of a Boeing Flying Fortress set a new record by downing 12 Nazi fighters during the October 8th American Air Force raid on Bremen, Germany. His plane, with 800 bullet holes in the fuselage and two engines shot out, barely made it back to the English coast. Damage had forced the B-17 to descend from 24,000 to 900 feet as crewmen, five of them wounded, frantically tossed guns, ammunition, navigation equipment and even the bombsight overboard. The engines sputtered through the last drops of gasoline as they crash-landed. Captain Blakeley's only injury was bruised shins.

November 1943

Washington State Wartime Business News

The Boeing Airplane Company continued to make headlines. On November 2, President P. G. Johnson announced that the October output of Flying Fortresses broke all records. No numbers were given because such information was considered a military secret. United Press reported that all U.S. aircraft factories produced 8,300 planes during the month of October. During the previous two months, Boeing increased its number of employees by 1,900 at the Seattle plant, 1,500 at Renton, and 1,000 at branch plants and sent hiring teams to the Midwest and South to find still more workers.

On November 4 Boeing paid an estimated $1,450,000 in retroactive wages. The War Labor

This Boeing Company B-17 tail section assembly area was located in the Seattle plant. Dozens of these Flying Fortresses were completed every month. The photo is dated September 21, 1943. Seattle P-I Collection, MOHAI.

Board agreed that employees who had been on the payroll since March 3 should receive $78 in back pay. On the same day the Army's "worst-kept secret" officially emerged from under wraps. For the first time it was all right to say that the B-29 existed. General H. H. Arnold issued a formal statement:

> We now have a super-bomber, the B-29. It evolved in secrecy during the past several years. The Boeing Company's large engineering staff at Seattle, which originated and developed the Flying Fortress, accomplished the engineering of the B-29 design. First experimental models of the B-29 were built at Seattle. Engineering and production information has been turned over to other major aircraft manufacturers, who also will produce the plane through final assembly. This battleship of the air is armored heavily with multiple-gun and power turrets. It can fly at very high altitudes. We will not discuss its performance capabilities before it enters combat, but it does have a range substantially greater than the maximum effective range of today's longest-range heavy bomber and will carry sizable bomb loads for that distance.

The Max Kuner Company, whose nautical instruments directed ships to many ports, stepped up production at a new location. At the request of the Navy Department, which needed the company's space, 26 truckloads of the firm's equipment were moved to a new factory. "With the increase in shipping, the demand for nautical instruments has become enormous," President Thomas R. Williamson, said. "We get many rush orders for instruments that require very careful work. We make range finders sized from 180 centimeters to 26 feet in length. The small instruments are used in planes and the large ones by coast defense fortresses."

The Bellingham Marine Railway and Boatbuilding Company, formerly producers of pleasure craft and purse seiners, manufactured minesweepers, patrol boats, salvage ships and rescue tugs between 1940 and 1943. They had earned the "E" for excellence in industrial production three times.

Dave Beck, vice president of the Teamsters'

Union, on November 24 spoke to a meeting of taxicab owners at the New Washington Hotel. Beck earlier had met with taxi drivers where he reportedly "gave them hell." He told the owners, "It's a dirty, stinking, rotten mess. Drivers overcharging as much as five times the legal amount — steering kids in uniform — your kid, my kid — to gambling houses and houses of prostitution, selling booze to 'em. It's got to be stopped. We'll expel every man caught and convicted. But we need the help of you owners." Beck suggested the owners launch an educational program to acquaint the public with legal prices and work to prevent the charging of "extra" fares.

On November 20, the University of Washington and the Seattle Chamber of Commerce announced a joint enterprise, a new approach to postwar planning. The economic and business research facilities of the University were pooled with the Chamber's committee on economic development. Dr. Nat H. Engle, director of the University's Bureau of Business Research, was loaned to the Chamber to direct the joint undertaking.

Shortages Persist

The national shortage of new tires resulted in a 30 percent reduction in the State's quota of truck tires and a 14 percent cut in passenger car tires. To compensate, the quota of used and recapped car tires was increased by 26 percent.

After the government reduced gasoline rations for commuters, the Seattle Transit System usage rose to all-time highs for three successive weeks in November. General Manager Lloyd Graber predicted the cars would be jammed full during the Christmas season. During the week that ended November 6, transit busses carried more than 3 million passengers. "Should another gasoline reduction come in December," Graber warned, "this thing is going to get entirely out of hand." On November 16, an order from the Petroleum Administration for War reduced by 17 percent the amount of gasoline allotted to the five West Coast states and Alaska and busses became even more crowded.

In Spokane, the housing situation improved considerably after 90 percent of the scheduled 7,168 dwelling units were completed. These new homes were centered in the High Bridge Park, Victory Heights and Garden Springs neighborhoods. Ray Bell, Manager at the War Housing Center, reported they were moving in 10 families per day.

The housing bureau in Spokane's city hall was open weekdays from 10 to 4 p.m. to gather information on what homes, apartments or individual rooms were available. The Red Cross staffed a special desk to aid commissioned officers and their families to find living quarters.

In Ellensburg, the army took over two downtown buildings, the old city hall and the Reed Building, for use by the quartermaster corps as a supply depot for army establishments in Central Washington.

Deer hunters in Eastern Washington and country families who did their own slaughtering were asked to help the fat salvage campaign by saving waste suet and turning it in for the war effort. In September, 13,114 pounds of grease was rendered in Spokane from public donations.

Even Thanksgiving turkeys were in short supply in Washington. The Army, Navy and War Shipping Administration continued to buy most of the birds. A Washington Cooperative Egg and Poultry Association official explained, "We are filling orders for Fort Lewis and other military stations. Last spring's hatching was late due to unsettled weather and many orders normally filled by Thanksgiving will not be filled until Christmas. Also we cannot find help to dress the fowls. Furthermore, with meats rationed, demand for fowl is heavier this year, especially from restaurants." Dealers advised housewives to order early or agree to split a large bird with a neighbor.

People In the News

Lieutenant Colonel C.E. (Cal) Butterworth and a small group of Americans overcame many obstacles to recover the bodies of men killed in action in the jungles of New Guinea and to see that they were buried with full military honors. Colonel Butterworth, president of a Seattle funeral home and a veteran of the World War 1, was placed in charge of the 41st Division's memorial section. Their duty was to make certain that fallen fighting men ultimately lay in a cemetery under the Stars and Stripes. His unit's efforts to recover bodies included such trials as an 80-mile search for bodies on horseback and a need to locate natives who could dive to the wreckage of a plane sunk deep in the sea to retrieve bodies. Most of the personnel in the group were embalmers or undertakers in civilian life. Few military dead remained unidentified since the burial parties were equipped with identification kits to take fingerprints and sketch dental charts. Soldiers who died in battle in the jungle usually were first buried where they fell. The graves were marked and maps made of locations to facilitate rapid recovery once the fighting had moved on, allowing Colonel Butterworth's men to transport the bodies to the nearest of eight United States cemeteries in New Guinea. Many later were reburied in the United States.

Frances Cameron, 26 year-old soda-fountain clerk, thought she would be different and join the WAVES. She explained to the recruiting officer that her parents had produced 24 children in their Kansas home. Three of her brothers were in the Navy, two in the Air Force, four in the Marine Corps, and two in the Army. Eight of her sisters were Army Nurses.

Mrs. Margaret Murrow was living in Spokane when she received a call from the WACS inviting her to join the Women's Army Corps. She was the wife of Colonel Lacey V. Murrow, former State Highway Director, who was serving on the staff of General Millard F. Harmon in the southwest Pacific. Mrs. Murrow was active with the Spokane Red Cross before heading south for basic training with the first Washington WAC unit to train at Fort Oglethorpe, Georgia.

Washington's Barbara Jane Erickson, Women's Auxiliary Ferrying Squadron pilot and commanding officer of one of four squadrons

The Boeing B-17 "Flying Fortress" became known as the workhorse of the U.S. Army Air Force. Thousands of them unloaded bombs over enemy factories and the battlefields of Europe, drastically punishing the Nazi war efforts.
Boeing Management Co.

the Northwest Football League, was "dangerously" injured when he crashed in a night flyer near Lincolnshire, England, in April 1942. Fractures of both ankles, head lacerations, serious burns and shock kept him in the hospital for seven months. But now Sprinkle was at his Seattle home on a 30-day leave before reporting back to the hospital for further operations on his ankles. He insisted he would hobble around on his casts to see friends and relatives. Two of his brothers — Don, a Seattle traffic patrolman, and Dick, a Marine — also were noted football players.

Not many "boys" at age 20 are first lieutenants credited with 25 bombing missions over France and Germany. Such was the case of Lieutenant Robert C. Greene of Seattle. A bombardier and gunner on Flying Fortresses, he was home on leave in early November for the first time in two years. He showed his folks his Distinguished Flying Cross and Air Medal with three Oak Leaf Clusters, but said he was most proud of the fact he had demolished three enemy fighters and that his plane was credited with a direct bomb hit on Nazi submarine pens at St. Nazaire. The most common desire among Yanks overseas, he said, was to return home.

Three seasoned veterans of bitter South Pacific air combat were home in Seattle for reassignment in early November. All were members of Marine Fighting Squadron 124, the first group to fly the new Vought Corsair in combat. Major William A. Millington, Jr., Technical Sergeant Arne A. Jacobsen and Master Sergeant Victor Mroz were with the squadron when it operated out of Guadalcanal, the Russell Islands and Munda, destroying 68 Japanese aircraft with certainty and probably 20 more. Major Millington, 30, a graduate of the University of Washington, was the son of Dr. William A. Millington, a Seattle plastic surgeon, who himself was on active duty with the Army. Sergeant Mroz, 28, a former transit operator,

of ferry pilots in the United States, enjoyed her first furlough in 14 months during November. She told a reporter, "I've logged 1,600 air hours, about 500 of them Army time. We fly on a 24-hour schedule, seven days a week, and I've piloted every kind of airplane the Army uses, flying them from factories to bases throughout the United States and Canada." Miss Erickson was a 1942 University of Washington graduate.

A Few of the Many Heroes of November

The War Department on November 19 listed three American soldiers from Washington State as dead of disease in Japanese prison camps. They were Pfc. Garth Ginther of Seattle, Pfc. Carl R. Capes of Bremerton, and Corporal Robert A. Settergren of Yakima. Listed as Missing in Action in the Mediterranean area and later reported dead was Raymond H. Mills of Chewelah in Stevens County.

Flying Officer William A. Sprinkle of the Royal Canadian Air Force first saw his five-month-old daughter on the morning of November 10, soon after being released from an Ottawa hospital. The pilot, 26, who had played football for the Renton Athletic Club in had also attended the University, and Sergeant Jacobsen, 22, was a graduate of Seattle's Lincoln High School.

December 1943

Business News Items

On December 2, Admiral S. A. Taffinder, Commandant of the 23th Naval District, approved a plan to recruit 8,000 additional workers for the Puget Sound Navy Yard in Bremerton. The 29,000 employed at the Navy Yard were too few to perform the necessary work. Since 1940, when shipyards were considered minor businesses in the state, the industry had grown to become the State's leading employer. Seventy-eight of the 164 ships delivered by U.S. yards in November 1943 were built on the Pacific Coast. Washington shipyards, in addition to producing new vessels, were busy repairing Army transports, tankers, freighters, Coast Guard vessels, barges, tugs, ferries and fishing vessels. Pacific Coast shipyards had repaired a total of 321 vessels during the two years since Pearl Harbor.

The Seattle Real Estate Board chose Philip G. Johnson, president of the Boeing Company, as "Seattle's First Citizen" for 1943. He was selected to receive the annual award because of his "outstanding civic services, his impressive role in the development of aviation, and the high honor he has brought to Seattle and Washington State through his activities as head of the firm that produces the world-renowned Flying Fortress."

The Coast Guard was again seeking manpower. They needed 300 men to join the Coast Guard Reserve to promote and preserve port security. The Coast Guard also was fighting oil pollution. Commander J. B. Calkins, Captain of the Port, said, "There has been an unusual increase lately in the number of oil-spills caused by carelessness. And there has been an increase in the amount of debris and refuse dumped into Seattle's harbor." He warned that such actions increased fire hazards and caused accidents. As an example, he told of a Liberty ship loaded with vital war material that reversed from a Seattle slip into refuse that fouled its propeller. Repairs delayed delivery of the war material for more than a week.

The government fought inflation throughout the war years and kept a close watch on prices. Frequent news reports told of retailers caught posting prices above the government ceiling. On December 13, a news item reported how a pair of stockings sold for $5.50 above the ceiling price resulted in the merchant being fined $100 and costs in U.S. District Court. He had charged $8 for a $2.50 pair of nylons.

More Hospital Space to Care for Wounded

The Fort Lewis Station Hospital became the largest Army hospital in the United States in December when a $5 million addition of 58 buildings was completed. The new space accommodated 1,567 beds, increasing the hospital's total capacity to 3,806 patients. All buildings were built as permanent structures connected by covered walkways.

People in the News

During the month, Tom and Fred Summerill established an employment record at the Boeing Airplane Company. They were the first brothers to retire after both had worked there 20 or more years. Fred, 72 years old, passed the 20-year mark in December and brother Tom, 73, had been with the company 23 years. On their last days on the job, they reminisced about when The Boeing Company turned to manufacturing bedroom furniture and sea-sleds after aircraft orders declined following World War I.

Soon after General Dwight D. Eisenhower was named supreme commander of all allied forces in Europe, a number of persons in Seattle and Tacoma proudly explained why they had avidly followed his career. They were all relatives. Eisenhower's brother Edgar and family lived in Tacoma, and six cousins — Mrs. Clarence B. Rogers, Mrs. Goldie Thompson, Arthur Stover, William Stover, Wesley Stover and Mrs. D. L. Hanson — were Seattle

Headlines: December 1943

December 1-30:
U.S. AND BRITISH BOMBERS UNLOAD 12,000 TONS OF EXPLOSIVES ON BERLIN, LEIPZIG, FRANKFURT, AND ON GERMAN FLYING BOMB LAUNCH SITES

December 2-3:
GERMAN NIGHT BOMBERS DEMOLISH AN AMMUNITION SHIP IN THE HARBOR AT BAIRE, ITALY, CREATING AN EXPLOSION THAT SINKS 18 ALLIED TRANSPORTS LOADED WITH 38,000 TONS OF SUPPLIES

December 13:
ALLIED BOMBING PROCEDURES ARE IMPROVED WHEN NEW LONG-RANGE MUSTANG FIGHTERS ACCOMPANY BOMBERS TO TARGETS

December 17:
U.S. FORCES INVADE NEW BRITAIN ISLAND, NEW GUINEA

December 24:
GENERAL EISENHOWER IS NAMED SUPREME COMMANDER FOR INVASION OF EUROPE

December 26:
THE BRITISH NAVY SINKS GERMAN BATTLE CRUISER SCHORNHORST

Service personnel always welcomed touches from home. In 1943 Seattle Red Cross volunteers filled thousands of gift boxes with candy, gum, cigarettes and dried fruits for overseas delivery. Seattle P-I Collection, 23621, MOHAI.

residents. In addition to family members, the general had many friends in the Northwest who met him while he was stationed at Fort Lewis in 1940-41.

Mrs. Lun P. Woo, the Japanese wife of a Seattle Chinese-American, was permitted to return to her home and husband in Seattle after a year in a Japanese relocation center. An Army spokesman in Seattle, said that a new policy allowed Japanese-Americans in mixed marriages to return to the Pacific Coast to live with their spouses.

A Few of the Many Heroes of December

After graduating from the University of Washington, Miss Dorothy F. Scott learned to fly in her hometown of Oroville, Okanogan County, before joining the Women's Auxiliary Ferry Service. She was awarded the rating of instructor at Spokane and from there was sent to Palm Springs, California. Three months later, she and two Army pilots were killed in the midair collision of an Army pursuit plane and a trainer. Miss Scott was 23 when she died.

Lawrence C. Norman was born in Seattle in 1917. His father Charles was Executive Secretary of the Seattle YMCA and each summer for 25 years was Camp Director at the YMCA's Camp Orkila on Orcas Island. His

mother, a registered nurse, helped keep the youth healthy while at camp. Young Larry enjoyed working at Camp Orkila and as he matured progressed from camper to counselor and finally to business manager.

A graduate of Roosevelt High School, Larry Norman enrolled at the University of Washington and joined Sigma Chi. After graduation he was employed at Pacific National Bank and a month prior to the Japanese attack on Pearl Harbor, he enlisted in the Army Air Corps. He won his wings at Victorville Air Base, and by April 1943 was overseas as a member of the 8th Air Force. He survived the risky raids on the Ploesti oil fields in Rumania and bombing raids in North Africa and around Rome.

In 1943, as a member of a noted squadron called "Ted's Flying Circus," Larry told a friend that at times he was scared and miserably sad because of the many friends he was losing during raids on the enemy Axis war facilities. He had been awarded several medals including a Distinguished Flying Cross and the Air Medal with four Oak Leaf Clusters, the equivalent of five Air Medals.

On December 22, 1943, Lieutenant Lawrence Norman and his crewmates were declared missing over the North Sea. Their plane apparently was shot down and no trace of it or the crew was found. Many years later a crewmember's dog tag washed up on a Dutch island. Lawrence C. Norman was his parent's only child. He was 27 when lost.

Marine Lieutenant Theodore J. McKay, former University of Washington football player, president of the Senior class of 1942, and son of Major and Mrs. William O. McKay, was killed in action in the South Pacific. His father, a major in the Marine Corps Reserve was in charge of the Seattle District Marine Corps recruiting service. Young McKay, 23, was survived by his widow and a two-month-old son whom he had never seen.

Lieutenant William Bryan of Seattle appeared in an Associated Press wire photo from Stockholm published locally on Christmas

Day, 1943. He was shown with a group of American flyers who had crashed, parachuted or made forced landings in Sweden after raids on Germany. All were interned by the neutral Swedes. The flyers indicated that they were lucky compared to Americans in other prison camps in Europe and were leading the life of vacationists. However, every one of them was anxious to return to combat as soon as possible.

On Christmas Day, Lieutenant Colonel Alexander B. Swenceski, a veteran Marine Corps officer, was "really glad to be home for the holidays," even though he spent Christmas in the Seattle Naval Hospital recovering from wounds. During the battle of Tarawa he was shot four times as he led his Marine battalion in an assault on Japanese fortifications. Now, a little more than a month later, the 31-year-old University of Washington graduate was back in his hometown and described for the press one of the bloodiest battles of the war to take the Gilbert Island stronghold. A gaily decorated Christmas tree stood beside his bed as he told how the resourcefulness, sacrifice and just plain guts of American troops had wiped out nearly 4,000 of the enemy in three days.

Celebrating the Holidays in Wartime

Santa Claus carried gifts to servicemen in Alaska and returned with a full pack to the states. Thanks to the Women's Advisory Board of the Washington Athletic Club in Seattle, scores of sweethearts, wives and mothers received presents from their men folk serving in the Aleutians. Through a Military Shopping Service organized by the women during the weeks before Christmas, the Army and Navy sent mimeographed Shopping Service order forms to men at five Alaskan outposts. The forms included spaces for the serviceman to list a choice of gifts and the name and address of the recipients. There were also spaces for listing sizes. Each was to enclose a money order or check to cover the cost of the gift and postage. Any money remaining after the present was purchased was included with the gift in the form of war savings stamps.

Citizens went all out to make Christmas an enjoyable time for servicemen and women stationed in Washington State. The Home Hospitality Committee of the Civilian War Commission's Services arranged for families to invite service personnel into their home for "a dinner like mom used to fix." There were parties at the Seattle Service Men's Club with dances, dinners and carol singing. The Salvation Army, the Army Navy YMCA and many other organizations arranged to help soldiers, sailors and marines celebrate the season. The Rotary Clubs, Kiwanis Clubs, Knights of Columbus Lodges and several women's clubs helped furnish gifts and refreshments for the celebrations. On Christmas Day, the Armed Forces Division Music Committee arranged for carolers to perform for wounded men at the huge Naval Hospital. This committee also arranged for choirs to perform at Fort Lewis and Fort Lawton. Travelers Aid Society lounges provided Christmas refreshments and decorated trees so those traveling through the area could enjoy a bit of Christmas. On Christmas Day, the Civilian War Commission's Victory Canteen distributed 15,000 Christmas gifts to small local military units such as anti-aircraft groups and searchlight crews, Coast Guard stations and Navy ships in port.

In many homes in the state, one of the finest gifts was a telephone call to or from a family member stationed at some distant post. The Seattle office of Pacific Telephone and Telegraph Company reported that with Christmas falling on Saturday, more than 51,000 long-distance calls were placed over the weekend, a new record.

Most New Year's celebrations were based on patriotic themes. One example: the Seattle Tennis Club's premises were festooned with red and white decorations. Club members appearing in their military uniforms were the honored guests of the evening. A midnight buffet supper was served and dancing continued until 2:30 a.m.

CHAPTER THREE

Helping Turn the Tide

January 1, 1944 ~ December 31, 1944

A Boeing bomber was a complex piece of equipment with thousands of parts. These women work on the interior of a B-29 in the Seattle factory. Machinists, electricians and others worked carefully, mindful that safety of the crew depended on how well they performed their duties. Boeing Management Co.

In spite of news reports indicating sparse supplies of liquor, celebrations at the start of 1944 were upbeat. Both the country's leaders and the public in general saluted hopes of victory in 1944. In Washington State, the New Year arrived comparatively quietly, with fewer arrests than usual by law enforcement officers. Many citizens attended church to pray for the safety of loved ones on the war fronts. Most war plants operated as usual over the holiday with one exception; The Boeing Airplane Company gave their employees their first holiday off in more than two years.

Mr. and Mrs. R. Kline Hillman celebrated at the ladies' annex of the Rainier Club by entertaining 180 members of the Women's Reserve of the Coast Guard (SPARS). After a fine buffet supper, there was entertainment, dancing and singing.

At the Service Mens' Clubs and USO in Seattle, Junior Volunteer Hostesses greeted soldiers and sailors and joined them in dancing and singing and enjoying a festive table. The young hostesses were expected to follow the rules that insisted they arrive early and leave without a date. Barbara Dawkins, a pretty 20-year-old, five-foot-nine-inch brunette, said she did not sit down all evening. "Between dances, I walked around. How else can a fellow tell how tall I am?" The young ladies tended to agree that Navy men were the best dancers. One hostess explained, "If you don't jitterbug, you either sit out most of the dances or you learn." A petite hostess remarked, "Short boys jitterbug best, and so do short girls." One pretty blond at the Service Men's Club sighed, "Gosh, what a wolf pack. We had 127 hostesses on duty New Year's Eve and were mobbed with 1,611 service men. We loved being able to show them a good time!"

Business News of the Month

In January, 20 Washington State pulp and paper mills contributed half a million dollars to University of Washington research to find ways to utilize and neutralize mill waste liquid. Previous research at the University had suggested large quantities of lignin, (a by product of the production of alcohol from wood waste) sulfur, sugar, and other ingredients needed for the war effort could be extracted from the liquids.

The National Youth Administration ended its existence in January after eight years of helping one out of every seven Washington State youths aged 16 to 25 survive the Depression. A large NYA center in Seattle's Georgetown neighborhood and dozens of similar NYA efforts across the state trained youth for future employment and helped them earn high school diplomas. During World War II, many of the NYA trainees used their new skills in the armed forces.

Butchers were delighted when the Office of Price Administration validated Spare Stamp Number 2 in War Ration Book 4, allowing additional purchases of fresh pork between January 3 and 15. At the time the pork supply was more plentiful than forecast.

The Delinquency Problem

The state's surging population figures created more than housing and transportation problems. In January 1944, estimates indicated that Washington State's number of residents had increased from 1,719,143 in 1940 to 1,883,000 by the end of 1943, more than a nine percent increase in three years. In many families both parents were working and teenage delinquency rates were rising sharply. The Reverend Dr. Newton E. Moats, speaking from the pulpit of Seattle First Methodist Church, said, "Adults must shoulder the blame for Seattle's serious problem of juvenile delinquency and must take steps to remedy the situation." He criticized law enforcement organizations, social agencies, churches and parents for inadequate steps to solve the problem. He suggested combining programs instead of "working in driblets," and favored keeping schools open longer hours. He called on housing authorities to provide full-time programs and keep community houses open at night for youth activities. He said the police

Headlines:
January 1944

January 1:
GERMAN U-BOATS BEGIN TO LOSE BATTLE OF THE ATLANTIC

January 22:
ALLIED FORCES ESTABLISH BEACHHEAD AT ANZIO

January 22:
RUSSIAN TROOPS FORCE GERMANS TEN MILES BACK INTO POLAND

January 28:
ALLIES PROTEST JAPANESE ILL TREATMENT OF PRISONERS OF WAR

American wives following their servicemen husbands around the country often requested assistance from the Travelers Aid Society. Some were lost, some ran short of funds, and others had sick children. Transient war workers, especially the younger ones, faced similar travails, Miss McCall said.

Transportation Improvements

The Army announced that beginning immediately $1,700,000 dollars would be spent improving Boeing Field, including the paving of much of the airport property.

The Spokane Street Viaduct along Seattle's waterfront was dedicated on January 25. It lifted traffic over the many railroad tracks on the route to West Seattle. At the brief ceremony, Mayor William F. Devin thanked those involved for their years of dedicated work and planning. He introduced Robert Macfarlane, representative of railroads and thanked them for contributing $250,000 toward construction of the viaduct. After the ceremony, Army trucks and a 25-car caravan of West Seattle residents led the first traffic over the new highway.

Fuel rationing was strictly enforced during January. Investigators from the Office of Price Administration confiscated one-third of all coupon books they inspected in the state because drivers had failed to follow the directive to write their vehicle license number and the name of the state on each individual coupon. This was to help prevent theft and to check validity of the ration books. The inspectors also drove to the mountains to look for skiers wasting gasoline. Robert C. Finley, district enforcement attorney for the OPA, reminded motorists that 5,000 barrels of gasoline had to be saved each day in order to meet the state's gasoline conservation program quota.

Families found that living in wartime housing projects provided opportunities to develop friendships and to share homemaking chores. Monday washday in a Bremerton project is depicted here. Kitsap Regional Library, 2497.

should work harder to keep "victory girls" off the streets and check the ages of girls in taverns and at dances. He also thought it wise for war industries to check home conditions before hiring both parents.

Meantime, mothers and fathers in some of the housing projects were acting on their own. At Rainier Vista, the fathers donated funds to provide a Christmas party for all the youngsters living there. Youth in the High Point housing project were some distance from the nearest movie theater so parents found a way to bring films to the housing project. As one newspaper reported, such efforts showed "Seattle has gained some pretty worthwhile citizens."

Bertha McCall, general director of the National Travelers Aid Association, visited Seattle in late January. She told the press that "War brides now arriving in America from all parts of the world, might become a postwar problem." She mentioned the difficulty in finding interpreters for more esoteric languages spoken by some of them. Also, new legal problems were apparent because wives no longer automatically became citizens when they married a serviceman. Even young

The World War II Generals from Washington

An item in the *Seattle Times* in January listed 18 World War II Army Generals
who were born in Washington State. The War Department provided the list
but gave only the birthplace of the commanders, saying for security reasons,
their present residences could not be divulged. They also explained that due
to the swiftly changing war scene, some of the officers might have a higher
rank than indicated on the list.

First on the list was Lieutenant General Jonathan M. Wainwright, commander of the defenders of Bataan and Corregidor after General Douglas MacArthur left the Philippines for Australia. Wainwright, captured by the Japanese when Corregidor fell, was listed as missing until the war ended. He survived many years in Japanese prison camps and was among other officers on the battleship *Missouri* when the Japanese signed the surrender papers at the end of the war. Wainwright was born in 1883 in Walla Walla where his father was stationed as an army officer. He was presented the Medal of Honor after his release. (See the appendix on Medal of Honor recipients for more details.)

Another well-known officer with ties to Washington State was Major General James A. Ulio, the adjutant general of the Army. He signed the telegrams sent to families of servicemen who were killed, missing, wounded or captured by the enemy. He, too, was born in Walla Walla, but one year before Wainwright.

Major General Muir Stephen Fairchild was born in Bellingham in 1892 and entered federal service as a sergeant in the Washington National Guard in 1916.

Major General Frederick Gilbreath was born in 1888 in Dayton, Columbia County, north of Walla Walla. In 1941 he was assigned command of the San Francisco Port of Embarkation and was headquartered at Fort Mason, California.

Major General Alan Walter Jones was born in Goldendale, Klickitat County, in 1894. In February 1943 he took command of the 106th Division at Fort Jackson, South Carolina. Late in 1944, the 106th was badly mauled by the Germans in the Battle of the Bulge.

Major General Lowell W. Rooks, born in Whitman County in 1893, at one time served as professor of military science and tactics at Washington State College in Pullman. He later was named chief of the training division of the Headquarters Ground Forces in Washington, D.C. and in 1942 was given an unannounced overseas assignment.

He was awarded the Distinguished Service Medal in 1943 for his success in helping direct the defeat of the Axis forces in North Africa.

Brigadier General Ben M. Sawbridge, born in Port Townsend in 1890, was listed simply as having an "overseas assignment" during the war.

Brigadier General Charles M. Ankcorn, born in Palouse, near Pullman, in 1893, also was listed as having an overseas assignment.

Brigadier General Jesmond D. Balmer, born in Pullman in 1895, was named commandant of the Field Artillery School, Fort Sill, Oklahoma, in 1942.

Brigadier General Boniface Campbell, born in 1895 in Colby, Kitsap County, served with the 98th Division.

Brigadier General Frank Lewis Culen, Jr., born in Seattle in 1892, was assistant division commander at Camp Hale, Colorado.

Brigadier General Robert W. Harper, born in Seattle in 1900, was the assistant chief of air staff training.

Brigadier General George McCoy, Jr., born in 1904 at Napavine, in Lewis County, was an Air Force commander in the Southwest Pacific.

Brigadier General Samuel L. McCroskey, born in 1893 in Colfax, commanded the 55th Coast Artillery Brigade at Camp Stewart, Georgia.

Brigadier General Raymond F. O'Neill, born in 1894 in Port Townsend, was commanding officer of Chanute Field, Illinois.

Brigadier General Frank E. Stoner, born in Vancouver, Washington, in 1894, was serving as chief of the Army Communications Service in Washington, D.C.

Brigadier General Robert I. Walsh, born in Walla Walla in 1894, served in Brazil during part of the war.

Brigadier General John S. Winn, Jr., born in Walla Walla in 1898, was artillery commander of the 42nd (Rainbow) Division at Camp Gruber, Oklahoma.

Headlines:
February 1944

February 1-23:
AMERICAN FORCES INVADE MARSHALL ISLANDS, THE FIRST PRE-WAR JAPANESE TERRITORY TO BE CAPTURED

February 2:
GERMAN REINFORCEMENTS HALT AMERICAN ADVANCES AT ANZIO

February 3:
U.S. WARSHIPS SHELL KURILE ISLANDS IN FIRST ALLIED ATTACK ON JAPANESE HOME ISLANDS

February 4:
U.S. MARINES OCCUPY TWO KWAJALEIN ISLANDS

February 15:
ALLIED BOMBERS DESTROY MEDIEVAL MONASTERY ATOP MONTE CASSINO IN ITALY

February 18:
U.S. ARMY, NAVY, MARINES INVADE ENIWETOK ATOLL

February 20-27:
U.S. AIRFORCE LOSES 65 PLANES IN MASSIVE RAIDS ON GERMAN AIRCRAFT INDUSTRY

February 29:
AMERICAN FORCES CAP A MONTH OF ADVANCES IN THE SOUTH PACIFIC BY INVADING THE ADMIRALTY ISLANDS

A Few of the Many Heroes of January

Marine Corps Pfc. Page Warren, 28, a former employee of Seattle Trust and Savings Bank, was killed by a land mine as he rushed ashore in the first wave of attackers trying to recapture the Island of Tarawa from the Japanese. Warren had been active in sports before graduating from Queen Anne High School in 1935.

After two years in the merchant marine as a cook and steward, James C. Follett was invalided home with injuries received during two enemy bombing attacks in the South Pacific. The 32-year-old sailor arrived in Seattle encased in a heavy plaster cast that extended from his neck to below his hips. He recovered quickly and in January was loading transit buses each day outside Boeing Plant No. 2. Follett explained without bitterness that he had to work because, "No pensions of any sort are provided for wounded merchant marine sailors."

Commander Melvyn H. McCoy arrived at his new assignement on Bainbridge Island on January 28. An Annapolis graduate, class of 1927, McCoy was sent to the Philippines in July 1940 as radio materiel officer. When the Japanese attack overwhelmed the islands, he retreated to Corregidor and was captured when it fell. He was one of a handful of Americans who managed to escape from the Japanese prison compound. The Navy ordered him not to reveal the details of his capture and escape for fear it would provide information to the enemy. The Commander received the Distinguished Service Cross for his part in the only successful escape from that prison camp.

Staff Sergeant Frank Obzina was resting at his mother's home in Seattle after surviving 40 flying missions in North Africa, Tunisia, Sicily and Italy. "The flak is the worst," he said. "You can't shoot back. You just sit up in the sky and pray." On one of his missions, the Sergeant downed an Italian plane and another time he helped sink three enemy transports.

February 1944

The Twins of February

The month of February brought stories of three sets of twins born in Washington State while their fathers were serving overseas. Lieutenant Bernard Pulver learned of the arrival of twin sons while recuperating in an Army hospital in Africa from wounds received in Italy. He wrote to his wife in Port Angeles asking her to please count again. He expected to be a father, he said, but of one child at a time. He added, "I want to get home and see those babies. I wonder if they look like me."

Sergeant A. A. Naes of Seattle was in the Army Air Force stationed in Alaska when his twins arrived in early January. His wife mailed him a copy of their picture that had appeared in a recent edition of Seattle papers. In this case the twins were a girl and a boy.

The third set of twins belonged to Mr. and Mrs. Robert Odle of Seattle. Corporal Odle, serving in the Army Air Force in the Southwest Pacific, was elated with the news. His wife in her message neglected to inform him whether he was father to two girls, two boys, or one of each. He sent a message asking the question and his wife quickly cabled him that he was the father of Pamela Lois and Robert William.

Sample Business Stories of the Month

Ten Seattle First Avenue tailor shops that specialized in service uniforms were warned by the Office of Price Administration to comply with price regulations. Robert C. Finley, district enforcement attorney, used the example of Navy enlisted men who preferred uniforms made of serge, a finer material than that used in regular issue uniforms. Though the demand for tailored uniforms was high, tailors, by law, were not to overcharge service personnel, he warned.

During the month, a recruiting party of 46 shipyard workmen and four Navy officers combed five Midwestern states for workers needed at Puget Sound Navy Yard in

War workers long remembered the streamlined ferry Kalakala *that transported them between Seattle and Bremerton. It was a familiar sight on Puget Sound during the 1930s and 1940s.* Puget Sound Maritime Historical Society, 1298-38.

Bremerton. Lieutenant F. A Walterskirchen accompanied the group to North and South Dakota, Minnesota, Wisconsin and Illinois, where many prospective employees were signed up.

War Bond Sales Involve Everyone

With the Fourth War Loan campaign nearing the end of its schedule, State of Washington residents had purchased more than $155 million in bonds but the state quota was $183 million. Students in the schools were asked to help. At Warren Avenue School in Seattle, pupils in the sixth, seventh and eighth grades sold bonds to relatives and friends and when Principal H. V. Mattern asked how many of the students themselves intended to buy war bonds, nearly every hand was raised. And when he asked how many of them had fathers or brothers in the armed services, most hands were raised again. The pupils also paid tribute to Miss Edith Gordon, one of their teachers who recently had resigned to join the Navy WAVES. Jane Horsfall, a WAVE Lieutenant, dropped by to tell students about the rigorous training that all women in the Navy experienced. When the bond campaign concluded on February 17, the state had sold bonds worth more than $194 million, exceeding its quota by six percent.

The American people were constantly hungry for information about the war. At Boeing's invitation, more than 25,000 Boeing employees and members of their families attended two film presentations about the war shown at the Metropolitan Theater in Seattle. One film, *War Department Reports*, utilized captured Germans and Japanese photos and materials. The second feature titled *Fortress of the Sky* was a color film depicting the history of the Boeing Flying Fortress.

People in the News

Her Royal Highness, Princess Juliana Louise Emma Marie Wilhelmina, Princess of Orange, Nassau, heir to the throne of The Netherlands, resided in exile in Canada after the Nazis occupied her country. She visited Seattle on February 3, while en route home from San Francisco. In an Olympic Hotel room, she smiled and told the press that she thoroughly enjoyed her first visit to the West Coast. She mentioned her interest in the Boeing Aircraft Company and its B-17 production facilities. She also toured shipbuilding plants on Puget Sound. In late afternoon she met with members of The Netherlands Society of Seattle. When queried about her emotions concerning the war, she responded in her perfect English: "Isn't the war news good today though?"

Kent residents, many of whom had indicated they wanted no Japanese-Americans to return to their valley, were having second thoughts. A series of forums concerning the subject were well attended. The principal speaker, Dr. Frank Williston of the Far East Department at the University of Washington quoted Joseph C. Grew, former ambassador to Japan, who said: "We should remember that whatever happens to persons of Japanese ancestry as a racial minority, can possibly happen to any other minority." Professor Williston added that Americans must remember that "we have two problems: one, to defeat Japan as a nation, and two, to meet a difficult internal question in our own democracy."

Washington's Birthday, 1943, found greeters answering questions about Snoqualmie Falls depicted at the entrance of the Seattle Service Men's Club. Local residents served as volunteers to answer questions, suggest places to visit, and converse with the servicemen who were far from home. Seattle P-I Collection, 28224, MOHAI.

The Coast Guard announced that Captain William H. Munter, 64, would retire in April with the rank of Rear Admiral, after nearly 45 years of government service. The veteran officer first was stationed in Seattle in 1902 as a third lieutenant. In 1907 he was transferred to the Gulf Coast. His final tour of duty on Puget Sound began in 1938, as war fears were troubling the five-state 13th Naval District. Captain Munter ably directed wartime safety measures and managed a vast increase in the personnel under his command.

A front-page newspaper story reported the serious problem facing a young mother of four small children. She faced eviction from the small home she rented in Seattle. The Japanese on Bataan had captured her husband, Captain Leslie Zimmerman, an Army chaplain. With the eviction order adding to her distress, she took the matter to Superior Court, declaring that the landlady had agreed to rent her the house for the duration of the war. Now the owner demanded the home back for her own use. "I'm willing to move," Mary Zimmerman said, "but I must find a place to move to." Mrs. Zimmerman, who was employed at the Port of Embarkation, said she could afford to pay "a decent rent or would consider buying a home." Within hours of the story being published, she received several offers of help.

News of Service Units

The Northwest's 3rd Infantry Division, recognized as one of the "hardest fighting" divisions in the Army, had been involved in a half dozen amphibious invasions. Its most recent battles were on the beaches of Anzio during the invasion of Italy. The 3rd Division trained at Fort Lewis before leaving for overseas duty.

The Army reported the more than 1,200 members of the Women's Army Corps stationed in Washington State were performing 230 different tasks. About 450 of these young women in the Seattle area filled positions formerly held by men who were shifted to the war fronts.

A Few of the Many Heroes of February

World War II casualty numbers mounted rapidly on the increasingly active warfronts. Military experts on February 3 estimated allied and enemy casualties, including civilians, totaled more than 28 million. The United States armed services casualties totaled more than 146,000. Of these 33,153 were dead, 49,513 were wounded, 33,615 were missing and 29,898 were prisoners of war. The newspapers published daily lists of local casualties. Behind each casualty was a human story of promising youth lost to the future and of grieving families, many including young children who would grow up never having known their fathers.

The short descriptions of the casualties included here are selected almost at random from the thousands of stories published in the state newspapers between 1941 and 1946. The names of more than 6,000 Washingtonians killed in World War II are listed in the appendix at the back of the book.

Usually only sketchy information was published about those killed in battle, in part because some details were censored so as not to aid the enemy. Another reason: during the war newspaper space was greatly reduced by the rationing of newsprint. On February 3, 1944, the Navy Department added 145 men to the missing list. Associated Press duly sent the information on to its subscribers. *The Seattle Times* reported that "The Navy Department today listed 145 men as missing. Five are from this state." The five were listed with names and, where available, addresses of relatives: "Lorne William Jewett, fireman, third class, U.S.N.R., son of Joseph O. Jewett, 3508 Woodland Park Avenue, Seattle; Seaman 2/c Charles W. Greenshield of Langley; Seaman 2/c Kenneth

T. Harbour, of Tacoma; Chief Boilermaker James A. Harris, whose wife lived in Port Orchard; and Seaman 2/c Vernon G. Johnson, of Puyallup." No information was available about why or in what theater they were missing. A check of the list of State men killed in the war shows that all five of these men were later declared killed in action.

Once in a great while the stories of casualties ended happily. Staff Sergeant Leonard J. Kelly of Everett was reported missing in action in October 1943 while serving with the Eighth Air Force in England. Sergeant Kelly was an aerial gunner with five combat missions to his credit and had shot down a German plane shortly before being listed as missing. After a few months with no indication that he had survived, a memorial ceremony was arranged for January 31 at Paine Field, during which his parents were presented his posthumous Air Medal with added Oak Leaf Cluster. The day before the ceremony, a cablegram arrived from Sergeant Kelly assuring them that he was alive and well. The ceremony was held as scheduled, but with tears of relief in the eyes of his family.

Marine Captain Frank E. Garretson had learned the value of teamwork while playing football at the University of Washington before entering the service. During the first week in February, he led a group of marines through a heated 24-hour battle for Roi and Namur Islands in the Marshalls. The fighting was bloody and often hand-to-hand. Enemy sniper fire was deadly and Garretson's company faced a problem maintaining communication with battalion headquarters. Garretson told a correspondent how one marine raced through a gantlet of fire three times to maintain the flow of orders and information. "Hell," the Captain concluded, "There were so many heroes around me I didn't have time to count them." A reporter on the battlefield watched Garretson walk a few yards to the body of an American marine, gently turn him face up, than stand silent for a moment, shake his head and softly say, "It's another one of my men."

Lieutenant Hugh R. Burch, 23, whose hometown was Prosser, received the Air Medal in early February. Burch earned the award for exceptionally meritorious achievement while participating in five separate bomber combat missions over enemy-occupied Europe. Lieutenant Burch, co-pilot on a Boeing B-17, had worked as a Boeing machinist before the war.

Many service personnel were killed while in training in the United States. On February 27, Mrs. Helen B. Gray, raised in Olympia but living in Seattle while attending the University, took the train to Boise to visit her 22-year-old husband, Lieutenant Llewellyn Gray, co-pilot of a heavy bomber. When Mrs. Gray reached the airfield, she immediately was escorted to the office of the commanding officer where she was gently informed that her husband had died before daylight that very morning when his plane crashed five miles south of Gowen Field. Six others aboard the bomber also died in the accident.

Army technician Wesley J. Sieber listed his hometown as the village of Palmer, located near Auburn. Sieber and Sergeant Eckley Guerin from Juneau, crewmembers on an Army rescue vessel, were awarded Soldier's Medals for braving rough and stormy Alaskan seas to evacuate two soldiers in need of immediate medical aid.

Technical Sergeant Bjarne H. Nelson, a former University of Washington student and a well-known Northwest skier, was listed as missing in action in the Asiatic area. The 35-year-old sergeant enlisted the day after Pearl Harbor and was assigned to the India-Burma theatre during most of 1943 and had been awarded the Distinguished Flying Cross and the Air Medal. His commanding officer in a February letter to Nelson's sister in Seattle told her the Sergeant's plane was hit by flak while attacking an unnamed target and "went down an extremely long way from friendly territory." Bjarne Nelson later was listed as dead.

Technical Sergeant Leonard K. Reger, a 26-year-old radio operator and aerial gunner on a Liberator bomber, was a graduate of Seattle's Lincoln High School where he starred on the varsity golf team. He had earned a Distinguished Flying Cross for action over Messina, Italy, shortly before his family received word he had not returned from a raid on the Ploesti, Romania, oilfields. In February he was listed as killed in action and his family was presented the posthumous Air Medal with Oak-Leaf Cluster awarded for his involvement in the Ploesti raid.

On February 15, four Washington State men were listed as Marine Corps flying aces. Major Gregory L. Boyington of Okanogan, missing in action on that date, was listed as top ace with 26 Japanese planes to his credit. Boyington was liberated from a Japanese prison camp when the war ended. Captain William P. Marontate, whose parents lived in Seattle, was credited with 13 enemy planes. He was missing in action and later declared dead. Captain Edward O. Shaw of Spokane also had downed 13 Japanese planes. Captain James E. Swett, with 14 planes to his credit, brought his new bride home to Seattle in early February. The Marine Corps

Landing Ship Tanks, commonly called LSTs were the largest ships capable of grounding themselves when reaching the invasion beaches, lowering front ramps to allow equipment and men to disembark. Many were loaded with equipment on the Seattle waterfront for transport to Pacific war fronts. Beyond the LST in the photo, Army men dismount from trucks to board a transport ship bound for an overseas destination. MOHAI Collection, 999.

credited the improved range, speed, maneuverability and firepower of the new Corsair fighter plane with aiding the success of combat pilots.

Thomas H. Mutchler, 19-year-old former Seattle Cleveland High School student serving with the Marine Corps, was one of four survivors aboard an assault craft involved in the landing on Tarawa. Pfc. Mutchler later was wounded and from his hospital bed at Pearl Harbor described the battle.

> We went in with the first wave. The Japs had us covered with machine guns, mortar fire, and snipers. As we drew into shore, they threw hand grenades at us. I guess they used everything but rocks to try and stop us. Our driver was killed going in when one of the grenades landed in our boat. We made for the beach and found cover. I didn't have a scratch until the next day when we had to attack enemy machine guns and snipers. We set out to take an enemy strong point and that is when I got hurt. It happened while we were advancing. Someone stepped on a land mine. It killed one man and wounded several others including myself.

Marine Lieutenant Gerald Hoeck, of Seattle was on Kwajalein Atoll in the Marshal Islands in February when his belief that the spoken word could be important in battle was verified. He and his men were trying to force the enemy from an underground shelter, but hand grenades, smoke grenades and bullets did not do the job. Lieutenant Hoeck, who spoke a little Japanese, called down into the dugout that U.S. marines would not harm enemy soldiers who came out unarmed and ready to surrender. He heard a frantic whispered conference below and a few minutes later a brown-skinned Korean appeared with his hands in the air. After the marines gave him food and something to drink, he turned to Lieutenant Hoeck and said, "Now if you will pardon me." He strode to the mouth of the dugout and yelled in Japanese, "Boys, they really mean it, and the food is good" or words to that effect. Two more of the enemy crawled out and were given something to eat before being sent off as prisoners. At the time,

young Hoeck, a Roosevelt High School graduate with a few pre-war credits from the University of Washington, was all of 22 years old.

Commander James E. Kyes, graduate of Everett High School and the U.S. Naval Academy, was patrolling in the North Atlantic on Christmas Eve when he sighted a pack of Nazi submarines. He boldly maneuvered his ship, *Leary,* closer to the four hostile U-boats when the enemy released three torpedoes. One struck its target, mortally damaging the *Leary.* After ordering his men to abandon ship, Commander Kyes hurriedly inspected the sinking ship to be sure none of his men remained aboard. As he was preparing to abandon the vessel, a crewmember held up a life jacket that was torn and useless. Commander Kyes calmly removed his own life jacket and gave it to the man, then climbed over the side as the ship went under. He was listed as missing for several months, then as killed in action. For his selfless act he was awarded the Navy Cross.

March 1944

Local War Efforts

All during the war, one of the nation's most vital military installations sprawled along Seattle's waterfront. The Port of Embarkation, among the largest on the continent, was described as "the heart" of a great military machine, pumping equipment and men to fighting fronts. The number of troops and the tons of supplies passing through the port and even the number of employees were considered military secrets in 1944. Brigadier General Eloy P. Denson, commander of the effort, explained that the Water Division, formerly called the Army Transport Service, operated more vessels than the Navy. Transports, freighters, barges and small craft shuttled into and away from the piers with clockwork precision.

All supplies and equipment were carefully prepared for transport to prevent damage. Exposed metal parts were sprayed with rust preventives, damageable parts were crated, and

Headlines: March 1944

March 8:
JAPANESE ARMY ADVANCES IN BURMA

March 13:
U.S. COUNTERATTACKS OVERPOWER JAPANESE ON BOUGANVILLE

March 19:
NAZIS SEND HUNGARY'S JEWS TO AUSCHWITZ AS RED ARMY NEARS

March 29:
U.S. CONGRESS APPROVES $1.3 BILLION FOR UN RELIEF AGENCY

March 30:
U.S. FLEET ATTACKS PALAU NEAR THE PHILIPPINES

March 30:
A FURIOUS HITLER FIRES TWO GENERALS OVER RETREATS IN RUSSIA

bags of silica were positioned to absorb condensation. General Denson added that, "the port's job will not end until the last soldier had been returned to this country after storming ashore and conquering the islands of Japan."

Washington State Housing Administrator John B. Blanford announced on March 7 that 800 war-housing units were scheduled for construction during 1944. Of these, 500 were scheduled for Renton, 40 would be built in Auburn, 100 in Sunnyside, 120 in Forks, and 40 in other small towns.

Washington State Residents in the News

Coast Guard Lieutenant (j.g.) Edith F. Munro, flew from Seattle to Houston, Texas, to christen a ship named for her son, Douglas A. Munro of Cle Elum, the only coast guardsman in U.S. history to be awarded the Congressional Medal of Honor (see appendix on Medal of Honor recipients). Within a year of losing her son, Edith Munro had enlisted in the Coast Guard, and in March 1944 she was serving as commanding officer of the SPAR barracks in Seattle's Assembly Hotel.

Major Einer Prestrud received a commendation for meritorious service in Queensland, Australia, where he served with the Water Transport Division of the Army. Major Prestrud had spent two long years in the South Pacific. His wife remained in Seattle and their son, Stewart H., was attending the Navy Language School at Boulder, Colorado.

American Red Cross women from Washington State were being posted all over the world. Frances Jane Sellen was with the first unit of Red Cross workers to land in New Guinea, where she served as a secretary and recreation program assistant. Betty Jane Thomas served as a staff assistant in England. Barbara Munter, daughter of U.S. Coast Guard Captain and Mrs. William H. Munter, received orders to report to Washington D.C. in March to be trained as a Red Cross hospital staff aide.

Five brothers, the sons of Mr. and Mrs. Adolph Radtke of Redmond, were all in the Army by March 1944. Pfc. Lawrence A. Radtke, 32, was in Ireland; Sergeant Francis E. Radtke, 28, was at Fort Francis E. Warren, Wyoming; Corporal Robert L. Radtke, 21, was stationed at Camp Campbell, Kentucky; Pfc. William J. Radtke, 20, was with the Army Air Forces in Italy; and Pfc. Henry E. Radtke, 19, was in Southern England. Their father was the caretaker of Marymoor Farm near Redmond.

Lieutenant (j.g.) Gordon S. Williams served as staff photographer for the University Daily while attending the University of Washington. After graduating in 1941, he took pictures for the Boeing Aircraft Company, and one of his photographs won a national award. In 1942, he joined the Coast Guard and was one of the first to be assigned as combat correspondent aboard a Coast Guard ship. In the South Pacific he photographed the most heated battles including the conquest of Tarawa in November 1943. Many of his photos were syndicated nationally.

Five Washingtonians were among 524 Americans repatriated in New Jersey when the ship *Gripsholm* arrived on March 13. Lee Murray, veteran U.S. Embassy attaché had been stationed in Paris when France fell. Lieutenant George Balkema, a World War I medic in France, had remained in Paris to study music and deal in antiques but had visited Seattle several times during the two decades between the wars. Balkema was serving as a liaison officer with the American Volunteer Ambulance Corps in France when the Nazis conquered the country. Eunice Taylor joined the staff of the American Embassy in Paris in 1937 and later moved to Vichy with the consular staff, then was sent to a German internment settlement. The other two Washington residents aboard the ship were Sophie Peterson of Bow, Skagit County, and Ethel Keysergot of Seattle.

Mrs. Inez Boswell of Snohomish received several letters from servicemen on different battlefronts praising her after they read in armed service newspapers how she worked 16 to 18 hours a day at Boeing and on her valley farm. She arose at 2 a.m., milked three cows, fed chickens and ducks, and prepared milk for shipment before leaving for the Seattle Boeing plant. On her return to the farm, she did the evening farm chores, cooked dinner and cleaned house. She'd been following the schedule for 19 months. One of the many letters sent to her was from a Marine Air Corps Lieutenant in the South Pacific: "Lady, you would make a good marine. Every day you prove our motto, 'Nothing is impossible if you won't believe it is.' It's good to know that a lot of you people back there in the States are working as hard as any of us."

Dr. James H. Mathews, president of the Seattle College Club, on March 20 presented a $250 check to Mrs. Percival K. Nichols, Jr. of the Red Cross Motor Pool. With 250 of their members in uniform, most serving on war fronts, the College Club was eager to help the Red Cross. Two of their members, Ensign Louis M. Love and Lieutenant William C. Haas, had been killed in action. Though many of their members were away in the services, about 2,000 service personnel assigned to the area had registered as members. The club location at Sixth and Spring was convenient for transient Army and Navy men who appreciated the excellent food, the squash courts, the bar, the fine library and College Club parties.

On March 25 the 13th Naval District for the first time transported WAVES by airplane from one duty station to another. Thirteen of the uniformed young women arrived at Sand Point Naval Air Station from the Naval Airfield in Pasco. For seven of the WAVES, this was their first experience of airplane flight. Among the new arrivals were three residents of Washington State: Betty Jo Edele of American Lake, Evelyn Skagg of Rochester in Thurston County, and Ellen Champoux of Yakima.

The Junior Chamber of Commerce selected Edward C. Wells as "Seattle's Young Man of the Year" for 1944. Wells, a 34-year-old Boeing chief engineer, was an expert on four-motored bombers. He had worked at Boeing for 10 years and was credited with the basic design of the Flying Fortress and for the exhaust-driven turbo-supercharger that provided Fortresses with high-altitude capabilities. He also was involved with development of the B-29 "Superfortress." The selection committee consisted of Mayor William F. Devin, U.S. District Judge Lloyd L. Black, Chamber of Commerce President Charles Clise, labor leader Dave Beck, and H. J. Gillie.

During the month, two old World War I buddies unexpectedly met on New Hebrides Island in the South Pacific. Captain Edgar C. Lockman, commander of an Army Quartermaster unit, recognized Harold Maysent, performer with a USO Camp Show touring in the South Pacific. Maysent and Lockman had served together in France 25 years earlier. Both were members of the University Post of the American Legion in Seattle. Maysent had polished up an old World War I vaudeville routine, "Alexander the Fust's American Expeditionary Force" and was traveling with an USO unit entertaining American soldiers in Alaska, the Aleutians and in the Pacific. Captain Lockman, an official with Bonneville Power Administration, had been recalled to active duty in 1941 at Camp White, Oregon, before being sent to the South Pacific.

With the increasing manpower shortages, avoiding the draft became more difficult in 1944. Howard Lacey of Bellevue, a 27-year-old shipyard worker, was charged on March 4 with failure to appear for induction the previous December. Lacey explained he had been living in a hotel and then moved to a farm and his mail had not been forwarded. After he originally had registered with a Montana draft board, the Army turned him down "because of having only one eye." After the hearing, Lacey was released on $500 bond and the assistant U.S. attorney on the case said another attempt would be made to induct him into the Army.

During the month, Selective Service officers, needing to locate more draftable males, reviewed the deferment papers of 17,000 farmers and agricultural workers in the state. County war boards were instructed to cooperate with the state extension service in investigating every case in which a farm

deferment had been granted and to forward the information to local Selective Service boards.

Planning the Post-War Years

The Seattle Times on March 5 published a major report on post-war planning. Reporter Doug Willix began with these telling paragraphs:

> There won't be any post-war planning needed for the Ballard kid who leaped into the surf on a South Pacific Island and whose gun flew out of his hand as machine-gun bullets spun him around.

> Nor will peacetime adjustments ever trouble that chap from Queen Anne Hill whose fingers were glued to the controls of a Flying Fortress over Germany when a concentration of flak caught his ship.

> They had cherished plans for the days after

peace. But, because of such men, Seattle — and every other American city — today is able to at least try to look into the future, even though its people know that the war is still far from having been won.

> The death of every Seattle man who has fallen places upon the city's citizens just that much more responsibility to do their utmost to see that the thousands of servicemen who will return have full opportunity to resume productive civilian lives.

The article continued with a description of how the machinery of unified post-war planning included contributions of various community groups. The Washington State Planning Council, a state-supported advisory group, stimulated practical research in many industries and prepared a post-victory employment program.

At least 20,000 discharged World War II veterans, many with wounds and physical disabilities, had already returned to civilian employment in the State. This vanguard quickly found jobs, but the situation was expected to change when war production was reduced. The serious planning was coordinated by an executive committee chaired by W. Walter Williams and with members Henry Broderick, Harry Carr, Frank West, Walter L. Wyckoff, Ben B. Ehrlichman and Dr. Nat H. Engle.

Among the questions being studied were these: How many service personnel will return to the State? Will they seek the jobs they left to join the service, jobs they have a moral and legal right to regain? How many instead will enroll for more education? How many women will leave industry and return to homemaking? How many newcomers will leave the area? How many war-born industries will be able to convert successfully to civilian production? How can industry use their war-learned techniques or efficiencies for peacetime production? What public works should be planned to create ready-made jobs? Though the war was far from over, Washingtonians were creating plans for the peaceful world of the future.

Business News Stories

The Seattle Chamber of Commerce on March 1 urged the House Agriculture Appropriations Subcommittee to approve $100,000 to fund experiments to find commercial uses of lignin, a by-product remaining from production of alcohol from wood waste. The Chamber explained that alcohol could be made from wood waste for about 16 cents a gallon and that the lignin residue could perhaps be used in production of plastics. If the process were perfected and the lignin sold for one cent a pound, the cost of producing alcohol would drop to 5 or 6 cents a gallon, whereas, at the time, the government was paying 96 cents a gallon.

A shortage of whiskey was projected in the state until two Kentucky distilleries signed a contract to supply 500,000 cases of Waterfill and Frazier bourbon. State liquor stores sold it at the regular price of $3.56 a quart plus a 10 percent state tax.

When Pearl Harbor was bombed, the farmers east of Lake Washington kept a firm grip on their plows but also picked up their shipbuilding tools. They came trekking out of Snohomish, Monroe, Snoqualmie, North Bend, Duvall, Redmond, Bothell, Woodinville, Bellevue and other small farm-fringed communities. Many accepted jobs at the Lake Washington Shipyard at Houghton. During the war that shipyard developed as one of the 15 largest shipbuilding plants on the West Coast. More than a third of the several thousand employees there were from nearby farms.

Grace Kaiser, 20, a swing-shift welder at the Houghton yard, once had the help of four brothers on their four-acre farm. Now all her brothers had gone to war and Grace and her mother tended to the farm's food production.

A great-grandmother, Mrs. Una Bernice Moffett worked in the sheet metal department of the shipyard. Five years earlier she and her husband had started to clear a 10-acre farm near Woodinville. Mrs. Moffett, using a stump-puller, lifted 183 stumps, roots and all, by herself and helped build a five-room house. When she finished work at the shipyard, she returned home to feed her 200 chickens, five goats and two pigs. Then if she had time she took a whack at clearing the remainder of the farm. "I guess these ships have to be built," she philosophized, "and everybody who can has to help build them."

Over on Bainbridge Island, at Winslow Marine Railway and Ship Building Company, another minesweeper was launched and by March 5 Navy trial runs were completed. This was the third of sixteen 180-foot welded all-steel ships to be built at the yard, and all were dispatched to far-flung battlefronts where they cleared water pathways of mines, marked channels with buoys and performed other vital services in the war effort. This shipyard previously had delivered four 220-foot steel minesweepers, two of which performed so well in the Tarawa invasion that officers aboard the vessels wrote commendations praising the shipyard's work.

A new $3 million shipping terminal building at the foot of Connecticut Street in Seattle was completed and turned over to the Army in March. The terminal included a double pier 1,000 feet long and 400 feet wide, making it the largest pier in Seattle with the exception of those at Smith Cove.

A fire at the Army depot in Auburn badly burned three men and injured three others. Started when a tar pot exploded, the flames swept through a $500,000 cold-storage plant at the huge supply depot.

A Few of the Many Heroes of March

On March 5, *The Spokesman-Review* carried a photo of Staff Sergeant Donel A. Novotney of Wilbur, WA, who had been missing over Germany since February 20. He was an honor student at Wilbur High School and had been an aerial engineer-gunner for five months. He apparently survived, perhaps as a prisoner of war, for he is not listed among those who died in the war.

First Lieutenant Samuel M. Bruce, a former Garfield High School football star in Seattle and a flyer with the 99th Negro Squadron, was killed on his 57th mission over enemy territory in Europe. A baby daughter, whom he had never seen, had been born on Lieutenant Bruce's birthday the previous December 7. After high school graduation, Bruce enrolled at A & T College in Greensboro. He received his commission from the Tuskegee Flying School of the Army Air Forces in September 1942 and had participated in the Italian campaign since the beginning.

Major Justus M. Home was expected home in Seattle the second week in March to meet his newborn son. Then word was received in early March that the 24-year-old flyer was killed in mid-February when his plane crashed in Italy. Mrs. Home told a reporter that she was planning an Army career for her 10-month-old son, Douglas, as a memorial to the father he would never know. "Perhaps he'll go to West Point as his father did," she said. She told the reporter that when the war was over her husband's body would be returned to the U.S.A. for burial either in Arlington National Cemetery or at the Military Academy at West Point.

Lieutenant Harold M. Bauer, a Zillah High School graduate and P-38 pilot, had his plane riddled with holes in a dogfight with the enemy. Then he ran out of gasoline just short of England, but managed to glide his plane down into the English Channel, an experience he described as "hitting the water with a tremendous shock, like hitting a stone wall." He had been in the water only about five minutes and was still attempting to inflate his rubber dinghy when a rescue ship arrived.

Marine Private John J. Murphy, from Spokane, was fatally wounded at the Tillamook, Oregon, Naval Air Station when another marine accidentally shot him in the chest when his pistol discharged while he was cleaning it. Private Murphy died the next day.

Sergeant Benjamin E. Craig of Tacoma, radio-gunner in a twin-engine bomber, and four other crewmen died when their plane crashed and burned on a mountain range in Arkansas. The plane, based at Barksdale Field, Louisiana, hit the crest of the mountain at 9 p.m. during an electrical storm.

Lieutenant Robert L. Watts of Seattle died during the invasion of Sicily while trying to turn the tide of battle. He was posthumously awarded the Distinguished Service Cross for his bravery. The citation read in part:

Under pressure of enemy counter attack, the left flank of Lieutenant Watts' company began to waver and give ground. Lieutenant Watts left his command post and made his way under terrific machine gun and mortar fire to his weakening flank. He personally captured an enemy machine gun and turned it around to fire at the attacking enemy troops. Realizing the need for more firepower, he then made the supreme sacrifice by advancing on another enemy machine gun, firing his carbine until the enemy gun was silenced.

Watts was a graduate of the University of Washington, and his wife was social hostess at the service club at Fort Lawton. She and their 2-year-old daughter Roberta lived with her parents in Seattle.

Lieutenant Charles F. Gumm of Spokane was noted for being the first Mustang pilot to shoot down an enemy plane over Europe. This occurred on December 16, 1943, and four months later he was attempting to land his plane after the engine failed and noticed the English village of Nayland ahead. He could have bailed out, but instead attempted to keep his plane from crashing into homes. He had nearly reached the open field beyond the village when a wing caught a treetop and flipped, throwing Gumm to his death. The townspeople of Nayland were deeply touched by his sacrifice and wrote to Gumm's family. Then they collected a fund to pay for a memorial to the pilot. His wife Toni and their 10-month-old daughter lived in Spokane.

Private Francis Conrad of Springdale, Stevens County, was killed in action while serving in Italy. The 20-year-old private was inducted into the Army in March 1943 and went overseas in September. His parents in Springdale received the Purple Heart Medal that was awarded to him posthumously.

Staff Sergeant Bruce B. Brown, 25, a tail gunner on a Flying Fortress, was listed as missing in action in the Central Pacific, the Army informed his mother in Seattle. Sergeant Brown, a Queen Anne High School graduate, enlisted in the Army on Christmas Day, 1942, and had been overseas since April. He later was declared dead. His brother, Staff Sergeant Frank H. Brown, a turret gunner and assistant engineer on a bomber stationed in England, was the first Seattle man to volunteer for army service after the Selective Service Act went into effect. Frank H. Brown also was later listed as killed in action. Their younger brother, Robert, served in the merchant marine, and their sister, Gladys, was employed at Sand Point Naval Air Station.

Private Ross Talbott of Oroville in Okanogan County, was one of four persons killed when a pilotless P-38 fighter plane crashed into the Camp Haan Post Hospital, California, on March 7. The pilot had parachuted to safety.

Ensign Richard E. Lockdam, a Queen Anne High School graduate and University of Washington student who dropped out a year before earning his degree, died in the crash of his Navy plane near Melbourne, Florida. Lockdam, 22 years old, was training to be a fighter pilot.

Lieutenant Donald V. Scavotto, son of Seattle City Councilman and Mrs. James Scavotto, died during a bomber raid on Kiel, Germany, his parents learned from a telegram received March 3. He previously had been listed as missing. Scavotto was not piloting his usual Flying Fortress, "Rat Killer," at the time of the raid but had volunteered to act as tail gunner with another Fortress that was short a man. During the raid the tail section of the plane was shot away, but hope was maintained that Scavotto had managed to parachute to safety. The lieutenant was 26 years old and wore the Air Medal with Bronze Oak Leaf Cluster. His wife, Kathleen, and their ten-month-old daughter, Susan, whom he had never seen, survived him. Scavotto was a graduate of Franklin High School and the University of Washington Law School.

Technical Sergeant Myron (Fritz) Schwab, 21, bombardier-navigator on a B-26 Marauder, was home in March on his first leave in 26 months. He wore a leather jacket with 40 bombs painted on its front, one for each bombing mission over enemy territory. On his last mission over Caprano, south of Rome, Schwab said he could see American soldiers facing great odds on the Anzio beachhead. "Those guys were fighting part of the time in muck and mud up to their arms," he said. "And the mountains, well, it would be like trying to take Mount Rainier with German machine gun nests on top. It's an inch-by-inch proposition." Then a smile spread over his face. "But it's grand to be home again with a good bed and good food. Gee, but I do enjoy Mom's cooking, and Pop's, too! I've been a lot of places and seen a lot of things. I saw the Leaning Tower of Pisa on one raid. It was surrounded by six batteries with 24 guns spouting at us." Schwab said he was going to try for aviation cadet training to become a pilot and had been ordered to Santa Monica, California, when his leave was over.

Staff Sergeant Clyde M. Lawrence of Seattle was reported missing in action in early March. Lawrence, 23, an engineer-gunner in the B-26 bomber called "Shady Lady," had been decorated with the Air Medal, the Distinguished Flying Cross and the Purple Heart, and had seen duty in Scotland, Ireland and England. A graduate of Ballard High School, he had enlisted in 1941 after working at the Boeing Aircraft Company. He was later declared killed in action.

Another Seattleite listed as missing and later declared dead was Navy Lieutenant Howard B. Berry, Jr., whose father was personnel officer for the 13th Naval District. Lieutenant Berry was an officer on the submarine *Cisco*, which the Navy announced was lost as sea. Berry was 27 years old and a graduate of the U.S. Naval Academy.

Major Edward M. Nollmeyer was home in Everett in mid-March after earning "nearly every award in the book for flyers." He had completed 88 missions over enemy territory in the China-Burma-India theatre. The major, only 23 years old, spent 23 months flying a P-40 fighter plane and was credited with destroying five enemy planes and four probables.

Lieutenant Ira C. Ide of Seattle was killed in the South Pacific area and was awarded the Silver Star posthumously. He previously had received the Air Medal and Purple Heart. His Silver Star citation read: "For meritorious achievement while participating as co-pilot from September 15 to 29, 1943, in sustained combat operational missions. He exhibited great courage and untiring energy; his services reflecting highest credit on the military forces of the United States." The lieutenant, 19 years of age, was a Queen Anne High School graduate.

Captain Robert P. Owen was home on 20-day leave in March after completing 40 combat missions during 14 months of duty with the Army Air Forces in the Mediterranean area. He entered the service two weeks after Pearl Harbor, was trained in California and later flew himself overseas. A B-26 Marauder pilot, Owen served as flight leader for the last 15 missions before his leave. He mentioned to a reporter that one day in the early part of the Italian campaign, 35 German fighter planes were shot down into the ocean. A veteran of battles in Algeria, Tunisia and Sardinia, Captain Owen added with a grin that he was finding his 20-day leave more tiring than combat.

On March 4 Lieutenant Frank L. McCallister of Omak, Okanogan County, was co-pilot of the first American bomber over Berlin when the Eighth Air Force mounted the initial American attack on the German capital. The crew reported satisfactory bombing results in spite of heavy flak. They proudly reported that no German fighter planes were able to pierce the U.S. Mustang fighter escort.

Captain Celon A. Peterson, a University of Washington graduate, received the Silver Star for gallantry in action, the Army announced on March 6. The award was presented at Camp Roberts, California, where he was stationed after his recovery from wounds received in Sicily. The citation stated that Peterson's company was on reconnaissance in Sicily when the enemy began sending in heavy fire. Without regard to personal safety, the Captain went ahead of his line of scouts to locate the enemy heavy weapons that were delaying the advance of his company. He located five enemy machine guns upon which he directed supporting mortar fire, putting the weapons out of action. Captain Peterson also received the Purple Heart for wounds suffered a month after the action for which he received the Silver Star.

The Navy announced on March 6 that the Air Medal had been awarded posthumously to Raymond C. Scott of Spokane. While serving as aviation chief radioman, Scott was killed when an enemy shell exploded in the radio compartment of his plane over the Bay of Biscay. The citation explained that when eight enemy fighters attacked Scott's plane, he immediately radioed his position to control base but was killed shortly after sending the message.

Lieutenant George A. Nunan, 26, co-pilot of the Flying Fortress "Shy Ann," was reported missing in action in November 1943. This was changed to killed in action on March 17. The bomber he was with disappeared in the English Channel with a full crew aboard. Young Nunan, member of a pioneer Seattle family, graduated from Oak Harbor High School. His survivors included his wife, Eleanor, and a baby daughter residing in their Burlington home.

April 1944

A Few of the Locals Who Made News

Two Seattle stage performers joined a USO unit to entertain the troops, not realizing how much of the world they would see. Paula Bane, a singer, was in the cast of the Broadway musical *Oklahoma* before volunteering for USO service. Card Mondor, a magician, was employed as a technical specialist at a Hollywood studio. Both were favorites of the service personnel they entertained overseas during the nine-month tour that took them to Alaska, Africa, Corsica, Sicily, and Sardinia. In April, near the end of their tour, they were flown to Italy and from there wrote home that they hoped to perform at the Wintergarden Theatre in Berlin before their tour ended. The two entertainers had not known each other prior to meeting as USO performers, though both were Queen Anne High School graduates.

The "sack-shaking department" at the Seattle Post Office terminal station was manned for the duration by retired businessmen, aged 67 to 85. Grandfathers and great-grandfathers, the seven men in years past had pioneered in their fields of business. Some had even ventured into Yukon Territory in the 1890s hoping to find gold. After years of retirement, they agreed to help the Post Office and to relieve younger men for war duty. These older volunteers worked three shifts a day, inspecting mail pouches, stacking usable sacks in neat piles and rejecting torn bags that would spill shipments of letters. "We manage to put in eight hours a day," 75-year-old Ben Ferguson declared proudly. The baby of the group was 67-year-old John Ratliffe. The oldest was Andrew V. Paulson, 85, who said, "It's really fun to be working again." Alfred J. Buzard, 70, said "All my life I never was really crazy about work, but I guess you have to do something." Other elderly men enjoyed their work there, too, often regaling one another with tales of long-ago exploits.

Charles F. Carroll, one of three Seattle brothers serving in the Navy, was home on leave after two years' service in World War II as a Chief Machinist. He compared notes with his brother George, a Navy chief motor machinist's mate, just returned from the Mediterranean theatre. The third brother, Joe E. Carroll, said he was "just listening-plenty." Charles told an intriguing story about Washington apples. On the beachhead of the Marshall Islands, he and friends toted five boxes of apples from the commissary to about 30 of the sailors from their outfit who were ashore enjoying a beach party. Then a bunch of soldiers saw what was going on and lined up behind the sailors. Charles said, "To men who had gone through 72 hours of fighting, those apples were passed out one by one, and the last few we split in halves to go around. I never saw food so appreciated. They said it was better than coffee, doughnuts or cokes. How they went for those apples!" The brothers Carroll were surprised at this unplanned hometown reunion, their first since February 26, 1942, the day both George and Charles enlisted.

Two Washington State defense positions were vacated during April. Irving S. Smith, executive director of the State Defense Council, asked the governor to relieve him so he could return to his position as vice president of a mortgage banking firm. Harold P. (Dick) Everest, director of the Northwest Sector Office of Civilian Defense, resigned to return to his

Headlines:
April 1944

April 10:
U.S. DROPS 43,500 TONS OF EXPLOSIVES ON EUROPEAN AIRCRAFT PLANTS

April 15:
U.S. FLYERS BOMB PLOESTI AND BUCHAREST, ROMANIA

April 17:
CONGRESS EXTENDS LEND-LEASE THROUGH JUNE 1945

April 22:
ALLIES LAUNCH MAJOR ATTACKS ON NETHERLANDS NEW GUINEA

April 28:
FRANK KNOX, NAVY SECRETARY, DIES OF HEART ATTACK.

faculty position at the University of Washington, where he soon was named chairman of the Journalism Department.

Commander Patrick H. Winston of Seattle was appointed planning officer for the National Selective Service System in April. A University of Washington graduate and former Seattle lawyer, Winston was executive secretary of the Washington Toll Bridge Authority before being called to active duty by the Navy in late November of 1940.

More than 600 of Seattle's "Victory Girls" had been hauled into Police Court since the first of the year. Some were arrested for violation of the city ordinance prohibiting unescorted women from loitering around a beer hall. But most were routed out of cheap hotel rooms where they had registered falsely as wives of the service man accompanying them. Judge James W. Hodson, who talked to as many as 23 girls a day before pronouncing their varied sentences, didn't consider all Victory Girls to be tough or hardened females. He explained that about two-thirds of them did not have a social disease and had simply made an unfortunate mistake. "This is a wartime problem," the judge said. "Perhaps they came to Seattle to meet a sailor boy friend, or maybe their husband. He may get orders to move to other locations before they meet him, and they're stranded without money. Instead of going to a welfare agency for aid, some of the girls wander down the Avenue and to the haunts where they feel most at home. After a few days, many return to their hometowns."

Navy Lieutenant Donald G. Brazier, 23, stepped from the train at King Street Station after 18 months in the Southwest Pacific as assistant gunnery and communications officer on a destroyer that participated in amphibious landings at Cape Gloucester and in the Admiralties. To meet him at the station was his bride-to-be, Susan Howard, and his brother Carl Brazier, Jr. on hospital leave from the Naval Training Station at Farragut, Idaho. The first order of business for the Lieutenant and Miss Howard was a wedding and then a honeymoon trip during the groom's 30-day leave. After seeing her betrothed for the first time in months, Miss Howard's reaction was to exclaim: "Gee, he *is* cute, isn't he?"

Mrs. Shirley Jean Grannell was inducted into the Marine Corps in early April, thereby becoming the first woman in Seattle to join her husband in that service. First Sergeant James B. Grannell had been a marine for nine years, was at Pearl Harbor when it was attacked, later fought at Bougainville, and was stationed in the South Pacific at the time his wife volunteered for the Marines.

Five German prisoners of war escaped from the prison camp at Fort Lewis during April. The front-page news story listed them as Helmut Wetzel, Hans Lermum, Herman Fischer, Alexander Gentersdorser and Walter Pherlicker, all in their early 20s. The State Patrol asked Seattle police to help search for the men who had escaped wearing blue denim or dark khaki fatigue uniforms. All five were apprehended, the last being Gentersdorser and Pherlicker who made it to Chehalis where they hid in woods for ten days, subsisting on a few cans of sardines they had smuggled from the fort. When their food ran out, they strolled into Chehalis and were quickly apprehended. Colonel R. S. Dicey, commanding officer of war prisoners at the fort, told reporters that the German POWs had been returned and punished in accordance with the Geneva Convention. Such punishments could be no stricter than those given American soldiers and could not extend for longer than 30 days. In addition, surveillance of the escapees was increased.

An April 30th Memorial Day service at Seattle's Cleveland High School honored nine former students who had died in World War II. A total of 494 former Cleveland students were in the service of their country. Parents and former classmates of the deceased were invited and many attended the service. Captain J. P. Forsander, district chaplain of the 13th Naval District, delivered the main address. He said: "Memorial Day can no longer mean just another day off, another holiday. Now it holds a new meaning — we are remembering and honoring persons we have known and loved." Jo Poore, standing before a new service flag with nine gold stars, read the nine names while the Cleveland a capella choir provided appropriate musical background.

King County's lone surviving Civil War veteran, 97-year-old Hiram R. Gale, occupied the seat of honor at Memorial Day observances conducted by veterans' organizations. Gale, in spite of his age, worked a 48-hour week at the office of his son because, as he phrased it, "This is every man's war." He was honored at Victory Square and rode at the head of the parade to Washelli for 2 o'clock services at Veterans' Memorial Park.

Captain Roscoe C. (Torchy) Torrance of Seattle, athletic and morale officer of the Third Marine Division somewhere in the South Pacific, boosted the morale of several families at home during April. He and Captain Porter DeRamus, division photographer, took photos of every Leatherneck in the outfit and sent them home for Mothers' Day.

Jack Benny and his wife Mary Livingston were en route to British Columbia to perform at the opening of a war-loan drive when their train pulled in at King Street Station for a ten-minute stop. During that brief time, they said hello to a large delegation of Army, Navy, Civilian War Commission, war industry and other officials who handed them an itinerary for their week in Seattle starting April 27. Mrs. A. Scott Bullitt, volunteer office chairman, settled a few details concerning their appearance at the Civic Auditorium on April 29. At that show, the Benny troupe, including band leader Phil Harris, black comedian Rochester, and radio announcer Don Wilson, honored 3,000 individuals who had worked a thousand hours or more as volunteers in the war effort. During their time in Washington State, Jack Benny's weekly radio comedy show was broadcast from the Puget Sound Navy Yard in Bremerton and the entertainers visited service men in hospitals and appeared at war-

plant rallies. In addition, Miss Livingston hoped to somehow find the time for a reunion with her aunt and uncle, Mr. and Mrs. Jules Glant, of Seattle.

Business Stories of April 1944

World War II veterans were returning to civilian jobs in Washington State at a rate of more than 50 a day, state manpower director A. F. Hardy reported on April 22. In March, 1,693 veterans returned, many of them recently recovered from wounds or illnesses. Special facilities were established in each of the state's 25 employment offices to serve returning veterans and several discharged veterans were hired by the State to work in these offices. Most common questions concerned ways to find a job or how to enter a training and/or education program. Hardy said employers were eager to hire the veterans and no difficulty was experienced in finding jobs for them.

In early April, negotiations began with owners of railroads and other properties the city needed for a four-lane highway to connect the Pacific and Sunset Highways in the Duwamish Junction area. The Boeing Aircraft Company said the shortcut would help speed deliveries between Plant 2 in Seattle and its Renton factory and would assist in the production of B-29 Superfortresses.

Radio was a major source of news and information during World War II. More than 60 million radio sets were in use in the U.S., 8 million of them in autos and 52 million in homes. During the war, no new radios were available for civilians because the armed services needed all radio parts being manufactured. In the 1940s radios operated with several different vacuum tubes that tended to burn out over time. As the months passed many families could no longer use their radios. After many complaints, the War Production Board announced in April that 18 million of the most needed tubes would be available for civilian use during the rest of the year.

Dr. E.A. Bryan, president of Washington State College for 23 years (1893-1915), was honored when a Liberty ship was launched at Richmond, California, with his name on the bow. The 4-H clubs of Washington State had sold war bonds to purchase the ship. Bryan's daughter, Mrs. Robert C. Hayes, was present for the christening.

The dispute over whether or not the Puget Sound area had a true labor shortage grew heated during the month. The War Manpower Commission decreed that until June 30, employers in the area were permitted to carry on their payrolls only the number of male workers they employed on April 9 minus the men drafted into the armed services. As a result only women could be hired to replace those drafted. On the same day, the Manufacturers' Association of Washington charged that Boeing, Puget Sound Navy Yard, and other large employers based the designation of Seattle as a "critical labor-shortage area" on exaggerated estimates of labor needs. A congressional committee chaired by Congressman Henry M. Jackson of Everett held hearings about the manpower problems of smaller war plants. After listening to various arguments, the committee agreed to recommend that Seattle be removed from the list of critical labor areas.

A survey released at the end of April reported that women were capable of filling 80 percent of the jobs in the nation. In other words, every woman hired freed a man to join the armed forces or to work in jobs requiring heavy lifting that women could not perform. Clarence R. Innis, chairman of the labor-supply committee of the Seattle Chamber of Commerce, released information on April 30, stating that 17 million of the 34 million women in the U.S. between the ages of 18 and 40 were already employed. Of the other 17 million, 11.5 million had children under 14 who required their attention, leaving 5.5 million who could serve their country by taking jobs. Innis said, "Every job nowadays is a war job. If the women of the Pacific Northwest would get on the job and stick to it, realizing the war in Europe is far from ended and the one in the Pacific has not really started, they will not only help bring the war to a quicker conclusion, relieve the manpower shortage and aid the government by investing part of their earnings in war bonds, but also will bring that father, brother, husband, sweetheart, or friend back to his loved ones much sooner."

Bremerton, a busy wartime city, was estimated in April to have increased its population to 70,000, ranking it the fourth largest city in Washington behind Seattle, Spokane and Tacoma. Much of the four-fold increase over just three years came from annexation of heavily populated residential centers, including wartime housing previously located outside the city limits. Vancouver climbed to fifth place with a population of 38,000, not counting a tremendous growth outside the city limits. Municipalities of the Yakima Valley from Yakima to Pasco, in the area affected by the Hanford engineering project, also showed marked growth over the previous year.

Leo Weisfield, chairman of the Civilian War Commission Salvage Committee, said glass was increasingly important as salvage and urged prompt return of glass containers and bottles that pay a refund. Persons with large stocks of non-refundable glass bottles were urged to call a charitable organization to pick them up. Conservation of glass was necessary, he said, because the millions of glass containers sent overseas to our service personnel are lost because ships have no space to bring the empties home.

The Seattle plant of the Boeing Aircraft Company in March produced more four-engine bombers than ever before had been built by a single plant in a single month. Boeing president P.G. Johnson announced that March production was 25 percent greater than February's and 34 percent greater than the mark established in January 1944, which was more than double that of January 1943. The number of planes delivered was not disclosed for reasons of security.

A Few of the Many Heroes of April

The news stories of heroic service by residents of Washington State were multiplying. From the news reports it appeared that hardly a battle was fought without men from Washington State being involved.

Pfc. Howard C. Foreman was decorated with the Silver Star medal for gallantry on Tarawa, the Marine Corps informed his parents in Spokane. The citation for his award read:

> Under intense machine gun and rifle fire, he removed two wounded marines from the water to the comparative safety of the beach, where he administered aid. Later, he succeeded, under intense fire, in neutralizing three enemy strong points with his flame-thrower. His devotion to duty under fire and his disregard for personal safety were in keeping with the highest tradition of the United States naval service.

Richard H. Klinge of Seattle had played football at the University of Washington 1937-1939 and served as assistant coach in 1939-40. Now, in April 1944, he was piloting a lumbering Navy Catalina flying boat north of Rabaul, New Britain. His objective was to rescue an Army pilot whose plane had been forced into the sea. With a dozen Corsair fighters covering his giant aircraft, he flew up St. George's Channel between New Britain and New Ireland Islands. At 12,000 feet, Klinge sighted the pilot's yellow life raft in Simpson Harbor. As he started down, Japanese machine guns and shore batteries opened up. He landed amidst a hail of lead and circled toward the pilot. A direct hit clipped all but one rudder control, but Klinge persisted in his rescue attempt, gunning alternate engines to swing his plane closer. The protecting Corsairs strafed the enemy guns without silencing them. Another Japanese shell

exploded almost on the Catalina's bow, drenching the plane. Concussion from enemy shells blew out both machine gun blisters and water poured through the holes. The rapidly rising water became an increasing hazard and Klinge feared both plane and crew would be lost. Gunning his motors he slowly took off through a storm of fire and rose to a scant 200 feet. He ordered his crew to jettison all heavy gear and bail the water out. With all rudder control gone, the former grid star and intercollegiate wrestler navigated his cumbersome plane back to its base for a safe landing. As for the Army pilot floating on the life raft, a second flying boat later rescued him unharmed.

A B-24 Liberator bomber had attacked an armament factory in Southwest Germany and was heading for its home field when enemy fighters forced it down into the English Channel. The eight crewmembers scrambled into their rubber dinghies in the choppy sea. One crewman died in the attack and a wounded man died as they tried to hoist him aboard a dinghy. They drifted for more than 48 hours before

Assembling the command portions of B-17s took great care and steady hands. Boeing Management Company. HS 3755.

sighting two small fishing boats. The fishermen cut away their nets to clear a way for the flyers to board their vessels. One of those rescued was Sergeant Richard Campbell, the waist gunner, whose wife and parents lived in Seattle.

Despite losing an engine on his Flying Fortress, Lieutenant Gordon B. Taylor of Bellingham successfully finished his bombing run over Cassino, Italy. Anti-aircraft fire had exploded a huge hole in the engine nacelle, taking the controls to engine No. 1 with it. This caused the engine to run at a constant speed. Next the crew discovered the landing gear would not descend. This forced them to circle for half an hour over their home field while Technical Sergeant Victor Poindexter of Grant's Pass, Oregon, the engineer, climbed into the bomb bay and cranked the wheels down by hand. Lieutenant Taylor then landed the plane safely, despite the extra power of the full-running engine.

Ensign Richard M. Einar, 22, formerly a member of the University of Washington freshman crew, was now a fighter pilot in the Navy's famed Skull and Crossbones Squadron that downed 154 enemy planes in the Rabaul-Bougainville area. In April Einer, home on leave, told a reporter that he didn't want to talk much about his war experiences or the records of his squadron in the South Pacific or about far-away places he had seen. Uppermost in his mind, he said, "was getting back to Kitsap County — its forests, hills, lakes and home." He did admit that the most beautiful sight he had seen in the war zone "was three burning Japanese Zeros falling headlong into the sea."

During April, nine Washington State servicemen were awarded the Silver Star, one of the country's highest awards for bravery. They were:

- Sergeant Gerry D. Bert, Jr., former Seattle city golf champion and co-medalist in the National Public Links Tournament of 1939 in Baltimore. He was cited for the part he played in cleaning out the enemy on Betio Island. He enlisted in the Marines in 1940 and had served in Iceland before being sent to the South Pacific.

- Pfc. Leonard A. Webber of Lilliwaup in Mason County was awarded the Silver Star for his bravery while acting as a runner between his tank unit and the infantry front line positions, "performing his duties under heavy enemy fire."

- Pfc. Milton R. Stephenson of White Salmon in Klickitat County was credited with killing ten Japanese and risking his life many times to stop enemy snipers from holding up the advance of his Marine buddies.

- Technician 4th Grade Mervin O. McKinstry from Castle Rock in Cowlitz County was presented an Oak-Leaf Cluster for the Silver Star he was awarded in July 1943. The second award was for gallantry in action near Tambu Bay, New Guinea.

- Technician 5th Grade Donald J. Bjorn, from Arlington, Snohomish County, received his Silver Star for bravery in action while serving as a Medic at Nassau Bay, New Guinea.

- Second Lieutenant Elmer D. Erickson from Burien was awarded the Silver Star for heroic action during infantry efforts near Salamaus, New Guinea.

- Field Artillery Staff Sergeant Frederick B. Lotspeich of Selah, Yakima County, was awarded the Silver Star for action at Tambu Bay, New Guinea.

- Staff Sergeant Oscar E. Klaas of Tacoma, also of the Field Artillery, received his Silver Star for bravery in the same battle as Sergeant Lotspeich.

- Sergeant Ronald L. Jones of Yakima, a Medic, received his Silver Star for helping save several wounded men on the battlefield near Mount Tambu, New Guinea.

Mr. and Mrs. Thomas G. Hammond, Sr., of Seattle had two major worries. Their daughter, Mrs. Elizabeth Damroach, wife of the Reverend

Leopold Damroach, chaplain at St. Lukes Hospital in Manila, was a prisoner of the Japanese. Their son, Lieutenant Thomas G. Hammond, Jr., was a prisoner in a German stalag luft. In April, the Hammonds and daughter-in-law Helen, were invited to a ceremony where they were presented the Silver Star, the Air Medal and Oak-Leaf Cluster recently awarded to her prisoner of war husband.

Lieutenant Floyd M. Calkins of Auburn was home after completing 50 missions over Europe. He brought with him German flak fragments in his eye and scars on his face and chest. He described a raid over Italy that almost "shelved" him.

> Our P-47s destroyed 35 enemy fighters, most of them just taking off from their airdrome, and during the half hour of enemy fighter plane attacks we got three Nazis definitely and one probably from our Fortress. We were flying out of Africa at the time, and our target was in Northern Italy. From the moment that coastline showed up, the fighters were on us. We thought they'd never let up. Then 15 minutes before we reached our target, anti-aircraft opened up. I saw three bursts almost in our plane. Then I knew I was hit. The co-pilot took over and I went back and lay on the catwalk. A piece of jagged metal about two inches long stuck out of my chest. The engineer helped me pull it out. He hovered over me — just like a mother. The crew kept asking how I was. I felt fine. I just didn't want them to have any more trouble, and to go ahead and finish the job. They did.

Calkins spent the next month in a base hospital. Other airmen wounded under similar circumstances usually were transferred to ground posts, but Calkins badgered his way back into the air. He flew a few missions as co-pilot before resuming his role as pilot. He completed 25 missions after being wounded thereby reaching the number 50 that made him eligible for home furlough. He brought his bride, a young lady from South Dakota, to Auburn with him. After his leave, Calkins reported for reassignment at Santa Monica, California.

Technician Ken Omura, a Seattle-born Japanese-American, drowned while on active duty in New Guinea in April. He was believed to be the first Nisei to lose his life in the South Pacific. Omura, 25 years old, a Garfield High graduate, joined the Army before Pearl Harbor. Volunteering for special service in a combat intelligence group, he was sent overseas in 1942. Omura's closest relatives — two cousins and an aunt and uncle, were in the Minidoka war relocation center at Hunt, Idaho.

Private Wayne C. Reed serves as an example of how Washington State soldiers saw the world. This Highline High School student was trained at Fort Lewis, Washington, and Fort McClellan, Alabama. He arrived safely in North Africa six months after entering the Army. From there he was sent to the Anzio beachhead in Italy. His parents received a telegram reporting their son had suffered slight wounds in Italy. However, young Reed, all of 18 at the time, wrote from the hospital that they shouldn't worry about him, that he was OK. His father added that Wayne, in his V-Mail letters, was more concerned about his mother, a Boeing employee who had been injured on the job shortly before their son received his wound.

The family of Lieutenant Nick G. Pantages, a navigator-bombardier with the Eighth Air Force in England, received word on April 20 that he had been missing in action since a March 11 raid over Germany. Young Pantages earlier had been awarded the Air Medal with Oak-Leaf Cluster. His was a familiar name at Renton High School where he served as captain and all-conference center on the football team. His wife, Elda, who resided with her husband's parents, Mr. and Mrs. George Pantages, reported that after receiving word her husband was missing, several letters arrived from wives of flyers stationed at the same field outside of London, expressing confidence that Pantages was safe, probably a prisoner of war. A few months later the Army reported he had been killed in action.

When a British bomber crashed during

take-off in Italy, three Americans rushed over to try to rescue the crew of the burning plane. A dispatch from the 15th Air Force said the Americans, using their coats as shields, approached the flames and rescued the gunner who had been thrown clear of the wreckage. They then returned to rescue a second victim, and as they placed him in an ambulance, the rest of the plane's bomb load exploded. One of the three American rescuers was Captain Philip M. Smart who lived in Edmonds with his wife and young son, Philip. Smart's mother, Mrs. Harry Smart, reported she had received a letter on April 20 in which her son remarked that "baseball season is under way over here." He said the food was "grand, now" and that one thing he had learned while in Italy was patience. He spoke highly of the Red Cross, Mrs. Smart said, then added, "and although Phil doesn't drink coffee, he surely likes doughnuts."

On April 21, the War Department listed 650 soldiers missing in action. One of them was James H. Keeffe, Jr., of Seattle. His parents received word he was missing on a March 12 raid over Germany. His parents told a reporter, "That was his 21st birthday." Keeffe had enlisted in August 1942, and earned the wings of a Liberator pilot. He was a graduate of Lincoln High School and a former student at Seattle College. He survived his experiences as a POW to return home to the Northwest.

When the new Selective Service Bill became law, one of the first Seattle men drafted was James C. Peterson. He passed eligibility examinations for both Officer Training School and the Army Air Corps and chose the latter. He received his wings in July 1943. His sister in Bremerton learned that Lieutenant Peterson, 26, was killed on March 15 while a passenger in a plane that crashed into the sea near the Island of Oahu.

Mrs. Hilda Kruger of Tacoma on April 21 accepted the posthumous Purple Heart awarded her only son, Captain Leo H. Kruger, a University of Washington graduate, who was killed in Italy in January. Captain Kruger, a member of an anti-tank company of the 30th Infantry Division, landed at Casablanca in December 1942, fought through the Tunisian, and Sicilian campaigns, and was wounded fatally while on reconnaissance on the Italian front when a shell burst near his jeep. The Captain, a 1936 graduate of the College of Economics and Business at the University of Washington, had been studying for his master's degree when the Army called.

Nearly 100 convalescent Navy men and Marines from the Seattle Naval Hospital, many on crutches, were guests of Seattle Lodge of B'nai B'rith in mid-April at a luncheon, theatre party and sightseeing tour. They all thanked their hosts, saying it was one of their most enjoyable days since arriving at the Navy hospital.

Private Jim A. Gordon of Seattle, a member of the American commandos, was wounded while in action in Italy. In an April letter to his father in Seattle, the young man said that doctors "took shrapnel from my left leg, shoulder and side." A later letter stated, "I'm already back doing my stuff." Private Gordon served in the Alaska campaign before being sent to Italy.

Sergeant Jack V. Davidson of Seattle, crewmember on a Liberator bomber, lived through a scary experience on April 23. While en route to raid the Japanese base at Truk, an electrical fire broke out in the bomb bay. The flames threatened to explode the 500-pound bombs just as the bomber was approaching its target. A crewmember managed to crawl into the burning bomb bay and jerk the electric wires loose, killing the flames. By then the bomber, named "AWOL," was just a couple of minutes from the target. Their bombs were released safely and landed accurately. During the return trip to their advanced base in the Marshall Island, the plane's hydraulic fluid began leaking and they had only drinking water to replace it. They reached their home field, touched down, and a wheel collapsed because of the low hydraulic pressure. The plane was damaged slightly, but no crewmen were hurt.

On April 24, Lieutenant Thomas W. Colby, a 21-year-old Thunderbird pilot with the Eighth Air Force, destroyed two German planes on the ground. All that day American fighter pilots over Southern Germany had a field day destroying 66 German aircraft. Lieutenant Colby already had earned the Distinguished Flying Cross and Air Medal with three Oak-Leaf Clusters for piloting his P-47 fighter, "Li'l Evey," on more than 30 sorties against the enemy. A Renton High School graduate, he attended the University of Washington for one semester before enlisting in the Army Air Force in 1941.

Lieutenant Damian R. Bourque, 25, of Seattle, and fellow crewmen of a Flying Fortress had an unforgettable experience on a bombing mission over Frankfurt, Germany, in early April. An Eighth Air Force news dispatch described what happened. Lieutenant Bourque was co-pilot of the bomber that received a direct flak hit, damaging both engines. As they left the target area, the crew learned that No. 1 engine could not be feathered and was causing a vibration that shook the plane, while No. 2 engine could be used only sparingly. They managed to keep the plane in formation until over the French coast where flak again smashed into the Fortress, forcing it to drop about 1500 feet a minute. Then a force of German fighters attacked, but the gunners aboard and the escorting fighter planes drove the enemy away with only slight additional damage to the B-17. Over a cloudy England the plane still was losing altitude too rapidly to reach base and the crewmembers were preparing to bail out when the thick clouds parted and the pilot spotted a possible landing site below. He set the ship down in the clearing, which, much to the crew's surprise, turned out to be an emergency landing field. Nobody aboard was hurt.

Posthumous awards for bravery given two Washington State men were announced April 28. A Silver Star went to Technical Sergeant Jack D. McMann of Walla Walla. The Sergeant was serving as radio operator and gunner on a B-17 bombing mission over Germany when he earned the award. The citation explained, "Just prior to the bombing run and while flying at an extremely high altitude, he overheard the pilot futilely trying to contact the waist gunners on the interphone. With utter disregard for his own safety, the Sergeant, after obtaining an emergency supply of oxygen, crawled to the waist of the plane to investigate. He found both gunners lying prostrate on the floor. He carried one man to the door of the radio compartment and returned for the second man, but apparently lost consciousness from lack of oxygen. When found a short time later beside his two comrades, whom he had tried in vain to help, Sergeant McMann was beyond all human aid. He had forfeited his own life in an attempt to save fellow crewmembers." His family received the Silver Star.

The second award, a bronze Oak-Leaf Cluster added to the Distinguished Flying Cross, went to the family of Lieutenant Warren W. Oakley of Seattle. Lieutenant Oakley had earned an Oak-Leaf Cluster while serving as a B-24 pilot on a bombing mission over enemy-occupied Europe late in 1943. Now awarded a second one, his citation read in part:

> Just after the bombing run, a 20 millimeter cannon shell exploded in the cockpit, wounding him and the co-pilot and rendering both unconscious. When Lieutenant Oakley regained consciousness, his aircraft had gone out of control and into a spin. While still struggling to regain control, he gave the order to bail out, and the two gunners abandoned the plane. Shortly thereafter, he returned his plane to level flight and regained a position in the formation, but only momentarily, as one engine had been knocked out and flak hits had started a fire in the right wing. Knowing that two members of the crew were too seriously wounded to bail out, he headed his crippled craft for the nearest friendly airfield, and upon reaching it, skillfully landed his plane without further injury to any member of the crew.

He survived the flight but later was killed in action. Both McMann and Oakley served with the Eighth Air Force in England.

Headlines: May 1944

May 18:
ALLIES FORCE GERMANS FROM MONTE CASSINO, ITALY

May 18:
U.S. 6th ARMY TAKES LAST OF ADMIRALTY ISLANDS

May 25:
ALLIED ARMIES LINK UP IN ITALY, MENACE ROME

May 27:
ENEMY RESISTS U.S. 41ST DIVISION LANDING ON BIAK ISLAND

U.S. Coast Guard SPARs served in many operational, administrative and support specialties during the war. Here two of them ensure that parachutes are properly packed.
Photo from U.S. Coast Guard.

After flying 52 missions over enemy territory, Lieutenant Albert E. Dowsing, Jr., navigator on a B-17, was home in April for a visit with his family, after which he would be reassigned. Dowsing had experienced a year in North Africa and the Mediterranean theatre. "We were lucky," he said. "None of the members of my crew was injured during the missions, but there were some narrow escapes. I remember one day when the tail of our ship picked up 281 holes. The gunner was in there, too, but his heated suit stopped the flak. They shot it up at us from an airdrome in Greece." He modestly added, "As navigator I didn't see much of the fighting. I was too busy charting a course and figuring out the weather." He told of one occasion when an engine of their ship went out. "The other planes in the formation went off and left us and 11 enemy fighters came at us. They stuck with us for about eight minutes, and that's a long time to have somebody shooting at you." Navigator Dowsing had been decorated with the Air Medal and nine Oak-Leaf Clusters and had requested assignment to pilot training when he reported back to duty at Santa Monica, California.

Infantry Lieutenant Charles W. Van Scoyoc, Jr., a former University of Washington student and member of a well-known Seattle family, was killed in action on the beachhead at Anzio-Netturno in Italy. In an earlier action there, Lieutenant Van Scoyoc managed to lead a group of 32 members of the 3rd Infantry Division back to the Fifth Army's front after they were trapped behind the German lines. Van Scoyoc's parents, his widow, Frances, and five-month old son, Stephen, whom he never saw, lived in Orting, Pierce County.

May 1944

Local Wartime Developments

A Washington D.C. dispatch on May 1 identified Bangor, on Hood Canal about 12 miles northwest of Bremerton, as the site for a new ammunition depot and shipping area. The dispatch explained that a new rail spur and other facilities for the ammunition depot were included in $18,700,000 of Navy-approved construction in the Puget Sound region.

War Bonds of a special kind were marketed at Victory Square on May 3. Sponsors of the event included the American Legion Auxiliary and the Women's War Savings League. The program opened the "Buy a Bond for Baby" campaign and launched a new bond owners' organization called "The Cradle Roll of Honor." Membership certificates for children under 14 years of age were presented by Sally O'Dell, youthful radio and stage star and head of the Junior War Savings League. The certificates issued by the Treasury Department were pink or blue with cartoon characters on the face.

Mothers' Day at Victory Square on May 13 was dedicated to the region's war mothers. Mrs. George B. Buchan, selected as Washington's representative 1944 mother, asked them "never to forget that our sons may be boys in years but they are men in strength, and in years to come they will use in peace the maturity they have won in war." State, civic and patriotic groups paid tribute to all mothers of the community. Officers of the women's

On a sunny May 25, 1944, cadet nurses from Schools of Nursing at Virginia Mason, Swedish and Providence Hospitals and the University of Washington and Seattle College (now University) assembled at Victory Square to receive diplomas. Seattle P-I Collection, 28272, MOHAI.

branches of the various armed services acted as honorary escorts to the war mothers. In the portico of the Square, with cloaks wrapped tightly to ward of chill breezes, stood many gray-haired gold-star mothers whose sons' names were included in the lengthening list of war dead inscribed on the tall white memorial pylon, a replica of The Washington Monument.

A recycling goal was reached on May 23 when the 100th railroad car was loaded with salvaged tin cans from Western states and sent to San Francisco to be reclaimed for the war effort. Since the recycling effort began, Seattleites had collected 2,756,420 pounds of rinsed and flattened cans.

Twelve Coast Guard Auxiliary SPARS became the new tenants of the large John and Anna Roosevelt Boettiger home on Mercer Island. Arrangements had been made during the spring for the SPAR officers to lease the home for a year. They could hardly contain their delight over their sumptuous quarters. They

exclaimed over the Spode china, counted the ten bedrooms and five bathrooms, praised the view and guessed at the cost of caring for the extensive grounds. They soon were acquainted with President Franklin Roosevelt's pet Scotty, Fala, who stayed with them for a short time. John Boettiger, publisher of *The Seattle Post-Intelligencer*, had accepted a position with the Allied Military Government Service and his wife, Anna, the daughter of the president and first lady, had moved to Washington, D.C., the previous December. The new occupants enjoyed off-hours in the knotty-pine recreation room, where they discovered a spinet piano. "Imagine," said one, "they left it tuned!" Bookshelves held hundreds of volumes and in a special cabinet was displayed a portion of President Roosevelt's collection of miniature animals. After the women were asked if they could maintain the plumbing, they began discussing which of them might know how best to use wrenches and install washers.

In 1944 the University of Washington graduated the smallest number of students in ten years. Only 400 graduates were listed in the May commencement program, and of these, 285 were women.

Few fraternity pins were seen on campus during the year. Men weren't allowed to pin them onto their service uniforms and the coeds had decided they preferred to wear Army, Navy, or Marine Corps insignia as romantic tokens. Approximately three times as many girls lived in sororities as during the prewar years. This was due, in part, to the fact that times were better; fathers had more money to spend on their daughters' education, while the armed forces were feeding their sons. Then, too, most coeds were earning money in defense jobs. In spite of having more cash, the young women were not pampered. The shortage of hired help resulted in the members of most houses performing all the housekeeping but the cooking. With dependable bus boys as scarce as a standing date on Saturday night, sorority sisters took turns waiting on table. And each sorority had a national and local war-work program and all invested heavily in war bonds. The girls worked their way through shoe ration coupons by dancing with servicemen at sorority parties and at the USO, the Naval Air Station, the Puget Sound Navy Yard, and other events for servicemen.

On May 22, National Maritime Day, the U.S. Maritime Service began a drive to recruit more young men. The age limit was lowered to allow youth aged 16 to 17 1/2 to join that service. The next day, with the consent of their parents, more than 200 Washington State youth signed up. They were sent to Catalina Island, California, for training in physical fitness, sea safety and their chosen specialty. The demand for merchant seamen had grown rapidly, explained Ensign T. D. Hurd, public relations officer in Seattle. "The Victory Ships coming off the ways in quantity must be manned. These ships are twice as speedy, sturdier, and better in all ways than the Liberty Ships. The Victory Ship is the post-war ship of the Merchant Marine."

On May 27, the War Production Board reduced the amount of newsprint available for civilian use. This forced local newspapers to reduce the number of pages. *The Seattle Times* reported that 1944 circulation increased 42 percent since 1941, mostly because of increased population in the Seattle area. The spaces dedicated to news and features were pared drastically and most national advertising was refused. Commencing May 28, the *Sunday Times* carried no classified advertising and dropped the editorial page. The Monday paper was reduced to 12 pages and corresponding reductions were made on other days.

Secretary of War Henry L. Stimson closed all aircraft observation posts on May 29 because danger of enemy air attack had diminished greatly. The 15,000 civilian warning service workers in Western Washington were disbanded. The Secretary warned, "This does not mean that the War Department is of the opinion that all danger of enemy bombing has passed. On the contrary, a small-scale sneak raid is still within the capabilities of our enemies. The calculated risk we are assuming in reducing our air-defense measures is justified by the offensive power we will thereby release."

Business News of May

Washington State shipbuilders were delivering a completely equipped warship to the armed forces every 11 1/2 days, a total of 32 vessels during 1944. The Navy had recently placed an order for 52 ships from Puget Sound Bridge and Dredging in joint venture with the Lake Union Dry Dock and Machine Works. In Houghton, the Lake Washington Shipyard earned high tribute from ranking officers of the Navy as they witnessed the colorful christening of the plant's 20th seaplane tender on May 13. Captain H. N. Wallin, supervisor of shipbuilding in the Seattle area, congratulated the yard and its workers on meeting their scheduled dates and "doing a fine job besides."

The Navy on May 13 allocated $191,000 for construction of a storage building, taxiway, access roads, and remodeling of four barracks at the Naval Air Station on Whidbey Island. The Pasco Naval Air Station was provided $176,000 for construction of public works, a transportation office and shops.

Seattle-Tacoma Shipbuilding Corporation celebrated national Maritime Day by launching the 30th $7 million destroyer built at the firm's Harbor Island plant.

Steamer passenger service between Seattle and Tacoma, abandoned back in 1930, was resumed in May 1944. The *Virginia V*, with a capacity of 340 passengers, was routed through the East Passage. Captain Howell Parker, co-owner, served as skipper. The vessel had recently carried soldiers from Puget Sound forts on scenic Puget Sound cruises.

Local motion picture theaters continued to provide a major portion of the recreation services in the state. In May, the top-drawing movie at the Palomar Theater at Third and University in Seattle, was a combination comedy and war story titled *Rosie the Riveter* starring Jane Frazee, Vera Vague, Frank Albertson, Frank Jenks and Lloyd Corrigan. The advertising explained "It has lovely ladies mixing rivets with rhythm, wrenches with revelry, and lyrics with love". The program also featured an hour of live vaudeville including singers, piano players, a card trickster and the Simpson Marionettes.

A Few of the Many Heroes of May

Early in the war Quartermaster Frank Patrick Huotte served on a Coast Guard transport in Alaska, then was transferred to the South Pacific where he participated in the Tarawa, Eniwetok and Kwajalein invasions. He described the Tarawa battle as one of the bitterest of the war. "Out of 1,500 marines who left our ship, we got only 400 back. The battle was expected to take eight hours, but it lasted eight days and cost

the lives of many fighting men." Huotte, a four-year veteran of the Coast Guard, had been home in Seattle in late summer of 1943 while his ship underwent repairs, but soon went back to sea. Then in early May he was given 30-day leave and arrived home just hours before his wife gave birth to their daughter, Patricia, at the Marine Hospital. After his leave, Huotte, reported to San Francisco for reassignment.

Two sons of Mrs. Bertha Larson of Seattle were wounded in Germany. Corporal Lawrence H. Larson, 28, was struck by shrapnel on the Western front in January and, after a time, was sent to Fort Lewis for treatment. He had seen three years of overseas duty and participated in the invasions of North Africa, Sicily, Italy and Southern France. He was an ordnance man with the First Division and previously had been wounded twice, both times in Germany. Mrs. Larson's other son, Corporal Raymond B. Larson, 19, was wounded on April 1 and was recuperating in a hospital in France. He had been an infantryman for three years and overseas since November 1943. Both sons were Franklin High School graduates.

The first time Private Jack Johnson's parents in Seattle knew he had suffered wounds was when they received a letter he had written while in a New Guinea hospital. He had been serving in the South Pacific since April 1942.

Here's just a line to let you know I'm still kicking, although I'm in the hospital propped up in bed writing this. I've been here several days now, but they've had me so full of dope until now that I slept most of the time. The nurses are swell and always kid the boys. My ward is a tent, but it has a radio and ice water in it, to say nothing of clean sheets and towels and a shower on the hill in back. The radio is Australian, and we receive only one station, and it is mostly organ music.

Marine Technical Sergeant Charles E. Wood was back home on Mercer Island on May 4, well and happy and telling about his "miracle"

The Boeing B-17 was a hardy warrior. Many of them returned to English airfields after being heavily damaged by enemy shrapnel and fighter planes. Nearly blasted in two, this plane was flown home by survivors of its able crew. Boeing Management Co.

survival. Sergeant Wood, 27, had volunteered for assignment on a torpedo bomber to photograph an attack on Kolombangara Island in the South Pacific. He explained that the plane circled low over the target, when:

We sent them a bomb which blew the whole point right off the island, and that was when our ship got hit. We headed out over Kula Bay and I supposed we were making a landing, but we went up instead. The bomber straightened, then started down, came within ten feet of the water once and, after a perfect back flip, landed in the bay going 207 knots. It wasn't until I crawled through the burning plane into the cockpit that I realized the ship was pilotless.

Sergeant Wood explained that he had failed to hear the "bail out" order because the radio was broken and the anti-aircraft fire was making a lot of noise. The ship had landed itself. Wood crawled out onto the wing wearing his life preserver and let himself into the water just as the plane sank nose first. After four hours in the water, a rubber boat was dropped to him. He didn't remember any more until he heard voices as they rescued him and took him back to the base. Badly burned, Sergeant Wood spent time in a tent hospital at Munda, then was

moved to Guadalcanal, and finally to New Zealand. He was given 11 pints of blood plasma and six quarts of saline solution during the early part of his struggle to live. Now he was enjoying a 30-day home furlough before reporting to a California base for reassignment.

The durability of the Boeing B-17 bomber became legendary during the war. Take the "Dottie Jane," as an example. The crew was releasing bombs on Berlin when flak began heaving and shaking the plane like a crazed bronco. While the pilot fought to hold it in formation, the engineer discovered that the radio operator was missing. The radio compartment and all the crew's parachutes that had been stored there were gone, too. In fact, the plane was almost blown apart in the middle. The crew managed to keep it airborne despite furious fighter attacks. The crippled hulk floundered 600 miles back to England, its fuselage and wings riddled with holes, with wreckage dangling. Observers described the B-17 as a skeleton of its former self, with a hole in the side of the fuselage large enough to drive a jeep through. Going in for the landing at the British field, the pilot used the jammed and frozen ball-turret's guns as a tail skid and made a near perfect three-point landing, bouncing

along the runway on a tire flattened by flak. The only casualty, besides the missing radio operator, was a wounded tail-gunner.

Commander Emmett L. Calhoun of Hoquiam, senior medical officer on the cruiser *Northampton* during five major engagements, was awarded the Silver Star for heroism. He had manned his station in the battle of Santa Cruz in 1942, six days after undergoing an appendix operation. During the engagement he suffered a concussion and a fractured hand but continued for five days, with little rest, to treat wounded survivors of the carrier *Hornet*. Commander Calhoun was wounded a second time when his ship was sunk in the Savo Island battle in November 1942.

Army Lieutenant Walter H. Campbell, former University of Washington student serving in Teheran, Iran, was credited with helping solve the problem of censoring mail and other communications concerning American military installations in North Africa. Lieutenant Campbell spoke and wrote 10 languages: Chinese, French, Spanish, Portuguese, Latin, German, Dutch, Italian, Russian and, of course, English. "Give me a few more months and I'll speak Iranian, too," he said. He obviously learned languages quickly, several of them while still in high school and at the University of Washington, and at Columbia and Yale Universities. He said he expected to teach foreign languages when the war ended.

In a tragic April accident, a Liberty ship blew apart in icy Alaskan waters, killing 55 of those aboard. However, details were not divulged until May 20, when official hearings were concluded in Seattle. Whether the explosion was ignited by the cargo of gasoline or by an enemy mine or torpedo remained unknown. The ship sank with startling speed as half-dazed men flung themselves into the oil-blackened sea. Almost immediately fire spread across the oil slick. "She went down in about 20 seconds," estimated Kenneth O. Baker of Olympia, an able-bodied seaman. Lieutenant Donald J. Moore, Navy gunnery officer, grabbed a life belt and dived off the bridge into the rolling water. Ensign Bruce S. Spang of Tacoma, third mate, was on the bridge at the time of the explosion. "The ship began to sink immediately," Spang said. "It was pitch dark. I made my way to the lifeboat station, but there were no lifeboats." As Spang started for the other side of the ship, he heard someone banging on a boat-deck door. He stopped to free the man trapped behind it. So swiftly was the vessel sinking that the Ensign was in icy water up to his waist by the time he got back to the pilothouse. "I jumped and swam to an overturned lifeboat," Spang said. "Thank God, I didn't have to go through burning oil to get to it." Spang and Moore reached the same overturned lifeboat and tried to aid other survivors. "It was bitterly cold," Spang said. "Our sole object was to hang to the bottom of that boat. We put the two men who were in the worst condition in the middle to help them hang on." At about 2 a.m. the lights of an approaching vessel were sighted but the ship did not see their lights or hear their whistles and turned away. At dawn, an Army rescue ship appeared but did not spot the survivors until about 6:30. She then immediately pulled along side and lifted them from the frigid sea.

Colonel Bernard D. Morley, former Army Air Forces representative at the Boeing Aircraft Company and commanding officer of Boeing Field, was killed on May 21 in a training plane crash at Muroc, California. The Colonel, 46, had been flying since World War I. At the time of his death he was commanding officer of the 730th Army Air Forces Base Unit at Muroc Army Air Field and was engaged in secret experimental work as test pilot of jet-propulsion planes. His plane, an A-24 trainer, crashed from unknown causes soon after taking off from the base. Morley was rated as an Army senior test pilot — next to the highest rating given in the service. While on duty in Seattle, he had piloted many Flying Fortresses on acceptance flights. He was survived by his widow, Marion, their daughter Patricia, 16, and a son, Bernard, Jr., 13, living in the family home in Seattle.

Joseph Driver, Army technician, fifth grade,

June 6:
**D-DAY! 150,000 ALLIED
TROOPS LAND ON
NORMANDY BEACHES**

June 11:
**U.S. PLANES ATTACK
JAPANESE BASES ON SAIPAN,
TINIAN, AND GUAM**

June 15:
**BOEING B-29S STAGE FIRST
RAID ON MAIN JAPANESE
ISLAND OF KYUSHU**

June 18:
**JAPANESE LOSE 400 PLANES,
3 CARRIERS IN BATTLE OF
PHILIPPINE SEA**

June 22:
**F.D.R. SIGNS GI BILL TO HELP
FINANCE VETS EDUCATION
AND HOUSING**

was reported missing in action and presumably lost in the Tunisian campaign. Then, later he was reported to be a prisoner of the Germans. His situation was altered a third time with the word he was wounded in action. On May 25, on a 10-day furlough, he appeared at the Seattle home of his brother and made plans to drive the next day to Yakima to see his mother. T/5 Driver, on limited service because of his wounds, was returned to the U.S. on the Army's rotation plan. He explained his experiences while serving as a command car driver:

I was driving a couple of majors and a captain through some Tunisia countryside and the major said he knew of a cut-off, so we tried it, but it didn't turn out so good. We'd hardly started on our shortcut, when machine-gun bullets started zipping all around. I got hit in the shoulder and ankle and one major and the captain were wounded, but the major who had the idea of the shortcut wasn't hurt.

The Germans took all four men prisoners, sending the uninjured man off to prison camp. The three wounded were placed in a Tunisian hospital.

We had been in the hospital five days when we could hear the hell of the front coming closer. At first the Germans started carrying out all their wounded. The worst hurt they left behind for junior corpsmen to take care of. They posted a German guard at the back door and a British guard at the front door and surrendered the hospital to a British doctor who had been captured and was helping out. The British doctor was in command for several hours before the place actually fell.

A message written by a Chinese-American prisoner of war in Germany praised a Seattle man for his work among the prisoners. Sergeant David H. Woo, a Broadway High School graduate, sent the letter on May 29. "I am writing a few words for you to pass on to the people of Seattle," he wrote. "It is about a certain son of our city, Tracy Strong, Jr., now with the European Student Relief Society in

Geneva. He is doing a wonderful job toward making life more comfortable for us prisoners of war. He has corresponded with most of us and is trying to secure for us any books we desire." Sergeant Woo, a gunner in a Liberator bomber, was shot down in March 1943. His father, the late Woo Gen, was a prominent Washington State Chinese merchant and cannery contractor. Tracy Strong's father was general secretary of the World Alliance of the YMCA and director of the war prisoners' aid committee in Switzerland. The Tracy, Jr. mentioned in Woo's letter, was a theological student aiding his father in his work with prisoners of war.

June 1944

Invasion of Europe

The long-awaited allied invasion of Europe brought enthusiasm and concern to Washington State, enthusiasm because it was a successful step toward defeating Germany, concern because hundreds of thousands of allied troops were involved in an invasion that everyone realized would cost many lives. In fact, 13,000 American aircraft and a naval force of 5,000 ships were involved with the invasion and by the end of the first day about 150,000 men of allied divisions had struggled ashore at Normandy. On some beaches, especially Omaha Beach, steep cliffs favored the defenders. Enemy artillery rained shells on allied landing craft full of soldiers, causing 2,500 American casualties during Day One. The families and friends of thousands of Washington service men known to be stationed in the British Isles fretted about their survival. The home front remained calm and prayerful with no cheering crowds. The Seattle Times editorialized:

More prayers in more hearts than ever in earthly history. And more courage and will to fight than man knew he could muster! For now we know that it was the terrible waiting that wrought nerves to the near-breaking point. Now we know that when the fight is on, our nerves don't crack — man becomes a nerveless being and his instincts to battle for preservation carry him through, oblivious to what had seemed such grievous worryings and plaints of a few hours before. That's the spirit of our boys — they're men, now — on European shores. And that's the spirit that moves us at home.

Three weeks later casualty lists began to carry the names of those killed or injured in the invasion. One of the first local men reported as a casualty on the Normandy beachhead was Corporal Donald R. Neal, son of State Senator and Mrs. M. T. Neal of Des Moines. Corporal Neal, a tank commander, was reported missing on D-Day and later declared dead. He had gone overseas in September 1942 and earned the Silver Star and the Croix de Guerre for bravery in North Africa. He was well known at Highline High School, where he excelled in football, basketball, and swimming.

Another Washington State man who lost his life in the invasion was Pfc. J. Allan Machan, 23, a graduate of North Central High School in Spokane. His mother received the fateful telegram at her home in Snoqualmie Falls, where she had lived for three years. Young Machan was a member of the Rangers, among the first to land on Normandy. He was engaged to marry Jean Crawford of Spokane, a member of the WAVES serving in Bremerton, when word arrived of his death.

Washington State Attorney General Smith Troy was a Major serving with an Infantry division involved in the invasion. In a letter to his wife, the Major wrote that he was penning the missive beneath an apple tree in Normandy, only a few feet from his slit trench, enjoying the first lull in 10 days of fighting.

On June 17, the Army announced that during the first 11 days of the Normandy campaign, 3,283 Americans were killed and 12,600 wounded. General Omar N. Bradley, when making the report, paid high tribute to the courage of the soldiers who established the beachhead on the European Continent. He added that casualties on the central beachhead,

where the American First Division and elements of the 29th Division landed, were higher than anticipated, but that casualties over the entire peninsula area were lower than anticipated.

Three destroyers built in Seattle by Todd Pacific, Incorporated, formerly known as Seattle-Tacoma Shipbuilding, played important roles in the D-Day establishment of the Normandy beachhead. The three ships moved in under the fire of shore batteries to cover the allied landings. As the battle opened at 5:30 a.m., one of the destroyers, the McCook, was assigned to eliminate a pillbox with concrete walls six feet thick. She blew it to pieces and then destroyed a battery concealed in a gulch curving away from the sea. The McCook fired 250 rounds in 25 minutes before moving on to other targets.

Major Leo Hawel, Jr., wrote to his father in Seattle about the buzz bombs the Germans were using over England. "Watching a plane with a man in it, hurtling through the sky in frantic pursuit of a plane without a man in it, causes one to wonder what the human race will be compelled to chase next. Can't you just imagine what kind of a world it would be to chase after radio-controlled office boys or the traffic cop on a robot motorcycle racing to pinch a speeding, short-circuited, artificial, magnet-stuffed man? What a world!" Major Hawel was recovering in an American hospital in England from wounds received over enemy territory. While flying back to England, he was forced to

Boeing Airplane Company rented small branch plants in several Washington towns. The upper floors of the Everett Auto Company was one such site. Boeing Management Co.

On July 4, 1944, youngsters and parents waited expectantly for the bands and service personnel to come marching down Seattle's Second Avenue. Seattle P-I Collection, 23301, MOHAI.

land in the Channel and then swim to land. He explained that allied bombers had been hitting the German buzz bomb launching platforms for a long time, but only a few higher-ups knew exactly what the target was. "If you hear that medium and light bombers hit installations in the Pas-de-Calais area, that is just what it means. Had the Germans been allowed to build their weapons unmolested, the damage would have been most appalling."

Puget Sound Bridge and Dredging Company, founded in 1889, invited all its old-timers and the queen and princesses of the Wenatchee Blossom Festival to the mid-June launching ceremonies of two 180-foot steel minesweepers. All employees of the yard and their families were invited to attend the launching of the *Execute*, which was the first vessel in the company's minesweeper program. Then at 9:30 p.m. the *U. S. S. Facility* slid down the ways, ready for the Navy to take control. A few days earlier the Navy had announced that Puget Sound Dredging, half-owner of Associated

Shipbuilders, would receive contracts to build 27 steel vessels costing several million dollars. The vessels included floating workshops, floating barracks, and auxiliary-powered landing craft.

Five Boeing branch plants had converted from manufacturing B-17 parts to making them for the B-29. The factories in Chehalis, Bellingham, Tacoma, Aberdeen and Everett began delivering these parts in early June.

The War Labor Board refused to grant a general wage increase to 130,000 Pacific Northwest pine and fir lumber workers, stating "that no evidence had been found that a general increase would solve the industry's manpower problem."

People in the June News

Surprised glances followed two young Frenchmen as they walked Seattle streets in their colorful French navy uniforms and wearing broad-banded flat hats inscribed "Marine Nationale." Lucien Francois Godet, 31, and Max Fischl, 22, both veterans of General Charles de Gaulle's fighting French Forces, explained they were on furlough from an airbase at Alberta, Canada, where they were being trained for the French Navy air arm. They hoped to "do a bit of Yankee hiking" with the aim of seeing the "entire Pacific Coast" during their 14 day leave. Godot, speaking in English with a pleasing accent, said, "We got off to a bad start. The immigration authorities were astonished. They could not understand why French sailors, carrying Canadian Air Force identification cards, should have any business crossing the border into the United States." At the Service Men's Club on Second Avenue the entertainment secretary made arrangements for the two to tour Seattle and supplied them with candy.

On June 24, the National Director of the War Manpower Commission, Paul V. McNutt, announced the appointment of Fay W. Hunter of Longview as director of the Commission's Region 12 that included California, Oregon, Washington, Nevada and Arizona.

A Few of the Many Heroes of June

The War Department on June 8 listed 504 soldiers killed in the sinking of a transport ship in the Mediterranean. Two Seattle men died in the disaster. Private Anthony T. Felice, who had managed the fruit and produce department of a grocery store for eight years before joining the Army, was survived by his wife and his mother. Corporal Seth E. Griggs, a graduate of Ballard High School, had worked for Boeing before entering the service. His wife and mother survived him.

Ensign Hugo C. Cloud, 24, was among 17 men killed in early June when a Liberator bomber crashed through two buildings at Camp Kearny Auxiliary Air station in Nebraska. The ensign, a 1938 graduate of Puyallup High School, had served for seven months in the New Hebrides Islands. He had received his commission six months before his death.

The Frank Rose family of Seattle received bad news over May and June. The latest message to arrive from the Army told them that their youngest son, Lieutenant Robert A. Rose, bombardier on a B-24, who had been reported missing, was killed in combat over Germany. Their other son, Lieutenant Adrian W. Rose, co-pilot on a B-17, had earlier been reported missing. Then the first week in June he was reported to be a prisoner of war. Both sons were honor students at Queen Anne High School and prominent in student affairs at the University of Washington.

Mrs. Evelyn Naher, widowed mother of five sons, worked as chief auditor at the Army Service Forces depot in Seattle. On June 24 she stood on the after deck of a new destroyer at Todd Pacific Shipyards to receive the Purple Heart awarded posthumously to her 19-year-old son, Robert, who was fatally wounded when his ship, the *U.S.S. Monssen*, was lost in the Third Battle of Savo Island. Captain H. N. Wallin, Navy supervisor of shipbuilding in the Puget Sound Area, presented the medal after reminding the audience that the ship on which young Naher had served and died was built at the Puget Sound Navy Yard. He added: "Mrs. Neher is a Gold Star Mother who knows the meaning of sacrifice and that it is necessary to win peace and victory. She is carrying on as a war worker and is setting a high example for others to follow." Mrs. Neher was accompanied by her two youngest sons, Allen, 14, and Jack 11. Her two other sons were involved in the effort, Edward as a corporal in the air corps in Alaska and Richard, 16, as an employee in a war factory.

On June 27 it was announced that four Washington State residents had been awarded the Distinguished Flying Cross for accomplishments while flying in the South Pacific. They were Technical Sergeant Charles F. Dudley of Seattle, Sergeant James L. Gregg of Seattle, Lieutenant Wilson B. Hazlam of Tacoma, and Technical Sergeant James C. DeGroat of Spokane.

Private Harold E. Dupar, Jr., of Seattle was killed in action in Italy, the Army announced late in June. His late father had been manager of the New Washington and other Western Hotels. Young Dupar, while a student at Lakeside School, earned both athletic and scholastic honors. He had enrolled at the University of Washington, then joined the Army and was sent overseas with an armored division three months before his death.

Lieutenant Harriet Thomas of Olympia, graduate of the Swedish Hospital School of Nursing in Seattle, was presented the Air Medal for flying 104 combat hours while caring for wounded soldiers. She was the third nurse working in the Southwest Pacific area to earn the coveted award.

July 1944

Celebrating July 4 in Wartime

Thousands of people lined Seattle's streets to view an impressive Independence Day parade of uniformed men and women, machinery of war and decorated floats. The greatest applause was given the many marching units of women in uniform. Military bands were interspersed among the parading units. Citizens

Headlines: July 1944

July 1:
44 NATIONS DISCUSS POST-WAR ECONOMICS AT BRETTON WOODS, NH

July 9:
U.S. FORCES COMPLETE THE CONQUEST OF SAIPAN

July 18:
ANTI-WAR SENTIMENT GROWS IN JAPAN; PRIME MINSITER TOJO OUSTED

July 20:
GERMAN ARMY OFFICERS ATTEMPT BUT FAIL TO ASSASSINATE HITLER

July 20:
RUSSIANS FORCE BROAD GERMAN RETREAT IN EASTERN EUROPE

July 21:
GUAM FALLS TO U.S. FORCES IN SIX-DAY BATTLE

July 31:
ALLIES PUSH GERMANS OUT OF NORMANDY, BEGIN TO LIBERATE FRANCE

This detachment of WACs from Spokane's Baxter General Hospital marched down Sprague Street as part of the parade celebrating July 4, 1944. Cheney Cowles Museum, Spokane L89-137.5.

of every major city and many smaller ones turned out in big numbers to view Independence Day events and show their support for the nation's fighting forces.

On the evening of the Fourth, a crowd of 10,000 gathered at the University of Washington stadium for an invasion demonstration. They heard the mournful whine of a submarine siren, saw the glare of subchaser searchlights, heard the roar of exploding land mines and the chatter of machines guns, as troops invaded the football stadium. They saw flame-throwers fling geyser streams of orange and white flame. Two sergeants fired bazookas at targets mounted at the open end of the stadium. They observed how war could be dangerous when one of the bazookas flared back and slightly injured the soldier who fired it. Navy planes roared overhead and infantrymen simulated an infiltration, while Chris Gilson, assistant general manager of the Seattle Chamber of Commerce,

narrated an account of the show over loudspeakers. The major speaker, Lieutenant General Alexander A. Vandergrift, Marine Corps Commandant, told the audience, "It's all over but the fighting." Most of the audience was clad in summer clothing for it was a warm holiday with the temperature in the 80s.

One of the happier July 4 events for service personnel was the announcement that President Roosevelt had signed legislation boosting the pay of trained Army infantrymen. A $5 a month increase was given to foot soldiers not in combat areas and $10 was added to the pay of men in combat groups, provided they met qualifications established by the War Department.

Military Education in Washington State

In early July the Navy dedicated a $4 million Navy school at Smith Cove where thousands of officers and men would be trained to man the new attack transports carrying personnel and equipment to Pacific combat areas. Rear Admiral Francis C. Denebrink, director of the Navy's training activities in the Pacific, traveled to Seattle as principal guest at the ceremony. Also in attendance were officials of construction firms that completed the training school buildings in record time. The installation included large receiving barracks, bachelor officers' quarters, classrooms, mess halls, laundries and a brig, all built on an acreage that fewer than four months earlier had been low-lying swamp land.

On the University of Washington campus, 400 young men with high IQ test scores streamed through Lewis Hall to register for the summer V-12 classes in the Navy accelerated college program. Many Marine Corps and Navy veterans were mixed with recent high school graduates and V-12 transferees from other colleges, all enrolling in University engineering and communications courses.

Local Names in the News

Colonel Lacey V. Murrow, former Washington State director of highways, returned to Seattle after 18 months in the South Pacific, reluctant to talk about the exploits that won him the Legion of Merit. Colonel Murrow, 40, served as director of the engineering division of the Army Services of Supply in the South Pacific. The citation praised his "vigor and resourcefulness," and credited him with developing a protective shield for tractor operators and for organizing an amphibious truck unit for a program of intensive research leading to improved combat performance.

A Liberty Ship belonging to the Alaska Steamship Company was unique in that its officers were all members of the same family. Four brothers — Amigo, Rupert, Dewey and Milton Soriano — arrived back in Seattle on July 1 after several months at sea. Amigo, 29, master of the ship, went directly home to see his new two-week-old daughter. Rupert, 25, the chief mate, and his wife spent several evenings visiting friends. Dewey, 23, second mate, former

pitcher for the Seattle Rainiers, was busy moving into a new home with his bride of three months. The youngest brother, Milton, 21, the third mate, got stuck with duties aboard ship. Amigo said the ship's officers were called by title since to call "Soriano!" resulted in four responses. He added with a grin that on the Alaska run the ship was known as the "S.S. Soriano."

Speaking of people, the resident population of the "Puget Sound congested area" — King, Kitsap and Snohomish Counties — increased 20.7 percent between April 1, 1940 and mid-June 1944. About 990,000 persons now lived in the three counties, 170,000 more than on April 1 four years earlier.

Seattle Postmaster George E. Starr issued an urgent appeal on July 8 for women to help deliver mail. "There is no alternative but to enlist the help of women for this work if the mail service is to be maintained," he said. "We have revised the routes so women carriers will have lighter loads to deliver and shorter distances to walk." He estimated that mail loads given to women would not exceed 15 or 20 pounds.

Workers at "the huge secret government war project at Hanford" opened a drive to buy

Survivors of the 7th Division that pushed the Japanese off Attu in the Aleutians in May 1943, these men arrived in Seattle in July. More than 600 U.S. troops died and 1,200 were wounded in the bloody month-long campaign. Seattle P-I Collection 28177, MOHAI.

war bonds, not just to "sponsor" a B-17 Flying Fortress but to purchase it outright as a gift to the Army Air Force. The idea originated with Max K. Blanchard, a carpenter, after he received a letter from his son, a Navy flyer, who suggested the project. Blanchard told his fellow workers that it was no sacrifice to buy "several million dollars worth of war bonds because they are the safest investment in the world. Let's show we're behind the war effort by giving at least a day's pay."

The state's "by-line" war correspondents were featured on Press Day at Victory Square July 17. Vern Haugland, 36, former University of Washington student and the first civilian to be decorated with the Silver Star Medal, was interviewed at a typical press conference conducted by reporters and photographers from three daily newspapers. He was questioned about his six weeks of wandering in the New Guinea jungles that he described in the book *Letter from New Guinea.* Coast Guard seaman Art Barduhn, a Seattle vibraharpist, was featured musician with Coast Guard bandsmen, many home on leave after performing on extended overseas tours.

Men wounded in the May 1943 battle on the Aleutian island of Attu arrived by train in Seattle on the way to hospitals. Seattle P-I Collection, 28178, MOHAI.

Philip G. Johnson earned another headline in July when the Security Exchange Commission disclosed that his salary was $50,000 per annum. He held two titles: president of The Boeing Airplane Company and general director of the subsidiary Boeing Aircraft Company.

A Few of the Many Heroes of July

Mr. and Mrs. C. J. Conover of Seattle learned on July 4 how their son Lieutenant Charles M. Conover, a 25-year-old M.P., was wounded on D-Day. They previously had been notified that he was recovering from wounds in an English hospital. An article in the Army newspaper, *Stars and Stripes,* reported that Lieutenant Conover's division was directing traffic and aiding wounded during the first landings on Normandy. Conover was shot in the shoulder as he left a landing craft, but carried on with his work for three hours, refusing to quit until he collapsed from loss of blood. The Lieutenant wrote home that he was "feeling fine" and expected to rejoin his division soon. Conover previously was awarded the Soldier's Medal with Oak-Leaf Cluster for rescuing a drowning officer during the invasion of Sicily and for saving the life of another officer caught in an ammunition truck explosion. He was a graduate of Roosevelt High School and the University of Washington.

Sergeant Harry Lewis, Jr., 23, was left gunner and engineer on one of the first Boeing B-29s to drop bombs on the Japanese home islands. He wrote his father describing the raid on the steel works at Yawata. In the letter, which arrived on July 3, he described the situation as "really hot when we came in. I counted over 40 searchlight beams, and could see strings of tracer shells coming up toward the planes ahead of us." Lewis said his plane was over the target for 12 minutes. As soon as the bombs were released, Lewis began searching the sky for enemy fighter planes, but none appeared. However, he described the flak as being "so heavy we could almost have landed on it." All four members of the Lewis family were helping win the war. While Harry was flying on the B-29, his brother Bill, 21, spent 22 months in the Aleutians and was with the first group of Navy men to land on Adak. His mother was in the nation's capital waiting to be sent overseas to take charge of a Red Cross rest home for combat-weary service men. Only his father, Harry, Sr., remained in Seattle.

Corporal William H. Bowker, 21, of Seattle, was killed in action in France on June 8. His mother said that in one of the last letters she had received from him he called himself a "sentimental soldier" and paid tribute to his family, home and country.

> This is one time in a fellow's life when he would like to be near his loved ones. It won't be long until I'll have been away from home for a year. Back home, a person would think nothing of it, but now it seems like eternity. I miss all of the things, no matter how large or small, I used to be able to do. The American people don't realize the privileges and freedoms they are able to enjoy in the grandest country in the world. Believe me, Mom, I say it from the bottom of my heart. I love the good old Stars and Stripes and I would gladly give my life if the people back home would realize they have more to be proud of than a new hat.

Army Air Force Major John G. Evans, 26, was listed as missing in February. On July 13 his wife in Bremerton received word that he was dead. Major Evans' commanding officer wrote that while leading a group of Air Transport planes on one of the longer daylight over-water hops between Ascension Island and Roberts Field, Liberia, Major Evans saw they were approaching a weather front of many thunderheads. "Johnny went down to 4,000 feet trying to find a place to take the formation through. Being unable to do that, he decided to break up the formation and go through on instruments. The clouds looked a little darker where Johnny went in. Nothing was ever seen or heard from him again." Evans had graduated from Roosevelt High School and the University of Washington where he served as president of his class, senior crew manager, and a member

of the Varsity Boat Club. His wife and seven-month-old son, Todd, survived him.

Corporal Lawrence L. Crotts, 24, a member of the Third Army Signal Corps, was killed in action on May 31 according to a War Department notification sent to his parents on July 13. They believed he died on the Anzio beachhead. The Tacoma-born Corporal enlisted in 1940 and was trained at Fort Lewis. He landed in Northern Africa in 1942 and participated all through the African campaign, then went to Sicily and finally to Anzio. He was a graduate of Snoqualmie High School.

Lieutenant John J. Egger, Jr., considered himself one of the luckiest paratroopers alive. What he called the longest 35 seconds of his life occurred when he "hitched" a ride for 700 feet atop the parachute of another soldier. This happened on training maneuvers in England. On a practice jump, he was the last of nine men to leap from a plane cruising at 700 feet. His parachute failed to open. A few seconds later, after dropping about 100 feet, he fell onto an open parachute and hung on for dear life. He realized two men could not depend on the same parachute to safely lower them to earth. John Egger told his wife that, though he outranked the legitimate wearer of the parachute, he did not want him injured, so at about 25 feet above ground, he rolled off and lit hard. In July he was convalescing with a fractured leg and bruises at Barnes General Hospital in Vancouver and enjoying occasional visits from his wife who was living in Ellensburg.

Sergeant Philip S. Kinoshita's parents, originally from Seattle, were in the Japanese relocation center at Hunt, Idaho, when they received word that their son had died of serious wounds. Sergeant Kinoshita, an infantryman, lost his life in action on the Italian front. He was a graduate of Maryknoll School and Broadway High School and had attended the University of Washington.

Captain Floyd Oles, former manager of the Washington Taxpayers' Association, was serving in England with the Army European

August 1-31:
THOUSANDS OF TONS OF ALLIED BOMBS CASCADE ON EUROPEAN CITIES

August 10:
AMERCIAN BOMBERS HIT NAGASAKI, JAPAN

August 14:
MANUFACTURE OF DOMESTIC APPLIANCES RESUMES IN USA

August 25:
FRENCH TANKS LEAD ALLIED FORCES INTO PARIS

August 27:
AN ESTIMATED 1.5 MILLION POLISH JEWS KILLED BY NAZIS

August 28:
ALLIES LIBERATE SOUTH COAST OF FRANCE INCLUDING MARSEILLES

August 31:
RUSSIANS CAPTURE BUCHAREST AND NEARBY OIL FIELDS

Civil Affairs Division when he was hurt by what was believed to be a German robot bomb. He wrote to his wife Helen Louise in Seattle that he was only slightly wounded. His wife, a concert pianist, was herself recovering from a serious auto accident when she received the information.

The parents of Pfc. Don R. Houghton received word late in July that their son had lost a leg and received serious hand injuries in a South Pacific battle. Since these wounds prevented him from writing, Red Cross scribes penned notes to his parents for him. "He's coming home, and that's wonderful news," his mother said. Houghton, their only child, had attended Roosevelt High School and Edison Vocational School before joining the National Guard in 1938. He transferred to the Army in 1940 and when wounded was serving with the field artillery.

Lieutenant Frank R. Moran, son of the founder of the Moran School and grandson of Robert Moran, pioneer Seattle shipbuilder and industrialist, was killed in action in France. While no details were included in the July 28th telegram to his father, the family believed the 23-year-old officer was among parachute troops making early landings in Normandy. Lieutenant Moran graduated from Roosevelt High School and completed his education at Washington State College and Hillsdale College in Michigan. His wife, Evelyn and a daughter who was born on her father's birthday, survived him. At the time of his death, his sister, Mary A. Moran, was a WAC first sergeant at Fort Knox, Kentucky.

Stanley C. Newell, 22, didn't want his family to worry about him. He wrote home that he was in the hospital "with skin trouble." However, his mother in Seattle had already received a telegram stating that her son had been wounded in action on Saipan. Young Stanley explained that he felt he had to make up something because his letter had a hospital return address. The young marine was a Lincoln High School graduate and had two brothers in the Army.

Captain Isabel Kane, commander of the first WAC detachment to reach Europe after D-Day, found that camping 17 miles behind the lines was a lot easier than hiking on pack trips in the Olympic Mountains. The officer, who called Tacoma home, was formerly a dancing instructor at Central Washington College in Ellensburg. She said, "The girls here are living the same life as the GIs. They are up by 6 o'clock every morning, walk half a mile for mess and do their laundry in their helmets." GIs had erected a recreation tent for the women and even though they could hear the guns in the distance they had scheduled a movie for that night. Captain Kane was a University of Washington graduate and had a master's degree from the University of California.

August 1944

Business News

Northwest shipyards held recently signed contracts for a wide variety of vessels including a $200,000 steel tuna-fishing vessel to be built by Reliable Welding Works of Olympia. Two wooden food-supply ships of the tuna-clipper type had been ordered from each of the following shipbuilders: Bellingham Marine Ways, Tacoma Boat Building Company, Petrich Shipbuilding of Tacoma, Martinac Yards of Tacoma, Ballard Marine Railway Company, Sagstad Shipyards of Seattle, Seattle Building and Drydock Company, Everett Marine Ways and Chilman Shipyards of Hoquiam.

In August the Bellingham Iron Works was awarded contracts to build 15 additional all-steel navy lighters and received its fourth Navy "E" for excellence for past production success.

On August 5, the Navy announced that Todd Pacific Shipyards in Tacoma received contracts to build a new type of aircraft escort carrier. More than 20 of the $15 million vessels were on the shipyard's schedule and 3,000 more employees were being sought.

The dogfish shark, found throughout Puget Sound, was long considered a pest by fishermen. However, during the war, it became the country's prime source of Vitamin A. The U.S. Fish and Wildlife service announced that between January 1 and June 30, 1944, livers of dogfish accounted for 9.7 trillion units of Vitamin A, while livers of the soupfin shark, long the principal source, produced only 8.6 trillion units. During the first half of the year, producers of vitamin oils purchased 2,816,000 pounds of dogfish livers valued at $1.5 million. This dogfish market was centered in Seattle where fishermen were paid an average of 54 cents a pound for the livers, compared to the 38 cents a pound received the year before. An entire fleet of boats began specializing in harvesting dogfish in waters from Puget Sound to Southeastern Alaska.

Dr. L. A. Walford, Fish and Wildlife Service biologist and specialist in the pilchard fishery, during the summer sailed on naval vessels on routine cruises through the fishing area of the Pacific Coast to test the Navy's new echo-sounding instruments as a means of locating schools of fish. Another of his tests was to find ways to track fish at night when they left a phosphorescent trail.

In August 1938, the first of 74 Boeing clipper passenger planes had taken off from Lake Washington to test the remodeled twin-rudder. Over the next three years, the Seattle factory produced 12 of the huge airliners for Pan American Airways. Now, six years later in 1944, eight of the twelve were still flying the Atlantic and the Pacific. During the war, among other newsworthy feats, they transported President Roosevelt and other notables to and from overseas meetings. One of the planes, stranded in the South Pacific at the outbreak of war, flew more than 31,000 miles around the world, near the equator, to reach homeport New York safely.

The war resulted in a use being found for most sawmill wastes. Two plants in the Northwest, one in Bellingham, the other in Oregon, began using wood waste as a source of sulfite liquor, a basic ingredient in synthetic rubber.

August Wartime Events in Washington State

Several thousand helmeted men and women in overalls who built Navy ships at the Puget Sound Navy Yard in Bremerton were given time off late on Saturday, August 12. They gathered at a huge dry-dock to hear President Roosevelt speak. While standing on the forward deck of a destroyer docked near them, he told of his trip to Honolulu and the Aleutians. Those in the audience, each wearing his or her identification badge, many carrying lunch buckets, stood close enough to notice the blue of the President's tie and the little upstanding ears of his Scottie, Fala. The speech was broadcast live across the nation at 5 p.m., as shift changes were underway, allowing more workers to hear the President. At one point, the President thanked the press and radio for their voluntary censorship that was a protection for him. At times on his recent trip in the Pacific, he explained, he was within reach of enemy action. A quiet but appreciative Kitsap County crowd listened intently to their wartime President.

The Fifth War Loan Drive was an overwhelming success in Washington State, the media reported on August 18. State residents purchased $284,880,000 worth of war bonds, $56,880,000 above the quota, thanks in part to the women of the state. The Women's Division of the King County War Finance Committee sold nearly $13 million worth of bonds during the drive. This Division included more than 70 women's groups with representatives in every neighborhood in the county. One of the largest projects, aided by women bank employees, was to raise the funding to purchase a hospital ship, the *U.S. Marigold,* on which a plaque was attached reading: "This Ship Sponsored and Made Possible by the War Bond Purchases of the Women of Seattle." During the drive, the Allied Florist Association arranged gardenia corsages that included war bonds hidden among the flowers. These sold well at large retail outlets.

A new Federal Revenue stamp was to be displayed on all automobiles starting July 1. In mid-August the Internal Revenue collectors began tagging Washington State cars without the stamp. Any driver tagged was fined $25 if he did not obtain the $5 revenue stamp within 24 hours.

Early in the war, many breakfast conversations concerned whether the woman of the house should accept a war job. Most Americans agreed that it was a patriotic duty to fill one of a multitude of positions open to them. Before the war, working outside the home had not been an accepted practice, but now the opposite was true; it was common for unemployed women to be asked why they weren't working. Another factor entered into the equation. Two-income families allowed savings to accumulate and many dreamed of purchasing a new home, or a new car, or paying off the existing mortgage early.

Six members of a Boeing flight crew were injured when a B-29 Superfortress was forced to land in Puget Sound near Redondo, 25 miles south of Seattle, about 6 p.m. on August 29. All crewmembers survived though one had a broken leg and others suffered shock, exposure and minor cuts. Redondo residents saw the big plane falter and slip into the water and used their motor boats to rescue the crew. O. J. Lattimer, foreman of a garage at nearby Des Moines, said the plane went into the water about a quarter mile from shore after its power seemed to fail. The plane did not sink and was later towed to shore by the Coast Guard.

A noticeable number of discharged veterans appeared in the State during August. Military rehabilitation offices, veterans' organizations, business and community clubs were anxious to help the veterans, many of whom were released from hospitals after being wounded. Most veterans just wanted "a home and a job." But after a few months, many with skills learned in the service discovered their potential exceeded the demands of their prewar employment. Others enrolled in college under the GI Bill. The discharged veteran, often a kid who'd been too young to vote but who had survived enemy bullets or Nazi flak, realized the discharge button in his lapel (soon known to servicemen as the "ruptured duck") was a symbol that he had served honorably during the war. Most soon developed career objectives and began striving to reach them.

The popular movies of the month included war stories such as *Wing and a Prayer, the Story of Carrier X*, starring Don Ameche and Dana Andrews. Another was titled *Four Jills In a Jeep* and featured Kay Francis and Carole Landis. One of the popular comedies of the month, *Up in Arms*, featured Danny Kaye and Dinah Shore.

Lieutenant Vance Haldeman, a navigator, knew what it meant to be rescued. He was asleep on a plane that crashed in December 1943 and awoke to find himself floating uninjured in the Pacific. He later learned that two officers and four enlisted men died in the crash. Haldeman, a 1942 graduate of Washington State College, had recently married and he and his bride were staying at the Camlin Hotel for a few days before he reported for reassignment at Whidbey Naval Air Station.

Aviation Ordnanceman Richard F. Raper, a widower with a 6-year-old daughter, flew long tiresome patrol missions as an aerial gunner. He was credited with rescuing 11 airmen whose planes had been downed in Pacific action. He had accumulated 3,100 combat air hours since Pearl Harbor and had participated in searches for enemy submarines and in night bombings of Japanese troops.

Two other Seattleites were involved with a unit that patrolled convoy lanes, performed search and rescue missions, provided anti-submarine escort, night harassment of the enemy and convoy coverage. Commander David Perry, Jr., in early August was honeymooning in Montana with his bride of 10 days. The 30-year-old flyer, a veteran of nine years of Navy duty, had attended the University of Washington. Wendell J. Panter, an aviation metalsmith, was enjoying his leave at home in Seattle with his wife after nine months in the Pacific.

In Europe, Captain Edmund H. Torkelson of Seattle witnessed an unusual surrender of two Germans. He and other front-line medics had bedded down for the night in an old French farmhouse. One of them suddenly sat up and asked, "Did you fellows hear anything?" The Captain said, "No, it was just one of our men moving around upstairs." The group then fell asleep but early the next morning unusual noises again woke them. They jumped up to find two German soldiers attempting to crawl from their hiding place in a closet. When ordered to halt, they surrendered to the unarmed medics.

Sidney D. Spear, a former University of Washington official and Harvard Law School graduate, died of wounds received on Wake Island. He had graduated from Cashmere High School and from the University of Washington with scholastic honors. His wife Nancy, who lived in Seattle, received a telegram in August telling her of his death. His brother, Captain Manion Spear, wrote a letter to her saying that those with him when he died proudly told him, "Sid got several Japanese after he was wounded."

Navy Lieutenant Malcolm Lawty of Woodinville, died in a plane crash at sea. The pilot of a torpedo-bomber, Lieutenant Lawty had been involved in overseas action for more than a year and among several exploits had survived eight days on a leaky raft after his plane crashed near Guadalcanal. Lawton was born in Corfu, Grant County, and had graduated from Bothell High School. In 1937 he enrolled at Annapolis, but when war broke out, he left to join the Canadian Air Force. In 1942, he transferred to the U.S. Navy. After eight months duty in the South Pacific, Lieutenant Lawty returned to Seattle to marry Lillian Pool, whose father was County Superintendent of Schools. He then returned to the South Pacific battle zone. Just a week before being notified of her husband's death, Mrs. Lawty gave birth to their baby daughter.

With many of the state's Japanese-Americans fighting in the U.S. Army in Italy, casualty lists began arriving at the Hunt Relocation Center in Idaho where their families had been relocated. The papers of August 8 listed 24 young Nisei who had been killed or wounded. Killed in action were former Seattle residents Sergeant George Sawada, and Private John Kawaguchi, graduates of the University of Washington. Also listed as dead were Private Satoru Onodera, and Pfc. William Kenzo Nakamura (see appendix on Medal of Honor recipients), both Garfield High School graduates; and Pfc. Matsusburo Tanaka, a Franklin High School graduate.

Marvin J. Bockle, 21, an aviation machinist's mate with Fleet Air Wing Four was decorated with the Air Medal on August 3. As captain of a Ventura medium bomber, Bockle volunteered in January for the first night photo reconnaissance bombing mission by a land plane, flying from Alaska to the Northern Kurile Islands. With full knowledge of hazards such as adverse weather, the limited range of the aircraft, and probable enemy opposition, he undertook the pioneer mission to demonstrate the feasibility of conducting offensive air operations against the Japanese home islands with the limited equipment available. Bockle flew three photo-bombing missions to the Kuriles before receiving an eye injury that sent him to the Naval Hospital in Seattle. He found the situation not all negative because his wife and nine-week-old son lived in Seattle. After healing, he was assigned limited shore duty.

Colonel Charles P. (Bert) Burnett, Jr., chief of foreign military government on the staff of General George C. Marshall, was responsible for forming civil governments in newly freed territories of the South Pacific. He was on the way home to visit his wife and three children in Seattle when his plane went down somewhere in the Pacific. Before the war, Colonel Burnett, 40, was a Seattle lawyer. His wife Francis was the daughter of Seattle pioneer and banker Joshua Green and his wife. The Colonel had graduated from Broadway High School and the University of Washington. He later was listed as dead.

Lieutenant Daniel R. Simpson, following a narrow escape in the North Sea, wrote to his wife in Seattle, "It was a terrific experience and one I don't want to go through again." The B-17 he was on was returning to England after a raid on a Leipzig aircraft factory when three of its four engines were damaged. The bomber was forced to drop from the formation and splashed to an emergency landing on the sea. The crew scrambled onto two rubber lifeboats, and prayed the accompanying P-38 fighter pilots would notice their plight and radio for rescue operations. As the first rescue boat arrived, so did two German Messerschmits. They attacked the rescue craft killing several of the crew and setting their boat afire. Lieutenant Simpson was wounded in the arm, hip and shoulder in the attack. The flames from the burning launch caught the attention of P-40 Thunderbolt pilots flying overhead who dove down to investigate. They called for a second rescue launch. The B-17 survivors, including Simpson, were taken to England where he spent five weeks recovering in a hospital before returning to combat. He was awarded a Purple Heart and the Air Medal.

Lieutenant P. Allan Fisher, 27, was killed in action two weeks after the D-Day invasion, the press was informed by his father-in-law, C Hoyt Watson, president of Seattle Pacific College. Lieutenant Fisher graduated from Seattle Pacific in 1939 and had completed some postgraduate work at the University of Washington before joining the Army in March 1940. He married Lola Watson in June 1941 and at the time of his death they had two daughters, one 2 years of age and the other 10 months old. His parents lived in Arlington, Washington.

On July 28, the same day that Mrs. Stephen Mills became the mother of a daughter, word was received that her husband, a bomber pilot, was missing in action over Austria. Her mother-in-law intercepted the telegram and did not relay the bad news to her on that day. On August 7, when Mrs. Mills was preparing to take her baby home from the hospital, she was told that her husband was missing. A graduate of Roosevelt High School, he had been in the Army Air Forces nearly two years and had piloted a B-24 bomber on more than 30 missions over enemy territory in Italy. Lieutenant Mills

apparently survived, for he is not listed among Washington State's war dead.

Corporal John R. Hale, the only son of Mr. and Mrs. John F. Hale of Poulsbo, was killed in action on the Normandy front on June 20, his parents were notified on August 9. A paratrooper, Hale was awarded his wings at Fort Benning, Georgia. Born in Bremerton, he had attended school in Aberdeen and Montana. He was an honor student at Carroll College and later enrolled at Seattle College for a short time after his parents moved to Seattle. His commanding officer told his parents that John Hale "was one of the finest scouts in the demolition platoon. He died a soldier's death."

According to an August press release, Brigadier General Nathan B. Forrest was killed on a bombing raid over Kiel, Germany, on June 13. His widow, Frances Forrest, was a Red Cross worker in Bremerton. General Forrest graduated from West Point in 1928 and was the great-grandson and namesake of Confederate General Nathan Bedford Forrest of Civil War fame.

The father of Staff Sergeant James T. Stuart always remembered how his son came home in 1942, proudly displaying his newly acquired high boots and Silver Wings of the U.S. Parachute Infantry. On August 12 a message arrived addressed to the father, who had died two months earlier, informing him that his 27-year-old son had been killed in action on July 7 during the invasion of Normandy. His mother had died several years earlier, so a sister received the information. A graduate of Broadway High School in Seattle, the Sergeant joined the service in 1942. While home on leave before going overseas, he told his father, "The way we feel is that once you're in this war you might just as well go after the best there is. They tell you that you're as good as five men. They do that because, you see, once you get over there and parachute down, there'll be five against each of us."

Private Will O. McLeod was wounded on June 13 while serving in the infantry in Italy.

His family in Seattle received word in August that he had died of his wounds two days later. They were presented the Purple Heart he was posthumously awarded. Young McLeod, a graduate of Seattle's Garfield High School, had been overseas for only four months when killed.

Not all deaths on the front were caused by enemy action. Patrick M. Murphy, Jr., a Navy cook serving in New Guinea, died on July 23 after a brief illness according to a Navy Department telegram received by his widow in Seattle. He had attended Roosevelt High School before enlisting in the Navy.

The War Department notified the mother of T/4 Clarence E. Danbom, that he had been killed in action in France. Danbom, a Franklin High School graduate, had entered the service in 1941. His widowed mother, confined to a wheelchair, had received his last letter shortly before the telegram arrived. In it he had written: "Mother, just keep your chin up and I'll be coming home soon." His mother added, "I could tell from his cheerful letters that he must have been a good soldier."

Lieutenant John M. Miller of Vashon Island was killed August 1 on the Normandy front his family was told on August 22. He was a 1940 graduate of Vashon High School and began his Army career in the National Guard. He was stationed at Fort Worden with the 248th Coast Artillery for a time, then was commissioned a Lieutenant in the Infantry after training at Fort Benning, Georgia. His widow and 15-month-old daughter survived him.

Lieutenant Colonel Jack Therriault, a 70-mission fighter pilot, on August 22 was home in Seattle for the first time in three years. He pulled his rods and reels from storage and began planning an excursion to the Methow Valley where he used to fish before the war. He figured that excursion would help him forget memories of the bloody action in Normandy. He told a reporter he had crowded more action into 40 hectic days on the Cherbourg Peninsula than he expected to experience in his lifetime. He explained how aviators helped the ground forces capture Cherbourg. "We were partners with the boys below. We worked in close liaison with the Infantry — bombing and strafing enemy troops and gun installations. We mussed up targets just ahead of the doughboys. In a way, we were long-range artillerymen. And we flew in more than a few paratroopers." A former Gonzaga University student, Therriault and his wife, who was from Spokane, visited his parents in Seattle. When his leave was over, the colonel expected to return to duty overseas.

Lieutenant Charles E. R. Blair, base operations officer at Paine Field near Everett, was killed instantly on the afternoon of August 22 when the P-39 fighter plane he was piloting crashed a short distance west of the field. At the time the Lieutenant was on a combat training flight. He was born at Index in Snohomish County 29 years before his death and had graduated from Longview High School. For a time he was based on Ascension Island, a highly secret base in the South Atlantic. A young son survived him.

A freak accident took the life of Lieutenant Orland L. Kuhr of Clayton, in Stevens County. The 22-year-old pilot was flying an AT-6 training plane in a dogfight scene being filmed in Arizona for the motion picture *God Is My Co-Pilot*. The AT-6, camouflaged as a Japanese Zero, was to approach a B-25 bomber but the plan went awry and the two planes collided, killing young Kuhr and three men in the bomber.

Lieutenant Douglas W. Mortensen, wounded in action over the North Sea while piloting a Liberator bomber later died from his injuries, his parents in Port Orchard told the press on August 31. The Lieutenant had been stationed in England. Before entering the service, he was an engineering student at the University of Washington. Survivors included a brother, Sergeant Richard G. Mortensen, stationed at Camp Gruber, Oklahoma, with the 42nd (Rainbow) Division.

For a short time Pfc. Maurice F. Scranton, whose parents lived in Seattle, was missing in action. However, Private Scranton wrote home that he was back with his company. He had been captured by the Germans during the battle for Cherbourg, but after a few days American forces liberated the city and freed him. In his letter he told his parents: "I haven't slept in a bed for 40 nights." He described the war as a "hard deal and pretty hot." Scranton had served in North Africa and was involved with the paratroops during the invasion landings at Sicily and Normandy. He also was involved in establishing the beachhead at Salerno.

September 1944

Life in Washington State

The Seattle Council of Churches announced on September 1 that the day Germany surrendered they would announce a day of prayer. "While V-E Day will bring deep joy to all, it should be observed not primarily by hilarious celebration but by rededication to our unfinished task," council president Reverend Harold V. Jensen said. The special service of worship planned for First Methodist Church would be open to all races and creeds. With the apparent progress of the war in Europe, many believed the fighting there would end soon. However, bloody battles continued in Europe for eight more months.

Families were discussing whether their servicemen might be home for Christmas if the battlefields on the Continent suddenly went quiet. On September 6, the Army explained that the average GI had only a small chance of being sent home when the war in Europe ended because most would be shifted to the Pacific or involved in the Army of Occupation in Europe. The services emphasized that those serving in Europe had no better chance for early discharge than did soldiers involved on other war fronts. The plan was to first release soldiers who had been overseas and in combat longest and who had small children at home. Army units would not be released intact. Soldiers with special qualifications needed on Pacific fronts would not be discharged, no matter their length of service and combat record. The biggest initial reduction would be in infantry and artillery

units, but some of these men would be transferred to Air and Service forces or trained as replacements for men who had earned a higher numbers of points toward discharge.

One of the most experienced units fighting in the Southwest Pacific was the Fighting 41st Division, manned largely by men from the Pacific Northwest. In August, an officer from the unit, Captain Ralph Westin, former Seattle dentist, returned home on a 30-day sick leave to heal an infected hand. During two and a half years overseas, the Captain helped preserve the teeth of the 41st Division engineers and recalled treating an ailing molar of a GI seated in a foxhole on the front line. He said, "Men from Washington, Oregon, and Idaho make up the bulk of the Division and have done an excellent job in the long campaign in the Pacific. The people at home can well be proud of their achievements."

The readjustment allowance section of the new federal GI Bill of Rights became effective on September 11. It paid unemployment benefits of $20 a week to veterans who had no job and smaller weekly amounts for "partial unemployment." Veterans were expected to be available for suitable positions upon referral by the Employment Service.

Later in September, the Seattle Civil Service Commission established a precedent when they ruled that a veteran of World War II was entitled to reinstatement in the position he held before entering the service, even if challenged by the interim office-holder. The commission directed that Colonel Clair A. Hulslander be reinstated as junior cashier in the Seattle Transit System, the position he held for 18 years before obtaining military leave and serving four years in the Army.

The popular Army weapons demonstration at the University of Washington Stadium in October 1943 had resulted in some damage and the University requested the Army pay for the repairs. After several meetings where blueprints and photographs were studied, the Army agreed to pay $18,893 to repair the University football practice fields and running tracks that were scarred during demonstrations by tanks, trucks and artillery.

On September 13, young men from high schools who were members of the Air Corps Enlisted Reserve visited Paine Field where they were introduced to the roles of air combat crews. The 80 youth examined sleek pursuit planes and felt the backwash of a P-39 propeller. Youth of 17 could enlist in the reserve program but were not called to active duty until age 18. Following a tour of the hangars and airstrip, they were guided through barracks, recreational quarters and the gymnasium. After lunch, they were taken to the chapel and later viewed a film explaining the indoctrination of airmen. Their final assignment was at the skeet range for shooting practice. A few of the youth were invited to experience actual flight in fighter planes but lowering clouds prevented takeoffs.

The Census Bureau reported that between 1940 and 1944 more than 250,000 war workers and their family members moved to King, Kitsap, Pierce, and Snohomish Counties. That number, when added to the natural increase from excess of births over deaths, and reduced by the loss of men to the armed forces, resulted in a population increase of 170,000 persons in the four counties. The labor supply increased 35 percent, principally due to employment of newcomers and housewives and others normally not in the labor market. The report also noted an increase in the ratio of workers to dependents and an increase in the percentage of employees from minority races.

During the month 225 additional names of King County war dead were added to the Victory Square pylon, raising the total to more than 525. The Seattle Chapter of American War Dads had charge of the program that recognized the sacrifices of the youth killed in battle. Fathers, mothers, wives and families of service men whose names were added were invited to attend the ceremony.

Later in the month, the Girl Scout Organization was honored at a Victory Square program. Scout executives and girl members

received Office of Civilian Defense citations from Mrs. A. Scott Bullitt for their work as hospital aides and for other war efforts. Mrs. Charles Clise, long active in Girl Scouts, was the major speaker.

People of the State of Washington mourned the death of Boeing President Philip G. Johnson who died September 14. He had risen from a $25 a week draftsman to the pinnacle of the aircraft industry. On the way home from a business trip to the East Coast, he had stopped off in Wichita to confer with officials at the Boeing branch factory there and suffered a heart attack. He was 49 years old. His body was returned to Seattle on a B-17 Flying Fortress accompanied by Mrs. Johnson and their children, Esther Mary and Philip, Jr., and Mr. and Mrs. J. E. Schaefer. Schaefer was general manager of the Wichita Division of Boeing. Philip Johnson was buried in Lake View Cemetery alongside many Seattle pioneers.

Native Americans were valued on all war fronts. The Swinomish Tribe in Skagit County took pride in the part they were playing in the war effort. The Sagstad Shipyard at LaConnor was located on property leased from their reservation. Furthermore, 30 of the 85 shipyard employees were Indians. And more than 30 of

The battles in the jungles of Bougainville were bloody affairs. The U. S. Marines landed on the Japanese held island in November 1943 and firefights ranged until the final Japanese attack failed six months later. The photo shows two Native Americans, members of a Marine Corps signal unit, operating a portable radio set just a few yards behind the front lines. The dense jungle can be seen behind them. U.S. Marine Corps photo.

the tribe's young men were serving in the Army and one of them had given his life for his country on a battlefield in Italy. The shipyard workers all were buying bonds under the payroll-deduction plan.

Master Sergeant Chester Stewart, the Army's "oldest sergeant," had held the rating longer than any other soldier, more than 26 years. He had enlisted in 1914, helped American troops hunt for Pancho Villa in Mexico, and served with the Second Engineers and in the Army of Occupation during World War I. His ten hitches had taken him to all parts of the world. On September 1, he turned in his equipment at the Army training center at Fort Lewis and retired to Ridgefield, near Vancouver. The Sergeant hoped to become reacquainted with his four sons. Two of them were in the service, one a corporal in the Air Corps and the other studying under Navy sponsorship in Minnesota. He, his wife and their two other sons managed a small farm and the sergeant was considering starting a surveying business.

Two news photographs appearing in newspapers depicted Washington State servicemen in the front ranks. The result was a deluge of phone calls to their families. One picture of American troops marching through the Arc de Triomphe in Paris focused on Lieutenant Donald S. Douglas, who grew up in Deming, near Bellingham. His wife Myrle who was from Sumner, and their 3-year-old daughter, were living with her brother and sister-in-law in Seattle. She could hardly believe her eyes when she saw the picture. She said she had not heard from her husband for two weeks but knew he was in France, though not exactly where. She expressed her delight at knowing he marched in the Paris liberation parade.

The second photo showed 10 men and women from Seattle on a Coast Guard-manned assault boat. It was published in newspapers early in September, and led to a ringing telephone in the home of Captain H. C. W. Klein, veteran master mariner for the Alaska Steamship Company, and his wife. Their daughter Alberta was not identified in the photograph but her face was clearly shown and some who knew her were soon on the phone. Miss Klein, a graduate of Roosevelt High, had volunteered for overseas service with the Red Cross and was serving as a staff assistant in the India-Burma theatre.

Never in the history of the United States had there been so many war veterans. Most were of high school and college age and thousands of them had interrupted their studies to take up arms for their country. The universities of Washington State in 1944 began developing programs especially for veterans. Mort Frayn, president of the UW Alumni Association, stopped to chat with a couple of recently discharged students on the steps of Clark Hall. He asked them what men fresh from the battlefronts hoped to receive from college. Sergeant Duane Eckols had seen action in the battle of Midway and Ralph Passman had fought at Tarawa. Both were enrolled as marine V-12 trainees. They discussed their hopes with Mr. Frayn who took notes, then he moved on to chat with other veterans about their college expectations. . George Carter, a graduate of Roosevelt High School, after serving three and one-half years in the Army's 41st Division, including a year in Australia and New Guinea, was discharged as a staff sergeant and immediately entered the University of Washington as a freshman with plans to major in accounting.

A Few of the Many Heroes of September

The mother of Lieutenant John O. Lockhart of Seattle received word that her son was one of more than 1,000 American flyers freed from German stalags in Romania by advancing Russian armies. Young Lockhart, a 22-year-old co-pilot, had been a prisoner of war since his plane was shot down in flames during a raid on the Ploesti oil fields 13 months earlier. The Lieutenant was one of only three crewmembers to escape the burning plane.

Few Washington State service personnel experienced war in both the Pacific and

European theatres. Colonel Charles Ross Greening of Hoquiam was one who did. He was involved in the Doolittle raid on Tokyo in April 1942. In July 1944, the Germans captured Greening after his plane went down in Italy. His wife and sister received a letter from him on September 1, the first they had heard from him since his capture. He said he "was whiling away the longest year of his life."

Mrs. Doris L. Moore of Seattle, an Army Air Force inspector at Boeing, received a War Department telegram notifying her that her son, Ensign James E. Neale, 23, had been killed in the South Pacific. A 1943 graduate of the U.S. Naval Academy at Annapolis, he piloted a C-47 until he was transferred to bombers shortly before his death. Mrs. Moore found it difficult to accept the telegram. Just a year and a half earlier, her husband, Commander Sam Moore, also an Annapolis graduate, had been killed in action while serving on an aircraft carrier in the South Pacific.

Lieutenant Gust J. Damascus, 22, died in action while serving with the Ninth Air Force in France. His mother in Seattle received the fateful telegram in mid-September. Just a week previously, she had received her son's last letter in which he had requested she locate a French woman living in Seattle and tell her he had met members of her family in Paris and they were well. Mrs. Damascus did locate Germaine Courbot in Seattle and immediately sent messages back to Paris for her son to relate to the Courbot family. Unfortunately he was killed before the task could be accomplished. In 1942 young Damascus had graduated in civil engineering with high honors from Washington State College, where he had participated in boxing and fencing. He had turned down a teaching contract to enlist in the Air Force.

The 95-foot Army Transport Service Freighter F-14, operated by a crew of 16, was seven days out of Honolulu when its reduction gears were stripped and all power was lost, shutting down machinery and navigation equipment. The ship floated at the mercy of the winds, the currents, and enemy submarines.

The tropical heat was terrific and sunstroke began to take a toll. After several days, heat and strain temporarily incapacitated both the captain and the first officer. Second Officer John W. (Jack) Maier, Jr., of Bellingham, took over as skipper and navigator. For 32 days the F-14 drifted, its lights blacked out at night to avoid detection by the enemy. With rations nearly depleted, Maier, after studying ship's charts, asked for volunteers to help him row the 85 miles to the closest American-held islands. They began rowing but sharks suddenly surrounded their little boat and the wind started to blow them toward enemy-territory, forcing them to return to the ship. After a time the freighter drifted near an island in the southern Gilberts and was sighted by natives, who pulled it into a safe anchorage. The various tribes of natives then adopted the crewmembers and made them comfortable. After a month on the island, 64 days after their ship was disabled, the crew of a passing PBY saw the message of rocks the crew had placed on the white sand beach. A few days later, a ship steamed into the harbor and rescued the merchant sailors that had been given up for lost for two months. In mid-September Maier was home in Bellingham on a 60-day furlough, after which he returned to the Army Transportation Corps.

The Navy in September reported Lieutenant Commander Carl B. A. Holmstrom of Arlington was missing in action. After finishing high school, Holmstrom attended the U.S. Naval Academy at Annapolis, receiving his commission 1938. He transferred to naval aviation in 1940, became a dive-bomber pilot and was named executive officer of his carrier-based squadron. Shortly thereafter he failed to return from a mission in the Southwest Pacific. He later was declared dead.

Six men from Washington State were among members of a Navy combat demolition group awarded the Presidential Unit citation for heroic action in clearing enemy obstacles from the Normandy invasion beaches while under devastating enemy fire. The six were:

Storekeeper William R. Wren of Seattle, Shipfitter James N. Barker of Spokane, Carpenter William C. Thompson of Bremerton, Lieutenant William M. Jenkins of Everett, Ensign Wade A. Peterson of Bellevue, and Machinist's Mate Gilbert P. Luttrel of Bremerton. The dispatch reported that 31 of the 171 men in the unit were killed and 60 wounded, including the above Barker and Thompson.

Lieutenant Tom Potts, 28, from Tacoma, died in action in France in August. He had acted in several motion pictures before enlisting in the Army soon after Pearl Harbor. Among the pictures in which he had parts were *Golden Boy* and *The Little Adventuress*. He was the nephew of Minnie Maddern Fiske, the famous stage actress, and his mother was a Tacoma schoolteacher. He was survived by his wife who lived in their home in Hollywood, California.

Pfc. William C. Westlake of Seattle was killed in the South Pacific, after serving there nine months. He was only 15 years old when he died. He had fibbed about his age so that he could join the Marine Corps at the age of 14.

The parents of Sergeant Stewart M. Holloway were told their son was missing in action over Austria. The 26-year-old waist gunner on a B-17 had completed his 48th mission on August 28, leaving two more to go before being eligible for furlough. Holloway, a Ballard High School graduate, had served four years in the Navy before joining the Army Air Forces in 1943. His mother told a reporter, "I am sure he is safe, somewhere. I'll let you know the minute I hear from him." Unfortunately the Sergeant had been killed in the skies over Austria.

Lieutenant David G. Schwartz of Vashon was listed as missing after his P-38 fighter named "Seattlelightning" was involved in aerial combat with a group of enemy planes. Then a few months later, his family heard that he had escaped from German-held territory, but for security reasons, the Army would reveal no details. Three weeks later, the Lieutenant arrived home and explained that his plane's controls were damaged while flying at 8,000

feet. He parachuted into an apple orchard 30 miles behind the German lines, injuring his back when he landed. He managed to hide his parachute and began trying to sneak toward the advancing American front line in Normandy. An elderly French farmer spotted him and provided some tattered clothes. Schultz said, "He looked terrified and I could see he wanted me to leave." So the Lieutenant made his way to another farmhouse where a man gladly offered to help him. For two weeks Schwartz hid in a barn while his injured back healed. His French protectors fed him and helped him improve his high school French. A 16-year-old French boy was anxious to be of assistance. He explained that the Gestapo had shot his father and his mother had died. The boy offered to find a way to lead Schultz toward the Yanks. For four weeks Schwartz lived in the garret of another farmhouse, waiting for the boy to arrange the escape. When they began to move, the boy saved his life a few times by doing most of the talking when they met German soldiers. As they approached the front lines, they bypassed some Wehrmacht soldiers and suddenly realized they were in no-man's land between the Germans and the Americans. When artillery shells began landing near them, they managed to dig a shelter. After surviving three days of bombardment, Schwartz spied a Yank corporal approaching and he and the French lad "joined up" with the American patrol. A few days later, when he reached England, Schwartz was advanced in rank to Captain and was given furlough. In late September, he and his wife were staying with his sister in Seattle, just across the Sound from his alma mater, Vashon High School.

The War Touched Every Hamlet, Village and Town in Washington State

Though the population of the cities and suburbs increased rapidly all during the war years, the smaller towns felt the effects of war, too. In towns where everyone knew everyone else, when a resident was killed or wounded on some distant battlefield, concern swept the town. The names that follow were selected from the long daily listings of war casualties carried in the newspapers across the state. Because of the numbers of casualties, often just name, branch of service and sometimes the hometown and theater of operations were included. These are but a few of the hundreds of small town names found in September 1944 listings.

- Oroville, Okanogan County: Corporal Herbert O. Price, Marine Corps, wounded.
- Poulsbo, Kitsap County: Sergeant Frank E. Olsen, Jr., Army, wounded (Mediterranean area).
- Dabob, Jefferson County: Private James F. Jones, Army, wounded (European area).
- Kirkland, King County: Staff Sergeant Joseph W. Hoyt, Army, wounded (European area).
- Sequim, Clallam County: Seaman First Class Glen Wilson Cays, Navy, wounded.
- Ridgefield, Clark County: Frank H. Dodge, metal-smith, Navy, missing, later declared dead.
- Edmonds, Snohomish County: Stephen R. Hendricksen, gunners' mate, Navy, wounded.
- Zillah, Yakima County: Pfc. Jack L. Hill, Marine Corps, wounded.
- Opportunity, Spokane County: Floyd W. Maier, hospital apprentice, Navy, wounded.
- Waitsburg, Walla Walla County: Pfc. Elmer W. Seagraves, Marine Corps, wounded.
- Dishman, Spokane County: Pfc. Laverne E. Sullivan, Marine Corps, wounded.
- Ashford, Pierce County: Pfc. Gordon W. Worden, Marine Corps, killed in action.
- Camas, Clark County: Private Nicholas E. Duback, Army, wounded.
- Hanford, Benton County: Private Robert E. Hankel, Army, wounded (Central Pacific).
- Ferndale, Whatcom County: Lieutenant Paul E. Larson, Army, wounded (Central Pacific).
- Colbert, Spokane County: Pfc. Eugene S. Long, Army, wounded (Central Pacific).
- Darrington, Snohomish County: Sergeant

Clarence H. Marshall, Army, wounded (Pacific area).
- Glenoma, Lewis County: Pfc. Felix O. Meade, Army, wounded (Pacific area).
- Oak Harbor, Island County: Sergeant Larry C. Boyer, Army, prisoner of war (Germany).
- Ellensburg, Kittitas County: Pfc. Darrel O. Borg, Army, prisoner of war (Germany).
- Monroe, Snohomish County: Lieutenant Robert M. Cook, Army, prisoner of war (Germany).
- Battle Ground, Clark County: Private Milton E. Winston, Army, wounded (European Area).
- Auburn, King County: Pfc. Harley H. Bren, Marine Corps, dead.
- Tonasket, Okanogan County: Pfc. Coburn J. Johnson, Army, wounded (European Area).
- Clayton, Stevens County: Lieutenant Jesse J. Groff, Army, wounded (European Area).
- St. John, Whitman County: Pfc. Harry O Martin, Army, wounded, (European Area).
- Suquamish, Kitsap County: Pfc. John E. Lemieux, Jr., Marine Corps, wounded.
- Omak, Okanogan County: Lieutenant Winston G. Emert, missing, (European Area).
- Concrete, Skagit County: Sergeant Leonard I. Hornbeck, Army, missing (European Area).
- Otis Orchards, Spokane County: Lieutenant Wm. A. Thurston, Army, missing, (Europe).
- Waterville, Douglas County: Sergeant Vernon R. Leming, Army, missing (Mediterranean Area).
- Colville, Stevens County: Pfc. John W. Hoppe, Marine Corps, wounded.
- Washougal, Clark County: Pfc. John D. Howard, Marine Corps, missing, later listed as dead.
- Electric City, Grant County: Pfc. John B. Denny, Army, wounded (Pacific Theater).
- Elma, Grays Harbor County: Private Johnny W. Tauscher, Army, wounded (European Theater).

- Lynden, Whatcom County: Private Gordon Van Leeuwen, Army, wounded (European Theater).
- Lowell, Snohomish County: Sergeant Robert H. Buckley, Army, killed in action.
- Bow, Skagit County: Pfc. Dixon W. Hobson, Army, killed in action.
- Harrah, Yakima County: Sergeant Leonard Boyle, Army, wounded (European Theater).
- Wapato, Yakima County: Pfc. Fred Estep, wounded (European Theater).
- Deep River, Wahkiakum County: Technician Tolvo Hokkanen, Army, wounded (Europe).
- Farmington, Whitman County: Pfc. Paul Felker, wounded (European Theater).
- Toutle, Cowlitz County: Corporal Harvey J. Holcomb, wounded (European Theater).
- Forks, Clallam County: Lieutenant Murry N. Maconley, wounded (European Theater).
- Ajiune, Lewis County: Pfc. Norman H. Blankenship, Marine Corps, killed in action.
- Dallesport, Klickitat County: Lieutenant Robert C. Fulton, Army, wounded.
- Moxee City, Yakima County: Pfc. Martin A. Cesaro, Army, wounded.
- Camas, Clark County: Private Curtis R. Barnett, Army, killed in action.
- Roslyn, Kittitas County: Private Frank Cheha, Army, killed in action.
- Nine Mile Falls, Spokane County: Pfc. Joseph W. Childs, Jr., Army, killed in action.
- College Place, Pierce County: John B. Goodman, technician, Army, killed in action.
- Selleck, King County: Private Martin A. Guerrini, Army, killed in action.
- Raymond, Pacific County: Lieutenant Harry Holech, Army, killed in action.
- Endicott, Whitman County: Pfc. Wilbur E. Stover, Army, killed in action.

- Castle Rock, Cowlitz County: Private Joseph M. Bowman, Army, killed in action.
- Boyds, Ferry County: Private Robert Arnold, Army, killed in action.
- Woodland, Cowlitz County: Sergeant Elmer Mattila, Army, killed in action.
- Ilwaco, Pacific County: Technician Elroy A. Nort, Army, killed in action.
- Port Orchard, Kitsap County: Private Harold W. Tiedemann, Army, killed in action.
- Buckley, Pierce County: Pfc. Keith E. Nearhood, Marine Corps, wounded.

The list provides some indication of why families worried about young Washingtonians serving on the war fronts of the world.

October 1944

Washington Residents Featured in the News

World War II was an emotional time for Washington State families. Miss Jo Ryan, a Red Cross worker in Italy, wrote her parents, Mr. and Mrs. L. J. Ryan of Seattle, a letter, parts of which were published in *The Seattle Times*. She told of a bomber pilot named Ed, a likable 22-year-old flyer, "young, but old, too, with a soft voice, perfect manners and always at ease, but underneath he was a bundle of nerves. He's had some pretty rough missions — brought a plane back with one engine, crash landed another, brought ships back a number of times that were badly hit." She described him as "plenty scared but he felt it was his place to fight this war so the married guys could stay home." She added that he had wanted to be a doctor, but the war came and he took to the air.

When the first crews from the mission came in and headed for the coffee and doughnuts, Jo was there to serve them. They began talking about Ed's plane and how it was shot down. They felt he had little chance to survive. Then they became pretty silent, she said. "I began to think of all the things he had said. His poor folks — I remember him telling once about losing his young brother in the South Pacific… Wives,

The U.S. had been at war for more than three years before the Puget Sound region had its own center for collecting, processing, and typing blood for medical uses. The King County Central Blood Bank opened in October 1944 in temporary quarters at King County Hospital. Dr. and Mrs. S. Maimon Samuels donated two lots at the corner of Madison and Terry in Seattle and citizens raised $200,000 for construction. In this photo of the ground breaking on October 11, 1945, Dr. Samuels is sitting in the earthmover and the first blood bank director, Dr. J. Richard Czajkowski, is standing second from the right. Seattle P-I Collection, 23607, MOHAI.

sisters, mothers, fathers are going through this every day." She talked about the harm done to the men on these missions and how most of them would never talk about it when they got home. She added, "Things that people squabble about on the home front seem pretty small."

A few days later, Miss Ryan's parents received a happy sequel to the first letter. "I was awakened this morning by a friend who was shouting that our lost pilot Ed was O.K. It's a very interesting and exciting story, and we may see him soon. It was a wonderful feeling and the world looked all bright."

Walter F. Clark, managing director of Clark's Restaurants, had three sons, all of whom attended O'Dea High School. Now all were in the service. Private Lawrence Clark, 26, was somewhere in France as an Army chaplain's assistant. Marine Lieutenant Walter F. Clark, Jr., 21, was a fighter pilot stationed at Mojave Air Base in California. Sergeant Eugene F. Clark, 20, had dropped out of classes at Washington State College to join the Army Air Force and was serving as an upper turret gunner on the Flying Fortress named "Something for the Boys."

The Blood Bank nearest to Washington State was located in San Francisco until October 12, 1944, when the King County

Central Blood Bank opened on a modest scale in Harborview County Hospital. The fear of attack during the first months of the war made obvious the need for a local blood supply. Physicians around the state regarded a Blood Bank essential to provide blood for transfusions in the region's hospitals. In 1944, a group of local citizens formed committees to found a King County Blood Center. Dr. J. Richard Czajkowski, hired as director, was a man with extensive experience in blood work. His objective was to supply blood and plasma to patients as needed, at the lowest possible cost, while eliminating the cumbersome "person to person" methods of transfusion previously used. A permanent building was soon completed at Terry Avenue and Madison Street in Seattle.

The first detachment of Transportation Corps WACS arrived in Paris by air on October 13 after a six-day stay in England. The commander of the detachment was Captain Joy E. Fincke, former WAC staff director at the Seattle Port of Embarkation. Also in the detachment were: Sergeant Frances G. Leicester, Sergeant Mary C. O'Toole, and Corporal Jennie Mae Turner of Seattle; Private Mabel C. Tjehaland of Port Townsend; Private Lorene A. Smith of Tacoma; Corporal Geraldine

L. Raymond of Yakima; Sergeant Gladys W. Prunty of Olympia and Pfc. Marjorie R. Would of Everson, Whatcom County.

In 1935, 9-year-old George P. Weyerhaeuser had been kidnapped for ransom. His father, a wealthy lumberman, paid $200,000 to secure his freedom. The kidnappers later were arrested and most of the ransom recovered. Now, nine years later, the 18-year-old young man was smiling cheerfully as he reported for induction at Fort Lewis. He was assigned to the Navy. Young Weyerhaeuser had completed a year at Yale University before being called into the service. His father, in one of his first public statements in a decade, said, "George will now go where Uncle Sam sends him."

Jack Startup, 20, a Navy cook, was startled as he walked through the door of the Seattle USO Club, at 1011 2nd Avenue. He found himself surrounded by officials, hostesses, photographers and reporters, for he was the one-millionth guest of the club. The bewildered Startup protested, "I just was hoping to take a shower." Instead he was showered with gifts — orchids, chocolates, a war bond, the key to the club and a free long-distance telephone call home. Accompanying Startup on the round of activities was attractive USO Junior Hostess Ruth Coffee who sighed: "I'm glad he wasn't a service woman!" The pair visited Mayor William Devin, and were guests at the Fifth Avenue Theatre. Startup, from Los Angeles, was stationed at Point No Point in Kitsap County.

Completed in mid-1946, the original King County Central Blood Bank stands in the shadow of St. James Cathedral. Today's Puget Sound Blood Center and Program has been rebuilt and now extends over much of the block. It is considered one of the most progressive blood banks in the country. Seattle P-I Collection, 23609, MOHAI.

A Few Business Stories of the Month

Ten thousand Christmas gift packages for servicemen in the Aleutians and South Pacific were sent on their way on October 16 thanks to Boeing Aircraft Company employees. More than 20,000 Boeing workers contributed to a gift fund sponsored by women's activity representatives at Boeing plants in Washington State. Contributions were used to purchase articles recommended by the Army, including thousands of cigars, tobacco, toilet articles, games, books and tons of snack food. Each gift had a personal message enclosed and was identified with stickers portraying the Boeing B-29 Superfortress. Boeing officials said some of the gifts were destined for the 41st Division in the South Pacific, an Army unit that included a large number of Washington State men.

Speaking of the Superfortresses, the price for the first one was $3,392,396, including the costs of years of engineering experiments, tests and changes. But by November the huge planes were rolling off Boeing production lines at a cost of $600,000 each.

State liquor stores had been selling liquor to servicemen during their regular store hours, but the Army and Navy imposed new regulations on October 16. Service personnel were allowed to purchase liquor only between noon and 8 p.m. Normally state liquor stores remained open until 10 on Friday and Saturday nights.

The Puget Sound war effort in shipbuilding, airplane manufacture and transportation of supplies vital to war zones had attracted much attention in the East and South, Colonel W. C. Bickford, Manager of the Port of Seattle, told local businessmen. He had toured East Coast and Gulf ports and found they were well aware of the Seattle area's postwar possibilities.

Because men without shipboard experience were urgently needed for training by the United States Maritime Service, Selective Service boards were notified in early October that men aged 18 through 26 could now join the United States Merchant Marine instead of the Army or Navy.

Serious efforts to control prices were apparent all during the war years. During one October week, 29 Seattle taverns were fined $4,890 for overcharging on beer and wine. In addition, three restaurants paid $115 for overcharging on their menus.

A Few of the Many Heroes of October

U.S. Army and Navy casualties since the start of the war totaled 453,375 as of October 1, whereas two weeks earlier the number had been 417,085. The large increase, the government explained, was due in part to "a revised and improved statistical system that permits a more up-to-date picture of the situation. However, there inevitably remains a time lag of about 15 days before actual casualties and the receipts of individual reports can be accumulated at the War Department."

Several Washington State flyers, members of Navy Squadron 144, arrived home on leave October 17 after a year in the Central Pacific. They had bombed and strafed enemy positions and flown reconnaissance and photographic patrols from Tarawa to Roi, and up and down the Gilberts and Marshalls. They dropped 26 carloads, about 780,000 pounds, of high explosives from twin-engine bombers. Every one of the squadron's Ventura bombers was damaged by enemy fire at one time or another, yet only one plane failed to return to a friendly base. The men who arrived home on leave were Lieutenant Donald M. McAusland, Lieutenant Russell F. Craig, and Ensign Rollin Ayers of Seattle; Lieutenant George King of Edmonds, Lieutenant Eugene Rowe of Toppenish, and Lieutenant Fred O. Like of Longview. Lieutenant McAusland, the executive officer of the group, said,:

> We found humor everywhere. I remember the time we came in with all our instruments gone and one half of our landing gear shot away. Naturally we were scared, but we decided to crash-land. When we hit the ground, the radio operator was first out. He ran along the wing and jumped to the runway, then turned, looked, and suddenly fell into a heap. We were worried,

because most all the fellows had been hit or nicked and we thought sure he was gone. When they got over to him he opened his eyes and looked around and then went out like a light again. It turned out that he was the only one in the outfit who wasn't wounded. The funniest thing of the whole affair was when the airport officer announced: 'You can't land on this field with your landing gear up.' But there we were in a heap on the runway.

When a reporter asked what was planned for their military leave, one of them responded, "That's a military secret." When furloughs were over, they all expected to be assigned to further training. One of the fliers added, "Then we'll go back and get it over with!"

The liberation of European countries resulted in a flow of Americans being freed from prisoner of war camps. After Romania capitulated to the United Nations, the Fifteenth Air Force in Italy sent a Flying Fortress to Bucharest to carry out a load of former prisoners of war. Among the men on the plane were three from Washington State: Sergeant

Three months prior to Christmas 1944, presents for overseas service personnel needed to be mailed. This booth at a bus stop near the Boeing Airplane factory took prepaid orders and wrapped and mailed the packages. Seattle P-I Collection, 23423, MOHAI.

Vernon E. Leming of Waterville, a radio operator-gunner; Sergeant D. C. Zelta of Port Townsend, an armorer-gunner; and Lieutenant Jess W. Coppedge, a pilot whose wife Velma resided in Pullman. They were among more than 1,000 American airmen evacuated from Bucharest.

First Lieutenant Isaac N. Alhadeff of the Army Air Force was listed as missing on August 6. Then on September 18 the War Department informed his family in Seattle that the International Red Cross had learned he was a prisoner of war. A graduate of the University of Washington, Alhadeff during two years had piloted a B-17 on 27 missions. Before entering the service he was associated with his brother in the Palace Fish Company and other business activities. The Lieutenant survived his experiences and returned to Seattle after the war.

Lieutenant Elton Dickens was listed as missing in early August. A bombardier on a B-17, he wrote to his wife shortly before his plane was lost on a raid, "We are making a couple of missions a day now. Not much time to write or eat." After receiving the telegram saying he was missing, his wife, Helen, said, "We thought maybe he would be home for his birthday in November. Lana Marie [their 11-month-old daughter] and I traveled to Tennessee to see him before he left for overseas. We are so glad that we did." Lieutenant Dickens had been in Europe since April and held the Air Medal and several Oak-Leaf Clusters. He later was listed as killed in action.

Shortly after Captain Lucius S. Davis had been advanced to the rank of Captain and awarded the Silver Star for gallantry, he was mortally wounded by enemy fire in France. He had been overseas with the Third Division for a year and had fought in the Tunisian campaign, the Anzio beachhead, and the drive through Rome and Northern Italy. Captain Davis was a graduate of Sedro-Woolley High School and the University of Washington. His widow, Violet, and small son Michael lived in Seattle.

The mother of Marine Corporal Orville E. Kitchen was notified in October that her son had been wounded. Later, a delayed dispatch from Guam described how Corporal Kitchen and a buddy on their knees in front-line foxholes managed to crush Japanese attacks during an all-night battle for Guam. The 30-year-old marine and his companion were credited with killing 32 of the enemy in that one night. Kitchen earlier had participated in the Empress Augusta Bay campaign on Bougainville.

Seaman Robert A. Duncan, who attended high schools in Deming, Whatcom County, and Coupeville, Island County, enlisted in the Navy at age 17. He had served on the destroyer *Warrington* for more than a year without receiving a wound, when on September 14 an Atlantic storm with hurricane force winds battered the destroyer so badly it sank, as did two Coast Guard cutters, a light ship and a minesweeper. The Navy announced on October 13 that 344 Navy personnel, including young Duncan, had died in the roiling seas. His mother said, "He had written me that he was serving below decks as fireman, so when I read that his ship had been lost, I didn't feel there was much hope." In addition to his mother in Alderwood Manor, the teenaged sailor left three brothers and a sister.

Charles A. Byxbee, water tender first class, a Navy veteran of major Central Pacific invasions at Kwajalein, Saipan and Tinian, was home on leave, worrying that he was missing the big show in the Philippines. Byxbee was serving on a minesweeper, one of the first vessels to arrive near the beachheads to clear away the mines and keep an eye out for submarines. Byxbee recalled, "Those landings were something to watch. Kwajalein was all smoke and dust, because of the coral. But at Saipan we could see our lines as they advanced from the beaches step by step. We could follow the flame-throwers, which were quite a sight. I have to give all credit to the Marines. That island was really tough to take. It was supposed to be impregnable and it almost was." He explained that when enemy snipers holed up in caves, the marines would send a bulldozer to close up the entrances and exits. "Then they go away and leave them. A gentle, but effective method." Byxbee, a veteran of World War I, had returned to Navy duty in 1942.

On October 25, the wife of Major Donald W. McCoy received a telegram informing her that her husband had been missing in action over Germany since September 27. McCoy, a squadron commander with the Eighth Airforce, was shot down a few days after being promoted to Major. The 23-year-old Seattle man was a graduate of Seattle's Franklin High School and was a sophomore at the University of Washington when he entered the Air Force in January 1942. His wife, Carmen, and five-month-old daughter Sheila, later received a second telegram informing them that their husband and father had not survived.

Army Lieutenant John Veblen was an old hand at risking his neck. In October, at a Fifteenth Air Force landing field in Italy, a bomber, returning after a successful combat mission, was approaching the landing strip when a 1,000-pound bomb was seen dangling from the bomb bay. It was too late to abort the landing and as the plane's wheels touched, the bomb skidded along under the ship at 150 miles per hour. The ground crew ducked, expecting a huge explosion, but the bomb broke free and bounced to a stop while the plane continued on down the runway. The following Liberator bomber continued in for a landing and rolled over the bomb without touching it. That was when Lieutenant Veblen directed the rescue. He and four ordnance men dashed onto the field. Catching hold of the small propeller of the bomb that controlled the firing mechanism, Veblen pulled it free. The five men then rolled the heavy explosive to the side of the runway, just as a third plane eased in for a landing. This was the second time Lieutenant Veblen was commended for a disregard for personal safety. Earlier he was praised for efforts in helping rescue the crew of a plane that had crashed and caught fire while taking off with a load of bombs. Veblen, a graduate of Roosevelt High School and Harvard University, had served in Italy for eight months. While Veblen was in the service, his wife and son, John, lived with her parents, Mr. and Mrs. Ford Q. Elvidge, in Seattle.

American troops fighting battles to reclaim the Philippines freed 83 American prisoners of war, including three from Washington State. The men had escaped from an enemy transport taking them toward Japan. After swimming ashore, they had connected with a Filipino guerilla group. The Washington State men were Corporal Ralph Person of Seattle, Pfc. Paul L. Browning of Centralia, and Pfc. Walter N. Alexander of Spokane.

In October, the United States Maritime Service awarded Donald H. Erickson, 26, of Seattle, the Mariner's Medal for bravery during enemy action. Shortly after Pearl Harbor, Erickson was aboard the steamship *Arcata* when a Japanese submarine sank her with a torpedo off Attu Island in the Aleutians. He was seriously wounded in the battle but survived the sinking. After receiving treatment in a hospital in Kodiak, he spent seven months in Seattle's Marine Hospital. When he had recovered, Erickson shipped out again, sailing back and forth in the Western Alaska battle zone. Then he was transferred to the steamship *George Himes* that traveled to the South Pacific where it was torpedoed by a Japanese submarine off Guadalcanal. Again a survivor and this time uninjured, Erickson immediately looked for another ship and found a berth as third assistant engineer on the *Alcoa Planter* that soon sailed for the Pacific war zone. Young Erickson deserved his Mariner's Medal.

Paratrooper Pfc. Robert Gates had been overseas 18 months when he received his third battle wound. The telegram informing his family of this wounding arrived in late October. Two days later a letter arrived addressed in his handwriting to his father, Seattle lawyer Cassius E. Gates. In the letter young Gates insisted he was not seriously wounded, that he had been hit in the knee with shrapnel. During the war years, his wife Jeanne and their young son Robert, Jr. lived in Los Angeles with her mother and sister.

Marine Lieutenant Howard A. Scholz, whose wife lived in Seattle and whose parents lived in Colfax, was killed in the Palau Island campaign on September 15, his family was informed a month later. Lieutenant Scholz, a Washington State College 1943 graduate, was the only member of his class to receive a Marine Corps commission. In a letter to his wife written just before he was killed, he said that he would be wearing battle campaign ribbons by the time he could write to her again. He added, "But don't worry, most of the fellows are quite calm, although they know that some of us won't come back."

The 13th Naval District honorably discharged 1,293 persons in October, District Commandant Admiral S. A. Taffinder reported. About 1,000 of these discharges were granted for medical reasons. The Seattle Naval Hospital discharged 334 and the Puget Sound Navy Yard hospital in Bremerton discharged 106. The others were released from Navy hospitals in Sun Valley and Farragut, Idaho.

November 1944

Some Local Wartime Events

Despite rainy, windy weather, 7,500 curious residents viewed captured Axis planes and aircraft parts displayed on vacant lots in Seattle's Denny Regrade area on November 9. The Army Air Corps' three-day exhibit called "Shot From the Sky" included two barrage balloons of the type used at Normandy. Band music helped attract viewers to the event and visitors were reminded of the current war bond drive. John W. Gordon, War Department director of the exhibit, explained that Axis war materials captured in Europe would be presented to purchasers of $1,000 bonds. Those that purchased $100 bonds were entitled to a Japanese helmet and those buying $25 bonds were offered a ride in a Link Trainer, the ground-based equipment in which pilots

learned to fly through bad weather.

The Army-Navy USO Club at the YMCA invited servicemen to help prepare the club for the holidays. Several soldiers offered to create new candles from drippings of partially burned candles. They melted the wax, colored it with bits of wax crayons and poured the results into molds. All the volunteers were from other states and expected they would be assigned to overseas stations by Christmas. They agreed their volunteering was a pleasant way to celebrate the holidays a little early.

Local American Legion posts joined the national drive to prepare 10,000 "Purple Heart" Christmas gift boxes for members of the armed forces hospitalized in the U.S.A. Women of local Legion Auxiliary units sold the $5 gift boxes in special booths at Frederick and Nelson and Bon Marche Department Stores. Each box included a variety of useful or entertaining items suitable for convalescing men. After each purchase, the Legion women wrapped the gifts and delivered them to the "40 and 8" Veterans' Club where Christmas stickers and seals were added. These gifts were distributed before Christmas at armed forces hospitals.

Of six warships lost in a recent battle near the Philippines, two had been constructed in Washington State. The destroyer *Johnstone*, was christened at Todd Pacific Shipyards in October 1943. The second ship lost was the *Gambler Bay*, an escort carrier, completed by Kaiser Shipbuilding Company in Vancouver. Another ship destroyed in the battle, the destroyer escort *Samuel B. Roberts*, was commanded by Lieutenant Commander Robert W. Copeland of Tacoma. His wife received a letter from him in mid-November reporting that he was in an advance base hospital, but was "all right." Commander Copeland was a University of Washington graduate and former Tacoma lawyer.

The Bon Marche management hosted store employees at a Sixth War Loan breakfast rally on November 20 to promote bond sales. Store workers were to sell bonds to their customers and friends and to invest as much as possible themselves to reach the storewide quota of $600,000, enough to purchase a fully equipped Army hospital train to transport wounded men to hospitals near their hometowns.

On Thanksgiving Day, Thursday, November 23, Washingtonians gave thanks for their many blessings and prayed that peace and goodwill would spread across the world. Tables were overflowing with appropriate foods, a pleasure few humans other than Americans experienced during those months of war. Men and women turning out the ships and planes for fighting fronts worked even harder on the holiday, hoping that would speed return of their loved ones. Visiting military personnel were welcomed at hundreds of homes in the state. Ambulatory patients and their attendants at the Seattle Naval Hospital, were guests of members of the Navy Mothers Club and their friends. Stores, banks and government offices were closed for the day, but most war agencies, including the ration boards, remained open for business.

A Few of the Business Stories of the Month

Todd Pacific Shipyards, located on Harbor Island in Seattle, was an extremely active place all during the war. On November 4, the last of 35 speedy destroyers slid down the Todd shipways. More than just another launching, it was a milestone never before reached by a Seattle shipyard — 35 destroyers in five years. The last destroyer was christened *Stormes* by the widow of Commander Max C. Stormes, who lost his life in November 1942 when the destroyer *Preston* was sunk during the Battle of Guadalcanal. The Commander had begun his long and distinguished naval career in Seattle after graduating from the Naval Academy in 1924.

The Boeing Airplane Company successfully tested the military version of its new Stratocruiser on November 15. Boeing Chairman C. L. Egtvedt announced that the new super-airliner, designated the Boeing 377, carried 72 to 100 passengers with extreme range and the highest airline speeds, and with the lowest operating cost of any land plane transport then being built. Four 3,500-horsepower engines powered the plane at takeoff and produced a top speed of 400 miles per hour and a cruising speed of 340 miles per hour. Direct operating costs were said to be about one cent per passenger mile. Built in secrecy, this military prototype of the new plane was the first of the improved postwar super-transports to be completed by any aircraft company. All Boeing 377 models being produced at the time were destined for military service.

During November the Navy opened the last of its 20 material redistribution centers on a pier at the port of Bellingham. These centers processed equipment and supplies returned from overseas or accumulated from domestic production.

Washington State People in the News

Walter A. Moore, Jr., of Seattle was the first member of the American Field Service to be cited by the Italian government. Italy, until a few months earlier, had been an enemy country, but was now an ally. Moore was awarded the *Il Cuore di Rincaino* in recognition of his work with Italian troops on the Adriatic battlefront.

Harry P. Cain, mayor of Tacoma, was on military leave in France. A fellow officer reported that Colonel Cain received his present assignment as assistant chief of staff of an airborne corps "through superior performance as a staff officer for General Eisenhower." Colonel Cain recently had announced he would be a Republican candidate for a Washington State Senate seat in the next election.

It wasn't only humans who helped win the war. Smarty was given an honorable discharge after 18 months with the Coast Guard. Now she waited quietly in a crate at the Railway Express warehouse at Seattle's King Street Station. Smarty was 3 years old and nearly half of her life and been spent in the service. When two boys, Herbie Allen, 15, and his brother, Joel, 10, scrambled through the Railway Express doorway yelling, "Where is she?" she retreated to the back of her crate. When Herbie spotted the tawny coat of the big German Shepherd, he raced over and fumbled with door latch. "You do recognize me, don't you, Smarty?" he asked. "Sure you do." Smarty promptly licked his cheek, then again retreated to the back of the crate. Herbie went on talking to her and rubbing her ears. Joel also crowded in to pet her. Little by little Smarty remembered them and suddenly she was out of the crate, joyously rubbing against the boys' legs and leaping to lick their faces. The boys' parents, Mr. and Mrs. Herb Allen, watched the reunion happily. "Look at her," Mrs. Allen said, then explained, "She's fat as a butterball. She's just had two months of rehabilitation at a center in Nebraska to prepare her for civilian life again. Smarty served with the Coast Guard in California on beach patrol. When her honorable discharge was due, they told her they would send her home as soon as they curbed her aggressiveness." Mrs. Allen added, "I can't imagine Smarty ever hurting anyone."

Jimmy Havacan was a 22-year-old marine with a problem. Granted a 30-day leave, his plan was to visit his parents and two young brothers in Savage, Minnesota. Then he lost his wallet with his savings of $130 in it. *The Seattle Times* printed an article about his situation and a "Send Jimmy Home" fund was started. Two days later the fund totaled $356.45 and Jimmy was studying train schedules. "It's going to be good to get home," he said happily. "I couldn't have made it if it hadn't been for all the swell people around here who helped." The shy farm boy from a town of fewer than 300 population wouldn't talk much about his two years of combat experience in the South Pacific, but the battle stars and campaign ribbons on his blouse were ample evidence that he had "been there." So it was that young Jimmy headed home with nearly three times the cash he had when he landed in Seattle.

A Few of the Many Heroes of November

Lieutenant Clark N. Rauth, flight engineer on a B-29 Superfortress, was killed over China on October 17, the War Department notified his family in Seattle. Rauth, 24, the only child of Mr. and Mrs. F. B. Rauth, had participated in the first B-29 raid on Japan in June 1944 and several later raids as well. The lieutenant was a Roosevelt High School graduate and had attended the University of Washington. His widow, Kathleen, and 1-year-old daughter lived in Seattle.

Sergeant Edgar R. Attebery, Jr., a paratrooper with the Army in France, was killed in action, his mother was notified on November 3. His father, Lieutenant Colonel E. Raymond Attebery, had died in New Guinea a few months earlier while serving as chaplain with the 41st division. The 20-year-old paratrooper was a graduate of Garfield High School where he distinguished himself in scholarship and starred in track. He had attended the University of Washington for two quarters before enlisting in the Army. When a portrait of his father was unveiled at Seattle's Grace Methodist Church, where he had served as pastor, his son Edgar debated coming home for the memorial service. Then he wrote to his mother, "Father realized the cause was great enough to leave civilian life and go into the jungle and lay down his life. I think Daddy would want me to be where there is the most to be done, and I'll stay here and try to make a difference as he would have wanted."

Milton Warshal was reported missing in action in France on August 7. In early November the Red Cross reported he was a prisoner of war in Germany. The Seattle soldier, member of a tank destroyer battalion, had been in the Army since January 1942, and was sent overseas to take part in the invasion of France. The last letter received by his family was dated August 4. He wrote it, he said, while in a foxhole in France, "with the ground shaking like an earthquake and shells dropping all around." Before entering the service, Milton Warshal owned a clothing store on Second and Washington in Seattle. Two brothers, Adolph and Bill Warshal, owned Warshal Sporting Goods Company. Private Warshal did not survive his experiences in prison camp.

Sergeant William N. May, 21, a radio-gunner stationed in England, was listed as missing in October, then on November 6 was declared killed in action. Sergeant May graduated from Tonasket High School in Okanogan County and enlisted in the Army Air Forces in February 1942. Over Europe on his 22nd mission, May's plane developed engine trouble. After he turned back toward his home field, the plane kept losing altitude and crashed into the North Sea. According to the telegram delivered to his parents in Seattle, May was given a military funeral and was buried in the American Military Cemetery at Cambridge.

Air Corps Lieutenant Bert Butterworth was home for a visit in Seattle in early November. During his 15 months service with the India-China wing of the Air Transport Command, Lieutenant Butterworth flew 73 round-trip flights over the rugged Himalaya Mountains. He had been decorated with the Distinguished Flying Cross and Air Medal and wore the Presidential Unit Citation that his outfit was awarded for overcoming severe hardships while transporting supplies over the mountains during the difficult winter season. The high altitude necessary to cross the world's highest range of mountains required the flyers to use oxygen masks on every trip. Bert Butterworth's father, Colonel C. E. Butterworth had been stationed in the South Pacific for more than two years.

Pfc. Francis E. Noland had been a prisoner of the Japanese for two and a half years when his captors decided to move him and hundreds of other American prisoners. His mother in Seattle had received one post card from him saying that he hoped for a quick reunion and urged her to "keep your spirits up." The Americans were forced into a ship's hold where the portholes and hatches were sealed shut. The interior soon became overheated and the oxygen supply low. The Japanese freighter was not marked with a Red Cross or any sign that prisoners of war were aboard. After allied planes attacked it, the War Department announced the freighter sank off the

Philippines on October 22 with heavy loss of life. Of the American men and officers who made it to shore, 83 were aided by Philippine guerillas. As soon as they physically were able, all but two of these Americans joined these underground fighters until the American Army invaded and began re-taking the islands. As soon as they were in U.S. hands, the former prisoners were transported to Australian hospitals to recuperate before being sent home. Unfortunately, Francis Noland had not escaped the sinking ship. When told she had lost her son, his mother said, "That's about all I can stand, to have him undergo all that suffering for so long and then have him lost on that ship. I heard from another mother who had a son on that ship, but her son was rescued. He said our boys were packed in that death ship like sardines."

Lieutenant John B. Graham of Seattle, a 23-year-old Army bombardier-navigator, had been overseas less than a month when he was awarded the Air Medal. Then his parents were notified in November that their son was killed in action over Italy on October 17. Details of his death were not revealed, but his folk's last letter from young Graham told of bombing tank concentrations in the vicinity of Vienna, in support of Russian forces. Lieutenant Graham, an only son, was born in Yakima but came to Seattle with his parents in 1923. He graduated from Roosevelt High School where he played center field on the baseball team. He had enrolled in the School of Journalism at the University of Washington, but decided to drop that plan in order to enter the service, but planned to complete his education after the war.

Three former Washington residents of Japanese ancestry were wounded in action in France according to word from the Minidoka Relocation Center at Hunt, Idaho. Pfc. Selieni Motoki, 23, and Pfc. Yoshito Mizuta, 30, were wounded October 17. Both had lived in Seattle. Pfc. Siego Shimoyama, 26, formerly of Kent, was reported seriously wounded on October

16. He had three sisters serving in the Women's Army Corps.

Army Lieutenant Robert C. Feuerstein had been missing in action since September 2 when his mother in Seattle received a few details of what had happened. The bomber in which he was flying during a strafing mission in the Southwest Pacific was damaged by anti-aircraft fire. Crewmen of other planes witnessed it landing on the sea. Two of these planes circled the area for a time and crewmen saw one man in the water, two on a wing and another helping the fifth out of the hatch. A short while later a life raft was observed with the occupants waving. An extensive rescue mission started immediately but no survivors were located. The tragedy occurred on Lieutenant Feuerstein's 50th mission that would have made him eligible for home leave. He had made plans to be married October 8 in Australia and to take his bride home to Seattle.

Captain William E. McClain was killed in action in June in France. A flight surgeon, he had been overseas since January. He had graduated from the University of Washington and had earned his medical degree at Creighton University in Omaha. After two years of interning at Harborview Hospital in Seattle, he served as a resident surgeon there until he joined the Army two years later. His wife Kathryn and his parents, Dr. and Mrs. William E. McClain, Sr., survived him.

First Lieutenant Robert A. Naylor, 34, a member of the glider infantry, landed in Holland with invasion forces from England. On November 17 his parents received word that he had been killed in action. Naylor was a Seattle native, graduated from Lincoln High School, and received an R.O.T.C. commission when he graduated from the University of Washington. His widow, the former Anita Loomis, lived with her parents in Seattle while he was in the service.

Alfred A. Skinner, a graduate of R. A. Long High School in Longview, was killed while flying over the Bonin Islands in October. Lieutenant Skinner enlisted in the Army Air Corps a month before Pearl Harbor. After receiving his wings, he served as a bombardier-navigation instructor in New Mexico until early 1944 when he transferred to combat training. He arrived overseas in May and had completed 12 missions before his death.

A war correspondent wrote that Staff Sergeant Harold C. Spring was the unluckiest man in France. As a result his buddies kidded him about the difficulties he encountered in battle. Spring was awarded the Bronze Star Medal twice for gallantry in action. The Sergeant had lived in Seattle for several years before entering the army, but had no relatives in the area. His friends here were notified in November that Harold Spring had been killed on the European front.

Lieutenant Donald DeLisle, pilot of a Flying Fortress and holder of the Air Medal with five Oak-Leaf Clusters, had twice managed to fly a crippled plane out of German territory. Once, when his motor failed, he was forced to land in the English Channel. The Lieutenant was a graduate of Chehalis High School where he excelled in football and later was intramural lightweight boxing champion at the University of Washington. He arrived in England just before D-Day. Two years had passed since he last had seen his family. He wrote to his wife, Margaret, that he had seven more missions to complete to reach the number 50. Then he would be home on furlough. The letter arrived at his wife's residence in Seattle on the same day that she received a telegram saying he had died in a hospital in England.

Lieutenant John Bosko from Seattle managed to fly his B-17 back to England after a direct hit over Germany had blasted the plane almost in two. An anti-aircraft shell exploded inside the bomb bay, blowing out the right side, wrecking the radio room and severing controls to the ailerons and elevators. The superchargers of all four engines were destroyed, part of the wing structure was missing. Seconds after the shell hit the plane, it was over its target. The crew released two bombs but the others stuck in the rack. A fire broke out but was extinguished. The Fortress gradually lost altitude down to 7,000 feet. Over the Channel one of the crew managed to free the jammed bombs with a pair of pliers and they fell harmlessly into the sea. The plane sputtered its way to its home airfield. After the plane was safely on the ground and the crew evacuated, Lieutenant Bosco reported to his superior office, "You should have bailed out," declared the officer, "It's a miracle that you made it."

Lieutenant Joseph A. L. Fournier saw more action that most servicemen. He joined the Marine Corps in 1939 and rose up through the ranks. He was on the original Aircraft Carrier *Lexington* when it was sunk. He survived that experience and was transferred to England to be trained as a commando. He was granted home leave in the U.S. in June 1942, then was sent to the South Pacific where he was involved in several invasions. Lieutenant Fournier was twice wounded and his decorations included the Purple Heart, the Bronze Star Medal, and the Navy-Marine Corps Medal. He was also recommended for the Silver Star and Legion of Merit. His pre-invasion reconnaissance work on New Britain right under the noses of the Japanese was mentioned in press dispatches, as was his work as commander of a Bazooka team that blasted pillboxes on Palau. On November 27 his wife, Lilah received a telegram reporting that he had been killed in action on September 19. "I have the telegram," she said, "but I'm hoping it might be a mistake. He had never even seen our 13-month-old daughter, Jolene."

Colonel Ted S. Faulkner, 31, commander of a B-29 bomber group in the Asiatic Theatre, was one of the state's recognized war heroes. Then, in late November the War Department informed his wife, who was staying with Faulkner's mother in Kirkland, that the Colonel had been missing in action since November 5. Colonel Faulkner, a University of Washington graduate, was at Pearl Harbor as a second Lieutenant at the time of the Japanese attack. He had been in almost constant action since then, winning rapid promotion and many medals. He had participated in B-29 raids on Japanese-held Formosa, on the Japanese mainland, and on Sumatra, Manchuria and Singapore. His wife told a reporter on November 28 that after hearing he was missing, she was startled to see him, "big as life" in a newsreel in a Seattle theatre. The Colonel was shown with other flyers studying a rough map drawn in the dirt at a B-29 base in the Pacific. The army later confirmed that Colonel Faulkner had been killed in action.

As a youngster, Gordon W. Fox grew up in China, Guam and other outposts where his father, a Marine Corps major was stationed. The father had retired in Seattle by the time Gordon graduated from Roosevelt High School. On a single day, March 1, 1944, young Fox achieved three goals: he graduated from the University of Washington, was commissioned a Navy ensign, and married Peggy Lindsey of Bellevue. Six months later, near the Philippines, the Japanese sank two U.S. destroyers, one destroyer escort, and an escort carrier. But before those four ships were destroyed, they somehow had managed to divert a larger attacking Japanese fleet. Ensign Fox was aboard the destroyer *Johnson* when it sank beneath the waves. On November 28, his mother, father, and wife received the dreaded telegram saying he had been killed. He was 22 years old.

December 1944

A Few Local War-Related News Items

Two million passenger car tires were produced in the U.S. in December, the highest output since the war began. Even so, most motorists with low priority, those with the "A" sticker on their windshields, had to wait until spring for new tires because the Office of Price Administration diverted some production to turning out needed jeep tires. The Seattle district was allotted 18,700 auto and motorcycle tires and 4,000 truck tires for December.

The First Meritorious Civilian Service Award to be given by the Seattle Port of Embarkation was presented to Miss Eleanor

Headlines:
December 1944

December 15:
GEORGE MARSHALL, DOUGLAS MACARTHUR, DWIGHT EISENHOWER AND HENRY ARNOLD BECOME THE FIRST U. S. 5-STAR COMMANDERS

December 16:
FAMOUS BAND LEADER GLENN MILLER, FLYING FROM ENGLAND TO FRANCE ON USO TOUR, IS LOST IN THE ENGLISH CHANNEL

December 16:
GERMANS BEGIN ATTACK IN THE ARDENNES (BATTLE OF THE BULGE)

December 29:
GERMANS SURROUND BASTOGNE, DEMAND SURRENDER; U.S.GENERAL McAULIFFE RESPONDS WITH SINGLE WORD-"NUTS"

December 31:
U.S. FORCES ON LEYTE CRUSH VICIOUS JAPANESE COUNTERATTACK

Stata, 22, for her outstanding performance and diligent study of Signal Corps Army Regulations. The award stated that at times Miss Stata, chief clerk, assumed almost full responsibility for the operation of the Port Signal Office. A Queen Anne High School graduate, she had finished a year of pre-med at the University before accepting a job at the Port.

A Liberty ship launched at the Todd-Houston Shipyard in Texas in December was christened with the name of the late William R. Lewis of Seattle, a fireman and water-tender who was lost when the freighter *M.H. DeYoung*, was torpedoed in August 1943. T.D. Hurd, public relations officer of the U.S. Maritime Service, earlier had presented the Mariner's Medal to Lewis' mother in Seattle at National Maritime Day ceremonies in Victory Square. Young Lewis had worked at Todd Shipyard's Seattle Division before going to sea.

When Todd Pacific Shipyards in Tacoma launched the ninth of a series of large escort aircraft carriers, the Navy decided to name it *The Puget Sound*. Originally the ship was to be named *Hobart Bay*, but when subscriptions in Washington State's Fifth War Loan campaign totaled enough to pay for the vessel, the name was changed.

The first girl child born in the City of Longview was a mature young woman when in December she christened a Victory freighter named for her birthplace. Edith C. Midthun christened the first of a new series of 63 Victory freighters being built at Oregon Shipbuilding in Portland. Longview Mayor C. C. Tibbetts, in a brief speech, described how Longview, founded by logging companies in 1922, had mushroomed so rapidly that the 1930 census gave it the largest percentage population increase of any city in the United States.

The 13 original Flying Fortresses, model YB-17, built in 1936 by the Boeing Aircraft Company for the Army, were retired in December. These planes led the way toward development of heavy bombers. After eight years of useful service, ten of the bombers were dismantled at Amarillo Field, Texas. Eight of them flew there on their own power, two were sent there in pieces, and records of three had been lost. The YB-17s made news from the outset, gaining renown before the war for a mass good-will flight to South America where they were used to drop food, supplies, and serums to flood victims. Many of the top officers in the Army's bomber command received their first four-engine plane training on the YB-17s.

Seattle's wartime battle against venereal disease was more successful than that of most other Pacific Coast cities, according to a December 7 report from the Federal Security Agency. Part of the success stemmed from close cooperation among law-enforcement agencies, the City Health Department and social groups. Barent Burhans, the field representative of the agency, said that Seattle's rapid treatment center was considered "the most outstanding in the country." He added that the chief remaining problem was pick-up girls, whom he described as "prosticuties." Closing the houses of prostitution, source of 80 percent of the infections before the war, achieved the initial success. Control of the pick-ups rested with the police, and they were doing a fine job, he said. An average of 300 girls per month were being arrested and of these about two in ten were found to be infected.

At the Minidoka Relocation Center near Hunt, Idaho, governmental officials interviewed 1,900 Japanese-American families about their hopes for the future. Of these about 900 expressed a desire to return to homes in the Seattle area. Only three said they wished to return as soon as possible; the others indicated they preferred to delay their return until suitable preparations had been made. One of the problems concerned land ownership. Most of the Japanese-Americans had leased or rented the land they farmed because of long-standing laws preventing them from purchasing property. Several other families said they did not plan to return immediately because their sons were in the service and it would be impossible to resume their normal farming pursuits until young family members were available to help.

Pfc. George R. Gibbs, Jr., of Seattle and Pfc. George Hornyak of Cleveland, Ohio, met at Pearl Harbor on the way to the South Pacific and quickly became buddies. The two 19-year-old marines were side by side during many battles for the Marshall Islands. Young Gibbs wrote to his parents about his best buddy Hornyak and sent his parents a photograph of the two of them together. The two were side by side fighting the enemy when a Japanese bullet killed George Gibbs. Not long after, the strains of battle struck George Hornyak and he began to shake with fatigue. The Marines ordered him sent to a hospital for medical treatment. When Hornyak found himself a patient at Seattle Naval Hospital, he immediately tried to reach his buddy's family, but he had neither their address nor phone number. "I just started calling," he said. "I called all the Gibbses in the telephone book, and I finally found the right ones. It was wonderful when they came out to see me."

The feeling on the part of his late buddy's parents was the same. "Such a load has been lifted from my mind," said Mrs. Gibbs. "All the terrible things I had imagined about how my son died were not true, and George was able to give me answers. This boy is everything that a boy should be, and when he puts his arms around me and calls me 'Mom' it is almost like having my own son with me again." George spent every weekend with the Gibbses and sat in his buddy's chair at the Thanksgiving table. On December 2 he was seated in the Gibbs' living room as he recalled for a reporter the times he had spent with young George Gibbs in the Pacific. George Hornyak's own mother had died four years earlier but now he had found another mother who had affection to spare. "She made me feel like I was home," he said.

Senator Warren Magnuson on December 28 reported that the Navy was allotting $322,000 of public-works funds to provide living quarters for transient naval personnel in Washington State. Magnuson said 12 of the housing units would be erected at Quillayute in Clallam County at a cost of $71,000 and that 40 othe units costing $251,000 would be built on Whidbey Island.

During the war, undermanned garbage collection crews had their hands full. To assist them, householders were asked to watch for the disposal trucks and to toss extra household waste that wouldn't fit into the garbage cans into the large containers attached to the rear of all trucks. Josie Razore, head of Seattle Disposal Company, explained that he and associates "are lying awake nights probing for new ideas that would beat the manpower shortage and maintain the regularity of service."

During the last days of December, shoe stores were thronged with hundreds of customers after the Office of Price Administration warned that it might be necessary to delay validating the new shoe-ration stamp until sometime in the summer. This would delay use of the new stamp, resulting in three pairs per person every two years instead of the existing rate of two pairs a year. The public misread all this activity to mean footwear would be in short supply during the next few months. The OPA countered with a statement that shoe stocks in most stores were sufficient to redeem all shoe stamps unless there were a run on the stores. The dealers echoed this message and the crush of frantic shoe purchasers subsided.

An engineers' unit at Fort Lewis developed a vaudeville-type Army show called "Sons of Bridges" that attracted crowds when performed in Seattle. It returned early in December as a means of gaining support for the Sixth War Loan effort. Anyone investing in a $100 war bond received a ticket; a $1,000 bond earned the investor a loge seat to view this all-Army music and comedy show. Prior to donning Uncle Sam's khaki, many of the performers were musicians with "name" bands, players in leading vaudeville acts, or noted radio or nightclub stars. The show's action and comedy took place not only on stage but also throughout the house. The Orpheum Theater was sold out on the night of December 5 and more than $10 million in bond sale pledges were credited to the Army show, an amount that shattered records for war-bond premiers across the country.

War bond sales were successful in the small communities of the state also. From Auburn, then noted as "the center of a busy farming section," War Loan Chairman Del B. Price announced the area had passed the half way mark toward its quota and sales continued at a brisk rate. In the south end of King County, "a broad territory of scattered residential areas and small business communities," businesses clubbed together to provide prizes to be auctioned at war-bond rallies or at community motion picture bond premiers. In Enumclaw, S. B. Lafromboise, the war loan chairman, reported his town would reach its $300,000 quota ahead of schedule. Hans Forster, Issaquah chairman, reported that clubs and merchants had devised several unique methods of calling the public's attention to the necessity of attaining their town's quota of $75,000.

Late in December at Smith Cove on Elliott Bay, where in prewar days crates of canned salmon were stored, two huge piers and warehouses had been transformed into a great naval supply depot that purchased, received, and stored thousands of carloads of all kinds of war materials. From this depot supplies were sent to Navy shore installations in the Pacific Northwest and to bases and ships in Alaskan and Central Pacific areas, including Pearl Harbor, Guam, and the Philippines. More than 20 double-deck warehouses, three of which held 750 carloads of freight each, had been constructed on the site. Nearby were workshops and numerous barracks and classroom units that housed a pre-commissioning school for attack transport crews.

Two of the Month's Business Stories

Most small firms in the Pacific Northwest were extremely busy during late 1944. More than 500 prime contracts valued at more than $50 million had been awarded to 350 firms in Washington, Oregon and Montana by the Small War Plants Corporation. The regional director, W.A. Castleton, announced from his Seattle office that "The little plants are the unsung heroes of the home front. We so often hear of the Kaisers, the Boeings, and the Douglases. It is true that these giant firms have done a wonderful job, but without the little fellow fabricating, machining intricate parts, producing castings and valves and the various items so necessary in the building of ships and planes, the records of the big fellows could never have been made."

In an effort to promote citizenship education and human relations, Dr. U.S. Mitchell, Pacific regional director of the National Conference of Christians and Jews, and Rabbi Raphael Levine of Temple De Hirsch, Seattle, traveled to Alaska at the invitation of the commanding general. Dr. Mitchell described their purpose as "promotion of citizenship education with emphasis upon basic religious and democratic principles essential to harmonious human relations." These tours were part of a national effort to counteract inter-group tensions of a racial and religious nature. Happy to be included in the tour, Rabbi Levine expressed satisfaction at the progress being made by the conference in the service camps. "It gives the men a proper basis for putting into practice the principles for which they are fighting," the Rabbi said.

A Few of the Many Heroes of December

Lieutenant Clifton H. Alford, a former Central Washington College music instructor and talented violinist, was reported missing in August. Four months later his parents in Ellensburg were notified that he was killed in action on a mission over Germany. Lieutenant Alford piloted a B-17 bomber that was shot down two weeks after he went into action. Besides his parents he was survived by three sisters and three brothers, two of whom were in the service.

Mr. and Mrs. John Erickson, pioneers in the Richland area, received the dreaded telegram in December. Their son, Flight Officer Carl Erickson, 29, was reported killed during the Sicilian invasion. After graduating from Washington State College in 1937, he joined the Army and learned to pilot a glider. The War Department told his parents that the towline on the glider broke when they were about 40 miles off the coast of Algeria. Heavy fog prevented the tow plane pilot from observing what happened to the glider and no trace of those aboard was ever found.

Pfc. Willard J. Robinson, born in Pullman in 1911, was killed on the German front on November 17, his parents in Pomeroy and his wife in Seattle were notified in December. He had enlisted twice during the course of the war and had gone overseas with the 104th (Timberwolf) Division in September. Just two days before he died, he wrote his mother that as of November 15 he was sleeping with a roof over his head for the first time in four months. He was survived by his widow and two small children, his parents and two sisters.

Three other members of that 104th Division from Washington State were luckier. Pfc. Howard J. Basanko was in his second major battle in Holland when he received his wound while in a foxhole. Shrapnel hit him in both shoulders and both legs. Pfc. John D. (Mickey) McDonaugh was wounded November 17 on the front lines in Germany. Private Leo F. Sharkey, Jr., was injured October 19 in a truck convoy moving up to the front in Northern Belgium. Sharkey and McDonough were buddies before they went into the service in April 1943. Both had played football for Seattle Preparatory High School. After graduating, they both enrolled at Seattle College. Privates Sharkey and Basanko were recovering in Paris hospitals, and McDonough had been flown to England for treatment.

Lieutenant Wilson B. Weber of Spokane was reported missing in August 1944. In December his parents were informed their son, pilot of a P-51 fighter plane that went down over Metz, France, was killed. He was a graduate of Lewis and Clark High School and Spokane Junior College, and had been a member of the National Guard and was sent to Hawaii with the 161st Infantry before being transferred to the air corps.

Five North Central Washington homes felt the cold hand of war during December. Ralph Henry Smith of Beaver Creek had been in the army for three years when he was killed in battle on Leyte, the Army informed his parents, Mr. and Mrs. Bill Smith. Mr. and Mrs. Roy Weltman of Omak were informed their son, Sergeant Lee Roy Weltman, died of pneumonia in Paris on November 28. He was a graduate of Omak High School and had served with the signal corps in Africa, England, Belgium and France. Three Omak youth were reported as wounded on the western front. Pfc. James Schindler was struck by an enemy bullet in Germany. Privates Thomas J. Winger and Eldon H. Reed were wounded on that same day, November 28, on the European front.

Hundreds of nurses tended the wounded on the front and in transit aboard planes and ships. Lieutenant Emma Lou Taylor, formerly of Wapato, wrote to a nurse friend in Yakima praising the wounded soldiers she helped care for. "They are wonderful. Knowing we are busy, they wait patiently on litters or beds until you can get to them. The tents are warm and dry to fellows who have been in foxholes for days at a time. They are so appreciative of any small kindness, and God bless their sense of humor. Some of them really need it now." She described the frontline hospital where she worked as somewhere in Belgium and serving as an evacuation unit. "We admit the patients, give them emergency treatment, such as surgery, plasma and transfusions. Then we feed them and wash them, if time permits, and evacuate them farther back. By that time a new group has arrived."

James T. Daly, 23, a Coast Guard fireman, was home in Seattle in December after 27 months of combat duty in the South Pacific. A

Wounded service personnel were moved as soon as possible to hospitals in the United States. Many were evacuated by air, with flight nurses and medical technicians to care for them during the journey. Here an army flight nurse tends to a badly wounded soldier. National Archives 86-wwt-56-3

story he related to friends concerned how they struggled to deliver gasoline to invading forces on Pelellu. They had carried First Division Marines ashore in an LST and were aware Marine casualties were heavy because the Japanese released a hail of mortar shells and machine gun fire from hidden tunnels and caves on ridges above the beach. The marines badly needed gasoline, but a treacherous coral reef hindered the delivery. The Coast Guardsmen decided the only way to get those 55-gallon drums to the Marines was to strip down to shorts and float the gasoline ashore. This they succeeded in doing. At a previous invasion, Daly recalled his LST weathered 19 air raids in eight days before a Japanese pursuit plane dropped a bomb squarely on her stern, wounding six

men. At Tinian a few weeks later, enemy shellfire struck the deck of his LST about 20 feet from a high-octane gasoline tank, causing four casualties. Daly recalled that he and other crewmen "got our biggest laugh when we put into Honolulu after one of our invasions. They thought we were ghosts. Our ship had been announced as sunk with all hands lost. But here I am."

After Mr. and Mrs. Erling H. Hoveland of Seattle lost two sons in the war, their only remaining son was returned from overseas. Lieutenant L. B. Hoveland, a B-17 Flying Fortress pilot, was 26 when he was shot down during a raid on Kassel, Germany, in July 1943. Aviation Cadet Vernon N. Hoveland was 22 when he died in the crash of his training plane in Texas in September 1942. Private Earl Hoveland, 19, was with an infantry unit in England. In December he was recalled to the United States in accordance with a new policy adopted by the Army requiring the sole surviving son of any family that had lost two or more children in the war to be returned to the continental United States.

Pfc. Horace Engle was killed in action with the infantry on December 3 in France. His parents, living in Marlin near Odessa, displayed a six star service flag in their window. Now one of those stars was changed to gold in honor of their dead son. His five brothers were: Pfc. Forrest Engle, serving with the Signal Corps in the Philippines; Private James Engle at Camp Wolters, Texas; Robert Engle, radioman in the U.S. Navy; Sergeant Harvey W. Engle with the quartermaster corps in India and Seaman C. Fay Engle, on sea duty with the U.S Navy out of San Francisco.

Lieutenant Kenneth Dirkes, 22, son of Spokane City Commissioner and Mrs. Otto Dirkes, had been missing in action since December 3 his parents were informed on December 28. He was a graduate of Washington State College and had been serving as navigator on a B-29 operating from Saipan that had participated in several raids over Tokyo. He later was declared dead.

Captain Clair W. DesVoignes of Spokane was reported missing in July over Belgium. In December he was declared dead. DesVoignes had enlisted in the Marine Reserve at age 16. When honorably discharged from the marines, he immediately enlisted in the Army Air Forces. He was trained at Williams Field, Akansas, and took tactical training at Paine Field in Everett, Washington. Among survivors were his widow, Lois, and his mother. His brother, Calvin, was home for a short leave from South Pacific duty when word arrived that his brother was dead.

Pfc. Lewis L. Ray, Sr., 30, was killed on December 18 in Belgium. His wife, Catherine, in Vancouver, received the War Department telegram only a few days after receiving word he was missing in action. Private Ray, between 1936 and 1940, was stationed at Vancouver Barracks with the 7th Division. Sent overseas in March, he fought in the Brest and Normandy campaigns with the Second Infantry Division. He was survived by his wife and their son, Lewis Ray, Jr., and five brothers and a sister.

Pfc. Kenneth L. Knapp was killed in action in Europe the day after Christmas. Knapp, born in White Salmon, Klickitat County, had lived most of his life in Vancouver. He and his wife had two children, a son, Teddy, 20 months old, and a new daughter, Gail, born just 13 days before her father was killed. Kenneth Knapp was a graduate of Vancouver High School and was employed by the Pointer-Willamette Company in Portland before entering the service. While fighting in France, Knapp was wounded on September 4, but was returned to duty in November, only to be killed the next month.

Lieutenant Russel E. Harry, 23, was killed in action over Europe on November 22. His parents in Vancouver received the information in early December. He had enlisted in September 1941 after graduating from Vancouver High School and had been overseas since June 1943, most of the time as a pilot with the 389th bombardment group. In July he began serving as a photoreconnaissance pilot for the 25th bombardment group.

Talk about bad luck! Fred M. Chapman, 27-year-old son of Mr. and Mrs. Emery E. Chapman of Vancouver, died in the crash of an airliner at Billings, Montana, on December 8. The 27-year-old had spent nearly four years in the army and was heading toward a furlough after overseas duty when he was killed just a few hundred miles from his family home.

After serving with the Women's Army Air Force Service Pilots (WASP) for a year, Miss Marcella Mae Fried, 22 years old, whose parents lived in Spokane, was home in December. After training in Texas, she was transferred to the Army base at Greenville, Mississippi, where she served as a test pilot, then to Peterson Field, Colorado Springs, where she flew twin-engine cargo and transport planes. Now that victory was nearly achieved, the WASPs were being deactivated, and the Army Air Force presented her with an honorable discharge.

Lieutenant Loren G. Hampton, whose father lived in St. John, Washington, was decorated with a third Oak Leaf cluster on his Air Medal, the Eighth Air Force announced in December. Hampton piloted a B-17 Flying Fortress through many daylight precision

Women Air Force Service Pilots, were known as WASPs. Between September 1942 and December 1944 more than 1,000 women were accepted into the program and flew nearly every aircraft in the U.S. inventory. They ferried these aircraft from factory to military fields, towed targets for gunnery practice, and performed many other vital missions. U.S. Air Force and Smithsonian Institution Photo.

Black Women Army Corps members served overseas when requested by the theater commander. Here a group sorts packages that have been emptied from mail sacks by French civilian employees at the 17th Base Post Office in France. National Archives, 11-SC-337995.

bombing assaults on industrial and military objectives in Germany and Nazi-occupied Europe. He graduated from St. John High School where he was a member of the football team and then studied mechanical engineering at Washington State College.

Christmas Efforts in Wartime

Shortly before Christmas, thoughtful Seattle residents donated gifts to the thousands of service men and women stationed near Seattle and scheduled to ship off to new assignments over the holidays. The Seattle Junior Chamber of Commerce supported the effort. Robert K. Rolfsness, chairman of the Chamber's "High Seas Committee," was helped by F. E. Smallidge, Faye O. Snelson, Wilfred Woollett, Ronald A. Olson, Basil Fawthrop, and Ralph Benaroya. For $1 donors purchased a package containing inexpensive but useful gifts such as stationery, pencils, books, hand lotion, camphor ice, soap, and razor blades. The donor's name and address written on a greeting card were attached to the package. Red Cross volunteers under direction of Mrs. Ralph Schoenfeld wrapped the gifts at the Seattle Merchant

Marine Victory Canteen. The "Buddy" presents, as they were called, were delivered to ships to be distributed to servicemen and women on Christmas Day.

By mid-December the Seattle Post Office had handled 36,000 mailbags of Christmas packages addressed to servicemen overseas. Much of the mail was routed through Army post offices in San Francisco and New York City. Mailbags bound for Alaska went through the Seattle Port of Embarkation. For the third year, more than 200 soldiers were assigned to assist the Seattle post office during the holiday rush. They helped unload mail from railroad cars and trucks, drove Army trucks filled with packages, and worked at distribution tables. The mail was so voluminous that the basement of the Civic Auditorium was rented by the post office as parcel distribution headquarters and many soldiers were assigned there. The soldiers received only their regular Army pay for this work.

Mrs. Andrew Gilbert was the only woman parcel post mail-truck driver in Seattle. When a newspaper reporter stopped to interview her, she gave her slacks a hitch, her cap a tug, flexed her muscles, and with hardly any effort tossed a bag of Christmas mail into her truck. "I've always been athletic," she explained. Hoisting mailbags and 70-pound boxes of apples from her truck was no major effort. She added, "I went to the post office two years ago when they advertised for help. I got this job and I stayed. I like it." She said that at first when she knocked on doors women would open it only a crack and peek at her until she told them she had a package for them. "I guess they thought I was selling something." Full of pep and ready answers, Mrs. Gilbert, during the busy holiday season, came to work at 6 a.m. and stayed until the job was done. Her husband, an Army private, had been overseas for nearly two years. She said that at the end of the day, she leans back and rests her feet in her home on a street whose name she liked — Victory Way.

For the first time in three years, most residents of the state of Washington did not work on Christmas Day. The shipyards, airplane factories, and virtually all other war plants closed for the holiday. Employees at transportation facilities, restaurants and a few other businesses worked their usual hours. Cities in the state were flooded with service personnel eagerly seeking transportation home. For many it was their first Christmas at home in two or three years. This heavy movement of men and women in uniform resulted in standing room only at rail and bus facilities. Most civilians, recognizing the nation's defenders had first call on public transportation, did not attempt to travel during the 1944 holiday season.

CHAPTER FOUR

Victory at Last

January 1, 1945 ~ December 31, 1945

Families of U.S. war dead had the option of final burial of loved ones in overseas military cemeteries or in this country. Some now lie in hometown graveyards, some in service cemeteries such as Arlington in Virginia, and some in veterans' sections of local cemeteries such as Seattle's Evergreen-Washelli. The bodies continued to arrive for reburial two years after the war's end. Here, on November 16, 1947, two non-commissioned officers guard 24 coffins unloaded at the Seattle Port of Embarkation. Seattle P-I Collection, 28188, MOHAI.

The 1945 New Year dawned brighter than the previous three; the smell of victory was in the air. Still, Americans across the land realized many battles still lay ahead. The New Year's Eve parties were well attended but comparatively quiet. The Seattle Tennis Club party was colorful with many of Seattle's leading citizens in attendance, several of them in uniform. Lieutenant and Mrs. Howard Richmond, Lieutenant and Mrs. George Barclay Parry, Mr. and Mrs. Robert Brinkley, and Mr. and Mrs. Aubrey Naef were listed among the attendees. Since New Year's Eve fell on a Sunday, many of the families attended church services before celebrating the arrival of 1945.

Even the newspaper comics mentioned the holiday. In Gasoline Alley, Sergeant Skeezix Wallet wished one of his men a Happy New Year. The friend reminded him that they were on a battlefront beyond the international dateline and that yesterday had been New Years Eve. Skeezix responded, "I don't care what day or what time it is here. What matters is what time it is back home!"

Business News

A Boeing C-97 troop and cargo transport, the military prototype of the postwar Stratocruiser, broke the coast-to-coast nonstop flight record on January 9 when it flew the 2,323 miles from Seattle to Washington National Airport in 6 hours, 3 minutes and 50 seconds, with an average speed of 383 mph. A Lockheed Constellation previously held the record at 6 hours, 57 minutes and 51 seconds. Elliott Merrill, Boeing test pilot, reported approximately 1,000 gallons of fuel remained in the tanks when they landed, in part because the pressurized cabin allowed them to fly at about 30,000 feet.

The Seattle Chamber of Commerce presented the Boeing Aircraft Company with the 1944 Paul Bunyan award for having brought Seattle more fame and national recognition than any other firm or individual. Honorable mentions were awarded *The Seattle Times*, *The Post-Intelligencer*, and the Frederick and Nelson Department Store.

On January 5, Puget Sound Bridge and Dredging Company launched the 55th ship constructed at its Harbor Island plant, a "barracks ship," described as "in the nature of a war-zone floating hotel." The 260-foot steel vessel was designed to take care of battle-weary men and to replace stationary shore buildings. Each barracks ship contained sleeping quarters, baths and recreation rooms where crews from submarines and other vessels could rest after long hours of battle duty. Mrs. Charles F. Frankland, wife of a banker, was sponsor. Charles F. Clise, President of the Seattle Chamber of Commerce, was principal speaker, and H. W. McCurdy, president of Puget Sound Bridge and Dredge, was master of ceremonies at this occasion.

Persons in the News

Rabbi Raphael Levine of Seattle's Temple de Hirsch and Reverend Dr. U.S. Mitchell of San Francisco, director of the National Conference of Christians and Jews, reported that while touring Alaska they found service personnel to be less prejudiced than civilians in the lower forty-eight states. For example, not a single serviceman they talked with advocated discrimination against loyal citizens of Japanese ancestry. The soldiers, the two churchmen reported, have learned the necessity of teaming together in total disregard of a man's religious or racial background.

One of the state's most famous citizens, Edward R. Murrow and his wife, Janet, were back in the Pacific Northwest in mid-January for one of their rare visits with his parents in Bellingham. Murrow had earned fame during his eight years broadcasting "This is London" that described the German blitz. He was raised in Washington and was a Washington State College graduate. After recording his daily network broadcast from Seattle, he departed for the East Coast, then flew on to London. From there he planned to commute to Paris,

Headlines: January 1945

January 6:
B-29s STRIKE NEW BLOWS AT JAPANESE IN TOKYO AND NANKING

January 9:
U.S. TROOPS INVADE LUZON IN THE PHILIPPINES

January 9:
ONE OF THE LAST MAJOR GERMAN ATTACKS THREATENS STRASBOURG

January 15:
U.S. TROOPS RETAKE TOWNS IN HEART OF BELGIAN BULGE

January 20:
FDR IS INAUGURATED FOR A FOURTH TERM

January 30:
U.S. LAUNCHES DRIVE ON SIEGFRIED LINE

the Italian front and other war fronts. Murrow told newsmen that he had flown 16 combat missions and felt a need to laud the ground crews he had seen working. He said they had 16-hour-a-day jobs, keeping the planes operating and changing bomb loads as often as eight times a day, regardless of whether it rained, froze or snowed.

On January 21, *The Seattle Times* carried an article about a Seattle youth who had faced adversity with typical American spirit. Hugh Klopfenstein, a senior at the Naval Academy at Annapolis, was rated an excellent student until stricken with infantile paralysis. He was sent to Warm Springs, Georgia, for treatment, and there he met President Roosevelt who was being treated for his polio problems.

Miss Ruth Ellis, director of nursing recruitment for the American Red Cross, arrived in Seattle in January to help recruit women to be trained as nurses. Because of

heavy casualties on the war fronts, the Army badly needed to add another 10,000 nurses to the 50,000 already serving the Army and the Navy.

George Coplen of the National Housing Agency announced early in January that public housing funds had been pledged to build 125 dormitory units to house war workers in the Puget Sound area. These were in addition to the 400 temporary family dwellings in Seattle, the 432 dormitory units in Renton, and an undisclosed number of housing units in Bremerton.

Mr. and Mrs. Fred Kinoshita, their daughter Mary, 18, and son Charles, 17, were the first Japanese-Americans to return to Seattle after the evacuation. They arrived on January 12 and moved into a house adjacent to their Catholic Church. The Kinoshitas emigrated from Japan in 1906 and had lived in Seattle since 1908. Mr. Kinoshita had served as bellman at the Rainier

Club for 22 years and had managed a Seattle apartment house from 1937 until his family was evacuated to Minidoka Relocation Center. They placed a gold star in the window of their home in memory of their son, Tsukasa, who was killed in action in France in August 1944.

Colonel Ivan W. Meyer, former chief of intelligence with the 41st Division, was enjoying a furlough at his West Seattle home after 29 months in the New Guinea area. The 42-year-old Colonel offered high praise for the Nisei interpreters and translating teams assigned to Army Intelligence. "I had a dozen Nisei boys with me all the time and they always did a splendid job and were never too tired to keep going. If there is any argument about them here at home, you can put me down as being 100 percent for them. They are playing a large part in the successful furthering of our Pacific campaigns and are certainly good Americans." The Colonel, an architect in civil life, enjoyed a short leave with his wife and two young sons before reporting to Santa Barbara for reassignment.

With servicemen from Washington State scattered all over the world, unplanned meetings of friends were rare. In mid-January two Seattleites linked the First and Third Armies in the Battle of the Bulge in the Ardennes Forest in Belgium. Sergeant Lawrence F. Becker was leading a Third Army four-man patrol sent out to establish contact with the First Army. Captain Brooks Norman was leading a First Army routine scouting expedition. Becker scrambled across a wrecked bridge on the Ourthe River just as Norman stepped out of the woods with weapons at the ready, not expecting to meet Americans in that area. The two men exchanged identification cards and shook hands. Both were ski enthusiasts and had been overseas since December 1943. Becker left Seattle when his little daughter was only a week old. Wounded during the landings near Cherbourg, he stayed in a field hospital only three days, then left for the front "on his own." He wrote his wife to tell their daughter that her Daddy would be home

soon to give her that first skiing lesson. Captain Norman was wounded when shrapnel ripped into his right leg and fractured his left foot. He had rejoined his outfit a few days before the meeting with Sergeant Becker.

Gordon L. Edris, a full colonel at age 27, returned home after 30 months in the Mediterranean Theatre as a troop carrier pilot. He had served in England, Africa, Sicily, Italy, Greece and Southern France. He told of dropping troops behind enemy lines in France and following up with supplies. He said, "My group is a wonderful bunch, and I hope we stick together until the war is ended. We want to fly home together when this thing is over." The colonel, a graduate of Tacoma's Lincoln High School and the University of Washington, was enjoying a reunion with his wife Esther and with his parents. After his furlough, he expected to return to his unit.

War Experiences Described in the Press

Captain Philip H. Luther was at the wheel of a big Army transport that was bucking a 65-mile an hour gale. Giant waves crashed against the steamer, cascading tons of green water over her fore deck. Captain Luther noted the hatch on her weather deck swing open while an Army private, homeward bound after more than a year in the Aleutians, emerged with his life belt in hand. Luther shuddered as he watched the

New Guinea is the second largest island on earth after Greenland. Japanese military occupied the western and northern coasts during the war. This was the farthest point south to be occupied by Japan. Allied counter offensives checked the enemy advance and by May 1945 had driven the enemy from the island. African American troops were involved and wounded were cared for at the 268th Station Hospital in New Guinea. The photo shows some of the black Army nurses treating patients in the surgical ward. National Archives, 111-SC-287482.

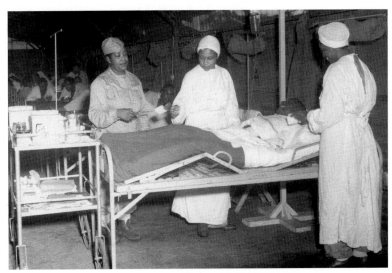

private suddenly slide down the steep pitch of the deck toward the railing and crash full speed into the rail. He saw the soldier's feet fly up as he turned a complete flip and disappeared over the side. When Luther saw the soldier's cap floating behind the ship, he grabbed the lever to signal the engine room to stop all engines. For an hour and a half the sea was searched but there was no trace of the missing soldier. A roll call was ordered of all aboard to identify the man who had fallen into the sea. Luther was about to give up the search when an Army officer appeared on the bridge accompanied by a pale and shaking Pfc. named John C. Coulson. The youthful soldier explained how, as he flipped overboard, he had grabbed back over his head and his hands hit a rail that he managed to grasp. He hung on until two of his buddies pulled him to safety. He then scurried below to change into dry clothes. His rescue had occurred between two life rafts and out of Luther's view. Luther said, "It was one of those freak occurrences that happen once in a million times."

Sergeant William H. Whiteside, Jr., thought he was dreaming when he awoke in his own cozy bed that January morning. The 25-year-old artillery liaison sergeant, a 1938 graduate of Seattle's Lincoln High School, two months earlier had been on the front in Alsace-Lorraine. Stationed with infantrymen on the Maginot Line, Whiteside and his radio operator were looking for a safe place to sleep. They entered a pillbox, found a German candle and a Nazi bayonet that the Sergeant decided to keep as souvenirs. Then they noticed a circular stairway. With the candle lit, they descended 14 flights and found a maze of tunnels with a light at the end of one of them. "Allo," called out a voice with a German accent. Whitehead responded, "Allo, Hans." A figure started striding toward them. Whiteside snuffed the candle and hid in a doorway. As the German officer strode by, he jabbed the bayonet against the German's back and grabbed the Luger from his belt. Whiteside then motioned for the German officer to turn around and lead them

back down the corridor. The German motioned to a door and indicated Whitehead should enter. Inside 18 German soldiers stood up and surrendered. After the 18 were escorted outside and turned over to American soldiers, the Seattle sergeant decided to hunt for more souvenirs in the depths of the fortifications. But again he was interrupted by German voices. He fired a couple of warning shots at the ceiling and pulled open a door. Out rushed 45 more prisoners with their hands elevated. Whiteside admitted he was uneasy when he saw the number of enemy soldiers that were surrendering. He had been twice awarded the Bronze Star for bravery while keeping battlefield communications open. He was most grateful for the furlough that followed these exploits and truly enjoyed life at home with his wife, Peggy and his nearby parents. In mid-February he reported back to the Army for reassignment.

Lieutenant George E. Thompson, whose parents lived in Seattle, was pilot of a Liberator bomber named "Battling Bachelor." Thompson and his crew held the Southwest Pacific record for the most damage to the enemy in the shortest time. The 13th Airforce reported the "Battling Bachelor" sank four Japanese ships in three weeks while on seven missions. All these missions were "lone wolf" flights beyond the previous limits of heavy bombers flying out of The Netherlands East Indies. Thompson and his crew also held the record for distance flown into enemy territory. One day, off the northern tip of Borneo, they sighted two enemy ships sneaking along the coast and damaged one and sank the other. Later on this same flight, they were the first to sight and report a large enemy task force of battleships, cruisers and destroyers headed toward the Philippines to attack Allied landing operations. They also earned the record for sending the briefest message on record. Over the China Sea, after sighting a large enemy tanker and a cargo vessel they radioed their base, "Sighted ships. Will sink." A few minutes later, they added a single word, "Sunk."

A Few of the Many Heroes of January

Mr. and Mrs. Charles F. Jones of Seattle displayed a banner with four blue stars in their window indicating they had four sons in the service. On January 5, after their son, Private Dan G. Jones, 19, died in a Paris hospital of wounds received two months earlier, a gold star replaced one blue star. Dan, a graduate of O'Dea High School, had been assigned to an M.P. division in England then was transferred to an infantry unit in France. He was in combat less than a month when killed. One of his brothers, Corporal Charles A. Jones 22, with the 4th Marine Division in the South Pacific, had survived the invasions of Saipan, Tinian and the Marshalls. Another brother, William H. Jones, 24, was serving as a Navy storekeeper in the Pacific, and oldest brother, James F. Jones 27, a chief commissary steward in the Pacific Theatre, had been in the Navy three years.

Lieutenant Thomas A. Bacchus, one of four Vashon Island brothers in the armed forces, was killed in the South Pacific battle area while piloting a Hellcat fighter plane. He had served aboard an aircraft carrier for seven months and earned several citations. He had served 18 months in Alaska before being sent to the South Pacific.

Sergeant Eugene H. Harris walked into his Seattle home in mid-January, surprising both his wife and his mother. The Army had informed them he had been awarded a furlough for distinguishing himself in battle and would be home for Christmas, but December came and went with no sign of Harris. He explained that wartime transportation from Europe to Seattle took longer than anticipated. The exploit that earned him a furlough and a Bronze Star occurred on a foggy day in France. Harris was gun commander of a two-vehicle tank destroyer unit traveling through open country when they came under direct enemy artillery fire. When the gun commander of the other vehicle was killed, Harris held his ground, returned the German fire and succeeded in wiping out the concealed enemy installation. Sergeant Harris had been on the front lines for 135 days and could hardly believe he really was home with the wife he wed one day before leaving for overseas duty. Now they were planning a belated honeymoon. When his 30-day furlough ended, Harris reported to Fort Lewis for reassignment.

Robert Jackson was one of the national guardsmen in the 1930s chosen to unveil the monument to World War I veterans at the Capital Building in Olympia. On January 12, his parents were advised that their son, a Lieutenant in the Army, had died of battle wounds received on the European front. Now his name is listed on the memorials to Washington State's World War II dead.

Infantryman Eugene L. Cummings suffered severe wounds while serving in New Guinea and spent a number of months in hospitals in the South Pacific. After recovering, he was sent to the Philippines where he was involved in the battle to retake Leyte. His family received word in January that Eugene Cummings had died of wounds received in a battle there. He was remembered at Seattle's Cleveland High School and Poulsbo's North Kitsap High School as a fine football player.

James R. Kestle, Navy motor machinist's mate, was listed as missing in action in mid-January and later reported as dead. He was aboard the destroyer *Spence* when it and other vessels were lost in a typhoon in the Pacific. The 19-year-old youth had been home in Seattle on leave four months earlier, after having served 13 months overseas. He was a Ballard High School graduate.

Private Yeu Louie, 22, was killed in action on the European front. He had been in the Army more than a year and had served in France since July. The China-born private had lived in Seattle seven years with his father, Sing Louie. Two brothers in China survived him.

James K. Ryan, the only son in his family, was killed on the French Front on January 3. He had graduated from Roosevelt High School in 1943 where he was a member of the scholastic honorary and the golf team. He joined the Army after passing tests with scores high enough to make him eligible for the Army Specialized Training Program at the University of Cincinnati. The Army canceled this program in March 1944 and the 19-year-old Ryan was sent to an armored division. By November he was on the front line in France fighting with the U.S. Seventh Army and was killed in action when the Germans attempted to recapture Strasbourg.

Lieutenant Robert M. Kennewick was piloting a B-17 on his first mission over Germany in December, when killed in action. Kennewick, 21 years old, was a popular student at Cleveland High School where he was president of the senior class, a basketball star and a member of the Coordinating Council. After graduation, he worked at Boeing while attending classes part time at the University of Washington, but rather than be drafted, decided to enter the Army Air Corps. Also killed when the plane went down was Sergeant Turrell A. Benson of Seattle, a member of the crew.

Lieutenant Eric J. Zackrison, 22, died in action over Italy in December 1944. Pilot of a B-17 with the 15th Air Force, the graduate of Seattle's Cleveland High School had been in the service since February 1943. His wife, Marianna gave birth to Richard Eric on December 1, just five days before his father was killed.

The parents of Lieutenant Robert J. Kiebler, 23, learned in mid-January that their son was killed in air action over Leyte on December 17. Kiebler, a former student at Seattle Prep and Washington State College, joined the Army Air Force in March 1943. The Lieutenant's last letter home, dated 11 days prior to his death, told how he had walked three hours in the mud before finding a church where he could attend mass. He finally located a cathedral and heard Filipino priests of the Order of the Divine Faith conduct the service. On January 30, a Solemn Requiem Memorial Mass was conducted in Robert Kiebler's memory at Seattle's Blessed Sacrament Church.

Captain H. J. Montgomery, an Army pilot, was en route home after serving a year as leader of a troop carrier squadron in the China-Burma-India Theatre. He held the Distinguished Flying Cross, the Air Medal with Oak-Leaf Cluster and the Presidential Unit Citation. Prior to entering the service in 1941, Captain Montgomery, a graduate of Central Washington College of Education, had taught music in Dayton, Washington, schools. Now, as he headed for home, tragedy struck. While between Egyptian Sudan and Nigeria, the plane on which he was a passenger crashed and he was killed. His parents, living in Enumclaw, received the fateful telegram in late January.

Lieutenant Starr Sutherland, Jr., a former University of Washington football player and pre-med student, died in battle in Luxembourg on January 4. Overseas for four months, he had been promoted to First Lieutenant 12 days before his death. Survivors included his father, a Lincoln High School history teacher, his mother and an 18-year-old brother, George, serving in the South Pacific with the Marine Corps. A few weeks after his death was announced, four history classes at Lincoln High School collected donations to be presented to the King County Central Blood Bank in Lieutenant Sutherland's name.

William Van Well Muche, Navy electrician's mate, was reported missing when the aircraft carrier *U.S.S. St. Lo* was sunk in the Second Battle of the Philippines on October 24, 1944. He had joined the crew of the carrier when it was commissioned and was with it during convoy duty and four major battles. Muche, 21, a graduate of Seattle's O'Day High School, had two brothers in the service. After being missing for months, he was declared dead.

On January 26, Mrs. Mary C. McLeod received the Bronze Star Medal awarded posthumously to her son, Pfc. Otto W. McLeod who died in June 1944 of wounds received in the European Theatre. The citation with the award stated that young McLeod took charge of a platoon after the commanding officer was killed. Private McCloud, braving heavy enemy fire, made his way to the top of a building from where he fired down on a vastly superior force of Germans, causing their surrender. He held the position until reinforcements arrived and they attacked the enemy. During the ensuing hand-to-hand combat, Private McLeod was mortally wounded. His mother and two brothers (one serving in the Army in Europe) survived the former Garfield High School student.

Sergeant Gerald Luther, former coxswain of the University of Washington lightweight crew, was killed in action January 7. Sergeant Luther enlisted in the Army Air Force in 1942 and was transferred to the Army Specialized Training Program at the University of Utah. When that program terminated in 1944, he was sent to an infantry division that went overseas in December. He was on the front lines only a few days when he was killed. A West Seattle High School graduate, he had completed two years at the University before enlisting in the Army. His parents, a sister and a brother survived him.

Lieutenant John V. Griffin was reported missing in action in Belgium on Christmas Eve. A fighter pilot, young Griffin, 22, had married in March and was sent overseas in May where he quickly earned the Air Medal and two Oak-Leaf Clusters. He had written his parents in Seattle that he expected to be home in time to celebrate Easter. His father said, "All of us feel he will return safely to us." Unfortunately Lieutenant Griffin later was reported to have died in the skies over Belgium.

John J. Riley's dad was a Colonel and a West Point graduate, so young Riley hoped to be appointed to West Point, too. After graduating from Seattle's Garfield High School, Riley passed intelligence tests making him eligible for the Army's Specialized Training Program at the University of Utah, a program that promised to graduate him as an officer. After a few months studying there, Riley and other students in the ASTP programs were told the program had been canceled and all were sent to the infantry. After a couple of months, Riley, now a Sergeant, was

reported missing in action in Europe. Two days after his missing status was received, the Army was informed that Senator Warren G. Magnuson had appointed young Riley to West Point. Several days later his father, Colonel Ernest J. Riley, serving in Southern France, was notified by cable that his son had been killed in action.

Another Washingtonian whose Intelligence Quotient made him eligible for the Army Specialized Training Program was Jack W. Rowland. A Queen Anne High School graduate, Private Rowland attended the University of Washington for a year before entering the Army in 1943. When the ASTP program was canceled, along with thousands of other cadets he was transferred to the infantry. A few months later, while manning a machine gun on the front lines during the Battle of the Bulge, he was killed.

John G. O'Neal, Jr., an only son, attended high school in Spokane. After graduating, he enlisted in the Army and was sent to Officers Candidate School at Fort Sill, Oklahoma, where he was commissioned a second lieutenant in the Field Artillery. He was sent overseas in September 1944 and was killed two months later. His parents and sister, who had moved to Seattle, survived him.

The parents of Pfc. Floyd E. Christensen, 18, were notified in January that their son had been killed in action near Aachen, Germany. Young Christensen moved to Bremerton with his parents in 1940 from Grand Coulee and graduated from Bremerton High. He worked at the Keyport Naval Torpedo Station, prior to entering the Army in September 1943. He earned the expert marksman badge with both rifle and machine gun and had seen action in France and Belgium before his unit crossed into Germany. In addition to his parents, three brothers and two sisters survived him.

William H. Shurts joined the Army in February 1940, almost two years before Pearl Harbor was attacked. He had earned sergeant's stripes as he fought in the North African and Sicilian campaigns and took part in the D-Day invasion of France. He had fought in the front lines for more than three years until late in

1944, when his luck ran out. His wife in Port Orchard received word in January that her husband had been killed in action in Germany in mid-November.

Pfc. Keith M. Callow, an honor student in high school, was a cadet in the Army Specialized Training Program until the program was suddenly canceled. In October 1944, young Callow, leader of an automatic rifle unit, was on the front lines during the Battle of the Bulge. His parents, Mr. and Mrs. Russell Callow, received a telegram in late January informing them their son had been wounded. He quickly recuperated and was sent back to the front, but a short time later he received a second wound, this time in the chest. He was in the hospital until the war ended in Europe. His father, a noted crew coach, during the war served as a Seattle war plant executive.

Navy Machinist's Mate James L. "Jimmy" Hartsoc was born in Palmer, a village near Enumclaw, in 1925 and was reared in Bremerton where he graduated from high school in 1942. A letter received by his parents on January 15 from his commanding officer revealed that Jimmy, the Hartsoc's only son, was seriously injured in October when his ship, the *Gambier Bay* went down in the South Pacific. For two days, Jimmy was kept alive aboard a life raft and was among those rescued, but he died a few days later at 20 years of age.

Not only young people died in the war. William Henry Gates, dean of ship officers on Pacific routes, was chief engineer of the American Mail Line freighter *Capillo* when it sailed on October 17, 1941. The ship and crew were in Manila Harbor when the Japanese bombed the port. The *Capillo* was set afire and settled to the bottom. Gates was captured and sent to a Japanese prison camp a short distance north of Manila. He died there on January 20, 1944, after more than three years as a prisoner of war. It took nearly a year for the word of his death to reach his wife and daughter in Seattle. William Gates, 70 when he died, had crossed the Pacific more than 200 times during his long seafaring career.

The Navy announced on January 30 that Lieutenant Dean O. Timm of Centralia was awarded the Air Medal for action in the South Pacific. The citation read: "During operations of the United States naval forces against enemy-held Marianas Islands on June 14, 1944, after completing his routine assignment, he voluntarily and in the face of intense anti-aircraft fire attacked parked aircraft on an enemy air field, destroying four parked planes." Lieutenant Timm, who survived the war, was 22 years old at the time.

Another Navy pilot from Washington State, Lieutenant Yates Hickey, Jr., was shot down behind Japanese lines on Luzon on December 15, 1944, and survived. He told an Associated Press reporter:

I didn't have time to destroy my carrier-based plane but other flyers saw me go down and soon two squadrons came over and destroyed the plane. Two civilians helped me to a village where I met a couple of Army men who knew of a railroad bridge that connected an enemy garrison with Manila. That was the only railroad access to the Japanese camp. The Army guys had a radio and we sent a message off to American forces on Leyte and flyers came over and dropped us explosives. With crude tools we grubbed out a reasonably smooth runway. After we blew the bridge, we sent another message to Leyte. They immediately sent two Cub planes, escorted by four P-38s. The little planes landed and took all three of us out.

Lieutenant Hickey's parents in Seattle were notified he was missing and later that he had been rescued.

Seattle physician Captain Jack L. Culp had his share of experiences on the front. He was on a landing craft headed toward the Normandy beach on D-Day when a direct hit by a German shell sank the craft 50 yards from shore. The Captain's jeep went down with the LST but divers were able to hook chains to it and a caterpillar dragged the waterproofed vehicle and its load of medical supplies ashore. He managed to establish contact with the 82nd Airborne Division, to which he had been assigned. "We didn't get much sleep," the captain reported. "We set up a medical center in the hedgerows by digging a deep ditch with causeways into the shelter so casualties could be brought in on litters. We were right in the middle of the battlefield. Some allied soldiers were wounded behind us." He remembered hundreds of cases where the medical personnel treated badly wounded men in those primitive conditions. After 125 days as a front line doctor, Culp's weight had dropped from 185 pounds to 130. Near Metz on the border of Germany, the Doctor dropped in his tracks and was carried from the front lines on a stretcher. The black-haired 33-year-old surgeon, a former University football player, spent two and one half months recuperating in an army hospital before being sent home to Seattle and to his wife Billie for additional rest before being reassigned.

Pfc. Donald L. Karney, orphaned at an early age, was reared by his grandparents, Mr. and Mrs. J. W. Amber, in Seattle. Karney had been an Army paratrooper for 16 months when his grandmother remembered he was due a birthday greeting. As she was writing the V-Mail greetings, the doorbell rang and she was handed a telegram reporting that her 19-year-old grandson Don had been killed in the Battle of the Bulge on January 7.

February 1945

Daring Raid Frees Prisoners in the Philippines

The major story in February 1 newspapers described a commando raid by 400 picked men of the 6th Ranger Battalion and Filipino Guerrillas that freed 513 prisoners from a Japanese prison camp located 25 miles behind the front lines. All Japanese guards were taken by surprise and not one was left alive. Within minutes, the prisoners were on their journey to freedom; the ambulatory walking and the incapacitated carried on the backs of husky Rangers, or riding in carts. Nearly 100 were so weak from malnutrition, disease and three-year-old wounds that they were immobile. Two died

in the excitement of the rescue, their feeble hearts flickering out at the sight of Americans. The rescue effort cost the lives of 27 Rangers and Filipinos who fought off a tank-led enemy attack along the escape route. In the process they killed 523 Japanese and knocked out 12 enemy tanks.

Several Washingtonians were among those rescued, including Marine 1st Sergeant Stanley E. Bronk, whose mother lived in Seattle. He had been a Marine for 18 years and was taken prisoner on Bataan. He was an only son and his father was deceased. His mother wondered how to plan for his arrival home and tried to remember his favorite dishes. She said "He certainly is going to have everything he wants to eat after what he's been eating over the past three years in that prison camp." She said she expected to fix up his room. "Stanley was born in this very house, you know, and lived here until he joined the marines."

Another Seattleite rescued was Marine Platoon Sergeant Milton A. Englin. His mother was at work in a cleaning establishment when notified that he was free and she promptly fainted and was carried to the first aid room. Later at home a reporter interviewed her. Tears rolled down her cheeks as she explained that three years of pent-up emotions were "sort of getting away from me." Her son was an only child and she had not told him his father had recently passed away, because she felt he had enough to worry about.

One of the Ranger officers in charge of the raid on Cabanatuan prison camp was a Captain from Seattle. A Sergeant Julian Brown from Florida told a reporter that he was one of the first prisoners to be helped out of the camp. "The first thing I knew I was standing outside with a great big Yank. His name was Captain Robert Prince of Seattle. It was really dark. I looked at this man, and realizing it was a Yank, the first thing I did was to grab the captain, hug him and kiss him on the cheek right there." Captain Prince was a graduate of Garfield High School and Stanford University.

As the allies advanced through the

Headlines: February 1945

February 1:
U.S. RANGERS AND FILIPINO GUERILLAS RESCUE 513 AMERICAN SURVIVORS OF THE BATAAN DEATH MARCH

February 2:
THOUSANDS OF ALLIED PLANES BLAST WIESBADEN, KARLSRUHE AND BERLIN

February 4:
GERMANS RETREAT FROM BELGIUM

February 11:
CHURCHILL, ROOSEVELT AND STALIN AT YALTA PLAN FINAL EUROPEAN BATTLES

February 14:
DRESDEN DEVASTATED BY ALLIED BOMBS

February 17:
U.S. FORCES LIBERATE MANILA AND FREE 5,000 ALLIED POWS

February 23:
IN FOUR DAYS OF BLOODY FIGHTING, MARINES TAKE IWO JIMA ISLANDS

February 23:
FIRST BOATLOADS OF U.S. FOOD REACH HUNGRY FRENCH CIVILIANS

During the war years most Washington citizens instantly recognized these leaders of Allied Nations known as The Big Three—Winston Churchill, Franklin D. Roosevelt, and Joseph Stalin. They are depicted here at the Yalta Conference in February 1945 making final plans for the defeat of the Germans. National Archives photo 111-SC-26048.

Philippines, several other camps were liberated and more Washingtonians set free. Lieutenant Ethel Thor of Tacoma was one of a group of 69 Army nurses rescued. She was a graduate of Lincoln High in Tacoma and of St. Joseph's Hospital. Others listed were Joseph Tremblay and Mrs. Vera Tremblay, Lester A. Anderson, and Lieutenant Dean K. Wood, all of Seattle. Wood, a graduate of Queen Anne High School, had been awarded a Distinguished Service Cross for bravery and a Purple Heart for wounds received before Bataan fell. Others freed were: Frank O. Bacon of Olympia, Private Louis E. Remark of Tacoma, George W. Weedon of Elberton in Whitman County, Corporal Lester H. Houdyshell of Granger in Yakima County and Pfc. James J. Palmer of Port Orchard.

Apparently fearing an invasion of Formosa by allied forces, the Japanese moved 177 important prisoners from the Taiwan Camp in Formosa to Hoten Camp, Mukden, Manchuria. Seattleites among the number were General Joseph P. Vachon, Colonel Donald B. Hilton, Colonel Louis J. Bowler, Colonel Napoleon Bourdeau,- and Colonel Ray M. O'Day. Seattle-born Colonel Loren A. Wetherby also was reported with the group, though listed with an East Coast home address. Others from the state moved by the enemy were Colonel Nunez C. Pilet of Tacoma, Colonel Malcolm V. Fortier,

Spokane and General Jonathan M. Wainwright, a native of Walla Walla.

Washingtonians in the News

Colonel William A. Millington of Seattle commanded the first Marine Corps Corsair squadron assigned to an aircraft carrier in the Pacific Theater. These fast, maneuverable planes helped provide fighter cover during Third Fleet attacks ranging from Saigon to Okinawa. Millington was the first marine officer to take complete command of a carrier air group and the first marine pilot to shoot down an enemy aircraft while operating at sea. The 31-year-old Colonel participated in the task force strike in the South China Sea in January, during which he and his flyers accounted for 10 planes destroyed on the ground, 24 others damaged, and one cargo ship sunk and two damaged. Millington graduated from Garfield High School and the University of Washington. His father, William A. Millington, a Seattle physician, served as a Major with the Medical Corps in Europe.

Lieutenant Philip Schallo, a Mustang pilot from Seattle, downed three enemy planes north of Weimar on February 10. Furthermore he saved enough ammunition to allow him to knock an ME-109 out of the air while on the way home to England. The 16 Mustangs in the raid found an undefended German airdrome where they destroyed 38 Nazi planes and four hangars. Major M. B. Nichols of Bellevue was leader of the squadron, but did not fly on this mission.

Thorbjorn Gronning, chairman of the American Relief For Norway Committee for Washington and Alaska, announced that more than 20,000 pounds of new and used clothing, quilts and other articles most needed by the war-distressed people of Norway had been collected and prepared for shipment.

Two Army evacuation nurses, Lieutenants Harriet Thomas of Olympia and Dorothy Field of Snohomish, were home after 22 months in

On February 3, 1945, heavy equipment maneuvered through mud at the Seattle Port of Embarkation. In the background an LST awaits a cargo for the Pacific War Theater. MOHAI Collection, 871.

the South Pacific. When asked what they wanted most, they responded: "a bath, a soft bed, and a hamburger sandwich." They reported that wartime transportation up the coast from San Francisco was one of the worst battles they had fought. Lieutenant Thomas said, "Finally, after we were almost reconciled to spending our 21-day leave in San Francisco, we squeezed onto a train and got as far as Portland. Then we couldn't get out of Portland. All one night we sat on those hard benches in the station, drinking coffee. At last we caught a bus to come on home." As members of the Fifth Air Force, the two nurses had taken care of wounded being flown to medical care from battlefields all over the Southwest Pacific. After their leaves, the nurses reported to the Miami, Florida, reassignment center.

Navy Lieutenant Commander Douglas S. Egan mailed a letter home from "somewhere in India" that arrived on February 10. He wrote: "By looking at the map, you will see that I am just about as far away from Seattle as I can be. Naval duty out here has been very interesting. I have been fortunate in traveling a bit and seeing a good part of this great continent." Egan, who had worked in the traffic department of General Steamship Company, added, "I look for some great times for Seattle in the postwar shipping world. There should be plenty of trade

with the Far East whenever things in the Pacific are over."

Three Seattle men took command of Navy ships in mid-February. Commander Harry Smith assumed the captaincy of the new 2,200-ton destroyer *Frank E. Evans*, commissioned at the Brooklyn Navy Yard. His wife, Grace, lived in Seattle. Lieutenant Commander Martin N. Chamberlain, a 1936 University of Washington graduate, was placed in command of the destroyer *Earle*, an escort vessel. Lieutenant Howard K. Smith of Seattle took over the Fleet tug *Chawasha* at her commissioning at the Charleston Navy Yard.

February Business Items

During February the War Manpower Commission hoped to recruit an additional 5,000 Seattle area women to work in the war effort, especially the aircraft and shipbuilding industries. Employment openings existed also in the transportation services, laundries and dry cleaning, food processing, and hospitals. In addition, the army was recruiting 8,000 nurses and the Navy needed 4,000. The Red Cross Military Welfare Division was calling for 250 more women employees in the Seattle area, and nationally the WACS, WAVES, SPARS and Women Marines were seeking recruits.

On February 12, Colonel Walter J. DeLong,

State Director of Selective Service, predicted that virtually every physically qualified male under 30 years of age in the State of Washington would be in uniform by July 1. "This is going to raise hob with Boeing and some of our other most essential industries, including logging," the Colonel said, "but we've been ordered to fill our draft quotas, regardless, and the young men with occupational deferments are about the only remaining source of manpower."

Todd shipyards in Seattle reported it had repaired, overhauled or converted 576 ships for war service during 1944. They also produced 17 destroyers, five of which were involved in the D-Day invasion. Todd Shipyards in Tacoma built 11 escort aircraft carriers during the year, completing its original contract to build 49 of the baby flattops, and had started a new program of constructing a larger type of carrier.

During 1945, the Seattle Western Union offices were busier than at any time in their history. Automatic machines typed out thousands of telegrams a day, including many that began with the dreaded words, "We regret to inform you... ." Telegraph companies estimated that one telegram in a thousand carried notification of a war casualty. Because such telegrams were apt to cause emotional reaction on the part of the recipients, certain staff members were especially trained to deliver them. Miss Gladys Hoxsie was one of those trained to hand deliver such messages. "So much depends on the way it is presented," she explained. "Usually I ask a woman if she is alone, and if she would like to have a member of the family or a neighbor with her when she opens the telegram. If it's a telegram about someone missing in action, I say, 'Well, this isn't as bad as it might be.' Most persons are able to steel themselves to hard news," Miss Hoxsie said. "Only rarely does a person break down."

A Few of the Many Heroes of February

Ray J. Scott rose through the ranks from private to be commissioned in the field. On February 2 he was visiting his mother in Seattle and feeling lucky to be alive. He had survived the invasions of Africa, Anzio and Salerno before taking part in the landings in Southern France. "We were about 150 miles into France," Lieutenant Scott related. "We were battling on top of a hill. One platoon had been sent up there and their leader was killed immediately. So I was ordered to take over. We were facing a crack Nazi armored-infantry outfit. I found only eight men of the platoon still in fighting condition." Soon after Scott reached the hilltop, a grenade shattered his arm, severing nerves and digging a small hole near his elbow. Scott said:

I knew my wounds would keep me out of it. I spied a deserted French farmhouse and slid down the hill into the backyard. I stayed overnight there but knew I needed a doctor or I'd lose my arm. At daylight, I took off trying to reach the American lines. I heard voices approaching and realized it was a German patrol. I hid in grass by the path, but a German soldier saw me. I was captured and taken to their headquarters where German officers interrogated me. Then they ordered me taken to an emergency hospital where doctors operated on my arm. They did a swell job, too. Soon I was moved to another hospital a couple of towns back — a place called Valence. There were 13 other American prisoners there and we talked about what might happen to us. We soon found out. Our troops began a big push. The Nazis, fearing the constant American bombardment, moved out, leaving us and 78 German wounded behind. All night long, the shelling continued, blowing off a corner of the building and breaking all windows. At daylight, U.S. troops moved in. Only 36 of the 78 wounded Germans were still alive. But all 13 of us Americans pulled through.

Lieutenant Scott was flown to Naples, then to the U.S. He faced more operations on his arm at McCaw Hospital in Walla Walla. He earlier had been awarded a Silver Star for "fortitude and bravery" and a Purple Heart in Italy. Now he added a Presidential Unit Citation ribbon and a second Purple Heart.

Lieutenant Donald E. Painter was pilot of a B-24 bomber that carried him safely through 37 missions before he turned up missing in the

Pacific Theatre. He had earned the Distinguished Flying Cross and held a citation for leading American destroyers to a Japanese warship that was trying to escape. In his last letter home, he told his parents he was listening to Japanese propaganda. "The little broadcasting station goes off at 10 o'clock, but the enemy in front of us keeps us entertained all night. Some of the enemy station's records are pretty good and everybody gets a kick out of their propaganda, some of which is really terrible. The other night they said they had shot down 500 of our B-29s. I don't think that even the people in Japan could believe that." Lieutenant Painter was reported missing three days after his 27th birthday, and later was declared dead. He was an Olympia High School graduate and had been a member of the Centralia Elks Lodge. He enjoyed sports, was a champion bowler and loved to ski.

Marine Lieutenant David F. Evans, 21 years old, died February 5 on Guam while being treated for wounds he received in November on Peleliu Island. Evans joined the Marines after graduating from Seattle's Roosevelt High School in 1943. The day he joined, his older brother, Major John G. Evans, departed the U.S. for overseas service. Major Evans was later missing over the Atlantic and declared dead. Thus Mr. and Mrs. Stanley R. Evans of Seattle lost both their sons in the war.

Pfc. Robert M. Starr was 20 years old when killed in action in Alsace-Lorraine on February 5. He was serving with the armored infantry attached to the Third Army, and had been overseas nearly three years during which he was involved in the African campaign and in Italy at the Anzio beachhead. He had attended high school in Yakima. His father, Robert F. Starr, was a music teacher in Seattle when he and his wife lost their only son.

Four Washington State men wounded in the Battle of the Bulge arrived at Madigan General Hospital south of Tacoma in late February. They were Sergeant Archie E. Hoefer of Seattle, Private Erik C. Torland of Edmonds,

Pfc. Marvin F. Allen of Selah and Private Dean E. McFarran of Olympia.

Lieutenant Perry J. Dahl at age 21 luckily knew how to play dead. He was forced to parachute into the Pacific after his plane was rammed during a battle with 12 enemy fighters over the Philippines. The collision set Dahl's plane afire and as he bailed out he burned his face, right arm, and neck. He landed safely in the sea, inflated his rubber dinghy, pulled himself onto it and looked around. He was startled to find himself in the midst of four Japanese destroyers. The nearest one strafed him with a machine gun and pulled up so close that he could hear the crew talking. Dahl played dead, practically stopped breathing, lay limp, his badly burned naked arm trailing over the dinghy's side. His flesh was burned black and he appeared lifeless, so the Japanese ship steamed away. Hours later his rubber boat floated onto a beach where Filipino civilians found him and provided treatment and food. After hiding for several weeks, Dahl had recovered sufficiently to walk into the surprised headquarters of his air group known as Satan's Angels. Dahl originally had been a member of the Washington National Guard 41st Division but transferred to the Air Corps in 1943. Before the war he lived on Mercer Island and worked as a professional jockey, a dude-ranch cowboy and a semi-professional hockey player.

This Army wounded soldier from the South Pacific war front is being carried on his stretcher down the gangplank of a hospital ship that landed at the Seattle Port of Embarkation about six months before the war ended. The soldier holds two crutches under his right arm. In spite of his wounds, he is smiling happily at being a step nearer home. Seattle P-I Collection, 28182, MOHAI.

Headlines:
March 1945

March 6 :
MAJOR GERMAN CITY OF COLOGNE FALLS TO U.S. FIRST ARMY

March 8 :
U.S. TROOPS CAPTURE RHINE BRIDGE AT REMAGEN BEFORE IT IS DESTROYED

March 10 :
300 U.S. B-29s RAIN FIRE ON TOKYO, KILLING 100,000

March 18 :
JAPAN CLOSES ALL SCHOOLS; ORDERS YOUTH OVER AGE SIX TO WAR SERVICE

March 19 :
HITLER ORDERS SCORCHED EARTH POLICY AS ALLIES ENTER GERMANY

March 27 :
13 SMALL NATIONS DECLARE WAR AGAINST GERMANY

Sergeant James Pratt of Rochester, Thurston County, was wounded at St. Lo shortly after D-Day. He spent months in hospitals in France, England, Scotland and the U.S. While he was recuperating in England, the Queen stopped to chat with him during a tour of the hospital. When she found out his hometown was in Washington State, she reminded him that she and the King had visited the West Coast in 1938. In February, Sergeant Pratt checked into Madigan General Hospital, not far from his home, for more rest and recuperation.

Private Fred Butler told a reporter he was saved "through the miracles of modern medical science." On the battlefield in Holland five months earlier shrapnel had passed completely through the lower part of his body. In February he was returned to the United States and called his parents, Dr. and Mrs. Fabius M. Butler, to let them know he would be home on furlough before long. "I will be all right now, "he said. "If I had spent $1,000 a day, I couldn't have had better treatment. They gave me 30 pints of blood plasma in the first ten days." Young Butler was a paratrooper who fought in some of the hottest battles of the war. He made his first combat jump on D-Day. His second jump occurred over Holland five days before he was wounded. A graduate of Seattle's Franklin High School and a former student at the University of Washington, he had been overseas more than a year. His wife, Jean, a quartermaster in the SPARS, was granted leave from her duties in Florida to be with her husband during his furlough.

Lieutenant Roy Hammarlund was wounded slightly on Christmas Day in France. A month later he was wounded again in Belgium. In a letter to his parents received February 6, he said, "I am glad that I am living in an age of medical miracles, otherwise I would not be alive today." The Lieutenant was wounded in both legs with shrapnel that crushed his kneecap. He told his parents, "Five hours later I was on the operation table of a well-equipped hospital in Belgium." He later was moved to England. Lieutenant Hammarlund was following in the footsteps of his grandfather, Professor Charles W. Johnson, dean emeritus of the College of Pharmacy at the University of Washington. Young Roy had been majoring in pharmacy when called into the Army.

Lieutenant Joseph Boltan, 25, of Port Orchard, Kitsap County, was a member of a B-29 crew that failed to return from an eight-plane raid on Tokyo, the Associated Press reported on February 5. While over Japan, about 100 enemy fighters attacked the formation and the number one engine of Boltan's bomber was damaged. The plane, when last seen, was losing altitude but appeared to be under control. Lieutenant Bolton had attended Washington State College from 1936 to 1939. He later was listed as dead.

John Cosper, Jr., of Seattle, couldn't say much about his experience because of military secrecy. He was bombardier on a plane that was attacking a target in Southern Germany, when heavy flak damaged the aircraft. Cosper was credited with taking over the duties of navigator and successfully guiding the plane to neutral territory in Switzerland. During his seven months of internment, Cosper tried to escape three times before managing to reach allied assistance. In early February he was on furlough enjoying visits with his parents and friends. He had attended the University of Washington before joining the Air Force in March 1944.

March 1945

Fort Lawton Plays Important Role in the War

The Army called them staging areas, those last camps before soldiers embarked for overseas. The staging area for the Seattle Port of Embarkation was Fort Lawton, a busy post during the war. The soldiers were transported by rail from training facilities to a Seattle depot. There they were loaded into Army trucks for the short ride to the Fort where they were housed in large temporary barracks. During their few days there, they completed a complex processing that prepared them for overseas duty. Though every man had completed training and supposedly was in fine physical condition, they all underwent final physical examinations. Any that had picked up contagious or infectious diseases were dispatched to the hospital and a replacement substituted from a pool of men maintained for that purpose. Each man's inoculation record was checked to be sure he was protected against smallpox, typhoid, typhus, tetanus and, depending on where he was going, other diseases. Lectures explained how all letters would now be censored and what information would not pass the censors. Processing concluded with the issuance of clothing appropriate for the climate at their destination. A large casual mess at Fort Lawton fed thousands at each meal. The post also provided theaters, bowling alleys, service clubs and churches. When the men were placed on alert, passes were no longer available, visitors were no longer permitted, and no communication was allowed with persons off the Fort. They left carrying full backpacks and barracks bags and were transported to the pier where their ship was waiting. As the Port of Embarkation band played lively tunes and Red Cross workers provided coffee and doughnuts, the men marched up the gangplank. It was an experience that every soldier remembered.

Some of the People Making News in March

The Palmason brothers held a reunion in the Pacific in March after a two-year separation. Victor, former University of Washington track star, and accomplished violinist, now an Army sergeant, was tracked down by his brother, Edward, a physician, vocalist, and Navy lieutenant aboard an attack transport. Ed wrote home this description of their meeting:

> Every place we stopped I asked for Vic, and all I heard was, sorry, his outfit has moved on. Finally we got to a place where his outfit couldn't go farther without climbing Fujiyama, and that's where I found him. I hiked four miles into the hills and located his encampment in a beautiful valley that, not many months ago, was scene of a sanguinary battle. Vic is brown as a native from the sun, and enjoys the healthful outdoor life in the salubrious climate. I invited him aboard ship and he stayed a few days with me until we pushed on.

The letter was read more than once by Vic's wife, Frances, and their son Stephen, who lived in Aberdeen, and by Edward's wife, Vivienne, and son, Palmy, living in Auburn.

In 1945, the Red Cross was facing its greatest year of worldwide service. More than 5,000 volunteers in King County worked during March to raise a quota of $1,167,000 to be donated to the Red Cross to provide vital services around the war-torn globe, according to Frank W. Hull, the Seattle-King County campaign chairman. He added, "Contributors can feel they are allied with the more than 10,000 Red Cross workers serving overseas to maintain that invaluable touch of home for our fighters of every race, color, and creed. It costs $6 per second to maintain the Red Cross organization. Possible contributors should recall that the Red Cross operates at the specific request of the armed forces and that Red Cross field workers undergo the same hardships as our servicemen."

Joanna Andrew was a favorite among members of a USO troupe presenting *Hellzapoppin* for service personnel in the Philippines. Miss Andrew was warmly welcomed at an advanced base where the show entertained hundreds of men of the Army, Navy, Marine Corps and Sea Bees. The pretty and talented Miss Andrew, 22, had appeared for two years in the New York presentation of *Hellzapoppin*. Her parents lived in Seattle, the city she called home.

In March, Navy Lieutenant Commander Willard Bergh was enjoying home leave with his wife Bea and 5-year-old daughter Gwendolyn after 20 months of overseas duty. Before entering active duty, Bergh had been a journalism instructor at the University of Washington and public relations director of Seattle Public Schools. His most recent duty was as supervisor of operations at a Naval Air Base on Tinian. He told a reporter that the last enemy soldiers on the island "lived back in the hills in caves, coming out only at night to wander through the sugar cane, their major food. The only way to capture them was by ambush." The 36-year-old officer told of one cave deep in the hills that Americans bombarded daily with grenades. "One fellow figured he'd cleared out the Japanese, but the next day he found a fresh batch of laundry hanging in the sun." In April Bergh returned to the Navy to be reassigned.

Dr. K. K. Sherwood went overseas with the 50th General Hospital that was formed in Seattle. In March he wrote to his friend Dr. George H. Davis of Kirkland, "Looking back on the experiences of the past 12 months, the 50th General Hospital has had an eventful year. The first event, and the lowest point in morale and comfort, was the staging camp before we boarded the ship on the East Coast. Everything about it was dirty. The trip across the ocean is now an enjoyable memory, including the novelty of eight senior officers to a small stateroom." Dr. Sherwood told of the stay in England and the transfer to France during the summer of 1944. He continued: "Then came the hustle and bustle and enormous work of setting up a general hospital in tents, followed by the thrill of learning that we could function both in quality and quantity in such an environment." He told of large multiple lines of starving bees, so fierce that the men dared not take jams, jellies or any sweets outside on one's mess gear. He continued:

> Two items that we feel we have become well versed in are beds and food. We have slept on floors, on ground, in pup tents, in ward tents, on litters, and on most types of common, poor beds. In food we have become quite critical. Dried eggs are probably nutritious, but if anyone thinks they are appetizing we would suggest that he eat them every third day or oftener, especially when prepared for a group of 100 or more. Dehydrated potatoes may be kindly described as edible if fried. Nevertheless, we all eat our ration quota, are gaining weight and both officers and enlisted personnel are deservedly popular.

Terrance James at age 22 was elected commander of the George W. Farwell Post 2713 of Veterans of Foreign Wars in Seattle, the youngest man to hold that office. James was a Guadalcanal veteran who had joined the National Guard at 15 and was in the Army when 17. He served three years overseas, attaining the rank of corporal before contracting malaria. He received a medical discharge in April 1943. During his term as commander, his wife, Mary served as a color bearer in the post's auxiliary.

Major William J. (Wee) Coyle, post adjutant at Fort Worden, was a World War I veteran. When he was president of the Young Men's Business Club of Seattle in 1925, the service organization signed him up for a 20-year endowment life insurance policy payable to the Children's Orthopedic Hospital. On March 22, 1945, at a meeting of the Business Club in the Roosevelt Hotel, he presented the check for $1,011.08 to Mrs. Henry B. Owen, president of the Hospital association board of directors. He said, "I've lived the necessary 20 years to collect this, but I'm getting old. The doctors say I'm too old to be donating any more blood, but I've already made donations ten times, and it's a great feeling. All of you should try it. The coffee and doughnuts you are served afterwards are the best food you've ever tasted." The insurance check represented the maturity value of the paid-up endowment policy plus accumulated dividends. It was one of several such checks presented to the hospital during the year.

The first American escapee from a German prison camp to return to the Northwest arrived at Boeing Field on March 27. Major Jerry M. Sage of Tacoma, a tall 27-year-old with a head of curly blond hair, spent almost two years as a prisoner of war. The Germans considered him a troublesome prisoner. He attempted to escape six times before he succeeded. He told a reporter of an attempt to escape from Stalag Luft 3 on July 23, 1943. "There were several of us being taken from the prison in an ambulance to get X-rays. I had heard that the little window in the rear of the ambulance might be removable, and if the window was gone, the outside grill might be removed and that then a man might reach through the opening and open the door. I got the window and grill off, but the door wouldn't open. I knew the ambulance had to go through one woodsy area and it was then or never. I felt I might be too big to squirm through that tiny window but decided to try." While the ambulance rolled down the highway, two of his friends who had been shoved into the vehicle with him, helped push him through the small opening, and he fell to the hard highway behind the moving ambulance. He was free three days before being recaptured by a Gestapo member. His successful escape was the easiest, he explained. "We were in a camp at Szubin, Poland. They alerted us the night of January 20 that we would be marched back into Germany. The Germans were jittery, because the Russian front was drawing close. A few of us dropped out of the column and faded into the woods." Some friendly Poles hid the Americans for a few days until the Russians arrived, took control of them and later turned them over to American forces. When the major's wife, Barbara, and their two sons, Mike, 4, and Terry, 2, met him at the airport, Major Sage scooped up his two sons who stared at their father in awe. Mike summoned the courage to ask, "Are you my Daddy?" And then the whole Sage family went into a collective hug. The major reached up and rumpled his wife's hair and said softly, mischievously, a line obviously out of their courtship: "Sa-a-y! You're pretty!" Major Sage had been president of the senior class at Washington State College when he met his future wife who was president of the school's women students.

Philip Cravat of Spokane, when rescued from a Japanese prison camp in the Philippines was so hungry for sweets that he wired a hotel restaurant to have a three-layer chocolate cake ready for him when he reached home. Hotel officials said the order specified a nine-inch chocolate cake with a filling of cream, figs, and raisins. "You have no idea how hungry we are for sweets after years on a starvation diet," Cravat wrote.

Ernest E. Johnson arrived in Seattle in 1905 as an oiler on a steamship. He enrolled in business college, then started a career in shipping that led to a job as a noted international trade expert. As a United States Maritime Commissioner and State Department representative he investigated Japanese trade practices which he said were unfair to the U.S. His criticisms were published in a book. When the Japanese took the Philippines, they captured Mr. Johnson and placed him in Santo Tomas prison. His friends in Seattle had heard rumors that he was killed but had no details until March 14 when new information arrived. On January 14, the Japanese dragged elderly Ernest Johnson from the prison camp hospital and accused him of being a spy. Without a trial, he was executed by firing squad on that day, shortly before American forces invaded the Philippines. His son, Navy Lieutenant Thor Johnson, discovered his father's grave after the invasion.

A Few of the Many Heroes of March

Sergeant J. Richard Winquist, a radio operator in a mechanized reconnaissance squadron with the Third Army in Germany, was awarded a Bronze Star for meritorious service during a particularly intense barrage. The citation reads in part: "Disregarding his own safety, Winquist raced fully 500 yards to an aid station to obtain medical help for a seriously wounded comrade. Though the shells were bursting all around him, he managed to get to an ambulance and lead it back through the barrage to the wounded man. The alertness and utter fearlessness of Sergeant Winquist doubtless saved the life of his fellow soldier." A graduate of West Seattle High School, Winquist had enlisted in the Army in 1942.

Coast Guard Lieutenant Samuel J. Lord of Redmond was one of the men whose courage and knowledge helped save the assault transport *Callaway* after a fierce Japanese aerial attack during the invasion of Lingayan Gulf. Several Coast Guard members of the crew were killed and many wounded when a plane scored a hit on the superstructure of the ship, starting a fire that flared down to the engine room. Lieutenant Lord's knowledge of fire-damage control was instrumental in controlling the blaze and saving the ship. The Lieutenant's wife and their two children, Francis, 13, and Ruth, 12, had saved the present they bought him for the previous Christmas. The Lieutenant had been in the Pacific war zone for 14 months.

A Flying Fortress was badly damaged by flak while bombing Haganau, Germany. After losing altitude and with one engine smoking, the pilot, co-pilot, navigator and bombardier agreed the plane was doomed and gave the order to bail out. Sergeant Charles H. Borland of Seattle was tail gunner on the plane. He saw four parachutes open and realized four men still remained in the waist of the plane, so he crawled up to join them where the door for exiting the craft was larger. Realizing they were still over German territory, Borland grabbed the engineer and they crawled to the cockpit where Borland took over the co-pilot's seat and the engineer the pilot's seat. Borland switched off the automatic pilot and began to fly the plane himself. He said he was wandering all over the sky until the engineer yelled, "Grab that stick hard." They decided to try reaching friendly territory before bailing out. Luckily a couple of P-54 fighter planes noticed them and flew over to check their situation. Borland made radio contact with one of the pilots who shouted back, "You're flying the wrong way. You're headed back toward Germany." He then helped him find the correct heading. Borland said he was surprised the damaged ship kept going. After about an hour, they were over Free French territory and the plane was rapidly losing altitude, so they all decided to bail out. Borland, the last to leave the ship, landed in a tree near the town of Avatte, France. By the time he climbed to the ground, the whole town was there to greet him. The Flying Fortress circled the area then smashed into a field, spreading metal for a thousand feet when it hit. The following day Borland made it to Paris and was

flown back to his Eighth Air Force base in England. In March he was home on leave and told his parents, "I'm glad to be alive, my only gripe being that we lost the plane on my 46th mission. It was a brand new plane and had been on only two flights. I'm really burned up to have lost it."

Harold F. Reese of Seattle was mining for gold in the Philippines when the Japanese invaded. His mother, living in Kenmore, had not heard from him since the start of the war. Suddenly in early March she received a hastily scribbled letter which said he was fighting with the guerrillas behind enemy lines and held the guerrilla rank of captain.

> After many fights, many escapes, and traveling the unsafe trail for many miles, your son has finally gotten into a position where he can write you a letter of his whereabouts. When I promised you that I would be home for Christmas 1942, I did not know that there would be a war that would stop me from carrying out that promise. This letter is being written in one of the numerous headquarters of the guerrillas in the mountain fastness of the Island of Luzon, with the enemy only one and a half miles away and looking for us everywhere. They have not been chased out yet, but, like Yamashita says, the guerrilla is like a thorn in the flesh, you cannot suffer to dig it out as it has already worked down too deep, almost to the bone.

Reese added that he was about to leave on a mission but would make it through and planned to visit his mother as soon as the war was over. Reese, a Medic in World War I, had lived in the Philippines since 1933.

Sixty-five enlisted men, survivors of the Navy salvage ship Extractor that was mistakenly torpedoed and sunk in the Pacific by an American submarine, arrived in San Francisco on March 3. The submarine captain, upon learning the sinking vessel was American, surfaced to pick up survivors. Among them were four Washington State men: John R. Kirton, Jr., a carpenter's mate from Bothell; Clarence E. Hadlock, an electrician's mate from

Raymond; John J. Thompson, a seaman from Spokane and Richmond L. Marsh, a seaman from Centralia.

Pfc. Robert Lee Ellis, son of Mr. and Mrs. Floyd E. Ellis of Seattle, was killed in action in Germany his parents were informed on March 14. Private Ellis was with a 94th Division mortar crew during a drive on the Rhine at the time of his death. Robert and his older brother, Lieutenant James R. Ellis of the Army Air Corps, joined the service on the same day, March 4, 1943. Robert Ellis went overseas in July 1944 and was involved in the invasion of France. He was a graduate of Franklin High School, where he played on the football team and in his senior year was voted the most inspirational player. He was vice president of the school's Boy's Club and was elected to the Inter-School Council. He graduated with honors and had attended the University of Washington before entering the service. In addition to his parents and soldier brother Jim, a younger brother, John W. Ellis, survived him.

Lieutenant Vance McKinney was killed in Western Germany on February 1, his family was notified in March. A member of the 9th Division, Lieutenant McKinney had been in the European Theatre four months and in the Army for four years. Previous to his service in Europe he had been an instructor with the 104th Division at Camp Carson, Colorado, and had served ten months in Alaska. He was a graduate of Hoquiam High School and had completed three years at the University of Washington before entering the service.

Private Robert H. Piro of Seattle enlisted in the army in early 1943 and trained at Camp Hale Colorado as a ski trooper. He was killed in Italy on February 22 while serving with the ski troops of the 40th Mountain Infantry Division. This graduate of Broadway High School was a pre-med student at the University when he joined the service.

Lieutenant Jack T. Barrie was reported missing in action over Germany on February 19. A P-51 fighter pilot, he had completed 30 missions from his 8th Air Force Base in England. He recently had been awarded the Air Medal for action during a raid over the Ruhr Valley when he forced a Nazi plane to crash without firing a shot at it. He promptly sent the medal to his wife Martha in Buckley, WA. She received it two days before he was reported missing. Lieutenant Barrie later was listed as killed in action.

Navy Machinist Mate Edward A. Welfelt was aboard the *Houston* when it was sunk in a sea battle near Java in 1942. For three years he was listed as missing, but his parents in Seattle had not given up hope that their 26-year-old son might be alive. In March, two brief prisoner-of-war post cards arrived in the mail. They immediately recognized their son's handwriting. He said he was alive but a prisoner of the Japanese and interned in Thailand. Welfelt, a West Seattle High School, was not listed as dead on any casualty lists, so he apparently survived his ordeal.

Pfc. William H. Downey, 20, was listed as missing in action in Belgium on December 17. On March 23, his parents in Seattle received a penciled note on a German Stalag post card on which their son wrote:

> Dear Mom and Dad: I'm sorry to say I'm a prisoner of war, but I haven't a scratch on me. Go as soon as possible to the Red Cross to see about sending me food, clothing, and tobacco. I am in a camp with British fellows. There is no reason to worry. I'll be back home in no time. Please tell all my friends to write. I will probably write every week. Please don't worry, everything is all right.

Private Downey was a Lincoln High School graduate and attended Whitman College before entering the Army in July 1943. He transferred to the Army Specialized Training Program to study engineering until the program was suddenly canceled and all students transferred to the infantry.

Donald A. Medford was an all-city basketball and track star at Seattle's Lincoln High School in 1941. On December 4, 1944, at age 22, he was killed in action in Germany, a fact his family did not learn until March 1945. Medford had trained as a paratrooper with the 82nd Air-Borne Division, but was injured during a practice jump in England. After recovering, he was transferred by the Army to the 14th Infantry Division. In his last letter home dated three days before his death, Sergeant Medford wrote: "I ate my Thanksgiving dinner out of my helmet at the front and am in a hurry now as it sounds like a battle coming on." His wife Dorothy, baby son, Gary, and his parents survived him.

Private Richard H. Wille, a graduate of Seattle's Roosevelt High School, had attended the University of Washington before enlisting in the Army in 1942. He was a member of a tank-recovery unit advancing against enemy elements at Alsace, France, when he was killed in action. The 22-year-old soldier had received basic training at Fort Lewis and later received specialized training in small arms at the Aberdeen Proving Grounds. He was sent to Europe in November 1944 and landed at Marseille, France.

Ernest Kozlowski fought in the Spanish Civil War before joining the U.S. Army at the start of World War II. On March 27 his wife Mabel, who lived in Seattle, was informed that Private Kozlowski had died of wounds suffered on Leyte. She was sent his posthumously awarded Purple Heart Medal. Private Kozlowski, 36, was a scout with the 77th Infantry Division when hit by an enemy rifle bullet while leading the advance against the enemy on December 20. He died the next day. A letter to Mrs. Kozlowslki from General Douglas MacArthur read in part; "I cannot express to you the poignancy of my regret at the death of your husband. I have lost a gallant comrade-in-arms and with you mourn a splendid gentleman." Kozlowski was born in Prosser, Benton County, and had attended Seattle College before entering the Abraham Lincoln Brigade during the Spanish Civil War. He fought for two years with the Loyalist army but suffered not a wound. Among his survivors was a brother, Sergeant Frank Kozlowski, a veteran of both World Wars, who was serving in France, and four sisters.

Pfc. Ralph D. Spies, born and schooled in Peshastin, Chelan County, was 20 years old when killed on November 19, 1944 on Leyte. Trained at Camp Beale, California, he was sent overseas in October 1942 without receiving a furlough home. He served in the New Guinea and Netherlands East Indies campaigns before being shipped to the Philippines. A letter from his commanding officer to his parents stated, "Ralph was acting as a scout in advance of a patrol attacking an enemy machine-gun position. The patrol had almost reached the objective when it suddenly came under fire from both flanks and several members of the patrol were killed or wounded."

Lieutenant Martin Faust was killed over Italy in 1943 but his parents in Seattle had never received any details about his death. Then on March 28, a letter was received from Mrs. Mariana Young in Oakland, California, the mother of Richard Young, an Army Air Force captain who had been a close friend of Lieutenant Faust. She explained she had been seeking their address for some time. She wrote:

> My son, Richard, went overseas with your son. In fact, the evening they left Oakland, Dick brought Martin to our home. It seems that when the boys passed the Statue of Liberty on their way over, they made some very solemn vows to each other. One was that in case either was lost, the other would carry on for the one gone. When Dick had finished his 100 missions, and had an opportunity to return to the States, he stayed on to try to fulfill the pledge. He always said, 'I must make many more missions to carry on for Marty.' So he completed 196 missions in all.

In another part of her letter, Mrs. Young wrote, "Our son Richard has a piece of an Italian plane. A fellow who claimed to have shot down the plane that struck Marty gave it to Dick. He wanted you to have it." Lieutenant Faust, born in Seattle in 1918, had graduated from Lincoln High in 1936 where he was prominent in baseball and basketball. In 1941 he graduated from the University of Washington, went into the Air Force, was sent overseas in April 1943, and served in Africa and Sicily. He was shot down on his 28th mission while returning to his Sicilian base from a raid in Italy. He was awarded the Air Medal with three Oak-Leaf Clusters and the Purple Heart. His wife, Jerrie, lived in California, and he had two brothers also in the service.

The wife of William H. Poston received word in late March that her 27-year-old husband, a member of the Merchant Marine, was reported lost at sea and presumed dead. He was aboard a tanker blown up in the South Pacific by a Japanese plane. Posten, born in Port Townsend, attended schools there where he played both baseball and football. He later enrolled at the University of Washington and taught sheet metal engineering at Todd Pacific Shipyards. He went to sea nine months before he lost his life.

Ivan L. Munns of Walla Walla enlisted in the Navy in 1944 and went through boot camp at Farragut, Idaho. The thought of killing even an enemy bothered him, but he wanted to help win the war. He eventually became a medic, a Navy Corpsman assigned to the U.S. Marines, with the rank of Pharmacy Mate 3rd Class. On March 6, while trying to rescue a soldier wounded in the battle to take Iwo Jima, he was killed three weeks before his 20th birthday and was buried with full military honors at Mountain View Cemetery in Walla Walla. He had been awarded the Navy Cross, Purple Heart, and a Presidential Unit Citation.

To end this report of state war news of March 1945, here is a bit of sunshine that foretold the future. The number of discharged veterans enrolled at the University of Washington passed the 300 mark as the new semester opened March 5. The University had planned for twice that number but not until fall quarter of the next school year. Dean Newhouse, director of student affairs, predicted that as many as 3,000 ex-servicemen might eventually be enrolled on the campus. He had warm praise for the veterans in the student body. "They are extremely efficient leaders," he said. "I can't compliment them too highly. They have brought maturity and experience to the school that is a real influence. They do not wish to be regarded as a group apart. As one fellow put it, 'It doesn't matter now whether I was a Marine, a Navy man or in the Army. Now I'm an engineering student, and I'm looking ahead, not backward.'"

April 1945

Local Business Stories of April

Boeing's last B-17 rolled out of Seattle Plant 2 on April 7 signifying the completion of the conversion of the plant to the production of B-29 Superfortresses. From that date on, Boeing facilities in Seattle, Renton, Vancouver, B. C., Wichita and eight Western Washington branch plants were devoted entirely to building B-29s. The last B-17, the 6,981st Flying Fortress produced at Plant 2, was decorated with bombs of many colors, each bearing the place and date of raids made by B-17s. A B-29 likewise was on display with bombs and dates indicating B-29 raids. A formation of six Boeing bombers flew over the city at 4 p.m. to commemorate the changeover. Other U.S. airplane companies continued to produce B-17s.

The Pacific Northwest Regional War Labor Board ordered Bremerton restaurants to abide by wage scales authorized by the government. In some restaurants cooks were paid as much as $16 a day when the top allowable wage was $8.64 a day. Some waitresses also were being paid above the legal limit of $3 a day. The manpower shortage and paying above the legal limit had resulted in widespread pirating of restaurant help. After being warned, the restaurants and union representatives agreed to bring wages into compliance with War Labor Board dictates.

Personal Experiences of Local Citizens

The shortage of hotel rooms complicated life for returning service personnel. Lieutenant Jim Hannon went overseas in April 1943 to serve

Headlines:
April 1945

April 8 :
RED ARMY DRIVES 3 MILES INTO VIENNA

April 12 :
FDR DIES SUDDENLY AT WARM SPRINGS, GEORGIA

April 15-30 :
AMERICAN TROOPS FREE INMATES OF SEVERAL DEATH CAMPS

April 19 :
U.S. FIRST ARMY TAKES LEIPZIG, 300,000 GERMAN TROOPS SURRENDER

April 23 :
RED ARMY BLASTS INTO BERLIN

April 25 :
UN DELEGATES IN SAN FRANCISCO FORM AN INTERNATIONAL ORGANIZATION

April 27 :
YANK AND RUSSIAN ARMIES CONVERGE AT ELBE RIVER

April 28 :
ITALIAN PARTISANS KILL BENITO MUSSOLINI

April 29:
GERMAN ARMIES IN ITALY SURRENDER

April 30 :
ADOLF HITLER COMMITS SUICIDE IN BERLIN BUNKER

As they battled their way up the boot of Italy, the American Nisei soldiers took many German prisoners. Here several Japanese-American soldiers escort a dozen German soldiers through an Italian village on the way to a prisoner-of-war camp.

as a paratrooper on the Italian front. German troops captured him in February 1944. After 11 months in a Nazi stalag, he was freed and four months later arrived in his hometown Seattle with his wife. A former student at Seattle College and a graduate of Ballard High School, the lieutenant called on the Officers' Information Bureau at the Olympic Hotel for help in obtaining a hotel room. They were sent to a small hotel and shown to their room, where they washed up and went to visit friends in Madison Park. About midnight they returned to the hotel and asked for their room key, but the clerk told them that someone with a higher priority was in their bed. Remembering his days as a prisoner of war when he was provided no real bed, the Lieutenant was not too upset. He called some friends who knew some friends with a spare bed. The Hannons stayed with Mr. and Mrs. William Wallace for a couple of days and while there enjoyed a visit with the lieutenant's mother, formerly of Seattle, who had traveled down from Winnipeg to be with her son. When his leave ended, Lieutenant Hannon reported for reassignment at the redistribution center for former prisoners of war that was located in Santa Barbara, California.

Mary Kenna was a businesswoman with several different interests. She was a landlady renting space to three couples, a legal secretary to a Seattle lawyer, and she operated the "Wedding House" in her home on Queen Anne Hill. The last mentioned, she said, was a hobby originated after she realized service personnel and their girl friends sometimes needed a place for a home-like wedding. During the eight months prior to her own marriage to a Navy ensign, she had arranged 42 weddings. In April, after her own honeymoon, she was back helping young folks become man and wife.

The Seattle USO Council, chaired by Stephen F. Chadwick, worked with a committee of Seattle women, chaired by Mrs. A. Scott Bullitt, to open a fine new Service Women's Club in a four-story building at 214 University Street. At the opening ceremony, all four branches of the service were represented.

Ross Taylor and Charles Lovett were among several recently honorably discharged veterans who had dropped out of high school to join the services. Now they and 22 others were enrolled at Broadway High School to earn credits needed for graduation. The program was the first in Seattle designed for veterans needing a high school diploma. The veterans appeared to be little different from other students until the effects of battlefield experiences were noticed. The hand of one student was partially shot away. Another was sightless in one eye. A few were still attempting to control their occasional battle fatigue palsy. They tended to stick together and at first did not mingle with the other students. They considered themselves to be more mature than their fellow students and talked of plans for the future now that the war appeared to be nearly over.

An April visitor to the large Seattle Naval Hospital in April found 15 well-known Seattle physicians working there as Navy officers. Most of them had seen overseas service. Their civilian shingles were in the closet until the war was won, but their names were familiar to thousands of their Seattle patients. Rather than speak of their own exploits, they preferred to tell of the spirit of young Americans, the gallantry of the men who died in the field, of men mended and returned to action, or wounded and returned home to recuperate. The fifteen M. D.s were: Captain C. E. Watts; Commanders Clyde Jensen, Albert C. Ohman, E. A. LeCocq, H. L. Leavitt, John F. Ramsay and Frank H. Wanamaker; Lieutenant Commanders Hale Haven, Kenneth B. Brilhart, J. L. Ash, J. A. Duncan, Carl D. F. Jensen, Norman W. Clein and Austin G. Friend; and Lieutenant W. A. McMahon. Commander Walter Voegtlin served at the hospital for a time but had returned to sea duty. Commander Leavitt was most impressed by the spirit of the wounded men. More than one of them, when resting in a bed next to a wounded comrade, told him, "Take care of him first, Doc. I'll be all right."

Charles Weil of Vashon Island was one of the older Americans imprisoned by the Japanese. A marine engineer, he was captured when the American Mail Line freighter *Capillo* was sunk in Manila Harbor at the outbreak of the war. He was 74 when he arrived home after 38 months in Santo Tomas prison camp in the Philippines. Weil arrived with a gray beard hanging nearly to his waistline. He told how his whiskers began growing in January 1942 when he was herded with 5,000 other prisoners into the camp. They never saw a razor, knife or pair of scissors during more than three years of internment. Freed from prison in February 1945, he decided to keep his whiskers until his wife "could pull them out personally." Weil weighed 219 pounds before the war, but lost 91 pounds during his imprisonment.

He told how the Japanese turned meaner as the war began going against them. The daily prison routine was roll call each morning at 7, with all prisoners hoping for food; another line up at noon while again hoping for food; and the same at 5 p.m., when prisoners were each provided three or four ounces of rice cooked without salt. The rescue came almost too late, he said. The wounded were carried out on stretchers and when Weil was helped out to climb on an allied tank, he was too weak even to carry the small packet of his personal possessions including the 150-page diary he had kept during his incarceration. "We were all skeletons. I could hang my hat on my shoulder blades. But many were worse off than I," the aged engineer said. He added that he intended to get a thorough medical overhauling. Confronted with three meals a day, he had to forego at least one of them. His body simply could not absorb that much food. And after years of little exercise, his legs refused to follow his brain and he could walk only with difficulty. Now his wife Minnie daughter Olga and granddaughter Roberta were taking good care of him on Vashon Island.

On April 17, it was reported that Mrs. L. E. Lippe's husband, a civilian Navy employee, was killed when the Japanese bombed the Navy Yard at Cavite in the Philippines. The couples' only child, Mary Ellen, was born after his death and Mrs. Lippe and Mary Ellen were captured along with her son by an earlier marriage, Marvin, 6, and held at Santo Tomas prison. Another son Myron, 11 years old, was kept in a separate building with the men and older boys. When American forces appeared, Japanese soldiers entrenched in a camp building held Myron as a hostage for two days while the battle raged. He later was rescued. Mrs. Lippe said she considered Seattle to be her hometown since she and her husband were married there in 1930. She and her three children were treated at the Treasure Island Naval Hospital in San Francisco before returning to Seattle.

Mr. and Mrs. Arthur E. Hughes from Seattle were also at Cavite Naval Base during the Japanese bombing of December 10, 1941. They were treated at Treasure Island Hospital after being liberated. Arthur Hughes worked as a traffic clerk at the base and his wife as a clerk-typist. Captured by the Japanese, they had survived three years of privation and near-starvation. However, their joy at being freed was short lived because they quickly learned their son, Lyle Hughes, a radioman in the Navy, had been captured and was believed to still be in a Japanese prison camp.

Miss Yoshike Tsuji of Auburn, a Japanese-American who had been evacuated to the Hart Mountain, Wyoming, relocation center, received a federal payment of $9,260 for 20 acres of land owned by her family. The Army needed the acreage as part of the site for the huge Auburn Army Depot. Harold Anderson, special attorney for the lands division of the Department of Justice, announced the payment.

As the first few relocated Japanese-Americans returned to King and Pierce Counties, protest groups became active. This caused Seattle Mayor William F. Devin to form a local civic unity committee to work with the Civilian War Commission to ease the situation. Seattle banker George H. Greenwood, chairman of the committee, called movements against the Japanese-Americans "deplorable," and condemned such activities. More than 150 University of Washington students crowded into an anti-Japanese meeting on Beacon Hill to distribute pro-Nisei pamphlets. They branded as "undemocratic" the threats shouted at them as they handed out the pamphlets and in return shouted questions at members of the "Remember Pearl Harbor League" and asked how the league differed from Nazi persecution groups. A few days later, about 700 persons gathered at another meeting of the same League but soon found the audience overwhelmingly favored return of the Nisei and strongly supported the principal speaker Dr. Linden A. Mander, Political Science Professor from the University of Washington. He reminded the audience that all returning Nisei had been given Army clearance and had proved their loyalty. Mrs. Mary Farquarson, a former state senator, asked, "Is it not true that no Japanese-American ever has been convicted of sabotage and that the dozen convictions of saboteurs on the Pacific Coast and in Hawaii were white persons, not Nisei?" This brought a roar of laughter followed by applause. John L. Hamilton told about a Nisei youth, a neighbor of his on Yarrow Point, who recently had returned from Italy after being wounded in action. "He still cannot walk. I was in this war, too," Hamilton said, "and I have far more respect for that boy than for some young Americans who avoided the draft with one flimsy excuse or another."

Madigan General Hospital Keeps Growing

A $3 million addition to the Fort Lewis Station Hospital was begun in 1943. Actually it was built outside the boundaries of the fort but still on the military reservation near where Pierce and Thurston Counties meet. The 58 brick and tile buildings were constructed under the direction of Seattle District Engineers. The added space was needed because sick and wounded soldiers were being returned from overseas at the rate of 36,000 a month. Under the Army's improved treatment schedule, patients were being sent from Army hospital advanced reconditioning classes back to active duty at the rate of 6,000 a week. About 2,000 others who were too badly wounded to resume active duty were discharged each week. Madigan had become one of the three largest Army hospitals in the United States and was a center of activity in the "speed-up" reconditioning program. As one doctor said, "Hospitalization no longer means a rest cure during which uninjured muscles became soft, the patient's mind idle, and his spirits increasingly depressed." Under the new reconditioning program, the period of convalescence was reduced by up to 33 percent by incorporating a program of progressively tougher physical exercise, starting with bed calisthenics. The program, inaugurated in March 1944, was increasingly successful in rehabilitating the wounded and ill at Madigan.

A Few the Many Heroes of April

Marine Lieutenant Robert W. Sherman of Seattle, a Roosevelt High School graduate, was awarded the Distinguished Flying Cross posthumously for heroism in aerial action with Marine Torpedo Squadron 233. On the night of February 14, Sherman was assigned an aerial mine-laying mission in Simpson Harbor, Rabaul. Over concentrations of heavy automatic anti-aircraft weapons, he made a long, level flight at slow air speed, at a precariously low altitude. Caught in enemy searchlights as he was approaching his object, Sherman maneuvered his plane through intense, accurate anti-aircraft fire. He managed to remain on course despite severe damage to his plane, and released his mine in its assigned location. However Lieutenant Sherman never arrived back at his home base. Young Sherman had trained at the Pasco Naval Base, graduated among the highest in his class, and was the first cadet to complete flying tests in Pasco. His parents, a sister and a brother survived him.

Staff Sergeant Frank R. Goulet, 22, a native of Sunnyside, was killed in action in Germany on March 1 and buried in Belgium. He had been in the Army six years, most recently as a member of General Patton's Third Army. The Sergeant's widow, Jean, and 1-year-old daughter, Alice Marie, lived in Minnesota with her parents. Also surviving him were a brother and 3 sisters.

Captain Frank O'Laughlin, former traffic officer in the Seattle Police Department, died in action on Palawan Island in the Philippines on March 6. His mother and his wife, Marjorie, and their three-year-old son, Philip, all in Seattle, survived him. Infantry Captain O'Laughlin had served in Australia and was wounded during the invasion of New Guinea. Besides the Purple Heart, he held the Bronze Star Medal for bravery.

Lieutenant Colonel A. T. Greathouse, 41, former detective in the Seattle Police Department, was home in mid-April after 32 months in Japanese prison camps. "I've lived through it once, I don't care to live through it again," he told reporters in explanation of his reluctance to talk about his experiences. Colonel Greathouse was an executive officer with the Philippine Army when taken prisoner. For a time in Bilibid prison he was confined to the prison hospital with beri-beri, the result of living on 700 calories of cereal a day, about one-quarter of an average diet. While there, the colonel followed reports of the approaching American invasion on a clandestine radio set. An Army engineer officer constructed the radio in a canteen cup that sat in plain view on a table. The Japanese knew a radio was in the hospital somewhere and literally tore the boards from the floor searching for it. They never found it. After returning to the U.S., Colonel Greathouse convalesced at Madigan General Hospital while regaining some of the more than 50 pounds he lost during his imprisonment. Then in late April, after four years away, he began enjoying life again at his Seattle home with his wife and their daughter, Betty.

Lieutenant Tor Torland, a well-known Seattle skier and newsman, was among the first to cross the Rhine on the Remagen Bridge after it was captured by American troops. Here are a few paragraphs from a letter he wrote to his parents in Woodway Park:

> The M.P. waves us on: 'O.K., go ahead. Five miles an hour.' We are on the bridge and creep slowly ahead. Nobody says a word. Suddenly a sighing hiss, followed by two more. Three little clouds of dust float up at the other end. A miss. Two more shells scream over. We jolt to a stop, and a combat engineer runs out and levers our wheel over a rough spot with a pole. He's just a kid, but he doesn't seem fazed at all. Along the side

In city, town and hamlet across Washington State residents quietly celebrated the victory in Europe. All realized the war in the Pacific was yet to be won. These three employees of the Bremerton Navy Yard hopefully display the morning news headline. Kitsap Regional Library, 2661.

of the roadway on the bridge we see the twisted corpses of G.I.s who were caught in the open. At last the wheels of our jeep bump onto the down ramp. The crowd in the tunnel lets out a cheer. An M.P. stands there waving us down the road. We are among the first Yanks across the Rhine. When it's done, we feel good about it — now that it's over.

Master Sergeant Virginia E. Stacy had followed the war from Pearl Harbor to Italy. But she was enjoying being home after her adventures with the first WAC contingent to be assigned overseas duty. Her parents picked her up at the War Department Personnel Center at Fort Lewis, their first meeting in 27 months. "It's good to find home like you left it," she said, "and you don't have to be back on American soil to know why you were over there. When I saw Pearl Harbor, I knew there was just one

thing for all of us to do — to help as much as we could in every way possible." Sergeant Stacy added, "I can't get used to seeing the bright and shiny automobiles here, and the ice cream and pudding! It doesn't seem possible. Being overseas really magnifies these things in your mind."

Robert Reece, 21, a Navy gunner, and Russell Reece, 18, a coxswain, had not seen each other for a year and a half when they held an impromptu reunion at Pearl Harbor. The brothers were assigned to the South Pacific. They wrote their mother in Seattle that they hoped their father, a merchant mariner in the South Pacific, could join them at their next get-together. Both Reece sons had attended Eatonville High School.

Marine paratrooper Mike Pizzuto of Sedro Woolley was killed on Iwo Jima on February 21, the Navy Department informed his mother on April 6. A graduate of Sedro Woolley High School, he was a member of the schools 1939 champion football team and won letters in wrestling. He also was a popular musician with his accordion and participated in dramatics. His parents, three brothers and two sisters survived him.

Private Berl O. Schmidt, 21, was killed in action in Germany in late February, the Army notified his parents in Bremerton. Young Schmidt went overseas in April 1944 and was stationed in England until July when his field artillery battalion helped the allies fight through France, Belgium and Holland. Shortly after entering Germany, Schmidt was killed. The young man was a graduate of Central Kitsap High School at Silverdale before being inducted into the Army. His parents and two sisters survived him.

Many casualties occurred in the United States during training exercises. Donald G. Biggs, 21, was one of eight Navy men killed in an April crash of a Martin Mariner plane into San Diego Bay. His parents received the telegram at their Kirkland home. Young Biggs, an aviation radioman first class, was a graduate of O'Dea High School, where he was active in sports and journalism. For several months before his death he had been attached to a naval rescue squadron at San Diego while training for overseas duty. He was the 16th O'Dea graduate to die in the war.

Lieutenant Paul S. Ostrander, 20, had been missing in action over Europe since March 31 his parents were informed in mid-April. A few weeks later they were told he had been killed in action. The Lieutenant, a Mustang fighter pilot, was credited with shooting down at least six enemy planes and held the Air Medal with four Oak-Leaf Clusters. In March he was among the 45 Mustang pilots who destroyed 32 of 39 attacking enemy planes as they escorted bombers deep into Germany. Before joining the Air Force, Paul Ostrander had graduated from Roosevelt High School and attended Pacific University at Forest Grove, Oregon. His father, the Reverend Dr. Clinton E. Ostrander, was pastor of University Congregational Church in Seattle.

Technical Sergeant Emil J. Anhoury, 29, was killed in action off New Guinea in late March when the Japanese launched a surprise air attack. Sergeant Anhoury entered the service in 1941 and was with the Army Air Force Air Transport Command at the time of his death. In 1942, while stationed in Seattle, he won the Northwest G.I. handball singles championship. His wife, Eleanor, and year-old daughter, Susan Marie, in Seattle, and his mother in Portland survived him.

Lieutenant Arthur (Jerry) Fallon was killed in action on Luzon in early April. He had been in the service four years and was a member of the 1st Cavalry Division at the time of his death. He was a graduate of Franklin High School and the University of Washington, where he majored in interior decorating and was an accomplished pianist and pipe organist. He was one of the first 100 men drafted from the Seattle area. On the day he left for overseas, Lieutenant Fallon had a telephone conversation with his brother, Lieutenant Commander Walter E. Fallon, whom he had not seen for 18 months. The brothers were

only a few miles apart in San Francisco but did not have time to meet in person.

Mr. and Mrs. W. A. Carton of Seattle learned on April 27 how their son, Staff Sergeant Richard E. Carton, gunner on a B-24 Liberator bomber, died on February 8. Sergeant Carton's squadron left early in the morning to bomb Iwo Jima. They released their bombs and had started the return trip to their base on Guam when an enemy fighter rammed into their B-24. Both planes burst into flames and the Liberator exploded. None of the crew was seen to escape. Sergeant Carton held the Air Medal with Oak-Leaf Cluster and the Distinguished Flying Cross. His parents in April received his Purple Heart and two citations, one from General Arnold, and a unit citation signed by President Roosevelt. Richard Carton died on his 37th mission, four months before his 23rd birthday.

Sergeant William Imamoto, a member of the Medical Corps of the 422nd Infantry Regiment, was killed in action on the Italian front on April 9. Born in Seattle, he graduated from Port Orchard's Union High School. At the time of his death, his mother, Mrs. Su Yeko, and sister, Mrs. Leo Fiyinami, were living at the Japanese Relocation Center at McGhee, Arkansas. The last letter the Sergeant sent his brother in Seattle said, in part, "Greetings from someone in old beat-up Italy. I guess you heard of us rescuing the lost battalion in the Vosges Mountains in France. While in France, I had a chance to visit the city of Nice, really a nice place, and the gals were lovely. Well, as I have lots of letters to write, I'll say bye for now and good luck."

May 1945

Victory in Europe (V-E) Day

The 19 draftees waited at the Harrison Street Armory in Seattle for the bus that would take them to the Fort Lewis receiving center. The date was May 7, the day the newspapers said the Germans would surrender. These men, most of them family men in their late 20s and early 30s, showed

May 7:
GERMANY SURRENDERS TO ALLIES, EUROPEAN BATTLEFIELDS FALL SILENT

May 8:
PRESIDENT TRUMAN WARNS AMERICANS "VICTORY IS BUT HALF WON"

May 11:
KAMAKAZI PILOT SMASHES INTO USS BUNKER HILL, KILLING 373

May 12:
U.S. ENDS LEND-LEASE PROGRAM TO SOVIET UNION

May 26:
B-29s DEVESTATE TOKYO, HIT ROYAL PALACES

their delight at the news. One remarked, "What a day to get inducted. At least we ought to be able to take one crack at the Pacific enemy." Another said, "I have a twin brother in Burma. It's sure swell news about the Germans. Now maybe I'll be able to give him a hand." Another, grinning like a schoolboy said, "It shouldn't be long now."

Men of the Fleet, some of them veteran survivors of ship sinkings, voiced a common concern, the hope that Americans planning to celebrate the German surrender would remember that "the hardest part of winning the war is yet to come."

The joy at the news of the German surrender was tempered for thousands of Washington families with kinfolk or friends listed as missing, or as prisoners of war, or as killed in action. Judy Robinson of Seattle, whose husband, Colonel Charles Gordon Robinson, was a Marauder pilot lost over Germany, was hoping that the end of the war would see her husband come home or at least solve his disappearance. She knew other families in the State with members missing on the war fronts. "The surrender buoys our hopes," she continued, "but then we fear we'll find out at last the whole end of things has come, but you keep pushing that thought away. But I am glad for all the people who will be coming home now."

Mrs. Floyd E. Ellis of Seattle, whose son, Bob, gave his life during the Third Army's bitter drive for the Rhine, felt a bit of resentment at the jubilation over the victory. "Your first reaction is that glorification of this victory is sowing the seeds for the next war. It seems that at a time like this, the casualties should be emphasized. It's been such a deadly business and we've sacrificed so much for the victory. Of course, I can't blame those who still have someone over there being relieved. I would be too. The main hope we have to look forward to is accomplishments such as the San Francisco conference to form a United Nations."

A Seattle bombardier, Lieutenant Earl Fisher, Jr., was credited with dropping the last bomb delivered by the Eighth Air Force against German defenders of "Fortress Europe." According to the news release, Fisher's epochal final bomb dropped on the Skoda Munitions Works at Pilsen, Czechoslovakia, at 11:16 a.m. on April 25. Young Fisher had graduated from Queen Anne High School and the University of Washington. His father was serving as a warrant officer in the South Pacific.

On May 10, the U.S. casualties in the German fighting during the month of April were reported: 5,324 killed in action, 25,407 wounded, and 3,867 missing, a total of 34,598 casualties. The war department reported that since Pearl Harbor American combat casualties (killed, missing, wounded, prisoners of war) had surpassed 1,000,000.

On May 9, German prisoners of war being held in a compound at Fort Lawton were assembled to hear the official U.S. Army proclamation that Germany had surrendered and that their government had ceased to exist. The prisoners, most of them captured during the Normandy break-through, had access to newspapers and radio and had known for some time that the collapse of Germany was imminent. Only a few seemed to be visibly affected as the proclamation was read. The prisoners worked at the Port of Embarkation preparing vehicles for overseas shipment.

On May 10 the War Department issued an explanation of the point system for discharging veterans. Service personnel were polled and 90 percent believed those who had been overseas and in combat longest and those with children should be discharged first. One point was given for each month of service since September 16, 1940. Another point was earned for each month served overseas. Five points were awarded for the first and each additional award, such as the Army's Distinguished Service Cross, Legion of Merit, Silver Star, Distinguished Flying Cross, Soldier's Medal, Bronze Star, Air Medal, Purple

Heart and battle participation stars. Also five points were awarded for the Navy Cross, Distinguished Service Medal, Legion of Merit and other Navy decorations. Twelve points were awarded for each child under 18 years of age up to a limit of three children. Men with the highest point totals became eligible for release first except for those possessing special skills required in the war against Japan for which qualified replacements were not available.

On May 12, the first three Washington State soldiers released under the point system at Fort Lewis were Sergeant Stanley V. Snow of Cusick, Pend Oreille County; Corporal Louis Brechemin of Seattle; and Corporal Marcel Aurestouilh of Richmond, Benton County. Snow and Brechemin had been on duty at Hickam Field, Hawaii, on December 7, 1941, when the Japanese first attacked. Across America on May 12 more than 2,000 cheering American veterans of World War II who had given three or four years of their lives to the armed services, happily hurried out of Army camps and back into civilian life. Their discharges under the point system came as a surprise to many of these men. More than 1,000 had just returned to camp from 45-day furloughs, fully expecting to see combat in the Pacific Theatre.

Civilians, too, began to be rewarded as a result of the war in Europe ceasing. On May 14, the War Production Board announced a 50 percent increase in passenger car tire rations for the month. This added a half million tires to the number to be distributed by the Office of Price Administration. Furthermore, the promise was made that in the future tires would be available in increasing numbers because of decreasing military demand. Since most American families were driving on well-worn rubber, this was considered very good news.

As if to remind Americans the war in the Pacific was not yet won, on May 5, a woman and five children died in the woods near Lakeview, Oregon. These fatalities were the only recorded World War II deaths within the U.S. mainland caused by enemy attacks. For several months Japan had been sending balloons across the Pacific on wind currents. Attached to the balloons were bombs that exploded if moved. The War Department kept the Oregon tragedy secret until May 31, not wanting the enemy to know their balloons were successfully crossing the ocean. Killed were the wife of a pastor, and five children she and her husband were escorting on a fishing trip. All the dead were from Bly, Oregon.

Persons in the News

Staff Sergeant Henry H. Gosho, whose parents had operated a Seattle drugstore before the war, served 16 months in the Burma-India Theatre working with an Army Combat Intelligence unit attached to Merrill's Marauders. He volunteered for duty in November 1942 while living at Minidoka Relocation Center. The sergeant had been awarded the Presidential Unit Citation, Bronze Star, Pacific Ribbon with three campaign stars, the Combat Infantry Badge, and the shoulder patch of Merrill's Marauders. When Gosho enlisted, Army doctors had declared him flat-footed and physically not qualified for combat. However he wore out four pairs of shoes walking more than 1,000 miles and contracted malaria seven times and survived several other tropical diseases. On May 2 he was convalescing at Fitzsimmons General Hospital in Colorado before receiving a medical discharge.

Colonel Donald E. Hillman, 27, of Seattle, a former prisoner of war in Germany, arrived in Washington, D.C. on V-E Day escorting two German officers. A Thunderbird pilot with many decorations, Colonel Hillman was taken prisoner in October 1944 and incarcerated at Stalag Luft 3. As the Allies drew close, the Germans marched the prisoners across Germany to Moosburg where Hillman escaped.

Headlines:
June 1945

June 5:
GERMANY DIVIDED INTO U.S., RUSSIAN, BRITISH AND FRENCH ZONES

June 7:
GERMAN CITIZENS FORCED TO VIEW CONCENTRATION CAMP HORRORS

June 14:
BRITISH TROOPS LIBERATE BURMA

June 19:
AMERICANS FORCE JAPANESE BACK ON OKINAWA

June 26:
50 ALLIED NATIONS SIGN HISTORIC UN CHARTER IN SAN FRANCISCO

June 28:
FORD COMPANY COMPLETES FINAL WAR CONTRACT; HAS PRODUCED 8,600 BOMBERS, 278,000 JEEPS, 57,000 AIRCRAFT ENGINES.

Hillman obtained the help of two German officers with the understanding that they would be his prisoners and he would try to ease their situation after Germany lost the war. The three hid in farmhouses until the colonel managed to contact his old outfit, the Ninth Air Force. He and the Germans were flown to London, then on to Washington. Colonel Hillman told his parents by phone that he lost 35 pounds in the march across Germany, but had regained most of it since his escape.

Major Chandler R. Thomas of Seattle led a group of 17 American soldiers off an Army transport at San Francisco on May 31. They had survived nearly four years of war since the Philippines fell to Japan. Some had been in enemy prison camps while others survived in the jungle as guerrillas. They were among more than 1,000 soldiers and several hundred Navy men returning on rotation or as hospital patients aboard the transport.

Navy Lieutenant James R. Crosby, commander of the destroyer escort *Frederick C. Davis,* was killed just a few days before Germany capitulated, when a German submarine sent his ship to the bottom of the Atlantic. The Navy reported a heavy loss of life among the nearly 200 men aboard. Crosby, a Seattle resident and former University of Washington student, was survived by his father and sister.

Pfc. Jack McKenna of Kirkland distinguished himself with gallantry in action while his unit was establishing a beachhead on the Kyll River in Germany. He went to the aid of a wounded man and carried him to safety despite constant machine gun and mortar fire. He was promoted to Sergeant and continued front line duty until he was killed on March 4 at age 21. He was told he had been awarded a Silver Star medal for his bravery but had not yet received it when he died. It was awarded posthumously to his parents, Mr. and Mrs. Horatio McKenna. Their son had graduated from Kirkland High School in 1941 with outstanding grades and was awarded a Harvard scholarship. He completed two years at Harvard before being called into the service.

June 1945

The Washington State National Guard's 161st Regiment

The original 161st Regiment was manned with youth living in towns ranging from Walla Walla to Bellingham. Having fought through many battles, by June 1945, a procession of new faces had replaced men wounded, dead, ill, or reassigned. Still, many of the old-timers remained as commanders and platoon leaders. They were all exhausted from years of war and dreamed of going home to the wheat fields of the Palouse, to the orchards of the Yakima and Wenatchee valleys, to the golf courses of Spokane, to the fishing streams of Western Washington. They hopefully discussed rotation plans and how the new point system might affect them. The big question was, "When are we going to get home?"

Still these men fought on doggedly with their machine guns and rifles, demolition charges and grenades, rooting out determined Japanese from their caves on Luzon. General MacArthur considered them among his top troopers. They had crossed innumerable mountain ridges and served on the front lines without rest for 120 consecutive days.

The 161st Regiment started out as part of 41st Division but was moved to the 25th Division early in the war. Most of the officers and men were from the Pacific Northwest. Colonel James L. Dalton II, led the 161st through the Solomons campaign and was in command at San Manuel. The triumph there brought a "well done" salute from General MacArthur. Later Colonel Dalton was promoted to assistant division commander and given the rank of brigadier general, only to be killed a few months later by a Japanese sniper. Colonel Victor Johnson, a West Point graduate of 1939, and the Sixth Army's youngest full colonel at age 27, was the new 161st commander.

The men paid tribute to Staff Sergeant

Wilbur Triggs of Tacoma, a regimental hero who was awarded the Distinguished Service Cross for the Battle of Bryant Hill. Members of National Guard companies originally from Walla Walla and Yakima scaled steep slopes on hands and knees to reach Japanese positions. Triggs, a hefty, unassuming youth, was credited with killing 25 of the enemy in the battles of San Manuel and Bryant Hill. One buddy said "He's quick on the trigger and he seems to be able to smell the enemy." Sergeant Gordon Gettman of Walla Walla said, "Triggs saved my life on the hill. I was in a shell hole with a Jap soldier rolling grenades down at me. I couldn't get a shot at him, but Triggs spotted him and bumped him off."

The Battalion commander was Major Thorkel M. Hasland of Tacoma, formerly a Washington State College student. His executive officer was Major George H. Russell of Bellingham, a Western Washington College graduate. Literally hundreds of instances of bravery were reported about men of this unit and other units of the Washington State National Guard.

The Long Road Home from Europe

Le Havre, France, was the port through which many weary American soldiers began the journey home from Europe. The rusty steel docks and gray cement rubble of the war-damaged waterfront structures would be remembered by the men who gazed for long hours at the scene as they waited to board a ship. They did not complain. They laughed and even sang because home was not far beyond those slow-moving lines.

The young privates and slightly older colonels stood in lines together and up to 7,000 were loaded on a ship that in peacetime carried perhaps 2,000 passengers. Once aboard, they heeded signs that read, "Do not waste water. Due to the number of troops on board, the water situation has become serious. When washing, shaving or taking a shower, think of the man behind you in line." A three-basin

washroom served 200 officers and the water was turned on only three hours a day. Bunks were stacked four high in the hold and the aisles were filled with barracks bags and battle souvenirs.

Aboard were airmen shot down over Germany and infantrymen captured in the Battle of the Bulge. Folks at home would call them heroes, but they didn't consider themselves as such. They just laughed and joked their way through the 10 days it took to cross the Atlantic.

Doctors aboard were worried that only two meals a day could be served, while 3,000 skinny RAMPs (Recovered American Military Persons) were on the ship. They had been rescued from German Stalags and Work Camps, men who survived death marches from camp to camp. Many were known to have bad stomachs and other health problems but they happily consumed whatever was served. One of them complained, "They told us they would give us six meals a day and special foods, but there are too many of us and they can't do that. Besides, this way we get home quicker. We all agree that we want to be home quick as possible." One officer remarked, "None of these young kids who were prisoners of war are kids any more."

In the holds they napped, thousands of them in the hot and stuffy atmosphere. At night the lights were turned off at 8 o'clock, leaving them with nothing to do. The men were supposed to get four hours of fresh air each day on deck, but they grew bored looking at the sea and many returned to the hold or to the washrooms, or to the corners of passageways where poker games were underway. Some found a corner by the hatch where red exit lights allowed them to read at night. A lieutenant warned one soldier who was crouched under an exit light that he would ruin his eyes. He closed his book until the officer walked away, then started reading again, because he hungered to read anything, and besides there was nothing else to do.

Many arguments developed over minor

subjects such as whether the Springfield or the Garand rifle was the best, which non-coms were most considerate, and whether the G. I. Bill would really help one through college. But the conversations invariably returned to dreams of arriving home, seeing loved ones and planning for the remainder of their lives.

Father's Day, June 17, arrived with thousands of men still on the war fronts. Many had children at home they had never seen. William F. McDaniel of Carnation, Washington, was an aviation electricians' mate with the Navy in the Pacific. His son Donald had arrived on May 31. Lawrence O. Hamilton of Seattle, an ensign who had been in the South Pacific area for three months, was father of a new daughter, Kathleen, born March 14. William D. Bailey of Redmond, a Marine Pfc. serving with an engineer unit in the South Pacific had a new son, William Donald, Jr., born April 30. Charles Nabel, a Sergeant with the Army in Italy, had been wounded twice. His son, Charles Robert Jr. was born November 2, 1944. Fathers such as these were anxious to be back in the Pacific Northwest with their offspring and their wives.

Marcia Katz was at a movie with her 7-year old son, Kenneth, when her husband and Ken's father, Captain Solomon Katz, telephoned from New York. She had not seen her husband for 29 months and when a neighbor called the theater to ask for her, she was summoned to the foyer and she and Kenneth rushed home to return his call. Captain Katz, professor of ancient history at the University of Washington, had been on leave from the University since September 1942 while serving as squadron intelligence officer with the Twelfth Air Force. He had seen action in the North African, Sicilian, and Italian campaigns and had been awarded the Bronze Star Medal for "meritorious service in direct support of combat operations in the Mediterranean Theatre." Now he had furlough papers in his pocket and would be headed home when transportation became available. Kenneth had heard his mother say many times that his daddy might be on the way

home and remained skeptical when she told him that the phone call was from his dad who would soon be home. "You've said that before, Mom," he said. He eventually became convinced that he would soon see his father. His younger sister, Cynthia, 2 years old, had never seen her father. Mrs. Katz said Cynthia became excited too, although she didn't understand quite what the excitement was all about.

Signs the War might be Ending

Washington Senator Hugh Mitchell announced that a board had been created to consider the release of medical officers who were no longer essential to the Army. This brightened the situation at King County's Harborview Hospital where a critical shortage of physicians existed. In fact, there was a countrywide shortage of civilian doctors. Secretary of War Henry L. Stimson said that with the war ended in Europe, his department had requested the early return of Medical Corps officers to civilian status. Only where there was military necessity, were medical doctors to be retained in the service.

The 500th Boeing B-17 built in Seattle, named the "Five Grand," was retired in June after 78 missions. As it rolled from the factory on May 13, 1944, scores of the Boeing employees who built it signed their names on the fuselage. As a result, the plane became a symbol of home-front production. As the Flying Fortress went into action, many of the combat and ground crews added their names. During its combat service, the "Five Grand" knocked two German fighters out of the sky and participated in attacks on chemical plants at Ludwigshaven, submarine pens at Hamburg, and tank and communications targets at Berlin. One of her feats was to fly 12 missions against the Nazis in 13 days. On her maiden bombing run over Germany, she was damaged by flak and forced to make a belly landing at her Eighth Air Force base. This historic bird was assigned to the command of Colonel Harley S. Jones, Army Air Forces Technical Service Command representative at Boeing. On hand to meet the plane on its return to Seattle was Captain P. E.

Kimerer, the pilot who tested "Five Grand" on its Army acceptance flight. Since then the big bomber had been riddled with about 60 flak and bullet holes. Earl Cruzen, 24, a flight test mechanic, one of the workers who signed his name on the famous Flying Fortress, inspected the scarred plane and said, "I never thought she'd be back when she left here. She's been through a lot. Still in good shape, though, considering everything. It's surprising."

Casualty Lists Grow Longer

The pylon-replica of The Washington Monument standing at the east end of Victory Square where University Street meets Fifth Avenue in Seattle had been erected as a memorial to King County servicemen and women who gave their lives in the war. The sides of the pylon rapidly filled with names. On June 3, another 500 names were added, bringing the total of King County war dead to 1,041. Many more names would be added before the list was complete.

Pfc. Ernest H. Columbus, 32, of Seattle was awarded the Bronze Star medal for bravery in action in October 1944. The citation noted that when powder bags near a howitzer caught fire, Columbus acted with alacrity and seized the blazing camouflage net and tugged it away from the cannon. He then fought the flames menacing the ammunition. Though danger of an explosion was imminent, he fought the blaze until it was under control. Pfc. Columbus had not received his medal before being killed by a German bullet in Italy. He was buried at the base of the Italian mountain on which he died, and to honor their fallen comrade, his friends in Cannon Company during May officially dedicated and named an athletic field in honor of Private Columbus.

Lieutenant Donald Sculati was listed as missing in action on May 30. A Mitchell B-25 pilot in the Philippines, the 25-year-old Marine was a graduate of Seattle's Ballard High School and Willamette University at Salem, Oregon. He was prominent in high school student affairs and was elected president of the student body. He also starred in football and received the Nelson award as a leader in athletics. He had been in the service three years and had completed over 150 combat hours before being reported missing. He later was listed as killed in action.

Staff Sergeant Leonard F. Olson, 21, of Edmonds, died in England of wounds received in action three months earlier in Luxembourg. The sergeant had graduated from Edmonds High School in 1942. He was a member of the 26th (Yankee) Division and had been awarded the Expert Infantryman's Badge and the Purple Heart with an Oak-Leaf Cluster, indicating he had been wounded twice.

In late June the parents of Captain John W. Thompson, received tragic word. In October 1944, their 26-year-old son was one of 1,775 prisoners of war forced onto a Japanese ship to be transported away from advancing Allied forces. The ship was unmarked and an American submarine sighted and sank it, killing all those aboard. Captain Thompson, a pharmacy graduate of the University of Montana, had completed R.O.T.C. training on campus and entered the Army in 1939. His parents and a sister in Seattle, and an Army Captain brother in the Philippines survived him.

Lieutenant (j.g.) Charles J. Lightfoot of Seattle suffered a similar fate. A prisoner in the Philippines, he was being moved northward when on September 7, 1944, the transport on which he was a prisoner was sunk. Lieutenant Lightfoot was born in Honolulu and was a grandson of a former governor of Hawaii. He attended the University of Washington and entered the Navy Supply Corps in 1940. He was sent to China in October 1940 and was stationed on a river gunboat and survived it sinking on May 4, 1942. He was taken prisoner when Corregidor fell. His mother survived him, as did three brothers, two in the service and one employed at the Naval Air Station at Sand Point.

Captain William MacDonald, veteran Seattle master mariner of the Alaska run, and half a dozen merchant seamen were rescued when their ship, the *Canada Victory,* was sunk in early June while carrying supplies to

Okinawa. One merchant crewman and two members of the armed guard were lost when the vessel went under. A Navy hospital ship rescued the Captain and other survivors. The War Shipping Administration announced that a Japanese suicide pilot dropped a bomb in the ship's hold before crashing his plane into the vessel.

Europeans Thank Local Red Cross Chapters

During the month many messages from destitute refugees in liberated Europe flooded into the Seattle-King County Chapter of the American Red Cross. Some thanked volunteer seamstresses for the home-sewn garments they sent to French families. One example: Mme. Helies and her family, forced to flee from Brest, thanked the Red Cross for the warm clothing sent for her children. She wrote:

> My happy children entreat me to thank you. I am learning English at school. Excuse me if you please if I make some mistakes. I have seen the American soldiers who have fought against the cruel Germans who burned my house, and where it will be impossible for me to return. I have lost a great quantity of clothes. I thank you very much for the pajama you have send to me. Thank you. Sincerely, Christiane Botharel, Finistere, France.

July 1945

The Fourth of July Celebration

A brilliant sun warmed the thousands lining Second and Third Avenues in Seattle watching the Independence Day parade led by Admiral Marc A. Mitscher and other military and civic dignitaries. About 7,500 marched in uniform, their units interspersed with floats and military equipment. Programs attracted hundreds to Victory Square at noon and in the afternoon to Woodland Park where Admiral Mitscher spoke. He urged speedier repair of Navy ships in West Coast yards. "I'm sure you wish to see a quick end to this war just as earnestly as I do," he said. "But a speedy conclusion and a complete victory are possible only if we pledge ourselves wholeheartedly to

the task ahead." He told of kamikaze attacks on Navy ships and predicted that final victory would come only after fierce fighting on Japanese soil.

Three Italian Prisoners of War Escape in Seattle

Vincenzo Calazzo, Nicola Gambicchia, and Antonio Maddalena, three Italian prisoners of war, climbed over the stockade fence of the Seattle Italian Service Unit on East Marginal Way at night. They had prearranged to meet two Seattle women on the Des Moines Highway. The women hid them in their home and in woods near South Park for eight days, then drove them down to Oregon. A state patrolman halted their auto when he saw four people riding in the front seat. All five were returned to Seattle where the women were prosecuted under a new law providing severe penalties for aiding prisoners of war to escape. The women were indignant that the men were "branded" prisoners of war, because as one exclaimed, "We never considered them prisoners because they were free to come and go from their Service Unit in Seattle, just as American soldiers were."

Names in the News

Captain Peter F. Butler, master of the steamship *S. Hall Young*, on July 1 received a special letter of commendation from the Navy. It read:

> Before dawn on the morning of April 30, 1945, the steamship loaded with inflammable and explosive cargo, was attacked by an enemy plane. Structural damage to the ship and a potentially serious fire resulted. The ship's personnel, ably assisted by nearby naval vessels, fought the fire with energy and skill. The fire was prevented from spreading, ultimately was extinguished, and the vessel and most of her valuable cargo saved. The cool conduct and courageous leadership of the master in these successful efforts to save his ship are worthy of high commendation.

Marine Lieutenant Alfred H. Clise, 23, was wounded June 10 on Okinawa, his parents were informed in July. He was struck on the chin by shrapnel when a 90-mm. shell exploded five feet

During the later war years, irrigation began converting the arid Columbia Basin from sagebrush to bountiful farm fields. The water came from the recently completed Grand Coulee Dam. The July 19, 1945 photo of Cedargreen Farms near Quincy, Washington, indicates a healthy crop of potatoes would be harvested. Seattle P-I Collection, 22102, MOHAI.

from him. Lieutenant Clise had been in the service two years, a year of that overseas. He enlisted while enrolled as a student at Whitman College.

WAC Violet Pinsley spent 18 months overseas in Italy as an Army telephone operator. At the age of 47, she was the oldest woman in her unit and the only grandmother. When she received a bulletin stating that WACs over 40 could apply for discharge, she decided it was time to return to Seattle to see her new granddaughter. She no sooner had arrived than her daughter decided to enroll at the University of Washington and her son-in-law, Corporal Richard Albert, stationed in Alaska, sent her a bouquet of roses. Pfc. Pinsley suddenly found herself a true grandmother taking care of a two-year-old granddaughter, a job she described as enjoyable.

Captain Albert J. Schaffler telephoned his wife Mildred that he was finally at Fort Lewis after three years in Europe, and on the final lap of the journey to their Seattle home. Mrs. Schaffler rushed about sprucing up 4-year-old Margaret and 7-year-old Albert, Jr., to meet their daddy and, she added, prettied herself up extra special as well. Then she and the two children sat on the front porch and waited. The neighbors, who knew Mrs. Shaffler and the children, also kept an eye out for the Captain whom they had never met. Late in the afternoon he strode up the walk. Margaret recognized her

dad from photographs and rushed down to meet him. Albert just kept saying "Hi, Dad," over and over. Captain Shaffler had commanded an Army engineer general service regiment through France. After a 30-day leave with his family, he reported for re-deployment to the Pacific.

Mrs. Nora Doherty while walking down the hall of her apartment house noticed a man in uniform and figured he was visiting one of her neighbors. As he passed he grabbed her and said, "Mom, don't you know who I am?" It was Lieutenant John Doherty, 25, a marine fighter pilot, back from Okinawa. When Mrs. Doherty realized her son was home after 17 months overseas, she nearly collapsed from surprise. The next day Lieutenant Doherty took the ferry to Bremerton to see his fiancee, a nurse in the Naval Hospital there who did not know he was in the vicinity. When she walked into the reception room and saw him, she started to sway like she'd lost her balance. The Lieutenant grabbed her and hugged her, and promised never to try to surprise people again. The tall lieutenant wore a Distinguished Flying Cross with Oak Leaf, the Air Medal with four Oak Leaves, and two Presidential Unit Citations. A former student at Gonzaga University in Spokane, Doherty had been a civilian pilot before entering the service.

Saul Haas, Collector of Customs, took leave to work as a war correspondent. On July 18 he cabled his wife in Seattle that he had arrived in

Paris. He stayed in Europe about six weeks, then went on to the Red Sea and then to the Pacific Theatre before returning home. Meantime, his assistant collector of customs, Roy L. Ballinger, took charge of the office.

Irena Prokopik McGillivray and Zgmunta Wellesczcuk Jenski were born in Poland. They arrived in Seattle in mid-July with their American Army husbands shortly after marrying the men in Tehran, Iran. The two young women were excited about arriving in America, a land they had only read about, and were proud of their new citizenship. But they carried some terrible memories accumulated over the previous five years. Zgmunta, who had served as a translator and censor for Anglo-Persian-Russian relations, spoke beautiful English. She explained how she and her family were shipped to Siberia. Thirty of them were herded into a boxcar and were not allowed out for four weeks. Their only food was the small rations they had brought with them. Two

children and four elderly people died on the journey. When they were allowed out of their stinking railroad car, the Russians herded them into the forests where they worked 14 hours a day chopping trees.

Irena told how the Russians took her father prisoner in Lithuania and locked her up for three days without food. They questioned her over and over about her father and said they would kill her if she did not tell them. She was 14 at the time. Later her father was released but died shortly thereafter. She and her mother were then shipped to Siberia where they worked two years in the fields while living on bread and water. After being freed, the girls made their way to Tehran. Zgmunta, 22, married Sergeant William H. Penski and Irena married Warrant Officer Colin D. McGillivray of Seattle. When asked why they were treated so badly by the Russians, Zgmunta responded, "They said because we were too rich."

A group of 290 Pacific Northwest infantry

officers and men who fought in France, Germany, and Austria with the 44th Division, arrived at Fort Lewis on July 26 and soon were on the way home for 30-day furloughs. Then they were to be re-deployed for training in Pacific warfare tactics. Among the soldiers was Sergeant Channing D. Elson, 26, who could hardly wait to visit his wife and her parents in Seattle. "It was pretty tough at times," Elson said, "but I think the next job we have to do will be tougher. I think I'd travel 10 million miles to get back to Seattle, the best city in the world."

The WAVES celebrated their third birthday on July 30 with a call for 20,000 more patriotic young women to join the Women's Reserve of the U.S. Navy. The hospital corps, alone, was calling for about half of that number. More than 80,000 women were already serving in Navy uniforms at more than 500 naval establishments in the U.S. and the Hawaiian Islands, and within a few weeks, some would be sent to Alaska, the Panama Canal Zone, Puerto Rico, and Bermuda. The 2,000 WAVES serving in the 13th Naval District in the Puget Sound area observed their anniversary with religious services and a Victory Square celebration.

With the surrender of Nazi Germany, the office of the Coast Guard's shipping commissioner was inundated with merchant seamen hoping to be transferred to ships in the Pacific Theatre. More than 6,000 seamen were being signed on or paid off each month in the Seattle office. Governor Mon C. Wallgren announced that "Seattle can handle up to 350,000 tons more of shipping each month." The stream of supplies that sailed westward out of Seattle demonstrated that his statement was no exaggeration.

A Few of the Many Heroes of July

Private Bruce A. Mitchell of the First Marine Division was killed in action on Okinawa on June 15, five days before his 18th birthday. His mother received the sad information on July 1. Young Mitchell was a student at Seattle's Lincoln High School when, anxious to help win the war, he dropped out to join the Merchant Marine and Army Transport Service. A few months later he volunteered to serve as an U. S. Marine. He had two brothers and a sister in uniform: Private Donald Mitchell in the South Pacific, Storekeeper Lawrence Mitchell also in the Pacific, and Sergeant Ruth Schmidt, a WAC at Camp Hood, Texas.

Pfc. Thomas J. Coyle was killed on Luzon, in the Philippines, on January 17, 1945. On July 18, in a simple ceremony, Major Arthur Kroeger of the 9th Service Command presented the posthumous Silver Star he was awarded for bravery to his mother, Mrs. Patrick Coyle. The major said, "I want to give you this as a token of the American people. I wish there was more I could say." The citation accompanying the Silver Star read:

> For gallantry in action against Japanese forces on January 17, 1945. Private Coyle, ammunition bearer of an infantry mortar platoon, was assigned the duty of transporting ammunition to his gun during an attack by three enemy tanks that approached from the rear. Private Coyle courageously performed his duties until killed by the ignition of ammunition in his arms, exploded by enemy shellfire. The unselfish devotion to duty displayed by him in the face of almost certain death served as an inspiration to the other members of his platoon.

Private Coyle, 19, had attended O'Dea and Franklin High Schools in Seattle and had been overseas for a year.

Colonel Jasper E. Brady, Jr., was captured by the Japanese in the Philippines when Bataan fell. He was a World War I veteran who had enlisted April 6, 1917, the day the U. S. entered that war. He received his commission while serving overseas and remained in the Regular Army. During World War II he was a regimental commander in the 31st Infantry Division in the Philippines when the Japanese took the Islands. In that battle he earned the Silver Star for his efforts. His family was notified that he died on December 15, 1944, when a ship carrying 1,619 prisoners of war was sunk in Subic Bay during an American

Headlines:
August 1945

August 3:
AMERICAN MINES SEAL OFF ALL JAPANESE HARBORS

August 6:
AN ATOMIC BOMB RAVISHES HIROSHIMA

August 8:
RUSSIA DECLARES WAR ON JAPAN; INVADES MACHURIA

August 9:
A SECOND ATOMIC BOMB IS DROPPED ON NAGASAKI

August 9:
PRESIDENT TRUMAN TELLS JAPAN, "QUIT OR BE DESTROYED."

August 13:
400 B-29 BOMBERS RESUME ASSAULT ON JAPAN

August 15:
JAPAN SURRENDERS, V-J (VICTORY OVER JAPAN) DAY BRINGS END OF WAR

August 15:
U.S. ENDS RATIONING OF GASOLINE, FUEL OIL AND OIL STOVES

August 18:
U.S. GOVERNMENT ENDS 35-MPH SPEED LIMIT ON ALL HIGHWAYS

August 21:
PRESIDENT TRUMAN ENDS ALL LEND-LEASE ACTIVITIES

August 31:
U.S. REVEALS THAT 3 HIDDEN CITIES—LOS ALAMOS, N.M.; OAK RIDGE, TN.; AND HANFORD, WA.—HOUSED 100,000 WHO HELPED PRODUCE THE ATOM BOMB

bombing raid. When the ship went down, 942 prisoners lost their lives and 59 died later. Letters praising the courage and outstanding character of Colonel Brady were sent to his wife by some of those who escaped or were later liberated. His wife, a daughter of Mr. and Mrs. Reginald H. Parsons of Seattle, three children and two stepchildren survived him. One son, Pfc. Jasper E. Brady, was serving in Europe and a stepson, Private Geoffrey Tootell, was also in the Army.

Pfc. Griffith B. King, at the age of 19 died July 1 of wounds suffered on Okinawa, his parents were informed on July 17. A graduate of Queen Anne High School, King was a descendant of two Seattle pioneers, Thomas Mercer and Daniel Bagley. He went overseas in January with the 7th Division.

Pfc. Vernon Farmer of the First Marine Division was killed in action June 20 on Okinawa. He had joined the Marines immediately after graduating from Queen Anne High School in Seattle. His Platoon Sergeant wrote to young Farmer's mother with details of his death.

> If it's possible to ease your grief, and the grief of those most dear to him, I'd like to say that Vernon fought and died gallantly, and is listed with and among the heroes of the South Pacific. Whenever the enemy's fire was close at hand, or an almost impossible drive was to be made, it took a kid like Vern to give out with a joke and a laugh as though he weren't conscious of the danger. That spirit will never die.

Vernon Farmer was 19 years old when he was killed.

August 1945

Washington Servicemen Stream Home from Europe

With the war in Europe having ended nearly three months earlier, increasing numbers of Washington State veterans were returning home, most with 30-day furloughs, after which they were to report for reassignment in the Pacific area. Most of them expected to be involved in the invasion of the Japanese Islands.

Newspaper headlines generated widespread interest in the names of those returning. "Many Vets Discharged at Fort Lewis," "26 Washington Men Due Today in Boston," "Three Transports bring Veterans." Below such headlines were long listings in small print, naming those who would soon enter the doors of home. The Army also provided lists of local soldiers being discharged at Fort Lewis. Needless to say, families avidly studied these lists.

Preparing to Finish the War in the Pacific

As thousands of service personnel from Europe anticipated returning home after many months on distant war fronts, others were reassigned to units being trained for the invasion of Japan. Forty acres of the golf course at Jefferson Park on Seattle's Beacon Hill were taken over by the Army to store olive drab trucks, amphibious jeeps, and other mechanical equipment to be used in the Pacific War. The exact number of vehicles was a military secret, but the Army reported 790 civilians and German prisoners of war worked in the maintenance shop on Airport Way to overhaul and repaint vehicles and to convert some for amphibious operations. On the Seattle waterfront, many ships loaded with material headed out toward the Pacific warfront. Puget Sound shipyards were beehives of activity and The Boeing Airplane Company continued turning out bombers at a record pace.

A Secret Weapon Ends the War

Banner headlines and radio news flashes startled the world on August 6. The world's first atomic bomb, the result of scientific endeavor in the United States, had been carried to Japan in a Boeing B-29 bomber and dropped on Hiroshima. The explosion, the equivalent to 20,000 tons of TNT, and the firestorm it caused, destroyed 60 percent of the city. About 80,000 were killed by the bomb and more died later from the effects of radiation. Even so, it was not the war's most devastating bombing attack on Japan. The

O.F. "Ole" Scarpelli served on the battleship Alabama *in the South Pacific, which returned to the Bremerton Navy Yard shortly before V.J. Day. The 24-year old sailor and two buddies ferried to Seattle to celebrate the end of the war. They became separated amid the exultant crowd at Fourth and Pike, so Ole climbed a lamppost to try to locate them. He was too busy waving at women in the windows of a facing office building to notice the P-I photographer snapping his picture. Scarpelli, who served as sergeant-at-arms of the Washington State Senate in the 1980s, first saw this photo 40 years after it was taken. Seattle P-I Collection, 20001, MOHAI.*

March incendiary raids on Tokyo had destroyed more and killed more. But the economy of sending one plane on a mission to destroy an entire city indicated the power of the new weapon.

On the day the bomb exploded, one of the best-kept secrets of the war became public. For the first time, area residents were told what had been produced at the 400,000-acre Hanford Project in South Central Washington. There, amid sagebrush-covered hills and former farm fields, 17,000 workers had been involved in producing the ingredients of the atomic bomb. Secrecy was rigidly enforced at Hanford during the war. When workers asked what was being produced, they were told only that the result would shorten the war and bring an allied victory.

When the Japanese did not respond quickly enough to the demand for immediate, unconditional surrender, a second bomb was dropped on August 8. The explosion over Nagasaki killed 40,000, and President Truman threatened Japan with total destruction if its leaders hesitated longer.

Washington residents anticipated the end of hostilities after hearing of the atom bomb attacks. They expectantly returned to their jobs with a prayer on their lips. Retail outlets announced that they expected to be closed on the anticipated V-J Day holiday. Amid reported negotiations with Japan, a quietly jubilant Washington State citizenry on August 11 awaited official proclamation of the end of the conflict. Adding to the feeling that the war was truly over, the U.S. Navy canceled $1.2 billion in contracts to build or repair 95 ships. The Army predicted it would reduce its forces by three million men within a year.

On August 14, with the Japanese still not accepting surrender terms, more than 800 American Superfortresses escorted by 180

The Hanford plant on the Columbia River in Central Washington produced an ingredient vital in developing the first atomic bombs. The radioactive chemical element plutonium was successfully purified at this isolated secret plant where most employees wondered what the end product of their labor would be used for. They were not told until after the atomic bombs had been dropped on Japan. Washington State Historical Society, Tacoma, Album 51.

fighter planes dropped 6,000 tons of fire and demolition bombs on Japanese war industries. Emperor Hirohito then broadcast to the Japanese that they had lost the war. Many of his countrymen could not at first believe his words for tight governmental control had prevented civilians from knowing the truth about the damage Japan was suffering. On that day, August 14, word was broadcast that the long and bloody war was truly over. Japan formed a new government and the emperor issued a cease fire order to all Japanese troops wherever they were located.

As the word that peace had arrived spread across Washington State, air raid sirens sounded and citizens poured into the streets, whooping and shouting. Tons of paper streamers and confetti cascaded from high windows. Servicemen on the street grabbed passing women and gave them a hug and a kiss. One paper described it as "a demonstration to dwarf anything the metropolis of Puget Sound had ever seen." There were sober and tearful faces, too, for the celebration reminded many that it was a day when some loved one would have been coming home, but wasn't. By the afternoon of the 15th, Washingtonians were exhausted from nearly four years of war and from an all-night celebration of the arrival of peace. August

15 and 16, a Wednesday and Thursday, were declared State holidays. Most retail stores closed on both days, but grocery stores and meat markets opened on the 16th.

Word did not travel to all the war fronts as quickly as hoped. Twelve hours after President Truman announced the Japanese acceptance of Allied peace terms, two Japanese bomb-laden suicide planes crashed into the American base on Ihya Island, 30 miles north of Okinawa, injuring several Yank soldiers. This infuriated Americans and resulted in Tokyo radio explaining that headquarters was endeavoring to transmit the imperial order to every branch of their forces. Allied fleets and convoys were requested not to approach Japanese home waters until cease-fire arrangements had been made.

On V-J Day, the Army announced no more troops would be deployed from Europe to the Pacific. Instead five divisions, approximately 75,000 men, would be on their way home within 30 days. The next day, word was received from the War Department that enlisted men in the United States with "excessive service" would not be sent back overseas with the Army of Occupation. In addition, men still overseas who had experienced long and hazardous service would be returned to the United States as soon as possible.

Despite the civilian holiday on V-J Day, Army and Navy posts in the Puget Sound region remained on a wartime basis, though commanding officers gave leaves to as many soldiers and sailors as possible. Some units operated with small skeleton crews.

Winston Churchill spoke to the British Commons the day after V-J Day, telling them that the atomic bomb was responsible for the sudden ending of the Japanese war. He estimated it had saved one million American and 200,000 British lives that would have been lost trying to invade the enemy's home islands. He said, "There are voices which assert that the atomic bomb should never have been used at all." He added bluntly: "I cannot associate myself with such ideas. Six years of total war have convinced most people that had the Germans or the Japanese discovered this new weapon, they would have used it upon us to our complete destruction with the utmost alacrity." As he concluded, cheers sounded from both sides of the House of Commons.

After the Japanese had surrendered, several U.S. wartime secrets were revealed. One was that plutonium for the Atom Bomb had been purified at Hanford, Washington. Another report disclosed that Japanese balloon-bombs for months had been floated on the prevailing winds from Japan to North America. Washington State sustained the highest number of hits by these bombs; more than 20 of them landed in the state, most of them in the Yakima Valley area. In most instances the balloon's four incendiary bombs, one anti-personnel bomb and one flash bomb to destroy the balloon itself, were not recovered. The only deaths caused by these bombs occurred near Bly, Oregon, an event described above.

Within a week of V-J Day, headlines proclaimed that hundreds of war workers were quitting their jobs. Women were returning to careers as housewives and mothers. Some people were making plans to return to former homes elsewhere in the country. Others were anxious to return to professions they had given up for the duration of the war. At the Boeing plants, spokesmen reported that normal "quits" might nearly take care of the reductions necessary in personnel, though some layoffs would probably be necessary. Later in the month, Boeing explained that it expected to maintain a work force about three times larger than their peacetime payroll. Their plans called for a future workforce of 15,000 employees, a drop of about 19,000 from their war-end total of 34,249. Company personnel officers stated that 233 of the newest employees were laid off during the week following the Japanese surrender and another 1,509 persons had quit.

To help quell fears that Depression days would return, several economic forecasts were published in late August. Dr. N. H. Engle of the University of Washington, while testifying before a U.S. Senate committee meeting in Seattle, explained that all economic and business surveys compiled in the past year, both locally and nationally, indicated that the Pacific Northwest would be one of the financial bright spots of the nation in peacetime. He declared that even during temporary re-conversions there would be fewer unemployed in the region than before the war.

Will Lake Washington Become a Ship "Bone Yard?"

Early in August, when it appeared Japan would soon be forced to surrender, the Navy began suggesting that surplus ships be moored in Lake Washington. Immediately a "permanent organization" of Lake Washington residents was formed to preserve the lake against further industrialization. Leaders of community clubs in Yarrow, Evergreen, and Hunts Points, Medina and Houghton called the first meeting. They discussed opposition to the Navy's plan to moor 600 idle warships in Lake Washington. Other groups soon joined the effort to keep Lake Washington pristine. Some Chambers of Commerce and business leaders thought ships moored in rows from the Lake Washington Shipyard at Houghton to the end of Yarrow Point would be acceptable. The problem dissolved when the Navy decided to moor the ships elsewhere.

The battleship *Washington* brought home one of the standout battle records of the war when it arrived at the Puget Sound Navy Yard in Bremerton on August 21. One of the fastest, most powerful battleships afloat, she had sailed 277,085 miles since December 7, 1941. She escaped unscathed from the bitterest enemy attacks while her mighty cannon piled catastrophe upon the enemy. In one battle, assisted by another battleship and four destroyers, the *Washington* hurled her metal against an overpowering force of more than a score of Japanese warships in the Third Battle of Savo Island. The *Washington* was credited with sinking an enemy battleship and, with the

aid of the other ships, routing the remainder of the enemy force and turning the tide of the bloody conflict for the Solomons. Arriving home aboard her were 18 Washington State men who took great pride in the vessel commissioned in July 1941 and named for their state. She had been called upon to perform more duties of differing types than any other battleship in the history of the U.S. fleet.

Names in the News

The commanding officer of the 50th General Hospital received a special commendation in August. Colonel H. T. Buckner, a well-known Seattle surgeon, had helped form the hospital unit early in 1942. The commendation praised him for outstanding service in the European Theatre. Major General Paul R. Hawley, E.T.O. chief surgeon, sent tributes to the entire hospital staff through the Reverend Harold Small, S.J., president of Seattle College, sponsor of the hospital unit. (The Very Reverend Francis E. Corkery, S. J., was college president at the time the hospital unit was formed, but had been

moved to Spokane to take over as president of Gonzaga University.) The 50th General Hospital had gone to England in January 1944 and soon was considered one of the best in the United Kingdom. As a result it was one of the first to be moved to Normandy after D-Day.

Technical Sergeant Steve N. Nava had a more or less typical travel experience when attempting to find transportation home from Europe for a 30-day furlough. The engineer-gunner had flown 53 combat missions with a "lucky crew" on a B-26 Mitchell Marauder medium bomber that came through unscathed. He had been in Europe for a year and was anxious to see Seattle again. Though the war had ended on the Continent several months earlier, the 21-year-old told a reporter that he thought he would never make it home. His orders placed him on a plodding Liberty ship, big and seaworthy, but moving at an irritatingly slow pace. He said, "Faster ships were waltzing right on past us." But now he was happy to be home. Earlier Sergeant Nava had been mentioned in the news after he and six other Ninth Airforce men laid aside their air gear temporarily to join one of the first American infantry columns to fight its way into the beleaguered city of Bastogne during the Battle of the Bulge.

Major Wilson E. Hunt of Seattle commanded the first Marines to go ashore when U.S. forces occupied the deserted Japanese naval base at Yokosuka. His mother said "You know, I had sort of a feeling that he was taking part in that. He'd get a thrill out of something like that." Major Hunt was sent to the Pacific in January 1942, with the first marine detachments and participated in many South Pacific engagements. He had a month's leave in the summer of 1944 and then returned to the Pacific in November to command marines in the Okinawa campaign. The major's wife and their daughter and son were awaiting his return in Pennsylvania. Major Wilson had never seen his two-month-old son.

Corporal Ethel Verner of the Women's Army Corps arrived home on August 3 after 11 months in Europe. She was a member of the first WAC contingent assigned to overseas duty and served as secretary in the Paris office of the chief of transportation. She believed she was the first member of the original group to arrive home after flying from Paris to Wilmington, DE and traveling from there to Seattle by train.

A Few of the Many Heroes of August

Lieutenant Ted West, co-pilot of a B-17, was reported missing in action on July 13, 1944, and then was listed as killed in action in August 1945. His plane was shot down over Brussels, Belgium, en route to a raid on Munich, Germany. He had completed more than 25 missions and had been awarded the Air Medal and three Oak-Leaf Clusters. Before entering the service Ted West had graduated from Centralia High School and Junior College. His wife, Violet, was living in Seattle when she received the final telegram.

Another hero from Centralia was mentioned in the press in August. Sergeant Dexter J. Kerstetter was awarded the Congressional Medal of Honor. A cook's helper, he volunteered for front-line duty and performed heroic action on April 13, killing 16 of the enemy (see appendix for details).

Captain Thomas E. Crowley, commander of a company of Japanese-American soldiers of the 442nd Battalion, came to Seattle to speak at the invitation of the Seattle Knights of the Round Table. He and several Nisei veterans of the 442nd also were guests at a Washington State Press Club reception. Captain Crowley, whose home was in Madison, Wisconsin, described the fighting ability of the Nisei as "superb." He continued proudly, "Their heroism became a habit but they are quite disheartened because their families are sometimes not received well at home. They thought they were fighting for the principles of equality and justice at home as well as abroad. They were completely sold on the idea that we were in this war for all Americans, not just part of them." He mentioned four Nisei from the 442nd who were recovering from wounds at the Fort Lawton hospital. One of them, Private Stanley Serrkaku was at the Round Table meeting and explained that he had bunked for a time with two Seattleites, Bill Nakamura and Isao Okazaki. Both were killed in battle. "They were really tops," said Private Serrkaku. "There were a lot of guys from here in my outfit. They know about some of the difficulties their folks are having and some of them resent it, but most of them are resigned to it. They want to come back here because this is their home. I don't have to worry about that because I'm from Hawaii where there isn't any race distinction." Private Serrkaku was wounded by enemy artillery while fighting in Northern Italy. Also in the hospital was Pfc. Howard Fujita who had been wounded by shrapnel during the rescue of the lost Texas Battalion in France, an effort for which he earned a Bronze Star Medal. Captain Crowley, who helped to organize the combat team at Camp Shelby, Mississippi, in February 1943, said from the outset the men had resolved to show their real patriotism by

Headlines:
September 1945

September 2:
JAPAN SIGNS
UNCONDITIONAL SURRENDER
DOCUMENTS ON BATTLESHIP
MISSOURI

September 6:
PRESIDENT TRUMAN GIVES
CONGRESS PROGRAM FOR
RECONVERSION TO
PEACETIME ECONOMY

September 21:
PRESIDENT TRUMAN
ACCEPTS SECRETARY OF WAR
STIMSON'S
RECOMMENDATION
THAT THE WAR BE OFFICIALLY
DESIGNATED "WORLD WAR II"

becoming the "best combat team in the American Army. And I want you to know they did just that."

Ten Seattle soldiers, former prisoners of war in Germany, were recuperating at Madigan General Hospital at Fort Lewis in August. One of them, Sergeant John W. Moffat, was recovering from severe malnutrition. He was shot down over Aachen in September 1944 and was a prisoner for 14 months before being liberated by the Russians. Philip S. Sexton was one of 3,400 Stalag Luft IV prisoners who were chained in pairs and forced at bayonet point to run four kilometers while carrying full equipment. Guards bayoneted several who fell exhausted, he said.

Sergeant William J. Green of Seattle arrived home wearing a Purple Heart with two Oak Leaf Clusters, indicating he was wounded three times in combat. His first wound was received in the Battle of Leyte and the two others were for wounds received on Okinawa. Sergeant Green was in the first wave of the 96th Division to reach the beach on Okinawa on Easter Sunday 1945 and fought on the front for 45 days before an eye wound put him out of action. He was flown to the Marianas for hospitalization. In addition to his purple hearts he received the Bronze Star Medal for meritorious service on Leyte and an Oak Leaf Cluster to the Bronze Star for what he called "a little incident on Okinawa."

Lieutenant Gerald L. Perry, Jr., was awarded the Silver Star for gallantry in action against the enemy in the vicinity of Veiden, Germany. Commanding officer of Company B of the 66th Infantry Regiment, Lieutenant Perry "led his patrol in an advance that paused only after eight enemy soldiers had been killed, four machine guns captured and the rest of the enemy forced to withdraw," the citation said. Lieutenant Perry graduated from Roosevelt High School in Seattle and attended the University of Washington for three years before enlisting in June 1941.

Paul A. Howard of Auburn stood soldier-straight on August 7 to receive the Silver Star Medal posthumously awarded his son, Pfc.

Norman E. Howard. The elder Howard was a hero of World War I during which he won the Silver Star for conspicuous gallantry during the Battle of the Marne. His son was awarded the medal for helping compatriots on patrol behind the enemy lines in Italy. After the Germans discovered them, the 20-year-old radio operator, Norman Howard, dodged through enemy fire to a church, from where he began firing on the enemy. Out of ammunition, he threw all the hand grenades he and the others had. Then, with utter disregard for his life, he stepped into to the line of enemy fire, covering his companions by firing his machine pistol. The patrol managed to withdraw to American lines, directed by Private Howard's radio, while he stayed facing the enemy with indomitable courage until killed.

Sergeant Gerald Bonne almost made it through the war. A tail gunner on a B-29, the 20-year-old Seattleite was reported missing in action on June 13 somewhere over Japan. A friend of young Bonne who was aboard another plane in the same formation wrote to his mother in Seattle that he had observed all the men of the stricken plane bail out just before it crashed. Sergeant Bonne had been overseas only since the first of June and was based on Guam. He later was declared dead.

September 1945

A Sample of News Items from Post-War Days

Honorable Discharge lapel emblems were available from Army and Navy offices across the state for all veterans who presented evidence of an honorable discharge. Within days former service personnel were happily if irreverently referring to the gold eagle emblem as "the ruptured duck."

Senator Warren Magnuson reported the Pacific Northwest could look for some good days ahead. "I think our future is brighter than that for many other congested war areas," he said. "Take our shipyards for instance. The Puget Sound yards were built for naval construction. It looks like we are going to keep a big Navy, and many of the present ships are in need of repair. That means our industry should keep right on being pretty busy." He added that the Boeing plant appeared certain to be a contractor for Army planes, and that much experimental work would continue to be done by the builders of the Flying Fortress. "And the Northwest is looking forward to peacetime production of aluminum and other light metals," he added.

A September 3 newswire story introduced the concept of a potential airline that would tie the Orient to the Pacific Northwest. Paving the way was an Army Air Force four-engine transport plane that landed at Boeing Field 21 hours and 40 minutes after leaving Tokyo's Atsugi airdrome. The record-breaking flight was routed via Adak in the Aleutian Islands. The plane, with a crew of six, carried 16 passengers and the undeveloped photographs of the Japanese surrender ceremonies for the media. Major G. E. Cain, former Seattle resident and United Airlines pilot until he joined the army in 1942, commanded the plane on the flight. His co-pilot, Captain Lyle Spencer, was a West Seattle High School graduate. After an hour on the ground in Seattle, the plane left for Washington, D.C. Colonel Armin F. Herold, former commander of the Army's McChord Field and now head of the aviation department of the Seattle Chamber of Commerce, declared the flight showed that any route to the Far East should pass through Seattle.

Thousands of motorists jammed the State's highways and the ferry system in Puget Sound over Labor Day weekend, September 1-3. The weather was nearly perfect and attracted thousands to parks and other outdoor attractions. The Ellensburg Rodeo at its first post-war revival reported record attendance.

On the gray morning of September 5, a large ship nosed up to the Naval Support Depot in Seattle to deliver the last members of "Seattle's own" 41st Division from their duties in the Pacific. A Navy brass band welcomed them with the popular melody "In the Mood." On the pier near the bow of the ship, Captain

Robert Allen of the 41st Field Artillery announced he was happy to be home after 40 months in the South Pacific where he saw plenty of action on New Guinea, Zamboanga and Jolo. Down the pier, an Army sergeant leaned over the railing amidship and fondly patted the side of the vessel, yelling to those on the pier, "She's a lucky boat; she brought me home." He was promptly corrected by a grinning sailor, "She's a ship, you landlubber." Among the returning veterans were 25 men from Washington State.

Construction of a new American Legion Service Center for men and women war veterans began in mid-September on property purchased at Seventh Avenue and University Street by Seattle Legion Post No. 1. The original plan was to remodel the old Labor Temple on adjoining property, but the cost would have been higher than constructing a new building.

The wartime production record at Boeing's Seattle and Renton plants was published on September 6. Approximately 8,200 airplanes were built there between Pearl Harbor and V-J Day. More than 1,000 of these were B-29 Superfortresses and most of the others were B-17 Flying Fortresses. Wages and salaries paid at the Seattle, Renton and eight branch plants in Washington during those years totaled about $410 million. The peak employment reached in February 1945 found 45,000 persons on the payroll.

A group of Washington State mothers organized an effort on September 6 to seek immediate release from the military services of all men with children at home. The founders of the effort, including Mrs. Royal Frew and Mrs. Donald Crew of Seattle, received scores of calls from women inquiring how they might help in the effort.

The Office of Price Administration told congressmen that "most rationing would end during the last four months of the year." Rent controls would be scrapped in 75 to 100 cities within four or five months. Both meats and shoes would not be rationed by the end of 1945.

World War II had ended a few weeks before this transport ship arrived in Seattle with a load of service personnel from Pacific war fronts. Notice the smiles on their faces as they descend the gangplank to step on the soil of their home country. Seattle P-I Collection 28199, MOHAI

Fats and oils would be rationed into 1946 and the end of sugar rationing was impossible to predict. Price regulations would gradually be removed. Ceiling prices for basic metals would be removed early. Food prices would be decontrolled commodity by commodity. The program to reduce clothing prices would be vigorously pursued. With the great demand for new homes, no early removal of ceiling prices on building materials was expected.

Washington State College obtained 50 prefabricated homes originally built to house families of Hanford workers in Richland. The college used the structures to house married veteran students and their families. Large dormitories also were moved from Vancouver, Washington, shipyards to house veterans in Pullman.

The more than 5,000 women released at the Boeing Renton plant since V-J Day were not as sorry at losing their jobs as most citizens expected them to be. Mrs. Ida DuMars, general supervisor of women at the plant, said she was heading for a vacation in Central America. "Nearly all the women, who came from everywhere to do their war job, are gone," she said. "Only a few remained to finish planes under construction."

Sergeant Herbert Lobl, an Austrian-born Seattle soldier serving in Europe had searched for several months for his parents whom he had not seen for seven years. He finally found his mother in a concentration camp in Theresienstadt, Czechoslovakia, where she had survived 15-hour days of forced labor cutting stone. Sergeant Lobl's wife, who lived in Seattle, said he had written that there was no sign of his father. A refugee from the Nazis, Sergeant Lobl came to the United States in 1939, but was unable to bring his parents with him.

A Few of the Many Heroes of September

Major Robert F. Goldsworthy was rescued from a prisoner of war camp in Tokyo, his wife, Jean, in Seattle, was informed on September 1. Mrs. Goldsworthy immediately informed Robert, Jr., that his daddy was coming home. Though only two, the child seemed to understand. The Major was shot down over Tokyo on December 3, as he piloted a B-29 on a bombing raid. He was listed as missing in action until he was rescued after Japan surrendered. The Major, a Washington State College graduate from Rosalia, had been a Spokane radio announcer before joining the Air Forces cadet training school in 1940. His father, Harry Goldsworthy, was a Washington State College regent.

Lieutenant Frederic P. Vanderhoof was discharged from the Navy at Sand Point Naval Air Station during the first week in September. Shortly before his discharge, the Lieutenant was awarded four decorations: a gold star on his Distinguished Flying Cross, designated his second such award, and three gold stars in lieu of his third, fourth, and fifth Air Medals. The 25-year-old Grumman Hellcat pilot was credited with shooting down four Japanese planes. His second D.F.C. citation read: "He skillfully directed his division in an action with a numerically superior group of enemy planes. He led the division in a series of strafing runs that resulted in the destruction or damage of eight large enemy planes on the runway of a major enemy airfield." Lieutenant Vanderhoof and his wife, Joyce, lived in Woodinville. He had graduated from Olympia High School and attended St. Martin's College. After receiving his honorable discharge, he planned on finding a job with an airline.

Pfc. Leonard E. Blom, 22, of Ferndale in Whatcom County, was flown in a C-54 transport from Nichols Field on Luzon to Hawaii in an iron lung. Blom, the first patient in an iron lung to be transported by air, was stricken with poliomyelitis at Lingayen in the Philippines. From Hawaii he was taken to Letterman Hospital, San Francisco, and from there to Barnes Hospital, Vancouver Barracks. Two flight nurses, a flight surgeon and two medical technicians accompanied him on the flight. A third technician controlled the chest-type respirator.

The Air Medal was awarded Captain Charles T. (Ted) Scholl of Seattle, one of the crew that managed a daring glider rescue of a WAC corporal and two service men marooned at "Shangri-La" in New Guinea. Scholl piloted the plane that dropped the initial glider into the "hidden" valley ringed by the highest peaks in New Guinea and accessible only from the air. He then returned and made two successful glider pick-ups of the three service personnel and 15 Filipino paratroopers who assisted in the perilous rescue. A graduate of Roosevelt High School, Scholl enlisted in October 1940 and for a time was a trainer of glider pilots.

Lieutenant Adrian W. Rose of Seattle piloted a B-17 through 19 missions over Germany before ending up in a German prison camp. In mid-September he was home on leave and preparing to step into a civilian job as soon as he received his discharge papers at the end of his furlough. His new job involved helping "pilot" other veterans of World War II back into civilian life. His title was assistant manager of the Veteran' Information Center of the Civilian War Commission. Lieutenant Rose, when asked how his plane was shot down over Frankfurt, explained, "The control cables of our plane were cut by enemy fire and it crashed into a sister ship, cutting it in two. Eight of us got out of the ship," he said. "When our B-17 hit theirs, it knocked the tail gunner unconscious. He went down in the severed tail section, which seemed to sort of float down like a leaf. He got out of it with only a broken leg. I talked with him that night, and he felt pretty lucky."

Major Ralph D. W. Brown, former Seattle Methodist pastor and Army chaplain was captured by the Japanese on Bataan. He was the first Army chaplain of the war to receive the Distinguished Service Cross from General MacArthur personally for his heroic attempts to rescue the wounded during the first battles. Major Brown was stationed at Clark Field in the Philippines when the Japanese invaded. He was in Catabatuan prison camp for some time and later was placed on a ship to be taken to Japan, but the ship was torpedoed. Next the Japanese placed him on a second ship bound for Japan, but it was bombed. He was returned to prison camp and in January 1945, he died there. His family received the information on September 13. His widow, Margaret, their three children, and his parents survived Major Brown.

On September 19 in Kirkland, the Silver Star Medal was presented posthumously to Staff Sergeant Edward R. Kardong. His wife and their son Randall accepted the award from Colonel Jensen, executive officer of the Ninth Service Command. The words of Sergeant Kardong's citation were meaningless to 18-month-old Randall, but in years to come he would realize his father had died a hero. Kardong, a Bellevue High School graduate, had been in uniform 18 months and overseas only three weeks when he lost his life in France. The citation for his Silver Star read: "For gallantry in action January 6, 1945. In the face of heavy small arms fire from the well-entrenched enemy, he repeatedly led his platoon across open ground to take enemy positions. Behind his gallant leadership the platoon succeeded in routing approximately 100 of the enemy. Sergeant Kardong remained in front, rallying and leading his men forward until he was mortally wounded by enemy gunfire." Colonel Jensen added a few words of his own while presenting the Silver Star to Mrs. Kardong. "It does not seem adequate for what your husband has done, but it's the best we can do."

Lieutenant Roy Mitchell, Colonel Vernon L. Lewis, and two Technical Sergeants accompany the body of a veteran being returned from overseas for burial in a local cemetery. The photo is dated November 1947. The war had ended two years earlier. At the request of their families, the bodies of thousands of veterans were returned to the United States for reinterment. Seattle P-I Collection 28189, MOHAI

EPILOGUE

World War II officially ended on September 2, 1945, when the Japanese signed surrender papers on the battleship *Missouri* in Tokyo Bay. The conflict had been so all-consuming that it took years for Washington State residents to unwind from the effort.

Seattle's skyline hadn't changed much during the war, but beneath the surface much had changed. The Depression had disappeared and there were no hungry people begging on the streets or pawing through garbage. After four years of war during which no new automobiles were available, models on the streets were of 1930s vintage. Hardly any new construction was visible after years of building materials being reserved for the military or for companies manufacturing war materials.

With the arrival of peace, movement of human beings accelerated. Servicemen who had served for three years or more, those who bore the scars of wounds, or who had been awarded decorations for bravery usually had earned sufficient points to be discharged from the armed services. Thousands of service personnel began arriving from stations around the globe and happily started the process that would free them to return to the mainstream of American life. The State's colleges welcomed hoards of discharged veterans anxious to use the G. I. Bill to earn a degree. The marriage license bureau became a busy place. Many the families who had moved to the state for war jobs now packed their bags and headed for their old hometowns. Many of the women who had filled critical positions at war factories and offices decided home and family deserved their full attention.

Guards at the German prisoners of war camps in Washington State escorted their charges to railroad stations to board trains bound for the East Coast where ships waited to return them to their devastated homeland. Meantime, hundreds of the State's young men who had experienced life in enemy prison camps began to arrive home, many of them still gaining back the weight lost to malnutrition and untreated illnesses.

Hundreds of flag-draped coffins holding the bodies of American war dead arrived at Puget Sound ports for transshipment to hometown cemeteries. The names of thousands of Washington youth killed in the war were listed on plaques and monuments in schools, businesses, clubhouses, churches and in government buildings across the State. Eventually most of those names were inscribed on permanent memorials as a means of remembering their sacrifices.

To this day, many reminders of World War II are apparent in Washington State — army bases, airfields, navy facilities, hospitals, museum artifacts, veterans' organizations, military cemeteries and hundreds of historical publications about the war. And, of course, the most vivid reminders come from the decreasing numbers of the American generation who experienced those years in the armed forces or in producing on the home front what was needed to achieve the victory that preserved our freedom.

During the war, other than Boeing Field, the only public airfields near Seattle were small and used mostly by private craft. During the war, several large Army and Navy fields such as Paine Field were built, but it also was obvious that a major commercial airport was needed. Hangers were built during the war at what was called Bow Lake Airfield, and there, after the war, Seattle-Tacoma Airport was developed. It is shown in here on opening day, July 9, 1949. Seattle P-I Collection, 20340, MOHAI.

This aerial view of Seattle was snapped shortly after the war ended. The Smith Tower was the city's tallest structure, the streamlined Kalakala was a major Seattle icon, and on the distant shore of Lake Washington the towns of Kirkland, home to about 2,000, and unincorporated Bellevue were hardly visible from the Seattle side of the lake. MOHAI Collection, 11569.

By June 1946, nine months after the end of World War II, hundreds of German prisoners of war kept in Washington State were being sent home. They are seen here boarding passenger cars that carried them to East Coast ports where ships waited to transport them to their war-devastated homeland.

Vestiges of World War II gradually disappeared during the post-war years. The pylon at Victory Square, a replica of the Washington Memorial, it stood covered with rows of names of Washington State war dead until it was demolished in January 1949. Today a more complete list of Washington's World War II dead, a total of 6,252 names, is inscribed in the permanent veteran's memorial garden at Benaroya Hall. Those names are also listed in the appendix of this book. Seattle P-I Collection,

A shipload of American prisoners of war captured by the Japanese in the Philippines arrived to a warm welcome in Seattle on November 1, 1945. When freed several months earlier, most suffered from malnutrition and disease and were treated in hospitals and rest camps. Seattle P-I Collection, 28313, MOHAI.

APPENDIX

MEDAL OF HONOR
RECIPIENTS

Twenty-five Washington State World War II veterans were awarded the Medal of Honor, often called the Congressional Medal of Honor, the nation's highest award for valor in combat. These men were born in Washington State, or resided in the State before or after the war. The following brief biographies of these veterans are based on newspaper reports and the book *Washington State Men of Valor* by Donald K. and Helen L. Ross, published by Rokalu Press, 15870 Glenwood Road SW, Port Orchard, WA. 98366-9404. This book, written by a Medal of Honor recipient and his wife, contains detailed accounts of how the men earned the medal.

RICHARD BEATTY ANDERSON
Private First Class, USMC

The citation explaining how Richard Anderson earned the Medal of Honor describes his gallantry while serving with the 4th Marine Division on Roi Island, Kwajalein Atoll, in the Marshall Islands on February 1, 1944.

Entering a shell crater occupied by 3 other marines, Pfc. Anderson was preparing to throw a grenade at an enemy position when it slipped from his hands and rolled toward the men at the bottom of the hole. With insufficient time to retrieve the armed weapon and throw it, Pfc. Anderson fearlessly chose to sacrifice himself and save his companions by hurling his body upon the grenade and taking the full impact of the explosion. His personal valor and exceptional spirit of loyalty in the face of almost certain death were in keeping with the highest traditions of the U.S. Naval Service.

Richard Anderson was born in Tacoma in 1921 and attended high school in McLeary and Sequim. He entered the U.S. Marines in July 1942 at Oakland, California. The following January he was sent to the Marshall Islands with the 23rd Marines. His first day of combat was his last.

Rear Admiral S.A. Taffinder, then commandant of the 13th Naval District, Seattle, posthumously presented Anderson's Medal of Honor to his parents, Mr. and Mrs. Oscar Anderson of Tacoma.

ARNOLD J. BJORKLUND
First Lieutenant, US Army

Lieutenant Bjorklund's Medal of Honor Citation reads in part:

Near Altavilla, Italy, on September 13, 1943, when his company attacked a German position on Hill 425, the first platoon, led by 1st Lt. Bjorklund, moved forward on the right flank to the slope of the hill where it was pinned down by a heavy concentration of machine gun and rifle fire. Ordering his men to give covering fire, with only three hand grenades he crept and crawled forward to within a few yards of a German machine gun and while continuously exposed to enemy fire, he hurled one grenade into the nest, destroyed the gun and killed 3 Germans. Discovering a second machine gun 20 yards to the right on a higher terrace, he moved under intense enemy fire to a point within a few yards and threw a second grenade into this position, destroying it and killing two more Germans. The first platoon was then able to advance 150 yards further up the slope to the crest of the hill, but was again stopped by the fire from a heavy enemy mortar on the reverse slope. 1st Lt. Bjorklund located the mortar and worked his way under little cover to within ten yards of its position and threw his

third grenade, destroying the mortar, killing two of the Germans and forcing the remaining three to flee. His actions permitted the platoon to take its objective.

Arnold L. Bjorklund was born in Clinton, WA, in 1918. He entered the Army in Seattle in February 1941. Two and a half years later he led his men to victory in the Italian battle. He received his Medal of Honor from President Franklin D. Roosevelt in the Oval Office of the White House on August 31, 1944. He retired from the Army for medical reasons in March 1945 and accepted a position as a laboratory plant technician testing glue formulas, a job he enjoyed. He rose to be plant manager for Pacific Resin Chemical Company in Vancouver, Washington, where he and his wife Darle made their home. Arnold Bjorklund died on November 18, 1979. His wife, a son and daughter and four grandchildren survived him. He was buried at Willamette National Cemetery in Portland, Oregon.

ORVILLE BLOCH
First Lieutenant, US Army

Orville Bloch, born in Wisconsin in 1915, was raised in North Dakota. His family was of German ancestry and spoke German as well as English. He attended North Dakota State University at Fargo, then, still lacking a few credits for graduation, enlisted in the Army and earned a commission. He instructed for a time at Fort Benning before being sent to Italy with the 85th Division.

One of the first battles he experienced was near Firenzuola, a hill town that his battalion was ordered to take. Realizing a frontal assault would result in many deaths, Bloch and three volunteers from his platoon sneaked up a steep embankment behind the Germans and surprised a machine gun crew. Bloch leaped up while firing his carbine, wounding the gunner. He kicked the machine gun into the laps of four surprised Germans who surrendered.

Moving on he came across another machine gun crew in a building and tossed a grenade at them, it failed to explode but alerted the Germans. After an exchange of shots, the Germans scurried into the far corner of the building. Block crept to the opposite end of the structure and surprised the enemy by firing through a window, wounding a rifleman. Then Bloch moved on, motioning his men to follow. As his citation noted:

Lieutenant Bloch undertook the task of wiping out five enemy machine gun nests that had held up the advance for one day . . . Altogether he single-handedly captured 19 prisoners, wounding 6 of them, and eliminated a total of 5 enemy machine gun nests. His gallant actions saved his company many casualties and permitted them to continue the attack with increased vigor.

After Bloch received his Medal of Honor at a regimental review on February 6, 1945, he was flown home for a few weeks with his family and to take part in a tour to sell war bonds. In October, shortly after the war ended, he asked to be separated from the army but found no satisfaction working as a civilian. When offered a regular Army commission, he accepted and spent the next 20 years on active duty. He retired in 1965 as a Colonel after being diagnosed with coronary problems. At the time he was serving with the Washington State National Guard 41st Division. He and his wife raised their four children while living at Richmond Beach near Seattle.

Orville Bloch died in 1973 and was the first to be buried in the new Medal of Honor section of Seattle's Washelli Cemetery.

GREGORY BOYINGTON
Major, USMC

Gregory Boyington was born in Couer d'Alene, Idaho, in 1912. In 1927 his family moved to Tacoma. In 1935 he earned an Engineering Degree from the University of Washington and a commission in the Marine Corps. For the next half dozen years he took flying lessons and did so well at it that he qualified as a member of the Marines' exhibition team. (One of his flying teammates was Seattle native Robert Galer, who also received the Medal of Honor.)

In 1941, before Pearl Harbor, Boyington volunteered to join General Chennault's Flying Tigers that were helping the Chinese resist the Japanese invasion. Since the U.S. was not yet officially at war, Boyington's Marine Corps commission was filed in a drawer. Over the next half year he flew missions out of China, strafing the Japanese.

In July 1942, with the U.S. having declared war, Boyington asked to be returned to the Marine Corps and was sent to the Solomon Islands. There he was put in charge of a group of unassigned, hard-living marines considered difficult to manage. Boyington had much in common with them and soon molded them into the famed "Black Sheep" Squadron.

Led by the 30-year-old Boyington, they ferociously met the enemy in the skies Because he was the oldest among them, they called him "Pappy." Over the Solomons between September 1943 and January 1944, though constantly outnumbered, the Black Sheep inflicted crippling damage on the enemy. Boyington himself shot down at least 26 Japanese planes, which tied him for the record.

In January 1944, as Boyington was attempting to save his wingman from an overpowering number of Japanese planes, the fuel tank of his fighter was hit and exploded. Boyington managed to eject himself and his parachute opened just before he hit the water. Four Japanese Zeros then strafed him, leaving him badly wounded. He managed to crawl aboard his inflatable raft and was captured. In prison camp, he was starved and tortured but survived and was transferred to a prison camp near Yokohama. Meantime, the Marines had reported him killed in action. His captors had not recognized him until a newspaper somehow reached Japan with his photo on the front page along with an article about his receiving the Medal of Honor posthumously. Fortunately, by then the Japanese military realized they were losing the war and had improved their treatment of Prisoners of War.

Five days after the Japanese surrender, the prison camp where Pappy Boyington was held was liberated. By the time he arrived in the U.S. to a hero's welcome, he had regained some of the 70 pounds he lost as a POW. President Truman presented him the Medal of Honor on October 5, 1945.

In the years following, Pappy Boyington's life was full of successes and failures, the latter due in part to his fondness for alcohol. Two of his books were commercial successes, one of them titled *Baa, Baa, Black Sheep* was a best seller and became a popular television series in the mid-1970s. He also was an acknowledged artist and prints of his work sold well and his speaking tours attracted crowds.

Colonel Gregory Boyington, one of this state's most famous warriors, died in January 1988 at age 76 and was buried with honors in Arlington National Cemetery.

ROBERT EUGENE BUSH
Hospital Apprentice First Class, USMC

Robert E. Bush was born in Tacoma in 1926. His mother, a Registered Nurse, introduced him to medicine. He attended high school in Pacific County but joined the Navy before graduating. He was sent to Hospital Corpsman School for medic's training, then took a four-month internship at Seattle Naval Hospital, followed by combat training at Camp Pendleton, California.

In December 1944, he was sent to the Russell Islands. In May 1945, during the battle for Okinawa, he was serving with the First Marine Division, when Lieutenant James

Roache was placed in charge of an 11-man reconnaissance patrol. Within a half-hour, half the men were dead or wounded. The Lieutenant was hit but managed to roll onto a sunken ledge just 30 feet from enemy trenches.

Medic Bush was not ordered to rescue the Lieutenant but decided he had to try. With two other men, he raced across a field toward the officer. The two marines with him were killed immediately by Japanese fire. Bush dove down onto the ledge beside the Lieutenant and found him nearly dead from loss of blood. Bush inserted a needle into a vein and began administering albumin. The Lieutenant immediately responded and muttered about getting out of there. Bush insisted they were safer on the ledge until U.S. troops advanced, but the officer jumped up and, dragging tubing and bottle, lurched across the field under intense fire. Though badly wounded, he managed to reach the front lines and safety.

Bush found himself alone in a position that had been revealed to the enemy. A grenade bounced off his posterior and exploded. A second shattered his left arm, the concussion blinding him. A third grenade hit him in the stomach. With shrapnel in gut and buttocks, almost no vision, and a broken arm, he figured the only way to survive was to attack. With a carbine held down by his right hip, he dashed behind a hummock, and then careened into the open toward the enemy, firing at what he thought were their midsections. When his carbine ammunition was gone, he used his 45 revolver. The Japanese retreated from his fire.

Knowing he was bleeding badly, Bush turned toward his compatriots and limped back to where he could collapse onto a stretcher. He was rushed to a jeep ambulance that transported him to an Army hospital where several ounces of shrapnel were removed from his body. They also worked on his right eye that had been blown from its socket.

From the front line hospital, Bush was sent to a hospital ship, then on to Guam and Pearl Harbor and finally to a hospital in Oakland, California. Discharged in July 1945, he returned to his home at South Bend, Washington, and there finished his last year of high school. He was invited to the White House on October 5, 1945, the day after his 21st birthday, where President Truman presented him the Medal of Honor. He and his fiancée had moved their wedding plans ahead so the trip east could be their honeymoon. At the time, Bush was the youngest Navy man ever to be awarded the nation's Medal of Honor.

Robert Bush later enrolled in business courses at the University of Washington and then founded a hardware store and a lumber company to serve southwestern Washington residents. He and his wife developed a close-knit family and in retirement divided their time between homes in Olympia and Palm Springs, California.

JOSE CALUGAS
Sergeant, US Army

Mess Sergeant Jose Calugas had served with the Philippine Scouts for 11 years when on January 16, 1942, he was preparing lunch for the 126 Scouts of the 88th Field Artillery. The unit was still battling effectively, though forced into retreat by overwhelming numbers of Japanese invaders. To quote from the Medal of Honor Citation:

> The action for which the award was made took place near Culis, Bataan Province, Philippine Islands, on 16 January 1942. A battery gun position was bombed and shelled by the enemy until one gun was put out of commission and all the cannoneers were killed or wounded. Sergeant Calugas, a mess sergeant of another battery, voluntarily and without orders ran 1,000 yards across the shell-swept area to the gun position. There he organized a volunteer squad which placed the gun back in commission and fired effectively against the enemy, although the position remained under constant and heavy Japanese artillery fire.

The courageous mess sergeant was scheduled to receive his Medal of Honor from General MacArthur but the General was ordered to Australia and the allied troops were forced to retreat to Corregidor before that date. When Allied troops surrendered to the Japanese, Calugas buried his copy of the general order of the award, figuring that such information would make him a marked man. He survived the Bataan Death March and was imprisoned. Often beaten and suffering malaria, he nearly died before he was released from his cell in January 1943.

The Japanese put him to work in a rice mill. An acquaintance convinced the Japanese to release Calugas and he began spying for the Philippine guerilla forces. After U.S. submarines sneaked arms in to the guerillas in September 1944, Jose Calugas served as leader of a heavy weapons platoon. On April 30, 1945, General George C. Marshall presented the Medal of Honor to 1st Sergeant Calugas.

After the Japanese surrender, Calugas received American citizenship, was promoted to Lieutenant, and in 1945 was transferred to Fort Lewis, Washington. He retired from the U.S. Army in 1957. By then his family had joined him in Tacoma. Calugas, using the GI Bill, earned a Business Administration degree at the University of Puget Sound and became an expediter at the Boeing Company.

JESSE RAY DROWLEY
Staff Sergeant, US Army

Jesse Ray Drowley was born in St. Charles, Michigan, in 1919. He left home prior to his 21st birthday in 1941 to join the Army. After basic training he was assigned to the Americal Division's 132nd Regiment which, after the Pearl Harbor attack, was sent to New Caledonia, then to Guadalcanal where Staff Sergeant Drowley received severe wounds and a Bronze Star for courage in battle. After recuperating on Fiji, Drowley saw further action on Guadalcanal, then his unit was sent on to Bougainville. It was there Drowley lost his left eye and earned the Medal of Honor. The date was January 30, 1944. His citation reads:

> S/Sgt. Drowley, a squad leader in a platoon whose mission during an attack was to remain under cover while holding the perimeter defense and acting as a reserve for the assaulting echelon, saw three members of the assault company fall badly wounded. When intense hostile fire prevented aid from reaching the casualties, he fearlessly rushed forward to carry the wounded to cover. After rescuing two men, S/Sgt. Drowley discovered an enemy pillbox undetected by assaulting tanks that was inflicting heavy casualties upon the attacking force and was the chief obstacle to the success of the advance. Delegating the rescue of the third man to an assistant, he ran across open terrain to one of the tanks. Signaling to the crew, he climbed to the turret, exchanged his weapon for a sub-machine gun and voluntarily rode the deck of the tank directing it toward the pillbox by tracer fire. The tank, under constant heavy enemy fire, continued to within 20 feet of the pillbox where Drowley received a severe bullet wound in the chest. Refusing to return for medical treatment, he remained on the tank and continued to direct its progress until the enemy box was definitely located by the crew. At this point he again was wounded by small-arms fire, losing his left eye and falling to the ground. He remained alongside the tank until the pillbox was completely demolished and another directly behind the first was destroyed. He then returned alone for medical treatment.

He wandered into the American camp, a gruesome picture with part of his forehead shot away, an empty eye socket and his jacket soaked with blood. A doctor arrived seconds later, treated the wounds as best he could and sent Drowley to the hospital, where for a time his survival was questionable. He felt no discomfort when his eye socket was cleaned but suffered considerable pain after the anesthetic wore off. He heard that he might be court-martialed for disobeying an order not to leave his position. Then, he heard that instead he might receive a decoration.

Several operations followed, the final ones by eye specialists at Baxter Veterans' Hospital in Spokane. It was there that he met Kathleen McAvory whom he married that spring. The following September, bride and groom traveled to Washingnton D.C. where President Roosevelt presented Drowley with the Medal of Honor.

They decided to settle permanently in the Pacific Northwest. After sampling other employment, Jesse Drowley was named foreman of all heavy-duty equipment for the 92nd Transport Squadron at Fairchild Air Force Base in Spokane.

ROBERT E. GALER
Major, USMC

Robert E. Galer was born in Seattle in 1913 to a pioneer family for whom Galer Street is named. Galer graduated from Queen Anne High School and then earned an Engineering Degree at the University of Washington. He later was elected to the Washington State Sports Hall of Fame for excelling during his three years as forward on the University basketball team. He was named an All American in 1934. He served four years in Naval ROTC at the University and after graduation enrolled in Marine Corps Aviation Cadet training. An outstanding pilot, he was selected to fly a Boeing F4B4 biplane in the Cleveland Air Races with "Pappy" Boyington, another UW graduate who was awarded the Medal of Honor.

Galer fought in skies over the Solomon Islands, Midway, Okinawa, Iwo Jima and the Philippines. To quote from his citation:

> Leading his squadron repeatedly in daring and aggressive raids against Japanese aerial forces vastly superior in numbers, Maj. Galer availed himself of every favorable attack opportunity, individually shooting down 11 enemy bomber and fighter aircraft over a period of 29 days [over the Solomon Islands]. Though suffering the extreme physical strain attendant upon protracted fighter operations at an altitude above 25,000 feet, the squadron under his zealous and inspiring leadership, shot down a total of 27 Japanese planes. His superb airmanship, his outstanding skill and personal valor reflect great credit upon Maj. Galer's gallant fighting spirit and upon the U.S. Naval Service.

Galer received his Medal of Honor from President Roosevelt on June 15, 1943. He stayed in the Marine Corps after World War II, fought in the Korean Conflict, was shot down and when he bailed out was injured when the tail section smashed into his shoulder.

Robert E. Galer retired from the Marine Corps in 1957 as a Brigadier General. He and his wife moved to Texas where he was involved in several businesses and served on several museum boards.

WILLIAM DEAN HAWKINS
First Lieutenant, USMC

William Hawkins was born in Kansas in 1914. Appointed to the Naval Academy, he attended but did not graduate. However, his Academy credits gave him officer status in the Marine Corps Reserve. Prior to entering active service in World War II, he was employed by a Tacoma title company.

In November 1943, a Carrier Task Force assaulted Tarawa, an island taken by the Japanese early in the war. A formidable shore bombardment and aerial bombing was expected to make the invasion easy. However, although the island was pulverized, pillboxes and bombproof shelters remained largely undamaged and protected concealed Japanese warriors. These enemy machine gun nests at Betio Beach were preventing a Marine advance. That is when Lt. Hawkins and his 34-man Scout Sniper Platoon volunteered for a suicide mission. The Lieutenant and his men, under heavy fire, began an effort to silence the Japanese emplacements. With grenades and demolitions, he repeatedly risked his life to lead attacks on pillboxes and other installations. His platoon that day exterminated six enemy machine gun nests before the first wave of Army troops hit the beach. During this action, the Lieutenant was wounded in the hand.

Early the following day, Hawkins' platoon continued to clear the beachhead of the enemy. On his own initiative and under withering fire, the Lieutenant crawled to a nest of five machine guns and tossed in grenades and fired point blank at the enemy. He received a second wound, this time in his shoulder, but refused to be evacuated. Later that day, after receiving a third wound, the Lieutenant died from loss of blood. Three days later the Americans controlled the island.

Lieutenant Hawkins and nearly 1,000 of his fellow Marines who died in one of the bloodiest battles of the Pacific war were buried in a mass grave on Tarawa. The following March, the airport near the burial site was named Hawkins Field in honor of the Lieutenant. In 1946-47 the bodies in the mass grave, including that of Hawkins, were exhumed and reburied at the newly established National Memorial Cemetery of the Pacific in Honolulu, Hawaii.

William Dean Hawkins was awarded his Medal of Honor posthumously.

LOUIS JAMES HAUGE, JR.
Corporal, USMC

Louis J. Hauge, Jr., was born in Ada, Minnesota in 1924. After finishing high school, he moved west to work in a Tacoma shipyard and lived with his brother in Kent until he joined the Marines.

After training, he was assigned to the First Marine Division and while with them he survived heated combat on New Caledonia, New Guinea, and Peleliu. On the latter island, while serving as a message runner, he was promoted to Corporal for his bravery under fire.

On May 14, 1945 [Victory Day in Europe], the Battalion to which Hauge belonged came under heavy fire on Okinawa and was ordered to assault a heavily fortified hill. The Japanese responded with a mortar barrage on the American lines and followed this with intense machine gun fire. After locating the two gun positions, Corporal Hauge, carrying several hand grenades, raced alone across the enemy field of fire, tossing the grenades at the enemy mortar squads. Before reaching machine gun number one, he was seriously wounded, but managed to kill the members of the crew. He then continued forward toward the second gun, quieting it also, just as a sniper bullet took his life. By eliminating the two strategic machine gun positions the 20-year-old hero had made it possible for his comrades to quickly take the hill.

Louis Hauge's body was never recovered, but he is memorialized on the Wall of the Missing at Punchbowl Cemetery in Honolulu and in the cemetery of Ada, Minnesota, his birthplace, where his name is inscribed on a headstone using the gold lettering reserved for Medal of Honor Recipients.

JOHN DRUSE HAWK
Sergeant, US Army

On July 21, 1944, John Druse "Bud" Hawk landed in France as a replacement and was transported toward the St. Lo breakthrough. The next morning, before officially reaching the front line, his helmet was shot off his head by a sniper, but he was uninjured.

He was assigned to Company E of the 359 Infantry Regiment, of the 90th Division. On the night of August 19 allied troops took positions in an orchard bordering a large field. Because of the terrain, the heaviest weapons the men of Hawk's squad could carry with them were light machine guns and bazookas. They dug in for the night and after dark heard noises nearby that they concluded must be allied activity. At dawn they realized the sounds they had heard were Germans setting up their field guns not more than 100 yards away. The men of Company E commenced firing at the enemy position and the Germans soon realized the Americans lacked heavy weapons. They called up their tanks that began to advance with infantrymen behind them. Sgt. John Hawk fired away with a light machine gun, but the tanks did not hesitate. Hawk's platoon leader, Lieutenant M. H. Smith, reported:

> A tank shell disabled Hawk's gun and wounded him in the thigh but he secured a bazooka and, with a companion, kept the tanks in a small wood until two American tank destroyers arrived. Their shelling was ineffective until Hawk climbed to an exposed position atop a knoll to act as a human aiming stake. The subsequent fire of the tank destroyer knocked out the German tanks and forced the remaining Germans into the open to surrender.

The Citation for his Medal of Honor says Hawk, realizing he could not be heard from atop the knoll, ran back through a concentration of bullets and shrapnel to correct the range, then returned to his exposed position, repeating the performance until two tanks were destroyed and one driven off. The Citation concluded: "Sgt. Hawk's fearless initiative and heroic conduct, even while suffering from a painful wound, was in large measure responsible for crushing two desperate attempts of the enemy to escape from the Falaise Pocket and for taking more than 500 prisoners."

Hawk received other wounds in battles that followed. Just before the Battle of the Bulge, the concussion from a huge shell blew Hawk 90 feet into the air and his buddies apparently believed him dead. He regained consciousness alone and in an exposed position and immediately began looking for his unit. However, before the day ended, Hawk's five months of constant front line action caused him to collapse. That was the end of the war for him. He had enough points to be given a 45-day rest and recuperation. He reached home in Bremerton, incredibly tired from two years of Army service that included months of front line duty.

Then he had a visitor who told him: "I have the pleasure to inform you that you have been selected to receive the Medal of Honor. We'll make plans for you and your family to go by train to Washington, D.C. for the ceremony at the White House."

The 21-year-old war-weary soldier, with visions of fatiguing travel ahead, replied, "Nuts! I'm not going anywhere. They can send it to me parcel post."

When U.S. Senator Warren G. Magnuson heard this story, he arranged to have President Harry S. Truman re-route his itinerary to San Francisco to allow him to stop in Olympia. And so on the morning of June 21, 1945, 8,000 people witnessed the President hang the blue-ribboned Medal of Honor around the neck of Sergeant John Hawk.

John Hawk, born in San Francisco in 1924, had moved with his family when a year old to Seattle and finally to Bainbridge Island where he graduated from High School in 1943. After the war, Hawk married Natalene Crandall of Bremerton and they had three children. Hawk used the GI Bill to earn a Bachelor's Degree, plus teaching and superintendent certificates and became an educator noted for an easy sense of humor and strict discipline.

VICTOR LEONARD KANDLE
First Lieutenant, US Army

Victor Leonard Kandle (usually called Leonard) was born in 1921 at his grandmother's homestead near Roy, Washington. He attended schools in McKenna, Yelm and Puyallup and enjoyed fishing, backpacking and camping. After high school, he enrolled at Beutel Business College in Tacoma, often walking the 8 miles each way.

He joined the Army in September 1940 and received basic training at Fort Lewis where he recognized his grandmother's homestead. He served as the Commanding General's field secretary and was sent to Camp Rucker, Alabama, for further training. From there he was sent to Fort Benning , Georgia, for officers candidate training and was commissioned a 2nd Lieutenant. By then he had taken as his wife Marigene Lee of Tacoma.

Kandle was sent to Italy to join the 15th Infantry Regiment of the 3rd Division that had trained at Fort Lewis. The unit moved into France and early in October 1944, near the town of LaForge, Kandle earned his Medal of Honor. To quote from the Citation:

> Lieutenant Kandle, while leading a reconnaissance patrol into enemy territory, engaged in a duel at pointblank range with a German field officer and killed him. Having already taken five

enemy prisoners that morning, he led a skeleton platoon of 16 men reinforced with a light machine gun squad through fog and over precipitous mountain terrain to fall on the rear of a German stronghold in a quarry which had checked the advance of an infantry battalion for 2 days. Rushing forward several yards ahead of his assault elements, Lieutenant Kandle fought his way into the heart of the enemy strong point, and, by his boldness and audacity, forced the Germans to surrender. Harassed by machine gun fire from a position which he had bypassed in the dense fog, he moved to within 15 yards of the enemy, killed a German machine gunner with rifle fire, and led his men in the destruction of another machine gun crew and its rifle security elements. Finally, he led his small force against a fortified house held by 2 German officers and 30 enlisted men. After establishing a base of fire, he rushed forward alone through an open clearing in full view of the enemy, smashed through a barricaded door, and forced all 32 Germans to surrender. His intrepidity and bold leadership resulted in the capture or killing of 3 enemy officers and 54 enlisted men, the destruction of 3 enemy strong points and the seizure of enemy positions which had halted a battalion attack.

Unfortunately First Lieutenant Victor Leonard Kandle never knew that he would receive the Medal of Honor. He was killed in action near Colmar two months after his action near LaForge. He was 23 at the time. He was buried in Epinol Cemetery in France. General H.C. Pratt, Commander of the Western Defense Command, presented the Medal of Honor to Kandle's widow and two-year-old son, Terry, at the Presidio, San Francisco, on June 4, 1945. Kandle's other decorations included the Silver Star, the Bronze Star, French Croix DeGuere and several battle ribbons.

REINHARDT JOHN KEPPLER
Boatswain's Mate First Class, US Navy

"Reiny," as his friends called Reinhardt Keppler, was born at Ralston, Washington, in 1918. After graduating from Wapato High School in 1935, he enlisted in the Navy. He soon decided to make this service his career and advanced through the ratings to Boatswain's Mate First Class. His first four years at sea were spent aboard the battleship West Virginia and the heavy cruiser USS San Francisco. He participated in several actions against the enemy at Pearl Harbor, Bougainville, Salamauna and Guadalcanal. Then on November 12, 1942, in actions at Savo Island near Guadalcanal, Keppler's bravery earned him the Medal of Honor. His Citation reads in part:

When a hostile torpedo plane, during a daylight air raid, crashed on the after machine gun platform, Keppler promptly assisted in removal of the dead and by his capable supervision of the wounded, undoubtedly helped save the lives of several shipmates who otherwise might have perished. That night, when the ship's hangar was set afire during the great battle off Savo Island, he bravely led a hose into the starboard side of the stricken area and there, without assistance and despite frequent hits from terrific enemy bombardment, eventually brought the fire under control. Later, although mortally wounded, he labored valiantly in the midst of bursting shells, persistently directing fire fighting operations and administering to wounded personnel until he finally collapsed from loss of blood.

Medics at the dressing station found his uniform soaked with blood. He continued to direct others in their duties and called attention to other wounded while refusing aid for himself. With his last minute of consciousness, Keppler administered aid to an injured firefighter. When daylight arrived, Keppler was taken to a hospital on New Hebrides where he died on the fourth day after the battle of Savo Island.

Keppler was posthumously awarded the Medal of Honor and the Navy Cross. While on leave in May 1942, less than six months before his death, he had married Elizabeth West of San Francisco. His body was brought home from the New Hebrides in 1948 and buried with full military honors at Golden Gate Cemetery, San Bruno, California. In June 1946, with his widow and three brothers in attendance, at Bethlehem Steel Company in San Francisco, a new destroyer was christened the USS Keppler. In 1984 Keppler Hall was dedicated on hospital hill in the Puget Sound Naval Shipyard. They serve as reminders of the bravery of Reinhardt John Keppler.

DEXTER KERSTETTER
Private First Class, US Army

Dexter Kerstetter was born in Centralia, Washington, in 1907. Thirty-five years later, as a member of Company C., 130th Regiment of the U.S. Army's 33rd Division, his unit became involved in battles to retake the Philippine Islands.

On April 12, 1945, near the small town of Galiano, his company faced an enemy fortification atop a hill. At dawn the Americans attacked and immediately lost four men. Pfc. Kerstetter located a better route and led a squad up a steep ridge. The enemy spotted them but Kerstetter ignored their fire and forged ahead. Using grenades and his rifle, he forced the Japanese back, his fellow squad members following him.

Kerstetter spotted a hole and lowered himself into it to find himself in a cave. Moving carefully, he surprised four of the enemy and killed them. He crawled back out onto the trail where a machine gun was holding up the advance of his unit. He managed to creep forward and silence the gun. When a group of about 20 enemy suddenly attacked, he filled the air with bullets, killing several and scattering the rest. Out of ammunition, he lobbed his last grenades.

Having burned his hand on his hot rifle barrel, he raced back to the American lines for first aid, and while there encouraged a second platoon to join the attack. When the day ended Pfc. Kerstetter had dispatched 16 enemy soldiers and, thanks to his aggressive tactics, Company C commanded the hill.

In October 1945, Kerstetter received the Medal of Honor from President Truman. After the war he worked at Puget Sound Naval Shipyard and continued as a member of the Washington National Guard from which he retired with the rank of Colonel. In 1972, he accidentally drowned while fishing in Hood Canal, leaving a widow, two daughters and two sons.

JOE E. MANN
Private First Class, US Army

Pfc. Joe Mann may have more memorials named for him than does any other soldier from the State of Washington.

He was born in 1922 in Reardan, Washington, a town a few miles west of Spokane. There were nine children in the family that operated a 720-acre wheat ranch. His heavy farm chores did not hinder his playing football, basketball and tennis in high school. He also turned out for plays and debate. His friends describe him as a handsome and thoughtful youth who was always pleasant company.

Joe Mann enlisted in the Army in September 1942, was sent to Fort Lewis for basic training, then chose to join the paratroopers. He was sent to Europe with the 101st Airborne. On September 17, 1944, this Division took part in one of the biggest airdrops of World War II over the Netherlands.

Joe Mann, as first scout, was sent forward to help capture a bridge over the Wilhelmina Canal. By the time his platoon reached the bridge, German fire had killed many members. The enemy had also infiltrated the village of Best during the night. Surrounded by the enemy, the Lieutenant in charge, Joe Mann and a few others dug in on the bank of the canal and began seeking an escape route.

The Citation for Mann's Medal of Honor states:

On 18 September 1944, in the vicinity of Best, Holland, his platoon, attempting to seize the bridge across the Wilhelmina Canal, was surrounded and isolated by an enemy force greatly superior in personnel and fire power. Acting as lead scout, Private Mann boldly crept to within rocket-launcher range of an enemy artillery position and, in the face of heavy enemy fire, destroyed an 88-mm gun and an ammunition dump. Completely disregarding the great danger involved, he remained in his exposed position, and, with his M1 rifle, killed the enemy one-by-one until he was wounded four times.

He was hit twice in a shoulder by rifle fire. The medic treated his arm and placed it in a sling to stop the bleeding, but Mann refused to stay under cover and returned to the battle. He was then shot twice in his other shoulder. Now both arms were in slings and bound to his body. Still he insisted he would stand his turn at sentry duty. At dawn, the Germans crept forward to where they could toss grenades into the American position. American soldiers caught two grenades and throw them back at the enemy, a third missed their location, a fourth hit the machinegun and blinded the gunner, a fifth landed at the sightless gunners, feet but he felt around for it and tossed it away just as it exploded harmlessly. The sixth grenade sailed over Joe Mann's head. Helpless with his arms bound to his body, he yelled "Grenade!" and fell backward over it to protect his buddies. The explosion shattered his body and he died within minutes.

In 1945, the Medal of Honor was presented to Joe Mann's father by the Commanding Officer of Baxter Veterans Hospital in Spokane. In 1949, Mann's body was returned to the U.S. and buried in Spokane's Greenwood Cemetery.

In 1956 a Dutch journalist happened upon the story of this brave young American and the articles he wrote resulted in Joe Mann's parents being hosted at the dedication of a monument to him and the other Americans who fought at Best. Over the next few years, several structures were named for him, among them: the Army Reserve Training Facility in Spokane; Mann Theater at Fort Campbell, Kentucky; Mann Field at Fort Benning, Georgia; Mann

Avenue at Fort Lewis; and a naval ship was christened the USS Joe E Mann. In 1987 in Berlin, Germany, a Mann Fitness Center was dedicated. And to this day the residents of Reardan recall with fondness the young man from their town who lost his life saving his buddies and in so doing earned the Medal of Honor.

LLOYD G. MCCARTER
Private, US Army

Private Lloyd G. McCarter was born in St. Maries, Idaho, in 1917 and lived there through high school. After graduation in 1936, he entered Gonzaga University in Spokane on a scholarship. Shortly after Pearl Harbor was attacked he requested transfer from the Idaho National Guard to the U.S. Army. He was sworn in at Tacoma and assigned to the 503rd Parachute Infantry Regiment.

After battles on Noumea and New Guinea, his unit parachuted onto the island of Corregidor in the Philippines. The date was February 16, 1945, and the Americans were fighting to regain the islands from the Japanese. The Citation for his Medal of Honor states:

> Shortly after the initial parachute assault, he crossed 30-yards of open ground under intense enemy fire, and at point-blank range silenced a machine gun with hand grenades. On the afternoon of 18 February he killed 6 snipers. That evening, when a large force attempted to bypass his company, he volunteered to move to an exposed area and open fire. The enemy attacked his position repeatedly throughout the night and was each time repulsed. By 2 o'clock in the morning, all the men about him had been wounded; but shouting encouragement to his comrades and defiance at the enemy, he continued to bear the brunt of the attack, fearlessly exposing himself to locate enemy soldiers and then pouring heavy fire on them. He repeatedly crawled back to the American line to secure more ammunition. When his sub-machine gun would no longer operate, he seized an automatic rifle and continued to inflict heavy casualties. At dawn the enemy attacked with renewed intensity. Completely exposing himself to hostile fire, he stood erect to locate the most dangerous enemy positions.

McCarter's luck finally ran out and he was seriously wounded but refused offers to be taken back to a hospital. He kept urging his compatriots to fight on.

Lloyd McCarter never recovered fully from his severe wounds but in August 1945 was well enough to travel to the White House to receive his Medal of Honor. In 1948 he married Mable M. Montague and worked for the Veterans' Administration at Sand Point, Idaho. In constant pain and carrying a bullet near his heart, he died February 2, 1956, at the age of 38 and was buried with full military honors at Woodlawn Cemetery in St. Maries, Idaho.

RICHARD MILES MCCOOL, JR.
Lieutenant, US Navy

Richard M. McCool, Jr., was born in 1922 in Oklahoma. He graduated from the U.S. Naval Academy in 1944 and was assigned as Commanding Officer of *LSC 122*. A few months later he and his crew were off Okinawa when a kamikaze smashed into the destroyer *USS William D. Porter*. McCool directed his ship to the rescue. When it was apparent the destroyer would sink despite all efforts to keep it afloat, McCool eased the LSC up to the destroyer and took the crew and official papers on board and delivered them to safety. Then early in the evening of June 11, 1945, as his Citation reads:

> When his own craft was attacked simultaneously by two of the enemy's suicide squadron, he instantly hurled the full power of his gun batteries against the plunging aircraft, shooting down the first and damaging the second before it crashed his station in the conning tower and engulfed the immediate area in a mass of flames. Although suffering from shrapnel wounds and painful burns, he rallied his concussion-shocked crew and initiated vigorous fire fighting measures and then proceeded to rescue several trapped in a blazing compartment, subsequently carrying one man to safety despite the excruciating pain of additional severe burns. Unmindful of all personal danger, he continued his efforts without respite until aid arrived from other ships and he was evacuated.

While trying to shout directions to his men as they were dousing the fire, he realized he could hardly breathe. His right side, he found, was soaked in blood. He transferred command to his Executive Officer before allowing a medical corpsman to lead him away.

Richard McCool recovered sufficiently to receive his Medal of Honor from President Truman in December 1945 and returned to active duty the next year. He retired from the Navy in 1974 as a Captain and settled on Bainbridge Island, Washington, with his wife Elaine, in a home where their three children could visit them often and he could pursue his hobbies of gardening and the study of history and drama.

DOUGLAS ALBERT MUNRO
Signalman First Class, USCG

Washington is the home state of the only Coast Guardsman in U.S. history to be awarded the Medal of Honor. Douglas Albert Munro was born in Vancouver, B.C., in 1919. His family moved to Cle Elum, Washington, when he was a youth. He completed high school there and enrolled at Central Washington State College in Ellensburg where he served as drum major of the college band and excelled in swimming and skiing.

When he tried to enlist in the Coast Guard in 1938, they turned him down as underweight. With his mother's help he gained six pounds in ten days and again tried and was accepted. Four years later Munro, now a Petty Officer in command of 24 Higgins boats, protected a company of Marines in a manner that resulted in his being awarded the Medal of Honor.

The Coast Guard had landed the Marines on Guadalcanal in August and September 1942. Reinforcements were landed on September 27 on the western side of the island and ordered to establish a beachhead. Munro and his Higgins boats successfully delivered the men and returned to their base. Later that same afternoon, word came that the recently landed Marines were under heavy attack by superior Japanese forces. When a call for volunteers was issued, Munro was among the first to offer his services.

Placed in charge of ten boats, Munro led them successfully to the Marines on the beach. Eight of the boats loaded and were away in seconds. Munro's boat and one other stayed to rescue the small number of marines who had covered the other troops as they boarded the escape vessels. Enemy machine guns from the far side of a narrow stretch of water began firing at those last Marines. There seemed no way for them to reach the rescue boats except by crossing the open beach under a hail of lead. Munro recognized another possibility. He taxied his boat close to the shore as a shield between the beach and the enemy. Enemy machine gun fire wounded two of his men, but he kept his boat shielding those scrambling to the other Higgins boat. As the last marines dived aboard, Munro started to pull away, but just then a Japanese bullet mortally wounded him. He lost consciousness momentarily, but gained his senses and turned his head toward the shore, straining to see. His last whispered words were: "Did they all get off?"

President Roosevelt at the White House presented Munro's Medal of Honor to his mother on May 24, 1943. A short time later, Mrs. Munro joined the SPARS, the Coast Guard Women's Corps. Later, she was invited to christen a destroyer escort, the *USS Douglas A. Munro,* when it was launched in Houston, Texas. A second ship, a high-endurance cutter, was named for him in the early 1970s, and he was further memorialized when a barracks was named for him at the Coast Guard Academy in New London, Connecticut.

Douglas Albert Munro was temporarily buried at Henderson Field on Guadalcanal. After the war, his body was brought home to Laurel Hill Memorial Park in Cle Elum. In 1976, one of the new Medal of Honor headstones was placed on his grave during a special memorial service.

WILLIAM KENZO NAKAMURA
Private, US Army

William Kenzo Nakamura was born in Seattle on June 21, 1922, and graduated from Garfield High School in 1939. His education at the University of Washington was ended by orders sending local Japanese-American families to Minidoka Relocation Center at Hunt, Idaho. His mother had died of cancer shortly before the forced relocation.

Bill or Kenzo, he was called both, followed his older brother into the Army. Their thought was that this action might help overcome prejudices against Japanese-Americans. Both trained with the 442nd Regimental Combat Team made up of young Nisei. Early in July 1944, the unit was fighting its way up Italy's coastline against well-trained Wehrmacht troops, when on July 4 they bumped into Germans atop Hill 140 and a fierce battle ensued. As Nakamura's platoon neared the crest of the hill, concealed German machine gunners opened fire from 35 yards away. Captain William Aull, commander of the platoon, reported that Pfc. Nakamura, not waiting for orders, dodged his way among scattered shrubs, then crawled another 20 yards with bullets barely clearing his body. He rose to a kneeling position to accurately toss four hand grenades that wiped out the enemy position.

As his platoon moved toward the summit of the hill, a radio message ordered them back so that mortars could bombard the crest. As the platoon again approached the hilltop enemy machine-guns opened fire from a nearby farmhouse. For a second time, with no one ordering him to do so, Nakamura crawled toward the enemy, stopping at the edge of a grain field. From there he expended several clips of ammunition in his M-1 rifle, allowing his platoon buddies to withdraw without further casualties.

A short time later, when the platoon again advanced, they found Nakamura lying in his advanced position, still clutching his M-1. He had been shot in the head by a sniper. He was 22 years old when he died.

Nakamura had married Hisako Deguchi a month before being sent overseas. Their short honeymoon was their only time together. After the war, the body of Pfc. William K. Nakamura was returned to Seattle and interred beneath a small headstone in the veterans' cemetery at Evergreen-Washelli.

In May 2000, 56 years after his death, the Army announced that Pfc. Nakamura was being awarded the nation's highest award for bravery in battle, the Medal of Honor. Few of his family members and friends survived to learn how he lost his life and how his actions saved the lives of many of his buddies in the 442nd Regiment, the most highly decorated World War II Army unit. His simple headstone now includes the information that he was a Medal of Honor recipient.

JACK JAMES PENDLETON
Staff Sergeant, US Army

Jack J. Pendleton was born in North Dakota in 1918. Ten years later, the family moved to Yakima, Washington, where Jack graduated from high school. His father died in 1931 and Jack and a brother worked to support the family. In 1942, Jack was drafted at age 23.

After basic training, he joined the 30th Division at Camp White, Oregon, and Camp Claiborne, Louisiana, before the division was sent to Europe. On October 12, 1944, at Bardenberg, Germany, Jack Pendleton, now a Staff Sergeant, showed his mettle. To quote from the Citation for his Medal of Honor:

> When Company I was advancing on the town of Bardenberg, Germany, they reached a point approximately two-thirds of the distance through the town when they were pinned down by fire from a nest of enemy machine guns. This enemy strong point was protected by a lone machine gun strategically placed at an intersection and firing down a street which offered little or no cover or concealment for the advancing troops. The elimination of this protecting machine gun was imperative in order that the strong position it protected could be neutralized. After repeated and unsuccessful attempts had been made to knock out this position, S/Sgt. Pendleton volunteered to lead his squad in an attempt to neutralize this strong point. S/Sgt. Pendleton started his squad slowly forward, crawling about 10 yards in front of his men in the advance toward the enemy guns. After advancing approximately 130 yards under the withering fire, S/Sgt. Pendleton was seriously wounded in the leg by a burst from the gun he was assaulting. Disregarding his grievous wound, he ordered his men to remain where they were and, with a supply of hand grenades, he slowly and painfully worked his way forward alone. With no hope of surviving the veritable hail of machine gun fire which he deliberately drew onto himself, he succeeded in advancing to within 10 yards of the enemy position when he was instantly killed by a burst from the enemy gun. By deliberately diverting the attention of the enemy machine gunners upon himself, a second squad was able to advance, undetected, and with the help of S/Sgt. Pendleton's squad, neutralized the lone machine gun, while another platoon of his company advanced up the intersecting street and knocked out the machine gun nest which the first gun had been covering. S/Sgt. Pendleton's sacrifice enabled the entire company to continue the advance and complete their mission at a critical phase of the action.

Jack Pendleton was buried in a military cemetery in Belgium, then three years later his body was moved to Yakima's Tahoma cemetery. His brother, very fond of Jack, said that the action that resulted in Jack's receiving the Medal of Honor posthumously was typical of him, that if someone told him something couldn't be done, he'd insist that it could.

ALBERT HAROLD ROOKS
Captain US Navy

For ten months Captain Albert Rooks commanded the heavy cruiser *USS Houston*, flagship of the Asiatic Fleet. He welded his officers and crew into a strong organization with extraordinary ingenuity and stamina. As his ship was escorting a convoy from Australia to Netherlands East Indies, a superior force of Japanese ships attacked, forcing Captain Rooks to order the entire convoy to turn back.

In the next action, the Battle of Java Sea, the *Houston* led the way in a surface battle against a strong enemy force. The *Houston*, though severely damaged, managed to escape sinking. After repairs the *Houston* left Java with the Australian ship *Perth* to pass through Sunda Straits. At 11:15 p.m. Rooks heard a lookout report two enemy ships were at the entrance of the Straits. He gave orders to commence firing. Then the lookout reported nine more enemy ships dead ahead. Rooks altered course, but at 11:45 after two torpedoes sank the *Perth*, the Japanese concentrated fire on the *Houston*. For 45 minutes Rooks dodged his ship about in the dark.

Then at midnight, a hit on her forecastle started a fire illuminating the cruiser. Firepower rained down on the *Houston* but her gunners fired right back. They sank one large Japanese warship and drove four transports ashore and damaged other enemy vessels. But the Japanese Navy would not be denied. A salvo smashed the *Houston's* main battery and a shell hit the turret as powder kegs were being loaded. Three torpedoes punctured *Houston's* hull. Still the crew fought on.

At about half an hour past midnight on March 1, 1945, a bursting shell killed Captain Rooks and a gun crew standing near a machine gun mount. Still the other guns fired until ammunition was gone. The ship lost headway as Japanese destroyers gunned those on deck. The Houston lay dead in the water and "Abandon ship" was sounded. Ten minutes later she slipped beneath the surface taking with her the body of the Captain and 500 of her dead and wounded crew. Later 227 more died, drowning in the sea or dying in prison camp.

Captain Albert Rooks, born in 1891 in Colton, Washington, graduated from Walla Walla High School and in 1914 from the Naval Academy. He served on submarines, destroyers and battleships, instructed at the Naval Academy and served as Aide to the Superintendent. He advanced to rank of Captain on July 1, 1940. Captain Rooks was listed as missing in action on March 1, 1942 and declared dead nine months later. His widow, Edith, and two sons, all of Seattle, survived him. Mrs. Rooks with son Harold received the posthumously awarded Medal of Honor in June 1943 from President Roosevelt at the White House.

The Captain is memorialized on the Walls of the Missing in the Manila American Cemetery and a destroyer launched from a Seattle shipyard in September 1944 was named for him.

DONALD KIRBY ROSS
Machinist, US Navy

Donald K. Ross, a Navy Warrant Machinist, was the Engineering Duty Officer aboard the *USS Nevada* on December 7, 1941, the day the Japanese struck Pearl Harbor. The citation for his Medal of Honor reads:

> For distinguished conduct in the line of his profession, extraordinary courage and disregard of his own life during the attack on the Fleet in Pearl Harbor, Territory of Hawaii, by Japanese forces on December 7, 1941. When his station in the forward dynamo room of the USS Nevada became almost untenable due to smoke, steam

and heat, Machinist Ross forced his men to leave that station and performed all the duties himself until blinded and unconscious. Upon being rescued and resuscitated, he returned and secured the forward dynamo room and proceeded to the after dynamo room where he was later again rendered unconscious by exhaustion. Again recovering consciousness, he returned to his station where he remained until directed to abandon it.

The dynamo rooms were vital to the ship. They provided the power for the guns, fire-fighting equipment and general operations. Ross kept them operating. He also managed to rescue the Chief Machinist Mate.

The next morning the Doctor determined that Ross, still unable to see clearly and considerably fatigued, dehydrated, and shaken, should go to the hospital. En route, Ross recognized the chaos at the Fleet Landing. Someone needed to organize boat pools to deliver men and supplies to ships in the stream. Though he had very little sight, people told him what was needed and he used a pre-dial-model phone to send messages. On Wednesday morning, Ross was still on the dock telephoning, ordering, and organizing. Finally, they got him to the hospital where, after a time, his sight returned. Ten days later he reported back to his ship.

On April 18, 1942, Donald Kirby Ross was decorated with the Medal of Honor on board the *USS Vesta* in Pearl Harbor. Admiral Chester Nimitz performed the ceremony not far from where *Nevada* was moored that morning of December 7.

Ross was born in Kansas in 1910, enlisted in the Navy in 1929, completed machinist school first in his class and was assigned to the China Service. In 1940 he met Helen Lou Meyer of Chicago, a schoolteacher. They married in 1942 and produced four children. (It was Helen Lou Meyer Ross who, with the aid of her husband, wrote the book *Men of Valor*, the major source for these biographies.)

Don Ross stayed in the Navy until 1956, rising from Apprentice Seaman to Captain. When he retired, he, his wife and family established a dairy farm and developed a strain of polled cattle on the Kitsap Peninsula. Don Ross, a good speaker and noted storyteller, after his retirement, spoke all over the country about patriotism. On December 7, 1991, the 50th anniversary of the attack on Pearl Harbor, Captain Ross was honored by being asked to introduce President George Bush at the Arizona Memorial.

Donald Kirby Ross died on May 27, 1992. At this writing, his widow lives in Port Orchard, Washington.

WILBURN K. ROSS
Private, US Army

Allied armies invaded France on June 6, 1944. The 3rd Infantry Division of the Seventh Army by October 30 had reached a small village called St. Jacques. Company G of the 30th Regiment was ordered to attack a company of elite German mountain troops entrenched in the foothills of the nearby DuForez Mountains. A hot battle ensued. Of the 88 men who started the day, only 33 remained mobile at 11:30 a.m. Realizing drastic action was necessary, Private Wilburn Ross took the initiative. As the Citation for his Medal of Honor explains:

> Private Ross placed his light machine gun 10 yards in advance of the foremost supporting riflemen in order to absorb the initial impact of an enemy counter-attack. With machine gun and small arms fire striking the earth near him, he fired with deadly effect on the assaulting force and repelled it. Despite the hail of automatic fire and the explosion of rifle grenades within a stone's throw of his position, he continued to man his machine gun alone, holding off six more German attacks. When the eighth assault was launched most of his supporting riflemen were out of ammunition. They took positions in echelon behind Private Ross and crawled up, during the attack, to extract a few rounds of ammunition from his machine gun ammunition belt. Private Ross fought on virtually without assistance and, despite the fact that enemy grenadiers crawled to within 4 yards of his position in an effort to kill him with hand grenades, he again directed accurate and deadly fire on the hostile force and hurled it back. After expending his last rounds, Private Ross was advised to withdraw to the company command post, together with eight surviving riflemen, but, as more ammunition was expected, he declined to do so. The Germans launched their last all-out attack, converging their fire on Private Ross in a desperate attempt to destroy the machine gun which stood between them and a decisive breakthrough. As his supporting riflemen fixed bayonets for a last-ditch stand, fresh ammunition arrived and was brought to Private Ross just as the advance assault elements were about to swarm over his position. He opened murderous fire on the oncoming enemy, killed 40 and wounded 10 of the attacking force; broke the assault single-handed, and forced the Germans to withdraw. Having killed or wounded at least 58 Germans in more than 5 hours of continuous combat and having saved the remnants of his company from destruction, Private Ross remained at his post that night and the following day, for a total of 36 hours. His actions throughout this engagement were an inspiration to his comrades and maintained the high traditions of the military service.

Wilburn K. Ross was born in May 1922 in Strunk, Kentucky, and entered the Army there in November 1942. General Alexander Patch decorated him with the Medal of Honor in Hitler Stadium, Nuremberg, Germany, on April 14, 1945.

Ross retired as Master Sergeant on February 1, 1964 and settled in DuPont, Washington, near Fort Lewis, with his wife Monica and their five children. For twenty years he was employed at the Veterans' Administration Office at American Lake Veterans' Hospital. When he retired, he devoted many days and evenings to patriotic programs.

BRUCE AVERY VANVOORHIS
Lieutenant Commander, US Navy

On July 6, 1943, during the battle for the Solomon Islands, the U.S. decoded a Japanese message revealing that the enemy air group on Green Island planned a surprise attack on the U.S. airbase on Hare Island. The islands were located about 700 miles apart. The military feared that a mass flight to destroy the Japanese base would alert the enemy. However, if a lone plane could sneak in, the pilot might be able to deliver a crippling blow before detection. Such an attack might force the Japanese to drop their attack on Hare Island, but the chances for the plane crew to survive were considered very small. VanVoorhis and his men volunteered for the dangerous flight and took off in the black hours of the morning. The Citation for his Medal of Honor reads:

> For conspicuous gallantry and intrepidity at the risk of his life above and beyond the call of duty as Squadron Commander of Bombing Squadron 102 and as Plane Commander of a PB4Y-1 Patrol Bomber operating against the enemy on Japanese-held Green Island during the battle of the Solomon Islands, 6 July 1943. Fully aware of the limited chance of surviving an urgent mission, voluntarily undertaken to prevent a surprise Japanese attack against our forces, Lt. Comdr. VanVoorhis took off in total darkness on a perilous 700-mile flight without escort or support. Successful in reaching his objective, despite treacherous and varying winds, low visibility and difficult terrain, he fought a lone, but relentless, battle under fierce anti-aircraft fire and overwhelming aerial opposition. Forced lower and lower by pursuing planes, he coolly persisted in his mission of destruction. Abandoning all chance of a safe return, he executed six bold, ground-level attacks to demolish the enemy's vital radio station, installations, anti-aircraft guns and crews with bombs and machine gun fire, and to destroy one fighter plane in the air and three on the water. Caught in his own bomb blast, Lt. Comdr. VanVoorhis crashed into the lagoon off the beach, sacrificing himself in a single-handed

fight against almost insuperable odds, to make a distinctive contribution to our continued offense in driving the Japanese from the Solomons and, by superb daring, courage and resoluteness of purpose, enhanced the finest traditions of the U.S. Naval Service.

Bruce Avery VanVoorhis was born in Aberdeen, Washington in 1908. Appointed to the Naval Academy at Annapolis, he graduated with the class of June 1929. Two years later he completed flight training and served in flight capacity on several different aircraft carriers. He became Commanding Officer of Patrol Squadron 102 in 1942.

VanVoorhis was declared missing in action on July 6, 1943, the day of his attack on Green Island, and was declared dead on January 25, 1946. He left a widow and two sons. He and the five crewmembers of his plane were later buried in a group grave in Jefferson Barracks National Cemetery, St. Louis Missouri. A destroyer escort was named *The VanVoorhis* in his honor and a plaque to him was installed in Memorial Hall at the United States Naval Academy.

JONATHAN M. WAINWRIGHT
General, US Army

Jonathan M. Wainwright, IV, was born in 1883 while his Army officer father was stationed at Fort Walla Walla in Washington Territory. As did his father before him, young Wainwright attended West Point Military Academy, an appointee from the new State of Washington. He graduated in 1906.

During World War I he served in the 76th and 82nd Divisions. Between the two World Wars he held numerous staff and service school assignments. In September 1940 he was ordered to the Pacific to command a Philippine Division and to serve as Field Commander under General Douglas MacArthur. When MacArthur was ordered to Australia in May 1942, Lieutenant General Wainwright was given command of 76,000 troops in the Philippine Islands attempting to hold off 200,000 Japanese. Forced to retreat to Corregidor, the General and his troops fought off the enemy for 28 days. With food, water, ammunition and hospital supplies depleted, the defenders held the enemy at bay with hand-to-hand combat during the final 15 hours before surrendering.

The Citation for the General's Medal of Honor reads:

He distinguished himself by intrepid and determined leadership against greatly superior enemy forces. At the repeated risk of life above and beyond the call of duty in his position, he frequented the firing line of his troops where his presence provided the example and incentive that helped make the gallant efforts of these men possible. The final stand on beleaguered Corregidor, for which he was in an important measure personally responsible, commanded the admiration of the Nation's allies. It reflected the high morale of American arms in the face of overwhelming odds. His courage and resolution were a vitally needed inspiration to the then sorely pressed freedom-loving peoples of the world.

Wainwright and tens of thousands of his troops were captured and sent to prisoner-of-war camps where many died. Wainwright spent much of his time in a camp 150 miles north of Mukden, Manchuria. After more than three years, the half-starved Americans at Mukden were liberated by the Russians in August 1945.

General Wainwright was invited to participate in the Japanese surrender ceremony aboard the battleship *Missouri*. Later he returned to the U.S. to a hero's welcome, addressed a joint session of Congress, was raised to the rank of four-star general, and received the Medal of Honor from President Harry S. Truman.

Wainwright then commanded the 4th Army until his retirement in 1947. He died in September 1953.

MORE THAN NAMES ON A WALL

Washington State lost more than 6,200 of its young citizens on the battlefields of World War II. Their names are etched on the granite walls at the Garden of Remembrance outside Benaroya Symphony Hall in downtown Seattle and on various plaques and monuments and are included below. These were vital, active human beings filled with the potential of youth, most of them in their late teens or early twenties when they died fighting to preserve our freedoms, then under attack by dictators who had bloodied many countries in attempts to control the world.

Names on a wall? They are much more than that. Though they died more than a half century ago, surviving family members and friends remember them fondly. In high school and college annuals of the 1930s and early 1940s they are depicted as handsome youth looking out expectantly at the world. Their images exist in family photo albums, and on the walls of family homes. We should remember them, for they gave all they had to give, their young lives, while fighting to keep our country free. Names on a wall. Who were they?

When this book was first contemplated, someone suggested we contact high schools in the State of Washington asking if they would assign interested students to compile brief biographies of former students of their school who were killed in World War II. The thought behind the request was that such an exercise might build understanding about the war years and indicate that those who died in the war were little older than the students. We thought researching the school annuals and newspapers of the war years would provide a history lesson and indicate the tragic cost of the war. And we hoped it would develop the understanding that those are not just names on a memorial wall.

We mailed the letters to more than 100 Washington State high schools, both public and private, that existed during World War II. We explained the objective of the effort and offered to send a list of the war dead from the county in which the school was situated. Those that contributed biographies were to receive free copies of this book. The results forced us to conclude that this plan was not such a good idea. Fewer than 10 high schools responded and only half of them assigned students to prepare brief biographies of some of the war dead from their schools. We certainly do thank those students and teachers who did participate and include here some of their work.

ELLENSBURG HIGH SCHOOL

Two Ellensburg students prepared well-written biographies of former students killed in World War II. Vonchi Pimomo, who wrote several of them, indicated the Ellensburg Daily Record and the High School annual, Klahiam, were sources of information.

William Albert Rice, Seaman 2/c, U.S. Navy, died of burns received aboard the battleship *Arizona* when it was bombed during the Pearl Harbor attack. He was 23 when he died. Born in Walla Walla on April 29, 1918, to Mr. and Mrs. Harry Rice, his family moved to Ellensburg when he was a baby. His mother tragically burned to death in a house fire when he was a year old and he was sent to live with his grandparents, Mr. and Mrs. M. M. Marquis, of La Grand, Oregon. They later moved to Portland where he finished grade school. He then returned to Ellensburg to live with his father and graduated from Ellensburg High School in 1938. William Rice loved boats and water, so he joined the Navy to carry out his dream of seeing the world by the way of the oceans. His father and stepmother and his grandparents survived him.

Corporal Carl Rasmussen of the Army Signal Corps died of wounds in an Army hospital in Tunisia. This 1938 Ellensburg High graduate while a sophomore participated in track, while a junior turned out for football and while a senior served as track manager. All the males in his family served during the war. His father was in the Army transport service; his brother Henry was with the Army Air Corps; his brother, Leo was a Marine Corps sergeant-instructor in North Carolina and his third brother Earl served in the Merchant Marine.

Sergeant James French of the U.S. Army was listed as missing in action in the Sicilian campaign and later the Army confirmed his death. He was the son of Mr. and Mrs. Victor French and had lived in Ellensburg most of his life. While at Ellensburg High School he participated in various activities including the Spanish Club, the Harmonica Club, Hi-Jinks. He was a member of the Blue and White Staff. He graduated in 1935. His parents and three sisters survived him.

Corporal Edwin K. Brown, Jr., of the U.S. Army was killed in action on August 6, 1943, in Sicily at the age of 23. Corporal Brown was the only son and namesake of one of Kittitas County's best known World War I veterans, Colonel E. K. Brown. Young Brown graduated from Ellensburg High School in 1938 and from the University of Washington in 1942. He then immediately enlisted in the army. Corporal Brown served with the 1st Division (the division in which his father served as an artillery officer during World War I). Young Brown dropped from officer's training school when offered an opportunity for immediate active duty and was sent overseas in March 1943. He joined the 1st Division in North Africa in May and landed on Sicily in July. He fought through more than half the 38-day campaign to take that island. Corporal Brown's mother, a trained nurse, had returned to her profession after her husband went overseas in World War I. She returned to nursing again when her son enlisted in World War II. Corporal Brown was survived by his parents and two sisters.

Ferdinand Holmberg a pursuit pilot died in an airplane crash while in action in Italy on October 13, 1943. He was the son of Fred W. Holmberg of Ellensburg. Young Holmberg had lived in Ellensburg since he was 12. In high school he participated in football, track and the Chemistry Club. After graduating in 1936, he enrolled at Central Washington College for two years and at Western Washington College for one year. He was active in college sports, especially skiing. Before enlisting in the Army Air Corps he worked in Alaska for a few months. He received his wings in 1942 and was sent overseas almost immediately. He had seen action in the North African, Sicilian and Italian campaigns before his death.

Francis Raison a Navy fighter pilot died on April 27, 1945, of burns suffered in a plane crash in the Pacific Theater a month earlier. His family believed he was stationed in the Okinawa area. He had been a Hellcat pilot with a carrier-based squadron and had been promoted to assistant gunnery officer. Ensign Raison was survived by his wife Ruthanne, their four-month old son, and his parents Mr. and Mrs. Clifford Raison of Ellensburg.

Pvt. John Massouras: Not all deaths were in battle. Pneumonia claimed the life of Massouras on May 18, 1945, at the hospital at Randolph Field, TX. He was a prominent Ellensburg High School athlete and had enlisted in the Army air cadet program. He trained for a time at the University of Washington before being transferred to the Army Air Forces.

Erin Harries of Ellensburg High School prepared the following six biographies of former students who died in World War II.

Pfc. John (Jack) Kelleher, Jr., died on September 23, 1944, of wounds received three days earlier while fighting on the Siegfried line. He was 22 years old. He attended Ellensburg High School where he excelled in football,

John Raymond Smart graduated in 1937. He was an active student, singing in the glee club and acting in the junior play. As a senior he was elected president of the student body and was inducted into the National Honor Society. An avid sports fan, he joined the sportsman club and served as business manager of the annual staff. After Army Air Corps training he was sent to Europe. Lieutenant Smart was killed when his plane was shot down over Italy on October 20, 1943.

GIG HARBOR HIGH SCHOOL

The following two biographies of Tacoma students were written by Cambria Brighten.

Marine Private Richard B. Anderson was killed during the invasion of the Marshall Islands. It was a tragic death because it occurred as he attempted to save his comrades. As the enemy attacked, he threw a hand grenade but it caught on his ring and bounced down near his buddies. The Private, to protect his compatriots, immediately fell on the grenade. He died the following day on a hospital ship. His story is told in some detail in the list of state Medal of Honor recipients.

Private Ward M. Young was killed in action on November 16, 1944, during the battle for Aachen, the first German city to be taken by American troops. He was 31 years old. Young was born in Midland, a town south of Tacoma, and graduated from Tacoma's Lincoln High School. He was a member of the Tacoma Chapter of DeMoley, and had worked at the Todd Shipyard until entering the service in March 1944. Among his survivors were his daughter, Claudette, and his parents, Mr. and Mrs. I. G. Young of Tacoma.

NORTH MASON HIGH SCHOOL, BELFAIR

Jay Hultberg, a teacher at North Mason High School found several students to research the background of former students who were killed in the war. One of them, Adam Hendrickson, sent the following brief biographies.

Lieutenant Miles E. (Bus) Elliott of Shelton was a P-51 Mustang pilot who had brushed against death several times. Once, when attacking a railroad train at close range, the locomotive exploded, embedding fragments in the fuselage of his aircraft. He had received the Distinguished Flying Cross for his exploits. Before the war, Elliott was employed as a bulldozer operator. He was lost in action over Germany on June 20, 1944, and left a wife and a sister in Shelton.

Pfc. Chester Evans, a tank driver in an armored division, was killed on September 13, 1944, while involved in one of the first invasions of Germany. Evans was born in Iowa in 1925, and when two years old his family moved to Shelton where he graduated with the class of 1943. He entered the Army a couple of months later. At the time of his death, his two brothers and the husbands of his two sisters were in the service.

Corporal Ralph W. Ledrew, a radio gunner in the Army Air Corps, was killed in action in the South Pacific on January 12, 1945, when 21 years of age. His plane was forced down at sea as a result of heavy anti-aircraft fire off the Celebes Islands. His wife, Sally, and two sisters in Shelton survived Ralph, a 1944 graduate of Shelton High School.

Lieutenant James J. Rutledge was killed on July 13, 1945, when his plane crashed as he took off on a night mission from Chungking, China. He was 21 years of age. Born in Meridian, Idaho, on April 4, 1923, he moved to Shelton with his parents in 1925 and graduated from Irene S. Reed High School in 1942. He enlisted in the Air Corps after graduation and was sent overseas to India and China as a B-24 pilot with the Flying Tigers. Three brothers and a sister survived him.

Pfc. James F. Taylor a paratrooper, died in action on January 3, 1945, during the Battle of the Bulge. He had joined the Coast Guard in 1938, then transferred to the Army. After basic training, he participated in the invasions of Sicily and Italy and in the D-Day landing in France. He fought through Europe to Belgium where he lost his life. James was the son of Mr. and Mrs. Jon Taylor of Belfair.

Jaslyn Buckaloo of North Mason High School prepared the following biographies.

Army Pfc. Sidney L. Collins son of Mr. and Mrs. C. C. Collins of Shelton was killed in action in Germany on March 9, 1945. He had enlisted on March 28, 1944 and, after basic training, was sent overseas in October 1944. Born in Winchester, Oregon, in 1926, he had lived in Shelton for 15 years when he joined the service. Besides his parents, he was survived by two brothers and his grandfather.

Torpedoman Robert Emes Eads was inducted into the Navy on January 1, 1944 and was killed in action on June 12, 1945, while aboard a destroyer off Okinawa. A letter to Eads' father from his commanding officer provided some details of his death. Young Eads was born in Weston, Oregon, in 1922 and his family moved to Shelton when he was 15. He graduated from Irene S. Reed High School in 1942. His survivors included his parents, the Rev. and Mrs. George R. Eads.

Pfc. Clayton E. Gunter was killed in action in Italy on February 25, 1944, leaving his wife, Evelyn and two children, Larry, aged 2 and Patty, 1 , and his parents, Mr. and Mrs. Ernest Gunter of Shelton. Clayton Gunter joined the Army in November 1943 and served with Mark Clark's Fifth Army.

Private Clinton Hawk of Shelton died on Okinawa on July 16, 1945. He was born in November 1917 on the Skokomish Indian Reservation and went to school on reservations and at Chemawa, Oregon. Before entering the service, Clinton Hawk worked as a donkey engineer for Phoenix Logging Company, and then was employed for a time by Simpson Logging Company before moving to the Puget Sound Navy Yard as a machinist. He enlisted in the Army on October 13, 1942. The Army assigned him to the engineers and he served in the Aleutian Islands, the Philippine Islands, the Marshalls and Okinawa. He was survived by his parents, Mr. and Mrs. John Hawk, three brothers and two sisters.

Sergeant Warren Melcum was injured when the Liberator bomber he was on made a forced landing in the South Pacific. Melcum was transported to a hospital in New Guinea where he died of wounds on February 7, 1945. Three other members of the crew also were killed in the crash. Warren Malcum, the son of Dr. and Mrs. M.C. Melcum, was a 1941 graduate of Shelton High School and an Eagle Scout. He joined the Army Air Corps in the summer of 1942 and had served in the South Pacific for nearly two years.

Captain Harold J. Moore was on his way home to Shelton after the European war had ended when he tragically lost his life to diphtheria. He had served as Company Commander of the Fifth Division's 482nd Engineers. He and his troops had seen action from D-Day to the Battle of the Bulge, and now with the battles over, he was in Paris on his way home when he died on May 28, 1945. The Captain was born in 1918 in Canada and graduated from Shelton High School in 1936. He was employed in the logging business until he joined the Army in 1941. He was trained in California and was sent to diesel school in Columbus Ohio. From there he was sent to Officers Candidate School in Virginia. In late 1941 he was commissioned a 2nd Lieutenant and sent overseas in September 1943. His wife, Katherine, and his parents, Mr. and Mrs. Frank A. Moore, survived him.

Adam Temple of North Mason County High School provided these next two biographies of war dead.

Lt. Commodore R. Burnett, Army Air Corps, was the third Mason County resident to die in the service during World War II. He was killed when a training plane in which he was the instructor crashed at the Naval Training Station at Pasco, Waashington. He was a graduate of Irene S. Reed High School in Shelton where he was prominent in athletics. He then attended Central Washington College at Ellensburg where he played center on the football team. His widow and their infant son in Pasco, his mother in Shelton, and five brothers, and a sister survived Lieutenant Burnett.

Lieutenant Leonard H. (Bud) Walton, 23, of Shelton, joined the Royal Canadian Air Force in January 1941, then after Pearl Harbor was attacked, he transferred to the U.S. Army Air Force. He was sent to the Aleutians where he participated in many bombing missions over enemy territory. A 1937 graduate of Irene S. Reed High School in Shelton, he had not been home for more than a year when his parents, Mr. and Mrs. L .A. Walton, received word that their son had lost his life while flying with the Army Air Forces over Fort Richardson, Alaska.

When word spread that this book would mention some of the young people of our State who died in the war, several persons offered to help. Gloria Mack Cummings mailed an envelope full of clippings from newspaper notices of casualties in the Vancouver, Washington, area. Roy Compton sent clippings from the *Island County Times* about war dead from that county. Ralph Newman sent a full page of names from the *Franklin Tolo* listing that Seattle high school's war dead. Joy Lucas of the Broadway High School Alumni Association mailed a list of the former students of that Seattle school who died in World War II. Broadway was closed as a high school in 1946 and became Seattle Community College. When older school structures are torn down, the plaques listing the school's war dead frequently are lost or destroyed. However, the strong Broadway alumni organization preserves such items.

The American Legion bulletin mentioned that this book was being prepared and asked for any appropriate information. Bruce and Kathy Barker of Battle Ground, Washington, sent items about several men from that area who died in battle.

And down in Goldendale, Washington, Clara Ganguin West of the Louis Leidel American Legion Post wrote a letter that provides an appropriate introduction to the following list of Washington State World War II war dead. Mrs. West's letter described the trials of her family when her brother was reported missing in action:

Private Alvin A. Ganguin was born May 1, 1920, on a ranch 13 miles east of the small town of Goldendale, Washington. He graduated from high school in May 1939. He was always interested in airplanes and wished to join the Air Corps. On January 21, 1941, he enlisted at Vancouver Barracks, Washington, and was sent to Hamilton Field, California, where he was assigned to the 46th Air Base Squadron.

As a student in school, he was interested in art and music. The officer in charge planned to send him to photography school where he could learn map work and other types of art, but the final decision was delayed. He also expected 30 days of furlough time that would allow him to be home for the Goldendale rodeo and over Christmas. But he received no furlough. Instead his squadron was sent on conditioning hikes and maneuvers, and to the firing range.

After his unit was vaccinated for yellow fever, he wrote home that rumors were floating around suggesting they were about to be sent overseas. Alvin posted a letter home on September 13, 1941, in which he apologized for not having written for some time. His squadron had been on maneuvers for ten days "up in the sticks where there were lots of mosquitoes and sand fleas." In his next letter home, mailed on September 28, 1941, he informed his family that his squadron was being transferred overseas and would leave within a week under sealed orders. "Everyone thinks to the Philippine Islands or Panama," he said. Then he concluded with these words: "Don't worry. I'll be fine." His family never heard from him after that.

Clara West in the information she sent described the subsequent information they received from the government.

A letter from the War Department dated May 7, 1943, from the Adjutant Generals Office informed Mr. and Mrs. John E. Ganguin that their son, Private Alvin A. Ganguin was missing in action from May 7, 1942. On May 24, 1944, from the U.S. Secretary of War, Henry L. Stimson, came word that the Purple Heart Medal had been awarded posthumously to Private Alvin A. Ganguin of the Air Corps. On May 31, 1944, a letter was received from the Chief of Staff, General Marshall, extending sympathy. On Memorial Day, 1945, Headquarters of the Army Air Force sent a message of sympathy signed by H. H. Arnold, Commanding General.

On August 24, 1945, a letter arrived from General Headquarters, U.S. Armed Forces, Pacific, with vital information the family had been seeking. "Private Alvin A. Ganguin died May 26, 1942 from dysentery at Camp O'Donnell Prison Camp while a prisoner of the Japanese." The same day General Headquarters of the U.S. Army Forces in the Pacific sent a message from the office of the Commander in Chief, Douglas MacArthur, extending sympathy to families of those who died on Bataan, Corregidor, and in enemy prison camps.

April 4, 1947 brought a letter from the office of the Quartermaster General asking if the family wished Alvin's final interment to be in a local cemetery or abroad. The Ganguins decided to leave his remains overseas since it had been five years since he died and his body had already been moved several times. On August 10, 1949, the Department of the Army sent a letter containing information about their son's final resting place. "Private Alvin A. Ganguin, ASN 19 020 546, lies in Plot L, Row 10, Grave 100, at Fort McKinley U.S. Military Cemetery, Manila, Philippine Islands."

THE WASHINGTON STATE WAR DEAD

The Garden of Remembrance Second Avenue at University Street downtown Seattle. Photo courtesy Murase Associates.

—A—

PETER AADLAND
HELMER F AAKERVIK
ARNE O AALBU
DAVID L AARHAUS
ERLING A AASEN
CHRISTIAN S AASTED
GEORGE H ABBOTT
VICTOR H ABBOTT
DONALD ABEL
EDWARD F ABEL
JOSEPH N ABEL
RICHARD K ABEL
JAMES L ABERCROMBIE
WILLIAM E ABERNATHY
FRANCIS C ABRAHAMSON
SAMUEL C ABRAHAMSON
LLOYD L ACORD
HOMER A ADAMS
HOWARD W ADAMS
LYLE L ADAMS
RICHARD ADAMS
RICHMOND ADAMS
ROBERT H ADAMS
SILAS E ADAMS
WILLIAM H ADAMS

WILLIAM P ADAMS
ALFRED ADAMSON
MARVIN B ADKINS
DONALD ADLER
ADRIAN L ADOLPH
LOUIS B ADRIAN
HUBERT R AGIN
HAROLD E AGREN
FRANCIS G AHEARN
RICHARD M AHLMAN
VICTOR E AHRENS
GIDEON AICHELE
DONALD G AIKEN
LLOYD J AKINS
WILLIAM A ALBERT JR
WALTER F ALBERTY
ALBERT A ALBINO
HARRY ALBOHAIRE
LOUIS R ALBRECHT
CARL E ALBRIGHT
SIDNEY J ALBRIGHT
EARL E ALBRO
RICHARD ALDERMAN
RICHARD L ALDERMAN
PENNY ALDERSON
RICHARD J ALDERSON

ALLEN R ALEXANDER
GEORGE W ALEXANDER
RAYMOND C ALEXANDER
ROBERT L ALEXANDER
EDWARD J ALFANO
CLIFTON H ALFORD
LAVERN L ALLARD
ALLEN E ALLEMAN
BARNEY M ALLEN
EDMUND T ALLEN
FRED T ALLEN
GEORGE C ALLEN
JAMES D ALLEN
JOHN E ALLEN
PHILIP O ALLEN
RICHARD C ALLEN
ROBERT L ALLEN
VICTOR S ALLEN
MICHAEL R ALLESSIO
CHARLES R ALLIE
EDWARD C ALLISON
KENNETH W ALLMAN
PAUL E ALMON
WALTER T ALSETH
WALTER L ALSTROM
ALEXANDER ALUTIN

EUGENE T AMABE
RALPH AMATO
PAUL A AMBROSE
RICHARD D AMBROSE
JACK R AMENDE
CLYDE AMES
EDWIN R AMES
WILLIAM E AMES
WILLIAM F AMIDON
CHARLES M AMMONS
RUSSELL M AMUNDSON
AVEN M ANDERSEN
CLARENCE K ANDERSEN
EDWIN B ANDERSEN
HARRY E ANDERSEN
JOHN V ANDERSEN
VERN R ANDERSEN
ALVIN M ANDERSON
BENJAMIN W ANDERSON
CARL V ANDERSON
CLARENCE I ANDERSON
CLARENCE N ANDERSON
CLIFFORD J ANDERSON
DUANE L ANDERSON
ERNEST H ANDERSON
EUGENE O ANDERSON

FRANCE H ANDERSON
HAROLD E ANDERSON
HAROLD J ANDERSON
HAROLD L ANDERSON JR
HARRY ANDERSON
HARRY M ANDERSON
HERBERT E ANDERSON
INER W ANDERSON
JOHN F ANDERSON
LEONARD F ANDERSON
LEORNE W ANDERSON
MERRIL J ANDERSON
ORTON K ANDERSON
RICHARD ANDERSON
RICHARD B ANDERSON
RICHARD E ANDERSON
RICHARD H ANDERSON
ROBERT E ANDERSON
ROBERT S ANDERSON
ROY G ANDERSON
ROY W ANDERSON
STEPHEN E ANDERSON
THOMAS G ANDERSON
TRIG ANDERSON
VIRGIL L ANDERSON
VIRGIL O ANDERSON

WALTER V ANDERSON
WILLIAM H ANDERSON
WILLIAM L ANDERSON
RODGER D ANDREWS
WILLIAM E ANDREWS JR
WOODROW D ANDRUS
EDWARD ANDY
EARL E ANEY
CARL O ANGVIK
RAYMOND L ANSTENSON
CLARENCE R ANTHONY
CHESTER L APPEL
FRED O APPLEGARTH
WALLACE R APPLEGATE
THOMAS H APPLETON
ELWYN D APRILL
ANTHONY F AQUINO
DONALD H ARBOGAST
WILLIAM N ARBUCKLE
PERRY O ARCHER
VANCE M ARDEUNE
JAMES H ARMSTRONG
JAMES R ARMSTRONG
HOWARD R ARNDT
ALTUS L ARNOLD
JAMES W ARNOLD
RICHARD C ARNOLD
ROBERT ARNOLD
ROBERT L ARONSON
DARYLE E ARTLEY
CARL H ARVIDSON
CHARLES E ARWOOD
ADAM J ARZO
CLYDE E ASHBAUGH
CLARENCE D ASHBERGER
CHARLES O ASHBY
DAVID G ASHBY JR
HUGH R ASHBY
LEROY ASHBY
ROBERT A ASHMORE
BROOKS U ATCHISON
IVAN D ATKINS
EARL G ATKINSON
HUGH H ATKINSON
EDGAR R ATTEBERY SR
EDGAR R ATTEBERY JR
JOHN ATWELL
WILLIAM H AUBURN
CLIFFORD E AUDINET
GLENN E AULT
JOHN E AURE
NORVILLE J AUSEN
MICHAEL O AUSTIN
LAUREN E AUTIO

HAROLD W AVERY
ROXY A AVERY
ROBERT O AXFORD
WILMER A AYERS
— B —
WILLIAM E BAARS
DOUGLAS BACCHUS
THOMAS A BACCHUS
ROSCIUS BACK
EVERETT R BACKMAN
BEN L BACKSTROM
JAY D BACON JR
WILLARD L BACON
ESTON J BADEN
DONALD G BAERMAN
SIDNEY J BAESCHLIN
JOHN P BAGAN
RICHARD O BAGGOTT
WILLIS T BAILES
CARL E BAILEY
GARFIELD A BAILEY
GERALD J BAILEY
JAMES E BAILEY
JOHN D BAILEY
LLOYD E BAILEY
MERVIN E BAILEY
VINCENT W BAILEY
FREDERICK F BAIR JR
HOWARD L BAIR
RICHARD M BAIRD
ROBERT E BAIRD
JOE BAK
ALBERT R BAKER
BRADFORD W BAKER
CHARLES E BAKER
CHARLES H BAKER
CLIFFORD H BAKER
DAVID W BAKER
DONALD J BAKER
DONALD P BAKER
FRANK J BAKER
FREDERICK H BAKER
GLENN H BAKER
NEIL T BAKER
RAYMOND E BAKER
ROBERT G BAKER
VERLE J BAKER
WAYNE S BAKER
WESLEY M BAKER
SAM P BAKSHAS
JOE BALASKI
ROGER BALCOMBE
FERNIS R BALCON
ALBERT J BALDA

ANTHONY BALDASARE
JACK L BALDERSTON
ALLAN F BALDWIN
EDMUND J BALDWIN
HAROLD L BALDWIN
MARVIN A BALDWIN
MYRL F BALDWIN
PHILIP G BALDWIN
ROBERT G BALDWIN
THOMAS J BALDWIN
WALTER C BALDWIN
EUGENE E BALES
JOHN B BALL
JOHN W BALL
WALTER B BALL
HENRY L BALLARD
ARTHUR E BALSIGER
SAMUEL A BANAKA
MELVIN BANG
SIDNIE BANK
JAMES A BARBER
JOHN W BARBER
NED D BARCLAY
ANTHONY BARCOTT
MATTHEW A BARI
GORDON D BARKER
JAMES D BARKER
ALBERT M BARKUS
STEVE G BARNA
JOHN R BARNARD
ROBERT L BARNER
ARTHUR C BARNES
DONALD L BARNES
JOHN E BARNES
ORRIN H BARNES
PHILIP K BARNES
RAYMOND G BARNES
ROBERT C BARNES
ROBERT G BARNES
CURTIS R BARNETT
DOLPH BARNETT JR
GEORGE R BARNETT
RICHARD S BARNETT
ROGER W BARNEY
OTHAR C BARNHART
EMIL J BARON
EDWIN H BARQUIST
RUSSELL C BARR
WILLIAM G BARR
JOHN H BARRETT
MARSHALL C BARRETT
RALEIGH BARRETT
JACK T BARRIE
IRVIN J BARRON

THEODORE W BARRON
EDWARD M BARRY
HOWARD C BARRY
MAYNARD C BARSNESS
ILTON J BARTHOLOMEW
R H BARTHOLOMEW
PHILLIP E BARTLETT
DAVID W BARTLEY
MARTIN E BARTLEY
CHARLES D BARTLING
ROBERT C BARTON
PERCY F BARWELL
RAYMOND L BASEL
ROBERT C BASKETT
WILLIAM C BATCHELDOR JR
WILLIAM W BATCHELOR
LEO L BATEMAN
MARK BATEMAN
BUEL W BATES
CLAYTON E BATES
LONNIE C BATES
RAYMOND L BATES
STANLEY F BATES
JAMES M BATSON
H D BATTERTON
FREDERICK J BATTIG
JAMES L BATTLE
JAMES D BATY
BERNARD F BAUCH
GEORGE A BAUER
BERNARD F BAUGH
DAVID J BAUGH
JOHN T BAUM
ELDEN R BAUMBACH
EDWIN J BAUMEISTER
S F BAUMGARTNER JR
HERMAN J BAUR
RICHARD L BAY
RALPH W BAYER
LEROY K BAYLESS
JAMES B BAYNE
HIRAM W BAZE
WILLIAM O BEACH
STUART E BEALES
DALE E BEAN
HERBERT BEAN
GERALD A BEARG
JOHN W BEATON
ROBERT B BEAUDREAU
LOUIS N BEAUDRY
DONALD D BEAZLEY
HOWARD N BECK
LAURIE M BECK
LEWIS G BECK

ROBERT J BECK
WILLIAM BECK
WILLIAM J BECK JR
ROBERT BECKER
VERNON F BECKER
WILLIAM G BECKER
HAROLD S BECKLUND
RODGER H BECKMAN
VALMORE V BEDARD
DONALD E BEEBE
ELMER L BEEBE
HENRY C BEERMAN
DARL A BEERS
RAY C BEESON
LLOYD S BEGGS
AMOS H BEHL
WILLIAM W BEHRE
WILLIAM J BEIERLEIN
SIDNEY C BEINKE
RAYMOND C BELAIR
ROBERT J BELFORD
FRANK W BELFOY
GORDON A BELL
HOWARD N BELL
JACK A BELL
JUNIOR J BELL
MORGAN A BELL
ROBERT C BELL
ROBERT O BELL
WILLIAM E BELL
WILLIAM W BELL
KERMIT A BELLES
PAUL L BELLUS
SHELL BELSBY
ELMAN R BELSHE
SIDNEY G BEMIS
GEORGE C BENDER
JACK V BENDER
GRADY BENFIELD
JAMES J BENFIELD
WILLIAM R BENJAMIN
CARL I BENNETT
CHESTER O BENNETT
EDWARD E BENNETT
HAROLD D BENNETT
HENRY J BENNETT
RICHARD C BENNETT
RAYMOND E BENNY
FRANCIS J BENOLKEN
JAMES W BENSCOTTER
ARNE G BENSON
KENNETH L BENSON
PAUL C BENSON
ROBERT J BENSON

ROBERT W BENSON	FLOYD E BIBLE	DONOVAN W BLANTON	HERBERT D BORDERS	KENNETH G BRAKKE
TURRELL A BENSON	VERNON E BICKLEY	THOMAS A BLAUVELT	ANDREW J BORKLAND	LAWRENCE F BRAMAN
WILLIAM R BENSON	DALE D BICKNELL	RICHMOND F BLIEFFERT	AUSTIN W BORLEN	JOSEPH A BRAND
SIGURD BENTSEN	RUDOLPH P BIELKA	FREDERICK W BLIND	EDWIN A BORNANDER	FLOYD E BRANDFAS
ARTHUR O BENTSON	ALEX W BIGELOW	JOHN T BLODGETT	CHARLES B BORNSTEIN	JAMES B BRANDON
HAROLD BENVIE	ALEXIS W BIGELOW	LEONARD E BLOM	WALTER G BORST	JOHN A BRANDSTROM
SHELDON L BENWELL	DONALD A BIGELOW	JOHN H BLOMQUIST	ANDREW J BORTLAND	DUANE G BRANDT
KENNETH F BEPPLE	ROBERT E BIGELOW	ARTHUR A BLOOM	ROBERT W BORTNER	ROBERT S BRANSHO
DELBERT G BERCHOT	CHARLES H BIGGS	RUSSELL F BLOOM	DON A BORTON	LOUIS R BRANZE
DENNIE F BERDINE	DONALD G BIGGS	DALE E BLOOMFIELD	HERBERT E BORTON	WILLIAM J BRASCH
ALBERT E BERG	GEORGE E BIGGS JR	EDWARD R BLOOMGREN	RAYMOND L BOTSFORD	WALTER S BRASH
ALBERT H BERG	FRED L BIGHAM	LESLIE F BLOOMINGDALE	ELMER F BOTTKE	JAMES G BRASHEAR
ALFRED H BERG	RONALD C BILES	ROBERT J BLURTON	WESLEY M BOTTOMS JR	JAMES E BRAUNN
DAVID BERG	MARGARET M BILLINGS	RODNEY BOALCH	ROGER E BOTTON	FRED W BRAYFORD JR
DAVID D BERG	BEN W BILLINGSLEY	HUGH A BOARMAN	RONALD J BOUCHER	WILLIAM BRAZELL
JAMES R BERG	HOMER D BILYEU	JOHN K BOB	JOSEPH H BOURLAND	MELVIN F BREASHAW
JIMMIE C BERG	LAURENCE W BINDREIFF	CARL J BOCK	RICHARD R BOUTELLE	DONALD E BRECHT
M G BERG	JAMES K BINGAMAN	HARVEY A BOCKOVER	CHARLES D BOVEY	PHILIP W BRECHTEL
MELVIN BERG	LOUIS F BIRCHLER	STEPHEN L BODDY	ROBERT J BOVIE	OTTO P BREDAL
RICHARD H BERG	LEONARD C BIRDWELL	JAMES F BODINE	WILLIE C BOWDEN JR	ROBERT L BREEDLOVE
THOMAS D BERG	PAUL K BIRDWELL	ALVIN L BODVIG	KENNETH G BOWDISH	JAMES D BREITENSTEIN
GEORGE W BERGER	NORMAN R BIRKELAND	HAROLD A BOE	ALBERT P BOWEN	LEROY A BREITGHAM
LEONARD A BERGESET	FRANK E BIRKS	KEITH A BOEDCHER	CLARK O BOWEN	MARION W BREITHAUPT
GERALD A BERGLAND	FERDINAND BISHOP	LONNIE BOERGER	GUY J BOWER	FRANK BREN
HENRY N BERGLUND	GEORGE F BISHOP	ARNOLD J BOERS	EUGENE BOWERS	HARLEY H BREN
KENNETH B BERGLY	VERNON E BISHOP	JOHN H BOETTCHER	REUBEN M BOWERS	ERNEST M BRENDEN
FREDRIK S BERGMAN	CHARLES R BISSELL	HENRY F BOGER	ROBERT E BOWERS	HAYDEN F BRENDLE
HAROLD H BERGMAN	LEO D BISSON	WALTER H BOGGS	WILLIAM H BOWKER	AUGUST M BRENNAN
GLENN E BERGSTRESSER	EMIL S BITAR	GEORGE BOITANO	WILBUR E BOWLBY	THOMAS BRENNAN
GEORGE S BERGSTROM	FREDERICK D BITTERMAN	HARVEY G BOLIN	WILLIAM E BOWLER JR	DAVID BRENNER
CHARLES F BERKSHIER	JOSEPH P BIZEFSKI	JEFFERSON L BOLING	GEORGE M BOWMAN	HENRY F BRESCH
ALFRED R BERLAN	GROVER B BJARNASON	MARION BOLIO	JAMES S BOWMAN	HARTWELL T BRESSLER
JOSEPH L BERNARD	ERNEST G BJORG	HARRY A BOLLES	JOSEPH M BOWMAN	ORVAL B BRETTHAUER
FREDERICK A BERRONG	CLARENCE E BJORK	HOBERT BOLON	ROBERT B BOWMAN	DOYLE E BREWER
CAREY W BERRY	CURTIS E BJORKLUND	ROBERT C BOLSON	ROSCOE W BOWMAN	W O BREWER
CLYDE U BERRY	STUART C BJORKLUND	JOSEPH BOLTAN	CLAUDE B BOYD	WILLIAM H BREWSTER
GORDON R BERRY	CHARLES E BLACK	ORA E BOND	HERMAN BOYD	KENNETH E BRIDGHAM
HOWARD B BERRY JR	DONALD C BLACK	CHESTER H BONDE	J B BOYD	BERNARD D BRIGGS
THEODORE S BERRY	DONALD E BLACK	BENJAMIN A BONIFERRO	MARTIN BOYD	GEORGE W BRIGGS
THEO BERRYHILL	HUGH D BLACK	FRANK P BONKOSKI	ROBERT R BOYD	LOYAL A BRIGHT
GERALD D BERT JR	LEROY P BLACK	GERALD D BONNE	JAMES P BOYER	PRESTON BRIGHT
PHILIP M BESCH	JACK W BLACKBURN	JACK L BONNER	DUKE R BOYETT	RICHARD M BRIGHT
REYNOLDS BESS	ROLAND D BLACKBURN	WILBUR E BONSER	JOHN A BOYLAN	EARL E BRINES
PETER F BESSESEN JR	ARTHUR D BLACKRUD	ARTHUR R BOODE	BILL BOYLE	JACK E BRISKY
RICHARD R BEST	ARTHUR J BLACKWOOD	EDWARD H BOOKWALTER	CON BOYLE	EUGENE W BRITTON
JOHN F BETANCOURT JR	CHARLES E BLAINE JR	EARL S BOON	HUGH BOYLE	WARREN H BRITTON
RUDY R BETTIN	FREDERICK J BLAIR	STERLING D BOONE	HUGH L BOYLE	JOHN W BROADHEAD
KENNETH L BETTS	HARRY M BLAIR	EDWIN C BOOTH JR	BRUCE G BRACKETT	ARTHUR BROADLAND
MARTHA S BETTS	NORMAN H BLAKENSHIP	RALPH W BOOTH	WILLIAM H BRADBURN	ROBERT G BROCKMAN JR
RUSSELL A BETTS	RICHARD H BLAKLEY	ROBERT E BOOTHBY	LEWIS H BRADEN	ROBERT H BROKAW
DELBERT J BETZ	KENNETH S BLANCHARD	CREED C BOOTHE	GILBERT E BRADLEY	RALPH R BROMAGHIN
ROY E BEVER	WILLIAM E BLANCHARD	ELMER R BORDEN	JOHN A BRADLEY	GEORGE E BROMLEY
THOMAS W BEZONA	DAVID W BLANFIELD	WILLIAM P BORDEN	ELBERT J BRADRICK	JIMMIE BROMLEY
AL BIAT	ERNEST E BLANKENSHIP	ELDEN C BORDERS	JASPER E BRADY	GUNNAR A BROMS

ROBERT E BRONSON
AVOD C BROOKS
NOEL W BROOKS
ROBERT H BROOKS
ROBERT N BROOKS
ULYSESS R BROOKS
ELMER O BROSAM
WILLIAM F BROSAMER
JAMES M BROSHEAR
VERN C BROUILLET
ROBERT J BROWER
ROY W BROWER
ALBERT BROWN
ARCHIE E BROWN
ARTHUR D BROWN
ARTHUR L BROWN
BEDFORD BROWN
BERNARD C BROWN
BRUCE B BROWN
DAROL C BROWN
DAVID S BROWN
DONALD C BROWN
DONALD W BROWN
EDWIN K BROWN JR
FRANK H BROWN
GIFFORD G BROWN
HAROLD L BROWN
HOMER F BROWN
JOHN W BROWN
LAVERNE C BROWN
LUKE C BROWN
LYNDIAN W BROWN
RALPH W BROWN
RICHARD BROWN
ROBERT A BROWN
ROBERT D BROWN
STANLEY I BROWN
THOMAS D BROWN
SAMUEL M BRUCE
GERALD O BRUMBACK
ERNEST L BRUMITT
OMER C BRUN
EUGENE R BRUNDAGE
LOWELL W BRUNDAGE
CHARLEY W BRUNETTE
DONALD R BRYAN
SAMUEL J BRYAN
WALTER T BRYAN
ROBERT K BRYANT
RALPH E BRYNER
JESS C BRYSON JR
CHARLES R BUCE
LOUIS S BUCHAN
DALLAS N BUCHANAN

DAVID F BUCHHOLZ
ROBERT W BUCHHOLZ
VINCENT L BUCHMAN
REDVERS B BUCKETT
RAYMOND G BUCKLEY
ROBERT H BUCKLEY
ROBERT K BUCKLEY
GEORGE H BUCKMAN
ROBERT M BUCKNELL
EDWARD W BUDDY
HARLEY W BUECHLER
LONNIE BUERGER
ALFRED A BUFFONE
HERMAN L BUGG
ROBERT H BUGGE
ANTHONY L BUHR
GEORGE A BULGARELLI
CLIFTON W BULL
JOHN BULLA JR
HOWARD M BULLARD
JOE BULLINGTON JR
CHARLES R BULLOCK
EDWIN J BULMAN
SHERWIN E BUMGARNER
NORMAN E BUMPUS
KENNETH I BUNN
ROY M BUNN
WAYNE E BUNNELL
CHARLES D BUOY
CARL C BURCH
JOHN C BURDICK
ALBERT R BURGER
GERALD A BURGESS
HARLAND F BURGESS
SCOTT E BURGESS
WALTER K BURGESS
CHARLES L BURGHDUFF
RICHARD E BURGHER
ORIN V BURGMAN
OTTO O BURGSTAHLER
MARTIN J BURKE
MILO C BURKE
RALPH V BURKE
ROBERT W BURKE
JOHN F BURKEE
WILLIAM T BURLESON
EDWARD A BURMASTER
JAMES L BURNET
CECIL J BURNETT
CHARLES P BURNETT JR
CHARLES V BURNETT
DEAN R BURNS
FRANK BURNS
HOMER C BURNS

JAMES A BURNS
ROBERT B BURNS
DAVID J BURR JR
WILLIAM K BURR
CLIFFORD J BURRUS
EARL L BURT
ALFRED F BURTON
CLAUDE BURTON
CRAIG N BURTON
JACK E BURTON
NORMAN H BURTON
ROBERT W BURTON
THADDIUS BURZYCKI
JAMES E BUSKIRK
DAVID A BUTCHER
ALLAN C BUTLER
DANIEL J BUTLER
DAVID R BUTLER
HARRY J BUTLER JR
HOMER L BUTLER
JACK H BUTLER
LAWRENCE A BUTLER JR
MAURICE A BUTLER
WILLARD O BUTLER JR
FRANK J BUTORAC
LAWRENCE R BUTTERWORTH
JOHN R BUTTS
WALLACE H BUTZ
LLOYD L BYER
BILLIE D BYRD
CALVIN L BYRD
CHARLES R BYRKETT
ERVIN E BYRNES
THOMAS C BYRON

—C—

PEDRO CABADING
RICHARD E CADE JR
THOMAS M CAFFEE
TERRY D CAGLE
NORVELL A CAIN
VERN W CAIN
ROBERT J CALDER
RENWICK S CALDERHEAD
HUGH M CALDWELL JR
ELMO D CALKINS
WESLEY CALKINS
JOHN J CALLAHAN
WILLIAM K CALLISON
RAYMOND R CALVER
BERT E CALVIN JR
JACK C CALVIN
DONALD L CAMBRIDGE
DAVID R CAMERON
GLENN CAMERON

HOMER W CAMERON
LELAND R CAMP
ARTHUR C CAMPBELL
CRAIG F CAMPBELL
DOUGLAS N CAMPBELL
JACK R CAMPBELL
JAMES E CAMPBELL
JEROME R CAMPBELL
ROBERT E CAMPBELL
ROBERT L CAMPBELL
STUART CAMPBELL
WESLEY M CANFIELD
THOMAS J CANTLIN
CARL R CAPES
ALEXANDER S CAPLAN
MIKE J CAPPELLETTI
WARREN J CAPRAI
JOSEPH R CAPRON
HENRY F CARAWAN
RICHARD E CARBONE
DAN CAREW JR
CLARK A CAREY
WILLIAM J CARLI JR
ALBERT F CARLISLE
CARL CARLISLE
ALBERT A CARLOCK
CARL F CARLOCK
RALPH J CARLOCK
ALFRED M CARLSON
CARL G CARLSON
CARL W CARLSON
CLAUDE J CARLSON
CLEMENCE R CARLSON
HAROLD R CARLSON
HOWARD F CARLSON
JOHN A CARLSON
JOHN R CARLSON
LEROY A CARLSON
LLOYD S CARLSON
MARVEL L CARLSON
NEIL A CARLSON
PALMER H CARLSON
RICHARD O CARLSON
ROBERT CARLSON
RUSSELL E CARLSON
WALTER R CARLSON
WILLIAM O CARLSON
LEROY M CARLTON
JOSEPH F CARMAN
MERLE E CARMAN
JAMES L CARMICHAEL
LAURENCE CARMICHAEL
CORTLAND L CARMODY
CARL F CAROSINO

LEWIS W CAROW
DAVID W CARPENTER
DONALD F CARPENTER
EDWARD L CARPENTER JR
HAROLD L CARPENTER
HAROLD R CARPENTER
KEITH H CARR
ROBERT L CARRIER
ALAN D CARROLL
CHARLES L CARROLL JR
DARWIN J CARROLL
JOHN B CARROLL
CLARENCE M CARSON
CLARENCE W CARSON
GALE E CARSON
MYRON B CARSTENSEN
JOHN B CARTER
ROBERT E CARTER
ROBERT J CARTER
WILLIAM J CARTER
WALTER A CARTMELL
RICHARD E CARTON
CYRUS G CARY
THOMAS H CARY
FREDERICK E CASCO
JOHN R CASE
ROBERT F CASE
JAMES W CASEY
ROBERT J CASHIN
JON P CASHION
CLARENCE M CASKEY
LEONARD CASKIN
FREDERICK E CASO
LORELL L CASSELL
CHARLES H CASTLE
VERNON L CASTLE
JESSE L CATES
JAMES D CATTRON
LESTER A CATTRON
EMIL A CAVALERO
JOHN E CAVE
JACK M CAVERLY
ROY E CAVITT
PAUL R CHAMBERLAIN
ROBERT J CHAMBERLAIN
WILLIAM F CHAMBERLAIN
JACK J CHAMBERS
WALTER P CHAMBERS
CHARLES M CHAMBLISS JR
ROBERT E CHAMP JR
JOHN J CHAMPLIN JR
CHARLES H CHANDLER
GEORGE W CHANDLER
WILBUR W CHANEY

FRANCIS W CHAPIN

GORDON W CHAPMAN

CECIL CHAPPELL

MARCEL H CHARBONNIER

ROBERT W CHAREST

WILLIAM CHARLES

ROBERT F CHARLTON

MARVIN A CHARNELL

GEORGE P CHASE

JOHN N CHATTERTON

CLARENCE R CHEADLE

FRANK CHEHA

JOHN CHEHA

HARRY J CHEHOLTS

JOHN P CHEMERES

CHRIS Y CHEN

PATRICK L CHESS

WILLARD M CHESSMAN

PARK G CHETWOOD

LEE H CHEW

CLARENCE M CHEZUM

HAROLD R CHILCOAT

JACK S CHILDERS

JOSEPH W CHILDS

RICHARD W CHILES

LESLIE P CHILTON

BOK H CHIN

JOHN CHINN

WILLARD E CHINN

KENT S CHOLLAR

JOHN CHOPP

CARLSON CHRISCO

EVERETT CHRISCO

ROBERT M CHRISMAN

RICHARD CHRIST

ALBERT A CHRISTENSEN

ALBERT R CHRISTENSEN

FLOYD E CHRISTENSEN

HAROLD N CHRISTENSEN

LINNIE A CHRISTENSEN

WARD A CHRISTENSEN

LOUIS K CHRISTIAN

M S CHRISTIANSEN

ALEXANDER A CHRISTIE

JED T CHRISTMAN

ROBERT L CHRISTOPHER

R O CHRISTOPHERSON

RAYMOND W
    CHRISTOPHERSON

KENNETH L CHRISTY

PAUL J CHUEY

CLARENCE C CHURCH

FRANK CHURCH

WELLS R CHURCHILL

WINSTON L CHURCHILL

MARK J CINKOVICH

LAURENCE CLAIRMONT

KEITH L CLAPSHAW

OTTO A CLARDY

ARCHIBALD M CLARK

ARLIEGH B CLARK JR

CHARLES F CLARK

CHARLES L CLARK

CLARENCE L CLARK

DARWIN J CLARK

FRANK W CLARK JR

FREELAND G CLARK

GEORGE R CLARK

GOLLARD L CLARK JR

JOHN W CLARK

KING CLARK

LAWRENCE D CLARK

LEONARD B CLARK

LLOYD R CLARK

REDMON F CLARK

ROBERT L CLARK

ROLAND M CLARK

ROY S CLARK

JACK CLARKE

MILTON D CLARKE

WILLIAM M CLARKE

RICHARD C CLAUS

ARTHUR M CLAWSON

DAVID M CLAY JR

WILLIAM J CLEARY

JAMES E CLEAVER

R F CLEGHORN

WENDELL CLEMENSON

CARL C CLEMONS

OTIS CLEVENGER

EVERETT R CLIFFORD

GEORGE D CLIFFORD

WILBERT L CLIFFORD

JOHN T CLIFTON

MELVIN M CLINE

WILLARD C CLINE

JACK B CLINKSCALES

MARVIN S CLINTON

JAMES C CLORAN JR

CHESTER W CLOTFELTER

JACK E CLOUGH

LEWIS E CLOUGH

RAYMOND E CLOUTIER

ALFRED B CLUMPNER

ROLAND H COATES

ARTHUR G COATS

GUY E COBLE

JERRY W COBLE

FRANKLIN M COCHRAN

LLOYD N COCHRAN

MARSHALL K COCKRILL

DONALD B COCKRUM

DALE R CODE

LOUIS G CODEY

JOE B COFFEY

ROBERT COFFIN

ROGER F COFFIN

EDWARD K COGHLAN

HAROLD L COGSWELL

MAURICE H COHEN

LEONARD C COHENOUR

ANTONIO J COLARCO

CHARLES W COLE

DEWEY D COLE

EARL R COLE JR

HARRY L COLE JR

JAMES W COLE

KERMIT U COLE

ROBERT A COLE

ROBERT M COLE

ROY K COLE

WILLITT S COLEGROVE JR

DONALD A COLEMAN

FLOYD W COLEMAN

FRANK E COLEMAN JR

MELBURN T COLEMAN

ROBERT C COLEMAN

SAMUEL E COLEMAN

JESSE L COLLEY

KENNETH R COLLIER

ARTHUR E COLLINS

HAROLD A COLLINS

JAMES T COLLINS

LOREN D COLLINS

NORMAN E COLLINS

SIDNEY L COLLINS

THOMAS K COLLINS

VICTOR E COLLINS

CHARLES L COLLISON

LOYD E COLMAN

SPENCER W COLSON

ERNEST H COLUMBUS

RICHARD R COLVILLE

RALEIGH V COLWELL

YORK F COLWELL

WARREN F COLYER

SYDNEY P COMLEY

HAROLD W COMPTON

HAROLD K COMSTOCK

JACK B COMSTOCK

MELVIN K CONDER

LON E CONDIT

EDMOND H CONDON

GERALD M CONDON

JACK G CONE

KENNETH C CONE

JOHN R CONKLIN

GEORGE C CONNEALY

DONALD W CONNELLY

CALVIN W CONNER

DONALD CONNER

VERNON C CONNER

ARMOND W CONNERY

GLENN H CONNERY

JACK S CONNOR

PAUL E CONOVER

FRANCIS CONRAD

ROBERT I CONRAD

WALTER G CONRAD

GERALD A CONRADI

BENJAMIN R CONROW

TONY CONTES

ROBERT J CONVERSE

JAMES D CONWAY

LEONARD B CONWAY

WOODROW G CONWAY

RAYMOND O CONWELL

GEORGE R COOK

LAWRENCE R COOK

MORRIS B COOK

ROBERT L COOK

WALTER I COOK

CHARLES C COOKE

JACK W COOKE

ARNOLD A COOPER

CLIFFORD A COOPER

DAVID J COOPER

EDWARD O COOPER

ELMER W COOPER

ERVIN E COOPER

ROBERT P COOPER

WILLIAM H COOPER

FRANK R COPE

ALDWIN D COPENHAVER

CHARLES M COPENHAVER

IVAN B CORBIN

JON R CORCORAN

PATRICK F CORCORAN

JOHN P CORDOVA

NICHOLAS G CORDOVA

CLIFFORD J CORDRAY

ERNEST E COREY

EDWARD B CORKETT

HOWARD W CORLEY

EMERSON CORNELL

JOSEPH P CORNELL

RICHARD P CORNELL

DWIGHT W CORRIER

REVEL B CORRIGAN

QUINTIN D CORY

RALPH CORY

TERRENCE D COSGRIFF

ROBERT L COSMAN

DUANE L COSPER

EARL R COSS

ROSS COSTAIN

VICTOR J COSTANZO

WILLIAM E COSTLEY

LOUIS E COTTONWARE

ROBERT S COULTER

CLYDE W COUNTRYMAN

DONALD L COUNTS

ROBERT E COURTNEY

ANTHONY B COURTWAY JR

CHESTER COURVILLE

PETE E COURY

JOHN A COUTURE

JOSEPH V COUTURE

DONALD G COVEY

CLAUDE W COVINGTON JR

CHENEY COWLES

ALFRED COX

ALLEN H COX JR

CLIFFORD J COX

DELBURT F COX

GLENN E COX

JOHN F COX

PEARLIN G COX

BENSON F COYLE

MATTHEW L COYLE

THOMAS J COYLE

RAYMOND L CRABB

ALFRED H CRAIG

BENJAMIN E CRAIG

DAVID S CRAIG

JAMES J CRAIG

MELVIN W CRAIG

ROBERT O CRAIG

WILLARD H CRAIG

CLINTON E CRAIN

HARRY A CRAINE

FREDERICK W CRAMER

HAROLD CRAMER

LLOYD CRANEY

FRANK H CRANSTON

HUGH E CRAVEN

RUSSELL L CRAVEN

THOMAS M CRAVEN

DAVID CRAWFORD

DAVID W CRAWFORD

ROBERT A CRAWFORD
ROBERT S CRAWFORD
HARLEY D CREAMER
JOHN M CREECH
EDMOND P CREETY
CORNELIUS CREMER
ROBERT H CRESSEY
RAY J CREWS
ARTHUR W CRISPIEN
LESTER CROCKETT
AUBRY CROMWELL
JAMES R CROSBY
DAVID L CROSETTI
HERBERT A CROSS
LAWRENCE J CROSS
ROBERT C CROSS
DAVID W CROSSWHITE
LAWRENCE L CROTTS
HAROLD P CROUSE
DAVID L CROW
LEWIS W CROW
ROY E CROWE
ELLIS B CROWLEY
JOHN K CROWTHER
MAURICE A CROWTHER
MANFORD O CROY
LAWRENCE L CRUM
D C CUEVAS JR
DALE A CULHANE
CECIL R CULL
DAVID E CULLINANE
DONALD A CULP
CLIFFORD I CULVER
FRANKLIN H CUMMER
AARON S CUMMINGS
EUGENE L CUMMINGS JR
ORANGEY M CUMMINGS
RALPH W CUMMINGS
RICHARD J CUMMINGS
ELVIN H CUNNINGHAM
PAUL F CURDY
THOMAS J CURRAN
JACK G CURRIE
CLIFFORD C CURRIN
CLYDE F CURRY
CHESTER H CURTIS
GERALD W CURTIS
HOMER A CURTIS
JOHN CURTIS
NOEL S CURTIS
VANCE T CURTISS
JEAN C CUSICK
JOHN C CYPHERS
WALTER J CZARZASTY

—D—

ARTHUR H D EVERS JR
LEONARD F DA DEPPO
WILLIAM C DA SHIELL
WILLIAM D DABBS
WAITE H DAGGY
EUGENE E DAHL
HENRY O DAHLBERG
SIGVARD A DAHLBERG
HENRY O DAHLEN
WILLIAM M DAHLKE
JOE F DAILY
RICHARD L DAILY
MURL J DAIN
RICHARD H DAIS
EDGAR H DAKE
GEORGE C DALE
JACK F DALEY
EMIL U DALKE
JOHN J DALY
CHARLES H DAMAN
FRANK DAMAN JR
GUST J DAMASCUS
CLARENCE E DANDOM
CLAIR L DANIELS
FLETCHER H DANIELS
JOHN E DANIELS
OSCAR J DANIELS
F R DANIELSEN
RUSSELL H DANIELSON
DONOVAN D DANMIER
JAMES W DANNO
ROBERT R DANSFIELD
WILLIAM L DARNELL
CHARLES DARRAGH
HENRY C DARRAH
CHARLES E DARROW
FRANCIS R DAUNCEY
LEROY J DAVIDSON
RAYMOND H DAVIDSON
ROBERT R DAVIDSON
JOHN W DAVIE
GEORGE W DAVIES
EDWARD I DAVIS
ERNEST G DAVIS
HAL B DAVIS
JACK L DAVIS
JAMES W DAVIS
JOHN A DAVIS
L D DAVIS
LEE L DAVIS
LUCIUS S DAVIS JR
MYRON E DAVIS
RAYMOND L DAVIS

ROBERT R DAVIS
THRELKELD M DAVIS
WILLIAM H DAVIS
CHARLES M DAWES
WAYNE E DAWSON
CYRIL A DAY
ROBERT M DAY
WILLIAM J DAY
VICTOR E DE BLASIO
ARNOLD B DE BOLT
WILLIAM H DE FEYTER
JOHN DE FIORE
JAMES A DE GARMO
HARRY R DE HAAN
CLIFFORD K DE HART
DENNIS S DE LISLE
DONALD DE LISLE
RICHARD C DE MARIS
LOUIS L DE MARS JR
MARVIN L DE MARSCHE
DONALD L DE MERRITT
RAYMOND J DE METSENAR
JOHN A DE ROSA
LEO V DE SHAZER
MARIO DE SISTO
FRANCIS E DE SOTO
LEWIS E DE VOE
MARVIN H DE VOE
ALVIN F DE WALD
HUBERT S DE WITT
WILLIAM H DE WITT JR
JACK H DEACON
LEO S DEAL
CARROLL R DEAN
DALE DEAN
MAURICE F DEAN
WARREN M DEAN
ALLEN DEATHERAGE
JOSEPH O DEATHERAGE
RAYMOND DEAVER
LAWRENCE R DECKER
LEO DECKER
GALE A DEDMORE
JOHN M DEENIK
JAMES H DEERING JR
JAMES C DEGROAT
HENRY DEIFE
GEORGE D DEISSNER
JOHN T DEJONG
LORENTIUS C DEKKER
CHESTER A DELBRIDGE
JOHN T DELMORE
ROBERT L DEMING
KENNETH E DEMOREST

ADOLPH H DEMULLING
RICHARD E DENNEY
JOSEPH P DENNICK
JOHN A DENNING
BASSEL T DENNIS
CARL D DENNIS
ROBERT D DENNIS
DAVID K DENT
JUNIOR C DERAMO
ARNOLD B DERIFIELD
RUSSELL E DERITIS
DONALD P DEROSIER
HOWARD H DERR
JOHN L DERWENT
ARCHIE G DERY
CLAIR W DES VOIGNES
BOYD L DESART
WILLIAM D DESINGER
CYRIL A DESMARAIS
PAUL E DESMARAIS
JOHN E DESMUL
KENNETH G DETWILER
RICHARD W DEWS
JAMES C DEXTER
HARRY N DEYETTE
MARION E DHONDT
JOSEPH J DI CARLO
CALVIN DIAMOND
ACE H DIBBLE
HAROLD V DIBBLE
FRANCIS E DICK
ELTON DICKENS
FLOYD F DICKENS
NORMAN I DICKER
JOHN J DICKEY
NORRIS D DICKEY
STANLEY E DICKINSON
THEODORE N DICKSON
ALVIN W DIEHL
STANLEY E DIEHL
FRED DIGGS
CLARENCE W DIGH
CARL I DIGNES
WILLIAM R DIKEMAN
HOWARD B DILATUSH
JACK DILLENBURG
HAROLD D DILLON
RALPH G DILTZ
ELLSWORTH W DIMMITT
RALPH J DINDOT
WALTER M DINGS
ROBERT R DINNEEN
ALOLPH F DIPPOLITO
KENNETH C DIRKES

RAYMOND P DIRKS
JOHN J DISTTELL
ROBERT R DIVELBLISS
RALPH L DIVEN
LYMAN R DIXON
ROBERT M DIXON
EDWARD F DOANE
JOSEPH DOBIASH JR
JOSEPH J DOBLER
JOSEPH W DOBLER
JAMES S DOCKENDORF
BERTRUM C DODGE
FRANK H DODGE
FRED E DODGE
LESLIE DODGE
WILLIAM C DODGE
WILLIAM K DOHERTY
DORRANCE P DOHRN
RUSSELL E DOLAN
WILLIAM G DOLBY
LYLE E DOLE
STANLEY A DOMIN
MARSHALL L DOMPIER
HOWARD B DONALDSON
TROSE E DONALDSON
JAMES W DONLEY
JOHN J DONNELLY
MARTIN J DOOLEY JR
ALBERT E DOOLIN
ALFRED R DOOR
FRANK M DORAN
JAMES J DORAN
LEO J DORGAN
RICHARD J DORGAN
LESLIE A DORNBUSH
GEORGE C DORRIS JR
WILLIAM H DORTCH
WILBUR E DOSEY
CHARLES E DOUGHERTY
CHARLES E DOUGLAS
NORMAN W DOUGLAS
RAYMOND H DOW
LESLIE E DOWLING
DELAVAN B DOWNER JR
CLAYTON E DOWNIE
HOWARD R DOWNING
WENDELL L DOWNS
GERALD E DOYLE
GEORGE N DRAGNICH
HAROLD F DRAIN
DONALD L DRAKE
VINCENT R DRAKE
GEORGE A DRAPER
WILSON E DRAPER

PAUL M DREIER
EARL R DRESCHER
GERALD B DRESSEL
JAMES G DROLES
FRANCIS C DROTTER
LEROY R DRUFFEL
ROBERT H DRUMHILLER
DARRELL M DRUMMOND
DEAN L DU BOIS
EDWARD L DU GALLO
LOUIS J DUBEY
MARVIN J DUCHARME
GORDON M DUDA
DELMORE A DUDACEK
LUCIEN J DUFAULT
ELMORE E DUFF
DONALD J DUFFY
WARREN F DUFFY
HERBERT H DUGAN
GEORGE F DUGGAH JR
MICHAEL F DUGGAH
DAVID H DUNCAN
GEORGE F DUNCAN JR
LOREN E DUNCAN
ROBERT A DUNCAN
JACK E DUNDIN
BOBBY L DUNLAP
THEODORE E DUNLAP
RICHARD H DUNN
THEODORE R DUNN
THOMAS L DUNNE
PATRICK DUNPHY
HAROLD E DUPAR JR
JOHN G DUPAR
CASPER DURGIN JR
PAUL G DURHAM
EDWARD N DURKEE
FREDERICK H DURNFORD
WILLIAM J DWELLEY
KATHERINE DWYER
HOWARD B DYE
CLINTON E DYER
JOE C DYER
NATHAN J DYER
DENNIS W DYKES JR
—E—
MARSHALL W EADS
ROBERT E EADS
HENRY H EAGAN
JOSEPH O EARL
EARLE G EARLING
ARTHUR D EASTMAN
NORMAN EASTMAN
JACK W EATON

RICHARD F EBBS JR
DANIEL M EBY
GLEN S EBY
ALFRED E ECCLES
HENRY C ECHTERNKAMP
GILBERT H ECKERSON
ERVIN C ECKHOFF
JESS A EDD
THOMAS L EDDY
JOHN J EDEN
ROBERT S EDENS
TOMMY H EDENS
ALFRED W EDES
ROBERT W EDICK
CHARLES B EDLER
CHARLES W EDMUNDS
CHARLES B EDWARDS
CHARLES W EDWARDS JR
GENE S EDWARDS
JOSEPH R EDWARDS
NORRIS W EDWARDS
RAYMOND J EDWARDS
WARREN T EDWARDS
WALLACE R EEL
VIRGIL J EGGERS
MARTIN T EGLAND
JUNIOR K EGLOFF
HENRY O EHLERS
RUDOLPH I EHRLICHMAN
KENT E EICHENBERGER
JOHN H EICHMANN
KENNETH M EIDE
KENNETH W EIGHME
FREDERICK W EILMANN
ROBERT K EINAR
BRUCE H EK
ROBERT D EKINS
GEORGE E EKLUND
DAVID A ELDRED
JOHN ELDRIDGE JR
MORRIS L ELDRIDGE
WALLACE K ELDRIDGE
JEROME H ELLINGER
MILES E ELLIOTT
RUSSELL J ELLIOTT
EDWARD L ELLIS
GEORGE ELLIS
HOWARD L ELLIS
JAMES C ELLIS
JAMES L ELLIS
ROBERT H ELLIS
ROBERT L ELLIS
BRUCE H ELLISON
LEON W ELLSWORTH

HAROLD E ELSASSER
PHILIP H ELSBERRY
NOREL E ELWELL
ROBERT C ELY
ALBERT P EMANUEL
DONALD L EMCH
CHARLES H EMERSON JR
HAROLD W EMERSON
WINSTON G EMERT
THOMAS L EMEY
HOWELL A EMLEY
CALVIN H END
DALE M ENDERSON
MORTON K ENDERT
LESLIE J ENDICOTT
RONALD B ENDICOTT
ROBERT T ENDO
RAYMOND G ENGDAL
ARNOLD M ENGE
HADLEY R ENGELDORF
ROBERT J ENGLAND
ROBERT O ENGLAND
HORACE G ENGLE
JOHN R ENGLE
ROY ENLOW
JOHN M ENNIS
JOHN E ERET
CHRISTIAN V ERICKSEN
ARNOLD W ERICKSON
ARTHUR W ERICKSON
CARL J ERICKSON
CHARLES N ERICKSON
DELBERT ERICKSON
ELIZABETH J ERICKSON
GLENN V ERICKSON
RICHARD T ERICKSON
ROBERT ERICKSON
ROLAND V ERICKSON
STILSON L ERICKSON
BILL L ERKER
ARTHUR R ERNEST
WILLIAM F ERNEST
CHARLES G ERNST
NENHART S ERVICK
IVAN A ERVIN
LLOYD F ERWIN
WILLIAM T ERWIN
ARTHUR H ESPE
LUIS ESPINOSA
ALFRED ESPINOZA
FRANK C ESTEK
NORMAN B ESTES
AMOS F ESTRADA
LYLE C ETHELL

MAYER ETKIN
JOHN G EUTENEIER
BENJAMIN R EVANS JR
CHESTER M EVANS
DAVID F EVANS
DAVID G EVANS
HERBERT G EVANS
HOWARD P EVANS
JOHN G EVANS
KENNETH EVANS
THOMAS H EVANS
WILLIAM E EVANS JR
RUDY EVANSICH
CLIFFORD B EVANSON
CHARLES EVERETT
ROBERT E EVERETT
WILMER E EVERS
EARL C EVERSON
ORVAL N EVERTTS
EARL E EWING
ROBERT R EXLINE JR
MARVIN E EYERLY
—F—
PAUL J FADON
WALTER A FAGERNESS
KENNETH W FAGG
VERNON FAILER
HAROLD D FAIRES
KENNETH E FAIT
JOHN B FALCONER
ARTHUR G FALLON
ERVEN F FALQUIST
JOSEPH W FANAZICK
PHILIP C FANDER
DAHL M FANSLER
VERNON G FARMER
LLOYD D FARNELL
LOUIS N FARNSWORTH
HAROLD D FARRIS
LEONARD R FARRON
JAMES D FARROW
GLENN A FATELEY
ERNEST E FATH
TED S FAULKNER
MARTIN FAUST
ORVALL A FAWVER
LOUIS P FAYETTE
LARRY L FEENEY
ARTHUR FEIN
GEORGE A FELCH
ANTHONY T FELICE
IRVING A FELIX
JOHN FELLIPONE
WILLIAM R FELTON

FLOYD O FENNESSY
WALTER R FENSKE
ALDEN P FERGUSON
ALLEN J FERGUSON
FRANCIS W FERGUSON
ROBERT G FERGUSON
JOHN FERRARO
LEE F FERREIRA
ABRAHAM FERRIS
ALLEN O FERRIS
EDWARD P FERRY
ROBERT FEURSTEIN
RICHARD W FEUTZ
WILLIAM FICKER
WENDELL H FIDELE
HAROLD L FIDLIER
BENJAMIN E FIELDER JR
FREDERICK C FIELDHACK
ALFRED K FIELDS
LESLIE E FIELDS
EMANUEL FIESS
GEORGE FIEVEZ
ROBERT L FIFIELD
DAVID B FINCH
NED FINCH
ALFRED R FINCK
DALLAS M FINDLEY
JOSEPH FINKENSTEIN
JACK N FINLEY
LESLIE H FINLEY
JACK L FINNEY
ARTHUR E FINUCANE
CHARLES G FISCHER
RICHARD H FISCHER
FRED R FISHBURN
DAVID D FISHER
GORDON R FISHER
LEWIS B FISHER
PEARL A FISHER
RALPH B FISHER
WILLARD C FISHER
JACK Y FISK
JOSEPH M FISK
RAWLEIGH E FISK
ROBERT M FISKE
JOHN H FITCH
WILLIAM K FITZGERALD
WILLIAM P FITZPATRICK
GEORGE D FIX
PAUL M FLAGG
ROBERT J FLAHIVE
THOMAS E FLANAGAN
ROBERT R FLANARY
ALLMAN J FLEMING

CLYDE H FLEMING
EUGENE B FLEMING
ROBERT J FLEMING
CHARLES M FLENER
CLIFFORD C FLETCHER
WALTER A FLETCHER
THOMAS F FLINN
GLENN C FLOE
PAUL E FLOODEEN
HENRY C FLOREA JR
LELAND J FLOWER
RALPH L FLOWERS
JOHN R FLUETSCH
WILLIAM F FLYNN
RAYMOND A FOGARTY
LOUIS C FOGG
GERALD W FOLEY
ARTHUR E FOOTE
JAMES S FORBES
ROBERT E FORBES
FRANCIS M FORD
THOMAS A FORDYCE
CYRUS M FORELL
CLARENCE M FORMOE
ARNOLD A FORREST
VIRGIL A FORREST
HENRY E FORSLIN
ELDEN G FORSTER
EMMETT D FORT JR
JAMES L FORTIER
EDWIN O FOSMO
BENNIE A FOSS
CARL E FOSS
CLAYTON E FOSS
JOHN W FOSSUM
CARL E FOSTER
EUGENE L FOSTER
HOWARD J FOSTER
ROSS B FOSTER
ROY D FOSTER
THOMAS K FOSTER
FRANCIS R FOURMONT
LAURENCE E FOURMONT
JACK A FOURNIER
JOSEPH A FOURNIER
GEORGE V FOX
GORDON W FOX
HUBERT L FRAKI
MARCEL J FRANCE
LLOYD J FRANCIS
ROBERT F FRANCIS
RAYMOND H FRANCISCO
GALE B FRANK
HARRY D FRANK

HOWARD B FRANK
JOSEPH W FRANKLIN
MILBURN M FRANKLIN
LYLE E FRANTZ
ARTHUR FRANZ
ARTHUR W FRANZEN
DONALD H FRASER
TONY S FRASL
ROBERT H FRAZER
IRVEN L FRAZIER
CECIL E FREDERICK
LESTER A FREDERICKS
WILBERT H FREDRICHS
DALE L FREDRICKSON
CHARLES A FREECE
JACK O FREEL
CHARLES E FREEMAN
DELBERT V FREEMAN
HAROLD M FREEMAN
JAMES S FREEMAN
WILLIAM A FREEMAN
GEAROLD R FREES
JAMES H FRENCH
JOY C FRENCH
JULIUS E FRENCH
KENNETH P FRENCH
WARNIE L FRENCH
ROBERT W FREUND
HUGH D FRICKS
LUNSFORD D FRICKS JR
JOHN H FRIEDRICH
BEN FRIESEN
LESLIE V FRINK
HOWARD FRITZ
ERIC G FROBERG
NORMAN L FRODENBERG
ADOLPH T FROELICH
DONALD H FROEMKE
HEMAN A FROHNHAFER
MILLER L FROLAND
EUGENE J FROST
WARREN K FROST
ARTHUR E FROSTAD
JOHN W FRY
CARL FRYE
HARRY C FRYE
LLOYD S FRYER
LOUIS J FUHRMAN
JAMES E FUHRMANN
PETER Y FUJINO
PETER K FUJIWARA
EDWIN YUKIO FUKUI
BEN FULLENWIDER
HAROLD A FULLER

JAMES A FULLER
JAMES C FULLERTON
CHARLES N FULMER
ERNEST S FULTON
FREDERICK G FULTON
JACK FUNES
OLIVER A FUNK
WILLARD J FUNK
CLARENCE E FUQUA
JAMES A FUREY
ROBERT E FURSE
ROBERT C FUTRELL
NORMAN L FYKERUDE

— G —

EDWARD L GABA
ANDREAS GABRIELSEN
DUANE I GABRIELSON
ALBERT C GADD
LAURENCE E GADDIE
VICTOR M GADROW
JACK GADSBY
JOHN C GADSBY
ALLEN GAETZ
CHARLES S GAGE
GEORGE C GALBRAITH
WILLIAM S GALBRAITH
JAMES M GALE
LORIS GALE
NORMAN GALE
PEDRO GALICIO
HARRY GALL
EDWARD W GALLAGHER
BOYD H GALLAHER JR
VICTOR M GALLAND
JAMES T GAMBLE
IRWIN W GAMELGAARD
LAWRENCE M GANES
ALVIN A GANGUIN
GERAL J GANLEY
LUTHER L GANN
MARTIN W GARBER
AUGUST GARCEA
LEWIS V GARCEAU
HARVEY E GARDNER
JOHN T GARDNER
ROGER L GARDNER
MARK A GARLOCK JR
ROBERT D GARLOCK
DONALD H GARRISON
ROBERT L GARRISON
ROY GARRISON
ROY H GARRISON
EUGENE E GARST
DANIEL C GASKELL

OWEN D GASKELL
HAROLD C GASTON
ORVILLE E GASTON
ROBERT B GASTON
INOCENCIO M GATAN
JACK P GATES
NELSON N GATES JR
ROBERT T GATES
WILLIAM H GATES
WILLIAM F GAUDETTE
ALBERT E GAUMOND
HAROLD D GAY
JOHN E GAY
LOUIS E GEAR
JACK H GEBBIE
CARL C GEESE JR
DONALD C GEIER
FRANK D GEIGER JR
ALOYSIUS A GEIS
RAYMOND H GEIST
DAYTON M GENEST
RICHARD D GENTRY
WILLIAM H GENTRY
HENRY P GENZALE
THOMAS N GEOGHEGAN
DONALD R GEORGE
PATRICK H GEORGE
DIMITRIOS J GERANIOS
CECIL S GERDON
URSHELL P GERDON
ERNEST E GERLACH
FREDERICK J GERLICH
J K GERSTMAN
VINCENT GETTY JR
ROBERT B GIBB
ELWYN H GIBBON
FRANK H GIBBONS
GEORGE R GIBBS
GEORGE R GIBBS JR
KEITH S GIBLER
WILLIAM H GIBSON
JOHN H GIDLUND
ROY A GIERKE
WALTER H GIESE
HARRY M GIFFORD
JOHN I GIFFORD
ORVILLE K GILBERT
DON M GILDEN
D D GILDERSLEEVE
WILLIAM R GILES
JOSEPH A GILLAM
WILLIAM A GILLAM
EARL L GILLELAND JR
JOHN L GILLES

ELLSWORTH GILLESPIE
GLENN H GILLESPIE
JAMES GILLESPIE
HUGH E GILLETTE
FRANK W GILLIAM
HAROLD L GILLIAM
JACKSON H GILLIAM
BERNARD P GILLINGHAM
ARTHUR T GILLIS
EARL F GILLIS JR
PHILIP F GILLIS
ROBERT L GILLIS
WALDO M GILLMER
RUSSELL M GILMORE
ROBERT L GILNOUR
GARTH GINTNER
JULIAN H GIVENS
JOSEPH L GLACKIN
ROBERT L GLAISYER
RAY D GLASER
ROBERT R GLASFORD
THOMAS D GLASPELL
GAGE E GLASS
HUGH L GLASSBURN
RALPH H GLATFELTER
MORRIS C GLAZE
HAROLD P GLEASON
LLOYD E GLEASON
MELVIN E GLEN
ROBERT T GLENN
HARRY GLIDE
JAMES V GLOSNER
ALAN P GLOVER
DON D GOBLE
JAMES T GOBLE
ROY H GOBLE
JOHN E GODFREY
MAYNARD E GODFREY
WALTER W GOE
HOMER R GOEHRI
GEORGE J GOELLER
HARVEY L GOFF
GEORGE H GOHN JR
NEIL A GOLBERG
MERTON S GOLDBERG
RICHARD GOLDEN
PAUL S GOLDMAN
LEO O GOLDSMITH
RICHARD GOLDSMITH
A S GOLKE
GERALD J GONLEY
EDWARD M GOODALL
GORDON W GOODING
GERALD A GOODMAN

JOHN B GOODMAN

JOSEPH M GOODMAN

GEORGE E GOODNER

GLENN W GOODRICH

JOHN S GOODRICH

LEVERNE E GOODRIDGE

RALPH N GOODSELL

ROBERT J GOODWIN

HENRY F GOON

JOHN GOOSMAN

ALFRED L GORDON

JOHNNY W GORDON

LYNWOOD B GORDON

HOWARD W GORHAM

EDWARD D GORMAN

HALBERT E GORMAN

JOHN D GORMAN

ROBERT J GOTTHARDT

CASPER E GOTTINO

JACK P GOULD

WILLIAM J GOULD

GEORGE W GOULDTHRITE

FRANK R GOULET

JOHN R GOW

VERNON R GOWER

PAUL E GOWEY JR

ARTHUR M GOWIN

ANTHONY J GRABINSKI

EDWARD T GRACE

HOWARD L GRADER

JACK GRAHAM

JOHN B GRAHAM

ORVILLE C GRAHAM

OWEN L GRAHAM

SIDNEY W GRAHAM

JAMES D GRAHNERT

GEORGE A GRANDO

RODERICK N GRANGER

MAYO L GRANLUND

HARRY W GRANT

JACK F GRANT

THOMAS T GRANT

WILFRED GRANT

FLOYD GRAPENTHIN JR

ARTHUR J GRATIS

JAMES H GRAVES

JAMES W GRAVES

RICHARD D GRAVES

ALBERT J GRAY

ALVAN P GRAY

DELBERT L GRAY

ELVIN W GRAY

FRANK W GRAY

JOHN M GRAY

RICHARD A GRAY

ROBERT B GRAY

WILLIAM J GRAY JR

EDWARD C GRAYBILL

WILLIAM F GRAYSON

NICHOLAS J GRECCO

CARL E GREEN

EARL K GREEN

EDWARD F GREEN

ERNEST R GREEN

RICHARD E GREEN

WALLACE J GREEN

WILLIAM F GREEN

ARTHUR L GREENE JR

EVERETT A GREENE

GEORGE R GREENE

JOHN R GREENE

PHILO J GREENE

ROBERT L GREENMAN

CHARLES W GREENSHIELD

ROBERT W GREENSIDE

PHILIP I GREER

MATHEW J GREGORICH

CHARLES R GREGORY

WALLACE D GREIG

STANLEY GRENS

GEORGE H GRENZ

WILLARD J GRESS

JAMES L GREYERBIEHL

ERNEST R GRIBBLE

WILLIAM S GRIER

AMBROSE P GRIFFIN

CHARLES R GRIFFIN JR

EVERETT P GRIFFIN

HAROLD N GRIFFIN

JOHN V GRIFFIN

ROYCE E GRIFFIN

WINFIELD S GRIFFIN

SETH E GRIGGS JR

THOMAS F GRIGSBY

ROY R GRILLO

ARNOLD F GROSE

CHARLES G GROSHENS

STANLEY R GROSS

LEONARD D GROUT

HYMAN J GRUND

ROBERT V GRUNHURD

STANLEY A GRUNLUND

WALTER O GUDJOHNSEN

PETER GUDYKA

ROBERT D GUENTHER

WARREN W GUENTHER

WARREN H GUERNSEY

HENRI R GUEROUT

MARTIN A GUERRIN

ALFRED E GUHR

CLAUDE E GUIER

DON H GUILD

WAYNE A GUINN

DANIEL L GUISINGER JR

WILLIAM E GULLIFORD

ORDEAN H GULLINGSRUD

CHARLES F GUMM JR

CLARENCE M GUNDERSON

GILBERT GUNDERSON

ROBERT K GUNDERSON

VICTOR GUNDERSON

DONALD I GUNN

THOMAS W GUNN

WILLIAM R GUNN

ROBERT GUNNS

ADAM H GUNNYON

CLAYTON E GUNTER

WILLIAM E GUNTHER

WILLIAM G GUSE

BURTON A GUSTAFSON

DEAN W GUSTAFSON

ELMER W GUSTAFSON

GORDON GUSTAFSON

HAROLD D GUSTAFSON

WALFRED E GUSTAFSON

GUSTAV B GUSTAVSON

ALBERT J GUYER

WALDO M GYLLMER

ALBERT J GYORFI

— H —

ELI L HAAS

MARSHALL F HAAS

RAYMOND R HAAS

WILLIAM C HAAS

EDWIN HAASE

JOHN C HABA

HAL D HABENICHT

ROBERT S HACKETT

LEROY HACKMASTER

ROY C HACKNET

CARL O HACKNEY

ROY C HACKNEY

JAMES J HADALLER

WAYMAN

HADDOCK JR

GEORGE R HADDON

ROBERT L HADENFELT

PHILIP HAFFNER

ROBERT E HAGAR

ALFRED L HAGEL

EARL J HAGEMAN JR

EDWARD C HAGEN

WESLEY M HAGEN

JAMES F HAGENSEN

HAROLD P HAGERMAN

EDWARD H HAHN

WALTER R HAHN

BRUCE S HAIGHT

DAVID B HAIGHT

EUGENE E HAIR

LUTHER J HAIRRELL

EIICHI F HAITA

FRED E HAITA

TOM S HAJI

ENNIS D HAKE

ROBERT C HAKENSON

JOHN R HALE

BRIDGEMAN G HALL

DAVID C HALL

DAVID S HALL JR

DONOVAN G HALL

HARRY J HALL

HASSAN H HALL

JACK Q HALL

JOHN E HALL

RICHARD C HALL

ROBERT V HALL

THEODORE H HALL

WESLEY C HALL

WILLIAM W HALL

JOHNIE HALLMAN

EDWIN W HALLSTROM

FLOYD W HALONEN

DONALD E HALSEY

CLIFFORD M HALSTEAD

THOMAS W HAMBY

ROBERT E HAMER

ARTHUR S HAMILTON

CHARLES H HAMILTON

CLARENCE J HAMILTON

CLAUDE F HAMILTON

CLIFFORD B HAMILTON

DOUGLAS R HAMILTON

GEORGE HAMILTON

JESSE W HAMILTON

MONTE R HAMILTON

DALE R HAMLIN

GROVER S HAMM

ROBERT M HAMMARLUND

HAROLD E HAMMERS

R B HAMMERSCHMITH

JAMES P HAMMOND

ROBERT L HAMMOND

WILLIAM R HAMMOND

NEIL H HAMPTON

GILBERT T HAMRICK

FRANK W HANAN

LEON G HANCOCK

ROBERT D HAND JR

RAYMOND E HANDLEY

ARDA M HANENKRAT

HAROLD V HANER

JIMMIE A HANES

ALBERT N HANLEY

CLYDE D HANLON

ERNEST E HANLON

MILTON C HANLON

ROBERT HANSCOM

ADELBERT J HANSEN

CHESTER S HANSEN

CLAUDE H HANSEN

DONALD HANSEN

JAMES M HANSEN

JAMES P HANSEN

KERMIT R HANSEN

LAVERNE B HANSEN

RALPH R HANSEN

ROY W HANSEN

THOMAS HANSEN

WALTER HANSEN

GORDON H HANSHAW

ALVIN C HANSON

EUGENE O HANSON

HARVEY A HANSON

PAUL V HANSON

ROBERT J HANSON

LEONARD R HANSTEAD

BEN K HARA

WILLIAM E HARBERT

ELISHA J HARBISON

KENNETH T HARBOUR

GLEN O HARDEMAN

FRANK A HARDER

JAMES R HARDMAN

DEWEY L HARDY

WALDON R HARDY

KENNETH W HARGRAVES

LEE HARKCOM

HAROLD HARLAN

JOSEPH M HARLEY JR

ANDREW E HARLIN

ALBERT D HARLOW

HARLEY E HARLOW

LUCIAN A HARNEY

CHARLES A HARNISH

MILFORD M HARPER

DONALD E HARRIS

FRANKLIN R HARRIS

JAMES A HARRIS

JOHN M HARRIS

LEO V HARRIS	FREDRICK R HAUSS	JACK H HELLUMS JR	JAMES H HIBBARD	LAWRENCE O HOBERG
THOMAS W HARRIS	A A HAUZENBERGER	CHARLES O HELMER	PAUL R HIBBARD	ROBERT D HOBERT
WALLACE HARRIS	EDWARD C HAVEN JR	HERB E HELSTROM	ROY E HICKCOX	DIXON W HOBSON
WALTER C HARRIS	WILLIAMS S HAVENS	THOMAS HEMBREE	KEITH S HICKEY	EVERETT H HOBSON
WILLIAM J HARRIS JR	RAYMOND A HAVERFIELD	PAUL F HEMMELGARN	ARTHUR L HICKMAN	SHELDON L HOCKINS
BENJAMIN F HARRISON	CLINTON HAWK	RASMUS E HEMNES	HARRY S HICKMAN	LEROY A HODGE
CECIL L HARRISON	ROBERT C HAWKEY	DON C HEMPSTEAD JR	ELMER O HICKS	CHARLES L HODGINS
DONALD D HARRISON	VERN D HAWKINS	DARWIN J HENDERSON	LAWRENCE M HICKS JR	HOWARD L HODGSON
DONALD W HARRISON	WILLIAM R HAWKINS	THEODORE W HENDON	VINCENT T HICKS	HERBERT H HOEHN
FREDERICK W HARRISON JR	EUGENE E HAWKS	HARLEY J HENDRICKS	CHARLES W HIGGENS	ALLEN N HOEY
LAWRENCE K HARRISON	DALLAS E HAWLEY	JOHN D HENDRICKS	BOB E HIGGINS	JACK D HOFF
ROBERT F HARRISON	RICHARD L HAWSON	JOHN R HENDRICKS	LOUIS W HIGGINS	LESLIE W HOFF
WILLARD C HARRISON	WILLIAM C HAWSON	ROBERT J HENDRICKSEN	ROY D HIGGINS	GLENN J HOFFER
WILLIAM C HARRISON	FREEMAN M HAWTHORNE	JOHN V HENDRICKSON	WALTER K HIGGINS	ALBERT B HOFFMAN
RUSSELL E HARRY	EUGENE HAYASHI	LAURENCE M HENEGHEN	HOWARD A HIGH	PAUL HOFFMAN
ROY L HARSH	GEORGE H HAYES	FRANK HENNING	ROBERT W HILBER	WILLIAM F HOFFMAN
CLIFFORD M HART	JAMES F HAYES	DWANE O HENRY	HAROLD A HILDEBRAND	GABRIEL M HOFLACK
DONALD W HART	JOHN C HAYES	PHILIP L HENRY	JAMES T HILDEBRAND JR	RUSSELL G HOFLIN
GEORGE W HART	RICHARD	SAMUEL C HENRY	CHARLES R HILL	LESTER T HOFSTAD
JOHN L HART	HAYES	DONALD F HENSEY	CLAIR S HILL	JOHN D HOFSTEE
WILLIAM F HART	EDWARD C HAYNES	BARCLAY J HENSHAW	CLYDE C HILL	JONATHAN HOFTO
WILLIAM L HART	LAWRENCE H HAYNES	RICHARD G HENSLEY	EARL L HILL	GEORGE K HOGAN
JACK M HARTER	WILLIAM HAYNES	DONALD A HEPP	EDWARD L HILL	KENNETH HOGAN
WARD A HARTFIELD	CLIFFORD J HAYS	HARVEY C HERBER	FRANCIS J HILL	PAUL E HOGAN
VICTOR W HARTLEY	VERNON S HAYS	WILLIAM E HERBERT	GEORGE J HILL	RAYMOND A HOGAN
ACE HARTMAN	CHARLES D HAZLETON	GILBERT C HERING	KELMAR J HILL	WILLIAM J HOGAN
RICHARD S HARTMAN	GEORGE D HEALY	JOHN HERMAN	MARION G HILL JR	CHESTER W HOGANSON
JAMES L HARTSOC	FRANK S HEATER	WILLIAM HERMAN	MORSE G HILL	GEORGE R HOGSHIRE JR
BRUCE HARTZE	JAMES P HEATER	HANS W HERMANSEN	MORTON W HILL	THEODORE R HOKENSTAD
THOMAS HARTZELL	CHARLES HEATH	WILLIAM T HERNDON	PERRY R HILL	JOHN L HOLBEACH
ASA H HARVEY JR	FRANCIS E HEATH	DAMON N HERRELL	ROBERT HILL	RAY F HOLBROOK
JAMES R HARVEY	MARVIN B HEATH	CRYSTAL R HERRIMAN	RODERICK T HILL	ALLEN D HOLCOMB
JOHN C HARVEY	WILLIAM J HEATH	WALTER W HERRMAN	TOM B HILL JR	RUPERT R HOLCOMB JR
KENNETH A HARVEY	CLAUDE L HEATON	CLARENCE A HERRMANN	WILLIAM F HILL	RALPH J HOLDEN
LUCIAN A HARVEY	ERNEST D HEATON	JOHN H HERRON JR	CARL C HILTON	ROBERT E HOLDEN
RICHARD W HARVEY	SAMUEL J HEBRON	LYNN A HERRON	JOHN R HIMELRICK	CHARLES E HOLDON
WAYNE A HARWOOD	FORREST D HEDINGTON	WILLIAM J HERT	RAYMOND S HIMES	FRANK E HOLEC
HOWARD S HASBROOK	GLENDALE HEFLEY	ROBERT G HERTHNECK	GERALD D HINCHY	HARRY HOLECH
NORMAN F HASCH	HARRY C HEFT	EUGENE N HERTZ	ENGVALD S HINDRUM	RAY C HOLFORD
JOHN T HASHIMOTO	ROBERT H HEGG	LOUIS F HERZER	WARREN R HINER	EDDIE C HOLGADO
WILLIAM K HASLAM	ROYCE M HEGG	DANIEL S HESS	CECIL G HINES	ROBERT J HOLLADAY
WILSON B HASLAM	IRVIN A HEGLAND	JAMES R HESS	HARVEY D HINRICHS	PATRICK D HOLLAND
ALTON J HASSELL JR	JOHN N HEIB	RALPH C HESS	ADONIS C HINTON	ROBERT L HOLLAND
OSCAR A HASSON	GEORGE HEICHEL	WALTER J HESS	JAMES W HIRD	WALTER L HOLLEY
ROBERT C HATCHER	WILLIAM F HEIDRICH	ANTHONY J HESSDORFER	ROBERT W HIRST	GERALD E HOLLIDAY
PHIL W HATFIELD	ROY F HEIDT	GUSTAF HETZE	KEITH HITCHCOCK	JASPER L HOLLIDAY
ROBERT E HATFIELD	ARNOLD E HEIKKILA	MARVIN L HETZLER	FRANK R HITCHING	ROMAIN L HOLLIS
ERNEST C HATHAWAY	KENNETH O HEILIG	CARL R HEUSSY	JAMES C HITE	CLARENCE C HOLLISTER
ROY A HATLEN	JOHN HEIN	DONALD D HEUTON	FRANK S HOAG JR	ORIS R HOLLISTER
ALVIN R HATTON	JOHN P HEINZEN	EDISON C HEUY	HUGH L HOAG	STEWART M HOLLOWAY
CLIFFORD V HAUFF	ARTHUR HEISLER	JOHN R HEWLITT	CLEO A HOAGLUND	W T HOLLOWAY
LOUIS HAUGE	THOMAS B HEITSTUMAN	WALTER C HEYER	EDWARD M HOARE	CARL C HOLLSTROM
JOHN D HAUGEN	JOSEPH F HELGASON	WILLIAM R HEYER JR	MACEO M HOBBS	HERBERT C HOLM
ALBERT G HAUSLE	HERBERT C HELLAND	WILLIAM E HEYES	MELVIN D HOBBS	INGOLE K HOLM

JAMES D HOLM
JOHN W HOLM
WILLIAM I HOLMAN JR
FERDINAND W HOLMBERG
BURYL A HOLMES
GERALD B HOLMES
HARRY B HOLMES
WILLIAM A HOLMES
AXEL W HOLMQUIST
GEORGE V HOLMQUIST
HAROLD D HOLMQUIST
CARL B HOLMSTROM
ROBERT L HOLSBO
MORRIS E HOLSEY
JAMES R HOLSHOUSER
CLAUD C HOLSTEN
JACK D HOLT
JUSTUS M HOME
ERNEST HONTOS
FRANK E HOOD
HENRY L HOOPER
JOE H HOOPES
FRED G HOOVER
RAYMOND HOPE
GEORGE P HOPKINS
WALTER S HOPKINS
JOSEPH F HORA
ROBERT A HORA
JOHN W HORMAN
ROBERT A HORN
DONALD M HORNER
WILLIAM H HORNER
WESLEY A HORR
WALTER R HORTON JR
CARL HORTSMAN
JOHN HOSEK
DONALD F HOSKIN
WALLACE J HOSKYN
RUSSELL F HOSMER
ANDREW F HOUK
JOSEPH M HOUSE JR
ROBERT HOUSER
ALBERT L HOUSTON
HAROLD B HOUSTON
LAWRENCE B HOVELAND
VERNON M HOVELAND
CLARENCE A HOWARD
CURTIS W HOWARD
EARL F HOWARD
HOMER L HOWARD
IVAN E HOWARD
JOHN D HOWARD
LLOYD M HOWARD
NORMAN L HOWARD

ROBERT E HOWARD
ROBERT W HOWARD
WALTER V HOWARD
WILLIAM E HOWARD
GRANT M HOWE
HAROLD D HOWE
ROBERT L HOWE
WILLIAM R HOWE
JOE T HOWELL
RICHARD P HOWELL
WALTER T HOWELL
TED L HOWERTON
GEORGE A HOWLAND
ROBERT M HOWLEY
GLENN A HOYER
WILLIAM H HRONEK JR
LAMBERT J HRUSKA
CARL HUBBARD
JACK C HUBBARD
FRANK L HUBBS
LONELL H HUBER
GLENN E HUBERT
ALBERT L HUDSON
GORDON L HUDSON
HOWARD B HUESTIS JR
JOSEPH E HUFF
RAYMOND J HUFF
BILLY I HUFFMAN
HAROLD F HUFFMAN
FREEMAN B HUFFSMITH
ARTHUR M HUGHES
BILL D HUGHES
EMMETT S HUGHES
HARRISON S HUGHES
IRA P HUGHES
JOSEPH S HUGHES
RICHARD E HUGHES
RICHARD K HUGHES
HAROLD L HUKILL
WESLEY J HULETT
CHARLES T HULL
DONALD L HULL
MELVIN O HULL
HAROLD HULTENGREN
LORENTZ E HULTGREN
LLOYD E HUME
ROBERT A HUME
GLEN W HUMERICHOUS
JAMES M HUMMEL
CLYDE R HUMPHREY
JOHN W HUNSAKER
HANS A HUNSKOR
IVAN E HUNT
KENNETH L HUNT

LEON L HUNT
MARVIN R HUNT
WILLIAM B HUNT JR
BILLY G HUNTER
CHARLES W HUNTER
JOHN J HUNTER
ROBERT K HUNTINGTON
EUGENE L HUNTLEY
CLIFFORD W HURLEY
WILLIAM G HURLEY
RICHARD M HURRELL
DAROLD A HURST
ELDWYN E HUSE
JOHN W HUSE
HENRY J HUSEBY
ALBERT A HUTCHINGS
KARL C HUTCHINGS
DELMAR T HUTCHINS
HERBERT W HUTCHINS
LEONARD J HUTCHINS
ROBERT D HUTCHINS
ROBERT E HUTCHINS
RUSSELL R HUTCHINS
WILLIAM N HUTCHINS
GEORGE L HUTCHINSON
THEODORE F HUTER
BILLY B HUTTEBALL
GEORGE E HUTTON
DON E HYDE
HAROLD L HYINK

— I —

HAROLD K IDDINS
IRA C IDE
THEODORE M IHRIG
EDWARD IKEBE
MASAO IKEDA
CHARLES P ILGER
WILLIAM I IMAMOTO
RALPH R IMBERG
ROBERT C IMHOFF
SHUNICHI B IMOTO
MASAMI INATSU
JACK M INDAHL
ROBERT J INGERSOLL JR
ELVIN A INGLIN
GENE A INGRAHAM
JOHN S INGRAHAM
ROBERT H INGSTAD
RAYMOND Y IRBY
HENRY A IRONS
WALTER W IRVIN JR
LAWRENCE W IRVINE
NORMAN IRVINE
WILLIAM B ISAAC

WILHELM T ISAACSON
EDWIN C ISAKSON
MITSUO M ISERI
HARUO ISHIDA
ALBERT A ISRAEL
JACK E ISRAEL
WILLIAM C IVARSEN
ORVILLE L IVERSON
RODNEY B IVES
HISASHI IWAI

— J —

JEROME P JACKMAN
ALVIN J JACKSON
HAROLD H JACKSON
HAROLD W JACKSON
ROBERT A JACKSON
ROBERT C JACKSON
ROGER W JACKSON
WALTER R JACKSON
DAVID E JACOBS
JAMES R JACOBS
JACOB JACOBSEN
LEROY E JACOBSEN
RALPH G JACOBSEN
CARMAN J JACOBSON
NED E JACOBSON
MERLYN L JAKEL
CLAUDE P JAMES
EDWARD R JAMES
HERSHEL D JAMES
JOHN D JAMES
MARTIN JAMES
CLIFFORD D JAMESON
ELMER W JAMESON
THOMAS S JAMIESON
LADDIE J JANACEK
JAMES A JANZE
CARL E JAQUES
JOHN W JARDINE
BENJAMIN E JARED
JAMES E JARRELL
ALBERT C JASPERS
CARL L JAVORSKY
HOWARD K JAYCOX
MO S JEE
CHESTER J JEFFERS
LEE E JEFFERS
RICHARD JEFFERSON
LARS P JELLE
THOMAS R JEMISON
DONALD M JENKINS
THOMAS A JENKINS
JOHN A JENNA
ROBERT L JENNINGS

WILLIAM F JENNINGS
ALFRED S JENSEN
CLARK H JENSEN
DAVID A JENSEN
ERIK L JENSEN
ETLAR M JENSEN
JACK P JENSEN
JAMES JENSEN
MYRON R JENSEN
ROBERT G JENSEN
ROY T JENSEN
THEODORE JENSEN
WILLIAM L JEPSON
SAMUEL R JEROME
HAROLD T JERRUE
HAROLD H JESKE
ERNEST E JESS
WALTER M JETT
WILLIAM H JETT
HAROLD N JEVNING
LELAND D JEWELL
THOMAS E JEWELL
LORNE W JEWETT
RICHARD P JOBB
LOUIE JOE
RICHARD C JOHANNSEN
LLOYD R JOHANSEN
ANDREW M JOHN
GEORGE H JOHN
HERMAN K JOHN SR
MERLE W JOHN
FLOYD R JOHNS
LELAND L JOHNS
PAUL H JOHNS
MARVIN D JOHNSEN
ALFRED A JOHNSON
ANDREW N JOHNSON JR
ANDY W JOHNSON
BEAUFORD C JOHNSON
CARL JOHNSON
CHARLES E JOHNSON
CHARLES R JOHNSON
CLIFFORD E JOHNSON
DANIEL E JOHNSON
DONALD E JOHNSON
DONALD L JOHNSON
EMERY H JOHNSON
EMIL H JOHNSON
ERNEST O JOHNSON
EUGENE B JOHNSON
EVERETT A JOHNSON
FAY C JOHNSON
FLOYD W JOHNSON
FRANK JOHNSON

GEORGE M JOHNSON
GORDON A JOHNSON
GUNNARD M JOHNSON
HAROLD JOHNSON
HAROLD E JOHNSON
HAROLD R JOHNSON
HAROLD W JOHNSON
HARRY F JOHNSON
HENRY E JOHNSON
HOWARD E JOHNSON
IRA E JOHNSON JR
IRVIN J JOHNSON
JAMES A JOHNSON JR
JOEL M JOHNSON
JOHN C JOHNSON
JOHN O JOHNSON
KARL E JOHNSON
KENNETH L JOHNSON
LEIGH H JOHNSON
LEMOINE K JOHNSON
LEO O JOHNSON
LEROY A JOHNSON
LLOYD G JOHNSON
LOUIS C JOHNSON
MAYNARD E JOHNSON
MELVIN G JOHNSON
OSCAR C JOHNSON
OSCAR G JOHNSON
PETER C JOHNSON
QUENTIN W JOHNSON
RANFORD JOHNSON
RAYMOND JOHNSON
RAYMOND G JOHNSON
RICHARD H JOHNSON
ROBERT JOHNSON
ROBERT S JOHNSON
ROY C JOHNSON
ROY E JOHNSON
SAMUEL C JOHNSON
SIGWALD C JOHNSON
STANLEY L JOHNSON
STEPHAN J JOHNSON
STERLING C JOHNSON
STUART JOHNSON
THOMAS W JOHNSON
VERNON G JOHNSON
VINCENT L JOHNSON
WILBUR F JOHNSON
WILLIAM J JOHNSON
WILLIAM R JOHNSON
WILLIS R JOHNSON
WOODROW W JOHNSON
EARL B JOHNSTON
FREDERICK V JOHNSTON

GARNETT M JOHNSTON
KENNETH G JOHNSTON
ROBERT D JOHNSTON
HENRY JOHNSTONE
DAVID G JOLLY
WILBUR F JOLLY
MELVIN P JONAS
GERALD W JONER
ALFRED L JONES
ARTHUR W JONES
BENNIE F JONES
DANIEL G JONES
DAVID E JONES
DAVID L JONES
DOUGLAS M JONES
DWIGHT W JONES
ELLIS E JONES
ELMER R JONES
FOY A JONES
FREDERICK M JONES
HAROLD E JONES
KENNETH A JONES
LEO C JONES
LIONEL A JONES
LYLE S JONES
MARION E JONES
MARMON JONES
MERLE D JONES
NEWTON W JONES
PETE JONES
ROBERT D JONES
ROBERT E JONES
ROBERT F JONES
ROBERT J JONES
ROY E JONES
THEODORE W JONES
THOMAS A JONES JR
VAWTER E JONES
VICTOR JONES
MAX J JONIENTZ
CLAUDE W JONON JR
FREDERICK H JOPLIN
PETER F JORDAN
ROBERT E JORDAN
MELVIN R JORGENSEN
WALTER M JOSELYN
DONALD JOY
ROBERT E JOYCE
JOSPEH J JUANICK JR
HOWARD C JUBB
RALPH JUDY
PAUL F JUELING JR
RUDOLPH JUGO
CHRISTY R JULL

CHARLIE F JUMPER JR
CARL JUNDT
CLIFF H JUNGERS
JAMES A JUNKIN
FELIX JURASIN
PHILLIP T JURASIN

— K —

ROBERT E KAAP
EDWARD T KAAS
JOE Y KADOYAMA
ANTHONY KAHL
DEAN E KAIL
GEORGE E KAISER
LAURENCE H KAISER
PAUL L KAISER
EDWARD KALAMA
STANLEY R KALENIUS
EDWARD KALINOWSKI
HALVOR C KAMP
VERNON W KANE
WALTER M KANE
WILLIAM E KANE
JERO KANETOMI
DAVID J KANNITZER
DONALD J KANNITZER
AKIRA KANZAKI
ALBERT G KAPEL
DAVID M KAPHINGST
ALEX KAPLAN
EDWARD R KARDONG
RAINO C KARIKKO
CARL S KARLSSON
LYLE G KARNATH
DONALD L KARNEY
CLARENCE C KASCH
LOUIS R KASSEBAUM
YOSHIO KATO
EZRA A KAUFFMAN
HENRY J KAUFMAN
JAMES W KAVANEY
JOHN R KAWAGUCHI
LAWRENCE L KAY
SIRTHUR B KAY
WILLIAM R KAYE
RICHARD L KEAN
AMIEL J KEARNEY
FRED H KEELER
MARCUS E KEELER
DAVID L KEEN
JOHN E KEEN
JAMES F KEENE
JAMES F KEENER
RUSSELL E KEENER

CECIL M KEEP
JOSEPH R KEHL
MAX J KEHRER
RALPH H KEIL
HAROLD F KEISTER
JOHN J KELLEHER JR
JESSE B KELLER
RALPH F KELLER
RAYMOND C KELLER
STANLEY H KELLER
JOHN F KELLEY
MAYNARD C KELLEY
PAUL H KELLEY
RONALD L KELLEY
TALBOT D KELLEY
VIRGIL D KELLEY
GEORGE S KELLOGG
BERNARD T KELLY
DUDLEY R KELLY
IVAN C KELLY
JOHN J KELLY
RICHARD S KELLY
WALTER W KEMP
GILBERT T KENNAUGH
JAMES D KENNEDY
JAMES L KENNEDY
LAWRENCE E KENNEDY
RUSSELL T KENNEDY
THOMAS M KENNEDY
ROBERT M KENNEWICK
IRVEN W KENNEY
DALE O KENNINGTON
GEORGE R KENNISON
JACK F KENT
NOEL KENT
ROBERT K KENT
WILLIAM J KEOGH
ROBERT L KEOUGH
WILLIAM S KEPPLER
PAUL L KERMEL
JOHN A KERN JR
ERWIN A KERNDL
DONALD M KERR
JAMES H KERR
LEE D KERR
WALTER C KERR
CHARLES S KERRICK
THURLOW E KESNER
CALVIN C KESSINGER
RICHARD A KESSLER
ROBERT E KESTERSON
JAMES R KESTLE
ARTHUR F KETTEL
WILLIAM B KIBBEY

ROBERT J KIEBLER
FRED KIEFERT
WILLIAM F KIEHN
HARVEY W KIERSTINE
EMERSON H KIESWITTER
FRANK D KIESZLING
JACK N KIFFER
HAROLD E KILDEW
EARL C KILDUFF
DONALD K KILGORE
JAMES M KILGORE
JOHN R KILGORE
ALFRED C KILTAU
JOSEPH H KIMBALL
MURRY B KIMBALL
ORVILLE E KIMBALL
ROY E KIMBLE
HARRIS L KIMBLE
BERT F KIMES
ROY H KIMMEL
LEROY E KINCAID
ROBERT F KINCAID
DELBERT O KINDLE
EARL KINDLUND
ANDREW KING
ARTHUR R KING
EDDIE M KING
EDWARD M KING
GRIFFITH B KING
JOSEPH L KING
LEIF T KING
LEROY W KING
MERVIN M KING
MILTON E KING
RICHARD S KING
ROLLIE KING
WARREN L KING
DALE N KINGMAN
CLAYTON G KINGSTON
FREDERICK W KINNEY
FRANCIS T KINOSHITA
JAMES B KINYON
ALBERT J KINZEL JR
ERVEN KINZER
WILLIAM A KIPHART
EUGENE D KIRBY
JOHN T KIRBY JR
ROBERT J KIRK
ROBERT T KIRK
WALTER F KIRK
ELVIN T KIRKEDAHL
KENNETH W KIRKENDOLL
CHARLES N KIRKHAM
WILLIAM E KIRKLAND

ROGER D KIRKPATRICK
ROY D KIRKPATRICK
RUSSELL J KIRKPATRICK
JOHN D KIRKWOOD
CLIFFORD J KIRPES
LAWRENCE H KIRSCH
LEWIS A KIRSCH
LAWRENCE H KISKADDON
JOHN H KITTLES
RALPH L KIZER
HAROLD G KJARGAARD
EDWARD E KJELNESS
HENRY R KJEMS
GUSTAV D KJOSNESS
JOHN L KLADNICK
WILIAM A KLAMAN
JOSEPH P KLARICH
RAYMOND M KLEER
HARRY R KLEIN
LAWRENCE J KLEIN
JAMES E KLEMGARD
ANDREW C KLENK
STANLEY H KLESPER
DANIEL B KLINE
JOHN O KLIPPERT
CECIL F KLISE
F M KLOPFENSTEIN
CARL J KLOVDAHL
DON L KNAPP
EARL B KNAPP
KENNETH L KNAPP
JOHN A KNARR
RICHARD L KNAUTZ
GERALD W KNIGHT
HARRY V KNIGHT
MARVIN A KNIGHT
ROBERT L KNIGHT
ROY A KNIGHT
ROY W KNIGHT JR
KENNETH M KNISLEY
BYRON C KNOLL
CLARENCE KNOPH
CLYDE C KNOWLES
ARTHUR L KNOWLTON
JACK C KNOWLTON
LEAL P KNUDSEN
DARROLL E KNUDSON
ELWYN G KNUDSON
EUGENE H KNUDSON
TOM KNUDSON
MARVIN W KNUDTSON
ORVILLE P KNUTSON
RALEIGH W KOBLOTH
LAWRENCE F KOCH

THOMAS A KOCH
WALTER KOCH
JACK KOCHEVAR
JACK L KOEHLER
MARSHALL I KOEHLER
CLARENCE K KOENEKAMP
JOSEPH P KOENIGS
ALVIN W KOESTER
ROY C KOHLER
EDWARD R KOHLS
GEORGE KOHUT
PAUL KOHUT
WALTER A KOLLER
GEORGE A KOMEDAL
JAMES O KOMEDAL
DOW W KOON
LAWRENCE C KOPLIN
RICHARD A KOREIS
ELMER J KOSKI
LEONARD P KOSS
NORMAN KOSSIS
JOHN KOSTICK
ERNEST KOZLOWSKI
WARREN E KRAFFT
JOHN L KRALMAN
EUGENE L KRAMER
FRANK R KRAMER
JOHN A KRAMER
KENNETH L KRAMER
EDWARD C KRAMES
ROBERT A KRASSIN
RAYMOND C KRAUS
EDWARD G KRAUSE
LEON B KRAVIK
RODNEY H KREFT
WILLIAM M KREIDE
CHESTER W KREILING
LEO H KREUGER
DONALD P KRIEG
HOWARD L KRIPPNER JR
NORMAN C KRISTENSEN
FRANK H KROGER
ERVIN L KROHN
LEO J KROLL
MAX KROM
ROBERT KROMM
GLEN G KROOK
FRANCIS L KRUEGER
LEO H KRUGER
HERMAN J KRUICK
JAMES H KRUPP
DONALD D KRUSE
MILTON W KUBICEK
E C KUCHENBECKER JR

ERNEST KUEHN
BURTON J KUHN
JOHN KUIPERS
JOHN M KULLOWATZ
RALPH D KUNEY
ALVIN E KUONEN
DONALD V KURTZER
THEODORE A KUSSMAN
ADOLF X KUTCHERA
WILLIAM F KUZEL
JAMES A KVIS
JAMES E KYES
HAROLD L KYLE

— L —

DONALD C LA BOLLE
WILLIAM J LA CAFF
CECIL V LA FLEUR
FRANCIS A LA FOND
ROBERT E LA FONTAINE
DONALD A LA ROSE
JAMES L LA RUE
WILLARD D LA SALLE
JOSEPH LA TORRE
GUY R LABERS
STANLEY B LABO
THOMAS J LACEY
CLINTON J LACKEY
JOHN N LACY
CLARENCE W LADNIER
DENNY F LAGOUNARIS
MIKE LAGOZZINO
WILLIAM B LAING
RICHARD F LAIRD
MELVIN F LAKE
LAVERNE A LALLATHIN
THOMAS E LAMB
CARL H LAMBERT
DAHRL A LAMBERT
MITCHELL F LAMBERT
ROBERT S LAMBERT
WILFRED T LAMBERT JR
JAMES E LAMBETH
CHARLES A LAMKE
AUX D LAMONRE
DONALD L LAMONT
DONALD LAMOREAUX
EVART LAMPING JR
ARTHUR T LAMPMAN
CHARLES C LAMSEK
LA FELL LAMSON JR
JOHN T LANCASTER
EDWARD H LANDEIS
EDWARD R LANDER
DENNIS M LANE

DONALD C LANE
GERHARD A LANE
HERBERT E LANE
HORACE B LANE
GLENN J LANG
JACOB L LANG
RAYMOND K LANGBERG
JOHN H LANGDON
JERE H LANGE
LOYCE E LANGSTON
RALPH H LANKFORD
THOMAS R LANKFORD
CECIL M LANNIGAN
MERLE J LARAMEE
THURSTON W LARAWAY
JOHN A LARKIN
CECIL E LARSEN
EDWARD LARSEN
GEORGE C LARSEN
JOHN W LARSEN
MILLARD F LARSEN
ROBERT G LARSEN
DONALD A LARSON
EDWARD M LARSON
HALVARD L LARSON
HERBERT LARSON
LEONARD C LARSON
LLEWELLYN L LARSON
RALPH H LARSON
ROBERT L LARSON
ROGER C LARSON
VERNON A LARSON
VERNON L LARSON
WILLIAM T LARSON
WILLIAM A LASBY
STANLEY M LASSOK
BEN E LASSWELL JR
WALDON W LATHROM
MERWIN LAUFER
CHARLES C LAUGENOUR
HIRSCHEL V LAUGHLIN
CARL M LAURSEN
JOHN E LAVELLE
ROBERT M LAVEN
CHARLES A LAWRENCE
CLYDE M LAWRENCE
DOYLE R LAWRENCE
IRVIN H LAWRENCE
VERNON L LAWRENCE
EDWARD W LAWSON
MALCOLM LAWTY
ERNEST B LAWVER
GEORGE A LAYMAN
RALPH W LE DREW

DOUGLAS C LE GEAR
ELGIN G LE GORE
EDWIN N LE LAND
HERSCHEL W LEABO
DONALD C LEACH
EARL J LEADON
LESLIE H LEAF
ROBERT L LEAKEY
EMORY H LEAMON
STEPHEN D LECKENBY
HERBERT O LECKMAN
TILBERT K LEDBETTER
WILLIAM H LEDER
HARRY S LEE
JAMES W LEE
JOHN F LEE
ROBERT E LEE
ROBERT V LEE
THOMAS LEE
THOMAS H LEE
THOMAS J LEE JR
WILMON G LEE
RALPH J LEEFELMAN
WILLIAM R LEESE
JOHN G LEGGETT
GEORGE J LEHMAN
JAMES E LEHMAN
HEROLD W LEHMANN
WILLIAM D LEHTO
HAROLD E LEISE
ROBERT O LEISHMAN
EDWIN N LELAND
THEODORE H LELAND
ABE L LEMLEY
ERNEST E LEMLEY
JOHN W LEMLEY
DOUGLAS E LEMMEL
JAMES L LENEAU
LESLIE E LENHART
ELMER E LENT
NICHOLAS LEO
DAN M LEONARD
JACK R LEONARD
WARREN C LEONARD
WILLIAM T LEONARD
FRANK LEONETTI
ERNEST F LEPP
GORDON W LESTER
JAMES W LESTER
WILFRED A LETAURNEAU
CHARLES F LETSON
LEONARD W LEVANDER
GEORGE P LEVASSEUR
EDWARD N LEVINSON

ISAAC M LEVY
DUANE M LEWIS
FLOYD S LEWIS
GEORGE A LEWIS
HAROLD H LEWIS JR
JACOB J LEWIS
JAMES M LEWIS
KEITH C LEWIS
LEON O LEWIS
LLEWELLYN D LEWIS
RAYMOND F LEWIS
RAYMOND R LEWIS JR
RICHARD W LEWIS
ROBERT B LEWIS
WILLIAM K LEWIS
WILLIAM R LEWIS
GEORGE L LEWMAN
LLOYD L LEWMAN
ALGER C LIBBY
KENNETH T LIDA
VERNIE D LIEBL
MARION A LIEBMAN
CAROLUS P LIEROP
ALDEN H LIGHTFOOT
CHARLES J LIGHTFOOT
JAMES W LIGHTLE
HARRY A LILLARD
WILLIAM J LILLEY
ALBERT J LIMPP JR
GORDON E LINBO
DAVID E LINDBERG
LLOYD A LINDBERG
RALPH R LINDBERG
CHARLES G LINDEN
CHARLES F LINDER
NORMAN LINDJORD
BERNARD E LINDSAY
BERNARD L LINDSAY
RAYMOND LINDSAY
ROBERT A LINDSAY
SHERMAN T LINDSAY
STACEY J LINDSAY
DONALD H LINDSEY
J R LINDSEY
EMILY R LINDSTROM
HENRY LINKER
MARCUS C LINN
JAMES W LIPSAY
EDWIN C LISHER
NORRIS W LITCH
MERRILL D LITERAL
BENJAMIN H LITTLE JR
JOSEPH M LITTLEFIELD
ERNEST T LIVERMORE

ALBERT L LLOYD
RICHARD B LLOYD
ROBERT B LLOYD
TONY B LLOYD
GLENN A LOBDELL
KENNETH C LOBDELL
HAROLD D LOCHRIDGE
RICHARD E LOCKDAM
STANLEY N LOCKE
WILLIAM C LOCKETT
RAYMOND B LOCKHART
WILLIAM LODIK
EDWARD C LOE
FREDERICK A LOEHRL
FREDERICK LOENDAHL
WILFORD E LOFGREN
RALPH D LOFTUS
DANIEL S LOGAN
PAUL E LOGAN
PAUL F LOGAN
ALLEN F LOHMAN
HOWARD H LOHMAN
ALBERT C LOMBARDY
JOSEPH L LONDO
ARTHUR T LONG
CHARLES R LONG
GEORGE A LONG
PERRY J LONG
WILLIAM E LONG
WINTON J LONG
DONALD G LONGFELLOW
MERLE H LONGNECKER
CHESTER E LONGSHORE
HENRY LONNER
WILLIAM A LONNEVIK
FOREST C LOOMER
EVERETT W LOOMIS
GEORGE T LOOP
EUGENE LOPEZ
GORDON L LORD
THUMAN R LORD
LAURENCE J LORTIE
WOODSON W LOSLI
NORMAN A LOTZ
ROBERT L LOUCKS
HAROLD E LOUGHARG
PATRICK T LOUGHIN
YEU LOUIE
RALPH E LOUNSBURY JR
KENNETH G LOUTHER
DONALD E LOVE
HAROLD D LOVE
LLOYD G LOVE
LOREN E LOVE

LOUIS M LOVE
DONALD E LOVELAND
GEORGE E LOVELL
JAMES B LOVETT JR
CLARENCE E LOW
JAMES R LOWE
JAMES W LOWE
THEODORE G LOWELL
CHARLES E LOWER
GROVER M LOWERY
CLYDE D LOWRY JR
AUSTIN P LUBIN
WALTER E LUBKER
RICHARD C LUCAS
RICHARD L LUCE
LOUIS M LUCENTE
MICHAEL B LUDWIG
ROBERT E LUDWIG
ORLAND L LUHR
ROBERT H LULL
DELMER H LUMBERG
MURRAY LUND
OTTO N LUND
ROBERT E LUND
VICTOR LUND
DARWIN H LUNDBERG
RODGER W LUNDE
MALTE LUNDELL
CAROL E LUNDRIGAN
CARL B LUNDSTROM
JOE LUPO
LESLIE G LUSK
GERALD G LUTHER
DAVID M LUTHY
CHARLES R LUTTON
HAROLD L LUTZ
JACK D LUTZ
CHARLES R LYBBERT
LESTER E LYLE
CHAUNCEY LYMAN
DAVID LYMAN
FRANCIS J LYNCH
PATRICK J LYNCH
ESTUS L LYNN
ROBERT C LYNN
JACK H LYON
JARLATH J LYONS
RICHARD L LYONS
LLOYD E LYTLE

— M —

ADOLPH R MAASS
ALLAN M MAC DONALD
F W MAC DONALD
RONALD F MAC DONALD

PAUL A MAC WILLIAM
WALTER E MACE
JAMES A MACHAN
HOWARD J MACHIA JR
ALEXANDER W MACKIE
NORMAN M MACKIE
ARTHUR MACKRO
ELMER L MADDEN
JOHN W MADDOX
RAYMOND A MADISON
BILL M MADSEN
CHARLES D MADSEN
KAMEIL MAERTENS
CHARLES MAGAURN
RAY A MAGNEY
GERALD C MAGUIRE
GUS A MAGUNSON JR
JAMES F MAHANEY
JOHN R MAHRT
JOE F MAISSEN
ROBERT L MALBY
EDWARD T MALLOY
TERRENCE M MALOY
DANIEL J MANGAN
DEAN T MANGOLD
JOHN G MANLEY
WILLIAM E MANN
JOE E MANN
DAVID E MANNING
HENRY A MANNING
JAY D MANNING
JOHN C MANTHEY
CAESAR J MARANI
HERBERT F MARCH
WAYNE P MARESH
ROBERT E MARILLEY
HARRY W MARKEY
DONALD F MARKHAM
KENNETH J MARKLEY
ROBERT T MARKSHAUSEN
CLIFFORD O MARKUSON
ALAN C MARLOW
WILLIAM A MARMONT
WILLIAM P MARONTATE
DONALD K MARQUETTE
KENNETH A MARQUIS
DAVID C MARR
KENNETH M MARR
WILBUR P MARR
CLELAND G MARRIOTT
FRANK N MARRS
HAROLD M MARRS
GEORGE L MARSDEN
DEWITT MARSHALL JR

LARRY MARSHALL
RAYMOND B MARSHALL
ROBERT H MARSHALL
ROBERT J MARSHALL
ROBERT L MARSHALL
BERNARD W MARTENS
EDWARD MARTIN
HAROLD B MARTIN
HAROLD E MARTIN
JOHN A MARTIN
JOHN H MARTIN
LESLIE D MARTIN
PAUL MARTIN
TURNER MARTIN
HOLLIS MARTIN
KENNETH E MARTIN
LAWRENCE P MARTIN
ROBERT E MARTIN
TERRY J MARTIN
FRANK MARTINDALE
RAYMOND B MARTINSEN
THOMAS MARVICK JR
EVEREST A MASKELL
GLEN E MASON
VERNON W MASON
HANRI C MASON
MERLE V MASSAR
EDMON E MASSEE
JOHN A MASSOURAS
ROBERT E MASTEL
EDWARD W MASTERMAN
MERRELL M MASTICK
WILLARD B MATCHETT
THOMAS C MATELAK
ARTHUR M MATHENT
ARTHUR M MATHENY
WILLIAM J MATHERS
DONALD E MATHEWS
ROBERT L MATHIAS
STANLEY A MATHIASON
GLEN E MATHIESEN
GARY M MATHISEN
DONALD J MATHISON
ELVIN J MATT
CHARLES E MATTERN
FRANK G MATTES
JOE K MATTESON
OLIVER P MATTHEWS
CLIFFORD MATTHIESEN
ELMER MATTILA
THOMAS E MATTISON
CLAIR E MATTOON
HARRY R MATTSON
CHARLES W MATZGER

FRANCIS W MAUL

ROBERT W MAXFIELD

JOSEPH L MAXSIN

HERBERT C MAXSON

JACK L MAY

LEONARD W MAY

MICHAEL F MAY

WILLIAM N MAY

GEORGE M MAYEDA

JAY R MAYER

HAROLD A MAYHEW

JOHN R MAYNARD

GEORGE C MAZE

ROBERT C MC ABEE

PERRY K MC ALLISTER

DONALD F MC ALLISTER

MERVIN E MC ATEE

MILTON G MC ATEE

GORDON MC BRIDE

JOHN C MC BRIDE

WAYNE MC BRIDE

JOHN M MC CABE

EDWARD J MC CAIN

JOHN A MC CAIN

ROBERT W MC CALDER

MACK MC CALL

JOHN MC CALLUM

HAROLD E MC CAMANT

HAROLD J MC CANN

WILLIAM W MC CANSE

EDWARD F MC CARRON

EMMETT P MC CARTHY

HOWARD MC CARTIN

JOHN D MC CARTY

WILLIAM E MC CLAIN

LLOYD A MC CLANAHAN

DEAN E MC CLAY

LLOYD E MC CLEARY

KENNETH B MC CLELLAND

JACK MC CLINTOCK

JOHN M MC CLINTOCK

J M MC CLINTOCK JR

RUSSELL G MC CLOY

DALE W MC CLUNG

LEE MC CLURE JR

JAMES A MC CLURE

ARTHUR C MC COLLEY

JAMES R MC COMBS

DONALD W MC CONNELL

C A MC CONNELL

DALE T MC CORD

RAY J MC CORMICK

JOE MC CORMICK

RODNEY MC COURTIE

BERRY B MC COWEN

WILLIAM J MC COWN

WALTER G MC COWN

CARL MC COY

CHARLES F MC COY

DON W MC COY

FRANCIS T MC COY

HARRY R MC COY

KENNETH C MC CREADY

EMMETT C MC CREERY

ARTHUR W MC CULLOCH

HERMAN MC CULLOCH

ARIEL MC CUMBER

ARCHIE R MC CUMBER

HOWARD A MC CURDY

DOUGLAS C MC DONALD

EARL T MC DONALD

FRANKLIN G MC DONALD JR

ROBERT H MC DONALD

MARTIN MC DONOUGH

RAPHAEL C MC DONOUGH

DAVID MC DOUGAL

JAMES S MC DOUGALL

CLYDE K MC DOW

PHILIP L MC ENTEE

ARTHUR H MC FARLAND

RONALD R MC FARLAND

GORDON D MC GAFFEY

HAROLD E MC GAREY

VICTOR H MC GEE

ROY C MC GHEE JR

JAMES R MC GILL

R A MC GILLIVRAY

STUART S MC GILLIVRAY

KENNETH E MC GILVRAY

EDWARD E MC GINNIS

JAMES MC GOVERN

CAMILLE W MC GOWN JR

T J MC GRATH

KENNETH M MC GRAW

HAROLD A MC GUIRE

JAMES L MC GUIRE

MICKEY L MC GUIRE

ROBERT J MC GUIRE

ROGER A MC GUIRE

JOHN P MC HENRY

STANLEY L MC IALWAIN

SAMUEL I MC ILVANIE

JACK L MC INNES

CLYDE MC INTYRE

JOHN W MC KANNA

ROBERT L MC KAY

THEODORE A MC KAY

ALLEN F MC KAY

JOHN L MC KEAN

AMOS H MC KEE

HOMER D MC KEE

WILLIAM D MC KEE

MERWIN MC KEE

ARCH M MC KEEVER

JACK MC KENNA

FRANKLIN C MC KENNEY

HENRY M MC KENTY

DONALD R MC KENZIE

LOUIS F MC KERNAN

ROY R MC KINLEY

DONALD E MC KINNEY

JOHN C MC KINNEY

JOHN MC KINSTRY

ROBERT L MC KULLA

JOHN L MC LAUGHLIN

H W MC LAUGHLIN

CLAIR C MC LEAN

JOHN P MC LEAN JR

ALLEN I MC LEAN

EDWIN L MC LELLAN

ANDREW L MC LEOD

JAMES W MC LEOD

OTTO W MC LEOD

WILLIAM O MC LEOD

WILLIAM R MC LEOD

WILLIS J MC LOUGHLIN

WILLIS I MC MAHON

ROBERT A MC MANIMIE

JACK D MC MANN

MILTON L MC MANN

WALTER J MC MURRAY

ROBERT E MC NAB

JAMES G MC NAIR

WARREN L MC NETT

MALCOLM MC NIVEN

JAMES D MC PHEE

JAMES H MC PHERSON

R M MC PHERSON JR

JOHN L MC QUADE

ROBERT MC QUADE

THOMAS T MC RITCHIE

RAY R MC VAY

PAUL H MC VICKER

DOUGLAS J MC WEENY

BOYD C MC WETHY

ROBERT C MCABEE

CHARLES R MCALLISTER

JULIUS C MCCARTY

RUSSELL G MCCLOY

HARVEY J MCCLUNG

GERALD C MCCORMICK

CHARLES F MCCOY

ARTHUR W MCCULLOCH

FRANKLIN G MCDONALD JR

JOHN L MCDONALD

KENNETH G MCDONALD

KENNETH O MCDOUGALL

RICHARD C MCFARLAND

CLIFFORD E MCFARLANE

JAMES R MCGILL

ROBERT R MCGINNIS

LAWRENCE J MCGRATH

JOHN B MCHUGHES

STANLEY L MCIALWAIN

FRANCIS B MCINTYRE

THEODORE A MCKAY

LOUIS F MCKERNAN

ROBERT M MCLAIN

WILLIAM M MCLAREN

FRANCIS O MCLAUGHLIN JR

JOHN E MCLAUGHLIN

LAWRENCE E MCLAUGHLIN

DONALD C MCLEAN

MILTON L MCMANN

ROBERT C MCNAB

JOHN K MCNEIL

RALPH C MCNEIL

DONALD J MCNEILL

JAMES K MCNETT

WARREN L MCNETT

JAMES H MCPHERSON

JAMES F MCREYNOLDS

JOHN J MCVEIGH

ROGER D MCWILLIAMS

CHRISTOPHER J MEADE

DONALD G MEDFORD

VINCENT D MEEKER

JAMES C MEFFORD

VERNON R MEGIVERON

WILLIAM W MEIKLE

E H MEINHARDT JR

WARREN R MELCUM

RUBEN A MELTON JR

ROBERT G MELVEY

EARL S MELVILLE

FRANK W MENANE

WILLIAM MENARD

WILLIAM J MENARD

ROBERT W MENDENHALL

ANTHONY R MENSING JR

LOUIS MENZAGO

WALTER H MENZEL

MIKE P MERCADO

WILLIAM H MERCHANT

EDWARD C MERMOD

HENRY M MERRIAM

ROBERT F MERRITT

THOMAS C MERRYMAN JR

RICHARD B MERSON

EUGENE N MERTZ

RICHARD W MERZ

EDWARD C MESCHER

JAMES M MESERVEY

LEWIS T MESHISHNEK

DOUGLAS L METCALF

GLEN R METSKER

FRANK E METZGAR

JAMES P METZKER JR

ROBERT L MEUSCH

EUGENE R MEYER

FORREST E MEYER

MARX E MEYER

WILLIAM L MEYER

EDWARD N MEYERS

JOHN H MEYERS JR

VIVIEN D MEYERS

WALTER N MEYERS

HERBERT A MEYRING

PHILIP MICHEL

MARLET A MICHELSON

EDWARD N MICKEL

WALLACE MIFFLIN

DELMAR A MIKKOLA

JOE MILANO

CLIFFORD O MILES

EDWIN A MILES

ROBERT MILES

ORIE MILLARD JR

CECIL D MILLER

CLANCY R MILLER

DELMAR MILLER

EDGAR L MILLER

EDWARD J MILLER

EDWIN L MILLER

EUGENE D MILLER

FRANK L MILLER

GALEN C MILLER

GEORGE MILLER

GEORGE C MILLER

GERALD C MILLER

GLEN W MILLER

GLENN E MILLER

HERMAN MILLER

HOWARD R MILLER

HUGH B MILLER

JOHN L MILLER

JOHN M MILLER

JOSEPH C MILLER

KEARNEY E MILLER

LEONARD S MILLER

LESLIE O MILLER
LOUIS I MILLER
MARSHALL B MILLER JR
MAURICE L MILLER
MICKEY V MILLER
PAUL R MILLER
RALPH V MILLER
ROBERT A MILLER
ROGER L MILLER
SAMUEL D MILLER
TRUMAN F MILLER
VERNON MILLER
WAYNE C MILLER
WILLIAM L MILLER
STANLEY E MILLERD
CHARLES R MILLS JR
DELMAR S MILLS
EDGAR MILLS
JAMES W MILLS
RAYMOND H MILLS
RICHARD W MINCKLER
KENNETH F MINEARD
ARTHUR E MINER
JACK E MINER
WILLIAM P MINGST
EVERETT R MINKS
DOMINIC MINOTTO
LOUIS MIORI
RICHARD A MISEK
ALBERT E MITCHELL
BRUCE A MITCHELL
C B MITCHELL JR
HENRY M MITCHELL
JACK M MITCHELL
JOHN MITCHELL
KENNETH E MITCHELL
LOREN L MITCHELL
MATTHEW MITCHELL
ROBERT E MITCHELL
HAROLD E MITTS
ALVIN M MIX
HAROLD I MIZONY
WILLIAM S MIZUKAMI
RICHARD S MOCK
DONALD W MODESITT
WALTER E MODIN
ALVA H MOE JR
EINAR A MOE
JOHN F MOE
MELVIN G MOE
LAWRENCE H MOEN
STEPHEN A MOGENSEN
JAMES C MOHN
GERALD E MOHR

CACIL E MOMAN
FRITZ MON
OWEN W MONGER
RAY W MONOSSO
HENRY A MONROE
STERLING T MONROE JR
JAMES R MONSON
ALFRED C MONTAGRO
FREMONT D MONTEITH
ELMER F MONTGOMERY
H J MONTGOMERY
PAT L MONTGOMERY
ROGER J MOODIE
EDGAR J MOON
GEORGE R MOON
ROBERT A MOON
JOHN A MOONEY
WILLIAM E MOONEY
CLARKE B MOORE
CLAUDE T MOORE
CLIFFORD C MOORE
DALE C MOORE
DAVID H MOORE
EDWARD L MOORE
GEORGE A MOORE
HAROLD J MOORE
JACK C MOORE
JACKSON M MOORE
JESS M MOORE
JOHN W MOORE
JOSEPH F MOORE
LELAND C MOORE
ROBERT C MOORE
SAMUEL MOORE
VINCENT H MOORE
WILLIAM G MOORE
WILLIAM L MOORE
MILFRED J MORALES
CHARLES R MORAN
ELBERT F MORAN
FRANK R MORAN
HAROLD D MORAN
PAUL D MOREHOUSE
ARCADE M MORELAND
EVERETT B MORELAND
CHARLES J MOREY
ALBERT W MORGAN
BOYD W MORGAN
CLARENCE W MORGAN
DAVID B MORGAN
DONALD R MORGAN
JACK W MORGAN
KEITH M MORGAN
KENNETH C MORISETTE

JEFFERSON D MORRELL
GEORGE J MORRILL
WILLIAM E MORRILL JR
EUGENE L MORRIS
F L MORRIS JR
JOHN O MORRIS
JOHN N MORRIS JR
RICHARD E MORRIS
ROBERT F MORRIS
ROBERT J MORRIS
STANLEY E MORRIS
WAYNE E MORRIS
WHITNEY MORRIS
ARNOLD J MORRISON
BERNARD C MORRISON
H MORRISON
ROBERT W MORRISON
STEPHEN H MORRISON
EUGENE T MORRISSEY
THOMAS L MORRISSEY
ARTHUR J MORROW
CLARENCE R MORROW
CLETUS E MORROW
JAMES L MORROW
JOHN C MORROW
ROBERT L MORSE
DOUGLAS W MORTENSEN
ALBERT P MORTENSON
DOYLE D MORTON
ELLIS R MORTON JR
RICHARD C MORTON
JOHN R MOSBRUCKER
VINCENT U MOSCHETTO
DIX V MOSER
ERNEST C MOSER
ARLIE J MOSES JR
JOSEPH C MOSNER
ROBERT C MOTT
RICHARD E MOVOLD
CLARENCE S MOWATT
MICHAEL H MOYNIHAN
LOREN R MUCKEY
WILLIAM V MUEHE
DONALD K MUELLER
CHARLES J MULDERIG
HUGH P MULLIGAN
ROBERT E MULLINS
THOMAS L MULLINS
ELGIN K MULLOY
RANDALL M MUMAW
GORDON W MUNGER
ROBERT S MUNN
DOUGLAS A MUNRO
RAYMOND C MUNSON

HERBERT A MUNTER JR
KENNETH R MUNYON
WILLIAM F MUNZINGER
DAVIS D MURDOCK
ROBERT W MURDOCK
FRANK E MURPHY
FRANK T MURPHY
MICHAEL M MURPHY
PATRICK M MURPHY JR
DONALD B MURRAY
HOWARD M MURRAY
JAMES J MURRAY
EDWARD A MUSCUTT
DONALD G MUSSELMAN
GENE C MUSSON
JAMES E MUSTARD
DERVYN F MUTH
MURRAY E MUZZAL
EDWARD J MYERS
GEORGE A MYERS
JAMES D MYERS
JAMES G MYERS
WILLIAM G MYHR
RAGNAR J MYKING
DAVE T MYLER
JAMES M MYLER
RAFAEL Y MYLLY
ALLEN C MYRHOW
HAROLD L MYRHOW

— N —

HUGH K NAFF
MALCOM E NAFF
ANDREW J NAGEY
EBA F NAGLE
MASAKI H NAKAMURA
NED T NAKAMURA
WILLIAM K NAKAMURA
ROBERT E NAMANNY
RICHARD P NAMES
ERIC F NASBURG
ROBERT A NASH
KARL W NASSTROM
ROBERT A NAYLOR
DONALD NAZE
AMES NEAL
CHARLES J NEAL
DONALD R NEAL
JACK NEDELEC JR
LEONARD B NEDREBO
JAMES W NEEDHAM
LA VERNE J NEEDHAM
ROBERT E NEEDHAM
ANTONE W NEFF
GEORGE I NEFF

ROBERT J NEHER
ROBERT H NELLOR
GEORGE NELSEN
BJARNE N NELSON
CALVIN A NELSON
CARL A NELSON
CARL W NELSON
CLYDE E NELSON
DANIEL R NELSON
EDDIE B NELSON
GEORGE V NELSON
HAROLD F NELSON
JAMES S NELSON
JEROME G NELSON
JOHN L NELSON
JOHN Y NELSON
KENNETH W NELSON
LAVERNE O NELSON
LESLIE V NELSON
MARLYN W NELSON
NELS K NELSON
ORA NELSON
OSCAR B NELSON
RONALD L NELSON
THEODORE E NELSON
THEODORE R NELSON
WILLIAM H NELSON
LESTER V NEMCHICK
ALFRED NESS
JOHN K NESS
OSCAR R NESS
PAUL J NESS
RULDOLF N NESS
FRANCIS E NESTOR
WILFRED W NEUROTH
HAROLD C NEWARK
ARCHIE W NEWELL
KENNETH H NEWELL
WARREN J NEWGARD
ED H NEWMAN
WAYNE L NEWMAN
HORACE W NEWTON
JOSEPH R NEWTON JR
WILBUR L NEWTON
RALPH S NEY
JAMES NICHOLAS
WILLIAM C NICHOLAS
BETHEL A NICHOLS
GORDON H NICKELL
ORVAL R NICKS
LESTER D NIELSEN
ROY G NIELSEN
THEODORE D NIELSEN
WALTER E NIELSEN

LLOYD K NIELSON
HERMAN C NIEMANN
ROBERT H NIEMANN
HARRY P NILSEN
GEORGE W NILSON
BAN NINOMIYA
RALPH V NIPPER
JOHN D NIX
GEORGE W NIXON
LEONARD M NIXON
PAUL E NOBLE
EMMETT C NOBLES
EDWARD D NOE
MERLE J NOE
LOUIS C NOEL
WILLIAM O NOEL
FRANCIS E NOLAND
WILLIAM B NOLAND
JAMES D NOONAN
MAURICE A NOONE
RUSSELL E NORD
ARNOLD M NORDALE
LENNART S NORDLUND
YOSHITO NORITAKE
MELVIN F NORLUND
DONALD C NORMAN
LAWRENCE C NORMAN
ELMER A NORRIS
RAYMOND L NORRIS JR
ROBERT H NORRIS
ELROY A NORT
VINCENT W NORTH JR
HARRY L NORTHUP JR
ROY R NORTON
WILLIAM NOSER
JOSEPH H NOYES
DONALD R NUGEN
HARVEY L NUGENT
GEORGE A NUNAN
LEONARD E NUNLEY
EDWARD NUSSBASUM JR
WALTER H NYBERG
JACK O NYE
PAUL L NYE
JOHN H NYLUND
LOUIS S NYSEN
RAGNAR E NYSTROM

— O —

EUGENE V O BERG
CLIFFORD W O BRIEN
FRANK O BRIEN
ROBERT O BRYANT
ROBERT R O BRYANT

LEO L O CONNELL
EDWARD R O CONNOR
FRANK M O LAUGHLIN
EDWARD D O MALLEY
THOMAS R O MEARA
EUGENE G O NEIL
DONALD C O TYSON
WARREN W OAKLEY
EDWARD OANE
LAWRENCE B OBERG
ROBERT M OBRIEN
EUSEBIO OCHOA
HENRY F OCHOSKI
BOB OCHSNER
RAYMOND J OCONNELL
SIGVARD E ODDEN
CHESTER D ODELL
LESLIE E ODELL
ROBERT A ODELL
RUSSELL S ODELL
WILLIAM M ODELL
JACK L ODLIN
EDWARD C OFARRELL
EUGENE V OGLE
MICHAEL D OGRADY
WILLIAM G OHLER
STANLEY C OHLSSON
ROY C OHMAN
ANDREW A OJA JR
ISAO OKAZAKI
TAKAAKI OKAZAKI
KELLY A OKEEFE
PAUL D OKERT
FRANK J OLBERG
ROBERT OLDS
ROY M OLELS
CHARLES V OLESEN
ROBERT W OLESON
CLIFFORD A OLIN
ROLLIN E OLIVER
ERIK M OLLESON
FRANK H OLMSTED
ADRIAN V OLNESS
EMIL S OLSEN JR
FRED W OLSEN
FREDRICK C OLSEN
HANS C OLSEN
LARRY S OLSEN
THEODORE C OLSEN
VERNE R OLSEN
WILMER E OLSEN
EDWIN S OLSON
ERIC H OLSON
FRANK W OLSON

GLEN M OLSON
HAROLD W OLSON
HERMAN L OLSON
JAMES G OLSON
JOHN E OLSON
KENNETH H OLSON
KENNETH J OLSON
LEONARD F OLSON
WALTER E OLSON
WARREN L OLSON
WARREN R OLSON
CHARLES L OMAN
ROBERT E OMOTH
KEN OMURA
JACK H ONDRACEK
JOHN G ONEAL JR
JAMES M ONEIL
JAMES E ONEILL
JOHN J ONEILL
TED S ONEILL
CLYDE W ONN
SATORU ONODERA
KARL E OPPEN
JAMES R ORCHARD
JUAN N ORDANIO
FRANCIS J ORGAN
DONALD R ORKNEY
CHESTER L ORLOFF
RICHARD E ORR
WILLIAM H ORT
GEORGE C OSBORN
NORMAN D OSBORNE
OWEN A OSBORNE
RAYMOND D OSBORNE
THOMAS F OSBORNE
LEROY L OSBURN
HOMER V OSTENBERG
EDWIN E OSTER
HAROLD E OSTERGARD
F G OSTERHOLTZ
NICK OSTOFOROFF
PAUL S OSTRANDER
RUSSELL J OSTREM
DAVID P OSWALD
ESBURN D OTIS
HAROLD H OTIS
KEITH V OTIS
ROBERT S OTIS
RICHARD B OTT
ROY O OTTERSEN
KEITH L OUTCELT
NORMAN O OVERHOLT
HARRIS K OWEN
JOHN H OWEN

FREDERICK J OWENS
JOHN D OWENS
ROBERT W OWENS

— P —

LEONARD E PACE
ROBERT E PACHAUD
JAMES R PACKARD
DEWEY B PACKER
EDWARD L PADDOCK
ROGER B PADDOCK
JOHN A PAETZ JR
CHARLES W PAGE
GILBERT PAGE
ORIN L PAGE JR
WILLIAM PAINE
DONALD E PAINTER
JOHN D PALLELA
ARTHUR PALMER
GEORGE S PALMER
JAMES M PALMER
PHILIP E PALMER
ROBERT G PALMER
ROYAL D PALMER
RUSSELL PALMER
JOSEPH T PALMIERO
JOE J PANCOSKA JR
FREDERICK S PANETTO
NICK G PANTAGES
JUSTIN L PAPE
JOHN C PAPPAS
TONY PAPPAS
GEORGE L PARADIS
RAYMOND F PARADIS
GLENN L PARISH
THOMAS L PARISH
GILBERT N PARKER
ORIN S PARKER
RAY D PARKER
THOMAS R PARKER
WILLIAM H PARKER
LEO T PARKKI
RALPH I PARLETTE
KEITH E PARMENTER
ERNEST F PARRISH
DONALD C PARSHALL
ERNEST B PARSONS
JAMES J PARSONS
THOMAS A PARSONS
RAYMOND A PARTEE
WILLIAM H PARTIN
RAYMOND E PARTRIDGE
CONRAD PASCAL
CALVIN D PASCHICHI
EARL V PASLAY

FRED P PASQUAN
JOE PASQUAN
TOIVO W PATANA
CLIFTON F PATCH
HUGH A PATRICK
ROBERT A PATTEN
CLARENCE C PATTERSON
EDWIN H PATTERSON
HARRY J PATTERSON
JOHN G PATTERSON
MAURICE L PATTERSON
SYLVANUS B PATTERSON
LAVERN PATTON
MALVERN E PATTON
ARNOLD W PAUL
FELIX T PAUL
WAGNER W PAULSEN
LLOYD W PAULSON
MILLARD P PAULSON
WILLIS C PAULSON
FRANK J PAVELICH
BOB J PAYNE
BUELL F PAYNE
JAMES B PAYNE
ELMER H PEAL
JOSEPH J PEARCE
REUBEN V PEARCE
RICHARD W PEARCE
THOMAS J PEARCE
THOMAS E PEARCE JR
ALLEN H PEARSON
CARL E PEARSON
CARL W PEARSON
EDWARD W PEARSON
MATTHEW M PEARSON
WILLIAM J PEARSON
ERVIN C PEASE
LAWRENCE S PEASE
ALLAN E PECK
GEORGE W PECK
LESTER H PECK
ROBERT S PECK
PAUL J PECOLAR
NORMAN C PEDEN
ALLEN C PEDERSEN
VICTOR P PEDERSEN
WILLY PEDERSEN
ERLING W PEDERSON
IVAN J PEDERSON
NORMAN W PEEL
JOHN W PEHRSON
ELMER E PELLETT
ALDO L PELLINI
WILLIAM A PELTO

CLYDE W PELTON
JOHN PELTON
GEORGE E PENDARVIS
JOHN C PENDERGRAFT
CLARENCE S PENDERGRASS
JACK J PENDLETON
BERNARD T PENNIG
ROBERT G PEOPLES
NORMAN A PEPPER
DUANE L PEPPLE
FLOYD PERIN JR
JOHN A PERINGER
GEORGE W PERKINS JR
HOWARD F PERKINS
WARREN B PERKINS
WILLIAM H PERKINS
BRUCE F PERRIGO
HOWARD J PERRY
NORRIS PERRY
ROBERT L PERRY
WESLEY D PERRY
WILLARD O PERRY
CARL V PERSON
ARCHIE C PERU
WAYNE R PETAJA
CHARLES D PETERMAN
DONALD J PETERS
ERNEST PETERS
ERNEST E PETERS
LEVI P PETERS
RAYMOND PETERS
WYMAN L PETERS
ODIAN A PETERSEN
RALPH M PETERSEN
CARL L PETERSON
CHARLES B PETERSON
CHARLES L PETERSON
CLAIRE M PETERSON
DONALD E PETERSON
ELMER H PETERSON
ELMER R PETERSON
GEORGE H PETERSON
HARDY W PETERSON
JACK J PETERSON
JAMES C PETERSON
JOHN M PETERSON
LELAND PETERSON
LOUIS PETERSON
MELVIN E PETERSON
NORMAN E PETERSON
ROBERT G PETERSON
ROBERT N PETERSON
ROY H PETERSON
SAMUEL C PETERSON

WILLIAM PETERSON
GEORGE PETTENGILL
BOBBY N PETTICHORD
OTIS C PETTY
PAUL R PFAU
RAYMOND C PFIEFER
RAPHAEL J PFLIEGER
HERBERT L PHELPS
BRYON F PHILBRICK
WILLIAM J PHILBROOK
ARMOUR PHILLIPS
CLIFTON N PHILLIPS
DOMENICK PHILLIPS
FLOYD S PHILLIPS
GEORGE W PHILLIPS
JAMES A PHILLIPS
LLOYD S PHILLIPS
MILTON P PHILLIPS
ROBERT L PHILLIPS
WILLIAM A PHILLIPS JR
ROBERT L PHILLIRS
ROBERT W PHILP
HENRY R PHINNEY JR
JAMES N PHIPPS
ERNEST R PICCIN
JAMES L PICINICH
JAMES A PICKARD
CLAIRE A PICKEL
FRANK C PICKELL
ALONZO I PICKETT
STEPHEN G PICKETT
JAMES PICKRELL JR
ASWELL L PICOU
ARTHUR D PIERCE
BERNARD C PIERCE
WILLIAM M PIERCE
HOWARD S PIERSON
MILTON L PIKE
ROBERT F PIKE
FRANK J PILLER
PATRICK E PILON
CLARENCE L PINKLEY
RAYMOND J PINNEO
DONALD H PINSON
ROBERT L PIPER
PAUL E PIPPIN
ROBERT H PIRO
JOSEPH A PISZCEK
JAMES PITBLADO
JAMES W PITBLADO
CHARLES E PITSER
EDWARD H PITTMAN
WALTER PIVINSKI
MICHAEL A PIZZUTO

KNUT G PLADSON
ROBERT E PLAUT
RICHARD D PLETTE
CLAYTON E PLOPPER
PHILIP E PLOTTS
CLINTON L POE
GERALD H POEPPEL
WOODROW W POINTER
LLOYD C POLASCHEK
MARTIN L POLER
GORDON A POLESLEY
CHARLES E POLF
THEODORE POLING
MARLEY O POLK
HANS L POLLITZ
DONALD N POLLOCK
JAMES M POLLOCK
WESLEY L POLLOCK
WILLIAM M POND
WALTER H PONDER
JAMES R PONTET
FRED W POOK
ELMER C POOLE
GERALD W POOLE
RICHARD D PORENTA
LLOYD J PORSCH
CLIFFORD T PORTER
GRENVILLE N PORTER
JOHN V PORTER
MARK F PORTER
MORGAN R PORTER
ROBERT B PORTER
ROBERT R PORTER
THOMAS B PORTER
WILLIAM L PORTER
WILLIAM V PORTER
SIMON POST
WILLIAM H POSTON
CLARENCE W POTTER
LAFAYETTE L POTTER
NORMAN A POTTER
HELEN M POTTRATZ
THOMAS R POTTS
ALLAN C POWELL
MILES W POWELL
EDMUND C POWER
GEORGE J POWERS
THOMAS E POYNER
JOHN V PRAHIN
LOUIS PRATICO
WESLEY D PREMO
LEE A PRESTON
VANCE C PREWITT
CHARLES W PRICE

IRWIN G PRICE
SONE H PRICE
THOMAS D PRICE
WILLIAM J PRIESTLEY
CHARLES M PRINE
ORVILLE V PRINGLE
AMBROSE B PRISK
ROBERT G PRITCHARD
DEWEY T PROBST JR
DONALD G PROBST
GORDON E PROCTOR
MICHAEL PROKOPOVICH
STEVE PROKOPOVICH
JOE J PROTZ
EDWARD E PRYOR
FRANK J PUCHORAS
LESLIE C PUE
HAROLD E PULLIAM
DAVID A PULRANG
GEORGE A PULTS
JOHN E PUMALA
NATHAN L PUMFREY
BILLY D PURCELL
CHARLES R PURDON
ELMER B PURJUE
JOHN E PUTMAN

— Q —

JOHN M QUACKENBUSH
JESSIE O QUERY
ROY A QUESTAD
GEORGE H QUIGLEY
HOWARD I QUIMBY
JAMES T QUINLAN
JOHN L QUINN
WAYNE E QUINN
OTTO A QUIRING
THOMAS A QUIRK JR

— R —

WILLIAM B RAABE
IRVIN K RAATZ
ERVING W RABE
WILLIAM A RACH
GEORGE E RADFORD
FREDERICK H RADIGAN
KARL S RADMAKER
WILLIAM S RAE
CHARLES H RAFFERTY
FORREST E RAGAN
LEE C RAGSDALE
EVERETT W RAINWATER
FRANCIS C RAISON
ROBERT M RAKOS
DON E RALSTON
HARRY W RALSTON

OSCAR J RAMBECK
ARTHUR C RAMSDELL
MARVIN L RAMSDEN
MORRIS O RAMSEY
ROBERT L RAMSEY
JOHN E RAMSTAD
CHARLES L RANDALL
DELNO E RANDALL
JOSEPH P RANDALL
LEWIS D RANDALL
RUDY RANDALL
CHARLES L RANDELL
RONALD R RANDOLPH
ALFRED RANG
GEORGE R RANKERT
CHARLES W RANKO
WILLIAM V RANSON
CARL RASMUSSEN
HARLAND B RASMUSSEN
GEORGE W RASQUE
IRA T RATHKE
JOHN RAUEN
GLENN M RAUHAUSER
CLARK N RAUTH
JOHN L RAVEN
JULIUS A RAVEN
GLEN E RAY
LEWIS L RAY SR
ROBERT L RAY
HOWARD B RAYFORD
GEORGE G RAYMOND
WILLIAM O RAYNER
HARRY E READ
HERMAN R READ
JOHN H REAGAN
JOHN F REARDON
LAWRENCE E REAVIS
WILLIAM W REDDICK
JAMES R REDDIE
FLOYD J REDFERN
ARNOLD A REDINGER
MANLEY A REDISKE
JACK K REDMON
ADAM REED
ALLAN H REED
DONALD O REED
GARLAND J REED
MAXWELL E REED
RALPH H REED
RICHARD C REED
WILLIAM W REED JR
ROBERT C REEDER
WAYNE R REEDER
CLIFFORD J REEDHEAD

HENRY C REEDY
ALBERT J REESE
RICHARD W REESE
JAMES W REEVE
PATRICK P REEVIS
HAROLD E REGAN
LEONARD E REGER
WILLIAM W REHFELD
CARL REHN
CURTIS W REICHEL
ALAN O REID
GARRETT M REID
LYLE V REID
WOODROW W REID
HOWARD A REIGHTLEY
JOSEPH D REIHL
GEORGE E REILLY
JACK B REIMLAND
STANLEY T REINERTSON
ARTHUR S REINHARDT
TERHO E REINI
RICHARD D REINKE
LEO R REINS
LOUIS R REITAN
ALBERT C REITMAN
PETER T REKDAL
JOHN W REMINGTON
CALVIN A REMPEL
RONALD RENARD
THEOPHIL J RENK
CHARLIE C RENNIE
HENRY C RENSINK
PHILIP R RETHERFORD
RICHARD V REUSCH
GEORGE W REYMORE
ARTHUR J REYNOLDS
DUDLEY L REYNOLDS
ERNEST E REYNOLDS
GORDON V REYNOLDS
LEONARD C REYNOLDS
WILLIAM L REYNOLDS
HENRY R RHODES
LYON R RHODES
HAROLD W RIAL
BERNARD S RICE
HARVEY F RICE
JAMES F RICE
JEROME R RICE
JOHN D RICE
LEO W RICE
WILLIAM A RICE
OTTO V RICH
DALE I RICHARD
HAROLD H RICHARDS

GEORGE E RICHARDSON
JOHN W RICHARDSON
MARION S RICHARDSON
ROBERT O RICHARDSON
SCOTT RICHARDSON
WADE M RICHARDSON
KENNETH W RICHER
JAMES A RICHEY
REAY D RICHMOND
ALBERT W RICHTER
THOMAS C RICHTER
THEODORE RICKENBACK
RAYMOND K RICKLES
DONALD D RIDDLE
GORDON G RIDDLE
JOHN L RIDDLE
WILLIAM L RIDDLE JR
ALVIN E RIDER
ROBERT L RIDGE
FRED W RIFE
ARTHUR J RIKANSRUD
ANDREW W RIKER
DORMAN N RIKER
GEORGE E RIKER
JOHN J RILE
JACK L RILEY
JOHN J RILEY
WILLIAM A RILEY
ROBERT E RIMBEY
HOWARD D RINEHART
FREDRIC C RINGLE
GLEN R RINGS
RONALD RINGSTAD
JUAN RIOS
JOSEPH W RIPLEY
GILBERT E RISE
WILLIAM H RISSLER
ERNEST M RITCHEY
DAVID B RITCHIE
HAROLD E RITCHIE
ROBERT A RITCHIE
ROBERT G RITCHIE
RAYMOND W RITTEL
ROBERT D RIZZO
WESLEY J ROAGER
EDWARD F ROARK
GEORGE L ROBARGE
PAUL E ROBB
RONALD O ROBBERTS
PAUL E ROBBIE
ARTHUR D ROBBINS
VINCENT D ROBEL
GEORGE G ROBERSON
LEROY R ROBERSON

DARWIN A ROBERTS
FRANCIS E ROBERTS
HUGH H ROBERTS
IVAL H ROBERTS
KENNETH F ROBERTS
LELAND E ROBERTS
PHILIP W ROBERTS
PHILLIP W ROBERTS
ROBERT T ROBERTS
WARING ROBERTS
WILLIAM H ROBERTS
WILLIAM J ROBERTS
GORDON E ROBERTSON
MARK R ROBERTSON
RICHARD J ROBERTSON
CLARENCE I ROBINETT
DONALD D ROBINS
ARTHUR E ROBINSON
CARL V ROBINSON
HARRY J ROBINSON
JAMES K ROBINSON
MARVIN H ROBINSON
WILLARD J ROBINSON
CHARLES D ROCK
HAROLD R ROCK
JOHN M ROCK
PAUL P ROCKAS
JACK E ROCKHILL
GRANT T ROCKWELL
IVAN A ROCKWELL
PAUL M RODAL
ASA L RODDY
IRVING D RODENBERGER
THOMAS RODERICK
ADOLPH RODGERS
HAROLD M RODGERS
WILSON F RODGERS
LLOYD J RODIN
ORVILLE M RODLEY
MAURICE A RODRIGOS
ERNEST D ROE JR
HIRAM A ROE
CLARENCE E ROEDELL
JOHN O ROEDER
JOHN C ROELL JR
CHARLES H ROESS
HENRY E ROGER
ADOLPH I ROGERS
EUGENE O ROGERS
GILMER R ROGERS
HARRY R ROGERS
IVAN L ROGERS
VINCENT G ROGERS
VIRGIL A ROGERS

WILBUR A ROGERS
THOMAS ROGERSON
CARL M ROGOWSKI
ROBERT L ROHLAND
HARVEY B ROHRER
RICHARD R ROLFE
JEREMIAH B ROLISON
ROBERT L ROLLAND
DAVID M ROLLINS
FRED S ROMAN
FRANK J ROMANI
DONALD R ROMBALSKI
NORMAN W ROMINGER
EDWARD A RONAN
RICHARD D RONNE
ALBERT A RONNING
ALBERT H ROOKS
PHILIP M ROONEY
ROBERT G RORABAUGH
MILTON F ROSBACH
DEAN R ROSE
EZRA E ROSE
HENRY M ROSE
ROBERT A ROSE
RALPH R ROSEBAUM
ERIC Z ROSEN
PER R ROSEN
HENRY ROSENFELDER
EDWARD A ROSLEFSKE
BERT C ROSS
BOBB F ROSS
CALVIN E ROSS
GORDON A ROSS
HOYT ROSS
LUTHER O ROSS
MAX L ROSS
MELVIN ROSS
MERLE E ROSS
MILES S ROSS
JOSEPH W ROSSART
ELMER W ROSSBACK
GEORGE S ROSSNER
DALE R ROSTAD
MELVIN W ROTH
MELVIN F ROTHENBUHLER
JOHN B ROTHROCK
GEORGE H ROTTLE
THELMA ROUNDS
ROSCO S ROUNDY
MARION F ROUP
NAPOLEON J ROUSSEAU
ROBERT E ROUZE
WILLIAM R ROUZIE JR
REIDAR D ROVIG JR

ROLLAND R ROWE
JACK W ROWLAND
HARRY C ROWLEY
EDWARD E ROZANSKI
TED ROZMARYN
ERVIN E RUARK
FRED A RUBATINO
HOWARD M RUBY
JOHN D RUCKERT
REUBEN P RUDD
JAMES R RUDDY
LEO R RUDY
LOUIS E RUFENER
DONALD C RUFF
ALFRED N RUFFCORN
GERARD L RUGERS JR
EDGAR W RUHL
CHARLES J RUIZ
IRA C RUMBURG
JOHN V RUNNELS
LOREN A RUNOLSON
STANLEY RUNYAN
EDWARD RUPERT
LAWRENCE M RUSHING
JOSEPH J RUSKEY
BANFORD L RUSSELL
DELLIS E RUSSELL
JAMES B RUSSELL
JAMES F RUSSELL
JAMES W RUSSELL
PERRY O RUSSELL
ROBERT A RUSSELL
JOHN RUSSO
DAVID S RUST
WARREN N RUSTAD
JOHN T RUTHERFORD
JOHN C RUTHVEN
ALBERT E RUTLEDGE
JAMES J RUTLEDGE
PAUL E RUTLEDGE
PAUL S RUTLEDGE
WALTER C RUTT
EDWARD T RYAN
HARRY W RYAN
JAMES K RYAN
JAMES M RYAN
JOSEPH E RYAN
THOMAS G RYAN
ROBERT M RYNEARSON
PAUL K RYRKETT

— S —

CURTIS W SADD
GORDON P SADICK
PLINY G SAEGER

JOHN C SAEGNER	DONALD L SCHAY	FRANK J SCHULTZ	ROBERT E SELF	TETSUO SHIGAYA
WILLIAM C SAEMAN	LLOYD P SCHEEL	GUSSIE SCHULTZ	HENRY A SELFRIDGE	MASAO F SHIGEMURA
ROGER F SAFFORD	MARION A SCHEEL	LEE E SCHULTZ	JOHN E SELIN	JIMMY T SHIMIZU
SEDRIC E SALLEE	ALBERT E SCHEIB	NORRIS R SCHULTZ	MILAN SELLARS	JEAN P SHINDLER
JOE B SALSGIVER	REINHOLD SCHELL	BENJAMEN L SCHULZ	WILLIAM J SELLARS	DELBERT D SHOEMAN*
DAVID H SAMSON	ALEXANDER C SCHENCK	FALK SCHULZ	PETE I SELLBERG	DON K SHOGREN
FRANK S SAMUEL	CLARENCE E SCHENCK	KENNETH C SCHULZ	CLYDE K SELLERS	WOODROW E SHOLES
CYRUS H SAND	ERNEST G SCHENCK	WILLIAM C SCHULZ	ARTHUR SELLGREN	RAYMOND V SHOOK
WALLACE N SAND	RICHARD J SCHENEK	FRED W SCHUMAKER	DENNIS R SEMLER	JOHN E SHORE
ALBERT J SANDAINE	F J SCHEUERMAN	STEPHEN SCHWAB	JUDD C SEMPEL	ROBERT L SHOTAK
CLYDE W SANDBURG	PHILIP L SCHEURER	EARL O SCHWAGER	KARL L SENER	WALTER D SHOWERS
JACK S SANDERS	REUBEN SCHIERMAN	PAUL SCHWANTES	STEPHEN H SEPOTZ	LYLE E SHRADER
OREN B SANDERS	DWIGHT C SCHIFFHAUER	LUDWIG SCHWARZ	ROBERT L SERRETTE	LEROY A SHREINER
SIDNEY G SANDERS	ROBERT D SCHILDT	MAX J SCHWENNSEN	DOMENICO M SERVIDIO	FRANK C SHRINER
WILBUR C SANDS	JOHN SCHIMKE	WALLACE F SCHWIESOW	CHARLES K SESHE	CLYDE S SHROY
WILLIAM SANDY	CLARK H SCHINDELE	ERNEST C SCOFIELD	LAWRENCE C SESSOMS	ALFRED F SHROYER
LEWELLYN SANFORD	ROBERT H SCHIREMAN	BERT E SCOTT	JOSEPH E SETH	CARL D SHULER
RONALD J SANFORD	NORMAN R SCHLECHT	DORMAN L SCOTT	CLARENCE J SETKO	GERALD O SHULER
WALTER E SANFORD	GORDON W SCHLICHTING	EARL J SCOTT	BEVERLY L SETSER	LEE E SHULTZ
CLARENCE H SANSTOL	MARVIN J SCHMELLA	EDWARD J SCOTT	ROBERT A SETTERGREN	CHARLES W SHUMAKER
DONALD A SANTIC	BERL O SCHMIDT	FRED A SCOTT	JAMES P SEVERSON	ROBERT P SHUMWAY
GABRIEL E SANTORA	EDWARD F SCHMIDT	GEORGE H SCOTT	REX D SEXTON	JOHN W SHUPE
PARKER E SARE	EUGENE J SCHMIDT	GLEN W SCOTT	PAUL W SHAFFRATH	WILLIAM H SHURTS
MARSHALL F SARGENT	HERMAN A SCHMIDT	HOWARD C SCOTT	KENNETH W SHAND	GEORGE W SHURTZ
HOMER R SARTIN	HOWARD K SCHMIDT	LEONARD D SCOTT	LLOYD SHANGLE	JAMES R SHUSTER
LEROY F SASSE	RAYMOND C SCHMIDT	RAYMOND C SCOTT	CORWIN P SHANK JR	DAVID B SICH
SAMUEL A SATHER	RICHARD P SCHMIDT JR	RICHARD SCOTT	GERALD P SHAPLEY	LOUIE L SICKLES
TADAO SATO	ROBERT E SCHMIDTMAN	ROBERT M SCOTT	CURTIS J SHARP	LORENZ F SIEGEL
YUKIO SATO	ALFRED E SCHMITT	ROY F SCOTT	GERALD W SHARP	WAYNE E SIEMON
RALPH E SATT	HERBERT G SCHMITT	DAVID L SCOVELL	JOHN R SHARP	WESLEY D SIGERSTAD
GEORGE L SATTERQUIST	JOHN W SCHMITT	JACK R SCOVELL	EUGENE P SHAUVIN	CALVIN D SIGRIST
EARL F SAUCER	JOSEPH J SCHMOLKE	JACK S SCOVEN	GARETH L SHAW	STEFAN K SIGURDSON
LOWELL S SAUER	RUBEN O SCHNASE	JOHN P SCRAFFORD	HOWARD L SHAW	JOSEPH B SILER JR
ALAN E SAUL	ERNEST T SCHNEIDER	HARRY C SCRIBNER	TED C SHAW	PHILLIP G SILVA
EDWARD P SAUNDERS	FRANCIS J SCHOENMAKERS	HAROLD J SCRIVEN	ANEL B SHAY JR	WALTER L SILVA
FRANK J SAUNDERS	JOHN F SCHOETTEL	JACK F SCRIVEN	GEORGE W SHEARER	PETER P SIMICICH
WILLIAM E SAUNDERS	HOWARD A SCHOLZ	DONALD R SCROGGIE	ROBERT F SHEARER	WILLIAM H SIMMONDS
DORICK J SAUVAGEAU	NORMAN J SCHOOLCRAFT	DONALD C SCULATI	HENRY SHEFCHEK JR	FRANK L SIMMONS
ROLLAND J SAUVE	DAVID J SCHORTGEN	WALTER P SCURE	DALE V SHELLENBERGER	NORMAN SIMMONS
ROY H SAUVOLA	ARTHUR W SCHRAM	ALBERT W SEABERG	HARRY A SHELLY	ROBERT N SIMMONS
CHARLES W SAVITZ	ROGER W SCHREIBER	JACK R SEAMAN	KENNETH J SHELLY	STANLEY W SIMMONS
GEORGE K SAWADA	PAUL B SCHROEDER	JAMES P SEARGEANT	DONALD J SHELTON	ARTHUR D SIMON
PAUL J SAX	RAYMOND P SCHROEDER	EVERETT E SEARL	DAVID H SHEPARD	OAKLEY A SIMON
JAMES O SAXE	EDWIN B SCHUBERT	CHESTER E SEATON	GROVER C SHEPARD JR	WILLIAM C SIMON
DONALD W SAYER	EDWIN D SCHUBERT	GEORGE W SECORD	PAUL C SHEPARD	JACK E SIMONDS
MICHAEL SBARDELLA	JOHN H SCHUELKE	WALTON T SEED	JOE E SHEPPARD	RICHARD B SIMONS JR
ANDY R SCALERA	C F SCHUENEMAN	ARTHUR H SEEGER JR	MICHAEL SHERER	SIGURD J SIMONSON
DEAN L SCALLY	VERNER C SCHUETZLE	STANLEY L SEEHORN	BERTRAND J SHERIDAN	ANDREW F SIMPSON
GEORGE V SCANLON	LOUIS O SCHUFFENHAUER	VAN L SEELEY	JOHN D SHERMAN	ANTHONY J SIMPSON
DONALD V SCAVOTTO	PAUL H SCHUKNECHT	ALBERT L SEEMAN	ROBERT W SHERMAN	EARL R SIMPSON
LOUIS G SCHADEGG	NORMAN F SCHULER	MELVIN H SEEMAN	JAMES E SHERWOOD	ERNEST A SIMPSON
WILLIAM H SCHAEFFER	CHARLES R SCHULTZ JR	MARION A SEICK	CECIL N SHIELDS	FRANK A SIMPSON
WILLIAM H SCHAFFER	DONALD J SCHULTZ	MARION ADAM SEICK	JOHN F SHIELDS	LEWIS E SIMPSON
EARL F SCHAIRER	EDWARD C SCHULTZ	TOLL SEIKE	LLOYD P SHIELDS	RICHARD E SIMPSON

ROBERT E SIMPSON	DOYLE B SMITH	ROY W SNELL	RALPH D SPIES	EDWARD R STEVENS
JOHNNIE V SIMS	EDWARD L SMITH JR	DONALD E SNIDER	JAMES D SPILLANE	JAMES F STEVENS
RALPH E SINCLAIR	ELLIS L SMITH	PAUL H SNIDER	CLIFFORD R SPLAINE	OSCAR M STEVENS
JOHN SINES	ELWOOD SMITH	CORNELIUS SNOEY	THOMAS R SPOHR	WILBUR W STEVENSON
EDWARD N SINGERMAN	ERIC O SMITH	DONALD S SNOOK	RONALD E SPOONER	ALEXANDER W STEWART
FLOYD M SIPPLE	ERNEST E SMITH	HERBERT M SNOW	CHESTER R SPRAGUE	CHARLES R STEWART
BERNARD W SIREN	FLOYD J SMITH	CLARENCE Z SNYDER	EDWARD C SPRAGUE	DONALD R STEWART
HAROLD R SIRES	FRANCIS F SMITH	GENE B SNYDER	HALSEY L SPRAGUE	HARRY A STEWART
HOWARD E SIRES	FRED E SMITH	HAROLD W SNYDER	JOHN F SPRAGUE	KARL M STEWART
WENDELL H SIRES	GILBERT L SMITH	JOHN SNYDER	J W SPRIESTERSBACH	LEON R STEWART
CLARENCE F SITKO	GLEN R SMITH	WILLIAM A SNYDER	GLENN C SPRIGGS	ORVAL L STEWART
RALPH SITTER	GLENN A SMITH	W A SOBIERALSKI	HAROLD C SPRING	RICHARD M STEWART
QUENTIN R SITTON	GORDON J SMITH	CHARLES A SODEN	HAROLD E SPRINGER	RUSSELL C STEWART
HAROLD C SIVEN	HAMILTON A SMITH	THEODORE J SODERBACK	RUDOLPH J SRSEN	BRUCE STICE
PERCY R SIVITS	HARDING A SMITH	ELMER SODERQUIST	JAMES H ST JOHN	SHELDON E STILES
JAMES E SJOGREN	HAROLD D SMITH	DONALD A SOENS	EDWARD A STACK	FRANCIS R STILL
JAMES E SKEWIS	HARRY L SMITH	LELAND R SOLDERS	JAMES B STAFFANSON	GERALD F STILLINGS
ALFRED A SKINNER	HOUSTON T SMITH	RICHARD A SOLLE	ROY K STAIFF	JACK M STILTS
CURTISS H SKINNER	HOWARD E SMITH	PAUL R SOLUM	WILLARD D STAMBAUGH	WILLIAM G STILWELL
CURTIS J SKOGSBERGH	HOWARD F SMITH	RICHARD A SOLVER	QUINTON D STANDIFORD	LEE A STINGER
ARTHUR P SKULEY	JACK A SMITH	REGINALD C SOLWAY	DOROTHY M STANKE	ALLEN H STOCKDALE
HENRY E SLATER	JACK R SMITH	CLARENCE P SOMERS	OSCAR H STANKE	ARIEL STOCKLAND
JOHN C SLATER	JAMES SMITH	WILBUR E SOMERS	WINSTON G STANLEY	EUGENE W STOCKSTILL
WILLIAM H SLATER	JAMES R SMITH	EDWIN J SOMMER	MERVIN L STANTON	ELDRIDGE C STOCKTON
ELMER A SLATON	JOHN H SMITH	ROBERT L SONNENBERG	ROBERT G STAPLETON	ROBERT E STODDARD
RUDOLPH A SLAVICH	JOSEPH SMITH	RODNEY L SOOTER	B E STARKENBERG	WILLIAM H STODDARD
EDGAR F SLENTZ	LOGAN C SMITH JR	VERNON F SORENSEN	CHARLES STARKOVICH	AARON STOKKE
HENRY D SLOAN	LOWELL H SMITH	MILTON L SORENSON	JOSEPH STARKOVICH JR	CLARENCE W STOLTZ
WILLIAM SLOAN	LYLE U SMITH	DALLAS H SORRELLS	CHARLES L STARR	LAWRENCE E STONE
WILLIAM J SLOAN	MAX E SMITH	EINAR SORTUN	ROBERT M STARR	ROGER L STONE
RICHARD O SLOAT	MERLE A SMITH	ARTHUR W SOULE	FRED G STATHAM JR	EDWARD R STORAASLI
HERMAN R SLOBY	ONIE R SMITH	JOSEPH B SOUSLEY	ROBERT J STAUCH	GEORGE N STORER
CHARLES E SLONAKER	PAUL C SMITH	FRANKLIN W SOUTHARD	FREDERICK J STAUFFER	RICHARD W STORK
JOHN A SLOSAR	PRESTON J SMITH	EARL C SPACKMAN	ROBERT H STEAD	LOUIS STORNELLI JR
WARREN SMALL	RALPH H SMITH	THEODORE M SPANSKI	ALFRED H STEELE	ERNEST C STORY
JOHN R SMART	RAYMOND H SMITH	GEORGE A SPARKS	GARVIN G STEELE	WILLIAM G STORY
STANTON M SMART	RICHARD W SMITH	NEAL R SPARKS	HAROLD W STEELE	GERRY E STOTT
WILBUR K SMAWLEY	ROBERT E SMITH	WENDELL C SPARKS	PERRY M STEELE	WILBUR E STOVER
CLARENCE F SMELSER	ROBERT F SMITH	CHARLES C SPARLING	MARION L STEFFENSEN	WILLIAM STOVER
ALAN E SMITH	ROBERT W SMITH	DANIEL J SPARLING	EDWARD H STEIGER	WILLIAM T STOVER
ALBERT A SMITH	ROLAND F SMITH	JOHN H SPARRENBERGER	ROBERT H STEIGER	MERLE J STOWE
ALLEN T SMITH	ROY S SMITH	DONALD E SPAULDING	JESSE F STEINER	NAOMI J STRAIGHT
ARCHIE J SMITH	THEODORE H SMITH	JESSE E SPAULDING	ARTHUR A STEINKE	LEON E STRAND
CARL G SMITH	THOMAS L SMITH	EARL G SPAULDONG	ERNEST E STEINSEIFER	MAURICE STRAND
CECIL D SMITH	VERNON D SMITH	SIDNEY D SPEAR	STANLEY P STEMKOWSKI	GEORGE F STRANDBERG
CHARLES E SMITH	VERNON L SMITH	CLINTON A SPEENBURG	ELMER L STEMP	KENNETH L STRANDT
CHESTER A SMITH	WADE E SMITH	ROSS M SPEIRS	CARL E STENBERG	CHARLES R STRATTON
CHESTER C SMITH	WALTER D SMITH	CHARLES L SPENCER	ERLING A STENSLAND	ROBERT J STRAUCH
CLAYTON F SMITH	WILLIAM C SMITH	DONALD E SPENCER	RUNGWOLD K STENSLID	CLYDE M STREET
CLIFFORD D SMITH	WILLIAM L SMITH	JOHN W SPENCER	ODD M STENVIK	JOHN S STREETER
DAN SMITH	WILLIAM M SMITH	WALTER E SPENCER	WILLIAM H STEPHENS	MELVIN H STREETS
DAVID W SMITH	WILLIAM R SMITH	CHARLES E SPERRING	WOODROW W STEPHENS	WALTER A STREICH
DONALD M SMITH	KENNETH M SMITHEY	GLENN H SPERRY	CLAUDE B STEPHENSON	W E STREISSGUTH
DONALD R SMITH	WILLIAM R SNEED	JAMES F SPERRY	THOMAS G STEVEN	C H STRICKLAND

DONALD L STRIEBY
DAVID E STRONG
JAMES W STRONG
STANLEY L STROUD
CLARENCE J STROWBRIDGE
JAMES T STUART
THEODORE A STUART
MILES STUBBLEFIELD
BENNY J STUCZKO
EDWARD A STUMPF
HERMAN F STURMER JR
HERBERT F SUDMEIER
HANS E SUESSMUTH
DWIGHT T SULLIVAN
NORBERT M SULLIVAN
WELDON J SULLIVAN
GLEN A SUMMERS
GUY W SUMNER
JOHN C SUNDAHL
FRED L SUNDAY
BERNARD SUNDIN
BOB SUPERINA
LEWIS R SUPINGER
ADOLPH A SUPPLE
MERLE S SUPPLEE
MERLE D SURBER
MICHAEL M SURERUS
JACK D SUTHERLAND
S S SUTHERLAND JR
T N SUTHERLAND
WALTER V SUTHERLAND
CLYDE W SUTTON
ROBERT L SUTTON
FRANCIS F SUTTORA
JAMES W SVENSON
CATO H SWALLING
GLEN G SWAN
OWEN D SWANEY
CHARLES F SWANSON
HARLAN V SWANSON
HUGO W SWANSON
LLOYD C SWANSON
RICHARD E SWANSON
DAVID H SWARTZ
ROBERT W SWARTZ
CHARLES O SWEET
WALTER W SWEET
JOHN SWENSEN
MELVIN E SWENSON
PALMER O SWENSON
JOHN SWICK
STANLEY F SWICK
MATTHEW SWIMPTKIN
BARNEY SWOFFORD

WALTER J SYKES
LYLE B SYLLING
PHILLIP C SYMONS
GEORGE A SZENTE
MICHAEL H SZUCS
— T —
GEORGE A TABBUT
MORRIS F TABER
FREDERICK P TABERT
SANITAGA TACDOL
MON TAKAHASHI
JIMMY Y TAKETA
ROSS E TALBOTT
FLOYD B TALLMAN
RICHARD M TAMURA
MATSUSABURO TANAKA
WESLEY V TANG
RUSSELL A TANNER
GEORGE TATSUMI
JACK K TAWES
ARTHUR G TAYLOR
ARTHUR L TAYLOR
DONALD G TAYLOR
EDWARD A TAYLOR
GEORGE TAYLOR
GORDON B TAYLOR
JACK W TAYLOR
JAMES F TAYLOR
JOHN P TAYLOR
KENNETH R TAYLOR
RUSSELL G TAYLOR
STANLEY C TAYLOR
VICTOR V TAYLOR JR
WALTER F TAYLOR
WILLIAM G TAYLOR
WILLIAM L TELLER
GORDON R TEMPLETON
JEFF A TESREAU
SHELDON E TESSENDORG
LEON A TESSIER
HAROLD W TETER
ALBERT F TEWS
HARVEY G THACKER
VERNON B THATCHER
HOWARD C THEW
LENARD THIBAUT
ARTHUR C THIELEN
CLAIR P THOLSTRUP
CHARLES E THOMAS
GEORGE F THOMAS
HENRY O THOMAS
JACK T THOMAS
LARRY B THOMAS
ROBERT B THOMAS

ROBERT E THOMAS
WILLIAM A THOMAS
RICHARD E THOMMEN
ALLAN L THOMPSON
ARCHIE R THOMPSON
ARNOLD W THOMPSON
CLARENCE H THOMPSON
DONALD L THOMPSON
EDWARD THOMPSON
GEORGE E THOMPSON
GEORGE J THOMPSON
HOWARD B THOMPSON
IRVIN THOMPSON
JAY V THOMPSON
JOHN W THOMPSON JR
JOSEPH V THOMPSON JR
JOSEPH W THOMPSON
LESTER O THOMPSON
LLOYD E THOMPSON
LYLE W THOMPSON
MC DONALD THOMPSON
RAYMOND B THOMPSON
RICHARD R THOMPSON
RICHARD S THOMPSON
ROBERT R THOMPSON
WILFRED A THOMPSON
WILLIAM D THOMPSON
JOHN E THORGERSON
HAROLD F THORNBURG
WILBUR D THORNE
HOWARD D THORNSBURY
CLARENCE C THORNTON
PRESTON R THORNTON
CLAUDE A THORP
HAROLD O THORSON
DANIEL A THUMLERT JR
ARTHUR J THUMME
MAGNUS O THUNESS
WALTER R THURLOW
ERNEST S THURMAN
JAMES B THURMOND
ROBERT M THURSTON
CHARLES H TIBBATS JR
WILLIAM F TIBBITS
HENRY J TIDD
HAROLD W TIEDEMANN
DAVID L TIERMAN
ALLAN R TILFORD
MILTON B TILLMAN
ALLEN L TIMBOE
JACK E TIPLER
WILLIAM V TISDALE
RICHARD M TITUS
HARVEY M TJOSTELSON

CHARLES R TODD
FRANK H TODD
MERL H TODD
WILLIAM A TODD
NEIL M TOIVONEN
ARTHUR K TOKOLA
GLEN E TOLLENAAR
CARROLL R TOLLETT
DONALD J TOMCHECK
CARLOS TOMES
JOHN J TOMICH
FRANK TOMKIEL
BRUCE E TOMPKINS
JOSEPH A TONDREAU
PHILIP J TONER
ARTHUR S TOOTHMAN
JOHN A TORI
LEONARD J TORVINEN
GEORGE TOST
JAMES F TOSTEVIN
LOYST M TOWNER
TALBOT TOWNSEND
RICHARD I TRACY JR
ROBERT C TRACY
THOMAS H TRADEWELL
CARL B TRAGER
DONALD O TRAIL
WILLARD A TRANSETH
L F TRAPHAGEN JR
ANTON S TRASK
JOSEPH TRASK
MAURICE G TRAUGHBER
GAYLORD E TREAT
CHARLES H TREMBLAY
PETER M TRENKENSCHUH
PETER A TRICK
ALBERT R TRIPLETT
JAMES M TRIPLETT
JAMES F TROWBRIDGE
ROBERT E TROWBRIDGE
ROBERT B TROYER
GERALD E TRUBE
ALBERT TRUSCOTT
PERRY R TRYON
NICKOLAS TSIMBIDIS
CLIFFORD TUCK
SHEREL J TUCKER
JAMES W TUINSTRA
CHARLES C TULLY
EDWIN E TUMA
ORREN O TUPPER
LLOYD R TURK
HARVEY J TURNER
JOE J TURNER

RICHARD S TURNER
WILLIAM C TURNER
WILLIAM J TURNER
WILLIAM P TURPEN
GILVERT A TUSTY
IRVING J TWEDT
WALTER A TWEEDY
ROBERT R TWITCHELL
LAVERNE E TWOHY
RONALD L TWOMBLY
SAMUEL J TYREE
— U —
EARL H UERLING
ELMER H UITTO
DONATO UMALI
DONALD R UMPHFRES
WILLIAM D UNDERWOOD
WILLIAM R UNDERWOOD JR
FRANK UNGER
JOHN R UPHOUSE
OSCAR T URETA
RAYMOND URQUHART
TONY J USICH
WILLIAM A USKOSKI
DE LEAUGH W UTTER
WILBER J UTTER
— V —
ALVIN G VAARA
LEO H VALENTINE
C J VALIQUETTE
HARRY F VALLIERE
CLARENCE E VAMMEN JR
JOHN W VAN ALLEN JR
JOHN D VAN ARSDALE
WILLIAM J VAN DEHOVEN
DEAN E VAN DONGE
CLAUDE F VAN EMELEN
DONALD J VAN GELDER
JOHN N VAN HORN
JOHN R VAN HORN
ARTHUR F VAN HOUTEN
DONALD H VAN IDERSTINE
ROBERT VAN KLINKEN
ISSAC D VAN METER
WENDELL P VAN NIMAN
PERRY H VAN PATTEN
GARRETTE M VAN RIPER
C W VAN SCOYOC JR
FORREST R VAN SLYKE
A N VAN SLYKE JR
ERIC B VAN WERALD JR
WALLACE J VAN WIRT
HARRY M VAN ZANDT
GARNETT F VAN ZANT

EDWIN H VANCIL
LAWRENCE H VANDERBERG
JOSEPH W VANDERBUR
CECIL L VANDERPOOL
MARION F VANDERPOOL
VANE I VANDERPOOL
DICK R VANDERVEER
JOHN J VANDIVER
FRANK O VARNER
NELSON VAUGHN JR
ROBERT W VAUPELL
ROBERT R VEBERES
PRIESKO VERDERICO
MARION B VERMEER
JOHN E VERNON
WILLIAM H VERNON JR
GORDON V VESTAL
WALTER R VETH
LAWRENCE E VETTER
THEODORE H VETTER
RALPH H VICK
LAWRENCE VICKERS
CLARENCE VINCENT
MARTIN P VOAG
RICHARD VOEIKER
DONALD R VOGEL
SEBASTIAN G VOGEL JR
FRANCIS J VOS
EDGAR M VOSS
CLAUDE W VROMAN
JOHN W VYE

— W —

WALTER H WADDELL
BUY W WADE
EUGENE W WADE
OLIVER P WADLEY
HERBERT A WADSWORTH
HERMAN E WAGNER
IRVING J WAHL
KARL R WAHLBRINK
WAYLAND L WAIT
WILLIAM J WAITE JR
KEITH M WAKEMAN
GERHARD A WALBERG
ALBERT M WALCOTT
JAMES T WALDO
LEO K WALDON
DENNIS G WALES
EARL R WALFORD
CHARLES C WALKER
EFF C WALKER
HERMAN R WALKER
JAMES H WALKER
JAMES O WALKER

JAMES R WALKER
JAMES W WALKER JR
ROBERT B WALKER
ROBERT E WALKER
WILLARD L WALKER
CHARLES E WALKS JR
CLAYTON E WALL
EARNEST E WALL
ANDREW WALLACE
ERNEST WALLACE
FRANK C WALLACE
JAMES L WALLACE
LEONARD A WALLACE
EDWIN J WALLEN
FLOYD B WALLIN
PAUL W WALLIN
GEORGE F WALLMAN
ROBERT J WALLOCH
OWEN P WALLS
MARVIN E WALSETH
ARLEN A WALTER
SAM WALTERS
VIRGIL O WALTERS
JOHN R WALTIER
DONALD L WALTON
DONOVAN E WALTON
LEONARD H WALTON
ORSON L WALTON
HENRY L WAMBA JR
RONALD T WANGBERG
EARL H WANKE
DALE L WANLESS
WILLIAM WAPPENSTEIN
HAROLD O WARBURTON
DUANE P WARD
JOHN V WARD
LEWIS A WARD
THERON S WARD JR
FRED G WARDNER
IVAN F WARDRIP
CLYDE S WARFIELD
ALBERT L WARNER
BERNELL R WARNER
HAROLD E WARNER
WILBUR A WARNOCK JR
CARL S WARREN
JAMES V WARREN
PAGE WARREN
ROBERT L WARREN
HUGH N WARRING
MILTON WARSHAL
FRITZ WASCOWITZ
JOHN V WASSER
THEODORE R WASSON

WILLIAM D WATERS
R W WATERSTON JR
HARLEY M WATKINS
THOMAS H WATKINS
GORDON L WATKINSON
ANDREW S WATSON
CALVIN WATSON
JAMES F WATSON
ORIN H WATSON
ROBERT S WATSON
WARREN M WATSON
CHARLES W WATTENBARGER
ROBERT L WATTS
HARLAND R WAY
WILLIAM D WAYENBERG
HUELON WAYYS
RAYMOND W WEAK
BEN WEATHERLEY
CHARLES M WEAVER
MELVIN E WEAVER
DONALD H WEBB
JAMES N WEBB
NORMAN WEBBER
GEORGE WEBER
WILSON B WEBER
DWIGHT O WEDDLE
HOWARD F WEDDLE
WILLIAM T WEEKS
ERVIN WEIL
GERALD L WEIMERS
JAMES R WEIR
RUDOLPH P WEISEL JR
ARTHUR M WEISS
JOHN WEISZHAAR JR
LEEROY H WEITMAN
GEORGE C WELCH
WILLIAM E WELCH
WILLIAM R WELCH
MILTON R WELLER
WALTER G WELLER
CHARLES W WELLS
EDWARD R WELLS
GERALD L WELLS
HARVEY E WELLS
NICHOLAS P WELLS
ROY O WELLS
CLYDE L WELSH
LEWIS J WENDELIN
PAUL A WENDELIN
OREN K WENDT
ADOLPH M WENNERLUND
BOB WERNER
EDWARD I WERSEBE
EUGENE B WESCOM

ROBERT WESCOTT
EARNEST WEST
ERNEST WEST JR
GORDON M WEST
JAMES H WEST
LEO M WEST ORVAL E WEST
PAUL WEST
RAYMOND R WEST
THEODORE WEST
WARREN W WEST
MELVIN A WESTALL
ROY W WESTBERG
DOCK M WESTBERRY
MARION A WESTBROOK
ARTHUR H WESTBY
LORAIN O WESTENHAVER
A W WESTERHOLM
ROBERT E WESTERHOLM
WILLIAM C WESTLAKE
ROBERT N WESTLING
LE ROY G WESTON
ROBERT W WESTON
VICTOR H WESTRAND
ROBERT H WESTROM
ARTHUR N WESTRUM
LEO D WETHERBEE
RICHARD A WETZBARGER
RAYMOND H WETZEL
RICHARD S WEYER
GEORGE E WEYHING
JEROME D WHALEN
PATRICK E WHALEN
ROY W WHALEN
STUART D WHALEN
THOMAS S WHANNELL
SIDNEY F WHARTON JR
BILL WHEELER
CHARLES R WHEELER
EVERETT M WHEELER
GLENN C WHEELER
JACK M WHEELER
JOHN A WHEELER
LESLIE J WHEELER
ROBERT L WHEELER
ROBERT M WHEELER
WILBUR E WHEELER
WILLIAM E WHEELER
RAY W WHIDDEN
ARLOS A WHITE
CLYDE T WHITE
EUGENE A WHITE
FERGUSON B WHITE
FRED W WHITE
JAMES K WHITE

JOHN L WHITE
JOSEPH L WHITE
LAWRENCE W WHITE
RAYMOND B WHITE
RICHARD A WHITE
RICHARD B WHITE
ROBERT E WHITE
ROBERT S WHITE
ROBERT W WHITE
THERON N WHITE
CLAUDE E WHITEHEAD
L E WHITESEL
EDWARD A WHITFORD
ROBERT L WHITHAM
EARL W WHITING
RUSSELL E WHITMORE
CHARLES M WHITNEY
CLYDE O WHITNEY
FRANK L WHITNEY
ROBERT A WHITNEY
ALTON W WHITSON
LLOYD H WHITSON
KEITH B WHITTAKER
EUGENE H WHITTEMORE
ALBERT E WHITTINGTON
JOHN P WHITTLE
BILLY D WICK
FRANK H WICK
MAX M WICKLANDER
EUGENE WICKS
WAYNE W WICKS
KEITH W WICKSTROM
MARVIN J WICKSTROM
RALPH V WICKSTROM
NORMAN WICKSTRTOM
ALFRED C WIDENER
VERNON O WIELAND
ELMER J WIERSMA
ROY E WIGET
ROBERT A WIGHTMAN
EARL M WILCOX
HARRY E WILCOX
ROBERT A WILCOX
FLOYD E WILDER
VIRGIL D WILDER
HORACE V WILES
ARCHIE C WILEY
GEORGE M WILEY JR
ROBERT F WILEY
HARLEY F WILHELM
A E WILKERSON
ROBERT S WILKERSON
CHARLES M WILKINS
DONALD E WILKINS JR

FRANKLIN E WILKINSON
ROBERT S WILKINSON
FERRIS W WILKS
ARVEL W WILLARD
EUGENE F WILLARD
FRED H WILLCOX
ELMER E WILLCUTT
RICHARD H WILLE
HAZEN F WILLETT
ROBERT L WILLETT
ABEL J WILLIAMS
CARL T WILLIAMS
CHARLES W WILLIAMS
CHARLES T WILLIAMS JR
DALE O WILLIAMS
EMIL WILLIAMS
GLENN L WILLIAMS
HARLAN B WILLIAMS
JACK O WILLIAMS
JOHN D WILLIAMS
JOHN M WILLIAMS
LAWRENCE C WILLIAMS
LORRAINE C WILLIAMS
ROBERT L WILLIAMS
THOMAS J WILLIAMS
ULYSSES G WILLIAMS
WAYNE WILLIAMS
WILLIAM B WILLIAMS JR
FRANK E WILLIAMSON JR
GEORGE J WILLIAMSON
MELVIN D WILLIAMSON
WILLIAM W WILLIAMSON
ALBERT M WILLIS
THOMAS WILLIS
WILLIAM E WILLIS
JOHN S WILLMERT
RONALD G WILLOWS
WALTER N WILLS
HOWARD R WILLSON
MERLE R WILLUMSEN
CALVIN M WILSON JR
CUTHBERT WILSON
DOUGLAS M WILSON
EINAR WILSON
HENRY E WILSON
HOWARD A WILSON
IRA WILSON
JOHN D WILSON
JOSEPH M WILSON
LEE R WILSON
LESTER WILSON
LESTER A WILSON
LLOYD L WILSON
MEURNICE S WILSON

ORVILLE M WILSON
PAUL W WILSON
RALPH G WILSON
THEODORE B WILSON
WAYNE E WILSON
WILLIAM G WILSON
CHARLES H WILTON
LYLE S WINCHELL
MARTIN W WINGE
BERNARD WINGERTER
SEBASTIAN WINGERTER
RALPH G WINGFIELD
CHARLES M WINGHAM
ILEY D WINN
WILL R WINN
WILLIAM R WINN
GEORGE H WINNIE
HARVEY E WINOSKI
DAVIE J WINSLOW
MILTON E WINSTON
EDWARD WINTER
EDWIN R WINTER
HERBERT T WINTER JR
REGINALD D WINTER
RICHARD WINTER
ROBERT G WINTHERS
DWAIN A WIRGHT
LLOYD WISBEY
JOHN F WISE
RAY W WISEMAN
HAROLD J WISER
LEONARD WISNEWSKY
EDWIN F WISNIEWSKI
DAVID J WITT
ROBERT W WITTE
ARTHUR R WITTENBORN
LYNN E WOLD
REUEL J WOLD
CLARENCE F WOLFE
LOUIS R WOLFE JR
LOWELL J WOLFE
MERTON WOLFE
RICHARD C WOLFE
ARTHUR C WOLFF
HENRY F WOLFGRAM
MORRIS O WOLLAN
FREDERICK R WOLLENBERG
JACK E WOLSLEGEL
GLENN I WOLTERS
BING P WONG
BRADY M WOOD
CARSON K WOOD
CLAUDE R WOOD
DONALD H WOOD

FRANCIS E WOOD
GEORGE A WOOD
HERBERT C WOOD
HOWARD J WOOD
JOHN V WOOD
RICHARD W WOOD
WILLIAM N WOODCOCK
ANDREW H WOODHALL
ROBERT E WOODMANSEE
DONALD N WOODRING
DAVID P WOODRUFF
ROY W WOODRUFF
WINFRED O WOODS
CLYDE R WOODWORTH
JOHN R WOODY
WAYNE R WOODY
ROBERT E WOOLEVER
WILLIAM E WOOLUM
GORDON W WORDEN
DARBY M WORLEY
ROBERT E WORMAN
WARD K WORTMAN
EDGAR N WORTZKEY
EON R WRALSTAD
CLYDE L WREN
ROBERT S WREN
EARL W WRENN
ALONZO C WRIGHT
CHARLES E WRIGHT
DONALD L WRIGHT
EDGAR B WRIGHT
HOWARD C WRIGHT
HOWARD L WRIGHT
LEWIS W WRIGHT
WALTER G WRIGHT
WILLET H WRIGHT JR
WILLIAM O WRIGHT
WILLIAM V WRIGHT
VERNON L WUBBENS
EUGENE K WUNDERLICK
VICTOR WURZEL
ROBERT A WYGLE
GLEN E WYLEY
RALPH W WYNN
JAMES C WYNNE
PATRICK E WYNNE

— Y —

GUY T YACONETTI
JOHN T YACONETTI
WILLIAM J YAKE
SETSURO YAMASHITA
GORDON G YAMAURA
ROBERT A YANCEY
ROBERT H YANCEY

THOMAS W YAPP
RICHARD A YARROW
HIDEO YASUI
KENNETH L YATES
FRED R YEAGER
ALLEN M YEATS
DUNG N YEE
JAMES W YENNE
LEO P YENNY
LUKE T YEUN
MAX L YORK
SHIGEO YOSHIOKA
MELVIN S YOST
LAWRENCE H YOUND
CHESTER I YOUNG
DAVID R YOUNG
DONALD YOUNG
LAWRENCE H YOUNG
LESTER J YOUNG
ORMAN W YOUNG JR
ROBERT B YOUNG
STANLEY H YOUNG
WARD M YOUNG
WILLIAM J YOUNG
ROBERT P YOUNGCHILD
LAWRENCE H YOUNKIN
LUKE T YUEN
HAROLD N YURISICH

— Z —

ROBERT O ZACHAUS
PHILIP ZACHRISON
ARTHUR N ZACHRISSON
KAY P ZACK
ERIC J ZACKRISON
RICHARD D ZAMBARD
ROBERT J ZANCKER
ORVILLE E ZANDER
FRANK ZANI
FLOYD R ZAWISTOSKI
JOHN F ZEBLEY
DAVID ZECHMAN
RAYMOND F ZEIPERT
MARTIN H ZELLER
GEORGE W ZICKEFOOSE
PERRY W ZICKEFOOSE
PHILMER G ZIER
ROBERT W ZIMMERMAN
CEDRIC W ZINDORF
STANLEY ZISKA
MARCO ZOLEZZI
LESTER L ZORNES
MARVIN T ZWAINZ

BIBLIOGRAPHY

Bennett, Robert A. *Walla Walla, A Nice Place to Raise a Family,* Walla Walla: Pioneer Press Books, 1988.

Coman, Walt and Helen Gibbs. *Time, Tide and Timber.* New York: Greenwood Press, 1968.

Crowley, Walt. *The Continental Family.* Salt Lake City: Publishers Press, 1997.

Daniel, Clifton. *Chronicle of the 20th Century.* Mount Kisco, NY: Chronicle Publications, Inc.,1987.

Gates, Charles M. *The First Century at the University of Washington.* Seattle: University of Washington Press, 1961.

Hines, Neal O. *Denny's Knoll, A History of the Metropolitan Tract of the University of Washington.* Seattle: University of Washington Press,1980.

Humphrey, Robert M. *Everett and Snohomish County.* Norfolk, VA: The Donning Company, 1984.

Keve, Paul W. *The McNeil Century.* Chicago: Nelson-Hall, 1984.

Kirk, Ruth and Carmela Alexander. *Exploring Washington's Past.* Seattle: University of Washington Press, 1990.

Lombardi, Michael J. (project manager). *A Brief History of the Boeing Company.* Seattle: Boeing Historical Services, 1998.

McDonald, Lucile. *Bellevue: Its First 100 Years.* Fairfield, WA: Ye Galleon Press, 1984.

McDonald, Lucile. *The Lake Washington Story.* Seattle: Superior Press, 1979.

Morgan, Murray. *Puget's Sound.* Seattle: University of Washington Press, *1979.*

Morgan, Murray, and Rosa Morgan. *South on the Sound.* Woodland Hills, CA: Windsor Publications, 1984.

Nance, E.C. *The Daniel V. McEachern Story.* College Place, WA: The College Press, 1958.

Newell, Gordon. *The H.W. McCurdy Marine History of the Pacific Northwest.* Seattle: Superior Publishing Co., 1966.

Nordstrom, Elmer J. *The Winning Team.* Self Published, 1985

Office of Financial Management. *State of Washington 1997 Data Book.* Olympia: Washington State Department of Printing.

Prater, Yvonne. *Snoqualmie Pass.* Seattle: The Mountaineers, 1981.

Richardson, David. *Puget Sounds, a Nostalgic Review of Radio and TV in the Great Northwest.* Seattle: Superior Publishers, 1981.

Ross, Donald K and Helen L. Ross. *Washington State Men of Valor.* Port Orchard, WA: Rokalu Press, 1994.

Serling, Robert J. *Legend and Legacy, The Story of Boeing and Its People.* New York: St. Martin's Press, 1992.

Simpich, Frederick, Sr. "War Time in the Pacific Northwest," *National Geographic*, 1942.

Steves, James. *Green Power.* Seattle, WA: Superior Publications, 1958.

Stimson, William L. *Going to Washington State.* Pullman: Washington State University Press, 1989.

Warren, James R. *King County and Its Emerald City, Seattle.* Tarzana, CA.: American Historical Press, 1997.

Warren, James R. *An Illustrated History of Puget Sound.* Northridge, CA.: Windsor Publications, 1986.

Young, Brigadier Peter. *The World Almanac Book of World War II.* Englewood, N. J.: World Almanac Publications, 1981.

The World Almanac 1944. New York World Telegram.

NEWSPAPERS

1941-1946
The Seattle Times
The Seattle Post-Intelligencer
The Spokesman-Review
The Walla Walla Statesman
Big Y Bulletin. Yakima, WA: February-March 1942.

INDEX